DEVELOPMENTAL

PSYCHOLOGY

James E. Birren
University of Southern California

Dennis K. Kinney
Harvard Medical School

K. Warner Schaie
University of Southern California

Diana S. Woodruff
Temple University

Houghton Mifflin Company   Boston

Dallas   Geneva, Illinois
Hopewell, New Jersey
Palo Alto   London

DEVELOPMENTAL PSYCHOLOGY

A LIFE-SPAN APPROACH

To our families, who taught us so much about human development.

Credits for photographs appearing on front endpapers, reading from left to right:

Eve Arnold, Magnum / Jim Harrison, Stock, Boston / Constantine Manos, Magnum / Cary Wolinsky, Stock, Boston / Guy Le Querrec, Magnum / George W. Gardner / Cary Wolinsky, Stock, Boston / Charles Gatewood / Jean-Claude Lejeune, Stock, Boston / Richard Kalvar, Magnum / George Bellerose, Stock, Boston / Bhupendra Karia, Magnum

Quotations on pages 509-512 reprinted from *The Origins of Intelligence in Children* by Jean Piaget (M. Cook, Trans.) by permission of International Universities Press, Inc. Copyright 1952 by International Universities Press, Inc.

Cover photograph by Dave Wade.

Printed in the U.S.A.

Library of Congress Catalog Card Number: 80-82839

ISBN: 0-395-29717-6

CONTENTS

PREFACE

This book is the result of several years of extensive planning, discussions, and writing. It was written in response to the growing need for a text that presents a complete but comprehendible introduction to psychological development over the life span.

Life-Span Coverage

In past years, developmental psychology was for the most part limited to child psychology. It is now widely accepted that individual development does not stop at any particular age. Most certainly it does not cease at the end of adolescence, where past texts in developmental psychology have often stopped. Indeed, some of the most significant aspects of development occur during adult life when individuals are challenged by environmental circumstances.

More answers are now known to questions about optimum patterns of life and the biological and social conditions that influence development throughout life. As a result, the task of the developmental psychologist today is to examine the processes and the outcomes of development from the fetus to very old age. Our aim, therefore, has been to write more than simply another child psychology text with a chapter or two added on adult life. We have worked to create a truly modern book based on the principles and facts of development over the life span.

Topical Approach

We decided in our early discussions about the book that it was not satisfactory to present the chapters in a simple chronological order. Instead, we have treated each aspect of behavior developmentally so that sufficient depth of understanding is gained. Our goal is to present the reader with a picture of how different facets of an individual's behavior change with time, ranging from the effects of parents interacting with a smiling baby to the socialization of older adults into the role of grandparents.

Organization

Another basic premise of this book is that development is affected by the interaction of biological and environmental influences. Each individual is a product of a unique heredity and a particular social and physical environment. Developmental psychology is thus both a biological and a social science. The early chapters in this book, therefore, establish the principles of biological and social influences on development. From there the book moves into the details of the various aspects of behavior, from perception to personality, that comprise the repertory of human behavior.

Part I provides an overview to the field of developmental psychology, including basic concepts and theories, a brief history of the field, and career opportunities in teaching, research, and the helping professions. Part II discusses biological and biosocial influences on development: genetic influences, maturation, health, and nutrition. To conclude this part, Chapter 5, "The Biosocial Interface: Interacting Influences," provides important information about how different kinds of influences interact in shaping development and how we can be misled in our attempts to understand development if we fail to consider how these various influences work together. Part III explores some of the social and environmental influences on development: early experience and family as well as social and cultural influences. Part IV covers the various behavioral processes over the life span. In this section, the chapters progress roughly from more basic behavioral processes (sensation and perception) to more global ones (personality). This progression is obviously not a strict one for some of the chapters in between, and they can be covered in any order an instructor prefers. Part V discusses ways in which we can fulfill our potentials for human development, how the decisions we make in interacting with our environment will affect the quality of our experience.

All the chapters in this book are both interconnected and independent. They are interconnected in that each chapter brings out the interaction of biological and environmental influences on development. They are independent in that each chapter is a complete unit in itself. Because the text has been written from a topical approach, the later chapters do not depend on a chronological progression from earlier chapters. For example, the behavioral processes in Part IV could be covered before the social and environmental influences in Part III, and as much of genetics and maturation can be covered as the instructor desires. In this way the text can be made adaptable to the emphasis an instructor prefers.

Out aim has been to present students with a text that is intellectually stimulating, useful, and informative about the most important aspects of human existence.

Learning Aids

We have provided several features to aid students in mastering the material in this text. Each chapter begins with a list of key points in the chapter and an outline of the chapter. Every italicized word in the text has been defined in the glossary at the back of the book. A summary appears at the end of each chapter except the concluding chapter on potentials for individual development. The numbered items in the summaries have been carefully coordinated with the major sections within the chapters. We have also provided brief, annotated reading lists at the end of each chapter, except the first and the last, for students who would like to explore various subjects in more detail.

Within the chapters are boxed inserts containing items of interest that relate to material being discussed in the text. Some examples include "Can You Live to Be 100?" which is a test that readers can take to determine the outlook for their individual longevity, "Where Jobs Will (and Won't) Be in the 80's," "California's Children of Divorce," "Acting One's Age: New Rules for Old," "Breaking the Age Barrier to Friendship," "Are Old Folks Really Poor?" Many of these inserts are from books and current magazine and newspaper articles. Others have been written especially for this book.

A *Study Guide* is available that includes multiple-choice questions with answers, a programmed review with answers, vocabulary review, and essay questions. Text page numbers have been given for all except the essay questions, so that students can refer back to the text for any areas in which they need more study and review. The *Study Guide* also contains a section on study techniques based on what has been learned from psychological research in learning and memory. This section includes comments on factors and techniques of learning such as motivation, overlearning, the value of spaced practice, recitation, organizing the material to be learned, mnemonic devices, the serial position effect, and the importance of reviewing.

Acknowledgments

We would like to thank the following people who have read portions or complete drafts of the manuscript and provided us with useful comments and reviews:

Peter E. Comalli, Jr., Temple University

Joyce G. Crouch, Appalachian State University

Janet J. Fritz, Colorado State University

Carol Furry, Clemson University

Aline M. Garrett, University of Southwestern Louisiana

Charles D. Hoffman, California State College, San Bernardino

John L. Horn, University of Denver

Paul S. Kaplan, Suffolk County Community College

Norman Livson, University of California, Berkeley

Stuart I. Offenbach, Purdue University

Marion Perlmutter, University of Minnesota

Leighton E. Stamps, University of New Orleans

Lillian E. Troll, Rutgers University

Suzanne Tuthill, Delaware Technical and Community College

Mary Ann Watson, Metropolitan State College, Denver
Marsha Weinraub, Temple University
M. Virginia Wyly, State University College at Buffalo

J. E. B.
D. K. K.
K. W. S.
D. S. W.

I DEVELOPMENTAL PSYCHOLOGY: AN OVERVIEW

Developmental psychology is the study of how individuals develop and change throughout the life span. This subject has scientific importance as well as usefulness to all persons interested in learning more about their own development and the development of those around them. Although not an old science as compared with physics or anatomy, developmental psychology has its roots in the scientific developments of the last century. The first part of this book provides an introduction to some of the basic ideas of developmental psychology and their historical background. Chapter 1 discusses in detail some of the fundamental concepts of developmental psychology, and Chapter 2 examines the theories, research methods, and historical emergence of the subject. Most of the early research in developmental psychology was done on children. More recently, research has increased significantly on the adult phase of the life span. It has been said that our society has changed from being child centered to being adult centered in its emphasis. Research, too, has been influenced by an increasing interest in the outcomes of early development on the mature and older adult. Part I equips the student to proceed to study the different aspects of development across the life span.

Chapter 1

Some Basic Concepts and Their Usefulness

Developmental psychology as a field of inquiry: how the study of human development can help us to understand ourselves better and thereby gain greater mastery over our lives

The cultural value of developmental psychology: how the knowledge of similarities and differences in human development can give us a perspective on cultural differences and on age differences within the same culture

Developmental psychology as an aid to personal adaptation: how the study of human development can solve or relieve problems that occur during an individual's life

Career opportunities in developmental psychology

Developmental Psychology as a Field of Inquiry
>   Evolutionary Development (Phylogeny)
>   Evolution of Development and Aging
>   Development as Part of Culture
>   The Age Structure of Society

The Cultural Value of Developmental Psychology
>   Social Roles and Norms
>   Social Expectations
>   The Range of Individual Differences
>   Appreciating the Lawfulness of Change over the Life Span

Developmental Psychology as an Aid to Personal Adaptation
>   Personal Experience
>   Careers

Introduction

There are many reasons why research is done in developmental psychology, why courses are taught, and why students from various backgrounds take the courses and read widely. One basic value in studying human development is personal. By seeking knowledge about development, we may understand ourselves better and thereby gain greater mastery over our lives. A noticeable recent trend in our society is for individuals to avoid domination by a large system or establishment, seeking instead to cultivate their own uniqueness. This cultivation of the individual self can be pursued by developing distinctive hobbies or special skills and abilities, including spiritual and mystical ones. Additionally, of course, rational persons turn to evidence from the sciences in order to understand their own nature and potentials. That is, they turn to the type of information presented in this book.

Another value in studying developmental psychology is cultural. Along with knowledge of our cultural roots and mastery of our language, an acquaintance with developmental psychology—and the insight it gives us into the similarities and differences in human development—is part of every people's heritage. Such insight gives us a perspective not only on cultural differences but also on age differences within the same culture. It is not unrealistic to propose that as people come to understand the psychology of development, many tragedies of collective life can be reduced.

Yet another value in studying developmental psychology is that such information may solve or relieve problems that occur during an individual's life. Developmental psychology also has social and professional ramifications. Some students explore the subject to prepare for careers as psychologists, teachers, social workers, or health professionals. Some begin the study as a requirement for research careers. Indeed, the questions and problems relating to how we grow up and grow old are among the most basic and intriguing to pursue. Numerous adventures and benefits await those who seek to discover more about the forces and mechanisms that affect a person's development from conception to life's end.

Clearly, the cultural and professional aspects of developmental psychology are closely related. Informed people have higher expectations and demand more professional services. Informed retired people may seek counseling for problems arising from their situations, while college-educated parents may seek professional help for problems affecting their growing children. Children should be educated in ways that take advantage of our best knowledge about developmental processes. Educational psychology thus depends heavily on developmental psychology. As individuals in our society are increasingly freed from productive labor, they will be more involved in personal services of an educational, counseling, or therapeutic nature. Even now, large numbers of careers are involved in providing skills that develop an individual's potentials. Yet childhood is not the end of life but only its beginning. Clearly, new careers are aimed at dealing with matters of marriage and the family, midlife career changes, preretirement counseling, and other age-related problems. These issues will be taken more seriously in a society where individuals have been

5

Developmental psy-
chology provides a
perspective on cul-
tural differences as
well as on age differ-
ences within a
culture.

Ira Kirschenbaum, Stock, Boston, Inc.

freed from labor and have the time and desire to enhance their personal lives. The needs and wants of an informed society must be served by new institutions and professionals providing new services and knowledge that minimize the problems of growing up and growing old. The study of human development can help us all realize our potentials more fully.

Traditionally, the study of developmental psychology has focused on changes that occur in growing children, in their abilities, personalities, social behavior, goals and motivations, and other attributes. Early developmental psychologists tended to neglect adulthood and old age, as though an individual's growth ended in the late teens and the person was sent into life to act out a defined role in a plot already written. But modern developmental psychologists accept the principle that life is a dynamic process, from beginning to end. In their view, a grasp of the main elements of human behavior *throughout* the life span can be regarded as a requirement for every person who would be well informed. The study of developmental psychology over the life span contributes to our culture by providing us with a more realistic concept of ourselves than can be obtained solely from historical transmission through generations. Although the wisdom inherited from past centuries about human nature can leaven current knowledge, a grasp of research findings on the main biological and social forces that shape our lives is essential for both personal and practical reasons in today's society.

Developmental psychology is part of general psychology. As such, it is concerned with the elements and organization of human behavior, sensation, perception, memory, learning, and other aspects of our lives. These topics can be approached from the viewpoint of physiological psychology, which focuses on the biological processes involved in the organization of behavior, and that of social psychology, which focuses on our social behavior. General psychology can be subdivided further into even more specific areas. It is essential here, however, to note that developmental psychology complements all of these subdivisions by arranging our knowledge about behavior according to age. Developmental psychology examines in detail the behavioral changes that occur with age and the determinants of those changes. Thus while developmental psychology depends on physiological, social, clinical, and other areas of psychology for information, it in turn provides those fields with important principles and facts. For example, judgments about a child's behavior and appropriate treatment or learning experiences should be based on a knowledge of what is observed and expected of most children having similar intellectual, personality, and social backgrounds. Deviance can be judged only in relation to some norm.

Research in developmental psychology has included studies of individuals from birth to late adulthood. A characteristic such as intelligence can be examined over long periods of the life span. Beyond the study of single traits,

Developmental psychology studies individuals throughout the life span, allowing us to understand the interrelationships among physical, intellectual, and emotional growth.

however, we can explore the interrelationships among an individual's characteristics, such as personality, intelligence, motor behavior, and rates of growth. From the study of patterns in individual lives, we can learn which biological and environmental factors lead to competence in many important aspects of life, including school, career, and marriage. Not only are these matters important for each individual, but they also benefit society by providing information about the effects of deprivations on its members—both children and adults. Early deprivation may have costly consequences for society as well as limiting the potentials of individuals as they move into adulthood.

Having outlined the broadest benefits to be derived from the study of developmental psychology, let us look more closely at some specific concerns and how they affect our lives.

Developmental Psychology as a Field of Inquiry

Evolutionary Development (Phylogeny)

We can consider psychological development from the viewpoint of what we have in common as human beings or from the viewpoint of our individual uniqueness—how we resemble or differ from one another as we grow up and grow old. While our apparent differences command our attention daily, we still must realize that we are members of a single species, Homo sapiens. It is the evolutionary, or *phylogenic*, viewpoint that emphasizes the study of our development as genetically related organisms.

Were intelligent beings from outer space to land on earth and try to describe us, they would begin with what we have in common. Among the characteristics they might describe are the way we look and behave as we grow up and grow old. From this vantage point, human beings are quite similar, or *homogeneous*—more so, for example, than dogs or cats are. Granting our individual differences, humanity still would appear to be homogeneous with respect to size, form, and behavior. So similar are we that Leonardo da Vinci developed rules with which to draw pictures of babies, children, adults, and old people. Because our unique appearances usually occupy our attention, we take for granted our phylogenetic similarities. But even the development and aging of groups of people living under natural conditions—say the remote Philippine tribes or the Australian Aborigines—resemble patterns found in other human groups more than patterns found in other species near us in evolution. In contrast, consider how different a Saint Bernard dog is from the small, "hairless" Chihuahua. One even suspects that the drives, motivations, and concerns of people growing up in widely scattered places on the earth are perhaps more similar to each other than they are different. In a dog show, attention is paid to slight variations among the average characteristics of a type—the size of the ears, the shape of the tail, or the distribution of hair color. So it is with human beings: we concentrate on our differences, which in some cases are very small, forgetting the commonality among us. There is great social variation among our customs for expressing drives and motives, such as the rituals of eating, being educated, selecting a mate, mating, giving birth, and even dying. These rituals give us an identity with subgroups, making it possible for a space creature—after describing our phylogenetic similarities—to describe behavior characteristics that group us into tribes and even families.

Evolution of Development and Aging

If we accept that human development has a phylogenetic pattern that is genetically controlled, the question arises as to how this control originated. A religiously oriented person might believe that humanity was created as a special entity all at once and is distinct in all ways from other living things. A person with a naturalistic outlook might say, instead, that we appear to have many things in common with other species, particularly those with spinal cords. Human cells synthesize proteins from the same amino acids used by other animals. Our processes of respiration and the use of oxygen in releasing energy are remarkably similar to those of other animals in many respects, as are the processes of digestion and nerve and muscle activity. Such observations lead to the view that we have evolved from common ancestors and are a more differentiated species than those that have formed our ancestral line (see Figure 1.1). Although we have most in common with other human beings, in this view we also share a common biological ancestry with other species. Furthermore, the development and aging processes themselves are believed to have

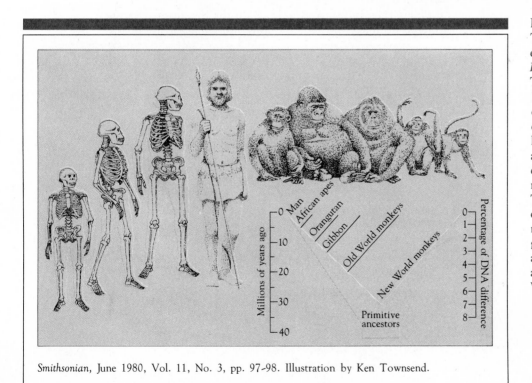

FIGURE 1.1
Time scale for evolution of *Homo sapiens.* This diagram illustrates the time of evolutionary development of human beings and the genetic distance between related species. The scale indicates that humans are closer genetically to the apes than are the apes to the New World monkeys.

Smithsonian, June 1980, Vol. 11, No. 3, pp. 97–98. Illustration by Ken Townsend.

evolved. This view leads to comparative research that aims to find similarities in, for example, how different species of mammals develop and age.

Development includes the process through which an individual organism grows from a single fertilized egg into a differentiated and complex adult consisting of billions of cells. This process itself can be seen as having evolved into a regular pattern. The progression is from a small size to a large size, from cells that do all things to organized groups of specialized cells such as nerve, blood, or muscle. Unlike single-celled organisms, the highly differentiated cells of the human body require the existence and cooperation of the other cells in order to survive. This cooperation we can call *integration*. Without it, the growth from fetus to adult would result simply in a large blob. Cells must be turned off after a required number have been developed, lest we die of overabundance. Such differentiation and integration are achieved by biochemical means that are only partly known. Much remains to be discovered about the regularity of our development, and why we do not randomly produce an eyeball growing out of a big toe or a toe in place of an ear.

The process of evolution is still going on—but indetectably slowly, compared with the rate of changes in our culture or in our individual lives. Cultural time is small, indeed, when compared with the millions of years required for the evolution of the species. One product of evolution is a specialized system for integrating complex organisms, the nervous system. Our complex nervous system appears to give us distinct advantages, such as the capacity to develop tools and to pass on culture through speech and writing. Yet the foundations of tool use and communication are seen in primates near us on the evolutionary scale. Observations of complex mammals reveal their capacity to learn, to modify their behavior through interactions with their environments and with others.

It is through evolution that we have developed a nervous system that is programmed partly on the basis of genetic information. Portions of the nervous system that evolved earlier regulate the vital vegetative systems of our bodies so well that by and large we are unaware of them and their efficiency. These portions of our nervous system appear to have much in common with those of other species. It is in the later-evolved portions of the cerebrum (which lies on top of the "older" brain) that complex learning, memory, speech, and thinking are organized. These portions of the nervous system are organized through experience. This plastic ability to be programmed by experience also comes to us through evolution.

Evolution has given us a nervous system that has the potential to learn and, indeed, to reorganize in the event of brain injury. Insofar as the results or content of individual learning are additive in a society, the society forms a culture so that we learn and transmit the necessary activities and rituals of living. This transmission across generations of culture is not accomplished by genes. Rather, information is passed along through speech and modeling behavior, since human beings need each other for sexual interaction, protection, and obtaining of food. Compared with the slow process of genetic evolution, changes in cultural directions can be very rapid. We can look within our cultural backgrounds for similarities in how we learn to grow up and grow old within a society.

Development as Part of Culture

Healthy children go through a period of puberty in which their adult reproductive capacity becomes established. This happens in all cultures, but the rites of celebrating the passage vary from group to group. The relatively stable part of every culture creates roles and expectations deemed appropriate at specific ages. Some cultural expectations are derived from a biological basis; that is, physical factors limit such functions as walking, talking, and other complex skills. Society's expectations for behavior are called *norms*, and they make it possible for families to know when their children are ahead or behind in the development of some socially approved behavior. Older individuals know whether they are ahead of or behind some norm, such as having a job at a particular level. Many norms of society are tied to age, and—although it is not always clear—there is an age status system to which we all are exposed. An *age status system* refers to the rights, privileges, and customs that are attached to particular ages. Along with the genetic programming of changes over the life span that controls our development, the programming of experience in our culture leads to norms and the age status system. One way of describing this cultural programming of change is in terms of developmental tasks.

A *developmental task* is a complex of stimuli and approved responses that give rise to expectations and norms. Starting school, dating, marriage, and retirement are all developmental tasks that we tend to face at characteristic times during our lives. Sometimes the transition through a developmental task is regarded as a *stage* of development. Thus an individual may be said to be in the "adolescent stage," implying that we can distinguish among the individual's

The extent of genetic and cultural influences on the development of sex roles and behavior is the focus of much current discussion and controversy.

Jean-Claude Lejeune, Stock, Boston, Inc.

behaviors before, during, and after the transition. A stage is a position in an ordered sequence. In terms of psychology, this sequence can be programmed or paced both by genetic development and by exposure to the developmental tasks of a particular society. Given a favorable environment, a butterfly will go through a developmental sequence from its larval stage to winged adulthood. There is a loose similarity between this biological metamorphosis, influenced by genetics, and our human behavioral development, influenced by a sequence of developmental tasks that we face as we grow up and grow old.

Part of our development as males and females results from genetic programming, and part results from cultural "patterning." The extent of each influence in determining particular sex differences in behavior is the subject of much discussion and controversy regarding sex differences and roles in society. One question being asked by developmental psychologists is precisely how much our culture encourages the development of independent behavior in boys and dependent behavior in girls. Also, the question must be raised as to why most cultures show a pattern of sex differences in behavior. Does sex-role differentiation have some utility for a society? What inherent temperamental differences exist between the sexes, if any? Such questions come to the fore as contemporary people examine their development and ponder their destinies.

The Age Structure of Society

One significant determinant of a society's needs is its age composition. A society made up mostly of young people has different emphases than one consisting mostly of older adults. America has been a young society in the sense that until recently it has had a high proportion of young persons. The situation now is different, and there are at least three causes for the "aging" of America. First, in previous decades the country attracted many immigrants who wanted to make their way in the New World. Immigrants tended to be young adults looking for a livelihood, and their influx tended to keep the country young. But immigration to America slowed and then stopped for a while during the Depression of the early 1930s. Recently, it has started to rise again. Two other changes in this century that have resulted in an older age structure are the dramatic fall in the death rate of infants and children during the first half-century, and the decline of the birth rate. If our desire to have a limited population prevails, then zero population growth will result in a still older population on the average. Figure 1.2 is a population pyramid that shows the size of populations in each age range and the relative size of male and female populations. From 1900 to 1980 there was a marked shift in the age structure of our society. Not only has the older population increased at a higher rate than the population as a whole, but beyond early adulthood there are more females than males, a difference that increases with age so that by age sixty-five there are 146 females to every 100 males.

Changes in the age structure of our society have psychological and economic effects. For example, teen-agers have different consumer habits than do middle-aged and older adults, so that industry will have to shift its marketing practices as older adults without children seek different products, services, and

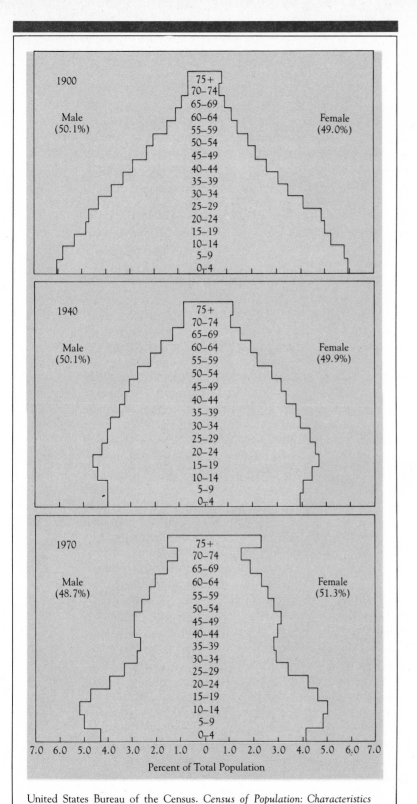

FIGURE 1.2
Population pyramids
showing percentage of
males and females in
each age group in the
United States.

United States Bureau of the Census. *Census of Population: Characteristics of the Population.* 1940, 1970.

13

leisure-time activities. There may be some benefits to this shift in age structure. As children become less common, they may be seen in more detail and may be appreciated more as individuals, rather than being lost in a sea of resented youngsters. Similarly, as more grandmothers and grandfathers live to later years, they may provide a perspective and emotional balance by which other generations may gain insight into their lives as a whole. Perhaps both young and old have been ignored somewhat in the population stampede of our pioneering society. In any case, we have arrived almost at the point of a stable state: society today has a low death rate, a low birth rate, and also a relatively low immigration rate. Not only is America older as a society, but it also is older in terms of age structure. This will affect behavior in future generations. However, as we have suggested, the consequences need not be bad. Freed from the pressures of ongoing population growth, we may come to appreciate in greater detail those of us who are here.

The Cultural Value of Developmental Psychology

Understanding one's origins in history is accepted as part of maturing. School systems require the study of history as a basis for understanding our institutions and the flow of important events and decisions. By learning about past mistakes and successes, a generation gains insight that increases its possibilities for wise decisions. But there is another reason for teaching history: to transmit respect for society's institutions. In this way we teach our young to carry forward the institutions and to adopt the social roles and behaviors associated with them. This process is termed *socialization*. Sometimes socialization is carried to a point where the young become convinced that their institutions are infallibly the best, and that they themselves are better in most respects than all other groups and are ultimately chosen for a special destiny. When a society has a state religion as well, it may teach its young that God has singled them out as favored children. Such socialization has a purpose different from the study of history, however. As a social science, history should portray as objectively as possible the flow of events leading to an understanding of society's processes.

Similarly, developmental psychology is concerned with the flow of events in the development of individuals. Its task is to describe these events as objectively as possible, leading to an understanding of the forces in human development. Individual histories are shorter than the history of a society. Also, within limits, we can perform experiments and controlled studies of human development. The results of this research lead to a body of knowledge that can rise above the particulars of any one group. Thus if adolescents need to become independent in their identities and move toward or away from adult controls, such a need—which in some instances can be expressed as hostile rebellion—can be generalized. It then becomes a matter of understanding the characteristic ways in which adolescents establish their identities. What institutions give adolescents the opportunity to act out this important drama?

There is considerable cultural value in knowing the underlying behavioral mechanisms in individual development that interact with the opportunities for growth. For this reason, life-span developmental psychology might be taught to high school students along with history so that each generation of students could increase the opportunities for all individuals to reach their greatest potential.

Social Roles and Norms

Individuals in society play or fill many different social roles. We may be spouse, lover, child, parent, teacher, student, doctor, patient, and so on. The significant thing about social roles is that rules go with them, often implicitly, so that they are acquired not by reading but through experience. For example, we expect different behavior from a physician than from the local bartender. And some rules are more clear than others. To become a physician requires specific training as well as an examination by a state board; in contrast, a bartender may need no educational prerequisite other than experience. In growing up, we come to differentiate the roles in society and to understand the rules that govern them. Children may not know the differences between the roles of a plumber or a city plumbing inspector, but homeowners do—including what to expect of each.

As mentioned earlier, social roles are associated with norms. Norms are like rules, except that they refer to what others expect. Thus an individual's performance or behavior may be judged to be below the standard, or norm, that is expected for a specific role. Children may be taken away from a mother if her performance is judged by a court to fall below the norm for maternal care. A physician may be sued for performance that is judged below standard for the treatment of a patient. Social roles and their rules and norms are central concerns of sociology and social psychology. How roles are acquired and how one

Roles, expectations, and norms—particularly age norms—are central concerns of developmental psychology.

George S. Zimbel, Photo Researchers, Inc.   Michael Abramson, Black Star comes to appreciate norms and expectations are important issues in developmental psychology. Particularly important, of course, are age norms.

Society has many age norms. Some are vague, whereas others are explicit enough to be written into law. For example, the age at which one becomes a citizen and can hold property without guardianship was changed in the last decade from twenty-one to eighteen. The age at which a child must have started school is usually between the sixth and seventh birthday, although children may enter nursery school or kindergarten earlier. (Nursery school and kindergarten are usually optional, in contrast to the required entrance into elementary school.) To enter school a child is expected to show some minimal physical and psychological maturity. Norms include such things as being able to use the toilet, being emotionally prepared to endure the separation from the mother, being able to use a fork for eating, and being able to talk and communicate with others. Other behaviors also may be considered when determining whether a child is near enough to the norms of the age group to be admitted without undergoing too much stress and without disrupting the group.

Norms for physical growth have been studied by researchers, and parents often use them in comparing their children with the average. For most purposes, a standard of growth or behavior that is accepted as "normal" includes statistically about two-thirds of the population. Pediatricians are often consulted by parents who wonder whether their child is normal. Some parents are not content even with normal development, wanting their child to be above normal in all respects. Such parents tend to be avid collectors of normative data about physical growth and the ages at which children usually begin to smile, turn over, crawl, walk, talk, speak in complete sentences, read, and so on—not to mention material about the social behaviors of adolescents. One well-known early researcher of development, Arnold Gesell (1943), published a book to guide parents through the early development of their children. By consulting the book, parents could find evidence as to whether their child was showing a typical profile of behavior, or "normal" behavior for the age level. There may be less preoccupation today about what is normal for four-year-olds or five-year-olds. Yet it seems likely that there will always be norms for professional persons to use in judging the appropriateness of a particular child's behavior and for many families to use in comparing their children with others.

The *intelligence quotient*, or IQ, is a common measure of intellectual development. As originally conceived, it was the ratio of a child's mental age (in months) to his or her chronological age (in months). This ratio was then multiplied by 100, so that children who were at the average for their age group had an IQ of 100. A child's mental age was determined by means of a battery of tests that required thought and concentration. By testing many children, researchers could construct norms by which a particular child's performance could be compared with the performance of other children in the group. On this basis they could assign a mental age—the age at which most children passed the tests. Among the more widely used measures of children's intelligence was the Stanford-Binet, an individually administered test. The normal range of intelligence for this particular test was 100 ± 16, or from 84 to 116.

These examples are offered not to assess the merits of a particular test but rather to illustrate that norms may be based on objective data. Intelligence tests were developed because of the need to distinguish between young schoolchildren who might be intelligent but acted as though they were retarded, and children who did not have the mental capacity to keep pace in a normal classroom. Before intelligence testing, it was more likely that the opinions of school administrators and teachers might cause even bright children with motivational and behavioral problems to be sent to an institution for the mentally retarded. Intelligence tests provided an objective way to assess children's competence for classroom learning.

The pressure for objective assessment rather than arbitrary rules also relates to other age groups. In the past, for example, individuals faced forced retirement at age sixty-five because of an employer's rules. Recently, however, the idea that one's functional age might be measured objectively and that such measures might be used to indicate an individual's ability to perform job duties has gained in popularity. If age is judged to be an artificial standard for retirement and its use is found by the courts to be illegally discriminating, then industry may have to shift to objective measurements of work capability. Nonetheless, social opinion will continue to play an important role in whether objective evidence is to be considered. For example, even though the United States government regards eighteen-year-olds as being of legal age, some states still do not allow them to purchase alcoholic drinks. Besides the legal age norm about drinking, informed opinion requires that other factors be considered as well, such as the capacity of the liver to metabolize the alcohol and the response of the nervous system in terms of impaired coordination and judgment. Then, too, a society simply may not wish to consider objective evidence, preferring to base its judgments on moral grounds. Thus in contrast to our general society, Mormons do not use alcohol, coffee, or tea. Similarly, the controversy surrounding marijuana—particularly by young adults and adolescents—is a mixture of moral judgments and objective evidence about its effects.

Norms, then, can have an objective character when used to assess the capacities and behaviors of an individual in comparison with others in the same age and sex group. Other reference groups also may be used, such as racial or ethnic groups and socioeconomic or educational levels. But norms also indicate a group's judgment about what is appropriate behavior for a particular individual in a given situation. In this sense, norms are established not by measurement but by what the *group expects* and what, therefore, is usual. Custom and the expectations of others greatly determine the norms we use in deciding what we should do and in judging the behavior of others. The process of acquiring these norms, or socialization, occurs within an individual; it is internalized. However arbitrary this powerful relationship between age and social expectations is, it exerts an important controlling force on our behavior.

Social Expectations

Throughout life there are strong reminders about our behavior in relation to our age. Young people in the armed services know whether they are ahead of or behind their class. They are bitter if they are passed over for promotion, and elated if they are promoted before others their age who entered service at the same time. Being on time, early, or late in one's career is something most

The Stages of Life: A Life-Cycle Calendar

ROBERT SELIM AND THE EDITORS OF THE FUTURIST

	Infancy and Early Childhood (0–5)	Late Childhood (5–12)	Adolescence (12–18)
Family	Mother is the center of universe. But child's behavior varies from complete devotion to unpredicability to outright rebellion. Dramatic changes in child's behavior can occur in only six months.	Still very dependent on mother, but goes to extremes of affection or dislike. Proud of father, family, and home. Generally good with siblings.	Family gradually becomes less important. Often, there is open rebellion; adolescents feel the need to break away from family. Occasional embarrassment over parents or siblings.
Education and Employment	Children are just entering school. Different children show a wide range of skills and interest in letters and numbers.	Children most often like school, sometimes devoted to teacher. Increasingly comfortable with the three R's. Behavior varies from studiousness to boredom to explosive activity.	Adolescents vary in opinion of school and teacher. Some very enthusiastic, others openly hostile. Many students concerned about college. Beginning to get part-time jobs after school and full-time jobs in the summer.
Entertainment	Infant's first activity is simple sight—then interest in toys and objects, crawling, throwing, exploring, toddling, eventually leading to the crayons and puzzles of nursery school and kindergarten.	Swimming, roller skating, climbing, swinging, bicycling, simple ball games, jigsaw puzzles. Children this age collect anything and everything. Growing interest in organized sports and activities.	Some of the same activities as in childhood, but more emphasis on organized sports. Growing interest in individual sports such as tennis and golf. Countless activities after school. Movies, parties, drug use.
Friends	Children make friends easily at about age three and grow more social, with occasional lapses, from then on. By age five many children are sure of themselves and at ease with almost everyone.	Considerable quarreling among friends, but some moments of good cooperation. Children this age begin to feel the importance of peer groups. Opinion of family members may be less valued than that of peers.	Friends become almost all-important. Prefer friends to family. Dating begins. Both sexes tend to socialize with large groups of friends. First sexual experience and increasing sexual activities.
Personal Growth	Children speed through the developmental stages at a dizzying pace. Growth is marked by alternating stages of equilibrium and disequilibrium.	Children go through stages of introversion and extroversion. Steadily becoming more self-assured and independent.	Important physical and pschological changes. Puberty. Extended periods of self-analysis and withdrawal give adolescents a firmer grip on themselves.

Source: *The Futurist*, February 1979, published by the World Future Society, 4916 St. Elmo Avenue, Washington, D.C. 20014.

Young Adulthood (18–25)	Adulthood (25–40)	Middle Age (40–65)	Retirement Years (65 and over)
Most people have left home. Many begin their own families.	Most people are married and have children. Many divorces occur in this stage. Single people often finally get married. Married couples may choose to have children before child-bearing years end.	Family size may decrease as children leave home. Parents of middle-aged people are dying. Some middle-aged couples become grandparents.	Many will be grandparents. Many may find themselves alone due to the death of a spouse. Women, especially, may spend many years alone.
Many young adults are in college; some continue education after college. Most begin working. Many unemployed or underemployed. Career choices assume special importance for some.	Some adults go back to school. Many change jobs. Married women may re-enter the work force. Increased emphasis on furthering career for bread-winners, who now have growing financial responsibilities.	Most workers are at the height of their careers. This is the stage of the most power and prestige at the work-place. For many, it brings the realization that their career can go no further. Some pick second careers.	Workers begin to retire. They may travel, resume education, develop new hobbies. For women who have stayed in the home, the job continues. Income will probably shrink.
Some organized athletics. Less recreation and more entertainment. Continued drug use, especially alcohol.	Spectator sports, travel, entertaining. Many start new hobbies such as pottery, painting, or photography.	Entertaining, travel, more expensive vacations. Hobbies may develop into second careers.	Increased opportunities to travel, entertain, spend time with relatives, concentrate on avocations, do volunteer work, etc., if money and health permit.
Friends and peer groups still very important. Single men and women searching for partners. Continuing emphasis on sexual activity.	Importance of friends declines as family size increases. Adults depend less on the opinions of peers to judge themselves.	As children leave home, friends may become somewhat more important. Sexual activity may decline.	Friends and peers are dying. There is more time to spend with those that remain. Old acquaintances are renewed.
The developmental pace slows and stages become less obvious. Psychologist Erik Erikson calls this the "intimacy vs. isolation" stage—a time for testing one's identity and growing further or hiding it and stagnating.	A stage of creation and production, often accompanied by dissatisfaction with past choices and an urge to change directions in order to build a new and more solid life.	A mid-life crisis may come as individuals confront their own mortality and the consequences of choices already made.	The individual comes to accept his past, his life, and the approach of death, or grows bitter and despairing.

people understand during their employment. While military service has a clearly defined age system, other occupations may have less clear signs of advance. Yet even artists, writers, and other creative persons may often compare themselves with some *internal standard* of where they are with respect to where they expected to be at a certain age.

Through experience, individuals learn the age-appropriate behaviors that are approved by society—as well as the consequences for violating the rules. For example, we use different speech patterns with people our own age than with people who are much older. Seated between two strangers at a lunch counter, we make judgments about their ages and select our speech accordingly. Although young people might use current slang with someone the same age to ask for the salt or sugar, they are more likely to open their request with "Excuse me, please" if the person is their parents' age.

While age norms are not the only norms used in our society, they are widespread and form an important topic for developmental psychology. As stated earlier, developmental psychology traditionally focused on socialization and the development of age norms during childhood and adolescence. More recently, socialization has been viewed as a process that continues throughout the life span. Learning to "act your age" by showing appropriate behavior is, therefore, an ongoing process.

Moreover, we are generally sensitive to what others expect of us. For example, a young woman usually knows when her family expects her to marry or to have a child, and she knows whether she is ahead of or behind this schedule. She may give her personal opinion about this and the extent to which she can violate what is expected. Neugarten et al. (1968) reported research indicating that there is general agreement among most people as to appropriate age-related behavior, such as when to marry, when to have one's top job, and when to retire. Personal opinions of individuals are less rigid, however; individuals may know what most people think but personally feel that they are more liberal with regard to age norms. Young women appear to be more sensitive to the demands of age norms than men, perhaps reflecting the dependency that is fostered in their upbringing. Nonetheless, both men and women clearly perceive society's age norms and how they affect behaviors that range all the way from knowing how to treat someone on a date to contemplating remarriage in later life.

The Range of Individual Differences

Besides identifying the social expectations that arise with age norms, we also recognize how we differ from these norms. One of the cultural values in studying developmental psychology is that we can perceive in even greater detail not only how we personally differ from the norms but also the wide range of individual differences in behavior.

Through developmental psychology we can alternate between the perspective of what we have in common—what we share with others as we grow and mature—and the perspective of how we differ from others. Clearly, every individual is unique. The circumstances of each individual's physical and social environments, his or her physical growth and development of behavior, and the sequences of experiences that affect that individual's goals, motivations, and opportunities will never be repeated for another human being. Even our genetic makeup is unique (Medwar, 1957). Acceptance of an organ transplant is difficult even from a brother or sister. Exceptions to genetic uniqueness are identical (one-egg) twins or multiplets, who do have the same genetic structure. But even for them, environmental differences before birth may bring about different fetal growth rates, depending on their share of the blood supply in the uterus.

The acceptance of our individual differences represents an important cultural advance. In the last century, children were regarded as willful if they did not keep in step with their class or adult expectations. With the advance of the concept of individual differences, we learned to accept not only different growth rates in young children but also different spurts in growth and maturation and different rates of aging in late life. At all ages there are early developers, late developers, and irregular developers. Acceptance of individual differences means that we do not expect others always to perceive the same event as we do and that this is not a matter of being right or wrong. Appreciating our differences provides us with an unlimited opportunity to learn from our fellow human beings. It also adds an important concept to the governance of society: by its nature a society must be pluralistic and provide opportunities for the wide range of individual differences among us.

Technically, the question may be raised as to whether human beings show a wider range of differences in one trait than in another. However, it is not possible to say statistically whether the range of differences in intelligence, for example, is greater or smaller than the range of differences in personality. Nonetheless, although we cannot technically compare the range of individual differences in behavior, conceptually an important advance was made when we first recognized that individual differences are to be expected and are the rule, not the exception, for all human traits.

Appreciating the Lawfulness of Change over the Life Span

Also of cultural significance is the observation that change rather than constancy marks the human life span. We expect that adolescents have different leisure-time interests than retired adults and that an open society should provide outlets for individual differences not only within age groups but also between age groups. The belief that change over the life span is predictable is what spurs developmental psychologists on in their research. In fact, a major puzzle of development is that, despite a large turnover in our chemical composition, we do remain the "same person." Not only is there a turnover in our chemistry as atoms come and go in our structure, but many body cells constantly turn over in the sense that old ones die and are replaced by young ones. Skin tissue is a prime example; old cells die and are sloughed off at the surface, while new ones are generated by cell division at the basic level of the skin. Blood cells and cells that line the digestive tract also are replaced continuously. What gives the human body and organism stability in the face of chemical and structural turnover?

Apparently, not all structures turn over. For example, a scar from a child-hood accident may remain for life. And the cells of the nervous system that integrate behavior—the neurons—do not divide after fetal life. These cells may grow larger, but they do not divide and increase their number or replace dead cells. Herein lies the natural lawfulness of change over the life span: some systems accumulate experience. Otherwise, change would be disorderly. Be-cause the cells of the nervous system are with us from birth and accumulate experience, we can recognize the uniqueness of our own history in comparison with others. The immunological system also has memory in the sense that recovery from an infectious disease may impart immunity if we encounter that disease in the future. Knowledge about the lawfulness of change in the human organism over the life span is by no means a finished business. Much remains to be discovered on the biological and psychological levels. But an appreciation of the need for such information is a mark of an enlightened society.

Developmental Psychology as an Aid to Personal Adaptation

Personal Experience

Knowing something about developmental psychology helps not only parents of growing children but also individuals of all ages. Understanding that similar developmental tasks face us at characteristic ages reduces the stress that may arise from those tasks. First, we can see that we are not unusual or abnormal. Second, if we know about the range of responses possible, we can choose behavior that best suits our personalities and lifestyles. Recognizing that retired people range from passive rocking-chair types to energetic, active individuals—and yet both derive high satisfaction from their lives—may help individuals realize they don't have to conform narrowly to what others expect or think, or lead a life that is unsuited to them. Similarly, adolescents identifying with sexual roles can adapt better if they understand not only the norms of society but also the range of individual differences from those norms. Such knowledge can reduce tensions at the transition points in the human life span, when specific developmental tasks may bring about undue stress and indecision.

Knowledge of developmental psychology also gives information about and insight into lifestyles outside one's family or personal experience. Awareness of individual differences increases the range of options for our own lives. This helps us to avoid undue pressures to conform to patterns that are not suited to our particular abilities and unique experiences. Indeed, it helps us to adjust to the demands of a changing society in which many options disappear while new ones emerge.

Knowledge about the different forces that shape people's lives also helps us construct productive and contented lives for ourselves. Insight into one's family background is enhanced by knowledge about other family patterns. For exam-ple, a family pattern that stresses achievement for school-aged children can be contrasted to a pattern that underplays achievement, allowing individuals to

The enormous range of individual differences frees each human being to express unique abilities and pursue personal goals.

Jean-Claude Lejeune, Black Star

evaluate and adjust to such influences on their own. The essential point is that by knowing about the norms of society, the range of individual differences, and one's own personality and abilities, an individual can exercise choice and control over life and avoid patterns that have a higher probability of bringing stress and despair.

Careers

As people become better educated, they want a higher standard of living. They expect educational and psychological benefits as well as material and physical gains. There is a vast range of problems for which our society and informed people everywhere want solutions. But solutions require painstaking, creative research by trained scientists. In terms of educational and psychological benefits, there is pressure to increase the school readiness and reading capability of all children, as well as the learning capability of retarded individuals. Society also wants knowledge that will reduce the problems for severely deviant children, such as autistic children who cannot or will not communicate and socially deviant children who set fires or hurt others.

The major transition points in the life span tend to awaken personal issues. A person who is faced with a particularly important task may not be able to

Where Jobs Will (and Won't) Be in the 80's

Listed below are the job prospects in selected categories through the mid-1980's. The list is based on unpublished data from the U.S. Bureau of Labor Statistics. The growth in the number of jobs expected in the coming decade in each field is indicated next to the job titles. In cases where jobs opportunities will drop—such as for secondary-school teachers—the change is shown with a minus sign.

Professional, Technical, and Kindred

Engineers 22.9
Aero-Astronautic 12.7
Chemical 18.4
Civil 21.6
Electrical 21.1
Industrial 25.6
Mechanical 19.3
Metallurgical 27.2
Mining 44.3
Petroleum 37.3
Sales 18.7

Life and Physical Scientists 25.8
Agricultural 27.5
Atmospheric, space 7.2
Biological 34.9
Chemists 20.5
Geologists 42.5
Marine 26.8
Physicists and Astronomers 15.8

Mathematics Specialists 25.9
Actuaries 23.9
Mathematicians 34.0
Statisticians 23.0

Science Technicians 25.9
Agricultural, Biological (except health) 6.5
Chemical 12.7
Drafters 28.2

Source: *New York Times*, October 14, 1979, p. 9.
Copyright 1979 by The New York Times Company.
Reprint by permission.

Electrical, Electronic 21.4
Industrial Engineering 29.7
Mathematical 49.0
Mechanical Engineering 24.0
Surveyors 38.9
Engineering, Science 11.7

Medical Workers 33.1
Chiropractors 30.1
Dentists 18.4
Dietitians 13.6
Optometrists 17.6
Pharmacists 14.8
Physicians, M.D., Osteopaths 36.6
Podiatrists 12.7
Registered Nurses 35.4
Therapists 47.3
Veterinarians 29.2
Clinical Laboratory Technologists 42.8
Dental Hygenists 118.9

Technicians (Except Health) 32.2
Airplane Pilot 30.4
Air-Traffic Controllers 32.9
Flight Engineers 31.2
Radio Operators 30.7

Computer Specialists 27.3
Computer Programmers 25.1
Computer Systems Analysts 30.5
Other Computer Specialists 30.4

Social Scientists 30.1
Economists 26.9
Political Scientists 22.7
Psychologists 33.8
Sociologists 28.2
Urban and Regional Planners 41.1

Teachers 3.7
Adult-Education Teachers 33.9
College and University 3.0
Elementary School 9.8
Preschool, Kindergarten 25.0
Secondary School -11.3

Entertainers and Other Artists 15.6
Actors 13.7
Athletes and Kindred Workers 13.1
Authors -3.2
Dancers 22.2
(continued)

Designers 20.4
Editors and Reporters 23.8
Musicians and Composers 17.8
Painters and Sculptors 4.1
Photographers 9.7
Radio and Television Announcers 29.8

Other Professional, Technical 18.6
Accountants 19.1
Architects 52.2
Archivists and Curators 6.4
Clergy 5.4
Religious (Except Clergy) 11.0
Foresters, Conservationists 14.5
Judges 6.8
Lawyers 18.9
Librarians 11.2
Operations, Systems Research 31.9
Personnel, Labor Relations 31.9
Research Workers −22.3
Recreation Workers 20.8
Social Workers 29.7
Vocation, Education Counselors 18.6

Managers, Officials, and Proprietors

Buyers, Sales, Loan Managers 35.2
Bank, Financial Managers 41.2
Credit Managers 13.2
Buyers, Wholesale, Retail 39.8
Purchasing Agents, Buyers 34.9
Sales Manager, Retail Trade 31.7
Other Sales Managers 32.9

Administrators, Inspectors 22.8
Health Administrators 45.0
Officials, Administrators, Public 20.8
Postmasters, Mail Supervisors −8.3
College Administrators 15.9
School Administrators 16.2

Other Managers, Officials 17.6
Funeral Directors 0.0
Building Managers, Superintendents 36.7
Office Managers 39.6

Sales Workers

Advertising Agents 30.6
Auctioneers 1.6

Demonstrators 6.7
Insurance Agents, Brokers 18.6
Newspaper Carriers and Vendors −19.4
Real-Estate Agents, Brokers 27.5
Stock and Bond Sales Agents 15.4

Clerical Workers

Secretarial 33.3
Secretaries, Legal 50.0
Secretaries, Medical 80.3
Secretaries, Other 37.3
Stenographers −22.0
Typists 20.0

Office-Machine Operators −0.1
Bookkeeping, Billing Operators 27.5
Calculating-Machine Operators 18.8
Computer, Peripheral Equipment 18.0
Keypunch Operators −26.8

Other Clerical 28.9
Bank Tellers 21.3
Billing Clerks 47.5
Bookkeepers 12.6
Cashiers 30.5
Collectors, Bill and Accounts 25.0
Counter Clerks, Except Food 23.8
File Clerks 19.0
Library Attendents, Assistant 17.5
Mail Carriers, Post Office 0.1
Postal Clerks −11.0
Real-Estate Appraisers 28.7
Receptionists 27.5
Teachers' Aides 54.4
Telegraph Messengers −50.0
Telegraph Operators −29.3
Telephone Operators 0.3

Crafts and Kindred Workers

Construction Crafts Workers 30.0
Carpenters and Apprentices 24.5
Brick and Stonemasons, Apprentices 18.1
Bulldozer Operators 49.6
Electricians and Apprentices 24.3
Painters and Apprentices 21.3
Paperhangers 50.0
Plumbers, Pipefitters and Apprentices 38.0
(continued)

Metal-Craft Workers   18.3
Machinists and Apprentices   16.8
Sheetmetal Workers and Apprentices   24.9
Tool and Diemakers, Apprentices   17.1

Mechanics, Repairers, Installers   19.9
Air-Conditioning, Heating, and Refrigeration
Mechanics   60.2
Aircraft Mechanics   25.5
Auto-Body Repairers   15.0
Auto Mechanics and Apprentices   16.0
Heavy Equipment Mechanics   13.5
Household-Appliance Mechanics   19.5
Radio, Television Repairers   31.6

Printing-Trades Workers   3.9
Bookbinders   6.3
Compositors and Typesetters   −7.9
Photoengravers, Lithographers   23.1
Pressmen and Apprentices   11.5

Other Crafts, Kindred Workers   11.5
Bakers   −1.5
Cabinetmakers   7.5
Crane, Derrick, Hoist Operators   25.8
Decorators, Window Dressers   23.0
Jewelers and Watchmakers   9.1
Shoe Repairers   −4.0
Tailors   4.2

Operatives

Operatives (Except Transport)   16.8
Semiskilled Metalworking   20.6
Grinding Machine   −1.5
Lathe, Milling Machine   26.5
Solderers   −24.9
Welders and Flame Cutters   26.4

Other Operatives   17.7
Assemblers   33.3
Dressmakers, Except Factory   −12.0
Garage Workers, Station Attendents   4.9
Meatcutters, Butchers   6.4

Transportation Operatives   11.4
Bus Drivers   −5.7
Delivery and Route Workers   11.9
Parking Attendants   6.3

Taxicab Drivers, Chauffeurs   0.0
Truck Drivers   13.5

Service Workers

Cleaning-Service Workers   20.2
Building-Interior Cleaners   28.6
Lodging Cleaners   78.5

Food-Service Workers   24.1
Bartenders   18.8
Cooks (except private)   26.6
Dishwashers   16.7
Food-Counter, Fountain Workers   35.2
Waiters   19.5

Health-Service Workers   42.3
Dental Assistants   47.6
Health Aides (except nursing)   52.9
Nurses Aides, Orderlies   35.0
Practical Nurses   54.6

Personal-Service Workers   26.4
Flight Attendants   79.3
Baggage Porters and Bellhops   −6.2
Barbers   1.6
Bootblacks   −54.6
Child-Care Workers   62.7
Elevator Operators   −25.6
Hairdressers, Cosmetologists   16.7
Housekeepers (except private)   11.6

Protective and Service   33.1
Firefighter   23.8
Guards   36.0
Police and Detectives   37.6

Farm Workers

Farmers and Farm Managers   −33.1
Farmers (Owners and Tenants)   −34.6
Farm Managers   56.0
Farm Laborers, Supervisors   −12.9
Laborers, Wage Earners   −43.3
Laborers, Unpaid Family   −15.3

resolve the crisis and its associated emotional stress and inability to meet the demands of others. Sometimes, the major transition points and life crises become so urgent that professional help may be sought or recommended. At such times, the professional services available must be based on solid research in developmental psychology. The expansion of such research and the careers that apply it will have increasingly important effects on society in the future.

Research Research in developmental psychology ranges all the way from studies of animal behavior and the neurochemistry of their developing and aging brains to research involving the social character of human subjects, including social roles, moral behavior, and group behavior. Indeed, new careers in research are created continually, as evidence is gathered about social and biological factors of development and aging. One important area concerns the effects of deprivation. Many people live their lives without realizing their potentials for effective behavior, contentment, and satisfaction. To understand a subject so complex as developmental psychology, we must break up the various elements of behavior into smaller units of manageable size for research. This often requires teamwork among various types of scientists and professionals. Thus it is not uncommon for developmental psychologists to work on a team with other scientists. For example, to study the early influences of deprivation on behavior, developmental psychologists may work with obstetricians and nutritionists to focus on the development of the fetus. So although the behavior

Developmental psychologists must share their research findings with sociologists, psychiatrists, educators, and other social scientists and professionals.

Cary Wolinsky, Stock, Boston, Inc.

of organisms and the manner of their development may be the focus of developmental psychologists, it is not their only concern. Increasingly it is recognized that neurobiologists, physiologists, geneticists, and other specialists have to cooperate in basic research, such as the development of communication among animals. Similarly, developmental psychologists must share their work in human research with sociologists, psychiatrists, and anthropologists, among others.

Prenatal behavior is one area of active research. How soon a fetus can respond to stimulation from the mother and from the outside environment has been a question of great interest to psychologists. Although we now know something about when response to stimulation is possible, we do not presently know enough about the importance of early stimulation. The effects of maternal diet, smoking, and drug use on a developing fetus also must be understood in greater detail. It is still difficult to separate the effects of maternal undernutrition from the effects of genetics and social deprivation.

One area of research thus involves those conditions of growth that provide a biological basis for optimal behavioral development. Developmental psychologists are concerned with the effects and interaction of inadequate nutrition and infectious diseases. Disease may change nutritional requirements so that a child on a normal diet may undergo a temporary deficiency state. Optimal protein in the diet is essential for the development of the nervous system. Between the extremes of deprivation—which in some areas of the world leaves children with a very low chance for survival—and the conditions for health are children whose lives can be improved to some extent. By examining the factors of physical development and how they affect behavioral capacities, we undoubtedly will discover ways to increase the number of persons who develop to their fullest.

New careers are being created in research into the effects of physical and social environments. Boring environments may be a form of deprivation in that they do not lead individuals to explore their surroundings. Severe environmental deprivation may lead to inadequate development of perceptual capacities, since early exploration of our surroundings seems necessary for development of these capacities. In examining the relationship of development to the environment, we probably will discover new influences on the limits of development, as well as recognize new diseases. It seems clear now that genetic defects, undernutrition, disease, and environmental influences result in a mixture that is associated with slow or abnormal physical growth, limited intellectual ability, and emotional and social disturbances. Future research in developmental psychology will have to separate these influences so that we can better control their undesirable outcomes.

Which personality traits and lifestyles seem associated with productive living and life satisfaction also needs further examination. With such knowledge, young people could be guided and helped toward the development of healthy lifestyles instead of the highly competitive, high-pressure patterns associated with the development of heart disease. Evidence is being gathered that behavior is related to the kinds of illnesses we develop as adults. For example, some lifelong patterns of behavior may be related to the environment of the fetus within the womb. Pregnant women and nursing mothers may respond to stress in ways that cause their child to acquire patterns of overexpression or underexpression of response to novel situations, such as in levels of hormones secreted by the adrenal gland, epinepherine or adrenalcorticoids (NICHD report, 1968, pp. 249-251).

As noted earlier, another important area of research lies in the basis of sex differences in behavior, both in developing children and in adults. In the past it often was assumed that behavioral sex differences—such as in social situations involving aggressiveness or dependency or in intellectual capacities such as verbal reasoning or spatial relations—were caused by the sex hormones, which, in turn, were influenced by genetic differences. More recently, research has shown that mothers and fathers give different stimulation to girls and to boys, which may influence the development of language, social behavior, and mental abilities. Much more research in the development of sex differences is needed in order to separate environmental influences from genetic effects. Such research will help us compare and understand inborn and acquired sex differences in behavior.

On the purely behavioral level, we need to know more about how the attitudes of parents are translated into their children's selection of opportunities to learn. Some early influences may result in later effects. By following individuals throughout the life span, we will be able to relate the effects of early and late development on competence and effectiveness in adulthood. For example, which early life experiences ease the transition of menopause and which make it traumatic? Which conditions of development are responsible for the differences between an active older person who at age ninety may be surfing and enjoying a satisfying personal and sexual life and the regressed older person who at age sixty has a failing memory and confused orientation? As more and more people live beyond age seventy-five, these and many related questions will be the focus of research. Growing older is a privilege of an advanced technological society, but it may not always be comfortable when families, industry, and public attitudes seem remarkably unprepared for an easy mixture of people of all ages.

We are also faced with basic questions about what supports the continuing growth of intellectual abilities from young adulthood through the adult life span. Large differences in abilities have appeared among the generations. Do these reflect improvements in education, or do they result from better physical growth, made possible by the elimination of many infectious diseases of childhood? New research careers in the psychophysiology of adult life will be directed at understanding the relationships of changing brain patterns and information processing in adults. Why do some adults lose their memories while others remain effective, creative, and intellectually rigorous? The greater tendency toward depression that comes with age requires new research insights, both from psychophysiological perspectives and from social and clinical approaches.

Much of this research may be conducted in the laboratories of medical schools and hospitals. Ideally, such institutions will have many positions for developmental psychologists, because such experts are needed to measure behavior differences in response to genetic, hormonal, or experimental factors. It is now impossible for one scientist to know all the relevant information and have all the research skills. Teams of scientists are required, and developmental psychologists will be essential team members. Some research will involve normally developing individuals, but in other instances it will be carried out with abnormally developing persons—for example, those with genetic defects that disturb normal sexual development in adolescence. Mental retardation is another area that requires the attention of teams of investigators. We have only begun to understand the influences of genetic defects, birth defects, and other factors that lead to impoverished behavioral development.

Besides the teamwork of people trained in the biological sciences, we need research that will involve the cooperation of developmental psychologists and social scientists with various backgrounds. For example, animal research suggests that early sensory stimulation and perhaps also social stimulation are necessary for the development of the fine structure of the nervous system. Apparently, the structure of the nervous system itself is influenced by early stimulation. Questions arise about the extent to which social and perceptual stimulation are related to some forms of mental retardation and to lifelong personality patterns associated with violent and aggressive behavior. More research will involve the real-life circumstances associated with proneness to alcohol and drug abuse, with expressions of sex-role differences, and with learning disabilities. Such research may be carried out in schools, in the community, or in various counseling centers.

At one end of the research continuum, we must examine in greater detail the effects of social deprivation; at the other end, we must consider environmental enrichment as well. Very likely, selected institutions such as schools increasingly will provide highly enriched environments that facilitate the development of motor, intellectual, and social skills. These skills are used by individuals whose personalities and temperaments greatly determine the choices and decisions made during a lifetime—decisions that in some instances will lead to improved standards of living and life satisfaction and in other instances to unhappiness and mental distress. Many people have mental health problems that are related to the emotional circumstances of their development, not to their abilities. Research in developmental psychology will increase the chances that future generations can better realize individual potentials for physical, intellectual, and personal development.

Clearly, future research will require many persons trained in developmental psychology. The knowledge gained will bring necessary improvements in educational systems, psychiatry, social work, and other areas. As society seeks more direct services from the helping professions, there will be an increased need for persons to enter the knowledge-building careers of research.

College Teaching   In the past, much experimental psychology was undertaken without regard for the development of individuals. Now more experimental work involves the processes of development itself, which will result in more teaching of the content of developmental psychology. In the past also, much college teaching of developmental psychology was related to the child, as though the child were an end in itself. Now more courses have a life-span orientation, such as is presented in this book. Sometimes the life span is cov-

As society has turned more and more to the services of the helping professions, the need has increased for trained professionals to pursue knowledge-building careers in research.

Peter Southwick, Stock, Boston, Inc.

ered in a series of courses—on the infant, child, adolescent, young adult, middle-aged adult, and aged adult. Besides specializing in one such phase, college teachers of developmental psychology should be trained to consider the life span as a whole. Another pattern that is likely to develop will require a life-span introductory course, offering a perspective on the forces that shape development throughout our lives. Following this, special courses will detail sensorimotor functions over the life span, intellectual abilities, personality and social roles, and more specialized topics in psychobiology. Few teachers now have the background needed to teach such courses, although the need for them is almost unlimited, given the large number of community colleges, four-year colleges, and universities in existence. As society turns more attention to the quality of life, research and teaching in developmental psychology will expand, providing new careers that carry with them the satisfaction that one is contributing to a better life.

Clinical Work   Many age-related problems need our attention, ranging from those of mute, deaf, blind, or spastic children to reading problems, adolescent maladjustment, child-parent conflict, job uncertainty, marriage problems, sexual maladjustment, difficulties adjusting to retirement, and many others. Individuals who find satisfaction in giving direct services to others will pursue more and more careers that help particular age groups. In addition, new kinds of clinical work are coming to the fore, such as helping the terminally ill to die with dignity or assisting the widowed to deal with their grief and develop new interests. Clinical work of this kind requires a thorough knowledge of normal development and change throughout the life span. Only by knowing the normal or usual patterns of behavior can we be sensitive to deviation. The widespread increase in the numbers of semiprofessional mental health therapists is evidence that many people seek advice and help. Clinical fields increasingly will need professionals who are well grounded in a life-span developmental psychology, and new areas in these fields will open as our sensitivity to issues increases.

Teacher Training Child psychology has always been taught to teachers in departments of educational training—using an approach that may lack the perspective that children are in the process of becoming adults. Education during childhood has long-range consequences for us as adults. By teaching children about development over the life span, we will help them in their personal development as well as in their interactions with siblings, parents, and grandparents. It is likely that more and more colleges will offer courses in this area. Furthermore, many adults are returning to school in middle age. Effective adult education requires that teachers grasp the abilities, motivation, and personalities of these mature students. Because of such trends, life-span developmental psychology will become more of an imperative in the curriculum of teacher training institutions.

Writing for the Public New careers also will become available for those who write well and know the principles of developmental psychology. Parents constantly search for written material to help them understand and deal with the problems of growing children. Similarly, professionally written self-help books are sought for a broad range of adult problems, from marital relations to motivational conflicts in one's job. Magazines are becoming increasingly popular outlets for material that is grounded in research—material that offers insights into developmental problems. Even movies that deal with developmental issues may offer career opportunities for writers. Also, college teaching uses much of this material, and consultants and writers are needed to translate technical research into interesting and understandable movies for classroom use.

Television is another medium that needs specialists in developmental psychology for its educational programming. Programs like "Sesame Street" and "Mister Rogers' Neighborhood" have increased the educational potential of television, and this potential will expand with cable and cassette television systems. More and more people will want to purchase cassettes for use at home. Increasingly, educational television series and privately owned cassettes will deal with developmental problems, providing even greater career potential for developmental psychologists in the preparation of scripts and exhibits.

Foundation Work Private foundations frequently give financial support to research and services in problem areas related to developmental psychology. Because private foundations often can work flexibly in helping to support research, they can respond to a problem quickly. And public foundations are also a feature of American society, as shown in the role played by the March of Dimes, the American Heart Association, and other such groups. These foundations collect public money to support research, training, and services in problem areas related closely to the concerns of developmental psychology. Such foundations are recognizing the importance of a developmental perspective, seeing the wisdom in Benjamin Franklin's adage, "An ounce of prevention is worth a pound of cure." Now that many major infectious diseases have been challenged or conquered, our major health problems represent disturbances of development and aging. For example, the March of Dimes now emphasizes prevention of birth defects, and the American Heart Association focuses on the prevention of strokes and heart attacks.

Effective prevention, however, requires knowledge about how problems develop and the critical periods at which we should intervene. Indeed, it seems reasonable to expect that in the future more foundations will deal with developmental problems throughout the life span. Foundations therefore will require persons with good training in life-span developmental psychology. They will seek professionals who are sensitive to the issues and problems, and able to design effective research projects and to translate financial investments into public benefits in training, research, and service projects. Those who seek such careers will find ample opportunities in foundation work.

Summary

1. There are many personal and cultural reasons for studying developmental psychology over the life span. Developmental psychology can offer insights into our concepts of ourselves and our development, as well as into issues relating to career planning. Knowledge of developmental psychology not only can lead us to help others but also may improve our own life adaptations.
2. The evolutionary, or phylogenic, viewpoint emphasizes the study of our development as genetically related organisms. Moreover, the processes of development and aging themselves are believed to have evolved over time.
3. Along with the genetic programming of changes over the life span that controls our development, the programming of experience in our culture leads to norms and the age status system. One way of describing this cultural programming of change is to view the events as developmental tasks.
4. An individual's performance or behavior may be judged in terms of social roles and norms. Of particular importance are group expectations regarding what is appropriate behavior for one's age and sex group. The process of acquiring these norms is called *socialization*.
5. Another cultural value in studying developmental psychology is that we can perceive in greater detail not only how we personally differ from society's norms but also the wide range of differences in behavior. Such knowledge can reduce tensions at the transition points in the human life span, when specific developmental tasks may bring about undue stress and indecision.
6. At times, the major transition points and life crises become sufficiently dominating that professional help may be sought or recommended. The professional services available must be based on solid research in developmental psychology. The expansion of such research and the careers that apply it will have increasingly important effects on society in the future.
7. The planning of future educational institutions and the control of the effects of social deprivation in our society require a perspective on the forces that operate on us throughout the life span. New careers will be created and will offer job opportunities of many types, ranging from research and teaching to clinical work and public service.

Chapter 2

History, Theories, and Methods

Early concepts about children and their development, and how these concepts evolved into the discipline of developmental psychology

The classification and uses of developmental theories, including their differences

The major developmental theories and theorists

The methods of research and their purposes

History

Early Concepts
Nineteenth-Century Concepts
Twentieth-Century Concepts

Perspectives on Developmental Psychology

The Range and Uses of Developmental Theories
The Classification of Theories
Differences in Developmental Theories

Major Developmental Theories

Cognitive Development
Psychoanalytic Theory
Learning Theory
Ethology
Organismic Point of View
An Overview of Developmental Theory

Methods of Research

Common Sense versus Science
Age as a Variable
Research Strategies
Realiability and Validity
Clinical Studies
Identical Twin Studies
Experimental Studies
Intervention
Research Designs
Bias in Measurement

Introduction

The purpose of this chapter is to give a perspective on developmental psychology by briefly reviewing its history. Over the last century there have been dramatic changes in our concepts of the nature of childhood and of the major social and biological forces that shape development. This chapter describes some major differences in theories and some of the leading scholars in the field. In addition, it examines the main research methods used to secure information. Finally, results from recent longitudinal studies are reported to illustrate how human behavior changes or remains constant from childhood to old age.

History

Early Concepts

Before the expansion of science during the nineteenth century, the main concepts and ideas about children were derived from religion. In fact, many schools were controlled by religious bodies, either under state religions or as church-connected schools. The emphasis was on correctness of behavior and on the discipline needed to attain well-behaved and respectful children. Thus in its beginnings child psychology was dominated by theology. But information eventually was sought about how children really *did* grow up, rather than how they *should* grow up. The naturalistic observation of children was undertaken when educated parents began to have time to observe their children's development and record it in baby biographies. Indeed, it became fashionable for a parent, a relative, or even a scientist to record the development of a child. Many baby biographies have been published—including the one Charles Darwin made of his child (Anderson, 1931)—and many remain unpublished. Sometimes these day-to-day records of a child's development were meticulous. To such records were added another source of information about development, the personal diary such as adolescents often keep. This detailed information about changes in individuals gave a practical basis to early efforts in child psychology.

Early thinking about aging arose from biological curiosity. In pursuing the development of modern science, Francis Bacon (1638) speculated on the biology of aging. And in 1835 a Belgian mathematician-astronomer, Quetelet, published a book in Paris under the title *On Man and the Development of His Faculties.* This important book contained many revolutionary ideas and included information about birth rates, death rates, and variations in development and aging. An important innovation of Quetelet's book was that it reported averages and ranges of the central tendencies of a group. It thus was an early example of the use of statistical data, and it advanced the concept of the *average person* around whom extremes are distributed. Quetelet viewed an individual as having characteristics that could be measured and found to conform with what we now call the normal curve. Furthermore, individual differences in the measured traits were related to social conditions. The belief arose that natural causes could be found for variations in how human beings grow up and grow old, in how they develop physically, intellectually, and socially. The publication of

Quetelet's book marks a clear break with the philosophical traditions of earlier centuries. Science became freer during the nineteenth century to speculate about natural causes in human phenomena, as earlier it had become possible to speculate about natural law in astronomy and physics (though not without some struggles on the part of pioneers).

Nineteenth-Century Concepts

After Quetelet, Charles Darwin contributed to the rapidly changing concept of humanity. Darwin placed our species in a chain of evolution in which we shared a common biological history with other species. No longer did people feel certain that they were created as a separate and special entity. Darwin's book, *On the Origin of Species,* was published in 1858, and the first edition was sold out in one day. Obviously, many people were ready for a new view of their position in the biological world. After Darwin, comparative research on other species could be used for clues about the biological and behavioral organization of human beings.

The conceptual revolution that resulted from Darwin's work needed two further elements to render the arguments more convincing: (1) a way of explaining the pathways of evolution, and (2) a mechanism for the transmission of characteristics. The explanation for the differentiation of species during evolution has become known as *natural selection*—the idea that those characteristics of plants and animals that aid survival within a particular environment will persist. Poorly adapted forms disappear. As environmental conditions change and mutations occur, new species develop. Thus humanity is seen as an evolving member of the animal kingdom that shares a common origin with other species. The mechanism for transmitting advantageous characteristics we now accept as being *heredity*. Shortly before publication of Darwin's book, Gregor Mendel, an Austrian monk, began experiments in crossing different strains of plants. He clearly showed that hereditary characteristics were carried by units that we now call *genes*. The mechanics and implications of genetic transmission are explored in Chapter 3.

Darwin's ideas influenced his cousin, Francis Galton, who might be described as the first English developmental psychologist. Galton was interested in individual differences among measured traits in populations of people. At the London Exposition of 1884, which was held for six subsequent years at the South Kensington Museum, Galton's assistants made a variety of measurements on nearly ten thousand visitors ranging from children to older adults. The analysis of these data required statistical techniques, some of which Galton himself attempted to develop. It was he who first measured the degree of association between two variables—the index of correlation—and he left his personal estate to establish the first professorship of biostatistics. This was created at University College, London. New statistical methods made possible the testing of ideas on an objective basis—another significant contribution of nineteenth-century thought.

Galton also began studies of twins, since observation suggests that twins are more similar in appearance and behavior than other children within the same

The publication of Charles Darwin's *On the Origin of Species* in 1858 revolutionized people's thinking about their place in the biological world.

Culver Pictures, Inc.

family. Twin studies are still used today for a variety of purposes, including attempts to establish the roles of heredity and environment in determining individual differences in intelligence, personality, and other characteristics.

The nineteenth century was a bubbling ferment of ideas. Educated people became convinced that measurement or systematic observation should be given more weight than personal opinion, regardless of the social standing of the person who held the opinion. People began to regard themselves as part of nature, subject to the forces of evolution and governed by genetics.

What was perhaps the first book on child psychology was published by W. Preyer in 1881, under the title *The Mind of the Child*. It differed from earlier diaries and records in that it replaced general observations or anecdotes with careful measurements of behavior—beginning with the development of reflexes from birth on.

The last century also had its excesses, particularly its emphasis on the theme *ontogeny recapitulates phylogeny*. This principle holds that the development of an individual goes through or repeats the evolution of the species. Indeed, the human fetus does appear to develop physically much as other mammals do. The basic thought is that our individual development retraces the steps in the evolutionary development of our ancestors, though even for physical development it may not be literally true.

It was an easy and enthusiastic jump for literal-minded scientists to assume that if individuals recapitulate the biological development of the species then they ought to recapitulate the behavioral development of the species as well. Looking back, we can see that this was an oversimplification. Nevertheless, well-informed persons held the view that the development of a human child follows the same pattern as the development of the species, in which there is a recapitulation of the behavior patterns seen in earlier species. In fact, some psychologists and educators held that, to grow up well, a child would *have* to go through the early, more animalistic behavior or bestial stages. Children were encouraged to do so, lest they remain incompletely developed or even mal-developed. (An early twentieth-century psychoanalyst, Carl Jung, showed somewhat similar reasoning by maintaining that individuals contain within them the history of the race, that there is an inherited *collective unconscious*.) Thus the concept of evolution influenced not only biological notions of development but also behavioral concepts. Both carry the theme that individuals must pass through predetermined stages.

Child biographies were useful in that they gave attention to the detailed changes that occurred in individuals as they matured. Charles Darwin's diary of his son's development was influenced greatly by his view that a child would retrace the evolution of humanity. Darwin was, however, a member of Britain's upper social class. In fact, it was only the upper classes that had the time and skill to record the development of their children, and we know relatively little about what it was like to grow up as a member of the lower social classes. Our ideas of family life during earlier periods are heavily influenced by the writing of upper-class persons—clergy, physicians, educators, and others of high status. Even so, embedded in these writings are often opposite philosophical views, such as the belief that a child is a nearly perfect organism that is more or less corrupted by the environment versus the view that a child is essentially an amoral animal that must be disciplined to show correct behavior. These opposing themes still exist today, and education is viewed sometimes as a process of permissively releasing the potentials of an individual and sometimes, alternatively, as the disciplining of an individual. Some of this thinking reflects the biblical belief that we were originally innocent but fell from grace in the Garden of Eden. Having fallen from that grace, we are now in the process of working, struggling, and disciplining ourselves to get back to the previous perfect life.

Family life has often been thought to have been more nearly ideal in the past. The nostalgic image is that of children and older adults bound happily together in the same household with the parental generation. The industrial revolution is often thought to have broken down the multigeneration family by employing both the men and the children at places remote from the farm. But the view that the industrial revolution led to the decline of the family and its idyllic life for children and old adults overlooks the fact that life was *not* easy or pleasant—particularly for the lower classes—in preindustrial rural society, where farms often provided only a meager living.

Children were needed as a source of labor in the preindustrial village or farm. Families took in the orphaned children of relatives because children

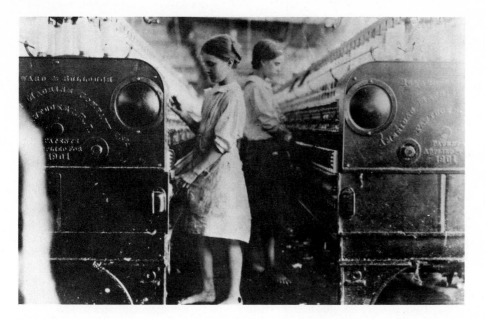

Although family life in the past has been pictured as idyllic, it was actually often quite difficult, especially for lower-class children who were expected to contribute to the economic production of the family both in preindustrial times and during the industrial revolution.

Brown Brothers

could do household chores. The larger the house, the more children and servants were to be found in it. For economic reasons, too, preindustrial households tended to have not only many children but also several young unmarrieds, sometimes relatives, who needed a place to live. Because the hard work required in those times could be odious, children often had to be beaten to hold them to the tasks of the household. The idea that children could be a source of pleasure from whom work and service were not needed came from the nobility and gentry.

Historical demographers are now attempting to reconstruct the life of preindustrial communities in England and France. The sources of data are old church records, which give household composition by name, age, and function. From these records, we can infer birth rates, death rates, characteristics of family life, and even the early practices of birth control. The eldest son inherited his father's property, and records indicate that he might turn even his aged mother out of the house, presumably because she could no longer contribute to the household's functions (Laslett, 1976).

The multivolume personal diary by Samuel Pepys of his life in England from 1660 to 1669 contains many details of family and household life during this period, including the treatment of children. This diary of a university-educated middle-class man gives us some insight into the concepts of the period. For example, if parents could not keep a child within their own house, it was a common practice for them to place the child in a larger household of a relative or friend. There the child could be beaten by the new master—for the child's good and to secure the performance of chores. Pepys describes beating his boy Will until Pepys himself was exhausted; he then threatened to send the boy back to his family, where the lad would again be beaten for losing his position. In another instance, when his cookmaid was to be promoted to chambermaid,

Pepys said, "after dinner did give Jane a very serious lesson against which we take her to our chamber-mayde; which I spoke to her that the poor girl cried and did promise to be dutiful and careful" (1976, p. 273).

Along with heavy physical punishment and verbal warnings there was the concept that children were often willfully bad. A willful child had to be broken to the task, like a colt to the harness. Furthermore, parents and masters were contributing to the downfall of those under their charge unless they disciplined them to their duties. The underlying concept can be labeled *voluntarism,* and it runs through much thinking about behavior. If children get poor grades in school, they are not putting their minds to it—as though good performance and grades were wholly within a child's control. Our social legacy still holds contradictory views about the nature of children, seeing them either as innocents corrupted by others or as primitive selfish animals requiring discipline, as unfolding organisms whose development is determined largely by genetic background or as a "blank page" on which environmental influences shape development.

The late 1800s saw the spread of the economic benefits of industrialization, and the middle class grew in size. More people became literate and had time to watch their children grow up. As photographic technology came within the reach of many families, photographs of the individual growing into adulthood became popular. Whereas the early phase of the industrial revolution encouraged children to work outside the home in factories, mills, and mines, the later phase moved them out of the labor force. Production became more efficient, and compulsory attendance in school became law. As the twentieth century unfolded, there was less social need to hurry children into adult roles. Children thus came to be observed in still greater detail by parents, teachers, and developmental psychologists.

Historically, there is a split in developmental psychology between the observations and thought about early development of children and those about adult development and aging. The study of developing children has different historical roots than does the study of adults and aging. Psychologists interested in aging had a more biological than educational perspective, and they focused on how long people live and the relation between this and behavior. Although the gap between the developmental psychology of the first quarter of the life span and the three-quarters spent in adult life is narrowing, there is a long history of different types of speculation. Gruman (1966) has written a history of ideas about the lengthening of life before 1800. Our concepts of aging lie close to our ideas about the life span and, of course, about death itself. Gruman traced our ideas about death and aging back to the Sumerian civilization of about 3000 B.C. The hero of an epic poem of that period was Gilgamesh, a vigorous young king who became sad when he realized, because of the death of a close friend, that he too would become old and someday die. The two alternative reactions in the epic of Gilgamesh are still with us today. Either we yearn for individual immortality, or we accept our mortality; either we rebel against the forces that shape our destiny, or we submit.

In the early 1600s Francis Bacon wrote *Cure of Old Age and Preservation of Youth.* In it he alludes to the concept that we were once in a better state of being and then slipped from virtue and well-being. The thought of linking childhood and adulthood in a common developmental process is particularly a twentieth-century idea. For example, we are now aware that diseases of childhood may affect how we age as adults, that fetal nutrition may affect the appearance of diseases in later life, and that the experiences of childhood form part of the history of an adult and interact with the demands of adult life. Whereas the later stages of the industrial revolution gave us the freedom to observe children in more detail, the new technological society gives us the methods and the time to look at our entire life span, including its psychological content in retirement.

Toward the end of the nineteenth century there began a wave of optimism about the progress of data-based psychology. Beginning in about 1879, when Wilhelm Wundt founded what is regarded as the first department of experimental psychology in Leipzig, Germany, psychology as a whole moved quickly toward an emphasis on gathering data through research. As departments of psychology were founded in rapid succession, psychologists became more assertive—if not hostile—toward philosophy. Measurement came to replace reflection as the cornerstone of psychology. There was also the widespread concept that psychology as a science would progress in the same manner as physics and chemistry; that is, the study of basic elementary processes would lead to an understanding of complex behavior much as the study of atoms and molecules leads toward the understanding of complex chemical reactions and structures. Tests and measurements replaced the daily records of children's lives as the information on which child psychology was based. Indeed, some psychologists today believe that, because of its split with philosophy, psychology has gone too far in ignoring introspection and intuition as sources of data.

Optimism about the new empirical psychology led to the founding in 1890 of the journal *Pedagogical Seminary* by G. Stanley Hall; and abroad, in 1893, the British Association for Child Study was established. In 1896 Witmer founded a psychological clinic for the study of maladjusted children at the University of Pennsylvania. As confidence in the new science of psychology and its contribution to the understanding of behavior spread, a second psychological clinic was founded, at the University of Iowa in 1910. The period from 1890 to 1900 was a golden decade for American psychology, and it brought an expanded interest in the objective study of children.

Twentieth-Century Concepts

G. Stanley Hall published his book *Adolescence* in 1904, offering the first psychology book on this phase of the life span. Hall had an evolutionary view of behavior that saw children's minds as evolving from an animal level to an adult level. In play, children were thought to recapitulate the evolutionary development of humanity from the anthropoid level, perhaps preparing themselves for adult activities.

Whereas philosophy's strengths lay in logic and theory, psychology's new strengths lay in systematic observation, description, experimentation, and measurement of the natural process of development. It is difficult to recapture the enthusiastic faith that psychologists at the turn of the century had in tests and measurements. In 1914 a compendium of tests was published by Whipple, the first volume of which was devoted to "simpler processes." Entitled *Manual of Mental and Physical Tests,* this volume was described as "a book of directions compiled with special reference to the experimental study of school children in the laboratory or classroom." A year later the second volume appeared, and it was devoted to psychologically "complex processes." Thirty tests were described in the first volume, and fifty-one tests were included in the second, together with results of studies in which large numbers of boys and girls were measured. A remarkable relationship between age and average level of performance can be seen throughout the results. Some topics are still relevant—for example, the age at which memory functions reach their maximum and the extent of sex differences on memory. The level of statistical sophistication and the objectivity of the writing are still impressive and illustrate the rigorous standards to which the scientific psychology and child psychology of the period were committed. Whipple makes an important distinction between an experiment and a test:

The primary difference between the research-experiment and the test-experiment is really one of aim. The test has a diagnostic, rather than a theoretical aim: its purpose is not to discover new facts, principles or laws for the science of psychology—though such a result may indirectly be attained—but to analyze, measure, and rank the status or the efficiency of traits and capacities in the individual under examination. (Whipple, 1914, p. 1)

Similarly, the data gathered in clinical studies are used to diagnose and treat the individual problem, whereas experimental studies are designed to shed light on a process in general as it occurs in most people.

A large step forward in the movement to test children was taken in France with the appointment of Alfred Binet to the Committee of Public Instruction. Binet and a colleague, Théodore Simon, devised a series of tests to determine the mental age of children in order to distinguish between lack of intellectual capacity and lack of motivation among French schoolchildren. The success of these tests in distinguishing between backward and unmotivated children led to the spread of the testing movement. Previously, even bright children had been sent to schools for the retarded because teachers could not differentiate between intellectual deficiency and the lack of motivation or the effects of other problems. The American translation of the Binet and Simon tests was published in 1916 and was known as the Stanford-Binet. Its 1937 revision expressed this expectation in the preface: "It is hoped that this revision of the Binet method will long provide a common standard by which to gauge the intellectual level of human subjects from early childhood to the end of life's span" (Terman & Merrill, 1937, p. x). By the First World War (1914–1918), the psychological testing movement had become so well developed that several million recruits into the American armed forces were given one or more tests. The analysis of the results of the tests showed age and ethnic differences in scores, the origins of which are still hotly debated.

The period between 1890 and 1920 was a prosperous one for developmental psychology, and many major contributors during this period had lasting effects on the thinking not only of scholars but of the general public as well. Some of these early ideas are not taken seriously today, such as Hall's theory that children recapitulate the evolution of the human mind. Nonetheless, the period bubbled with ideas. In 1915, Sigmund Freud wrote about instincts. He believed that instinctual drives were channeled by the environment, and he came to emphasize early emotional experiences in particular. His followers, who were active in the 1920s, were concerned with the psychoanalysis of children and the family. In a countertrend, J. B. Watson showed his dislike for introspective data and the verbal approach favored by psychoanalysis; he wanted instead to obtain data from visually observed behavior. In yet another trend, Jean Piaget began in 1923 to publish his books on the development of children's thought processes, although his work did not arouse lay interest until the 1950s in America. He wanted to describe the stages of mental development and the logical processes that become possible as a child matures.

By about 1925 there was a wide array of concepts about development. Supporters of biological determinism confronted equally strong environmentalists; those who saw validity in the concept of the unconscious mind had supporters and scoffers. Some believed that a child, if allowed to play and explore freely, would learn all the essentials of living. Generally, after 1920, emphasis shifted away from the biological determination of behavior to the importance of the social environment. Keeping this brief history of that shift in mind, let us now examine several theories in more detail, since they form the background of current thought in developmental psychology.

Perspectives on Developmental Psychology

The task of developmental psychology is to help us understand how behavior becomes organized. The key word in this statement is *becomes,* for it carries such meanings as coming into existence, evolving, coming to be, or undergoing change. The behavior of people and animals is not random activity such as we see in the particles of a dust cloud. Rather, behavior is organized into patterns, such as the nesting behavior of birds, the mating behavior of insects, or the game playing of children. As researchers and scholars study and think about how human behavior becomes organized, they develop theories.

Theories have several purposes:

1. To help us understand the organization of behavior
2. To predict the course of behavior
3. To enable us to control behavior
4. To suggest directions for further research

To *understand* means to know how the influences or variables interact in an organism. To *predict* means to forecast the behavior that is to be seen at a particular age under a particular set of conditions. This is an important distinction. For example, several thousand years ago early observers of the stars and planets began to be able to predict recurring patterns according to time of day and season. Their predictions became quite accurate and useful for navigation and agriculture. However, their accurate predictions notwithstanding, these observers tended to hold supernatural or demonic interpretations of the nature of the stars and planets and of the forces that led to their movement. Therefore, it is important to distinguish between the observations themselves and the statements used in explaining how the observations are related. Typically, understanding is incomplete; as it progresses, theories are replaced or modified. As people began to understand physics, their explanations of the movements of stars and planets shifted from supernatural ones to those of natural science, and so the sciences of astronomy and astrophysics came into being.

The cycle time of the stars is one year—much shorter than the human life span. Clearly, it is more difficult to become aware of regularities in human development than to note annual patterns of seasons or star movements. We can, however, rely on the observations of others, passed on from previous generations.

Developmental psychology consists of a collection of information (data or observations), predictions, and theories about how behavior becomes organized. The term *model* is often used as a synonym for *theory,* and for present purposes they can be used interchangeably. A theory and a model have some things in common. They both state a view of how variables are organized, and they both lead to predictions that can be tested. Researchers are concerned with comparing observations with predictions to see whether the conclusions of their theory are to be accepted or rejected.

A subject so vast as the development of human behavior tends to defy a single unifying theory. It is not surprising, then, that developmental psychologists have tended to have small theories to explain limited aspects of the development of behavior, such as perception, motor skills, learning, emotion, or personality. Put another way, developmental psychologists have tended to create theories explaining how *particular* aspects of behavior develop, rather than trying to explain the development of *all* behavior.

The Range and Uses of Developmental Theories

Axioms   Although developmental theory is not yet well organized with axioms and theorems, there are some self-evident principles that developmental psychologists accept and use as a basis for systematic research and reasoning. These principles are summarized in the following statements. Although they are not without some controversy, these statements illustrate the character of basic assumptions about the development of behavior.

1. Early life experience has an unequal influence on later development. This may be called the *primacy factor* in experience.
2. Although later development is founded on early development, it is not explained fully by early development or by the primacy principle. Thus adult differentiation—while proceeding from early development—responds also to the biological and social context of adulthood.
3. Early child development represents a transition from immature biological characteristics to complex behavior that is increasingly culturally influenced.

Early development involves a transition from immature biological characteristics to complex behavior that is shaped increasingly by culture.

Charles Gatewood

4. Individuals continue to differentiate psychologically and socially after biological maturity has been reached.

5. Individuals move toward increasing differentiation or distinctive characteristics over the life span in terms of biological development, behavioral capacities, and social behavior.

6. Individual differences in behavior tend to increase over the life span. These differences arise from the uniqueness of one's genetic background, variations in the supporting conditions for biological development, and differences in one's opportunities, which result in an increase in individual differences in behavior over the life span.

7. The important conditions for the development of behavior in childhood shift from biological to social variables; after midlife, biological and health factors emerge as important determining or limiting factors in behavior.

8. Individuals who are born at the same time and grow up in the same historical period form a cohort that may differ significantly from other cohorts in health, attitudes, and behavior. Cohort differences often become confused with changes within individuals.

9. The individual is a product of genetic and environmental interactions as well as both normative and nonnormative events. (*Normative events* are events that most individuals growing up in a culture are expected to face. *Nonnormative events* are accidents or events that occur so far away from

their expected time in the life course that there is little guidance for the individual in meeting the requirements of the situation.)

10. Culture, the human part of our environment, presents individuals with sequences of tasks and obligations at characteristic times in the life course. Whereas learning provides the basis for modifying behavior, culture provides the sequences and rituals that give rise to age-graded behavior, specialized sex-role behavior, and other social role differentiation desired by the culture.

The above principles or axioms are more or less explicit in theories of developmental psychology. Their special emphases can lead to excesses, however. For instance, the primacy principle can lead to the position that what happens in the first year or two of life is so important that this phase of life should be the exclusive area for research in developmental psychology. Another type of excess is an underemphasis on the kinds of skills young children must have in order to cope with their limited environments. In adults, childhood skills become incorporated into more complex skills wherein new principles emerge. Thus the mastery of language and early life socialization are necessary in order for adults to demonstrate highly differentiated moral behavior and wisdom in complex decision making.

Because developmental psychology attempts to explain how behavior becomes organized, it has become closely identified with the study of learning. However, there are important differences between the psychology of learning and developmental psychology. For example, the typical study of learning by psychologists usually occupies only a few hours or a short interval of time in the life of the learner. Learning may be defined as the modification of behavior as a result of experience. In learning studies, experience is distributed over a number of days or weeks, and the increase in mastery is analyzed in terms of the number and types of practice trials. Although the principles of learning so discovered are relevant to development, they are not identical.

Hypotheses Theories are useful, of course, in interpreting data already collected. But they also give rise to assumptions or predictions about the way facts yet to be gathered will be related. Such assumptions or predictions are called *hypotheses*; they are statements about what should hold true if facts are gathered and analyzed.

In daily life we generate many hypotheses about people and events, discarding them casually if they are proved wrong. The essence of scientific reasoning lies in generating hypotheses and testing them against observations. The difference between scientific reasoning and daily life is the degree of rigor or formality in the process and the standards used in accepting or rejecting hypotheses. For example, in daily life a single observation is often enough to change one's mind and cause one to reject a hypothesis. If you believe that a man is friendly but on your first meeting find him hostile, you may reject your original hypothesis about his being a "nice guy." In science, one usually requires many observations, made under standard or controlled conditions, before rejecting or accepting a hypothesis. A decision is made in terms of the probabilities that the hypothesis can be accepted or rejected as being due to chance or to some other cause.

There are three kinds of hypotheses: attributive, associative, and causal. An *attributive hypothesis* merely asserts that some thing or phenomenon exists and that it can be demonstrated. An *associative hypothesis* is a statement that two things go together, but it does not explain in detail why they are associated or vary together. For example, one might advance the unlikely associative hypothesis that children's body weight is related to their intelligence. A general *causal hypothesis* about such a relationship might hold that malnourished mothers tend to have premature or small, underdeveloped babies who—on a probability basis—may be more likely to be limited in the development of their nervous systems. A formal causal hypothesis would give a detailed account of the many variables that occur between the two observations of weight at birth and intelligence in childhood. In contrast with associative hypotheses, causal hypotheses attempt to specify the sequence of steps by which the causes are the necessary and sufficient conditions for the effect or outcome.

Descriptive and Experimental Research Besides giving rise to hypotheses that lead to new discoveries, theories also help scientists organize already existing facts and predict the outcome of circumstances that have not yet been observed. In the early stages of a science, research tends to be based on associative hypotheses, and the character of the research tends to be descriptive rather than experimental.

Descriptive research simply describes events and things that go together, occur at the same time, or occur in a sequence. Thus one might describe a child learning to walk. The description would be a history of the emergence of walking, but would not lead to an explanation of why the behavior developed or of what caused it to develop. Nor would the description tell what the development of walking was associated with, such as the opportunity to crawl, to see others walk, and so on.

Experimental research manipulates variables to study their effects. It is often difficult to do experimental research—particularly in developmental psychology—because of the moral and ethical issues involved. Researchers may not manipulate many aspects of a child's experience because the outcomes may not be reversible. For example, to prove experimentally that crawling is a necessary phase in learning to walk, one cannot ethically deprive a child of the opportunity to crawl, for that might produce long-lasting undesirable consequences for the child. An alternative would be to attempt to use "natural" experiments or to design animal experiments that closely approximate the conditions for human beings.

A *natural experiment* involves individuals who have been exposed to unusual developmental conditions, such as isolation, stress, or handicaps like congenital blindness or deafness. Much psychological and medical science follows the strategy of combining data from natural experiments with correlational studies on both human beings and animals. While this is often necessary, it is not ideal, for nonexperimental results are more likely to lead to misleading conclusions about cause and effect.

Limits on Developmental Psychology One factor in the relatively slow growth of developmental psychology as a science is the complexity of human behavior. Another is the lack of large masses of reliable data about behavior over the entire life span. Because an investigator's life is the same length as other people's, it is impossible for a single scientist to study many individuals over their entire life spans. Developmental psychologists thus tend to specialize in one age level or phase of the life span, such as the newborn, the preschool child, the adolescent, the young adult, the middle aged, or the aged. They also specialize in terms of methods and the types of behavior studied, such as motor skills, perception, intelligence, memory, learning, personality, and so on. Such specialization results in a picture of developmental psychology that is difficult to assemble, if we wish to account for the development of human behavior over the life span. Thus while developmental psychology has made dramatic progress since the last century—when impressions and dogma passed for fact—it is still, as a body of knowledge, a "young science." As such, it is characterized by associative rather than causal hypotheses, and its research is sometimes more descriptive than experimental in nature. Most important, perhaps, is the fact that it is difficult to get large masses of reliable data over long periods of the life span. For this reason, many important contributions remain to be made—an exciting prospect for those who have inquiring minds and are willing to be pioneers.

Ethics of Experimentation Researchers in developmental psychology have two obligations. One of these is to respect the rights of the individuals who are the subjects of the study. Investigators must explain to subjects the nature of the research, its likely effects during and after the experiment, and whether any benefits will result. The other obligation of researchers is to consider society, which may benefit from well-designed experiments. For example, many children, particularly boys, have difficulty in learning to read. For some, this is a turning point in their lives. While they may be quite intelligent, their school careers may be ended early, and they may end up in jobs that are well below their ability. Or they may drop out of the mainstream of society and become hostile gang members. If the possibility of conducting experiments or research on reading were denied because it would infringe on established ways of teaching or make "guinea pigs" of children, no progress in understanding could be made. What is needed is not less research into the psychological bases of human problems but more research that is well thought out. Research must respect the rights and dignity of individuals while providing us with the basic knowledge for improving our quality of life and realizing our individual potentials. A society that prohibits all animal and human experimentation is just as immoral as one that condones all research without questioning. We need the discoveries resulting from ingenious experiments carried out by well-trained investigators; without them, our ability to understand and reduce human problems will be held back dramatically.

When Jonas Salk and Albert Sabin did their work on polio myelitis, they believed that the terribly crippling and sometimes fatal disease was caused by a virus. They needed to inject living organisms in order to test their hypothesis and also to determine whether immunity could be developed and transmitted

The Ethical Obligation to Experiment

The experimental method is one of the most valuable tools we have for advancing knowledge. One important obstacle to increasing our understanding of human development is the widespread public opposition to experiments involving human beings. Underlying much of this opposition is a failure to understand the importance and ethics of experimentation.

For example, despite the many billions of dollars spent each year on education, and despite the strongly held opinions most of us have about the need for and nature of quality education, we have very little hard scientific evidence about what kinds of educational practices really work. There have been many small-scale educational experiments involving only a handful of classrooms. What is needed is not simply pilot studies to see if an educational innovation will improve achievement of students in a particular classroom or school, but more extensive studies to see if the new method or approach will work in a variety of classrooms and schools across the country. Only with this kind of

large-scale systematic experimentation in which many classrooms are randomly assigned to be taught by an experimental method or a control method are we likely to develop a set of educational principles and effective methods that have some degree of power and generality. To create an effective science and practice of education, therefore, we must educate the public as to the critical importance of rigorous and large-scale systematic experimentation in our schools.

People often assume that when researchers perform an experiment they tend to abuse or mistreat those involved in the experiment. For this reason, they say that researchers should not use human beings in experiments, and especially children because they could be more easily abused. However, experiments are actually performed haphazardly in the school system whenever new educational materials are used. The real "abuse" is that systematic records of such changes and their results are not kept, and educators thus lose valuable opportunities to learn the effects of new teaching methods and materials. If we want to find better ways of teaching, we have an obligation to experiment and to use the results of these efforts for the benefit of society.

by vaccination. To accomplish this, they needed to use living monkeys. Their work bore magnificent results, but it would have been blocked if public opinion had not permitted the use of monkeys in research. While an occasional mishap in an experiment may lie heavily on the conscience of an investigator, how much heavier should be the conscience of a society that would prohibit such experimentation?

The Classification of Theories

As we have seen, theories may be classified according to the type of behavior studied, the methods used, the phase of the life span studied, and the independent variables or determinants of behavior that the investigators use. For many

Without ingenious
experiments conducted
by trained investiga-
tors, our ability to
understand and allevi-
ate human problems
would be curtailed
drastically.

Van Bucher, Photo Researchers, Inc.

studies the independent variables are biological; for others they are social.
Hence theories may be classified as being primarily biological, social, or interactive—meaning that the development of a particular behavior results from
interaction between a particular genetic or biological background and the
environment.

Because of the wide content of theories, they are not usually contradictory;
rather they are directed toward explaining different developmental phenomena.
Thus a psychoanalyst and a student of experimental learning may appear to
have conflicting points of view because their theories lead them to study different things. Contradictions often arise because of claims of importance. That
is, different theorists may believe that their theories explain more important
aspects of behavior or are more relevant to human problems than other theories
are. But there are at least four criteria by which to judge the significance of a
theory: (1) how generally the conclusions of the theory apply to human behavior, (2) the ability of the theory to generate further development of concepts
and research, (3) the rigor of the theory, and (4) whether the theory leads to
practical applications for human welfare. The first criterion is scientific, because
it deals with the range of phenomena over which a theory may be applied.
Thus the best developmental theory is the one that explains the most about the
development of human behavior. This includes the idea that a good developmental theory should explain behavior over a long segment of the life span
rather than just a small age range.

Another possible reason that developmental psychology grew more slowly
than the natural sciences is that the latter describe the conditions of research in
a single system of measurement, the centimeter-gram-second system. This system enables natural scientists to interrelate their data. But behavioral scientists

must use various means of describing behavior, since it rarely can be measured in units of length, weight, or time. Behavior must often be described in terms of correctness, in terms of the number of attempts to achieve mastery, or according to a wide range of classification methods that suit the needs of a particular study and investigator. If basic or common units of behavior could be used to describe many different types of studies, the possibilities of generalization would be much increased.

Often investigators make implicit assumptions about behavior that are not stated in their theories, and we must be alert for such assumptions. Hidden assumptions in theory may involve concepts of "good" or "bad" or the goals of behavior. Some theories imply an assumption of social progress—the idea that the conditions of human life inevitably become better in succeeding generations. Such implicit assumptions are based on values that vary from investigator to investigator or from culture to culture. It is easy, for example, to slip into an assumption that the goal of development is the attainment of a behavior that one desires or admires. However, to assume that development is shaped by some purpose can be dangerous, for it can distort the interpretation of observations, causing investigators to explain phenomena in terms of the assumed purpose.

If a behavior or biological process is adaptive and helps organisms to survive, the process and the genes that bring it about will increase in the course of selective evolution. There probably are genes that channel development toward some adult form—although how long such guiding of development may persist is not known. However, the implication that some forms of behavior are superior or more adaptive than others has to be considered in the context of the particular environment in which individuals live. To say whether some forms of intelligence or of moral behavior are superior to others, we must know about the environment in which they are expressed.

Of great significance in developmental psychology is the possibility that there are qualitative stages in the intellectual, emotional, and social development of individuals. However, hypotheses about such stages are by no means proven as yet by research across the life span.

Differences in Developmental Theories

Besides varying in the extent to which they depend on a sequence of stages, developmental theories differ in at least three general characteristics. These are:

1. The type of behavior being explained
2. The age level being studied
3. Whether the theory emphasizes biological and genetic determinants or social and cultural determinants

Behavior can be graded roughly in terms of complexity—that is, from simple to complex. Some theories deal with elementary processes, such as how we receive information from the environment (sensation). These theories involve questions such as, At what age does an unborn fetus become aware of environmental sounds? or, At what age does the perception of visual forms become established? Often, investigators are interested in the conditions that accelerate or retard the development of perception. Thus a theory may focus on various areas of behavior, such as (1) sensation and perception, (2) motor skills, (3) memory, (4) learning, (5) thinking and intelligence, (6) drives and motivation, (7) personality, (8) social behavior, and (9) deviance, maladaptive behavior, and pathology. Thus while the basic principles of a theory may involve how memory functions, for example, development and change over the life span will bring different factors into focus, depending on the age level being studied. All the behavioral processes listed above can be studied over the *entire* life span— from the fetus to old age. And, of course, the theories vary in the extent to which they emphasize biological or social determinants of behavior.

Such considerations explain why theories seem to be more in conflict than they actually are. But there is also the logical question of whether an investigator is trying to explain the existence or nature of a process or of individual differences. For example, if we were trying to explain the *nature* of memory and how it develops, we probably would emphasize physiological changes in the nervous system. If we were interested in explaining individual differences in the *content* of memory, on the other hand, we likely would deal with differential experiences of individuals. The variables used to explain development and change in human behavior are not necessarily the ones used to explain individual differences in behavior. In short, developmental theories are less in conflict with each other than they are attempts to explain *different* facts or phenomena. With that in mind, let us investigate the major theories of developmental psychology.

Major Developmental Theories

It would be convenient if theories could be neatly packaged and described by the above principles. However, the content of research and theories often overlaps. It seems best, then, to describe developmental theories according to their main ideas and the people identified with them, along with a little of their history.

Cognitive Development

Piaget   One of the most influential thinkers in developmental psychology has been Jean Piaget, a Swiss psychologist. Although Piaget began publishing in the 1920s, he did not have a major impact on American developmental psychology until after World War II, around 1945. Piaget has been interested in the higher *cognitive*, or knowledge-acquiring, processes involved in thinking and reasoning in the solution of logical problems. He believes that there is a sequence of stages in intellectual development and that logical forms of thought are not available to young children, whose thoughts are dominated by egocentric thinking. Piaget's stages of cognitive development are described in Table 2.1. According to Piaget, the stage of formal operations is the most mature and highest stage of cognitive development, which not all adults reach.

TABLE 2.1
Piaget's Stages
of Cognitive
Development

Stage	Chronological Age	Main Characteristics
1. Sensorimotor	Birth to about two years	Capacity to move around and respond to the environment; elementary communication
2. Preoperational thought	About age two to seven	Use of elementary forms of speech in communication; beginning use and response to symbols; starts to play in groups; thinking is marked by egocentrism and precausal relations; use of *animistic thinking*, in which objects are regarded as being alive or aware
3. Concrete operations	About age seven to twelve	Reasoning about sizes, volumes, weights, and numbers
4. Formal operations	About age twelve and beyond	Ability to formulate general laws and principles; formulates hypotheses (tentative explanations of facts or phenomena)

Piaget and his followers hold that the stages of cognitive development occur in the same sequence for all persons, although the ages at which the transitions take place may vary depending on the biological maturation of the individual and on the timing and amount of experience. There is an interaction factor involved: Increasingly complex experience determines whether one will go through a stage earlier or later than others. For Piaget, cognitive development (thinking and learning) provides the basis for other behaviors. In his view, moral development is a progression of stages that depends on cognitive processes and that moves from egocentrism to rational idealism.

Piaget's writings introduce several terms with rather specific meanings. One of these is *conservation* of physical quantities, as shown in the child's ability to grasp that the total area of a piece of paper cut into small pieces equals the same total area of the uncut paper. Similarly, recognizing that a volume of water remains constant whether poured into a tall thin glass or a wide squat one involves understanding the principle of conservation of *volume*.

Another important Piagetian concept is that of *schemes*, which are organized thought processes or motor activities. These become elaborated into new and more complex schemes as a result of growth and interaction with the environment. In other words, individuals show *adaptation* to changes within themselves and in their perceptions of the environment. Adaptation depends on two other processes, assimilation and accommodation. Through *assimilation* an in-

In Jean Piaget's view, cognitive development involves a sequence of stages that provides the basis for other behaviors, including moral development.

Yves De Braine, Black Star

dividual incorporates new environmental experience into already existing cognitive structures. *Accommodation,* on the other hand, requires individuals to change their schemes and behavior in order to manage new situations.

One question that theorists usually have to confront is the source of drive or motivation in human beings. For Piaget, motivation is influenced by the balance between the internal and external forces operating on an individual. *Equilibrium* refers to this balance of forces; in fact, the lack of equilibrium is a source of motivation for learning and for the development of higher cognitive processes.

Piaget and his followers are essentially students of the structure of thought, and they believe there is an orderly sequence to its development. Also, the cognitive structures provide the basis for other complex behaviors, such as the use of language. One important controversy concerns the extent to which the learning of language determines the structure of thought, and how much the structure of thought develops by itself and influences the acquisition of language.

Piaget and his colleagues have mostly studied children and adolescents, but some scientists have begun to study what Piaget offers in understanding the intellectual operations of mature and aged adults (see Chapter 13).

Kohlberg An elaboration of Piaget's concepts of moral stages has been made by Lawrence Kohlberg, who described six stages of moral development. Later he added a seventh and most advanced stage, which few people reach. This last stage is characterized by reasoning through the implications of one's actions for other persons. Both in the cognitive sense and in the moral sense, Kohlberg's stages are marked by qualitative differences in an individual's behavior.

Psychoanalytic Theory

Psychoanalysis had an important impact on child psychology in the 1920s, at about the same time that Piaget's ideas were just beginning to be discussed in America. Whereas Piaget was interested in the development of logical thinking as a normal process, psychoanalysts were concerned with behavior problems and how to correct them. The founder of psychoanalysis, Sigmund Freud, was born in 1856. He became interested in behavioral phenomena after graduating from medical school and working for a period in a general hospital in Vienna. He began to study the structure and diseases of the nervous system. In 1886 he was impressed by the work of Jean Martin Charcot, who used hypnotism in the treatment and study of hysteria and other disturbances of behavior. Later, Freud substituted detailed introspection and free association for hypnosis as a better way of gathering information from a patient, since not all patients could be hypnotized. Introspection and its close ally, free verbal association, became the tools of psychoanalysis.

Arising as it did from medical treatment of patients with severe behavior problems, psychoanalysis took as one of its tasks the understanding of the origins of deviant individuals in society. There was also an underlying hope that the study of disturbed or mentally deviant individuals would lead to the identification of the basic mental mechanisms that all persons use. By contrast, Piaget sought to understand the developing intellectual processes of essentially normal or typical children. Although Freud attempted to recover by free association the early life experiences of his patients that led to adult behavior problems, for the most part he studied young adults. Thus his views of development were shaped by his patients' accounts of their development, rather than by direct observations of children.

An important difference between Piaget and Freud lies in the nature of the problems they studied. As a physician, Freud began with patients who had a variety of mental problems, and he sought to unravel the origins of those problems he regarded as being based on early life experience. This is a retrospective approach. In contrast, Piaget studied the development of the mind's capacity to reason by examining children's behavior at different developmental stages. In the following discussions, we can see that some of Freud's particular emphases arise from the fact that he studied disturbed patients and attempted to generalize from them to the more typical or "normal" person who adapts to life's demands without mental symptoms. Freud's expectations were that the same processes—though in different degrees—were involved in both abnormal and normal persons.

Freud Sigmund Freud posited three basic processes in the organization of behavior:

1. A motivation or drive system, called the *id*, that impels an individual into action to satisfy appetites
2. A rational system, called the *ego*, that learns how to handle or control the drives and impulses in relation to the environment
3. The conscience, or *superego*, which is responsible for our sense of guilt arising from violation of rules of relationships with others

In turn-of-the-century Vienna, where Freud did his work, societal prohibitions on sexual expression were extensive. Thus the battle between sexual drives (*libido*, for Freud) and conscience, or superego, was often intense in individuals. Repression and denial were common ways for middle-class adults in Vienna to control sexual impulses. Freud later came to believe that the most crucial task of individuals was to manage anxiety. In relation to sex drives, the anxiety was generated by actual or contemplated breaking of taboos against sexual activity. The taboos were usually learned from parents, and they often carried implied threats to control behavior. For example, children might be told that they would go insane if they masturbated. Earlier in this century it was more common than now to see hysterias, in which part of the body might be paralyzed, as mental symptoms—a result of severe repression. For example, soldiers in World War I might lose their hearing, become functionally blind, or develop a paralyzed limb as a result of battle exposure. They were caught in the severe tension between a basic fear of injury and an ethic that encouraged bravery. Similarly, a young adult might develop a hysterical paralysis in a hand that violated a sex taboo.

Psychoanalysis is a form of psychotherapy developed to relieve the symptoms resulting from inefficient or maladaptive ways of handling anxiety. It consists of retracing the experiences of growing up in order to gain insight into and recover the repressed experiences and feelings; this reduces the tension and releases the individual to show more effective forms of behavior. Both psychoanalytic theory and therapy are less dominant forces in contemporary thought than they were a generation ago. Other, briefer, forms of therapy are now considered equally useful (in comparison with the one-hour sessions that could go on three or four times a week for two or more years).

Critics of psychoanalytic theory have claimed that its reasoning is circular, so that no negative evidence can be generated to refute a psychoanalytic principle. For example, if a patient does not gain insight or denies a point, he or she is being defensive and resistant; if predictions are opposite to observed behavior in patients, the patients are acting out or showing an unconscious influence that led them to behave in a manner contrary to the way they said they wanted to behave. Nonetheless, psychoanalytic theory has had a widespread influence in society, affecting anthropology, social work, literary criticism, and other fields.

One reason for its popularity lies in its holistic approach to the person. No other perspective in developmental psychology has been so comprehensive.

Whatever appraisal we make of his theory, Freud did create a conceptual revolution by thinking about the behavior of people in everyday life. One of his ideas that found wide acceptance is that of the *unconscious,* an area of the personality from which come many of the dictates of our actions. Dreams, for example, are thought to reflect the workings of the unconscious mind, and events and objects in dreams are thought to be symbols of important events or processes. Indeed, interpretation of dreams has become a common topic of discussion as people try to understand the hidden meanings and significance of their dreams.

Adler   Another contributor to the development of psychoanalytic thought was Alfred Adler, who should indeed be regarded as holding a theoretical view of development. Like Freud, Adler believed that personality is determined largely in early childhood, but Adler gave less emphasis to the role of sex in the formation of personality. Rather than focus on the unconscious or the stages of personality development, Adler stressed the struggle of individuals to gain assertion over others. He contributed a phrase to daily speech as well as to psychology: *inferiority complex*—the concept of a lifestyle of self-depreciation. A prime example of Adler's concept of a continuing struggle for power can be seen in the short man who overcompensates for his size by becoming a dominating power figure. In Adler's view, this is an effective form of compensation for feelings of inferiority in comparison with a retreat into mental illness.

In the competition for attention and assertiveness that individuals face, Adler emphasized the birth order of children as being important. His theory begins with the observation that an infant is small, weak, and dependent and grows from a position of inferiority relative to the adult world to one of striving for dominance. Adler assumes that at the beginning of life there is a fairly general, deep-seated inferiority feeling. Thus the striving for superiority is universal, and one cannot understand individuals without taking into account their style of overcoming these inferiority feelings and asserting dominance over others. To adapt successfully to life, an individual must show some amount of social identification in striving for superiority. An individual's concept of self-worth thus depends on that person's apparent usefulness to the community and to others. Adler believed that an individual's mode or strategy of assertion is well established by the fifth year of life and remains essentially the same into adulthood. Thus a child of six has established a unique way to express strivings for superiority and to overcome feelings of inferiority. After that, there are three main problem areas for an individual: occupation, social relations, and love and marriage. Adler's emphasis on the striving efforts of an individual as the unifying force in personality development bears some relationship to contemporary humanistic psychology, with its emphasis on the directed behavior of self-actualizing individuals.

Jung   Yet another contributor to psychoanalytic theory is Carl Jung, who, unlike Adler, gave particular attention to the idea of an unconscious mind. In fact, Jung extended Freud's idea of the unconscious to include not only a personal unconscious but also a *collective unconscious*, which contains the beliefs and myths of the race to which an individual belongs. At the deepest level of this collective unconscious are the elements common to all humanity, which may be extended to our animal ancestry as well. Jung saw a similarity in the content of dreams, myths, and religious dogmas across various cultures, reflecting a collective unconscious that results in certain recurring themes, or *archetypes*, among different cultures. Unlike Adler and Freud, Jung believed that the period of youth lasts until the age of thirty-five or forty. In fact, he believed that real psychotherapy, in the sense of changing an individual's behavior, can be done only with someone who has reached the middle years. Jung also believed that the basic tasks of later life are to accept gradual biological decline and to expand one's inner awareness, rather than to regress to earlier simple forms of behavior.

Jung is perhaps best known for his classification of personality types. Everyday speech often includes a description of someone as being an *introvert* or an *extrovert*—the former being someone who is interested primarily in himself or herself, and the latter being someone who is interested in other people. Jung also outlined four categories that can interact with introversion and extroversion, thus giving eight personality types in all. These four categories are *thinking, feeling, sensorial,* and *intuitive.* Jung's classification system is often used for descriptive convenience without attributing exclusive boundaries, as one might classify types of animals in zoology.

Psychoanalysis originated just before World War I, and was elaborated on as converts spread the influence from Austria and Germany to England and America. Because the ideas of Freud, Adler, and Jung have spread through Western culture, it is important for students of developmental psychology to understand the basic terms and concepts involved.

Learning Theory

Many developmental psychologists concentrate on learning as a basis for development. Whereas Piaget and Freud stressed stages of development, learning theorists view the differentiations in behavior that occur with age as being gradual and due to the accretion of learning. Students of learning take for granted that children have the capacity to learn. They emphasize what is learned and the principles of learning rather than the maturation of structures by qualitatively different stages that make learning possible.

Obviously, not all aspects of development can be explained simply by Piaget's studies of cognitive development or by Freud's work on personality development. Similarly, not all individual differences in behavior development can be explained by learning theory. Still, much *can* be explained by the principles of learning, including the conditions in which learning takes place most effectively and the content of learning. That Russian children learn Russian and American children learn English can best be explained by environmental opportunity. However, how rapidly and how well they learn their native languages depends on the conditions of learning that can accelerate or retard the process. The capacity to learn complex material depends on the maturation of intricate neural structures. Although learning theory does not explain how the human organism develops the capacity to learn, it can help us to understand the conditions that can optimize learning. We will now examine several types of learning and related theories.

Pavlov   Russian physiologist Ivan Pavlov, who won a Nobel Prize in 1904, discovered that the salivation pattern of dogs was modified by anticipation of food. The process by which a basic reflex like salivation in the presence of food could become associated with some other stimulus, such as a light or a bell, was called *conditioning*. If a dog is presented with the sight of meat at the same time as a bell is sounded, the dog in time will come to respond to the bell alone in the same way as it responded originally to the meat. Furthermore, after conditioning has occurred, the bell can be paired with another neutral stimulus, such as a light or an object, which in turn will acquire the potential for eliciting the response. Thus by a process of higher-order conditioning, a neutral feature of the environment can acquire the potential for eliciting a response. One startling feature of conditioning is the fact that internal physiological events can be modified through acquired association.

Because of Pavlov's work and the research of others working in America at the same time, the acquisition of behavior through conditioning came to be regarded by some as the basis of development. Thus a countermovement to psychoanalysis began at about the same time Freud was developing his ideas, and this parallel movement was called *behaviorism*. In the 1920s, J. B. Watson emerged as the spokesman for this new approach, which rejected introspection as a method for gathering information and replaced it with conditioning.

Watson and others believed that conditioning could explain the development not only of normal behavior but also of abnormal behavior. *Phobias*, or strong fears, could be reduced by pairing the fear-evoking stimulus with a positive, rewarding stimulus. This is the basis of contemporary desensitization therapies for treating phobias. A child who is afraid of a dog, for example, can learn gradually to overcome that fear if a dog is introduced into the environment in controlled exposures while the child is eating or otherwise engaged in some relaxing activity. Watson and his followers in behaviorism rejected the use of subjects' verbal statements about themselves and substituted the study of observable behavior (hence the name *behaviorism*). Even today, some developmental psychologists insist that verbal statements from subjects have little value.

Behaviorists have been characterized by some as being overly optimistic about their ability to shape and control behavior through environmental stimuli. In America, the most recent and best-known proponent of behaviorism is B. F. Skinner.

Skinner   The name B. F. Skinner has been identified with behaviorism in American psychology from World War II to the present. Although the behaviorist movement has not given much direct attention to issues of behavioral development, by implication it suggests that we develop through the selective

In B. F. Skinner's
view, behavior is
shaped by selective
rewards and punish-
ments within an indi-
vidual's environment.

Christopher S. Johnson, Stock, Boston, Inc.

reinforcement of behavior. That is, some behaviors are rewarded by the environment and become dominant over behaviors that are punished or, at least,
not rewarded. Skinner's ideas about how a community or a society can be
organized around such principles are described in his book *Walden Two*. In
Skinner's view, an individual's behavior can be shaped by the selective rewards
and punishments presented by the environment. There is no built-in or genetic
plan of development and no goals of development. Skinner reasons that a child
is unprogrammed and learns essentially by reactions to stimuli and by reinforcement. This contrasts with Piaget's view, which holds that goals for behavioral
development come from within and are an expression of genetic programs.

One of the best-known pieces of equipment in today's psychology laboratories
is the *Skinner box,* a container that seals out extraneous light and sound and
houses one or more levers that animals can learn to press in order to get food or
turn off some noxious stimulus such as an electric shock. (Additional details are
provided in Chapter 11.) By forming chains of associations, animals can learn
rather complicated behaviors. For example, marine animals such as seals can
learn not only to juggle balls but also to play complicated games. Behavior is
reinforced by the reward of food, given to the animal when it shows the desired
response. The only "meaning" of the game for seals seems to be the securing of
food rewards; that is, animals would be unlikely to evolve such a game spontaneously. But do the same principles apply to human learning? Do children
learn to play games because of selective reinforcement and, if so, what rewards
are involved? One reward is being able to play with older children or adults.

Deborah Skinner: From Baby-Tender to Canvas

THOMAS SABULIS

In 1945 the newborn Debbie Skinner was the subject—many people claimed the victim—of national controversy. For the first 2½ years of her life she was raised in a "Baby-Tender," which was designed to cut down on parental chores during infancy. It was the invention of her ever-tinkering father, the author of "Walden Two."

Soon the story got out. The Ladies Home Journal yelped, "The Machine Age Comes To The Nursery." Newspapers, radio and Pathe News pursued the story. There was an air of uncertainty within the psychological community. Many people denounced Skinner as an ogre, but just as many wrote to ask how to build their own Baby-Tender.

Skinner explains the situation in the latest volume of his autobiography, "The Shaping Of A Behaviorist."

When Yvonne said she did not mind bearing another child but rather dreaded the first year or two, I suggested that we simplify the care of a baby. For our second child I built a crib-sized living space that we began to call the Baby-Tender. It had sound-absorbing walls and a large picture window. Air entered through filters at the bottom and, after being warmed and moistened, moved upward around the edges of a tightly stretched canvas, which served as a mattress. A strip of sheeting 10 yards long passed over the canvas, a clean section of which could be cranked into place in a few seconds. . . .

When Debbie came home, she went directly into this comfortable space and began to enjoy its advantages. She wore only a diaper. Completely free to move about, she was soon pushing up, rolling over and crawling. She breathed warm, moist, filtered air, and her skin was never waterlogged with sweat or urine. Loud noises were muffled (though we could hear her from any part

Source: *The Boston Globe,* June 15, 1979, p. 23.
Reprinted courtesy of *The Boston Globe.*

of the house), and a curtain pulled over the window shielded her from bright light when she was sleeping.

The baby is not at all isolated socially. She is taken up for feeding, of course, and at 6 months spends about 1½ hours per day in a play pen or teeter-chair. One whole side of the compartment is safety glass, through which we all talk and gesture to her during the day. She . . . greets us with a big smile when we look at her through the window. I cannot see that she is anymore isolated than in the standard crib. . . .

The baby sleeps in a variety of positions and changes posture during sleep with ease. The danger of smothering or strangling is entirely eliminated. . . . During the first six months her exercise consisted of a violent snapping action executed by lifting her legs at the hips and then suddenly straightening so that the feet strike the mattress with great force. This has developed strong stomach muscles. . . . The baby is obviously strong.

Deborah Skinner feels no resentment toward being brought up in the Skinner Baby Box, as it was sometimes called. Living in England, she doesn't think about it that often. "Fewer people have heard of my father there," she said. But one of her favorite lines comes from a London gallery owner who once asked, "Are you your father's daughter?" . . .

At 34, Deborah Skinner is a successful artist living in the Hampstead district of London with her husband, Barry Buzan, a lecturer on International Politics. . . .

One thing is certain. If the Buzans ever have a child it will be raised in a Baby-Tender. "Absolutely," she says. B. F. Skinner's invention is no longer on the market—it was once for sale as the "Heir Conditioner"—but another could always be built. Skinner's older sister, Julie, a psychologist in West Virginia, has used the Baby-Tender in the rearing of her two children.

According to Skinner, the original Baby-Tender was given to Twin Oaks, Virginia, a model of a utopian community influenced by her father's "Walden Two."

Young children observe those older than themselves, and, when motor capacities mature, they imitate the older children and try to play their games. That rewards are involved is suggested by the fact that younger children often cry when they are excluded from a game by older children.

Skinner and his followers do not speculate about the purpose of games and other behaviors. They instead concentrate on the observation of behavior in response to stimuli and controlled conditions of reinforcement. By emphasizing that the science of psychology can be advanced only by observing responses under controlled conditions, Skinner excluded from consideration inferences and speculation about what was going on within an organism. He ruled out attempts to explain behavior on the basis of internal events, whether physiological or mentalistic in character, if they involve such concepts as purpose and consciousness. The strength of Skinner's contribution lies in his method of studying behavior by means of controlling reinforcing rewards or punishments. Selective reinforcement has been applied in modifying the behavior of severely disturbed individuals, including criminals. And nonspeaking autistic children can sometimes be brought to speak through selective reinforcement. Later, however, such children may regress if removed from the reinforcing routine.

A limitation of Skinner's approach to behavior lies in its restrictiveness, for it excludes information that is derived from sources that Skinner considers mentalistic and therefore not to be taken seriously. In the physical sciences, for example, researchers often point to hypotheses, hunches, and intuition as leading to discovery. Yet Skinner would have us avoid all use of the word *mind* and all reference to internal states when explaining how behavior is organized.

Clearly, not all behavior is learned. Consider, for example, the playful behavior of kittens or puppies. It is difficult for a behaviorist to deal with such play behavior in animals, for it evokes concepts of an active organism that selectively seeks certain types of stimulation rather than acquiring a pattern of behavior by responding to external stimulation or reinforcement. Skinner and many other learning theorists make the convenient assumption that an organism is an empty box or, at most, a box filled with living clay to be molded by input from the environment. By contrast, ethologists such as Lorenz and Tinbergen have given considerable attention to inborn behaviors that are part of an organism's state when learning takes place. Yet another group, supporters of *observational learning,* points to the fact that individuals can learn by observing environmental events without making overt responses to them.

Observational Learning A surprising characteristic of monkeys and higher apes is their ability to mimic human actions. The evolution of the primate brain apparently has resulted in a high capacity for duplicating behaviors that are observed in others. It is difficult to explain mimicry or more complex observational learning on the basis of the reinforcement of overt responses. Some birds—like the mockingbird—can mimic the calls and songs of other birds. The capacity for accurate mimicry appears to be an evolved ability of a particular variety of birds, although the specific sequence of sounds is acquired from listening. Human beings also appear to have a rather marked capacity to duplicate movements and sounds by observing and listening. In fact, the observation of others is one important source of new behavior for developing children. Children learn to duplicate the behavior patterns of those who are older, particularly those who provide a model.

The important feature of observational learning as compared with Skinner's operant conditioning is that the sequence of behaviors is assembled internally, without an overt response that is rewarded or punished. Observational learning is probably an important aspect of human behavior throughout the life span.

Bandura Albert Bandura did considerable research in the 1960s on observational learning and children's duplication of behaviors shown by models. The extension of the results of his research to social learning suggests that children are selective regarding which persons they incorporate as models. Children attend more closely to the behaviors of people they admire. Parent-child relationships thus can be viewed in terms of their consequences for learning. Also, a slightly older, taller boy is admired by a smaller one, who watches what the older boy does and imitates it—sometimes to the annoyance of the older boy. Similarly, a little girl breaks into her mother's clothing to "dress up." Adult behavior is observed and mimicked by children.

Research into observational learning probably will contribute much to the future of developmental psychology, particularly since it provides a way of studying how children adopt complex behaviors. Very likely it will yield an understanding of how children come to adopt accepting or rejecting attitudes toward adult figures such as fathers and mothers, and it may show why deviant behavior or compliant behavior develops during adolescence and adult life. Adult socialization—by which young adults, upon entering careers, begin to observe and conform to behavior patterns of admired superiors—has yet to be studied in detail. Doctors, lawyers, teachers, and others not only are the products of social forces during childhood but also provide opportunities for observational learning and become models for others to adopt as adults. For example, it seems reasonable that future research will find that patterns of white-collar crime may result from the emulation of senior models by other adults. The Watergate scandal that rocked the nation in the early 1970s may thus continue to affect our society for a time.

Ethology

Unlike operant conditioning and observational learning, ethology is concerned with the behavioral capabilities that permit mimicry and other aspects of the development of complex behavior. One of the most striking forms of behavior ethologists study is called *imprinting*, which refers to the sensitivity of an animal at a particular time in its development to the formation of a strong bond with a "mother." This is, of course, a two-way process; the young animal is imprinted on the mother, and the mother is imprinted on her particular offspring.

Lorenz There is apparently a short period of unusually high sensitivity in newborn animals. Imprinting has been studied particularly well in fowl. If unusual circumstances are created during this phase of sensitivity, a gosling, for example, might come to follow a human being as though that person were its mother. One leader of ethological study is Konrad Lorenz, who received a Nobel Prize in 1973 for his research. Although there has been a long tradition in comparative studies of animal behavior, Lorenz, Tinbergen, and other ethologists have given particular emphasis to instinctual forms of adaptive behavior. The imprinting of an offspring on a mother object and the appearance of tag-along, or following, behavior are viewed as being biologically programmed. The adaptive value of these behaviors arises from the fact that they increase the chances of a newborn's being able to maintain a favorable relationship with its environment for food, warmth, and protection from predators. Ethologists try primarily to understand the instinctual and biological bases of the organization of such complex behaviors as food seeking, reproduction, and nesting, and specialized behaviors like the warning calls of birds. It is possible that human beings have inherited tendencies toward social behaviors that have evolved as part of our phylogenetic or biological history. Yet it is difficult to establish the extent to which a human baby's attachment behavior is equivalent to the imprinting of a duck on its mother. Nonetheless, ethologists have enriched our knowledge of behavior and have increased the likelihood that we will be able to link the behavior patterns of higher mammals with those of lower forms (Lorenz, 1952; Tinbergen, 1951).

An important contribution of ethologists is that they have discovered and elaborated on the details of a critical period in which an animal is unusually sensitive to forming a bond with some object in the environment. The response to the natural object—whether a mother or some substitute—is rapid, unlearned, and difficult to reverse. Such imprinting does not resemble typical learning in that the response is organized in advance, or "preprogrammed," and the bonding seems limited to a particular period of the life span.

Harlow Imprinted ducklings will follow a decoy rather than a real duck and will persist in this behavior for a long time; the decoy or other object might be called a *surrogate mother*, for the offspring will run to it when threatened. In the 1950s, Harry Harlow studied baby monkeys and their relationship to chicken-wire and terry-cloth figures that were shaped somewhat like an adult monkey. The baby monkeys formed a bond with the inanimate surrogate mothers and were able to mature. However, because their social experience was limited to interaction with the lifeless surrogate, their social development was found to be impaired when the monkeys were later placed in the company of other monkeys. Harlow's research has shown that bonding or imprinting does occur in primates and also that the character of early life experiences is important for the later appearance of mature social behavior. However, it is by no means clear precisely how much preprogrammed readiness for bonding exists in human infants and at what age or stage of maturation such readiness appears. Some psychologists believe that the second half of the first year is a critical period in this regard.

The ethologists who study the effects of maternal deprivation on children seem to have something in common with Piaget, who observes intellectual development. Their work and theories all seem to point to stages or periods in which a developing organism is ready to show an organized or partially organized pattern of behavior—when appropriate stimulation comes from the environment to release it.

Organismic Point of View

Heinz Werner is often characterized as having a broad, or *organismic*, point of view; that is, he considered an even wider range of behavior than did Piaget or Freud. Werner's concept of development was

not merely applicable to delimited areas such as child growth or comparative behavior of animals, but as a concept that proposes a certain manner of viewing behavior in its manifold manifestations. Such a developmental approach to behavior rests on one basic assumption, namely, that wherever there is life there is growth and development, that is, formation in terms of systematic, orderly sequence. (Werner, 1957b, p. 123)

Werner believed that developmental psychology needs to find the characteristics that underlie behavioral activity in the process of either progression or regression. He emphasizes developmental sequences that begin with a state of general activity and then lead toward increasing differentiation and articulation. Werner also uses the term *hierarchic integration* to indicate that a behavior is directed through steps toward some hierarchical goal. Such a principle of directionality in a sequence is usually unacceptable to those who approach development from the standpoint of learning. But it seems difficult in the face of daily experience to deny that children proceed toward increasing differentiation as they approach adulthood.

Werner and his students at Clark University have followed with particular interest the development of and changes in perception, which they believe moves from an undifferentiated or global whole into a more differentiated pattern. Werner has named this movement from undifferentiation to differentiation the *orthogenetic principle* of development, a term that refers both to normal development and to the typical pattern of change for the species. Unlike most students of developmental psychology, Werner also has expressed interest in data about adults. Still open to question, however, is whether many of the changes noted in adults after maturity can be explained by the principles and theories developed primarily from the observation of early life stages.

An Overview of Developmental Theory

By no means has this chapter discussed every major contributor to developmental theory. Only a very large book could adequately present a systematic view of the history and status of theory in developmental psychology. Because the basic task of developmental psychology is to explain how behavior becomes organized, theories appear to explain behavioral development in terms of (1) the unfolding of a biological sequence that is programmed on a genetic basis, (2) intellectual and social stimulation from the environment, and (3) an interaction between the readiness of an appropriately mature organism and environmental opportunities for accumulation and learning. One important issue is the relative contribution of these forces to changes—in particular, to behavioral changes over the life span. Additionally, developmentalists want to be able to specify the particular genetic and environmental influences precisely.

There are clear differences between how mature adults and young children behave, and there are impressive differences in the complexity of their intellectual processes, motor skills, and social behavior. At present, however, we do not know the consequences of many types of early childhood experiences. Generally, it appears that development proceeds from simple to complex. The lawfulness of this progression is a concern of theorists. As Quetelet said in 1835, "Man is born, grows up, and dies, according to certain laws which have never been properly investigated, either as a whole or in the mode of their mutual reactions" (Quetelet, 1835, p. 1). Discovering the details of the lawful relationships between a child's behavior and an adult's behavior requires considerable research on both animals and human beings. It is difficult, of course, to follow the effects of early life experiences because thirty or more years might elapse before consequences might be observed.

If we are to guide development and education, it is important that we know whether development is a continuous process such as going up an incline or a series of qualitative steps with rapid moves into more complex behavior. If maturational stages characterize development, then efforts to produce early increments in a process should not be undertaken until an individual is ready. It might be frustrating for teachers and even emotionally damaging to children to present learning tasks before a child's developmental stage is reached. On the other hand, if the bit-by-bit incremental learning model better characterizes our development, efforts at early acceleration should be profitable. New facts may enable us to identify which aspects of behavior development are better described by a stage theory and which are explained by an incremental theory. Research supplies the reliable facts about development that theories try to explain. Therefore, we must investigate the designs and methods of research in developmental psychology.

Methods of Research

Common Sense versus Science

Confusion often arises about the difference between the common sense of daily life and reasoning of scientists. What are the differences in the logic and in the kinds of interpretations made by scientists and by people in everyday life? What is the difference, for example, between the close observations of a child that are made by the mother and those made by a developmental psychologist?

There is no reason, for instance, why an Eskimo's observations and interpretations of the behavior of seals should be less accurate than those of a university-trained biologist. Yet although scientists may not be right in every particular instance, they have a higher probability of being correct because of the systematic way they gather information, consider alternatives, and correct inadequate explanations. Developmental psychologists have been taught to depend more on measurement and planned observations than on casual information. Because Eskimos have depended on seals for food and fur, they are intimately responsive to that animal's behavior, and they also have received useful information about seals from their ancestors. Yet scientists, on average, can solve more complex problems than the Eskimos for several reasons. Through education, scientists have greater access to information about the biology and behavior of seals, and their observational and recording skills are greater. For example, scientists might implant a small transmitter under the skin of a seal and track its movements while it is swimming freely, or they might use an implanted transmitter to broadcast physiological changes in the animals when they dive. Underwater cameras also might be installed to record the social behavior of young and adult animals.

Another powerful tool of scientists is their training in experimentation. They may do experiments in which they deliberately change some feature of the environment to see whether their predictions or explanations of the animal's behavior are correct. The process of adding to collected information would not be as organized without the systematic observations and testing of ideas that scientists go through.

A key advantage to scientific reasoning is its objectivity. A mother observing her child, for example, may be so intimately involved with the child that she may be more correct than a developmental psychologist in observing and interpreting some detail of her child's behavior. But being deeply involved with and responsible for her child's development, she is also more likely to be subjective,

The systematic observations of a trained psychologist bring objectivity to the study of human behavior.

Photographed by Marcia Weinstein, © 1975

to mix facts, desires, and feelings together. Developmental psychologists are less concerned with the behavior of a particular child than with generalizations about how most children behave under particular circumstances. Unlike mothers, psychologists make observations of many children and organize these observations in a systematic manner. Such systematic organization is what underlies theory, and it leads scientists to form questions and devise hypotheses about how things are related. Also, researchers use probabilities in deciding how likely an answer to a question is, or how likely they are to prove or disprove a hypothesis. Thus psychologists are armed with theories and questions that arise from the theories; they make observations of many children, think in terms of probabilities, and are less involved subjectively than are parents.

Science begins with observation. That is, something has been observed, and it appears to need an explanation. When many instances of the same thing have been observed, patterns of occurrence appear. If patterns of development occur, an inquiring mind begins to seek systematic explanations and to plan studies to test the explanations. Progress and conceptual revolutions in science can result from observations of new patterns or associations, from the emergence of a new concept, from new ways of observing, or from new ways of looking at old facts. Advances can also be made in the logic of research and in the way studies are planned. Let us see how some of these characteristics of scientific investigation are applied in developmental psychology.

Age as a Variable

Age is a powerful index to the development of behavior. Many predictions can be made about the likely behavior of an individual if we know his or her age. Age is also a good way of organizing information, much as one may organize a file of correspondence according to the dates the letters were written. The succession of events in correspondence is important, and to understand outcomes one must read letters in sequence to separate causes from effects. Thus the historical sequence of material—time—inevitably becomes important in explaining the flow of events. And though age is only an index and time itself does not cause anything, it is difficult to describe the development of behavior without regard to chronology. Without chronology, an event that occurs after an earlier event might be regarded as causing the first. Similarly, if we know that two events occur at precisely the same time, we know that one event cannot cause the other.

In observing the orderly progression in the development of a behavior over time, we soon want to replace time or age as the explanation of the behavior with some variable that can be regarded as its cause. That is, as developmental psychology becomes more sophisticated, age is used less and less as an index to behavior change. Nonetheless, age will continue to be used as a convenient index for describing behavior over the life span. For one thing, age is important subjectively in people's lives. Birthdays often are marked with considerable ceremony, and individuals attach significance to age, sometimes wanting to be older than they are and sometimes wanting to be younger. At times there are social advantages in being considered younger or older than one actually is.

Using age as an index, we can group various kinds of data about individuals into three categories. That is, we generally can see people as having three ages: (1) biological age, (2) psychological age, and (3) social age (Birren, 1959). Chronological age is related to all three of these, but it is not identical to any one. *Biological age* is an index to an individual's position within the potential life span. It indicates where an individual is between the beginning of life and the potential life span that remains. To measure biological age, one would pick a variety of measurements of important physiological functions, such as cardiovascular, respiratory, or endocrine.

Psychological age can be used to refer to an individual's adaptive capacities, such as perception, learning, and memory. Psychological age is related to biological age, but it emphasizes behavioral potentials and capacities to adapt to environmental change. To some extent our psychological capacities are skills, for they have to be exercised in interaction with the environment and are, therefore, partly the product of experience. For that reason, psychological development should be expected to proceed somewhat more slowly than biological maturation.

The *social age* of an individual reflects how that person behaves in interpersonal situations and in large groups. Social age parallels a person's biological and psychological ages to some extent, but not entirely. How old does an individual seem to look and act as a biological organism? How old does he or she appear in terms of thought processes, or in terms of mannerisms and customs that are expected from individuals in our society? Social age refers to people's social habits and to the types of roles they fill in society. It indicates the extent to which an individual has acquired or performs the various social roles expected for a person of that age.

It should be clear from this that an individual might be viewed simultaneously in terms of biological age, psychological age, and social age. But other types of ages have also been suggested. For example, *maturational age* might be defined as a person's level of maturation relative to other persons; *functional age* might be defined as an individual's ability to perform tasks; and *mental age* might be defined as a person's relative ability to think. The intent of all of these, of course, is to compare an individual's position to the average level for most persons of that age.

Research Strategies

Scientists can use a number of strategies in gathering information, analyzing it, and interpreting it. By its nature, research is empirical rather than philosophical. That is, it relies on experience or observation rather than on an effort to arrive at truth and wisdom only by logical reasoning. Empirical science aims to gain an understanding of phenomena through observation and controlled experience—as in an experiment. All experimental studies are empirical, but not all empirical studies are experimental; some are observational. Thus one research strategy is simply to observe a phenomenon in its natural setting, without interfering in any way.

Science begins with observations, usually of recurrent events. For example, early people became sensitive to the regularities of star patterns at night, and they learned to predict the patterns. Similarly, Polynesian sailors in the Pacific Ocean navigated between islands over two thousand miles apart without a compass. Indeed, they could travel for fairly long intervals without the orientation of the sun, moon, or stars. They did this by becoming sensitive to the wave forms and cross-currents on the surface of the Pacific Ocean (Lewis, 1974). Making such natural observations of recurrent patterns, systematizing them, and passing them on to later generations is similar to the methods used by trained scientists. Thus another strategy that can be used to scientific advantage is that of natural observation. Scientists, of course, must keep their observations as free as possible from personal bias and must separate their interpretations of events from the recording of them.

Reliability and Validity

Two terms often used in connection with observations and measurements are reliability and validity. *Reliability* refers to the accuracy of reproduction of data. Will other observers report essentially the same information under the same circumstances? For example, to measure intelligence, one should use a method that can be reproduced by a wide variety of users in a wide variety of situations.

Just because observations are reliable does not mean they are valid. *Validity* refers to the extent to which measurements—regardless of how reliable they are—truly measure or predict the thing under consideration. For example, a thermometer that measures body temperature might be very reliable, but if investigators use it to predict intelligence, they obviously would not have a valid measure of intelligence. Validity is the extent to which a measure reflects the concept or theory that it claims to reflect. While a thermometer may be a highly reliable instrument and may be a valid measure of temperature, it is not valid as a measure of intellectual ability. Similarly, an intelligence test may be a reliable, valid measure of mental ability, but it probably is not a valid index of a person's social adjustment.

Clinical Studies

Clinical studies combine observation with careful questioning, and they are a useful tool because they provide a kind of "natural experiment." Often, serious problems occur naturally to people, such as blindness, deafness, spasticity, or autism. Their study can be used not only to understand the problem of the disturbed development itself but also to provide insights into normal development. For example, a person who has been blind since birth and who later recovers sight through a surgical operation can be studied to provide information about how the visual process is organized. While it is not ethical to keep a child in the dark for long periods of time in order to study how recovery of visual function takes place, it is ethical—and important—to study the problem in someone who has had a natural affliction. Another example arises from the separation by surgery of Siamese twins—two individuals who are joined because

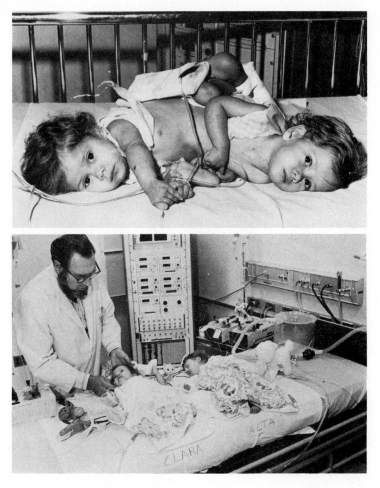

Clara and Alta Rodriguez, thirteen-month-old Siamese twins, are shown before and after the successful operation that separated them in 1974.

United Press International, Inc.

of an incompletely divided fertilized egg. In 1974, for example, thirteen-month-old Siamese twins who were born in Puerto Rico were separated by surgery at Children's Hospital in Philadelphia. The twins were joined from the chestbone to the pubis, and they shared internal organs. This situation provides an opportunity to study the effects of early life experience on development, for the separation of these twins at the age of thirteen months by unusual surgical procedures—literally, by sawing them apart—should result in individuals whose personalities and cognitive structures are dramatically different from those of most persons.

Identical Twin Studies

The phenomenon of Siamese twins, mentioned above, happens about once in every sixty thousand or more births. But most fertilized eggs that result in twins complete their division to give rise to separate identical twins. The

Twin studies allow us to compare the relative influences of heredity and environment on particular behavioral characteristics.

Photographed by Marcia Weinstein, © 1979

development of identical twins can be compared with the development of fraternal twins, who result from the fertilization of two different eggs that were in the uterus at the same time. This enables us to study the relative contributions of heredity and environment to particular behavioral characteristics.

Experimental Studies

The purpose of an *experimental study* is to manipulate what one thinks is the causative factor of some behavior. For example, if the lack of parental attention were thought to lead to emotionally disturbed children, one could attempt to alter the environment of children to increase the amount of personal attention.

Experimental studies attempt to manipulate the causal agent. A distinction is made between the *dependent variables*, or the outcomes, and the *independent variables*, which are the manipulated causes in an experiment. A cause (independent variable) always precedes an effect (dependent variable) and is always joined with the effect. If a change in one variable is the necessary and sufficient condition for a predicted outcome in another variable, a *cause-and-effect relationship* exists between them.

In observing children or adults over a period of time, intervening influences may disturb the validity of the experiment. The term *quasi-experimental* refers to research designs involving a number of factors that must be considered in interpreting research results (Campbell & Stanley, 1963). For example, if one is doing something to children over an interval of time, it is possible that the outcomes result not from what is done to the children but merely from the fact that the children have matured. Similarly, one must be certain that children are at a sufficiently advanced maturational level to respond to the treatment or experimental variable.

Since researchers often need to measure children or adults before and after exposure to an experimental variable, the initial pretesting may itself affect the subjects—either in practical or motivational terms. This may make it necessary to use a *control group* of subjects who do not receive the experimental treatment. It also may be desirable to use a second control group of subjects who do not receive pretesting but only get the second testing. In this way, researchers can be sure that a change between the pretest and posttest does not result from practice or from some motivational consequence.

Sometimes, observations or measurements themselves may alter an individual's performance of the behavior being tested. For example, after people's attitudes about something are measured, the people may begin to reflect on their attitudes and rehearse their views so that later measurements or interviews will reveal a shift. However, the shift does not result from the experimental treatment but from the fact that the subjects have been stimulated to think about the questions. Other factors also may influence the outcome of experiments, even though they have nothing to do with the experimental or treatment effects. For example, research often involves the study of volunteers. Under some circumstances volunteers may behave differently than nonvolunteers. Thus achievement-minded parents might be more willing to volunteer for experiments, or to encourage their children to volunteer, than would passive parents. It is important, therefore, to control the amount of attention given to subjects in a study so that the precise effect of a variable can be separated from the context of the experiment.

Intervention

One topic that comes up more frequently as educators and others discuss ways to minimize some of the problems in human development is *intervention*, which refers to steps taken to alter the course of events rather than simply allowing them to follow their natural course. Sometimes an institution might intervene on behalf of an individual even if he or she does not realize the need for such intervention. It has been suggested by Harsberger that "up to thirty percent of all elementary school children are in need of specialized intervention" (Harsberger, 1973, p. 340).

A wide range of human problems may warrant intervention long before the individuals involved may seek professional help. Among these problems are learning disabilities, emotional disturbances, marital difficulties, social problems arising from racial issues, and health concerns. Often the interests of professionals and their desire to intervene contradict the value system of individuals. Thus although a child's future survival may depend on some medical intervention such as immunization, the parents may not permit this because of a religious belief. Harsberger points out three types of prevention or intervention: (1) *primary prevention*, an intervention strategy designed to reduce the frequency or occurrence of specified problems; (2) *secondary prevention*, which is designed to reduce the duration of problems; and (3) *tertiary prevention*, which is designed to reduce the amount of time needed by a person to return to a relatively productive life.

Individuals are often reluctant to change behavior when the consequences of events exist far in the future. It is difficult, for example, to get dropouts to continue their schooling or smokers to give up smoking. While scientists are sometimes accused of being overcautious and slow in translating research results into useful applications, it is also true that society and individuals are not disposed to accept and put into practice what evidence shows to be good for them. Nevertheless, for human beings to realize their intellectual, emotional, and physical potentials, it seems desirable for our educational institutions, communication media, and social agencies to become more involved in experimentation and intervention.

Research Designs

The first and most common research design for developmental study is the *cross-sectional design*, in which investigators observe children or adults of different ages and then compare the average values of different age groups. For example, if researchers are interested in the relation of age to intelligence, they might initiate a study by giving a test of intellectual function to schoolchildren at every grade level and then examining the average values. Then they might begin to draw inferences about the course of development for a particular intellectual function studied. Although the cross-sectional design is the first approach to developmental study, it has limitations. The most obvious one is that no single individual is followed over the course of time. As a result, the average values that result from a cross-sectional study by age may not resemble any particular individual's course through time. That is, the detailed observation of an individual's course of development might have considerable ups and downs, whereas the average course might show a steady trend.

Once investigators have done a cross-sectional study, they may contemplate using a *longitudinal design*. In this, the same individuals are measured repeatedly over a longer part of their life spans. Results of longitudinal study obviously are easier to interpret than a cross-sectional design, especially when studying the course of individual development or aging.

There have been several large-scale longitudinal studies undertaken, and many of these have involved children, such as the Berkeley Growth Study and studies at the Fels Research Institute and Harvard. Other longitudinal studies have involved adults, for example, the Boston Normative Aging Study, the Thousand Aviators Study of the Naval Air Station in Pensacola, Florida, and other studies at such places as the Gerontology Research Branch in Baltimore, Duke University, and the National Institute of Mental Health. Sometimes these longitudinal studies become important resources in answering questions that come up after the research began. In 1921, Lewis Terman began a study of gifted children because he wanted to study the characteristics of subjects who were in the top 1 percent of the school population in terms of general intelligence. He studied children in grades 3 to 8 and eventually obtained 1,528 subjects (857 males and 671 females) who were regarded as intellectually gifted. Almost all subjects tested had an IQ above 140, though 55 subjects had IQs ranging from 135 to 139. These subjects are now in their late sixties and seventies, and they have been followed for their accomplishments and productivity throughout their lives.

Even longitudinal studies have limitations, however. We might question whether a study of gifted children today would yield the same results as Terman and his colleagues obtained. To answer such a question, we would have to obtain new groups of children at intervals to see whether, for example, eleven-year-olds have remained the same or changed in their characteristics. That is, a sequence of longitudinal studies could be used to determine whether there are changes in the characteristics of the population along with maturational or developmental changes. It has been observed, for example, that there is a tendency for subsequent generations of children to be taller and heavier than their parents. A similar trend has been reported for intelligence (see Chapter 13); that is, the average intelligence of children of the same age seems to be increasing.

Longitudinal studies may tell us something about the course of change within individuals, but there may be changes or drifts in the population that may necessitate new longitudinal studies. The *cohort effect* is one such effect. That is, individuals born at a particular time—even if followed longitudinally—may not represent the course of development of other groups. During World War II, for example, children in England were subjected to unusual living circumstances for a five-year period. Wartime consequences in terms of nutritional deficiences, trauma, and educational and emotional disturbances would produce a unique cohort of individuals. The educational and emotional experiences of subsequent cohorts might be quite unlike those of the war-period children. Obviously, the initial selection of subjects in a longitudinal study is an important issue.

Studies often have to use volunteer subjects, who may be different intellectually, emotionally, and socially from nonvolunteers. In order to generalize to the population as a whole, researchers must know the extent to which volunteers differ from nonvolunteers. Similarly, during the course of a study, there may be selective dropouts—whether the study is a short-term experiment or a long-range longitudinal one. For example, subjects who experience difficulty with a test or its measurements or who are hostile to its intent may tend to drop out. Of course, investigators may compare the average initial scores of the dropouts with the scores of subjects who stayed, thus securing a quantitative estimate of the bias introduced by dropouts. High achievers are more likely to volunteer and continue with a study than low achievers, who may be threatened by measurements and by having their results compared with those of other individuals—even though such information may be confidential.

When subjects are followed over a long period of time, there will be selective survival, particularly with subjects in the upper age ranges of adulthood. Thus there is a possibility that a positive bias will be introduced in studies of older age groups because of the fact that only healthy survivors are left to study. The survivors are more likely to be people whose socioeconomic level provided them with health benefits and who came from concerned, well-established families that had economic and social resources available. Thus the surviving older population would have a relatively high intial level of health. Because other characteristics (such as intelligence, achievement, motivation, and emotionality) may be related to health, researchers may get a highly selective population of old adults even in a longitudinal study.

Bias in Measurement

Even the methods of measurement used in developmental research are not necessarily free from bias. Cultural biases in the selection of test items may favor particular groups. For example, bilingual children who are growing up in a Mexican-American community may perform poorly on some measures of achievement and intelligence because the items favor children growing up in a homogeneous community with an Anglo-Saxon background. Cognitive measurements are especially difficult to free from bias related to the requirements for achievement in a particular culture. Instead of using global tests that measure overall functions, investigators can resort to reliable tests that measure specific areas of function. Instead of measuring IQ, they may use separate tests for various components of intelligence. Guilford (1959), for example, has suggested that there are 120 different factors or components of intelligence on which an individual might show differential strengths and weaknesses. Compared with global measures or performance, differential patterns may prove to be more valuable in the future in aiding individualized instruction in schools and in assaying the effects of experimental procedures.

As the content of developmental psychology has improved, so have its research methods. Improvements have been made in terms of the specific techniques used to gather information, in the logic by which experiments are designed, and in the methods used to analyze data. In all, however, there is no substitute for well-motivated, creative investigators, whether they are conducting a field observation of play behavior among children or a highly specific laboratory investigation under rigorously controlled conditions.

Developmental psychology has an important contribution to make in explaining developmental influences on individuals so that we can maximize the number of adults who realize their full potentials for making mature judgments. It should be possible for adults to engage in the complex interpersonal relationships required by our society in a way that increases individual effectiveness and reduces excessive tension and destructive behavior.

Summary

1. The historical beginnings of developmental psychology can be found in people's early thinking about children, from the viewpoint of a theologically based education system and through the parental descriptions of children recorded in baby biographies. In the last century there developed the concept of the average person, around whom individual extremes are distributed. Since then, variations in the course of physical, intellectual, and social development have been studied.

2. In the last hundred years, thinking about development has been influenced greatly by the theory of evolution, which places humanity within a long line of biological ancestors. The early part of the twentieth century also saw the rise of psychoanalytical concepts about child development, in which early experience was thought to play a particularly important role in shaping a child's personality and subsequent adult behavior. To some extent, undue emphasis was given to the early years, with little attention being paid to adult life. Later, the large increase in the proportion of the mature adult population brought attention to the neglected adult phase of the life span.

3. Individuals born within a particular period form a cohort and differ significantly from other cohorts in terms of health, attitudes, and behavior. Cohort differences resulting from unique historical periods of peace or war or prosperity or depression often become confused with changes that occur within individuals.

4. Culture, the human part of the environment, surrounds individuals with expectations and norms. *Normative events* are those that are typical and are faced by most individuals growing up and growing old within a culture. *Nonnormative events* are accidents or events that occur so far away from their usual time in the life span as to constitute a unique experience for the individual.

5. Culture presents individuals with sequences of tasks and obligations at characteristic times in the life course, giving rise to age-graded behavior, specialized sex-role behavior, and other social role differentiation typical of the culture. The capacity for learning provides the basis for modifying behavior in relation to the expectations of society. Recent years have seen much research on learning in developmental psychology.

6. Because ethical restraints prohibit experimentation, many important issues cannot be studied by manipulating the conditions of human life but have to be learned indirectly from natural experiments or observations. For this reason, the progress of developmental psychology as a science has been

slow. Recently, animal studies have been used increasingly to provide conditions analogous to those thought to be important in human development, such as the effects of perceptual deprivation, environmental enrichment, diet, and drugs.

7. There have been extreme points of view toward behavior. The behaviorists primarily study and emphasize the reinforcements an individual receives from the environment. Another group of researchers, the ethologists, have looked at the development of animals and have described the principles of development. More recently, advances in neurobiology have provided information about the organization of the nervous system and thereby have made it possible to take an organismic point of view toward development; this embraces, in a meaningful way, the observations of both social and biological scientists.

8. Longitudinal studies of children that were started in the 1920s have followed individuals from birth to middle age and are providing evidence about continuity and discontinuity of behavior within the same individuals over large portions of the life span. Casual impressions of important factors in development over the life span are now being replaced by detailed observations of the same individuals as they grow up and grow old.

Selected Readings

Baldwin, A. L. *Theories of Child Development.* New York: Wiley, 1967. A scholarly and useful statement about theories of development in the early phases of the life span. A well-integrated statement written by a single author.

Birren, J. E., and Schaie, K. W., eds. *Handbook of the Psychology of Aging.* New York: Van Nostrand Reinhold, 1977. A major reference source on the adult phase of the life span. Three chapters deal with issues of theories of aging, two chapters are devoted to research design and methods, and there is a separate chapter on the history of the subject.

Fisher, S., and Greenberg, R. P. *The Scientific Credibility of Freud's Theories and Therapy.* New York: Basic Books, 1977. Two psychologists review the scientific evidence bearing on the validity of Freud's ideas. The authors conclude that although many of Freud's ideas must be rejected in light of present knowledge, others have held up surprisingly well to various empirical tests. On the whole, a balanced and reasoned review of Freud's theories and the research stimulated by them.

Flugel, J. G., and West, D. J. *A Hundred Years of Psychology.* 3rd ed. London: Gerald Duckworth, 1964. A readable history of psychology that includes information on the early days of developmental and experimental psychology. Over a hundred pages are devoted to the period from 1900 to 1933. Behaviorism, psychoanalysis, and the mental test movement are among the aspects traced historically.

Grotberg, E.H., ed. *200 Years of Children.* U.S. Department of Health, Education, and Welfare, Office of Child Development. Washington, D.C., 1977 (DHEW Pub. No. OHD 77–30103). A collection of articles reviewing the history of children in America, and the historical changes in different factors influencing their development, including health, education, family, economics, recreation, literature, and the law. Brief, but well-written and authoritative, articles by historians and child development experts.

Murchison, C., ed. *A Handbook of Child Psychology.* Worcester, Mass.: Clark University Press, 1931. A good picture of early developmental psychology, with twenty-two chapters written by the then leaders in research and theory. Comparing the material on methods and design of research with that in Nesselroade and Reese reveals how much the subject matter has developed.

Nesselroade, J. R., and Reese, H. W., eds. *Life-Span Developmental Psychology: Methodological Issues.* New York: Academic Press, 1973. A collection of chapters written about methods and design of research in life-span psychology. Provides a good look at the basis of modern developmental psychology.

II BIOLOGICAL AND BIOSOCIAL INFLUENCES

Part II discusses how various biological factors influence development. Chapter 3 provides a background in the principles of modern genetics and how genetic factors shape intellectual and personality development. We also consider how genetic knowledge can be used to prevent illness and promote healthy development. Chapter 4 gives the reader a background in how the brain develops, along with a discussion of individual differences in bodily maturation and how these may influence behavior. We then consider how health and nutrition can influence psychological development and, conversely, how the behavior patterns one develops are among the most important determinants of health and long life in our society today. Chapter 5 is concerned with how different kinds of influences—ranging from genes to learning experiences and culture—interact in shaping development. Here we consider the scientific field of ethology, which is particularly concerned with this question. We also discuss how the learning process itself is shaped by genetic and maturational factors, and how easily we can be misled in our attempts to understand development if we fail to consider how different kinds of influences work together in shaping development.

Chapter 3

Genetic Influences

The basic concepts and principles of genetics

The impact of hereditary factors on developmental processes over the life span

The implications of genetic influences on development: the degree to which individual differences result from hereditary factors and the importance of genetic diversity

Genetic influences on personality and intelligence

How knowledge of genetics can be used to increase human welfare

Basic Concepts and Principles

The Nature of the Genetic Material
Concepts and Principles of Mendelian Genetics
The Application of Genetic Principles

Developmental Genetics

Pathways of Genetic Influence
Genes and Development over the Life Span

Implications of Genetic Influences on Development

Genetics and Mental Retardation
Heritability
Implications of Attitudes Toward Heritability
Genetic Influences on Personality Development

Using Genetic Knowledge to Improve Human Life

Prevention of Erythroblastosis Fetalis
Genetic Counseling
Amniocentesis
Genetic Engineering
Positive Eugenics
Interaction of Genotype and Environment

Introduction

Among the most exciting advances in human knowledge during the twentieth century has been our revolutionary progress in understanding the biochemical and cellular basis of heredity. Of all areas of science, perhaps the most significant breakthroughs now being made are those by molecular geneticists, scientists who are unlocking the mysteries of genetic material. Questions about the origins of life have baffled the human mind since thoughtful men and women first began to speculate about their nature. This chapter presents an overview of genetics and how heredity influences our development as human beings.

Basic Concepts and Principles

You, the reader—like every other human being—began life as a single cell smaller than the period that ends this sentence. You are the result of a union between two microscopic cells—an *ovum*, or egg, from your mother and a *sperm cell* from your father. As shown in Figures 3.1 and 3.2, the fertilization of egg by sperm created a tiny fertilized egg, or *zygote*. In its nucleus was packed the genetic material containing the hereditary blueprints for the incredibly complex psychological and biological organism that you represent. How is it possible that all the information needed to direct the growth and development of your trillions of cells could be contained in such a tiny bit of matter?

The answer is a miracle of miniaturization in which hereditary blueprints, or *genes*, are encoded by means of sequences of atoms on strands of the molecule

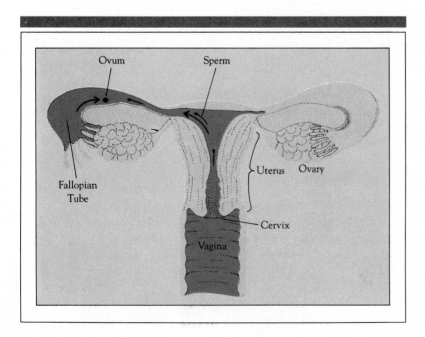

FIGURE 3.1
Female reproductive system during conception. This is a schematic drawing, and all the parts are not exactly to scale.

87

FIGURE 3.2
Fertilization of
egg by sperm

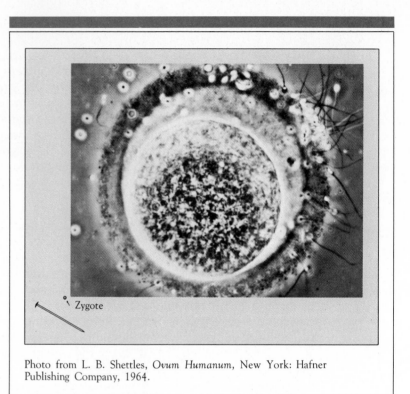

Photo from L. B. Shettles, *Ovum Humanum,* New York: Hafner
Publishing Company, 1964.

deoxyribonucleic acid (*DNA*, for short). In 1953, when American geneticist J. D.
Watson and his British biochemist colleague Francis Crick succeeded in building a model for the structure of DNA, they joyfully celebrated at a pub near
Cambridge University, shouting to their friends that they had discovered "the
mystery of life" (Watson, 1968). In a very real sense, they had; for in the
structure of the DNA molecule lies the hereditary basis for essentially all living
things on earth.

The basic structure of the DNA molecule is remarkably simple. Indeed, part
of the genius of Watson and Crick was that they saw that such a seemingly
simple molecular structure (1) could be self-replicating and (2) could store such
an enormous amount and variety of information.

The Nature of the Genetic Material

The key to the self-replicating property of the DNA molecule lies in its "double
helix" structure. As shown in Figure 3.3a, DNA is a kind of spiral staircase or
twisted ladder in which two long chains of phosphate and deoxyribose sugar
groups form the "uprights," and the "cross-rungs" are formed by pairs of ni-
trogenous bases tied together by loose chemical bonds. Altogether, there are
four different kinds of bases: adenine, guanine, cytosine, and thymine. The
chemical configurations of these bases are such that they can bond to one
another in only two combinations: adenine always pairs with thymine, and
cytosine always bonds with guanine (Watson, 1976).

The self-replication of DNA occurs in a fascinating manner, made possible by the double helix structure. The weak chemical bonds linking complementary bases in the chemical cross-rungs are broken, and the double helix "unzips." The two formerly linked chains of the molecule separate. Then, nucleotide units (consisting of one of the four bases hooked to a segment of the sugar-phosphate backbone) become bonded to the complementary bases that now are exposed on the two single chains. As shown in Figure 3.3b, the end result is the formation of two double-chained molecules that are identical to the original one.

The Genetic Code   How is hereditary information stored in the genes? As we have seen, the DNA molecule consists essentially of a structured "backbone" of phosphate-sugar units, along which is arrayed a long sequence of the four nucleotide bases. The sequence of these bases makes up the genetic code; different sequences spell out different sets of information. The four bases thus constitute a kind of four-letter alphabet. Triplet sequences of these bases form three-letter "words," or *codons*, in the genetic code. And because there are four basic letters, sixty-four different three-letter combinations, or codons, are possible.

To continue our comparison with the alphabet, it is a particular sequence of several codons that spells out a meaningful message and constitutes a gene. Each gene makes up the smallest functional unit of hereditary material, containing the information or blueprint for constructing a particular protein, or part thereof. More specifically, proteins consist of *polypeptides,* long chains that are composed of chemical building blocks known as *amino acids.* Each codon specifies a particular amino acid. Thus the sequence of nucleotides on a DNA molecule specifies a sequence of amino acids and hence determines the structure for a particular protein.

The production of a protein in the cell involves an intermediate step as well. In this step, the gene's information is "transcribed" into a second molecular form, *ribonucleic acid,* which acts as a molecular messenger to carry the information to another part of the cell. There, in conjunction with special structures and helper molecules, the molecular blueprint in the genetic code is "translated" into the production of a protein.

The Packaging and Transmission of Genes   Sets of genes are packaged together in structures known as *chromosomes.* A chromosome basically consists of a long stretch of DNA with associated molecules. A gene is thus a segment or portion of the DNA on a chromosome; it codes for a particular protein or part thereof. Each normal human being has forty-six chromosomes in most body cells.[1] The chromosomes occur in twenty-three matched pairs, and the two

---

1. The number of chromosomes normally present depends on the species of an organism. Although there is not perfect correspondence between the complexity of an organism and the number of its chromosomes, closely related organisms tend to have similar numbers of chromosomes. For example, chimpanzees, gorillas, and orangutans—species closely related to human beings—have forty-eight chromosomes. Recent analyses of chromosomes indicate that during human evolution two of the chromosomes present in these great apes fused to form a single chromosome (Chiarelli, 1973).

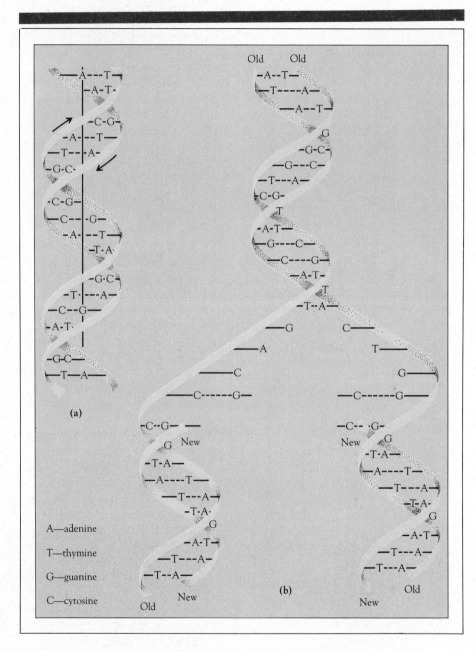

FIGURE 3.3
(a) The Watson-
Crick model of
DNA structure;
(b) the replica-
tion of DNA

(a)

A—adenine

T—thymine

G—guanine

C—cytosine

(b)

matched chromosomes in each pair are termed *homologous chromosomes*. One chromosome of each pair is inherited from the mother, and the other comes from the father. Two of the homologous chromosomes are termed the *sex chromosomes* because they determine the biological sex of the new organism. In the human species, males have an X and a smaller Y sex chromosome in each of their body cells, whereas females have two of the larger X chromosomes. The other forty-four chromosomes are termed *autosomes*. Figure 3.4 shows how the chromosome pairs differ in their relative size and shape. These differences, together with recently developed fluorescent-dye staining techniques, make it possible to distinguish the different types of chromosomes under a microscope. We thus can detect the presence of many chromosomal abnormalities.

A male's sperm cell and a female's ovum each contains half the number of chromosomes found in normal body cells. Hence the sperm and egg cells each contain twenty-three chromosomes. These unite during fertilization to produce a zygote with forty-six chromosomes. This not only determines the offspring's sex but also holds constant the number of chromosomes in the species. In other words, the halving of chromosomes in each parent's sex cells keeps the total

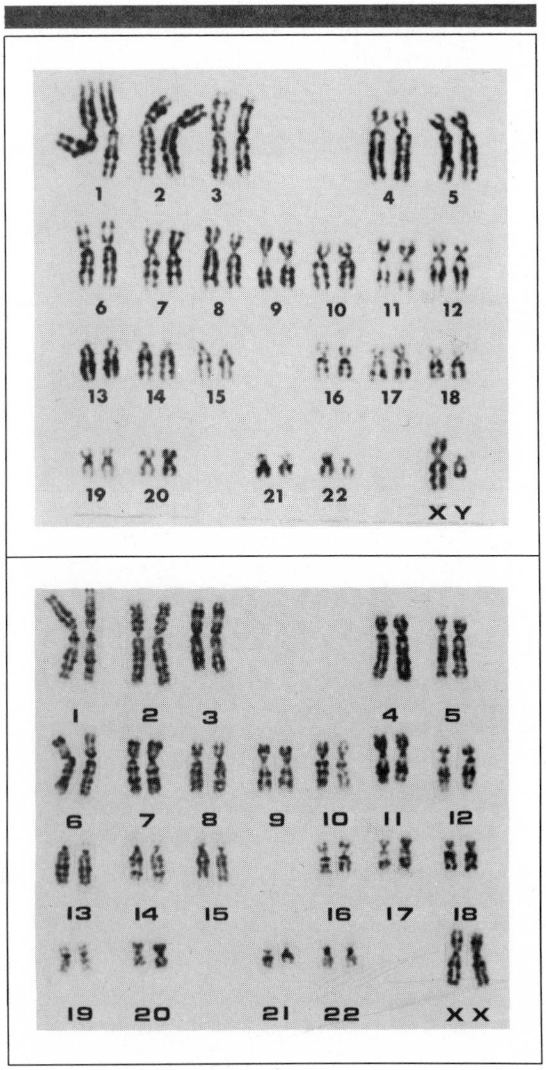

FIGURE 3.4
Human chromosome pairs. Pairs one to twenty-two are the autosomes; pairs twenty-three are the sex chromosomes, XY for the male and XX for the female.

number of chromosomes from doubling with each generation. The process by which this halving occurs is called *meiosis*.

Meiosis   Figure 3.5 illustrates meiosis, the process by which the chromosomes are sorted out during the formation of sex cells. Meiosis is orderly in the sense that a normal sex cell always receives one member of each chromosome pair. But there is also an element of randomness, for which one chromosome in a pair ends up in a particular sex cell is a matter of chance. This results in a variety of sex cells that contain different genetic combinations. Genetic variety is increased further because homologous chromosomes lie next to each other at one point during meiosis; at this time they may exchange stretches of DNA (called "crossing over" of genes). Finally, of course, the genetic variety is increased still further when the sex cells of the two parents are combined through fertilization (see Figure 3.5).

Note that the process of meiosis has some interesting consequences. For one thing, it ensures genetic variability, even among offspring of the same family.

FIGURE 3.5
Meiosis and mitosis.
(a) The body cells of each parent contain twenty-three pairs of chromosomes. (b) However, through *meiosis*, a member is taken randomly from each original pair of chromosomes. Each germ cell thus has twenty-three single chromosomes. (c) At fertilization, the single chromosomes from each parent's germ cell pair up and unite so that the zygote again contains twenty-three pairs of chromosomes—half from each parent. Then, through *mitosis*, the cells of the zygote divide and double, exactly duplicating the genetic material in each body cell.

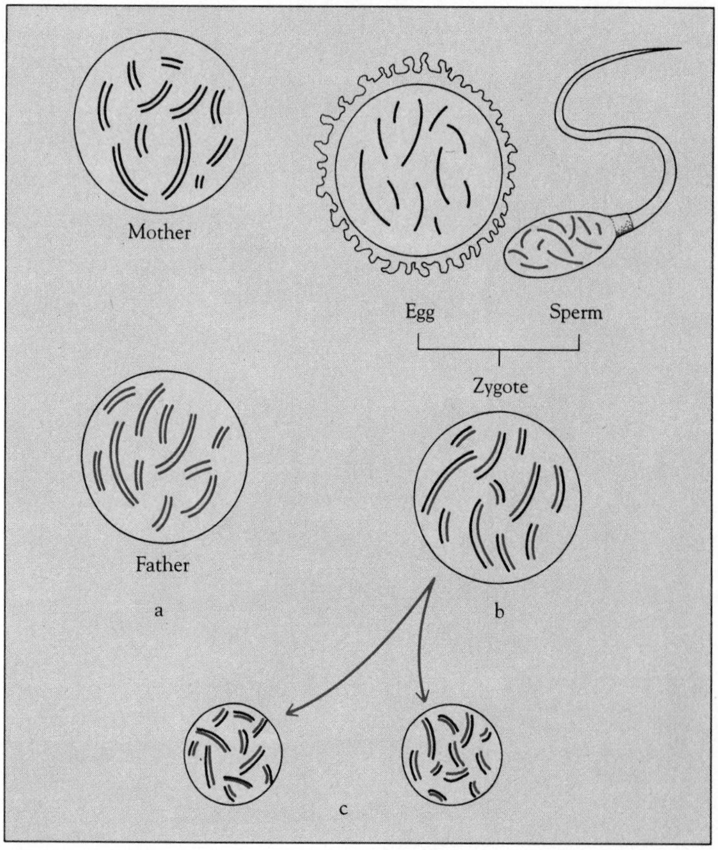

Family members are likely to resemble each other because their genes are drawn from the same pool, but because the off-spring inherit only one-half of each parent's genes, even brothers and sisters are certain to have differences.

Nina Leen, *Life* Magazine, © 1948 Time Inc.

To be sure, brothers and sisters are more likely to resemble each other and their parents than some biologically unrelated person, because their genes are drawn from the same pool provided by their parents. However, because the offspring inherit only one-half of each parent's genes—and because the subsets are drawn partly by chance—even children of the same parents are certain to differ considerably. Thus each individual is genetically unique (except when multiple births result from the splitting of a single fertilized egg). The likelihood that two individuals would inherit the same entire set of genes by chance is astronomically small.

Sex Determination Another interesting consequence of meiosis involves the determination of the offspring's sex. Because an XY sex chromosome pair produces a male and an XX pair results in a female, the sex of the child is determined by whether the sperm cell contains an X or a Y chromosome. (Because the mother's sex chromosome is XX, a normal egg cell will always contain an X chromosome.) A professor of gynecology at Columbia University, Landrum

Shettles, has suggested that this knowledge might be used to enable parents to determine the sex of their children. The X- and Y-bearing sperm should differ systematically in their weight (since the X chromosome weighs slightly more than the smaller Y), and perhaps in shape and chemical properties as well. Shettles has claimed (Rorvik & Shettles, 1970) to demonstrate in experiments with animals and in clinical trials with human couples that, indeed, it is possible to increase significantly the chances of having a child of the desired sex by using such methods as slightly altering the acidity of the mother's reproductive tract. (Shettles believes that acidity differentially affects the viability of X- and Y-bearing sperm.)

Shettles's work has been the subject of much criticism and controversy on both scientific and ethical grounds, and further research seems to be needed to establish the validity of his ideas and methods. One concern is that such methods may increase the risk of congenital defects. It may well be, however, that the not-so-distant future will offer parents reliable means of determining the sex of their children. This would be of greatest benefit when the risks of serious medical illness in a couple's offspring are known to be much smaller for children of a particular sex. Clearly, if such techniques do prove successful, they will also have important implications for such social problems as population control, the prevention of unwanted children, and the ratio of males to females in society. It is thus important that concerned persons begin to consider the possibility seriously, and to plan for its intelligent use.

Mitosis   Nearly all the cells in a particular person's body contain the same set of chromosomes and genes. (The few exceptions involve either errors or such cell types as red blood cells, which lose their nucleus and chromosomes during formation.) Most of the trillions of cells in the human body therefore contain the same genetic makeup as the single fertilized ovum from which they descended. Thus the original zygote and its descendants must undergo millions of divisions to produce this enormous number of cells. This cannot be accomplished by meiosis, in which the chromosomes are divided in half and then sorted out to form sex cells. Instead, a different process, called *mitosis,* occurs. In contrast to meiosis, mitosis involves the exact duplication of all the chromosomes, which are then sorted out into two "daughter" cells whose chromosome sets are exact duplicates of the original cell. As each cell divides and doubles, the hereditary blueprint is duplicated so that each body cell contains the same set of chromosomes and genes.

Concepts and Principles of Mendelian Genetics

Genes, like the chromosomes on which they are arrayed, occur in matched pairs. Genes found at the same spot, or locus, on homologous chromosomes are likely to contain similar strings of codons. They thus would be concerned with coding for the same type of protein, and they would affect similar traits. A gene at a given locus may have variant forms, called *alleles.* A person who inherits different alleles for a given locus is said to be *heterozygous;* if the alleles are identical, the individual is *homozygous* for that locus.

Inheriting two different alleles can have varying effects, depending on the particular genes and traits involved. The term *genotype* is used to refer to the genetic makeup of an individual, whereas the term *phenotype* refers to the actual physical or behavioral trait manifested (such as height, eye color, or intelligence). Suppose we identify the two allelic forms of a gene by the letters A and a. Given these two alleles, there are two possible homozygous combinations—AA and aa; and there is one heterozygous possibility—Aa. The effects of alleles A and a may be additive, in which case the phenotype corresponding to the Aa genotype will represent the average of AA and aa. Another possibility is that the inheritance of a single A allele may produce a phenotype equivalent to that of AA—in which case the A allele is said to be *dominant* and the a allele *recessive*. Or, if the A allele is only "partially" dominant, the phenotype may represent some value closer to that of AA than to Aa.

Interestingly, a number of the principles of genetic transmission were discovered around the time of the American Civil War by an Austrian monk named Gregor Mendel. On the basis of experiments in which he crossed different strains of plants such as garden peas, Mendel inferred several genetic principles. Among these are that each individual inherits two allelic forms of each gene (one from each parent); that genes affecting different traits can be segregated and then recombined to form new assortments during the formation of the sex cells; and that certain allelic forms can be dominant over other, recessive ones.

Mendel's work shows that the scientific mood often must be just right in order for the discovery of an important principle to have significant impact. His ideas were largely forgotten until the beginning of the twentieth century, when they were rediscovered and helped to inspire a new wave of scientific work on genetic processes (McClearn, 1970).

The Application of Genetic Principles

The random assignment of alleles at a given chromosomal locus to the sex cells during meiosis means that the genotypes inherited by a couple's children follow the rules of probability. For example, consider a case involving two allelic forms of a gene important in the metabolism of the amino acid phenylalanine. In this case, the allele that produces the enzyme responsible for normal metabolism is dominant over the recessive allele, which fails to produce a functional enzyme. An individual who is homozygous for the recessive gene thus suffers from an inherited metabolic disorder. Unless this is treated, it usually leads to a severe form of mental retardation.

Now consider a family in which both parents are heterozygotes who carry the recessive gene but are themselves phenotypically normal (since they also carry one normal, dominant gene). From this information we can calculate the chances that their children will inherit different genotypes and thus be either phenotypically normal or mentally retarded. Both parents in this case are carriers, and so their genotypes can be described as *Pp* (where *P* is the normal dominant allele and *p* is the dysfunctional recessive allele). Now, one-half of each parent's sex cells will contain the *P* allele, and the other half will contain the *p*. Which of these will actually unite during conception to form the zygote is a matter of chance. On average, one-quarter of the children will inherit the *pp* genotype and will be mentally retarded (unless treated); one-half will inherit *Pp* and will be phenotypically normal (through carrying a *p* allele); and one-quarter will not even carry the *p* allele. Clearly, the ability to make such probability statements is of critical importance in advising parents of their chances of having a child with an inherited disorder.

Developmental Genetics

Although the genotype is clearly necessary for the production of an individual's traits, there is rarely a perfect correspondence between a person's genotype and his or her phenotypic characteristics, for the phenotypic traits are usually influenced by environmental factors as well as by genetic inheritance.

Very briefly, genes seem to exert their control over development and bodily functions by regulating the production of proteins. One critical function of proteins—a function essential for life—is to serve as biochemical catalysts that control chemical reactions in the body. In many cases, the function of a particular gene is to provide the information for the synthesis of a particular enzyme, and each enzyme in turn regulates a specific chemical reaction or set of reactions. Genes thus influence physical and mental traits by means of their influence on biochemical reactions in the cells.

Pathways of Genetic Influence

The immediate products of genes are thus biochemical, and the ultimate effects of genes on mental and physical traits occur through biochemical mediators. Therefore, the pathways by which different genes affect behavior may be very complex. For example, Figure 3.6 shows how a genetic mutation that changes a single codon in a gene that codes for part of the hemoglobin molecule can lead to physical distortion or "sickling" of red blood cells. In turn, this can cause circulatory difficulties resulting in a variety of serious medical problems, including possible brain damage and paralysis (Neel & Schull, 1968).

The nature of the causal pathway linking genotype and phenotype also can take widely varying forms, depending on the gene and the behavioral trait involved. For example, when discussing genetic influences on intelligence, most of us probably think in terms of innate differences in brain structure and chemistry. This is certainly the explanation for some differences in intelligence. But genetic influences may also take less obvious and less direct forms. For example, there is evidence that some genetic factors may influence intelligence significantly via their impact on the quality of the intrauterine environment (Ahern & Johnson, 1973). Or genes may affect personality traits or even physical differences that, in turn, may influence such things as how much time a person spends studying intellectual material or how much opportunity the person has for higher education.

A final example illustrates the need for caution even in interpreting the nature of a trait in question. A classic study by Tryon (1940) selectively bred strains of rats that were high or low in "intelligence" as measured by the ability

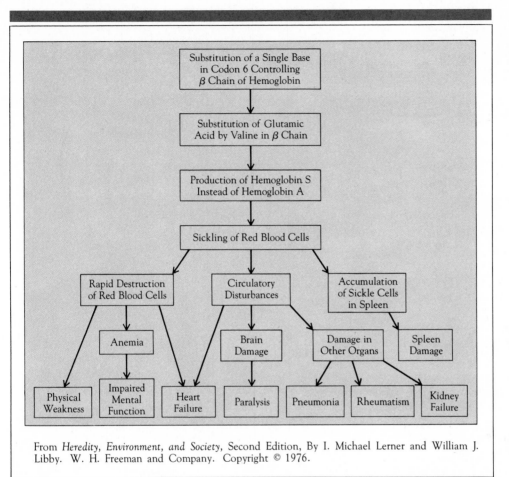

From *Heredity, Environment, and Society,* Second Edition, By I. Michael Lerner and William J. Libby. W. H. Freeman and Company. Copyright © 1976.

FIGURE 3.6
Simplified se-
quence of events
in sickle-cell
anemia

to learn certain mazes. However, analyses indicated that what distinguished the "dull" and "bright" strains of rats in this particular study was not learning capacity per se but sensitivity to such factors as the clanging shut of mechanical gates in the maze, which seemed more upsetting to the "dull" rats. Nonetheless, this should not be taken to mean that genetic factors do not influence learning ability or intelligence. For example, another study with rats was successful in selectively breeding for intelligence on maze tests because it excluded the kinds of emotional and sensory factors mentioned above (Fuller & Thompson, 1960).

Genes and Development over the Life Span

The impact of hereditary factors on developmental processes seems to be evident over the entire life span. This can be particularly striking in the case of physical traits, such as the resemblance between identical twins at different ages. Indeed, one can predict with about 98 percent accuracy whether or not twins of the same sex are identical by noting whether they are often confused for one another by their friends and relatives (Cohen et al., 1973).

Identical Twins Reared Apart

CONSTANCE HOLDEN

Bridget and Dorothy are 39-year-old British housewives, identical twins raised apart who first met each other a little over a year ago. When they met, to take part in Thomas Bouchard's twin study at the University of Minnesota, the manicured hands of each bore seven rings. Each also wore two bracelets on one wrist and a watch and a bracelet on the other. Investigators in Bouchard's study, the most extensive investigation ever made of identical twins reared apart, are still bewitched by the seven rings. Was it coincidence, the result of similar influences, or is this small sign of affinity a true, even inevitable, manifestation of the mysterious and infinitely complex interaction of the genes the two women have in common?

Investigators have been bemused and occasionally astonished at similarities between long-separated twins, similarities that prevailing dogma about human behavior would ordinarily attribute to common environmental influences. How is it, for example, that two men with significantly different upbringings came to have the same authoritarian personality? Or another pair to have similar histories of endogenous depression? Or still another pair to have virtually identical patterns of headaches?

These are only bits and pieces from a vast amount of data ... being collected by the University of Minnesota twin study.... The Minnesota investigators ... have processed nine pairs of identical or monozygotic twins (as well as several pairs of fraternal or dizygotic twins used as controls) and ... have managed to locate 11 additional pairs to take part in the study.

The Minnesota study is unprecedented in its scope, using a team of psychologists, psychiatrists, and medical doctors to probe and analyze every conceivable aspect of the twins' life histories, medical histories and physiology, tastes, psychological inclinations, abilities, and intelligence.... Each pair goes through 6 days of intensive testing, [including] ... detailed medical histories; ... electroencephalographs; ... several dozen pencil-and-paper tests, which ... cover family and childhood environment, fears and phobias, personal interests, vocational interests, values; ... three comprehensive psychological inventories; ... a slew of ability tests, [including] the Wechsler Adult Intelligence Scale (the main adult IQ test).... Mindful of charges of investigator bias in the administration of IQ tests in past twin studies, Bouchard has contracted with outside professionals to come in just for the purpose of administering and scoring the Wechsler intelligence test.

And the upshot of all this probing? Although the data have not yet been interpreted, there have already been some real surprises. Bouchard told *Science:* "I frankly expected far more differences [between twins] than we have found so far. I'm a psychologist, not a geneticist. I want to find out how the environment works to shape psychological traits." But the most provocative morsels that have so far become available are those that seem to reveal genetic influences at work.

Take the "Jim twins," as they have come to be known. Jim Springer and Jim Lewis were adopted as infants into working-class Ohio families. Both liked math and did not like spelling in school. Both had law enforcement training and worked part-time as deputy sheriffs. Both vacationed in Florida, both drove Chevrolets. ... Both like mechanical drawing and car-

Source: *Science,* Vol 207, no 21 (March 1980), pp. 1323-1326. Copyright 1980 by the American Association for the Advancement of Science.

pentry. They have almost identical drinking and smoking patterns. Both chew their fingernails down to the nubs.

But what investigators thought "astounding" was their similar medical histories. In addition to having hemorrhoids and identical pulse and blood pressure and sleep patterns, both had inexplicably put on 10 pounds at the same time in their lives. . . . Both suffer from "mixed headache syndrome"—a combination tension headache and migraine. The onset occurred in both at the age of 18. They have these late-afternoon headaches with the same frequency and same degree of disability, and the two used the same terms to describe the pain. . . .

Psychiatrically, according to Heston, who conducts personal interviews with all the twins, there has been remarkable agreement. "Twins brought up together have very high concordance in psychiatric histories," he says. (For example, if one identical twin has schizophrenia, the other one stands a 45 percent chance of developing it.) But what is surprising is that "what we see [with the twins in the study] is pretty much the same as in twins brought up together." By and large, he says, they share very similar phobias, and he has noted more than one case where both twins had histories of endogenous depression. In one case, twins who had been brought up in different emotional environments—one was raised in a strict disciplinarian household; the other had a warm, tolerant, loving mother—showed very similar neurotic and hypochondriacal traits. Says Heston, "things that I would never have thought of—mild depressions, phobias—as being in particular genetically mediated . . . now, at least, there are grounds for a very live hypothesis" on the role of genes not only in major mental illnesses, where chemistry clearly plays a part, but in lesser emotional disturbances. . . .

One of the greatest areas of discordance for twins was smoking. Of the nine pairs, there were four in which one twin smoked and the other did not. No one has an explanation for this. But, surprisingly, in at least one case a lifelong heavy smoker came out just as well on the pulmonary exam and heart stress test as did the nonsmoker. . . .

Lykken, who does the tests on the twins' central nervous systems, insists that when the mass of data has been ordered "there will be material that will make environmentalists very happy and material that will make hereditarians very happy." One thing that will not make the environmentalists happy is the fact that IQ seems to have a high degree of heritability, as indicated by the fact that of all the tests administered to identical twins separately reared, IQ shows the highest concordance. It is even higher than the introversion-extroversion personality trait, a venerable measure in psychological testing that shows higher concordance than other conventional categories such as sense of well-being, responsibility, dominance, and ego strength. . . .

The scores of identical twins on many psychological and ability tests are closer than would be expected for the same person taking the same test twice. Lykken also found this to be true of brain wave tracings, which is probably the most direct evidence that identical twins are almost identically wired. Several researchers also felt that there is something to the idea that identical twins reared apart may be even more similar in some respects than those reared together. The explanation is simple: competition between the two is inevitable; . . . many twins, in the interest of establishing their individuality tend to exaggerate their differences. . . .

Although the similarities are the most titillating to most observers, it is the discordances that will be the most informative. For any difference between a pair of identical twins is "absolute proof that that is not completely controlled by heredity."

Identical twins at different ages show the impact of hereditary factors throughout the life span.

A similar pattern is found for a number of psychological traits. On tests of intelligence, for example, identical twins have been found to be significantly more similar than fraternal twins—not only in infancy, childhood, and early adulthood but also in their sixties and seventies (Freedman, 1965; Jarvik & Cohen, 1973). Or, to consider an example in the realm of mental illness, Tay-Sachs disease and Huntington's chorea are both especially tragic degenerative diseases of the nervous system. Both typically result in the progressive psychological deterioration of a patient over a period of years, ultimately leading to death. And both diseases are caused by a defective gene or genes at a single chromosomal locus. But whereas Tay-Sachs usually strikes young infants soon after they are born and leads to death within a few years, Huntington's chorea usually does not set in until middle or old age.

The Timing of Gene Action   Genetic differences can also affect the timing and course of behavioral events, ranging from the age at which different behaviors first mature to the actual longevity of an organism. For example, Wilson (1978) has shown not only that the actual scores on motor and mental development tests are more similar for identical than fraternal twins but also that lags and spurts in mental growth also seem to be more similar for identical twins. Freedman (1965) has reported similar findings in the areas of social and personality development. Identical twin infants are more likely than fraternal twins to show similar ages for the onset of gazing into a human face, smiling at the mother's face, and showing fear of strangers.

Only a fraction of the genes in an individual's genotype are active at a given time. Different genes may be active at different times, and different sets of genes may be active at the same time in different cells of the body. (Recall that, with few exceptions, all cells in your body have the same set of genes—yet the properties of different cells vary greatly.) The fact that new genes are brought into play with increasing age has some interesting consequences. For example, because many genes that synthesize enzymes in an adult are not yet functional in a fetus or infant, the fetus or infant lacks many enzymes that an adult uses to metabolize various chemicals. As a result, many chemical substances (for example, drugs) that are relatively harmless for adults can cause serious harm to a fetus or infant. Furthermore, because different genes may manifest themselves at different times in the life cycle, behavioral characteristics that are absent in infancy or childhood but that appear in adulthood do not necessarily result solely from environmental factors.

How Gene Activity Is Controlled On the basis of the Nobel Prize-winning research of two French scientists (Jacob and Monod), it now appears that different stretches of the DNA molecule on a chromosome perform different functions. In effect, there are several different kinds of genes. *Structural genes* carry the actual blueprint for synthesizing a particular protein, and they direct the synthesis of that protein when they are "turned on." Other stretches of DNA, termed *operator* and *regulator genes,* do not themselves synthesize proteins but rather act to control the action of the structural genes. Operator and regulator genes thus provide a mechanism by which structural genes can be turned on or off at appropriate times, according to the developmental timetable of the organism.

The basic idea of gene action is that an active gene codes for the production of an enzyme that catalyzes chemical reactions in the cell, producing some necessary chemical product. But what prevents the gene from producing too much enzyme? What tells a gene to stop? The Jacob-Monod model suggests that regulator and operator genes act together to detect when a desired level of chemical production has been reached and to decrease production of additional enzyme by the structural gene. Although this model is based essentially on work with bacteria—and although genetic control mechanisms are likely to be even more complex in multicellular organisms such as human beings—it seems likely that similar genetic control mechanisms operate to influence our development.

Homeorhesis and Canalization of Development Most students of psychology are familiar with the concept of *homeostasis,* the idea that the body has regulatory mechanisms that maintain various critical physiological factors such as body temperature and acidity of the blood in a steady state that is compatible with life. These mechanisms act something like a thermostat, which maintains the temperature of a room at a steady level. But, as Jean Piaget (1970, 1973) has pointed out, a concept that is just as important for psychology—especially for developmental psychology—is that of *homeorhesis.* This refers to innate control mechanisms that serve to keep *developing* processes on a predetermined track, which is specified by the hereditary program in the genes.

Two examples involving physical growth may help to clarify this concept. Figure 3.7 illustrates evidence for the genetic control of growth between the

FIGURE 3.7
Genetic control of
growth for triplets
between ages six and
eighteen

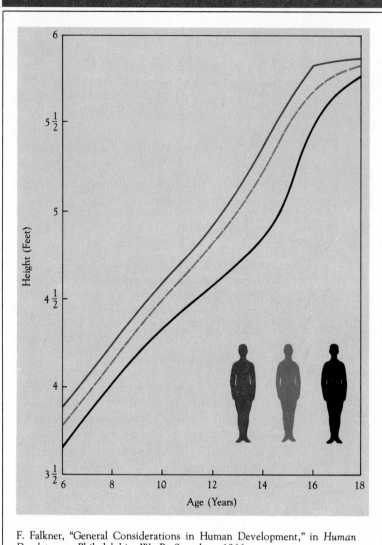

F. Falkner, "General Considerations in Human Development," in *Human Development*. Philadelphia: W. B. Saunders, 1966.

ages of six and eighteen. Note that two genetically identical members of a set of triplets showed very similar growth patterns, whereas the third triplet, who was descended from a separate zygote (but shared the same prenatal and postnatal environments), shows a dissimilar curve. Even more dramatic is the case of two single-egg twins who received very different amounts of nourishment through the placenta and then showed large corresponding differences in birthweights. With increasing age, the smaller twin tended to catch up with the large one in the years after birth (Falkner, 1966).

The idea, then, is that there are genetic factors that serve to channel, or *canalize*, development along certain predetermined pathways. This idea was

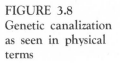

FIGURE 3.8
Genetic canalization
as seen in physical
terms

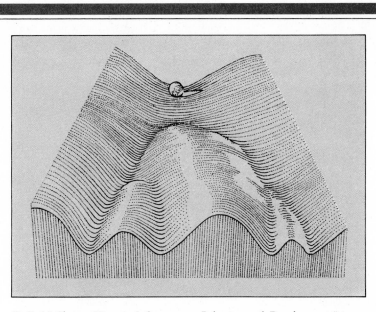

G. E. McClearn, "Genetic Influences on Behavior and Development," in *Carmichael's Manual of Child Psychology* P. H. Mussen (ed.). New York: John Wiley and Sons, 1970.

elaborated by the developmental geneticist Waddington (1957). The genetic canalization processes are thought to produce a kind of developmental equilibrium, so that if some environmental event temporarily pushes anatomical or behavioral development off course, the genetic mechanisms will tend to push it back on course. Waddington has proposed the analogy of a "developmental landscape" to illustrate the concept (see Figure 3.8). As McClearn (1970) has explained, development is in some ways analogous to a ball rolling down a landscape. In this analogy,

the contour of the landscape is determined by genotype, and the position of the ball represents the value of the developing phenotype. In the developmental process, represented by the ball rolling forward, environmental forces may act laterally upon the ball and displace it from its path. At crucial moments such a displacement can shift the system into a new channel of development. . . . A wide valley floor with gradually sloping sides represents a developmental pathway that is not well buffered, and permits environmental forces to displace the phenotype considerably. A narrow floor with steep walls, on the other hand, represents a highly buffered or canalized pathway. (p. 64)

Implications of Genetic Influences on Development

The concepts and principles we have examined so far provide a theoretical framework for understanding how genes influence development. For example, we have looked at how genetic material is duplicated, how it is transmitted within an organism and from one generation to the next, and how it acts via biochemical pathways. This section investigates some practical implications of genetic theory. Specifically, we will examine some ways that genetic factors can lead to mental retardation. Then, by examining IQ and skin color, we will discuss the degree to which individual differences result from hereditary factors, as well as the implications of genetic diversity. Finally, we will look at genetic influences on personality factors other than intelligence.

Genetics and Mental Retardation

It is possible to classify most genetic factors influencing mental development into three categories: major gene effects, chromosomal aberrations, and polygenic (multiple-gene) effects. Now we will discuss each of these categories in turn, illustrating them with an example of how each can lead to mental retardation.

Major Gene Effects   Many serious behavior disorders are known to be caused by the presence of a single defective gene. In such cases, a psychological defect results from the action of genes at a single locus on a chromosome pair. Such defects usually are termed *major gene disorders*.

Perhaps the best-understood example of a mental disorder caused by a major gene defect is *phenylketonuria,* or *PKU.* This is an interesting and important disease in its own right, for, if not treated, it is almost always associated with a severe degree of mental retardation. Several thousand Americans—about 1 percent of patients in institutions for the mentally retarded—are retarded because they have PKU. Moreover, because the disease is relatively well understood, it will serve to illustrate several points about major gene effects.

PKU was discovered in an interesting way. It seems that the father of two retarded children had mentioned to the children's dentist that, although the children were severely retarded, the doctors had been unable to discover any cause for the retardation. The dentist was intrigued by this puzzle and was particularly interested in whether the retardation might have something to do with the peculiar odor of the children. The dentist, in turn, interested a biochemist friend, who set about trying to determine the cause of the strange odor. He soon discovered that the culprit was a chemical substance in the children's urine—phenylpyruvic acid. This fortuitous discovery led to an understanding of the genetic basis of PKU, as well as to the development of a preventative treatment. More to our point, the story illustrates that inborn errors of metabolism often have odd diagnostic symptoms. A related example of mental retardation that is inherited through a single defective gene is *maple syrup urine disease.* Like PKU, this disease deposits an abnormal chemical in the urine, which—as its name suggests—smells something like maple syrup.

As might be suspected, there are a number of other forms of mental retardation that result from the lack of an enzyme needed to metabolize a particular amino acid. Typically, these forms of retardation also are characterized by the presence of an abnormal chemical in the urine, and they therefore are collectively called *amino-acid urias.*

People with PKU lack a particular enzyme—phenylalanine hydroxylase—that is needed to metabolize one of the amino acids, or building blocks of protein. Lack of this enzyme results in toxic levels of chemicals in the blood stream that seriously interfere with normal development of the nervous system. Because PKU is caused by a recessive gene, a person must inherit the same defective gene from *both parents,* resulting in a double dose of that gene (in technical terminology, the person is homozygous for that gene). Researchers have found that most genes that have an adverse effect on mental development are recessive. (There are exceptions to this; for example, Huntington's chorea is believed to be caused by a single dominant gene.)

Parents who are closely related biologically are more likely than distantly related parents to resemble each other genetically. Therefore, closely related parents are both more likely to carry the same defective gene and, therefore, to bear children who have a double dose of that gene. This principle, along with the fact that harmful genes tend to be recessive, means that closely related parents are more likely to have defective children.

That inbreeding tends to depress performance has been found to hold true for a variety of behavioral traits in both animals and human beings. This principle has been termed *inbreeding depression.* The extreme case of human inbreeding depression, of course, occurs in children born of incestuous relationships. Children conceived as the result of brother-sister or parent-child matings suffer a high risk of being stillborn or having a congenital mental or physical defect. Conversely, as kinship between the parents becomes increasingly distant, the probability increases that their children will be healthy, vigorous, and intelligent. The extreme example of *outbreeding* in human beings is represented by children of interracial unions. We might expect such children to show, on average, the benefits of *hybrid vigor.* This term originated in the observations of animal and plant breeders who saw that the hybrid offspring resulting from crossing two different strains were typically more productive and vigorous than either of the parent strains.

A gene usually has multiple effects, a principle that has been termed *pleiotropy.* A particular gene often contains the blueprint for a particular protein enzyme. A defective gene thus can lead to a metabolic block in the particular chemical reaction controlled by the enzyme for which the gene codes. But a particular chemical reaction in the body usually lies at the "crossroads" of a complex network of intersecting biochemical pathways. Hence an abnormality in the reaction controlled by a particular enzyme is likely to result in abnormalities in a number of chemical pathways and products.

Such is the case in PKU, where the failure to metabolize phenylalanine has the side effect of interfering with production of the skin pigment melanin. Hence people with PKU are likely to be blonder and lighter skinned than they would be without the defective gene. In addition to these tendencies, people with PKU also tend to have the odd-smelling urine mentioned earlier as well as small brains and bizarre mannerisms.

Besides having multiple effects, a gene is influenced by its genetic and environmental "background." PKU also illustrates the principle that a given gene's actual effects on the phenotype of an individual usually are modified both by the background of other genes in the person's genetic makeup and by the environment. Thus while most PKU patients are severely retarded, a small percentage show normal intelligence. The idea that the effects of even a "major" gene (that is, one with unusually strong effects on a particular trait) can be modified by a person's genetic background is also illustrated by pigmentation in PKU patients. For example, although European patients with PKU tend to be blond and blue-eyed, Japanese PKU patients typically have brown hair (rather than the usual black hair). Environmental factors also undoubtedly play a role, for PKU children who are kept at home seem to show higher IQs than those who are placed in institutions.

Treatment for PKU presently involves removing from the diet the chemical that tends to build up in toxic levels when the enzyme is missing. Thus PKU patients are put on diets that are low in phenylalanine. The *timing* of such dietary treatment is extremely important. The longer after birth that one waits to institute therapy, the greater the degree of permanent retardation the patient is likely to suffer. A low-phenylalanine diet seems to do little good if first given to children six years of age or older. (This may indicate that an important aspect of brain maturation is completed by around age six.) By contrast, children whose treatment is begun right after birth have a good chance of developing normal intelligence.

Because of the critical importance of beginning dietary treatment as soon as an infant with PKU is born, most states have passed laws requiring that all newborn infants be tested for the disease. It is estimated that about five hundred PKU babies are born in the United States every year. Fortunately, compulsory screening now allows medical experts to identify and treat most of these infants. Efforts are also under way to develop mass screening procedures for identifying infants with other amino-acid urias. Such measures would protect hundreds of additional infants from inherited mental retardation.

Chromosomal Aberrations Defects in the number or completeness of entire chromosomes represent a second type of genetic factor that has serious implications for psychological development. Recent technological advances have made it possible, through microscopic examination, to determine the number and types of chromosomes carried by a given individual. This has led to the discovery that several kinds of chromosomal aberrations are associated with serious mental disorder. About fifteen thousand babies born each year are deformed, mentally retarded, or sexually abnormal because of chromosomal abnormalities.

Perhaps the most serious form of chromosomal aberration occurs in *Down's syndrome* (formerly often referred to as "mongolism" because Down's syndrome patients often have a fold of skin covering part of the eye, thereby reminding some European observers of Oriental features). Patients with Down's syndrome carry an extra number 21 chromosome. Thus they have forty-seven chromosomes in all, and three are number 21 chromosomes (rather than the normal pair). Therefore, the term *trisomy-21* is often used for the disorder. Symptoms present in most patients include general retardation of growth, abnormal palm and finger prints, increased susceptibility to certain diseases such as leukemia,

Patients with Down's syndrome carry an extra number 21 chromosome and thus have forty-seven chromosomes in all.

© 1976 Bruce Roberts, Photo Researchers, Inc.

and severe mental retardation. As many as 10 to 15 percent of institutionalized patients with mental retardation have Down's syndrome.

There also are several forms of sex-chromosome aberrations associated with mental disorder. *Turner's syndrome* involves girls who have only a single X chromosome. Such girls usually fail to show normal sexual development, and about 20 percent are mentally retarded. *Klinefelter's syndrome* affects about 1 percent of institutionalized male retardates. The affected males have one Y chromosome and two or more X chromosomes (a normal male has one Y chromosome and one X). Males who carry an *extra* Y chromosome also may be at greater risk for behavioral problems. Men with this XYY set of sex chromosomes have been reported to be unusually tall on the average. It should be emphasized, however, that many—perhaps most—individuals with the XYY set develop as normal, responsible people.

It appears that defects involving chromosomes other than X, Y, or 21 are usually even more serious—so serious, in fact, that the fetus or infant who carries them typically dies very early in development. It is estimated that chromosomal aberrations result in about 100,000 miscarriages (spontaneous abortions) in the United States every year. This is about one-fifth the total number of miscarriages that occur—and a compelling reason to increase efforts to understand genetic influences on development.

Why Retardation Afflicts More Boys Than Girls

RICHARD A. KNOX

Scientists have recently stumbled on a new form of mental retardation, a discovery that begins to explain why more males than females end up in institutions for the retarded.

The disorder has been dubbed the "Fragile X Syndrome" because it shows up under the microscope as a defect in the X chromosome—one of the two sex chromosomes in every cell that determine whether a child will be male or female. It is characterized by retardation ranging from moderate to severe.

From early surveys, it appears that 2 to 3 percent of all males in institutions for the mentally retarded suffer from the newly recognized genetic defect. If this is borne out, it means that the disorder is second only to Down's Syndrome, or mongolism, as a known cause of mental retardation.

About 3000 US babies are born every year with Down's Syndrome, which afflicts males and females equally. Scientists are estimating that there are about 300 "Fragile X" babies (about one in 10,000 births a year), virtually all of them male.

Dr. Park Gerald of Harvard outlined "The Fragile X Story," as he called it, during a genetics conference at the Jackson Laboratories. . . .

From available evidence, it appears that the "Fragile X" syndrome is usually passed from mother to son—unlike Down's syndrome, which is almost always derived from a chance, one-time reshuffling of either parent's chromosomes rather than an inherited genetic defect.

Source: *The Boston Globe*, July 25, 1979, p. 3.
Reprinted courtesy of *The Boston Globe*.

The "Fragile X" syndrome is also unlike Down's and many other genetically caused forms of retardation in that it is associated with no gross physical abnormalities, though there is a tendency toward abnormally large testicles.

As Gerald explained it, scientists have puzzled for decades over the excess of males over females in institutions for the mentally retarded. Typically, 55 to 70 percent of institutionalized retardates are male.

The reason for this was a mystery until two Australians, Grant R. Sutherland and P. L. C. Ashforth, discovered in 1977 that the blood cells of many male retardates, but not in females, carried the "Fragile X." The defect showed up when the cells were grown in a special laboratory broth deficient in certain nutrients.

Other scientists soon began discovering the "Fragile X" trait. One important confirmation came from Gerald's laboratory at Children's Hospital Medical Center in Boston when he and his colleagues studied a family seen more than a decade earlier.

This famly, plus evidence from other labs, strongly indicate that the "Fragile X" syndrome is largely, if not always, an inherited defect passed on through the mother.

Daughters are usually spared the ill effects because they inherit one "good" X chromosome from their fathers, but sons (who inherit one X chromosome from the mother and a Y from the father) suffer the retardation if they get the mother's faulty X chromosome.

This pattern leads Gerald to suggest screening families for the "Fragile X" trait when there is an unexplained case of retardation. If the trait turns up, it probably means that future sons have a 50 percent chance of inheriting the defect and future daughters have a 50 percent chance of carrying the "Fragile X" defect.

Gerald said it is not possible to diagnose whether a fetus is affected.

Polygenic Effects.   As mentioned earlier, the term *pleiotropy* expresses the idea that a particular gene is likely to affect many different phenotypic traits. Conversely, the term *polygenic* refers to the idea that a particular trait can be affected by many different genes. Differences in some traits are determined mainly by whether individuals inherit one or another of the alternate forms (alleles) of a particular gene. However, individual differences in most traits that have been studied by geneticists are affected by many different genes; that is, the traits are polygenic. Human body height is an example. Some deviations from average height may result essentially from the action of a single gene; thus some forms of inherited dwarfism represent the effects of a major gene for height. However, most differences in height represent the cumulative effects of many different genes (and many different environmental events), each of which exerts a relatively small effect. Human intelligence, like height, seems to be largely a polygenic trait. That is, although a significant percentage of children may be retarded in physical or intellectual stature because of a single defective gene, *most* deviations from normal height or intelligence seem to reflect the combined action of many different genetic and environmental events.

Because they have relatively small individual effects, and because these effects may be masked by environmental factors, it is difficult to pinpoint individual "polygenes." It should be noted, however, that in the last few years, with advances in knowledge and methodology, researchers have begun to zero in on some of the polygenes affecting individual differences in intelligence. For example, one team of researchers using "marker genes" (genes known to have recognizable effects and to be located on a particular chromosome) recently produced evidence that a gene on the X chromosome affects cognitive styles related to intelligence (Goodenough et al., 1977). The difficulty in studying individual polygenes has led researchers to use various statistical techniques to study the impact of polygenic factors on such measurable traits as intelligence test scores.

Heritability

An important concept in genetic theory is that of *heritability*. The heritability of a trait like intelligence may be defined roughly as the proportion of the observed variation of the trait in a group that results from gene effects. In other words, heritability is a measure of the degree to which individual differences in a characteristic result from hereditary differences. Note that heritability refers to a group, or *population*, of organisms. It makes no sense to talk about the "heritability" of intelligence in a particular individual. In any individual case, retardation might spring from genetic factors, from some type of organic brain damage, from grossly inadequate learning opportunities, or from some combination of these. In addition to asking what role environmental and genetic factors may have played in the intellectual development of a given individual, we also may ask about the relative importance of these factors in an entire population. For example, if we were considering deviations from average IQ in all schoolchildren in a large city, we might ask whether these deviations resulted primarily from genetic or from environmental effects.

Heritability figures depend on the particular trait and population studied. For example, suppose we were interested in the heritability of skin color. If the population we studied consisted of all adults living in a Norwegian fishing village, we probably would find a low heritability—that is, most differences in skin color would probably reflect environmental factors having to do with amount of exposure to the sun rather than genetic factors. If, on the other hand, we took delegates to the United Nations as our population for study, we probably would find not only that the amount of individual variation in skin color was much greater but also that most of the variation was caused by genetic rather than environmental factors. Thus the heritability of skin color in *this* population would be quite high.

This point is worth emphasizing, because people often are tempted to take heritability figures for one population and try to generalize to another population—or even to make inferences about the causes of differences between two different populations. Such approaches can be misleading, however, as the following thought experiment illustrates. Suppose you took one hundred pairs of identical twins. Soon after conception you separated the members of each pair of twins, randomly assigning one twin of each pair to environment A and the other twin to environment B. All twins reared in environment A would receive uniformly good prenatal and postnatal care; all those in environment B would receive uniformly miserable care. Then you would test all the twins. If you looked at the scores for twins reared in environment A, the heritability would by definition be 100 percent; because you reared all these children under exactly the same conditions, any differences in IQ scores must reflect genotypic differences. Similarly, the heritability of the IQ scores for the B population would also be 100 percent. Because the heritability of IQ within both the A group and the B group is 100 percent, one might at first glance say that the differences in mean IQ between the A and B populations would also primarily reflect genetic factors. On the contrary—the differences between the A and B populations must reflect the differences between the good and bad environments that characterize the two populations, for we have designed this thought experiment so that the distributions of genotypes is exactly the same in each population (for every twin in population A, we have placed a matching identical twin in population B). What should we conclude from this?

The Practical Significance of Heritability   First of all, even a high heritability figure does not mean that the trait in question cannot be affected by environmental influences. For example, quantitative geneticist John deFries (1971) has pointed out that even in a population in which the heritability for IQ is 80 percent, one can expect to produce a twenty-point increase in IQ by rearing children in the best 1 percent rather than the worst 1 percent of intellectual environments in the population. Moreover, even a trait such as blood type, which now is 100 percent determined by genetic factors, can be affected by some new environmental treatment that does not yet exist (in this case, for example, by some new biochemical breakthrough).

What, then, does a high heritability figure for a trait suggest? First of all, it suggests that small to moderate changes in environment within the existing range are likely to have only slight effects on the phenotype in question.

Second, it suggests that in trying to improve the trait in question, it would be foolish to ignore the influences of genetic differences because they account for most existing individual differences. Third, and in particular, a high heritability figure indicates that the trait is likely to respond well to selective breeding. Indeed, the quantitative statistics of heritability were developed in large part to aid plant and animal breeders, because a heritability figure for a trait such as egg size or yield per acre gives breeders an indication of how rapidly and successfully they can breed for improvements in the trait. In fact, most psychological and physical traits in most species of animals and plants have some degree of heritability and will show response to selective breeding. One researcher (Thompson, 1954) was able to breed for a kind of "intelligence" in rats that involved the ability to solve a variety of different maze-running problems.

Is Average IQ Declining? In human populations, systematic and intensive artificial breeding of this kind is the exception rather than the rule. This does not mean that selection for particular genes does not occur—only that it usually does not take the form of deliberate public policy. (Exceptions involve the occasional attempts by governments—including some American states—to legislate sterilization of severely retarded individuals.) If, as seems to be the case, there is a significant heritability for a trait like IQ, and if persons with low IQs tend to have more children on the average than people with high IQs, then genes for low IQ tend to become relatively more frequent in the population. Thus the mean IQ would be likely to drop. For precisely this reason, when surveys showed that parents of low IQ do, indeed, tend to have larger-than-average families, many geneticists became alarmed, for it seemed possible that a disastrous drop in average IQ might result. Subsequent studies, however, indicate that the tendency for many retarded adults not to marry and not to have children at all more than compensated for those who do marry and have large families. In fact, taking this into account, two separate studies of white American populations suggest that, if anything, there may be a positive selection for genes for high IQ (see Figure 3.9). This is consistent with the findings of studies in both the United States and Europe that show a tendency for the mean IQ score to increase in the general population during the past fifty years (Bajema, 1966; Higgins, Reed, & Reed, 1962).

Heritability also depends on the particular trait being considered. Differences in some traits, such as blood type, are essentially determined entirely by genetic factors. Thus their heritability is 100 percent. However, most psychological traits manifest a much lower heritability than this. Of psychological traits that have been studied extensively, IQ score seems to show one of the highest heritabilities.

Evidence for High Heritability of IQ Scores Most estimates for the heritability of IQ range from about 40 to 85 percent, with the particular estimate depending on the particular population and test studied and on the method used in making the estimate. To consider the specific formulas used in making these estimates would involve a lengthy excursion into statistics, which is beyond the scope of this book. However, we can briefly survey some of the kinds of evidence that point to the high heritability of IQ.

FIGURE 3.9
Relationship between
fertility and IQ in
two samples of white
American populations.

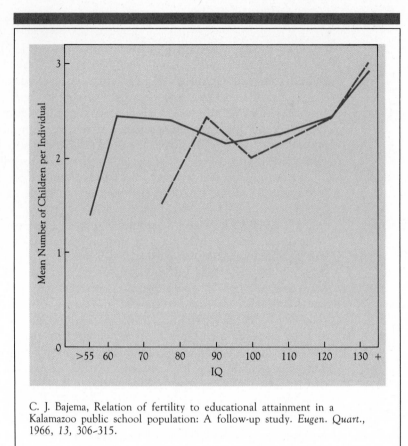

C. J. Bajema, Relation of fertility to educational attainment in a
Kalamazoo public school population: A follow-up study. *Eugen. Quart.*,
1966, *13*, 306-315.

First of all, there is the finding of literally hundreds of studies in many
different countries that the average similarity between two people in their IQ
scores increases in fairly direct proportion to the degree of their biological
relationship. That is, as illustrated by Figure 3.10, the IQs of biologically
unrelated individuals tend to be uncorrelated; distantly related relatives show a
slight positive correlation; close relatives show a moderately high similarity; and
identical twins show a very high degree of similarity in IQ scores (Erlenmeyer-
Kimling & Jarvik, 1963). Moreover, the exact way in which IQ correlations
increase with genetic similarity is very close to what one would expect according
to quantitative genetic principles. Although this is consistent with the idea of a
high heritability for IQ, it is not by itself conclusive because we would expect
the environments as well as the genes of closely related individuals to be more
similar. In an attempt to separate the effects of genetic and environmental
influences, researchers have turned to other kinds of studies.

Perhaps the most persuasive evidence for the importance of genetic influences
in accounting for individual differences in IQ comes from studies involving
twins and adopted children, respectively. Studies have repeatedly found that

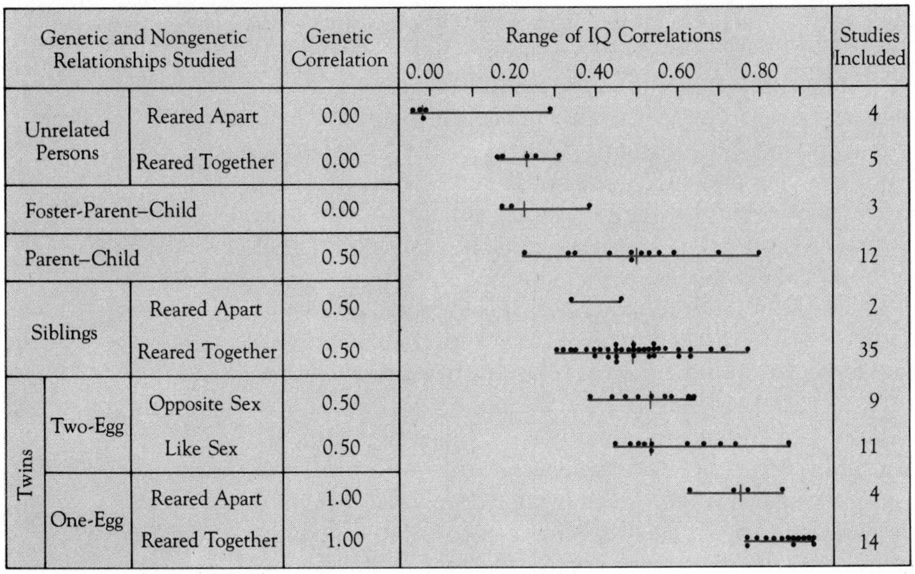

FIGURE 3.10
Summary of cor-
relation between
biological rela-
tionship and IQ

Genetic and Nongenetic Relationships Studied		Genetic Correlation	Range of IQ Correlations	Studies Included
Unrelated Persons	Reared Apart	0.00		4
	Reared Together	0.00		5
Foster-Parent–Child		0.00		3
Parent–Child		0.50		12
Siblings	Reared Apart	0.50		2
	Reared Together	0.50		35
Twins	Two-Egg Opposite Sex	0.50		9
	Two-Egg Like Sex	0.50		11
	One-Egg Reared Apart	1.00		4
	One-Egg Reared Together	1.00		14

Scale: 0.00, 0.20, 0.40, 0.60, 0.80

"Genetics and Intelligence: A Review," Erlenmeyer-Kimling, L., and Jarvik, L. F., *Science*, Vol. 142, pp. 1477-1479, Fig. 1, 13 December 1963. Copyright 1963, by the American Association for the Advancement of Science.

identical twins (who have identical genotypes) resemble each other much more closely in IQ than do fraternal twins (who genetically resemble each other no more on the average than ordinary siblings). Indeed, identical twins resemble each other more closely in IQ than fraternal twins even if the identical twins have been separated and reared by different families and the fraternal twins have been reared in the *same* family. By contrast, biologically unrelated children reared in the same household do not tend to resemble each other very closely in IQ. Most impressive of all, twins separated and placed in different homes right after birth resemble each other just as much in IQ as twins not separated until several years after birth (that is, who shared the same home environment for several years). Environmentalists still might argue that the greater resemblance of identical twins who have been separated might reflect a greater resemblance of their *prenatal* environments. However, the most careful studies of this question indicate that, on the average, the prenatal environments of identical twins actually tend to be somewhat more different than the prenatal environments of fraternal twins.

Studies of adopted children also point to the high heritability of IQ. The IQs of adopted children tend to correlate highly with the IQs of their biological parents but show little or no correlation with the IQs of their adoptive parents. And, most remarkable of all, one longitudinal investigation (Honzik, 1957) found that, with increasing age, the IQs of adopted children came to resemble more and more closely the educational level of their *biological*, rather than their adoptive, parents.

Studies such as these make a rather persuasive package, and some psychologists have been led to suggest on this basis that the heritability of IQ may approach 90 percent (Jensen, 1969). At the other pole are skeptics such as Kamin (1973), who point out that most studies are flawed by methodological weaknesses that make them less than conclusive. For example, the adoption studies reveal a troublesome tendency for adoption agencies to selectively place the children born to parents of higher socioeconomic status in better adoptive homes. Furthermore, adoption agencies conscientiously try to place all foster children in the best available homes. Since adoptive homes tend to be uniformly good, it would be difficult to show that differences between such homes have much effect on IQ. (In fact, in one classic adoption study, although there was no significant correlation between adoptive children's average IQs and the adoptive parents' socioeconomic status, the adoptive children's average IQs were significantly higher than those of their biological mothers.)

Kamin also argues that the twin studies are inconclusive, since statistical analyses suggest that much of twin resemblance simply may reflect the fact that the twins are the same age. Finally, Kamin notes that the studies of twins reared apart are somewhat misleading because the twins not reared by their own parents in these cases are often placed with a relative or family friend who is likely to provide a similar environment. Kamin concludes that there is little if any significant heritability for IQ.

What, then, are we to think? In the light of these conflicting arguments, can we conclude anything about the heritability of IQ? A balanced view suggests that the overall pattern of data is most consistent with a heritability estimate that lies somewhere between that of the hereditarian Jensen and the environmentalist Kamin. For although no single study seems immune to methodological criticism, the body of research on this question seems most consistent with a moderate figure on the order of, say, 0.40 (see, for example, Jencks, 1972). The basic problem, of course, is that all the data we are discussing are correlational rather than experimental in nature. As with almost any correlational study, it is usually possible to think of some alternative explanation (other than a causal linkage) for the association between two correlated factors.

Although this complex pattern of present evidence and arguments may not yield a conclusive answer, it is worth considering for two reasons. First of all, it is the best evidence we now have regarding the heritability of intelligence. And second, our discussion serves to acquaint readers with the kinds of ingenious though imperfect twin- and adoption-study methods that have been the primary tools used to try to establish the heritability of a whole range of critically important psychological processes, ranging from personality characteristics to serious forms of mental illness such as schizophrenia and depression. Clearly, we need some new methods for analyzing the genetics of human behavior.

Recent Approaches to Studying Genetics of Behavior   Until we can produce experimental evidence that genetic factors (aside from a few known major defects such as PKU and trisomy-21) affect individual differences in IQ, it will be hard to convince environmental skeptics such as Kamin. Is it possible, ethically, to conduct such genetic experiments on human intelligence? On reflection, the answer seems to be yes—if we apply enough ingenuity. One approach is to study children conceived through artificial insemination; investigators could assign sperm randomly from among donors who would be chosen in the usual manner. Any correlations between the IQs of sperm donors and their biological children would argue strongly for genetic influences on intellectual development (though it is technically possible for environmental factors, such as viruses, to be transmitted with the semen from the donor).

A complementary approach utilizes the natural experiment that is entailed in the random assignment of genes from the parents' genotype to that of the children. This approach, technically known as *linkage analysis,* works roughly as follows. Genes located close to each other on the same chromosome tend to be passed on together and are said to be genetically "linked." Geneticists now know of a number of genetic "markers," such as blood types, which are determined by genes on a particular chromosome. Thus if siblings who are identical for a certain genetic marker resemble each other more closely for a trait such as IQ than do siblings who differ with respect to that marker, that fact suggests that a gene close to the marker gene contributes significantly to similarity in IQ. One recent study used this technique to provide some preliminary evidence that a major gene influencing cognitive-perceptual style may have its locus on the X chromosome (Goodenough et al., 1977).

It seems likely that sophisticated and ingenious new techniques of analysis such as these will be needed to provide definitive evidence concerning the genetic factors that influence such vitally important psychological traits as intelligence and mental illness.

Implications of Attitudes Toward Heritability

Many people—and perhaps psychologists and social scientists most of all—are reluctant to accept the idea that genetic differences may be the most important or even *a* very important factor in accounting for individual differences in such psychological traits as mental health or IQ. Perhaps two sources of this reluctance involve past perversions of genetic arguments used to rationalize inhumane practices, and a feeling that genetic causation of a condition implies that little can be done to improve the condition. Let us consider these two propositions.

The history of inhumane policies has been associated with the misunderstanding of genetic principles. Most Americans are aware that unfounded beliefs about the racial inferiority of other peoples have been used to rationalize a variety of brutal social policies. For example, consider the slavery and racial discrimination that occurred in the United States, including immigration policies that until fairly recently discriminated against all nationalities except northern Europeans. Other examples include the colonial exploitation by Europeans of hundreds of millions of Third World people and the "Aryan supremacy" programs of the Nazis, which set out to exterminate entire groups of people such as Jews and Slavs, who were deemed racially inferior. Because basic misunderstandings of the nature of racial differences have led to such horrible and tragically misguided policies, we should examine our present scientific understanding about the nature and origin of races.

Racial Groups: Genetic Diversity Beneath Apparent Uniformity   Racial conflict and discrimination probably have been aggravated because appearances are somewhat misleading in the case of racial differences. That is, particular racial groupings of people are often remarkably similar—at least in terms of such physical aspects as facial features and color of skin, eyes, and hair. Moreover, these physical features are most obvious at first glance and are also strongly influenced by genetic factors. This often leads people to infer incorrectly that individuals of a given racial category are likely to be uniform as well with respect to other traits strongly influenced by genetic factors.

In fact, however, evidence suggests that—beneath the superficial uniformity of striking physical features—there is enormous genetic diversity. Recent biochemical research indicates that if two different members of the same racial group are chosen at random, they will be almost as different genetically, on the average, as two individuals chosen at random from *different* racial groups.

Racial Differences as Biological Adaptations   Anthropological research provides us with a good explanation for this finding. It appears that the striking physical characteristics that many people use in attaching racial labels to others show a high degree of uniformity because they represent important biological adaptations to climatic conditions that have exerted very strong and uniform selection pressures (see Howell, 1960). For example, the epicanthal fold (or fold of skin partly obscuring the eye) that accounts for the beautiful almond-shaped eyes characteristic of most Asiatic peoples is thought to represent a biological adaptation to extreme cold (see Figure 3.11). This belief is based on fossil evidence showing that most present-day Asiatic peoples are descended from a group of people who were isolated for tens of thousands of years in the northeast corner of Siberia. The characteristic facial features of Orientals, including the epicanthal fold and extra deposits of insulating tissue in the face, seem to represent a biological adaptation serving to protect the nasal and sinus passages from exposure to extreme cold.

Similarly, skin color seems to represent a biological adaptation to the average amount of sunlight present in a given geographical area. It seems that when ultraviolet rays in sunlight penetrate a certain layer of the skin, they induce a chemical reaction that results in the production of vitamin D. This source of vitamin D is important for good health and survival—especially if it is difficult for individuals to obtain enough of the vitamin through their diet. For this reason, it is advantageous for peoples living in regions that receive relatively little sunlight to have light skins because the skin pigment, melanin, serves to reduce the amount of ultraviolet light penetrating the deeper layers of the skin. Conversely, it is advantageous for peoples living in tropical regions to have dark skins, both to prevent them from accumulating too much vitamin D and to protect them against skin cancer. (Even in temperate zones, the risk of skin cancer is much greater for a blond than for a brunette.) Eskimos, interestingly,

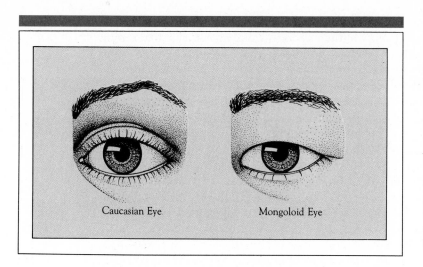

FIGURE 3.11
Racial differences as biological adaptations. The epicanthal eye of the Mongoloid races is one of the more recent anatomical human adaptations to the environment. The epicanthal fold protects the eye against the severe winters in Asia. Compare this with the Caucasian eye, which has a single, fatty lid.

are the exception that proves the rule in this case, for though their skin is certainly dark by comparison with Scandinavians, their diet is unusually rich in vitamin D. (Clinical signs of vitamin D deficiency have been reported in a number of Eskimo communities where the people have switched from traditional to more "modern" eating habits.)

A third example concerns the aquiline nose characteristic of many Semitic peoples. Like the epicanthal fold and skin color, the form of the nose is most likely a biological adaptation to particular climatic conditions. For example, an aquiline nose may confer a selective advantage in semidesert regions by helping to protect the lungs against dust and desiccation.

The three physical traits we have discussed (epicanthal fold, skin color, and aquiline nose) together have played a crucial role in the racial discrimination that has racked the world for centuries. It is especially sad and ironic that this should have been so, for each of these traits represents a particularly beautiful and valuable biological adaptation. Indeed, if biologists were forced to design one "ideal" human type most likely to adapt physically and mentally to a variety of conditions, they might well include all three of these traits.

The Value of Biological and Genetic Diversity   Of course, it would be a tragic mistake to try to design any one ideal biological type of human being (though some simple-minded racists have attempted to do just that). Diversity in the genetic makeup and biological traits of a species is virtually a necessity for survival itself over the long haul, because survival requires repeated adaptation to changing environmental circumstances. A rather striking illustration of this general genetic principle concerns the dangers of excessive genetic uniformity in crops. Plant geneticists have been remarkably successful in breeding "miracle" strains of crops that are unusually productive. In many cases, these crops have been of critical importance—literally saving thousands of people from starvation because of their increased yields. Unfortunately, however, many of these new strains carry with them an immense danger of catastrophe. Because plant breeders often work under great time pressures, they have not always been able to include much genetic diversity in the new high-yield strains. Thus in certain areas entire crops have been planted with seeds that essentially are identical genetically. This greatly increases the risk that the *entire* crop will be wiped out by an outbreak of some plant disease. (In a genetically diverse crop, only a fraction of the plants would be likely to succumb to the blight, for some would be genetically resistant to that particular disease.) An example of this phenomenon is apparently the reason why the English are today an nation of tea drinkers. It seems that, until about 150 years ago, most English men and women drank coffee. Then an epidemic broke out among the coffee plants on the island of Ceylon, from where Britain secured most if its coffee, that destroyed the entire crop and drove the price of coffee in Great Britain sky-high. The coffee plantations in Ceylon were replanted with tea plants, and the British began taking tea, instead of coffee, with their crumpets.

The human species would do well to preserve diversity in its own gene pool as well. Diversity is especially important with respect to genes that strongly influence psychological development. After all, the most important biological adaptation of Homo sapiens is our ability to survive by our wits.

The Genetic Irrationality of Racial Discrimination The fact that racial groups are genetically heterogeneous (with the exception of a few striking physical traits already discussed) has some important implications. It means, first of all, that although the *average* values of a particular quantitative physical or behavioral trait will not necessarily be exactly the same in different racial or geographic populations, the *distributions* of these vaules will almost always overlap. In other words, only rarely, if at all, will the striking physical characteristics we use in assigning racial labels to people be useful in predicting how a particular person stands on some other trait. For most purposes, then, racial categories are likely simply to distract us from the really important genetic differences among individuals (differences that cut across different racial groupings). The practical implication of this, of course, is that racial discrimination is both inaccurate and unfair.

The Danger of Ignoring Individual Differences Many American psychologists and educators have tended to minimize or ignore the question of how genetic differences may affect behavioral differences. Perhaps they fear that evidence of such differences might somehow be used to defend practices of racial or ethnic discrimination. But ironically, there is reason to think that, in the long run, *ignoring* the impact of genetic differences on psychological development is more likely to result in harm to members of racial minorities. For example, although the distribution of values of a trait are *likely* to overlap in different racial groups, there is no magical guarantee that the average value of this trait will always be *exactly* the same for both groups. In cases where the average value of a trait differs significantly between two racial or ethnic populations, and where individual differences with respect to that trait are ignored by educators or health professionals, the result is likely to penalize members of the ethnic minority.

An illustration of this idea is provided by research on the trait known as lactose intolerance. Adults with this trait tend to develop gastric distress when consuming lactose, the primary form of sugar present in milk and many milk-based products. Lactose intolerance seems to be inherited, and it is rare among northern Europeans but very common among many peoples of Africa and East Asia, who have not had a long tradition of using dairy products. A dietician who believes in equal treatment for all might well choose milk as a staple item for meals served in a college cafeteria because it is so nutritious for the majority of students. Although intended to be egalitarian, this rather simple-minded and misguided treatment would tend to disadvantage members of ethnic minorities whose ancestors came from regions of Africa and Asia where lactose intolerance predominated. A more enlightened dietician would take individual genetic differences into account and would give lactose-intolerant students a choice of readily digested, nutritious substitutes for milk.

A hypothetical example will illustrate how this principle might apply to psychological development. Suppose that there are two methods of teaching an important skill such as reading. Let us further suppose that some children learn better with method A and others learn better with method B. Finally, suppose that most children of the racial or ethnic majority learn best with method A and that most children of the minority racial group learn best with method B. If educators decided to ignore individual differences and utilize only one method, they naturally would tend to choose the method that works best for the most children, regardless of their ethnic or racial identities. In this hypothetical case, educators would choose the method that works best for the children of the majority racial group, since, by definition, there are more children in that group. At first glance, this reasoning might seem to argue that schools should be segregated along ethnic or racial lines. This strategy would miss the point, however, because it would simply create "new minorities"—that is, minorities of children in each of the racial groups who would do better if they were taught to read by the second method.

A proper scientific understanding of human genetics and individual differences suggests that we must avoid two dangers. On the one hand, we must eschew fallacious hereditary theories of racism that overlook individual differences and misguidedly attempt to type people according to certain simple-minded genetic categories. On the other hand, we must avoid the kind of simple-minded and fallacious environmentalism that tries to deny or ignore genetic influences on individual differences altogether.

Genetic Influences on Personality Development

Up to this point we have focused primarily on the genetics of intelligence and mental retardation, both because these traits are so important and because they have been the focus of so much research and controversy among developmental psychologists. It is important to emphasize, however, that genetic differences affect not only intellectual development but a wide range of other psychological processes as well. Experimental studies with animals have shown the effects of genotypic differences in such personality traits as activity level, emotionality, and hoarding; in such social behaviors as maternal care and aggression; in measures of learning ability or intelligence; and even in susceptibility to mental diseases or such abnormalities as seizures and alcohol addiction. Genetically controlled behavioral differences between different species and among different individuals of the same species may be even more evident among *non*mammalian animals that display a wide variety of instinctual behaviors in which the action of genes is well buffered against environmental changes. Thus geneticists have been able to demonstrate genetic control of such behavioral differences as the tendency for flies to avoid or approach light, for bees to remove dead or diseased larva from their hives, and for birds to engage in complex mating displays or nest-building activities (McClearn, 1970). Moreover, geneticists have been able in many cases to determine the number and types of genes mediating these behaviors—and even to map their locations on particular chromosomes.

Human Personality and Mental Illness   Do genetic differences influence a variety of psychological differences in human beings as well as in animals? The best evidence indicates that they can, although heritability seems to vary considerably from one trait to another. Briefly, genetic influences are known to affect differences in sensory processes, such as color blindness or taste acuity, as well as in personality traits and predispositions to certain forms of mental illness.

Although the present evidence for genetic influences on many personality variables is inconclusive (Nichols, 1969), one personality trait that consistently has appeared to have high heritability in a number of twin studies is the tendency toward introversion or extroversion. (*Introverts* show a greater tendency toward shyness in social situations, whereas *extroverts* are more outgoing and gregarious.) Hereditary factors also seem to play a role in mental illness, particularly in the more serious, or psychotic, forms such as manic-depressive psychosis and schizophrenia. In this discussion we will focus on *schizophrenia*, because it is among the most serious forms of mental illness and because it has been the subject of particularly extensive genetic research. Millions of people around the world are afflicted with schizophrenia, which involves a disturbance of logical thought processes, attention, emotional harmony, and social relationships. In more extreme cases, it may include such symptoms as hallucinations, delusions of grandeur or persecution, and bizarre postures or movements. Because the illness affects so many and often involves prolonged hospitalization, it has been estimated that until recently 25 percent of all hospital beds in the United States were occupied by schizophrenic patients.

Genetic Predispositions and Environmental Triggers   Evidence from a number of carefully conducted twin and adoption studies suggests that there is an important hereditary predisposition to schizophrenia (see, for example, Kety et al., 1973; Kinney & Matthysse, 1978; Rosenthal, 1970). Supporting evidence also comes from studies that indicate that infants who later became schizophrenic were more likely than normal babies to show deviations in their sensorimotor development—even within the first few months after birth (Fish,

1973; Mednick, 1972). However, evidence suggesting that genetic factors contribute to many cases of schizophrenia does not mean that environmental factors are not involved. Indeed, in some cases it appears that a severe environmental event such as a brain tumor or injury may precipitate symptoms indistinguishable from those of schizophrenia (Davison & Bagley, 1969). Moreover, it may be that even when a definite genetic predisposition is present, it still may take some adverse environmental factor to trigger the onset of the illness. Therefore, although it is three to four times more common among identical twins than fraternal twins for both members to be schizophrenic, it is still true that when one twin is schizophrenic the genetically identical co-twin will be schizophrenic only about half the time. It may be that several genes can contribute to this predisposition to schizophrenia. If so, then one could inherit varying numbers of such genes, and the degree of vulnerability (and, hence, the strength of the environmental stressors needed to trigger schizophrenia) thus might vary considerably. Another possibility is that schizophrenia, like mental retardation, is really a cluster of phenotypically similar disorders with different genetic and environmental causes.

Finding ways in which twins are consistently similar (despite being discordant for schizophrenia) is likely to point to the nature of the hereditary predisposition. Conversely, finding consistent environmental differences between the life histories of a sick twin and a well co-twin is likely to give clues about the nature of environmental stressors that trigger schizophrenia. Twin studies of this kind, as well as other data, suggest that environmental stressors triggering schizophrenia might include complications of pregnancy and delivery as well as social conflict and family dynamics. However, evidence concerning the exact nature of the genetic and environmental factors still eludes us.

It does seem likely that what is inherited in many cases of schizophrenia is not a disease per se but a genetic predisposition that makes a person more likely to develop a certain type of psychiatric illness when subjected to environmental stresses. If this general notion is correct, then it clearly is important that we be able to identify the nature of both the hereditary predisposition and the precipitating environmental stresses. If we could detect genetically vulnerable individuals at an early age, we might be able to protect them from precipitating factors and thus prevent them from developing schizophrenia.

Using Genetic Knowledge to Improve Human Life

As we noted earlier, one source of resistance to evidence for genetic causation of behavioral disorders is the incorrect assumption that genetic determination of a psychological condition implies that nothing can be done to improve the condition. To help clear up that dangerous misunderstanding, we will conclude this chapter by considering briefly some of the many approaches to dealing with genetic influences on psychological development.

Perhaps the most dramatic examples of the benefits of genetic research are provided by cases in which the nature of a genetic disorder is so well understood that a specific preventive treatment can be applied, as, for example, in the dietary treatment of PKU. Another such instance is the prevention of *erythroblastosis fetalis,* a disease resulting from an immunological incompatibility between a pregnant woman and the baby she is carrying.

Prevention of Erythroblastosis Fetalis

If a baby's blood is Rh positive (it has a gene that produces the Rh protein carried on the surface of the red blood cells) but the mother's is Rh negative (it lacks the genes for this protein), her immunological system will produce antibodies to attack this foreign protein should it enter her blood stream. Thus if any Rh positive fetal blood should seep across the placental barrier or enter the maternal blood stream as a result of hemorrhage during delivery, the mother will become sensitized against the Rh antigen and may produce antibodies that will attack and destroy the baby's red blood cells.

Approximately 15 percent of American women are Rh negative. Of the more than three million births every year in the United States, roughly 250,000 involve an Rh positive infant and an Rh negative mother. About 10 percent of these cases are likely to present a serious problem. As recently as 1967, perhaps ten thousand babies a year died in the United States from Rh disease, and thousands more suffered such mental disorders as paralysis and mental retardation.

Today, however, this illness can be prevented 99 percent of the time. The preventative treatment is as ingenious as it is effective. When a problem arises, it is usually because the mother has become sensitized to the Rh antigen during the birth of her first Rh positive baby, so that it is typically only later-born infants who are affected. If the mother somehow could be prevented from becoming sensitized, the problem could be averted—and that is precisely the approach used. Within seventy-two hours after birth (or an abortion or a miscarriage), most Rh negative mothers in the United States now are injected routinely with Rhogam, which contains Rh antibodies produced *outside* the mother's body. These antibodies help to destroy any Rh-positive antigens from the baby that may have seeped into the maternal circulation, thereby preventing the mother from becoming sensitized (see Figure 3.12). Thus because of advances in our understanding of human genetics, the potentially tragic effects of erythroblastosis fetalis can be prevented—if the Rh incompatibility between the mother and baby is recognized in time. It is therefore clearly important for prospective parents to consult with a gynecologist about taking appropriate precautions to protect their baby from this disease.

Genetic Counseling

Even in cases where such direct biochemical prevention is not yet possible, other methods are available for preventing genetic disorders. The simplest method is that of *genetic counseling*—providing parents with knowledge about the risks of their passing a genetic disease onto their children. For example, in cases of diseases caused by a dominant gene (such as Huntington's chorea), the

FIGURE 3.12
The cause and
prevention of
Rh disease

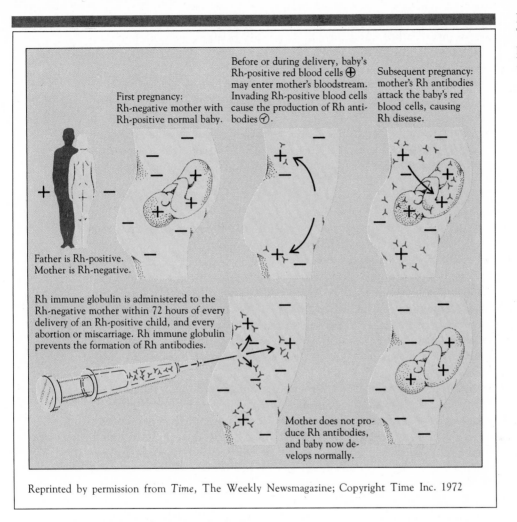

First pregnancy:
Rh-negative mother with
Rh-positive normal baby.

Before or during delivery, baby's
Rh-positive red blood cells ⊕
may enter mother's bloodstream.
Invading Rh-positive blood cells
cause the production of Rh antibodies ⊙.

Subsequent pregnancy:
mother's Rh antibodies
attack the baby's red
blood cells, causing
Rh disease.

Father is Rh-positive.
Mother is Rh-negative.

Rh immune globulin is administered to the
Rh-negative mother within 72 hours of every
delivery of an Rh-positive child, and every
abortion or miscarriage. Rh immune globulin
prevents the formation of Rh antibodies.

Mother does not pro-
duce Rh antibodies,
and baby now de-
velops normally.

Reprinted by permission from *Time*, The Weekly Newsmagazine; Copyright Time Inc. 1972

probability that a given child will inherit the disease is 50 percent in a mating where one parent has the disease. For a recessive disease, if both parents are carriers, the chances are 25 percent that a given child will inherit the defective gene from both parents and thus manifest the disease. Until recently, parents usually did not realize that they were carriers of recessive deleterious genes; they did not know that their children were in danger until a child was born with the disease. With recent advances, however, it is possible in many cases to detect whether a parent is a carrier. Such parents still face a difficult decision: either they risk having a child who may be born with a serious disorder, or they decide not to have children at all. Nevertheless, in cases where such a genetic disorder is relatively common among a well-defined group, medical geneticists are now making efforts to screen large numbers of potential parents so that they can be alerted about the dangers of having an affected baby. One example of this procedure concerns *Tay-Sachs disease* (also known as infantile amaurotic idiocy), a serious degenerative disease of the nervous system that usually sets in soon after the infant is born and produces a steady psychological decline, culminating in death when the infant is only a year or two old. The disease is thus an unusually cruel one, as the parents must watch helplessly as their young baby slowly dies. As it happens, Tay-Sachs disease is caused by a recessive gene and primarily affects Jewish children of northern and eastern European ancestry. For this reason, the Jewish medical community has been active in urging all American Jews who are prospective parents to have a simple test to determine whether they are carriers of the gene. Carriers thus could avoid marrying each other, or, if already married or planning to marry, they could adopt children.

Amniocentesis

For people who already are married and wish to have their own children, the knowledge that they are carriers of deleterious genes alerts them to the danger but does not solve their dilemma. However, a new procedure provides a partial solution. Called *amniocentesis,* this process involves inserting a long-needled syringe through the pregnant mother's abdomen and withdrawing a bit of the amniotic fluid containing cells sloughed off by the developing fetus. The cells and fluid can then be analyzed to determine whether the fetus is carrying the genetic defect. If so, a therapeutic abortion can be performed; if not, the parents can continue the pregnancy without fearing that their baby will inherit the disease.

The use of amniocentesis holds considerable promise for the prenatal detection of genetic diseases. It is estimated that one out of every five childhood diseases is caused by one of the more than 1,500 genetic diseases. A particularly prominent example is the case of trisomy-21, which shows a striking so-called maternal age effect. That is, the risk of having a baby with Down's syndrome increases significantly with the increasing age of the mother. It has been estimated that if all pregnant women over thirty-five were examined through amniocentesis, and if all those carrying babies with trisomy-21 received therapeutic abortions, the number of children with Down's syndrome could be cut in half.

However, even amniocentesis is hardly an ideal solution. For one thing, the process involves a slight but real danger of injury and infection to mother and fetus. In addition, of course, many people have strong ethical or religious objections to therapeutic abortion, regarding it as outright murder of the unborn child. What is needed is some method of preventing genetic defects from becoming a factor in pregnancy.

Genetic Engineering

The ideal solution would be a kind of magic scalpel that could be used to perform "genetic surgery," replacing defective genes with normal ones. Consider, however, the intrinsic difficulty of such a task—of somehow inserting an infinitesimally tiny bit of DNA into the nuclei of billions of different cells. Amazingly enough, scientists already have devised methods for doing this.

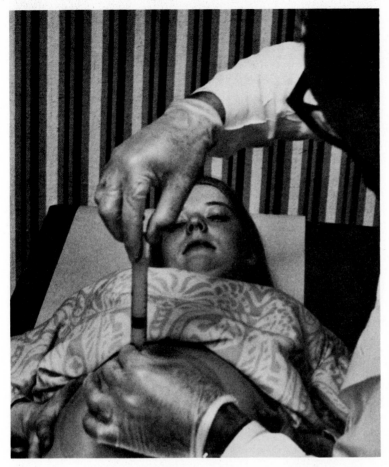

Through the process of amniocentesis, cells in the amniotic fluid can be analyzed to determine whether the fetus is carrying a genetic defect.

Leonard McCombe

One potential method involves the recent discovery that viruses consist essentially of strands of DNA or RNA, along with protein coats and enzymes that allow them to enter and reproduce within cells. Moreover, some viruses actually insert themselves into the genetic material. And some RNA viruses are thought to contain special enzymes that allow them to reverse the normal process by which DNA is transcribed into RNA, thus producing DNA copies of themselves.

Many viruses, of course, are deadly enemies of human beings, producing polio, rabies, and various forms of cancer. But recently geneticists have hit upon the ingenious idea of using innocuous viruses as "friends" to help carry missing genetic material into cells and insert it into the nuclei. The possibility of this method has been demonstrated in the laboratory and appears to hold enormous potential. However, not even this brilliant idea is without problems. Some scientists, pointing to ways in which the discovery of the atom has been misused, argue that genetic engineering also might be put to evil ends, and they have called for a halt to its development.

Positive Eugenics

So far we have been discussing examples of *negative eugenics* or attempts to decrease the frequency of harmful genes. In conclusion, we should consider the opposite side of the coin, *positive eugenics,* or attempts to increase the frequency of beneficial genes. One straightforward method would be simply to encourage talented people to have many children. But this has drawbacks, too. For example, it would be difficult to arrive at any formula for identifying such people that would be politically and morally acceptable. Moreover, caring for a large family is time consuming, and presumably we would like our most talented people to be as free as possible to devote their efforts to solving society's most pressing problems. However, the Nobel Prize-winning geneticist Herman Muller has made an interesting suggestion that avoids some of these problems. Muller notes that thousands of babies are conceived every year through artificial insemination, and that this constitutes a golden opportunity to disseminate the genetic material of unusually gifted individuals. At present, the fertility specialists who perform these procedures usually—perhaps rather immodestly—choose medical students to be the principal sperm donors.

Interaction of Genotype and Environment

A final practical step involves the application of the principle of genotype-environment interaction. The idea here is that the same environmental factor does not necessarily produce the same phenotypic effect in individuals of different genotypes. In fact, the same environmental factor may produce different—or even opposite—effects in genetically different individuals. One classic study (Cooper & Zubek, 1958) found that when two genetically different strains of rats were reared under normal laboratory conditions, one strain was much brighter than the other on a maze-running task. However, when both strains were reared in a more "enriched" and stimulating environment, the differences in maze-running performance largely disappeared. An even more dramatic example is provided by a study of the effects of rearing different breeds of puppies in social isolation (Fuller & Clark, 1968). Upon testing, it was found that rearing terriers in isolation made them more active, but it made beagles *less* so.

Pioneering educational and personality research has suggested that such interactions between genotypes and environment are probably also to be found in human beings. In other words, the child-rearing or teaching method that is best for one person is not necessarily best for another. For example, one researcher compared the effectiveness of two different methods of teaching children to read, using pairs of twins. One member of each twin pair was taught by the sight method, whereas the other was taught by the phonics method. Results indicated that although the phonics method was superior for average children, there was no real difference for gifted children (Vandenberg, 1965). Thomas, Chess, and Birch (1970) have also presented some interesting data suggesting that newborn infants show important and rather stable differences in temperament that are probably determined at least in part by genetic inheritance. This pattern of innate temperamental variables in turn affects which type of handling by parents and teachers works best for a child.

To sum up, the implications of this lesson for human behavior seem clear. Because each of us is genetically unique (except for identical twins), the more we learn about the genetics of human psychological development the more we will know how to provide environments that will help each individual to attain his or her greatest potential.

Summary

1. A person's life begins when a sperm cell fertilizes an ovum to form a zygote. Although it is barely visible to the naked eye, the zygote contains all the genetic blueprints, or genes, the individual will have. The genetic information is coded in terms of the sequences of four different bases in the DNA molecule.

2. A gene is the smallest functional unit of hereditary material. Genes are packaged together in chromosomes; in human beings there are normally forty-six chromosomes. Chromosomes come in matched, or homologous, pairs. One member of each pair is inherited from the mother, and the other comes from the father. Genes at corresponding loci on homologous chromosomes tend to be similar in structure and function. Forty-four of the human chromosomes are termed autosomes; the remaining two are known as sex chromosomes, because they determine an individual's biological sex. Normal females inherit two of the larger X sex chromosomes, whereas males inherit one X and a smaller Y chromosome.

3. During the formation of sperm and egg cells, the process of meiosis sorts out the chromosomal material so that each sex cell receives twenty-three chromosomes. One chromosome is chosen from each of the twenty-three pairs, but which member of a pair is selected is a matter of chance. Thus when the sperm fertilizes the egg, the new individual will have twenty-three matched pairs of chromosomes, just as the parents do. The egg cells produced by the mother will normally always have an X chromosome, whereas the father's sperm cells may carry either an X or a Y. The sex of the offspring thus will be determined by whether an X- or Y-bearing sperm fertilizes the ovum.

4. With a few exceptions such as mature red blood cells, most of the trillion cells in a person's body contain the same identical set of forty-six chromosomes. This duplication of the chromosomal material occurs through a process known as mitosis.

5. Genes, like the chromosomes on which they are arrayed, occur in matched pairs. Genes found at the same spot, or locus, on homologous chromosomes tend to contain similar strings of codons and thus to code for similar proteins affecting similar traits. A gene at a given locus may have variant forms, called *alleles*. The term *genotype* refers to the genetic constitution of an individual, whereas *phenotype* refers to the actual physical or behavioral trait manifested. The inheritance of many phenotypes follows principles discovered by the Austrian monk Gregor Mendel. These principles include the ideas that each individual inherits two allelic forms of each gene (one from each parent); that genes affecting different traits can be

segregated and then recombined to form new assortments during the formation of the sex cells; and that certain allelic forms can be dominant over other recessive ones in determining the phenotype. An important practical application of Mendelian principles is in genetic counseling to predict the likelihood that a couple will have offspring with certain genotypes and phenotypes.

6. Genes influence development via their effects on biochemical reactions in cells; effects on psychological development are therefore often complex and rather indirect. The same allele may influence may different phenotypic traits in the same individual. Conversely, the same phenotypic trait is often influenced by alleles at many different loci.

7. Genes can influence development at various periods throughout the life span. Most genes are not active all the time, and many are active for only a particular period during the individual's life span. Many genes that are active in an adult are not yet functional in the fetus or infant. One consequence is that many chemicals and drugs harmless to adults are harmful to fetuses and infants, who cannot yet synthesize the enzymes needed to metabolize the chemicals. Characteristics that first appear in later childhood or even adulthood are not necessarily environmental in origin. Conversely, traits present at birth may reflect prenatal environmental influences rather than genetic ones.

8. In addition to structural genes that carry the blueprint for synthesizing particular proteins, there appear to be operator or regulator genes that turn structural genes on and off at appropriate times during development. Such regulator genes may provide the basis for homeorhetic control mechanisms that act to channel or canalize development, so that even if some environmental event temporarily pushes it off course, the control mechanism will tend to push it back onto a genetically predetermined track.

9. Major gene defects refer to powerful effects on a phenotype caused by the action of alleles at a single locus. An example is phenylketonuria (PKU), a disorder caused by a recessive gene that can lead to severe mental retardation. It is now usually possible to prevent retardation by placing PKU infants on a special diet soon after birth. Most states in this country now require screening of all newborns for PKU.

10. Errors involving entire chromosomes represent a second important type of genetic influence on development. Such chromosomal aberrations cause an estimated 100,000 miscarriages each year in the United States, as well as thousands of cases of physical deformities and mental retardation. Perhaps the most serious chromosomal disorder is Down's syndrome, or trisomy-21, which results when an individual inherits an extra number 21 chromosome. This usually produces a number of serious developmental defects, including mental retardation.

11. Individual differences in most traits are polygenic, that is, they are affected by alleles at many different loci. Most deviations from normal height or intelligence seem to reflect the combined action of many genetic and environmental events. Because each gene has relatively small effects, it is difficult to study individual polygenes. Researchers usually have had to use

indirect kinds of evidence to study the polygenic influences on such traits as intelligence.

12. The heritability of a phenotype such as intelligence may be defined roughly as the percentage of the observed variation of the trait in a group that is caused by genetic differences. A heritability figure applies only to a particular phenotype in a particular population at a particular time. Most research—particularly twin and adoption studies—indicates that the heritability of IQ scores in white Americans is fairly high. This suggests that both genetic and environmental differences are important sources of individual differences in intellectual development. However, we need more knowledge about specific genes and how they affect cognitive development.

13. Misunderstandings about the nature and origin of genetic differences, particularly racial differences, have aggravated racial and ethnic prejudice, discrimination, and conflict. Better scientific understanding of these matters may help to prevent such inhumane behavior in the future. The striking physical traits that many people use in attaching racial labels to others often show a high degree of similarity within a group. Beneath the superficial uniformity of striking physical features, however, is great genetic diversity. If two different members of the same large racial group are chosen at random, research indicates that they will be almost as different genetically, on the average, as two individuals chosen at random from different racial groups. Such genetic diversity is important for the survival of a species over the long run, because it makes it more likely that some members of the species will be able to adapt to changing environmental challenges.

14. Some psychologists have tried to ignore the question of how genetic differences may influence behavioral development out of fear that evidence of such genetic influences might contribute to racial or ethnic discrimination. However, ignoring the impact of genetic differences on psychological development seems more likely to work to the disadvantage of members of racial or ethnic minorities, as the example of lactose intolerance illustrates.

15. Genetic factors influence individual differences in a number of psychological traits, ranging from color blindness to serious mental illnesses such as schizophrenia, for which adoption and twin studies indicate an important genetic predisposition is often involved.

16. Understanding the genetic basis for a disorder often makes it possible to develop practical steps to prevent or treat it. Genetic counseling can provide parents with better estimates of the likelihood that they will have a child with a particular condition. Mass screening can identify carriers of recessive genes for such traits as Tay-Sachs disease. Amniocentesis provides a basis for diagnosing the presence of genetic errors prenatally. Future approaches may include the use of viruses to insert missing genetic material into a person's cells, and positive eugenic measures to increase the frequency of beneficial genes.

17. Another use of genetic information is to design the best environment for a particular individual. Experiments with animals indicate that the same environmental treatment can produce different—even opposite—effects on behavioral development, depending on the genetic strain involved. Similar

relationships may well hold for human development. Infants seem to show important and relatively consistent differences in temperament, which in turn may affect the type of parental handling that is best for a particular child. Knowledge of genetic influences on human development is thus important even for those who would nurture development solely by improving environmental conditions.

Selected Readings

Fuller, J. L., and W. R. Thompson. *Genetic Basis of Behavior.* St. Louis: C. V. Mosby, 1978. A scholarly and rather comprehensive text regarding research on behavior genetics in human beings and animals.

Jarvik, L. F., and D. Cohen. "A Biobehavioral Approach to Intellectual Changes with Aging." In *The Psychology of Adult Development and Aging.* Eds. C. Eisdorfer and M. P. Lawton. Washington, D.C.: American Psychological Association, 1973. Includes discussions of research into genetic influences on aging and longevity, as well as chromosomal changes in body cells that some research suggests may be associated with aging processes.

Loehlin, J. C., and R. C. Nichols. *Heredity, Environment, and Personality.* Austin: University of Texas Press, 1976. Presents the results of a study of 850 pairs of identical and fraternal twins designed to investigate genetic and environmental influences on personality, ability, and interests. The book also presents a good review of other research into genetic influences on ability and personality.

McClearn, G. E., and J. C. deFries. *Introduction to Behavioral Genetics.* San Francisco: W. H. Freeman, 1973. Two eminent authorities in the field of behavior genetics have written a text that provides an introduction to the basic principles of genetics, psychology, and statistics needed for understanding behavior genetics.

Nirenberg, M. W. "The Genetic Code: II." *Scientific American, 208* (1963), 80–94. A brief overview at an introductory level by a scientist who won a Nobel Prize for work on this subject.

Rosenthal, D. *Genetic Theory and Abnormal Behavior.* New York: McGraw-Hill, 1970. (A shorter version entitled *Genetics of Psychopathology* is available in a paperback edition.) A very scholarly yet highly readable review of research into the genetics of various behavior disorders.

Watson, J. D. *The Double Helix.* New York: Atheneum, 1968. (Also available in paperback.) An autobiographical account by Watson of how he and Francis Crick made their Nobel Prize-winning discovery of the structure of DNA and the secret of the genetic code. The book provides an interesting look into the human side of scientific discovery, including a sense of the intellectual excitement involved.

Watson, J. D. *The Molecular Biology of the Gene.* 3rd ed. New York: Benjamin-Cummings, 1976. This advanced text will provide a detailed, technical, and reasonably up-to-date account of molecular genetics. It also includes an interesting section on genetics and cancer, which is the current focus of Watson's research.

Worden, F. G., B. Childs, S. Matthysse, and E. S. Gershon. "Frontiers of Psychiatric Genetics." *Neurosciences Research Program Bulletin,* 14 (1976). Boston: Neurosciences Research Program. This volume contains the edited proceedings of a symposium in which many of the world's leading researchers in psychiatry and genetics review the current state of knowledge about the genetics of psychiatric illness, particularly schizophrenia and manic-depressive illness. Of particular interest are the discussions of new research strategies for learning more about genetic influences on psychological development.

For the most recent research and theories about genetic influences on psychological development, readers are urged to consult professional journals in the fields of genetics, psychology, psychiatry, education, child development, and gerontology. Particularly recommended is the journal *Behavior Genetics*.

Chapter 4

Maturation, Health, and Nutrition

The principles and processes involved in brain maturation over the life span

Physical growth and development and how it affects psychological development

How health factors and nutrition affect development throughout the life span

How health is affected by behavioral influences, including personal habits, life events, and stress

Principles of Brain Maturation

Processes of Brain Development
Genetic and Hormonal Regulation
Synaptic Connections Among Neurons
Brain Maturation over the Life Span

Individual Differences in Maturation

Secular Trends
Causes of Secular Trends
Psychosocial Implications of Secular Trends
Implications for Sex Differences in Mental Abilities

Health and Nutritional Influences on Development

Effects of Obstetrical Complications
Malnutrition and Behavioral Development
Cerebrovascular Disease

Behavioral Influences on Health

Infant and Prenatal Mortality Rates
Accidents: The Leading Killer of Children and Young Adults
Sex Differences and Death Rates
Personal Habits and Good Health
Life Events, Stress, and Illness
Stress, Personality, and Coronary Heart Disease

Introduction

Relations among health, maturation, and behavior constitute some of the most important influences shaping human development over the life span. This chapter focuses on several such relations. After an overview of the principles and processes involved in brain development over the life span, we will discuss some examples of individual differences in maturation and their implications for behavioral development. Then we will consider the impact of health-related factors on psychological development, concluding the chapter with a discussion of how behavior and personality development affect health.

Increasingly, public health authorities are recognizing the crucial role of behavior patterns as causes of illness and death. Public attention to medical advances in recent years has focused largely on the most glamorous techniques and technologies, such as open-heart surgery and computerized x-ray scanning of the brain. Yet many health authorities believe that increased numbers of doctors and greater use of high-cost hospital-based technologies are *not* the most promising ways to improve health. As the late John Knowles, former head of Massachusetts General Hospital and the Rockefeller Foundation, has put it, the "next major advances in the health of the American people will come from the assumption of individual responsibility for one's health and a necessary change in life style for the majority of Americans" (Moore, 1975, p. 1).

The chapter concludes by reviewing research evidence that personal habits and attitudes are now among the most important determinants of health. Indeed, getting people to develop healthier behavior patterns may well be the most important step that industrialized societies can take to prevent death and disability.

Principles of Brain Maturation

Of all phenomena in the universe presently known to us, the human brain is perhaps the most complex and amazing. Above all, of course, it is responsible for conscious experience (what we call "mind" or "soul," if you will)—a mystery that modern science has only begun to fathom. Even considered simply as a feat of biological engineering, the human brain is miraculous. In its flexibility and miniaturization, our brain still far outstrips the most advanced computers we can devise. Most miraculous, however, is that this incredibly complex neural computer—composed of tens of billions of nerve cells and their billions of interconnecting nerve fibers—is, in effect, able to "wire" itself. How does this occur?

The process of brain development is incredibly complex, and perhaps we may never understand all its details. But we do understand some of the more general principles and dynamics. As with all organs in the body, the building blocks of the nervous system are, of course, cells. In this case there are two basic cell types: (1) The *neurons*, which, through their specialized processes—the *dendrites* and *axons*—respectively receive and transmit information in the form of neural impulses; and (2) the *glia*, which are thought to provide nutritive and structural support to the neurons, as well as forming the myelin sheaths that protect and insulate many nerve fibers and facilitate transmission of impulses along axonal processes. Glial cells also seem to play an important role in memory storage and learning, although this role is only beginning to be understood. Physiologist Victor Shashoua (1980) and his colleagues, for example, have found in experiments with laboratory animals that glial cells secrete specific chemical factors necessary for long-term memory. By forming antibodies to these factors and by injecting them into animals, Shashoua is able to block the retention of information learned at a particular time.

Figures 4.1 and 4.2 illustrate the basic structure of neurons and neuroglial cells. The glia form multiple wrappings around the axons of neurons, forming an insulating myelin sheath. This process of myelination facilitates the trans-

FIGURE 4.1
The structure of neurons. The neuron receives input from other nerve cells by means of the dendrites; it transmits output by means of the axon. The inset shows a segment of the apical shaft as it might appear under electron magnification (30,000 to 40,000 power). The spines form synapses with the axon terminals (boutons) of other neurons.

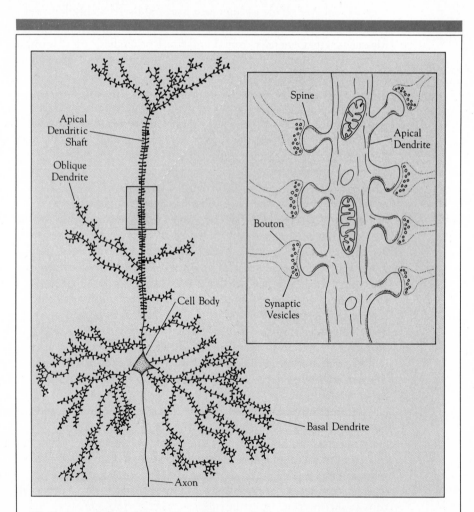

W. T. Greenough, Experimental modification of the developing brain, *American Scientist*, 63 (1975), 37-46. Reprinted in I. Janis (ed.), *Current Trends in Psychology*, Los Angeles, Wm. Kaufmann, 1977.

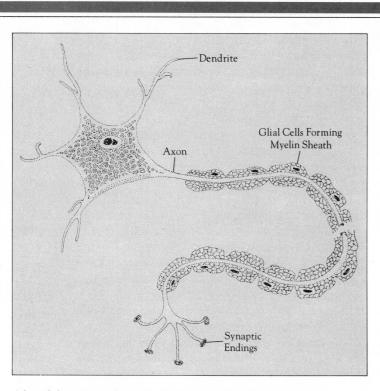

Dendrite

Axon

Glial Cells Forming
Myelin Sheath

Synaptic
Endings

Adapted from E. Gardner, *Fundamentals of Neurology*, 6th ed.
Philadelphia, W. B. Saunders Company, 1975. In Turner and Helms, *Life Span Development*, W. B. Saunders Company.

FIGURE 4.2
Glial cells form a sheath of myelin around the axons of many neurons. This myelin sheath provides a kind of insulation that aids the transmission of neural impulses along the axon.

mission of neural impulses. It is one of the important processes that occur during brain maturation.

Processes of Brain Development

Following are descriptions of several basic processes whereby nerve cells are able to sculpt themselves into a functioning nervous system (Altman, 1967; Cowan, 1979; Tanner, 1978).

Proliferation   First of all, of course, there must be cell division. The original founding line of primitive nerve cells must divide to form new "offspring" cells, and these in turn must divide, and so on, until the billions of cells in the developed brain are formed. The division and resulting *proliferation* of new cells, as the process is called, is explosive during the prenatal period in human beings. By the time of birth, or shortly thereafter (there is some dispute about the exact time), the proliferation of neurons is complete. Newborn babies, therefore, are born with virtually all the neurons they will ever have. The mature human brain has roughly 100 billion neurons. It thus can be calculated that new neurons must be produced during prenatal development at an *average* rate of 250,000 per minute. During the later months of gestation, when growth is especially rapid, the rate must be even higher.

Clearly, the prenatal period is a critical time for brain development. Any event that interferes with brain growth will likely produce a deficit in the number of neurons. Adverse factors such as malnutrition may produce permanent brain stunting if they occur during this time.

After birth, the human brain continues to grow rapidly, increasing from approximately 25 to 75 percent of its adult weight between birth and 2½ years of age, by which time the rate of growth has begun to slow considerably. This rapid growth after birth occurs even though neuronal proliferation is essentially complete.

Growth   Normal brain development requires that the cells, besides proliferating, undergo growth in size—not only in the main body of the cell but also in the axonal and dendritic processes that connect one neuron with others. In the case of some sensory and motor neurons in the spinal cord, to take an extreme example, nerve fibers extending into the toes of a tall person may be several feet long.

Davison and Dobbing (1966) have noted that the maximum rate of brain growth occurs in different species at different times in relation to birth (see Figure 4.3). In human beings, the most rapid period of brain growth extends from roughly the sixth month of gestation to the end of the first year after birth. Metabolic stresses such as malnutrition appear most likely to have permanent effects on brain size and composition if they occur during this vulnerable period of greatest brain growth. Human brain growth is particularly rapid right around the time of birth, when the brain is adding weight at the rate of 1 to 2 milligrams per minute. Therefore, interference with normal growth at this time might be particularly disadvantageous. Some biomedical scientists have suggested that this may explain why prematurity carries with it an increased risk of physical and psychological problems. (This is not to say that all or even most premature infants have major problems; on the contrary, most of them appear to be relatively normal in development.)

Differentiation   By themselves, of course, the processes of cell division and cell growth are not enough to form a brain. (Indeed, uncontrolled cell division and proliferation are characteristic of cancer.) Therefore, besides simply increasing in numbers, the primitive nerve cells, or neuroblasts, must take on specific sizes, shapes, and biochemical properties that will enable them to fulfill their specialized functions in a particular part of the nervous system. In a word, the neuroblasts must undergo *differentiation*, which results in an enormous variety of mature neurons. These range from sensory neurons, which may have only a few genetically programmed synapses, to some cortical neurons that have lushly branching dendritic "trees" with thousands of synapses.

Migration   In addition to being in the right number and the right form, nerve cells must also be at the right place—and at the right time. For this to occur, there must be large-scale, yet very orderly and precise, *cell migration*. Rita

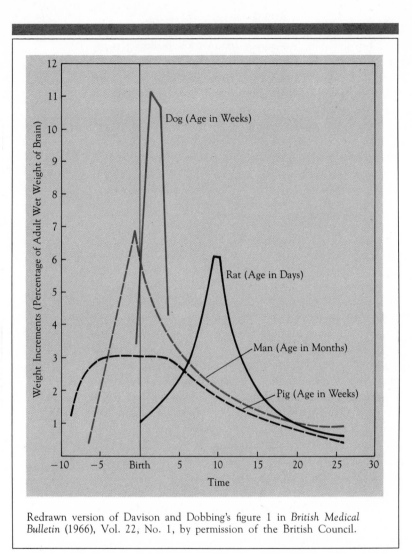

FIGURE 4.3
The timing of brain
growth in different
species, compared
from birth. Brain
growth is expressed as
weight increases
(adult wet weight of
brain) per unit of
time. Curves show
species variation in
timing of growth
spurt. Early growth
represents cell divi-
sion and increase
of cell size. This
period overlaps with
increases due to
myelination.

Redrawn version of Davison and Dobbing's figure 1 in *British Medical Bulletin* (1966), Vol. 22, No. 1, by permission of the British Council.

Levi-Montalcini is a developmental neurobiologist who has spent much of her life observing the development of the nervous system in organisms such as the chick embryo. Watching these cell migrations under the microscope, Levi-Montalcini has noted that it is as if one were watching an army of soldiers marching under orders, so orderly are the movements of these columns of migrating neurons streaming past one another in bewildering complexity. Yet each column punctually arrives at the correct location to lay the foundations for the necessary neural structure. It appears that migrating neurons may be directed in part by a kind of scaffolding of special filaments laid down by specialized glia cells (Cowan, 1979).

Death   Finally, some cells must undergo *death*. That is, the destruction of some cells, rather than resulting from any disease process, seems to be planned in the developmental genetic blueprint for the construction of the nervous system—much as the scaffolding used in the construction of a building is removed once the structure is complete. In those regions of the developing brain in which cell death has been studied most carefully, between 15 and 85 percent of the initial neuronal population died before maturation was complete.

Critical Periods   While all these processes occur at once, they peak at different times during development. The peak for the production of neurons occurs first, followed by the peak rates of brain growth and of myelination of nerve fibers. What we have, therefore, is not one but a *series of critical periods* for brain growth. Thus interference with brain development is likely to have different adverse effects, depending on when the interference occurs and which process is affected during its critical period of most active development.

Genetic and Hormonal Regulation

Having surveyed some of the basic processes underlying brain development, we now may ask what drives and directs these cell processes. Ultimately, of course, the answers lie in the genetic machinery of the cells, and neurobiologists have discovered many interesting genetic mutations that illustrate this point. For example, in certain strains of mice, a normal structure of the brain or nervous system develops abnormally or fails to develop at all (in one strain, the major bundle of fibers that connects the two hemispheres of the brain in mammals is missing entirely). In other mutant strains, neural mechanisms needed for a proper sense of equilibrium and coordination may be damaged, producing bizarre whirling, jerking, and shaking behaviors. Such mutant mice have long been observed and, in fact, were bred many centuries ago as a curiosity in the courts of Chinese emperors. Today, however, they provide an important tool for scientists in unraveling the mechanisms that control the development of the nervous system.

Genes direct cellular processes through their control of the biochemical machinery. Hormones, for example, play an important role, as was illustrated dramatically by the discovery of a specific kind of nerve-cell growth hormone (Levi-Montalcini, 1964). This "nerve growth factor" specifically stimulates the growth of fibers in sensory and sympathetic nervous system neurons. However, it also seems clear that there must be similar hormonal factors involved in regulating the amount and direction of cell growth in other parts of the nervous system.

Synaptic Connections Among Neurons

We have considered with amazement the proliferation, growth, differentiation, migration, and death of neurons and glia. Perhaps even more remarkable is the pattern of billions upon billions of interconnections that must be formed among these hundred billion or so neurons if they are to function at all. As we have noted, neurons transmit information to one another by means of their dendritic and axonal processes. The actual exchange of information from one neuron to another occurs at the *synapse*—a microscopically small junction or "cleft" that separates the transmitting neuron's axonal end (bouton) from the receiving neuron's cell body or from its receptive dendritic branches (see Figure 4.4). The transmission of information across this synapse involves the release of tiny packets, or *vesicles,* of molecules of the messenger chemicals (neurotransmitters), which are released from the bouton of the transmitting cell into the synaptic cleft. Once released, these neurotransmitter molecules can cross the synaptic cleft to interact with chemically receptive sites on the cell membrane of the receiving neuron. Depending on the type of neurotransmitter molecule and postsynaptic receptor site involved, a particular neurotransmitter released at a particular synapse may tend either to stimulate or to inhibit the receiving cell into "firing"—that is, into sending out neural impulses.

The essential function of the neurons is to process, transmit, and exchange information. To do so, they must communicate with other neurons by means of synaptic connections. Neurons—particularly the interneurons in the cerebral cortex—may connect with thousands of other neurons. To provide enough surface area for these thousands of synaptic connections, the neurons develop dendritic processes with lushly branching, treelike structures. The receptive surface area may be increased further by the sprouting of tiny budlike formations, called *spines,* along the surfaces of the dendritic branches. Microscopic examination of the developing brain shows an explosive growth of these dendritic trees and their spines—especially during the first few years after birth for human infants (see Figure 4.5).

FIGURE 4.4
Synaptic connections
between neurons

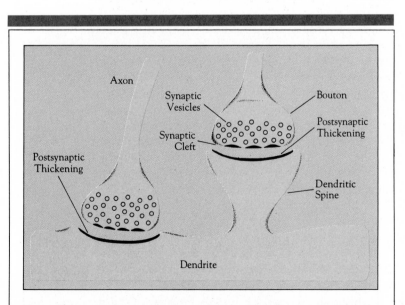

FIGURE 4.5
Development of den-
dritic "trees" and
"spines" in human
infants of
different ages

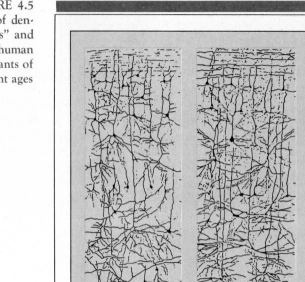

3 Months   15 Months   24 Months

J. L. Conel, *Postnatal Development of the Human Cerebral Cortex.*
Cambridge: Harvard University Press, Vols. I-VI, 1939-1963.

The critical importance of these synaptic spines is best illustrated by what
happens (or, rather, fails to happen) in their absence. Purpura (1974) has described cases of severe mental retardation in infants whose brains appeared on
examination to be perfectly normal. Not only were the gross anatomies of these
brains normal, but under the microscope it could be seen that their neurons
were beautifully formed. In fact, everything was normal, with one exception:
there were few if any normal dendritic spines. In other words, all parts of the
nervous system and its cellular units appeared normal and in their proper
places. The only problem was that the neural processes—without normal
spines—formed few synaptic connections, and so the neurons could not communicate with one another and were functionally useless.

To a considerable extent, genetic information specifies both the form of the
neurons' dendritic and axonal processes and the pattern of synapses those processes make with other neurons during development. For example, cells in the
retina of the eye are linked in a remarkably orderly and precise way to corresponding cells in the visual cortex of the brain. One of the most important and
challenging questions about brain maturation is how the neurons are able to
form the correct connections during development. The explanation that best
seems to fit present data is the *chemo-affinity* hypothesis, which posits that most
neurons become differentiated at an early point in their development, depending on the position they occupy in the developing brain. As a result, the

neurons manifest distinctive chemical labels that growing axons of other neurons are able to recognize. When the axon senses the appropriate chemical label on the surface of a neuron, it "knows" it has reached the target on which it should form a synapse. Finally, just as many cells die during development, so are many neuronal processes and synapses selectively eliminated during later stages of development, providing a mechanism for the removal of incorrect or excessive connections.

Brain Maturation over the Life Span

Now that we have examined some of the processes involved in brain development, let us briefly consider how these processes are orchestrated, and the form of the product they sculpt. Cowan (1979) noted that in the development of any part of the brain, one can identify eight major stages, which appear in the following order:

1. The induction of the neural plate
2. The localized proliferation of cells in different regions
3. The migration of cells from the region in which they are generated to the places in which they finally reside
4. The aggregation of cells to form identifiable parts of the brain
5. The differentiation of the immature neurons
6. The formation of connections with other neurons
7. The selective death of certain cells
8. The elimination of some of the connections that were initially formed and the stabilization of others (p. 113)

Prenatal Development   In its anatomical development, the nervous system begins as a *neural plate*—a flat sheet of cells on the outer surface of the developing embryo. This plate then folds into an elongated and hollow column, known as the *neural tube*. The tail end of this tube eventually becomes the spinal cord, and the head end develops into the brain. Defects in the formation of the neural tube at this stage can cause congenital defects in the formation of the brain or spinal cord.

From the head end of the neural tube, three major protruberances develop, which eventually become the three major parts of the brain—the forebrain, the midbrain, and the hindbrain (see Figure 4.6). The hollow core of the neural tube eventually widens to form the fluid-filled cavities (ventricles) of the mature brain. In the development of the human brain, the growth and maturation of the cerebral hemispheres—with their specialized capacities for language, reasoning, planning, and complex pattern recognition and problem solving—is especially marked. As can be seen in Figure 4.6, by the middle of pregnancy the cerebral hemispheres have begun to overgrow the midbrain and hindbrain. By the latter part of pregnancy, the characteristic convolutions of the cortex are already apparent. And by the time of birth, the rounded elevations *(gyri)* and furrows *(sulci)* of the cortex are clearly visible.

Human growth proceeds more rapidly in the brain than in other organs. From early in fetal development, the brain is closer to its adult weight than is

FIGURE 4.6
Development of
the human brain

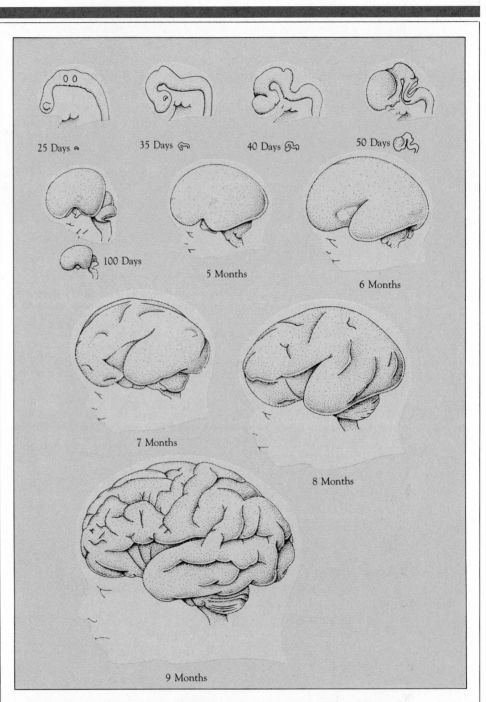

25 Days   35 Days   40 Days   50 Days

100 Days

5 Months

6 Months

7 Months

8 Months

9 Months

"The Development of the Brain" by W. Maxwell Cowan, September 1979. Copyright © 1979 by Scientific American, Inc. All rights reserved.

any other organ, except possibly the eye. This rapid growth of the brain relative to other organs can be seen in Figure 4.7. At birth the brain is already 25 percent of its adult weight; by ten years, it is 95 percent of the adult weight. By contrast, the weight of the whole body is only about 5 percent of its adult weight at birth, and about 50 percent at age ten (Tanner, 1978). This differential rate of growth is reflected in the dramatic changes in body proportions that occur during development (see Figure 4.8).

Prenatal development involves an amazing progression of anatomical transformations (Arey, 1974; Meredith, 1975; Rugh & Shettles, 1971). It begins

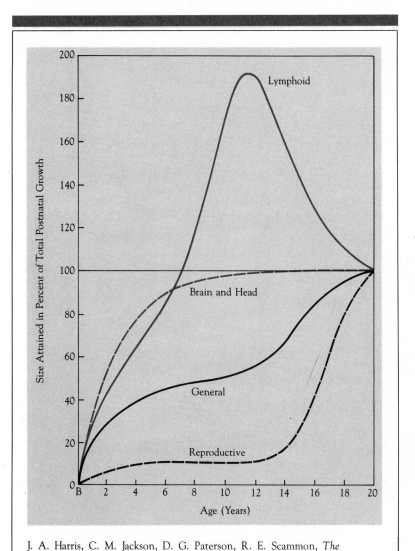

FIGURE 4.7
Growth curves of different body tissues (percent of total gain, birth to twenty years)

J. A. Harris, C. M. Jackson, D. G. Paterson, R. E. Scammon, *The Measurement of Man.* University of Minnesota Press, Minneapolis. Copyright © 1930 by the University of Minnesota.

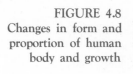

FIGURE 4.8
Changes in form and
proportion of human
body and growth

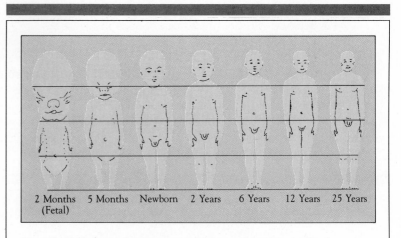

2 Months   5 Months   Newborn   2 Years   6 Years   12 Years   25 Years
(Fetal)

From C. M. Jackson, Some aspects of form and growth, in W. J.
Robbins, S. Brody, A. F. Hogan, C. M. Jackson, and C. W. Green (Eds.),
Growth. New Haven: Yale University Press, 1929, p. 118. By permission.

when the human egg, having been released from one of the mother's ovaries,
travels into the oviduct (Fallopian tube) and is fertilized by one of the father's
sperm cells. As it travels down the oviduct, the fertilized egg, or zygote, repeatedly divides, so that by the time it reaches the uterus, it has become a
blastula—a single-layered spherical formation of cells surrounding a fluid-filled
center. Cells on one side of the blastula then form a thickened mass of cells
known as an *embryonic disc,* from which the embryo and supportive structures
develop. Roughly a week after conception, the embryo, still only about 1/100
of an inch in diameter, implants in the wall of the uterus. Figure 4.9 shows the
progression in size and shape of human development in the weeks following.

   The nervous system begins to develop at about eighteen days after conception. By about twenty days, the foundations for the brain and spinal cord have
been laid. By three weeks, a primitive heart has begun to beat and pump blood
through the embryo. During the first two months, the basic shape and organization of many organs are being formed, and congenital malformations are most
likely to result from interference with developmental processes during this
period of prenatal development.

   At the end of two months, the embryonic period becomes the fetal period.
By this time, the embryo is only about an inch long, but facial features are
already beginning to form. As early as the ninth or tenth weeks, the fetus may
begin to display gross turning movements, though they will not yet be detect-
able by the mother. By eleven or twelve weeks, the fetus can show simple
reflexive behaviors in response to stimulation. (For example, at eleven weeks,
stimulation of the palm will elicit a closure of the fingers, marking the beginning
of the grasping reflex.)

   Prenatal development from conception to birth lasts an average of 280 days,
or about nine calendar months. Pregnancy typically is divided into three *tri-*

FIGURE 4.9

Graded series of embryos drawn to actual size

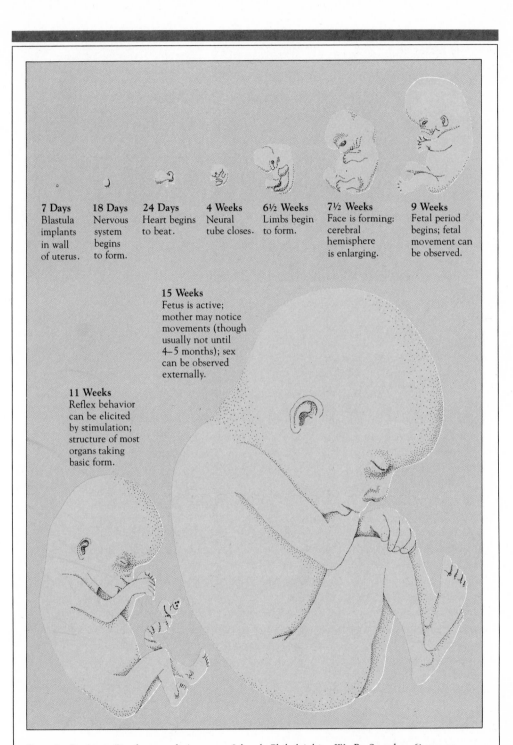

7 Days
Blastula implants in wall of uterus.

18 Days
Nervous system begins to form.

24 Days
Heart begins to beat.

4 Weeks
Neural tube closes.

6½ Weeks
Limbs begin to form.

7½ Weeks
Face is forming: cerebral hemisphere is enlarging.

9 Weeks
Fetal period begins; fetal movement can be observed.

15 Weeks
Fetus is active; mother may notice movements (though usually not until 4–5 months); sex can be observed externally.

11 Weeks
Reflex behavior can be elicited by stimulation; structure of most organs taking basic form.

From L. B. Arey, *Developmental Anatomy*, 8th ed. Philadelphia, W. B. Saunders Company, 1974.

Fetus at eight weeks (left) and at sixteen weeks (right). During this period the basic shape and organization of many organs is being formed; the fetus can show simple relexive behaviors in response to stimulation; and congenital malformations are most likely to result from interference with developmental processes.

mesters, or three-month periods. The first trimester is characterized by the formation of basic organ structures. The second trimester brings further differentiation and is marked by increased size (from about 1 ounce to 1½ pounds). The third trimester sees tremendous growth (typically, a gain of 6 to 7 pounds) and the onset of potential viability outside the uterus. (By late in the sixth or early in the seventh month, the fetus begins to have at least a slim chance of survival independent of the mother, given special medical care and support apparatus such as incubators.) With increasing age, the chances of the fetus's survival increase markedly.

Postnatal Development   The maturation of different brain areas proceeds at different rates during postnatal development. For example, the regions of the central nervous system such as the spinal cord, pons, and medulla—which are involved in the regulation of vital functions such as breathing—mature before higher brain structures such as the cerebellum (which appears to be involved in the regulation of fine motor movements) or the cortex. Within the cerebral cortex, the so-called primary sensory projection areas, which are the first to receive input from the sense organs, develop before the "association" areas of the cortex, which are involved in integrating information from different senses. Within the cortical areas involved with motor control or with sensory input, the cells concerned with the arms and upper trunk develop before those involved with the legs. As a result of such differential rates of maturation, behavioral capacities emerge over time as brain structures mature and begin to function.

The maturation of new brain areas, and the corresponding development of qualitatively new forms of psychological capacities, proceeds perhaps most rapidly and dramatically in the sequential development of different motor skills in infancy (see Figure 4.10). These skills tend to develop in the same order and at

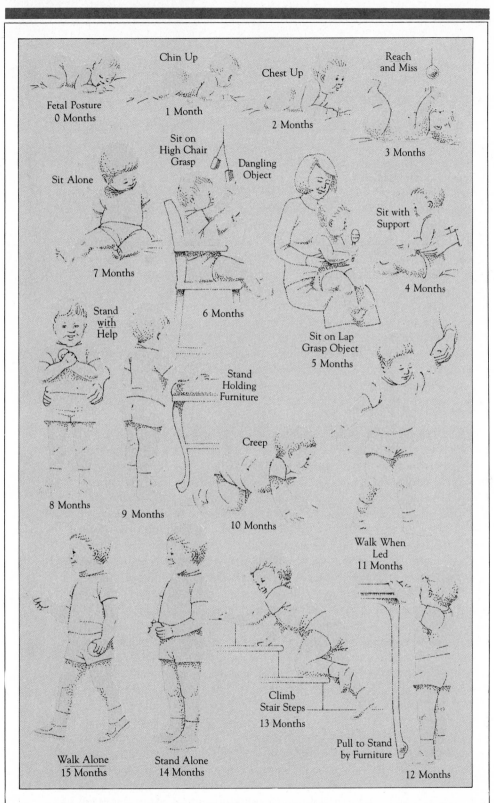

FIGURE 4.10
Sequence of
motor develop-
ment during
first fifteen
months

Mary M. Shirley, *The First Two Years*, Vol. II, University of Minnesota Press, Minneapolis.
Copyright © 1933 by the University of Minnesota.

roughly the same age in different children. The emergence of new and qualitatively different capacities also can be seen in other areas, such as cognitive development and language development.

Myelination   Research by neuroanatomists such as Yakovlev and Lecours indicates that brain maturation continues throughout life. The process of myelination, in particular, proceeds through adolescence into adulthood. Myelination of some areas of the cortex seems to continue even into old age. On the basis of studies of hundreds of fetal and postnatal human brains of different ages, Lecours (1975) and Yakovlev (Yakovlev & Lecours, 1967) have been able to identify the periods, or cycles, during which myelination occurs in different fiber tracts or regions of the brain. They have found that each fiber system has a particular *myelogenetic cycle,* or period of myelination. The ages when myelination begins and ends differ in different brain structures, as does the time it takes for the cycle of myelination to be completed. Moreover, Yakovlev and Lecours believe that the formation of myelin sheaths in a system of nerve fibers is a sign that the flow of nerve impulses has become committed to a particular pathway, and "correspondingly, the fiber system that has completed its myelogenetic cycle may be assumed to have achieved functional maturity" (Lecours, 1975, p. 122). It is therefore reasonable to assume, they believe, that the cycles of myelination reflect the functional maturation of different brain regions, which can then be related to the development of different behavioral skills mediated by those brain regions.

For example, myelination of some of the auditory pathways in the brain begins as early as the fifth month of prenatal development, whereas myelination of the optic pathways does not begin until the ninth fetal month. (This corresponds to evidence we shall consider in Chapter 6, showing that the human fetus seems able to respond to sounds in utero, whereas the fetus receives no external visual stimuli.) In the period shortly after birth, however, myelination of the visual pathways of the brain proceeds extremely rapidly, with this cycle being completed by the third or fourth month after birth. (This corresponds well with the rapid development of visual perception in the human infant during the first few months after birth.) By contrast, the myelination of the acoustic pathways, though beginning early in prenatal development, continues up to four or five years after birth—a period during which language development is proceeding rapidly. Lecours points out that various behavioral stages in language development (described in Chapter 12) have reasonable parallels in the myelination of different brain structures.

In general, neural pathways that conduct sensory information from the sense organs to the cortex complete their myelination rather early, as do neural pathways conveying impulses from the cortex to the muscles and other effector organs. Fibers that connect different regions of the cortex, especially those involved in making associations between stimuli from different senses, tend to be myelinated later. For example, in some of the large bundles of fibers that conduct nerve impulses between the two hemispheres of the brain, myelination seems to continue slowly even after age ten. And in certain association areas of the frontal, parietal, and temporal cortices of the brain, myelination seems to progress throughout adulthood. The end of myelination is "not definable except in terms of pathological demyelination as the expression of the stresses and strains of disease and senile changes in the brain" (Yakovlev & Lecours, 1967, p. 61).

Individual Differences in Maturation

Now that we have considered some aspects of brain development over the life span, let us examine some sources of individual differences in physical maturation and some of the effects of such differences on psychological development. We will consider several examples of maturational differences. First we will examine research on differences in physical growth. Then we will investigate the trend for females to reach puberty at an earlier age, including some psychosocial implications of this trend. Finally we will consider the average sex differences in rates of physical maturation and some recent research that suggests that such differences may influence the development of different patterns of mental abilities as a result of direct effects on maturation of the brain.

Secular Trends

Earlier Maturation   One of the more interesting developmental growth trends is a *secular*, or long-term historical, trend: the tendency toward more rapid maturation. The main evidence of this trend is the striking increase in the mean height of individuals that has taken place in industrialized societies in the last few generations. As biologist René Dubos noted:

One need only look around the world to know that the same is happening everywhere to human beings. We all know that Japanese teenagers are now much taller than their parents, not as a result of genetic change but because the postwar environment in Japan is very different from what it was in the past. One is quite familiar by now with the extraordinary changes that have occurred in the Israeli kibbutzim where children were raised under conditions very different from those experienced by their parents in the ghettos of Europe. Within one generation these children tower over their parents and are completely different from them in many behavioral characteristics. These changes in the rate of maturation in Japan and in Israel are but particular cases of a constant trend toward earlier maturation of children in all countries that have followed the Western way of life. (p. 17)[1]

Physical Stature   The most marked secular trend has been in the degree of early physical maturation. Individuals born more recently not only reach a greater maximum height earlier but also show an earlier growth spurt, so that they approach the maximum height at an earlier age. Thus in Europe and the United States from the turn of the century until the present, children growing up in average economic conditions have increased in height at age fourteen by 2

1. From *A God Within* by René Dubos. Copyright © 1972 by René Dubos. Reprinted by permission of Charles Scribner's Sons.

to 3 centimeters (about 1 inch) each decade. Over the same period, there has also been a steady increase in the final height of adults, which is less marked but still striking. In Western Europe, for example, records indicate that adult men increased in height hardly at all "from 1760 to 1830, about 0.3 cm per decade from 1830 to 1889, and about 0.6 cm per decade from 1880 to 1960" (Tanner, 1970, p. 145). Recent data from the middle 1970s indicate that this secular trend finally seems to be leveling off in the United States but is apparently continuing in Europe.

Menarche   It is not only the maturation of physical stature that has accelerated over the last century. In addition, *menarche,* or the time of first menstruation in women, has also shown a dramatic secular trend toward earlier onset. In Figure 4.11, which shows the data (Tanner, 1962), note that in Norway, after roughly a century, the average age of first menstruation has advanced nearly four years!

Causes of Secular Trends

What is causing these dramatic changes in maturation? The earlier onset of menarche seems to be linked both statistically and physiologically with the

FIGURE 4.11
Secular trend in age
at menarche

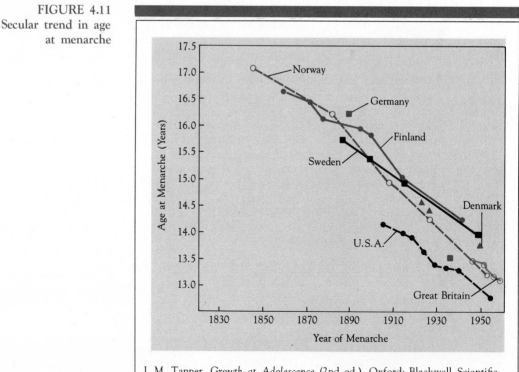

J. M. Tanner, *Growth at Adolescence* (2nd ed.). Oxford: Blackwell Scientific Publications Limited; Philadelphia: Davis, 1962, p. 146.

acceleration of physical growth. Frisch (1974), after analyzing data on longitudinal growth patterns in children, concluded that menarche is triggered by hormonal changes that occur when a certain body weight is reached. In addition, the ratio of body weight to stature is important, for girls who are heavier for a given height have an earlier onset of menarche.

Earlier menarche thus seems to be—at least in considerable part—a consequence of more rapid physical growth. But what is responsible for that growth in the first place? Almost certainly important are such environmental factors as the improvement in health care and nutrition, vaccination against diseases, better sanitation, and the like. But it is also likely that genetic factors have played an important role in these trends. As noted in Chapter 3, a large body of research suggests that genes that promote large physical stature tend to be dominant. Thus the crossing of two different genetic strains of animals tends to produce offspring who are larger, healthier, and more fit than either of the parent strains. Similarly, in human populations, genetic outbreeding tends to produce more heterozygotes and, hence, "hybrid vigor." Outbreeding in industrialized countries has been increasing ever since the invention of the bicycle. This seems likely to have made an important contribution to the secular trends.

Figure 4.12 illustrates the apparent impact of poverty on growth. Note that ten-year-old children in the United States in the early 1970s were several centimeters shorter in families below the poverty line than in those above it. This seems to indicate that poverty—and the poorer nutrition and health care that

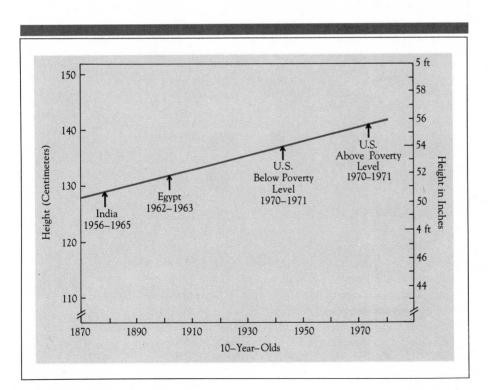

FIGURE 4.12
Increase in mean height of ten-year-old U. S. children during the past century, and comparison of the mean heights of Indian children (1956–1965), Egyptian children (1962–1963), and U. S. children by income level (1970–1971)

tend to go with it—is stunting the growth of poor children in the United States. However, note also that the *secular* increase in the height of the average ten-year-old is much larger than even that associated with the poverty gap today. Note too that United States children in the past century had an average height smaller even than children living today in developing countries such as India, which suffers from severe poverty.

In sum, the height of poor American children lags a generation behind that of children above the poverty level. The height gap is almost certainly the result of poverty rather than, say, racial differences, for black children are actually slightly taller than white children whose parents have the same income (National Center for Health Statistics, 1975, p. 387).

Psychosocial Implications of Secular Trends

These dramatic changes toward earlier physical and sexual maturity clearly call for concomitant changes in social attitudes and institutions. For example, most young women now can conceive by age twelve or thirteen, rather than at seventeen, as was the case a century ago. Although the current generation of twelve-year-olds may be somewhat brighter and better educated than their counterparts several decades ago, it seems questionable whether the rate of intellectual and emotional maturity has increased as rapidly as that of physical and sexual precocity. The sexual precocity of today's young teen-agers probably plays a role, for example, in the skyrocketing rates of illegitimacy and divorce—which are much higher than average among teen-age pregnancies and marriages. It seems safe to say that the psychosocial implications of the secular trends toward more precocious physical and sexual maturity have not been given sufficient attention. As Dubos put it:

It is a disturbing fact that our society tends increasingly to treat young men and women as children and to deny them the chance to engage in responsible activities precisely at the time when their physiological development is so markedly accelerated. There is a dissociation between social responsibility and biological development that is truly one of the most peculiar aspects of our society. (Dubos, *A God Within*, 1972, p. 17)

Implications for Sex Differences in Mental Abilities

In their review of research on sex differences in psychological processes, psychologists Eleanor Maccoby and Carol Jacklin (1974) concluded that two of the best-established sex differences in human beings were tendencies for females to excel in verbal ability and males to excel in visual-spatial ability. Maccoby and Jacklin note that although there are obviously large individual differences, most studies report higher average scores on various types of verbal tasks for girls than boys, beginning at about age eleven. The degree of female superiority increases at least through the high school years. Conversely, in tests of spatial visualization, average scores for males are rather consistently higher in adolescence and adulthood, though not in childhood. (Such sex differences are examined in detail in Chapter 15.)

Research by Waber (1976) suggests that these sex differences in ability may reflect differences in the organization of psychological functions in the developing brain. These, in turn, are related to differential rates of physical maturation. On the average, girls tend to mature more rapidly than boys, reaching puberty and their adolescent growth spurt earlier than boys (see Figure 4.13). Waber examined groups of girls aged ten and thirteen as well as boys aged thirteen and sixteen. For each age and sex, twenty children were seen—ten who were much more rapid in their physical maturation than most children their age, as judged by the development of secondary sexual characteristics, and ten who

FIGURE 4.13
Typical growth curves for girls and boys

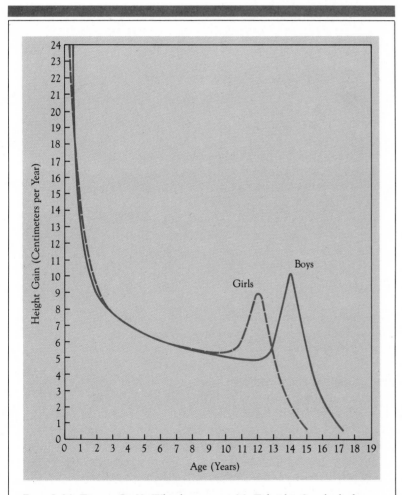

From J. M. Tanner, R. H. Whitehouse, and M. Takaishi. Standards from birth to maturity for height, weight, height-velocity and weight-velocity: British children 1965. Archs. Dis. Childh., 1966, *41*, 454-471; 613-635.

were much slower. Regardless of sex, early maturers were found to score *relatively* better on verbal than on spatial tasks, whereas late maturers scored relatively better on spatial tasks. Maturation rates were found to be highly related to spatial, but not to verbal, test scores. Results from other tests indicated that late maturers had a greater tendency for verbal abilities to lateralize—that is, for the right or left side of the brain to play a predominant role in particular functions.

Individual differences in physical maturation rates accounted for much more of the variability in test scores than did sex differences per se—suggesting that sex differences in mental abilities "reflect the differential distribution of the sexes along a physiological continuum more than a categorical difference between male and female" (p. 573). Waber also noted that, because physical maturation was related to differences in spatial but not verbal abilities in her sample, sex differences in these two kinds of abilities probably develop for quite different reasons.

Health and Nutritional Influences on Development

Among the most powerful influences on psychological development are health and nutritional factors. Unfortunately, these factors are often overlooked in investigating the development of behavior. Indeed, this is more than unfortunate, because such factors have been found to exert numerous significant influences on psychological development throughout the life span.

While we cannot review all the health-related factors that influence behavioral development, the following sections consider the most important influences during (1) prenatal and neonatal development, (2) infancy and childhood, and (3) adulthood. The factors we will investigate include, respectively, pregnancy and birth complications, malnutrition, and cerebrovascular disease.

Effects of Obstetrical Complications

Fetal or infant death is perhaps the most dramatic consequence of obstetrical complications. Such deaths, however, represent only the most visible damaging results of obstetrical complications. Medical epidemiologists such as Pasamanick and Knobloch (1960a) have pointed out that obstetrical complications tend to produce a *continuum of reproductive casualty,* ranging from death at the most extreme through varying degrees of injury, including brain damage, to the fetus. Complications that cause fetal or infant death often do so via mechanical or asphyxic injury that, though not fatal, produces brain damage with serious effects on psychological development. Obstetrical complications have been found to be associated with a number of serious behavior disorders, including mental retardation, reading disabilities, epilepsy, hyperactive behavior disorders, and cerebral palsy, which involves impairment of motor coordination related to brain injury (Pasamanick & Knobloch, 1960b).

Several studies also have found that pregnancy and birth complications are more common than normal in the obstetrical histories of persons with schizophrenia, perhaps the most serious form of psychiatric disorder (McNeil & Kaij, 1978). Jacobsen and Kinney (1981) found that the overall frequency and severity of pregnancy and delivery complications was significantly greater in a sample of sixty-six schizophrenics than in control subjects matched for age, sex, and social class of rearing parents. Extremely long labors, in particular, were much more common in the schizophrenics than in control subjects. This was true even among a subgroup of thirty-four matched pairs of schizophrenics and controls who had been adopted shortly after birth. It therefore seems unlikely that the association between schizophrenia and obstetrical complications resulted simply because the parents who provided poor prenatal environments also provided environments conducive to schizophrenia after birth. Rather, the results seem most consistent with the hypothesis that obstetrical complications are a causal factor in schizophrenia.

Other evidence suggesting that obstetrical complications contribute to psychiatric disorders comes from experiments in which laboratory animals are exposed to varying degrees of asphyxia. Obstetrical complications that severely restrict the oxygen supply to the fetus are especially suspect as sources of brain injury. Brain tissue has an unusually high metabolic rate and is particularly vulnerable to a lack of oxygen (anoxia). After only several minutes of total oxygen deprivation, nerve cells may begin to die.

To study the effects of anoxia on the brain under controlled conditions, physiologists (Myers, 1978) have delivered infant rhesus monkeys by caesarian section and then have clamped the umbilical cord for various periods of time so that the effects of varying intervals of anoxia can be observed. Such research suggests that acute and total deprivation of oxygen seems most likely to damage the brain stem, with perhaps most marked effects on such psychological processes as arousal and emotional responsiveness. Less severe but more prolonged periods of partial oxygen deprivation, by contrast, have the most serious effects on the cerebral hemispheres.

Prenatal and Perinatal Risk Factors Many different pregnancy, delivery, and neonatal complications increase the risk of prenatal or perinatal mortality. Birch and Gussow (1970), among others, present a careful review of research on this subject, showing how closely such risk factors are related to economic, social, and educational factors.

One way of looking at obstetrical risk is to move a step backward in the causal pathway leading to complications, asking what characteristics of the mother and her pregnancy place her at greater reproductive risk. Birch and Gussow (1970) review a number of such factors. They note that two of the most general maternal characteristics affecting pregnancy outcome are the mother's age and her history of previous reproductive problems. The general pattern of risk associated with a mother's age and the number of previous pregnancies can be summarized as follows: "relatively high risks of complication for the never-before-pregnant or the young too-often-pregnant mother, relatively lower risks for those in their twenties bearing second, third, or fourth children, and rapidly increasing risk for mothers who are over 30 or of parity over 4" (pp. 83-84). A particularly high risk is associated with mothers who have a large number of pregnancies in rapid succession. Poor nutrition and other adverse environmental conditions that impair or stunt a woman's physical growth also tend to increase her reproductive risk. The physical size, vigor, and bone structure of a mother—particularly aspects of her pelvic structure—can be important determinants of whether she can carry a fetus to term and whether the infant can pass through the birth canal without major complications. Women of shorter stature and abnormal pelvic shapes are at greater risk for obstetrical complications. The quality and amount of prenatal health care received by mothers also affect her risk. Women who delay seeking prenatal examinations are at greater risk for obstetrical complications.

At another level of causation, we may ask what environmental and public health conditions are responsible for such maternal risk factors as poor nutrition or poor health care during pregnancy, having many children in rapid succession, or having a child in one's early teens, before one's own body has matured. Obviously, one crucial factor is economics. Infant mortality and prematurity rates are correlated highly with income, both among different countries and within regions of the same country. Internationally, these rates tend to be extremely high in poorer countries. Even within relatively affluent countries such as the United States, however, there are marked regional differences in infant mortality rates. Rates are high in such poverty pockets as urban ghettos, Appalachia, Native American reservations, and poor areas of the rural South.

Income is not the only important factor, however. The distribution, quality, and accessibility of health care are also important. As noted earlier, a number of countries have lower infant mortality rates than the United States even though their per capita income is considerably less. These tend to be countries in which medical care is provided by the government so that access to health care is not restricted by the ability to pay. Even when health care is free, however, it does not necessarily reach those who need it most. Birch and Gussow (1970) reviewed a number of studies indicating that in the United States public health clinics often provide prenatal care in an impersonal, patronizing, and generally inconsiderate manner that discourages women from seeking such care. Moreover, it is the very women who most need early prenatal care—those on welfare, for example, or those with four or more children or having a child out of wedlock—who tend to wait the longest before seeking care. If women with high-risk pregnancies are to receive optimal care, it is likely that prenatal health care programs will have to reach out actively to help them and their children.

Colleges and universities also could do much more to foster healthy pregnancies and deliveries among their students, faculty, and staff. Better prenatal education and health care programs are important steps in this direction. In addition, colleges could do more to encourage female students to have children during their twenties and early thirties, when the statistical risks of obstetrical complications are lowest, and to create a more emotionally supportive environment for women who are pregnant. An increasing percentage of women are pursuing higher education and careers outside the home. Society as a whole, as well as individual women, will benefit from wider educational and career opportunities for women. An unfortunate side effect of such opportunities, however,

Even when quality health care is freely accessible, it does not necessarily reach those who need it most.

© 1980 Bernard Pierre Wolff, Photo Researchers, Inc.

is that women may delay childbearing beyond the statistically optimal years; or they may bear children in periods of great stress or forgo having children even though they would like to have them. Colleges could do much more to promote low-cost, high-quality day-care centers and more flexible educational programs that would encourage women to have children when they are under minimal stress and of optimal reproductive age.

Drugs and Childbirth The effects of medication given to women during delivery is a controversial topic. Most women experience some degree of pain and discomfort during childbirth, and some report childbirth as one of the more painful experiences of their lives. To help alleviate this discomfort, a variety of drugs have been developed. These include tranquilizing drugs to reduce the emotional response to pain signals, local anesthetics to deaden pain in the pelvic region, and general anesthetics to make the woman unconscious. These drugs and the techniques for administering them have been refined to the point that they appear to be reasonably safe for the mother. In recent years, however, concern has grown about possible harmful effects of such drugs on the fetus. There are several reasons for such concern. First of all, it is now recognized that such drugs pass across the placenta into the fetal blood supply within a matter of minutes. Second, these drugs tend to have sedating or depressant effects on the nervous system of the infant as well as the mother, increasing the risk that the infant will suffer hypoxic brain damage during delivery. Third, when the mother is anesthetized—and particularly when she is unconscious—she cannot participate fully in the delivery of her infant. To compensate, the obstetrician may have to use forceps or other means to carry out the delivery. Such methods may increase the risks to the fetus.

A number of studies have documented the fact that infants whose mothers have received sedatives or anesthetics during childbirth tend to be less alert for several days after birth, showing, for example, less active nursing (Brazelton, 1961) and reduced attention to visual stimuli (Stechler, 1964). Perhaps the most crucial question concerning the safety of childbirth medications, however, concerns their long-term behavioral effects on offspring. Bowes et al. (1970) compared infants whose mothers (1) received no delivery medication with those who received (2) local anesthetics and (3) general anesthesia. Infants born to mothers in the first group did significantly better than those in the second group, who, in turn, seemed more advanced than the third group. In other words, the greater the level of exposure to medication, the poorer the development, on the average. This was true even on tests given several weeks after birth. (For example, infants exposed to more medication showed slower habituation to repeated presentation of a loud noise.)

More recently, Dr. Yvonne Brackbill of Florida University and Dr. Sarah Broman of the National Institute of Mental Health examined the relation between obstetrical medications and development. For this study they used data from the Collaborative Perinatal Project, a longitudinal study of fifty thousand pregnant women and their children (Kolata, 1979). Besides studying information about the pregnancies and deliveries of these women, Brackbill and Broman followed the children over a seven-year period and periodically gave them physical, neurological, and psychological tests. They examined the relation between obstetrical medications received and test scores on various measures of development. Of course, a correlation between poor development and heavy exposure to delivery medication might arise because delivery complications both increased the risk for damage to the infant and caused the obstetrician to administer more drugs. To control for this possibility, Brackbill and Broman focused on a subsample of 3,500 children who had full-term pregnancies and births with the fewest complications. Even among this group, they found that children whose mothers had received childbirth medication did more poorly on tests of sensorimotor and cognitive development. The heavier the exposure to delivery medication, the greater the average retardation in developmental test scores. Moreover, this relation held not only for tests of young infants but also for tests administered several years after birth.

This report by Brackbill and Broman has led to heated controversy. Leading obstetricians and anesthesiologists have attacked the study for methodological flaws (Kolata, 1979). Critics of the study have noted that women with some important obstetrical complication (such as high blood pressure) were included in the sample studied. They noted further that approximately one-third of the neurological and developmental defects in the Collaborative Perinatal Project sample were associated with maternal high blood pressure and that women with hypertension are more likely to be given delivery medications.

Other studies have found significant relations between the mother's personality characteristics and the amount of anxiety she shows during prenatal visits, on the one hand, and the amount of sedative and analgesic drugs she subsequently receives during labor and delivery (Yang et al., 1976). Related studies have found that women who are more anxious tend to have infants who score lower on tests of mental and motor development (Davids, Holden & Gray, 1963). Such findings suggest that the correlations between birth medication and postnatal development may result from maternal characteristics rather than from the effects of the birth medications. The critics also are concerned that women who hear of Brackbill's and Broman's results may refuse delivery medication even when it is important for the health of the mother or her baby, and that those who accept medication may feel unwarranted guilt later.

One of the most important contributions to this debate is provided by Ronald Myers and his colleagues at the Laboratory of Perinatal Physiology at the U.S. National Institute of Health (Myers, 1980; Myers & Myers, 1979). These researchers agree that sedatives, analgesics, and general anesthetics used at excessively high doses during labor and delivery can be dangerous to both mother and child. However, they also argue that barbiturate drugs, when administered in appropriate doses, will not cause asphyxic brain damage and actually can provide lifesaving protection against such damage. Myers and Myers present evidence from both human and animal studies that barbiturates in proper doses can protect against asphyxia through at least four different physiological mechanisms. First, barbiturates depress fetal brain metabolism and prolong the brain's tolerance to oxygen deprivation. In addition, barbiturates dampen the activity of the mother's sympathetic nervous system, thereby increasing uterine blood flow and the supply of oxygen to the fetus. They also diminish the force of labor contractions, which can harm a fetus that already is receiving too little oxygen. Finally, barbiturates moderate high blood glucose levels produced by stress.

Myers and Myers believe that it is unclear whether barbiturates should be administered during uncomplicated births. However, they argue that present evidence strongly suggests that barbiturates, and possibly other delivery medications, may be lifesaving in deliveries in which asphyxia is known to be present. Barbiturates may also be helpful in preventing brain damage or death when the fetus is at high risk for anoxia. This view has become the subject of lively debate (Kron & Brackbill, 1980; Myers, 1980). Clearly, there is an urgent need for additional research to determine more precisely the risks and benefits of using different delivery medications.

Psychological Preparation for Childbirth   Another influential view in this debate is provided by lay groups promoting what is often called "natural" childbirth but is more accurately termed *prepared childbirth*. The essential idea is that proper psychological preparation for childbirth *(psychoprophylaxis)* can greatly reduce the need for drugs during labor and delivery.

The natural or prepared childbirth movement has been extremely influential for many years in both Western and Eastern Europe, and recently it has spread rapidly in the United States. The thinking of this movement has been influenced strongly by the writings of the English obstetrician Grantly Dick-Read and his French colleague Fernand Lamaze. Dick-Read and Lamaze argued that ignorance and anxiety about childbirth tend to increase the pain of uterine contractions and the perception of pain associated with childbirth. They believed that the birth process is a natural physiological process in which most women could participate without drugs. Several different types of preparation are taught in childbirth education classes. In addition to basic information about the biology of pregnancy and childbirth, pregnant women are taught techniques of muscle control. Breathing and massage techniques are used to divert attention from painful stimuli associated with childbirth. Emphasis is given to allaying the expectant mother's anxieties and involving the father as a source of emotional support during pregnancy and childbirth.

The movement for psychological preparation for childbirth would appear to present potential dangers as well as benefits. If Myers and his colleagues are right, harmful consequences might result if parents became so dogmatic or fanatical in their rejection of medications as to deny obstetricians the flexibility to use drugs when they are really needed. At the same time, techniques for reducing pain and anxiety during childbirth without the risks of drug side effects would clearly be of great benefit. However, the results of research concerning prepared childbirth are mixed. One study (Zax et al., 1975) did not find significant differences in anxiety between women who did and did not take prepared childbirth classes. Other studies have reported that participation in such classes was associated with less use of medication during childbirth and more positive attitudes toward it—particularly if the father was present (Henneborn & Cogan, 1975; Huttel et al., 1972). Tanzer (1967) concluded that personality differences among women who tend to choose prepared childbirth do not account for its beneficial effects. It is difficult, however, to exclude the possibility that parents who choose prepared childbirth differ in important ways that influence the outcome of childbirth. To provide definitive information about the effects of prepared childbirth, controlled experimental studies are needed—including follow-up studies of postnatal development and parental attitudes.

Malnutrition and Behavioral Development

If one considers the world as a whole, perhaps the most important adverse influence on psychological development is malnutrition. Myron Winick, Columbia University Professor of Nutrition and Pediatrics, noted that a recent study found that

about 50% of the children up to 4 years old in three districts of Uganda showed either biochemical signs of protein imbalance or growth retardation, or both. On a nationwide basis this would be more than half a million children. Findings such as this are unfortunately consistent in many developing countries throughout the world. They indicate that perhaps 300 million people alive today have suffered some degree of malnutrition early in life. (1976, p. 22)

Winick noted that children suffering from severe malnutrition typically belong to poor families living in crowded slum conditions in towns or cities where poor sanitation, parasites, and disease exacerbate the effects of poor nutrition.

Even in relatively affluent countries such as the United States there is a distressing amount of malnutrition. Surveys in the 1960s and 1970s found extensive malnutrition, particularly among the poor. Evidence of malnutrition generally increases as income levels decrease. Malnutrition in the United States tends to be particularly severe among many Native American populations. For example, one study (Moore, et al., 1972) of Navajo Indian children in Arizona found clear signs of malnutrition, often affecting large portions of the population. Nutritionist Winick noted that the causes of this malnutrition were the same as in poor rural populations of Latin America, Africa, and Asia: poor housing and sanitation, inadequate water supplies, unemployment, lack of education, and poverty. Most Navajo families simply cannot afford an adequate diet.

Effects of Malnutrition on Development   Severe malnutrition in children is traditionally classified as either kwashiorkor or infantile marasmus. *Kwashiorkor* results when protein intake is insufficient but carbohydrate supplies are adequate. Kwashiorkor is characterized by edema, skin lesions, and reduced synthesis of important proteins. It occurs most commonly in poor families when a young child is weaned from the mother's milk, thereby losing this source of high-quality protein. *Infantile marasmus* results from restriction of calories as well as protein intake. It involves severe emaciation from the wasting away of the body's tissues.

Perhaps the most striking effects of severe malnutrition are the visible bodily changes such as emaciation and *edema* (the bloating of tissue as the result of excess water retention). However, the most serious long-term effects of malnutrition involve retardation of growth. Severe malnutrition in adults can produce terrible emaciation as well as edema in some people. Yet an adult's metabolic processes permit the brain to receive preferential access to whatever nutrients are available, thus sparing the adult from some effects of malnutri-

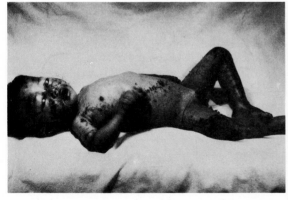

World Health Organization, Photo by Dr. Liem Tjay Tie

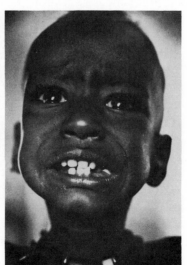

World Health Organization, Photo by R. Seitz

The effects of malnutrition in children usually cannot be reversed through proper nutrition; malnutrition impedes growth processes and may result in permanent stunting of the brain and other organs.

tion. Winick notes that terrible as the short-term physical and behavioral changes in adults may be, they usually can be reversed once proper nutrition is restored.

This is not the case in children. Malnutrition interferes with ongoing growth processes and can produce permanent stunting of the brain and other organs. Winick explains that in well-nourished populations, there is no significant correlation between head size and intelligence—except in cases of gross brain pathology. The situation is quite different in poor populations subject to malnutrition, however, where there is a high correlation between reduced head circumference and low intelligence:

Numerous studies have demonstrated that malnutrition, especially during gestation and the first two or three years of life, will retard the rate of increase in head circumference, and leave the older child or adult with a permanently reduced cranial volume. This reduction in cranial circumference has been reported in almost every developing country in the world. It was the first alarming sign that permanent brain damage might result from early malnutrition. The earlier the malnutrition, the more marked is the reduction of head circumference. . . . Moderate and even mild undernutrition very early in life may retard brain growth more than severe malnutrition later in life. Thus the time in life when malnutrition occurs is crucial to brain growth. This is an essential point because the pattern of undernutrition throughout the world is shifting in the direction of younger and younger children. (1976, p. 18)

Winick noted that experimental undernutrition in animals produces permanent deficits in the number of nerve cells and the extent of synaptic connections. In animals, the effects of undernutrition during the vulnerable period when nerve-cell production is occurring cannot be reversed after that period of vulnerability. The same seems to hold true for human brain growth; malnutrition during critical periods of neuron production and myelination in prenatal and early postnatal development is likely to result in irreversible deficits in the number of nerve cells and the extent of their synaptic processes.

As Birch and Gussow (1970) point out, the harmful effects of poor health and malnutrition on children's intellectual development need not be only, or even primarily, brain damage per se; rather, there may be several, less direct, effects. For example, children who are ill or malnourished generally are less responsive to their environment. They may be less able to concentrate in learning situations; delayed development may result simply from the loss of learning time. By making the child irritable or apathetic to social or intellectual stimulation, poor health also can reduce the amount and quality of child-adult interactions.

Rehabilitative Effects of Good Rearing   Experiments with laboratory animals have found that a stimulating environment as well as good nutrition can reverse many if not all of the behavioral deficits produced by a period of malnutrition early in development. A similar finding for human development was observed by Winick, Meyer, and Harris (1975) in a study of Korean girls who had been adopted by families in the United States by age two. Before being adopted, 42 of the girls had been severely malnourished during the first year of life; 52 had been marginally nourished; and 47 had been well nourished. The adoptions were made on a first-come, first-serve basis, and the adoptive parents had no knowledge of their child's nutritional history. The study thus makes use of a kind of natural experiment. The children were followed up when they were between seven and sixteen years old, and intelligence and achievement test scores were obtained through the schools. Upon adoption, the children were markedly below normal in height and weight for their age. By age seven, however, there were no significant differences in mean height or weight among these three groups of girls, and all were above average in both height and weight by Korean standards. The mean IQ scores for the groups that had been severely malnourished, marginally nourished, and well nourished were respectively, 102, 106, and 112; the difference between the first and the last groups was statistically significant. Achievement test results for the three groups showed a similar pattern.

The finding that the severly malnourished children scored ten points below the well-nourished children is consistent with several other studies suggesting that early malnutrition has lasting effects. At the same time, the study shows that, when reared in a middle-class home environment, even children who have experienced severe malnutrition in infancy can catch up in height and weight, and can attain normal levels of intellectual development and school achievement.

Poor Health, Impaired Learning, and Poverty   Poor health, educational failure, and poverty are linked by a number of vicious circles. Birch and Gussow (1970) have devised a schematic representation (see Figure 4.14) of how several

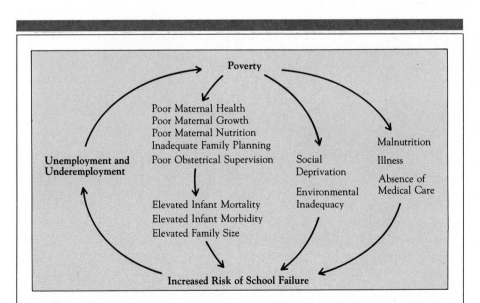

FIGURE 4.14
Environmental relationships between poverty and educational failure

Birch and Gussow, *Disadvantaged Children*. New York: Harcourt Brace Jovanovich, 1970, p. 268. By permission of Grune & Stratton, Inc.

causal chains act to bind generations of poor families into repeating cycles of educational and economic failure. Freeing disadvantaged children and adults from these cycles calls for long-term action on many fronts. Children from economically and educationally disadvantaged backgrounds usually face numerous adverse health and nutritional conditions throughout their development:

Mothers of such children tend to be less well fed, less well grown, and less well cared for before they reach childbearing age. When they reach it, they begin to bear children younger, more rapidly, and more often, and they continue to bear them to an older age. When such a mother is pregnant both her nutrition and her health will tend to be poorer than that of a woman who is better off, but she will be far less likely to get prenatal care and far more likely to be delivered under substandard conditions.

   Children of such mothers are smaller at birth, die more readily, and are generally in poorer condition in infancy than are children born to the more affluent. If they survive the first month of life, their mortality thereafter is excessively high and their illnesses more frequent, more persistent, and more severe. Their early nutrition is negatively influenced by their mother's health, her age, her income level, her education, her habits and attitudes, so that among such children in the preschool years frank malnutrition, as well as subclinical manifestations of depressed nutritional status (reflected in anemia and poor growth), are markedly more prevalent. (p. 267)

Cerebrovascular Disease

The average level of performance on tests of cognitive ability tends to decline in old age. Yet many elderly people maintain a vigorous and even superior level of intellectual and creative functioning into their eighties and even later. Longitudinal studies of intellectual change with aging have shown that the losses in intellectual functioning are not so great as was previously suggested by cross-sectional studies. Moreover, the amount of intellectual decline with age varied greatly among individuals. These findings suggest that average declines in intellectual functioning may arise from the impairment resulting from particular diseases rather than from something inherent in the aging process. If such a view is correct, it holds important and rather optimistic implications. It would mean that much of the intellectual loss and disability presently seen among the elderly need not be accepted as inevitable but could be avoided by better understanding and prevention of specific diseases. This viewpoint takes on particular importance in industrialized societies, where birth rates drop and life expectancy increases, resulting in a rapidly increasing population of the elderly—both as absolute numbers and as a percentage of the total population. Epidemiologists, psychiatrists, and gerontologists are increasingly warning that industrialized countries such as the United States are facing an increase of epidemic proportions in the numbers of cases of *senile dementia*—progressive mental deterioration occurring in the aged, marked by confusion, disorientation, and loss of memory, particularly for recent events (Clark et al., 1979).

   Cardiovascular and cerebrovascular disease are the leading cause of death for adults in industrialized societies today. But death is only the most severe end of a spectrum of disability caused by cerebrovascular disease. Jarvik and Cohen (1973) have reviewed several lines of research indicating that cerebrovascular disease is one of the most important contributors to intellectual losses in the aged. First, they note that, in longitudinal studies of intellectual changes over time in aging persons, it has been repeatedly found that individuals who died (or were otherwise lost from the sample and could not be retested) obtained lower scores on cognitive tests at the beginning of the study. The lower initial test scores of nonsurvivors appears to result from a more rapid decline in mental performance rather than from a lower level of ability earlier in adulthood. Other studies show that a rapid decline in mental test performance frequently precedes death. Indeed, a rapid decline, particularly in certain intelligence subtests, is a good predictor of individuals who are at high risk for mortality (Jarvik & Blum, 1971). Such intellectual test changes thus may serve as early warning signs of impending death—which might be averted by appropriate medical intervention. Since most deaths in these longitudinal samples resulted from cardiovascular or cerebrovascular disease, the observed declines in mental test performance may be an early sign of vascular disease affecting the brain.

Jarvik and Cohen (1973) also note that other research has shown that the level of cerebral blood flow is lowered in persons suffering from cerebral arteriosclerosis, and that the level of cognitive impairment is correlated with the levels of reduced blood flow. In one study, for example, twenty-four men and women aged seventy-one to eighty-seven were tested on the Wechsler Adult Intelligence Scale (WAIS) at the beginning and end of a twelve-year period. Those who showed the biggest drop in IQ scores over this period tended to have lower levels of cerebral blood flow at the end of the study. The decrease in cerebral blood flow seems to be rather widespread among patients with senile dementia, affecting frontal, temporal, and parietal lobes of the brain (Wang, Obrist, & Busse, 1970).

Finally, Jarvik and Cohen note that hypertension (high blood pressure) also has been found to be correlated with declines in mental test performance. In subjects aged sixty-nine to seventy-nine who were studied over a ten-year period, decreases in WAIS scores were associated with increased mortality. By contrast, elderly subjects without hypertension tended to have rather stable test scores over the period of the study (Wilkie & Eisdorfer, 1971).

Behavioral Influences on Health

At the turn of this century, the leading causes of death and illness were mainly infectious diseases. Over the last several decades, however, medical advances have greatly reduced many of the harmful effects of infectious diseases. This is particularly so in industrialized countries, in which life expectancy has increased significantly. Now other factors have become the leading causes of death and disability.

Joseph Califano, former Secretary of Health, Education, and Welfare, has noted that the first great revolutionary advance in public health was the fight against infectious diseases that occurred during the nineteenth century and the first half of our century. What is needed now is a new health revolution that will be equally effective against today's leading killers and cripplers. *Healthy People: The U. S. Surgeon General's Report on Health Promotion and Disease Prevention* (1979) concludes that the most effective way to combat death and illness is to prevent them, by getting people to stop cigarette smoking, eat more nutritious food, drink less alcohol, exercise more, and obtain better prenatal care. In the pages that follow, we will expand on and illustrate this general theme.

Can You Live to Be 100?

DIANA WOODRUFF

Take the test by starting with your current age on the life expectancy table and finding your beginning life expectancy age on the basis of your sex and race. Add or subtract years according to your answers to the following questions.

Life Expectancy Table

Age	Caucasian Male	Caucasian Female	Black Male	Black Female	Oriental Male	Oriental Female
10	70.9	78.4	65.8	74.4	72.9	80.4
11	70.9	78.4	65.8	74.4	72.9	80.4
12	70.9	78.4	65.8	74.4	72.9	80.4
13	70.9	78.4	65.9	74.4	72.9	80.4
14	71.0	78.5	65.9	74.4	73.0	80.5
15	71.0	78.5	65.9	74.5	73.0	80.5
16	71.0	78.5	66.0	74.5	73.1	80.5
17	71.1	78.5	66.1	74.5	73.1	80.5
18	71.2	78.6	66.1	74.6	73.2	80.6
19	71.3	78.6	66.2	74.6	73.3	80.6
20	71.4	78.6	66.3	74.7	73.4	80.6
21	71.5	78.7	66.5	74.7	73.5	80.7
22	71.6	78.7	66.6	74.8	73.6	80.7
23	71.7	78.7	66.8	74.8	73.7	80.7
24	71.8	78.8	66.9	74.9	73.8	80.8
25	71.9	78.8	67.1	74.9	73.9	80.8
26	71.9	78.8	67.3	75.0	73.9	80.8
27	72.0	78.9	67.4	75.1	74.0	80.9
28	72.1	78.9	67.6	75.1	74.1	80.9
29	72.2	78.9	67.8	75.2	74.2	80.9
30	72.2	79.0	68.0	75.3	74.2	81.0
31	72.3	79.0	68.1	75.4	74.3	81.0
32	72.4	79.0	68.3	75.4	74.4	81.0
33	72.4	79.1	68.5	75.5	74.4	81.1
34	72.5	79.1	68.6	75.6	74.5	81.1
35	72.6	79.2	68.8	75.7	74.6	81.2
36	72.6	79.2	69.0	75.8	74.6	81.2
37	72.7	79.3	69.2	75.9	74.7	81.3
38	72.8	79.3	69.4	76.0	74.8	81.3
39	72.9	79.4	69.6	76.1	74.9	81.4
40	73.0	79.4	69.8	76.2	75.0	81.4
41	73.1	79.5	70.0	76.4	75.1	81.5
42	73.2	79.6	70.3	76.5	75.2	81.6
43	73.3	79.6	70.5	76.6	75.3	81.6
44	73.4	79.7	70.8	76.8	75.4	81.7
45	73.5	79.8	71.0	77.0	75.5	81.8
46	73.7	79.9	71.3	77.1	75.7	81.9
47	73.8	80.0	71.5	77.3	75.8	82.0
48	74.0	80.1	71.8	77.5	76.0	82.1
49	74.1	80.2	72.1	77.7	76.1	82.2
50	74.3	80.3	72.4	77.9	76.3	82.3
51	74.5	80.5	72.7	78.2	76.5	82.5
52	74.7	80.6	73.1	78.4	76.7	82.6
53	74.9	80.7	73.4	78.6	76.9	82.7
54	75.2	80.9	73.8	78.9	77.2	82.9
55	75.4	81.0	74.2	79.1	77.4	83.0
56	75.7	81.2	74.6	79.4	77.7	83.2
57	75.9	81.4	75.0	79.7	77.9	83.4
58	76.2	81.5	75.4	80.0	78.2	83.5
59	76.5	81.7	75.8	80.3	78.5	83.7
60	76.8	81.9	76.3	80.7	78.8	83.9
61	77.2	82.2	76.8	81.0	79.2	84.2
62	77.5	82.4	77.2	81.4	79.5	84.4
63	77.9	82.6	77.7	81.8	79.9	84.6
64	78.3	82.8	78.2	82.2	80.3	84.8
65	78.7	83.1	78.7	82.5	80.7	85.1

Source: From *Can You Live to Be 100?* by Diana S. Woodruff. New York: Chatham Square Press, 1977. Copyright 1977 by Diana S. Woodruff. Reprinted with permission.

66	79.1	83.3	79.2	82.9	81.1	85.3
67	79.5	83.6	79.7	83.2	81.5	85.6
68	80.0	83.9	80.2	83.5	82.0	85.9
69	80.4	84.1	80.7	83.9	82.4	86.1
70	80.9	84.4	81.3	84.4	82.9	86.4
71	81.4	84.7	81.9	84.9	83.4	86.7
72	81.9	85.1	82.5	85.5	83.9	87.1
73	82.4	85.4	83.2	86.2	84.4	87.4
74	83.0	85.8	84.0	86.8	85.0	87.8
75	83.5	86.2	84.7	87.5	85.5	88.2
76	84.1	86.6	85.5	88.2	86.1	88.6
77	84.7	87.1	86.2	88.9	86.7	87.1
78	85.4	87.6	87.0	89.6	87.4	89.6
79	86.0	88.1	87.7	90.3	88.0	90.1
80	86.7	88.6	88.5	91.0	88.7	90.6
81	87.4	89.1	89.3	91.7	89.4	91.1
82	88.1	89.7	90.1	92.4	90.1	91.7
83	88.8	90.3	90.8	93.1	90.8	92.3
84	89.5	90.9	91.5	93.6	91.5	92.9
85	90.2	91.5	92.1	94.1	92.2	93.5

Heredity and Family

1. *Longevity of grandparents* Have any of your grandparents lived to age 80 or beyond? If so, add one year for each grandparent living beyond that age. Add one-half year for each grandparent surviving beyond the age of 70.

2. *Longevity of parents* If your mother lived beyond the age of 80, add four years. Add two years if your father lived beyond 80. You benefit more if your mother lived a long time than if your father did.

3. *Cardiovascular disease of close relatives* If any parent, grandparent, sister, or brother died of a heart attack, stroke, or arteriosclerosis before the age of 50, subtract four years for each incidence. If any of those close relatives died of the above before the age of 60, subtract two years for each incidence.

4. *Other hereditable diseases of close relatives* Have any parents, grandparents, sisters, or brothers died before the age of 60 of diabetes mellitus or peptic ulcer? Subtract three years for each incidence. If any of these close relatives died before 60 of stomach cancer, subtract two years. Women whose close female relatives have died before 60 of breast cancer should also subtract two years. Finally, if any close relatives have died before the age of 60 of any cause except accidents or homicide, subtract one year for each incidence.

5. *Childbearing* Women who have never had children are more likely to be in poor health, and they also are at a greater risk for breast cancer. Therefore, if you can't or don't plan to have children, or if you are over 40 and have never had children, subtract one-half year. Women who have a large number of children tax their bodies. If you've had over seven children, or plan to, subtract one year.

6. *Mother's age at your birth* Was your mother over the age of 35 or under the age of 18 when you were born? If so, subtract one year.

7. *Birth order* Are you the first born in your family? If so, add one year.

8. *Intelligence* How intelligent are you? Is your intelligence below average, average, above average, or superior? If you feel that your intelligence is superior, that is, if you feel that you are smarter than almost anyone you know, add two years.

Health

9. *Weight* Are you currently overweight? Find your ideal weight on Table A. If you weigh more than the figure on Table A, calculate the percentage by which you are overweight, and subtract the appropriate number of years shown on Table B. If you have been overweight at any point in your life, or if your weight has periodically fluctuated by more than ten pounds since high school, subtract two years.

(continued)

TABLE A
Weight, Height, Age Tables
(Ages Twenty-five and Over)

Desirable Weights for Men

Height
(in Shoes,
1-inch
Heels)   Weight in pounds
                              (in Indoor Clothing)

Ft. In.	Small Frame	Medium Frame	Large Frame
5 2	112–120	118–129	126–141
5 3	115–123	121–133	129–144
5 4	118–126	124–136	132–148
5 5	121–129	127–139	135–152
5 6	124–133	130–143	138–156
5 7	128–137	134–147	142–171
5 8	132–141	138–152	147–166
5 9	136–145	142–156	151–170
5 10	140–150	146–160	155–174
5 11	144–154	150–165	159–179
6 0	148–158	154–170	164–184
6 1	152–162	158–175	168–189
6 2	156–167	162–180	173–194
6 3	160–171	167–185	178–199
6 4	164–175	172–190	182–204

Desirable Weights for Women

Height
(in Shoes,
2-inch
Heels)   Weight in Pounds
                              (in Indoor Clothing)

Ft. In.	Small Frame	Medium Frame	Large Frame
4 10	92–98	96–107	104–119
4 11	94–101	98–110	106–122
5 0	96–104	101–113	109–125
5 1	99–107	104–116	112–128
5 2	102–110	107–119	115–131
5 3	105–113	110–122	118–134
5 4	108–116	113–126	121–138
5 5	111–119	116–130	125–142
5 6	114–123	120–135	129–146
5 7	118–127	124–139	133–150
5 8	122–131	128–143	137–154
5 9	126–135	132–147	141–158
5 10	130–140	136–151	145–163

Ft. In.	Small Frame	Medium Frame	Large Frame
5 11	134–144	140–155	149–168
6 0	138–148	144–159	153–173

Source: Metropolitan Life Insurance Company.

TABLE B
Risk to Life of Being Overweight
    (in Years)

Age	Markedly overweight (More than 30%)		Moderately overweight (10–30%)	
	Men	Women	Men	Women
20	−15.8	−7.2	−13.8	−4.8
25	−10.6	−6.1	−9.6	−4.9
30	−7.9	−5.5	−5.5	−3.6
35	−6.1	−4.9	−4.2	−4.0
40	−5.1	−4.6	−3.3	−3.5
45	−4.3	−5.1	−2.4	−3.8
50	−4.6	−4.1	−2.4	−2.8
55	−5.4	−3.2	−2.0	−2.2

Source: Metropolitan Life Insurance Company.

10. *Dietary habits* Do you prefer vegetables, fruits, and simple foods to foods high in fat and sugar, do you always stop eating before you feel really full? If the honest answer to both questions is yes, *add one year.*

11. *Smoking* How much do you smoke? If you smoke two or more packs of cigarettes a day, *subtract twelve years.* If you smoke between one and two packs a day, *subtract seven years.* If you smoke less than a pack a day, *subtract two years.* If you have quit smoking, congratulations, you subtract no years at all!

12. *Drinking* If you are a moderate drinker, that is, if you never drink to the point of intoxication and have one or two drinks of whiskey, or half a liter of wine, or up to four glasses of beer per day, *add three years.* If you are a light drinker, that is, you have an occasional drink, but do not drink almost every

day, add one and one-half years. If you are an abstainer who never uses alcohol in any form do not add or subtract any years. Finally, if you are a heavy drinker or an alcoholic, *subtract eight years.* (Heavy drinkers are those who drink more than three ounces of whiskey or drink other intoxicating beverages excessively almost every day. They drink to the point of intoxication.)

13. *Exercise* How much do you exercise? If you exercise at least three times a week at one of the following: jogging, bike riding, swimming, taking long, brisk walks, dancing, or skating, *add three years.* Just exercising on weekends does not count.

14. *Sleep* If you generally fall asleep right away and get six to eight hours of sleep per night, you're average and should neither add nor subtract years. However, if you sleep excessively (ten or more hours per night), or if you sleep very little (five or less hours per night), you probably have problems. *Subtract two years.*

15. *Sexual activity* If you enjoy regular sexual activity, having intimate sexual relations once or twice a week, add two years.

16. *Regular physical examinations* Do you have an annual physical examination by your physician which includes a breast examination and Pap smear for women, and a proctoscopic examination every other year for men? If so, *add two years.*

17. *Health status* Are you in poor health? Do you have a chronic health condition (for example, heart disease, high blood pressure, cancer, diabetes, ulcer) or are you frequently ill? If so, *subtract five years.*

Education and Occupation

18. *Years of education* How much education have you had? *Add or subtract the number of years shown on Table C.*

TABLE C
Education and Life Expectancy*

Level of education	Years of life
Four or more years of college	+3.0
One to three years of college	+2.0
Four years of high school	+1.0
One to three years of high school	+0.0
Elementary school (eight years)	−0.5
Less than eighth grade	−2.0

* Estimates based on data presented in E. M. Kitagawa and P.M. Hauser, Differential mortality in the United States: A study in socioeconomic epidemiology. Cambridge, Mass.: Harvard University Press, 1973 (pp. 12, 18), and in Metropolitan Life Insurance Company, Socioeconomic mortality differentials, *Statistical Bulletin,* 1975, 56, 3-5.

19. *Occupational level* If you are working, what is the socioeconomic level of your occupation? If you do not work, what is your spouse's occupation? If you are retired, what is your former occupation? If you are a student, what is your parents' occupational level? *Add or subtract the number of years shown on Table D.*

TABLE D
Occupation and Life Expectancy*

Occupational level		Years of life
Class I —	Professional	+1.5
Class II —	Technical, administrative, and managerial. Also agricultural workers, as they live longer than for their actual socioeconomic level	+1.0
Class III —	Proprietors, clerical, sales, and skilled workers	±0.0
Class IV —	Semi-skilled workers	−0.5
Class V —	Laborers	−4.0

* Estimates based on data presented in E. M. Kitagawa and P. M. Hauser. Differential mortality in the United States: A study in socioeconomic epidemiology. Cambridge, Mass.: Harvard University Press, 1973 (pp. 12, 18), and in Metropolitan Life Insurance Company, Socioeconomic mortality differentials, *Statistical Bulletin,* 1975, 56, 3-5.

(continued)

20. *Family income* If your family income is above average for your education and occupation, *add one year*. If it's below average for your education and occupation, *subtract one year*.

21. *Activity on the job* If your job involves a lot of physical activity, *add two years*. On the other hand, if you sit all day on the job, *subtract two years*.

22. *Age and work* If you are over the age of 60 and still on the job, *add two years*. If you are over the age of 65 and have not retired, *add three years*.

Lifestyle

23. *Rural vs. urban dwelling* If you live in an urban area and have lived in or near the city for most of your life, *subtract one year*. If you have spent most of your life in a rural area, add one year.

24. *Married vs. divorced* If you are married and living with your spouse, *add one year*.

A. Formerly Married Men. If you are a separated or divorced man living alone, *subtract nine years,* and if you are a widowed man living alone, *subtract seven years*. If as a separated, divorced, or widowed man you live with other people, such as family members, *subtract only half the years given above*. Living with others is beneficial for formerly married men.

B. Formerly Married Women. Women who are separated or divorced should *subtract four years,* and widowed women should *subtract three and a half years*. The loss of a spouse through divorce or death is not as life-shortening to a woman, and she lives about as long whether she lives alone or with family, unless she is the head of the household. Divorced or widowed women who live with family as the head of their household should

subtract only two years for the formerly married status.

25. *Living status as single* If you are a woman who has never married, *subtract one year for each unmarried decade past the age of 25*. If you live with a family or friends as a male single person, you should also *subtract one year for each unmarried decade past the age of 25*. However, if you are a man who has never married and are living alone, *subtract two years for each unmarried decade past the age of 25*.

26. *Life changes* Are you always changing things in your life; changing jobs, changing residences, changing friends and/or spouses, changing your appearance? If so, *subtract two years*. Too much change is stressful.

27. *Friendship* Do you generally like people and have at least two close friends in whom you can confide almost all the details of your life? If so, *add one year*.

28. *Aggressive personality* Do you always feel that you are under time pressure? Are you aggressive and sometimes hostile, paying little attention to the feelings of others? *Subtract two to five years* depending on how well you fit this description. The more pressured, aggressive, and hostile you are, the greater your risk for heart disease.

29. *Flexible personality* Are you a calm, reasonable, relaxed person? Are you easygoing and adaptable, taking life pretty much as it comes? Depending upon the degree to which you fit this description, *add one to three years*. If you are rigid, dogmatic, and set in your ways, *subtract two years*.

30. *Risk-taking personality* Do you take a lot of risks, including driving without seat belts, exceeding the speed limit, and taking any dare that is made? Do you live in a high crime rate neighborhood? If you are vulnerable to accidents and homicide in this way, *subtract two years*. If you use seat belts regularly, drive in-

frequently, and generally avoid risks and dangerous parts of town, *add one year.*

31. *Depressive personality* Have you been depressed, tense, worried, or guilty for more than
a period of a year or two? If so, *subtract one
to three years depending upon how seriously you
are affected by these feelings.*

32. *Happy personality* Are you basically happy
and content, and have you had a lot of fun in
life? If so, *add two years.* People with feelings
like this are the ones who live to be 100.

TOTAL _____

Infant and Prenatal Mortality Rates

Infant death rates vary greatly from country to country. As Figure 4.15 shows,
the most extreme differences exist between the industrialized countries with the
highest standards of living and the poorest developing countries, where infant
mortality rates are as much as ten times higher. Even among industrialized
countries, however, there are highly significant differences.

For example, the infant mortality rate in the United States is higher than in
most other industrialized countries. Indeed, our high infant mortality rate is
considered a national disgrace by many health professionals, for it represents an
enormous and needless source of death, illness, and psychological disability.
Note that the infant mortality rate in the United States is nearly twice as high as
that in Sweden, the country with the best record. Infant death rates have
declined significantly in all industrialized countries, including the United States,
over the last several decades. Yet the United States rate has been significantly
higher than that in most other technologically advanced countries. In fact, if
this country's infant mortality rate had been as low as that in Sweden in the
years since World War II, over a million infants' lives would have been saved.

Several lines of evidence indicate that much of the differential in infant
mortality rates between the United States and Sweden could have been prevented by better education and health care. Although infant death rates in all
industrialized countries have declined significantly in recent decades, the rate in
some countries has declined much more rapidly than in the United States. It is
also striking that many poorer countries can do so much better than the United
States. Clearly, we can do much more to provide good obstetrical and pediatric
care and, in particular, to see that good health care and nutrition reach all strata
of our society.

Within the United States there are great disparities in the infant mortality
rates among different ethnic and socioeconomic groups. Over the last fifty
years, for example, infant death rates have declined for both whites and nonwhites, but the rate for nonwhites has remained roughly twice as high as for
whites. Research suggests that much of this disparity reflects unequal access to
good health care. Moreover, within each ethnic group, mortality rates were

FIGURE 4.15
Infant mortality rates
per 1,000 live births

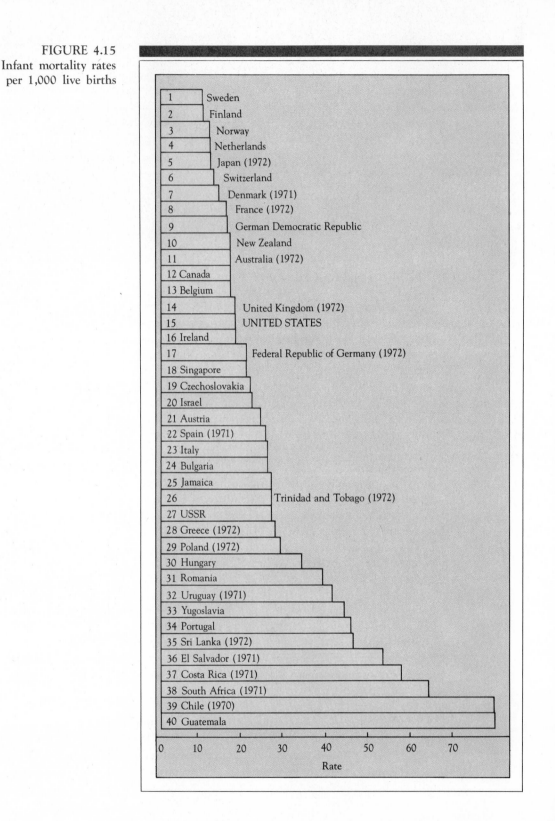

strongly asociated with the quality of health care received. Among several thousand New York City women of different ethnic groups and income levels surveyed in 1968, it was found that 38 percent of native-born white mothers were judged to be at some risk for obstetrical complications, compared with 71 percent of Puerto Rican and 75 percent of black mothers. On the other hand, 43 percent of native-born white mothers were judged to have received adequate prenatal health care. By contrast, less than 5 percent of black or Puerto Rican mothers received adequate prenatal care. Thus the mothers at the greatest risk for pregnancy or birth complications—and, therefore, those in most need of good prenatal and delivery care—were least likely to receive it (Kessner, 1973).

A related issue of equally tragic dimensions is the prenatal mortality rate (the number of fetuses lost through induced or spontaneous abortions). Judging from the long-standing and fierce debate over the legality and morality of induced abortions, it may well be more feasible to forge an ethical and political consensus to avoid preventable spontaneous abortions, which are on a scale comparable with induced abortions.

Determining the mortality rates during the prenatal period—particularly during the early months of pregnancy—is difficult. Miscarriages or spontaneous abortions are less likely than infant deaths to be reported. Moreover, a spontaneous abortion very early in pregnancy may not be recognized even by the mother, who may misinterpret the event as simply a delay in menstruation.

Some of the best data on prenatal mortality rates come from a prospective study conducted on the Hawaiian island of Kauai (Werner et al., 1971), in which a large group of expectant mothers were contacted early in pregnancy and the outcome of their pregnancies was carefully monitored. As can be seen in Figure 4.16, the known mortality rates in this group of pregnancies was highest during the earliest part of pregnancy. Even in this study, however, it was not possible to get reliable data during the earliest weeks. Nonetheless, extrapolation suggests that the mortality rate during the first several weeks after conception may be very great.

A major proportion of spontaneous abortions involves chromosomal aberrations or other genetic and medical conditions that cannot at present be prevented. However, a significant proportion is also the result of environmental conditions such as poor health care, emotional stress, and malnutrition, which *are* within our power to remedy. It seems clear that very large numbers of prenatal as well as infant deaths can be prevented—if only we are willing to expend the necessary economic and educational resources.

Accidents: The Leading Killer of Children and Young Adults

In the 1920s and 1930s, the chief killers of young children were infectious diseases such as influenza and pneumonia. Thanks to antibiotics, vaccines, and better medical care and public health measures, tremendous progress has been made since then. In 1925, of every 100,000 children aged one to four, 150 died from flu or pneumonia; by 1973, only 6 children out of 100,000 died from those causes.

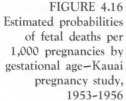

FIGURE 4.16
Estimated probabilities
of fetal deaths per
1,000 pregnancies by
gestational age—Kauai
pregnancy study,
1953–1956

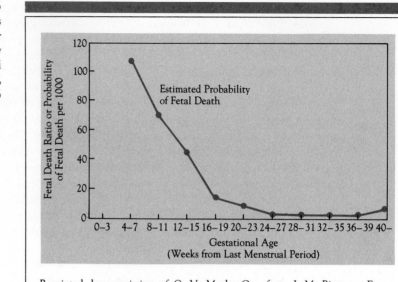

Reprinted, by permission of C. V. Mosby Co., from J. M. Bierman, E. Siegel, F. E. French, and K. Simonian. 1965. Analysis of the outcome of all pregnancies in a community. *American Journal of Obstetrics and Gynecology*, fig. 1, Vol. 91, 1965, pp. 37-45.

Today the leading killer of children in industrialized countries is accidents. In the early 1970s, accidents accounted for about one-third of all deaths among American children aged one to four, and about half of all deaths for children aged five to fourteen. The proportion of total childhood deaths due to accidents has increased steadily over the last fifty years (National Center for Health Statistics, 1978). In industrialized countries like the United States, accident prevention thus may be considered the highest health priority for children and young adults.

Among accidents, the worst killer is motor vehicle accidents, which are the leading cause of death for American children, teen-agers, and adults under twenty-five. By 1980, traffic accidents had killed over two million Americans—considerably more than all of the country's wars. Most traffic fatalities and injuries could be prevented by taking steps to apply present knowledge and technology. Let us very briefly consider just a few examples of such steps:

1. *Instituting better safety education for children.* Health agencies, in recognition of the fact that traffic fatalities are probably the single most important preventable cause of death in children, have recently begun to fund research by developmental psychologists into how children can be educated more effectively concerning traffic safety.

2. *Using seat belts and air bags.* The U. S. Department of Transportation estimates that about nine thousand lives and a half-million serious injuries could be prevented *each year* if all cars had air bags. This potential saving of

life will become even greater in the future, with more cars on the road and with a growing trend toward smaller cars in the interest of fuel economy. Recent studies estimate that an incredible 93 percent of small children in the United States are *totally unrestrained* when riding in automobiles. (Special restraints should be used at all times for infants and small children; standard seat and lap belts should be used for older children.) Tests by General Motors indicate that air bags offer substantial protection, even to children who are standing or in other unusually vulnerable positions (Carter, 1976).

3. *Buying safe equipment.* To ensure that car seats or other equipment such as cribs or infant seats meet the best safety standards, check state or federal consumer protection agencies or consumer publications in your library.[1]

4. *Reducing drunken driving.* Roughly half of traffic fatalities involve intoxicated drivers. The number of intoxicated drivers on the road could be reduced by stiffer penalties both for drivers and for those who provide them with liquor yet allow them to drive away while intoxicated.

Sex Differences and Death Rates

Why do women live longer than men? Biologist Ingrid Waldron (1976) has reviewed research on the major causes of death in American men and women. Waldron points out that the sex difference in mortality has increased markedly over the past several decades in the United States. In 1920, life expectancy for women stood at fifty-six—just two years longer than for men. By 1970, however, life expectancy for women had reached seventy-five, almost eight years longer than for men. In 1970, the death rate for American males exceeded the rate for females by 60 percent overall, and by 180 percent among people aged fifteen to twenty-four.

Genetic and hormonal factors may play a small role in producing these sex differences. For example, Waldron noted some evidence that females tend to be more resistant to infectious diseases, perhaps in part because the X chromosome carries genes that seem to enhance the production of antibodies. Some research also suggests that female sex hormones may lower the risk of coronary heart disease, but the scientific evidence on this point is inconsistent and unclear. Waldron concluded that intrinsic biological differences account for only a small percentage of the marked sex differences in death rates. Instead, most of the sex differential in mortality seems to result from cultural and psychological influences on the development of health-related attitudes, habits, lifestyles, and occupational choices. Table 4.1 shows those major causes of death in the United States for which the male death rate was at least twice as great as that for females. These seven causes of death account for three-quarters of the present sex differential in mortality. Each of these causes of death, in turn, can be related to differences in behavioral habits or lifestyles.

For example, the fivefold to sixfold increase in death rates among males from lung cancer, emphysema, and other serious respiratory diseases results largely

---

1. A useful source of information is *Good Things for Babies* (Jones, 1976); see selected readings listed at end of this chapter.

TABLE 4.1
Major Causes of
Higher Mortality
in Men

Ratio of Male to Female Death Rates	Cause of Death	Male Death Rate	Female Death Rate*
		(Deaths 100,000 population)	
5.9	Cancer of respiratory system, not specified as secondary	50.1	8.5
4.9	Other bronchopulmonic disease (including emphysema)	24.4	5.0
2.8	Motor vehicle accidents	39.4	14.2
2.7	Suicide	15.7	5.8
2.4	Other accidents	41.1	17.4
2.0	Cirrhosis of liver	18.5	9.1
2.0	Arteriosclerotic heart disease, including coronary heart disease	357.0	175.6
1.6	All causes	1081.7	657.0

This table lists all causes of death that had a sex mortality ratio of 2.0 or more and were responsible for at least 1 percent of all deaths in the United States in 1967. These causes of death are responsible for three-quarters of the sex differential in mortality.

*Female death rates have been age adjusted using the age-specific death rates for females and the age distribution for males to calculate the death rate that would be expected for a population of females that had the same age distribution as the male population. Thus the male and female death rates are directly comparable and are not affected by the higher proportion of females at older ages.

Source: Reprinted with permission from *Social Science*, vol. 10, I. Waldron, "Why Do Women Live Longer than Men?" Copyright © 1976, Peragamon Press, Ltd.

from the higher percentage of men who have smoked heavily for many years. The higher rate of fatal motor vehicle accidents among men results in part from the tendency for males to drive more recklessly and take more risks. An even more important contributor may be the greater consumption of alcohol by males; roughly half of all fatal motor vehicle accidents involve drunken drivers. The higher suicide rate for males partly reflects the greater stress on men resulting from competition for jobs. For example, when unemployment rates go up, suicide rates increase more for men than for women.

Alcohol abuse and the malnutrition that accompanies it are major contributors to cirrhosis of the liver, and to the greater death rate for men. Greater alcohol use and risk-taking also contribute to the higher death rates for men as a result of other kinds of accidents—which are five times more common among men. Finally, cigarette smoking is a major risk factor in coronary heart disease, which is associated with a 100 percent increase in fatal heart attacks among middle-aged adults.

Sex differences in smoking habits seem to be a major cause of the higher male death rates from heart disease, though another important factor may be the greater incidence among males of the so-called *Type A*, or *coronary-prone, behavior pattern*. The Type A person is said to be highly ambitious, competitive, time conscious, impatient, and achievement oriented. Some data suggest that coronary heart disease may be just as common among Type A women as Type

Bad News for Women Smokers

Since men have been smoking much longer than women, males have borne the brunt of smoking-related diseases like lung cancer and heart attacks. But women smokers have caught up rapidly and their health reflects their cigarette habit at an accelerating rate. Within three years, U.S. Surgeon General Julius B. Richmond predicted last week, more women will die of lung cancer than from breast cancer.

The bad news came in the Surgeon General's annual report on smoking and health which, for the first time, was devoted exclusively to the risks for females. "Cigarette smoking, an early sign of woman's social emancipation, is now the major threat to her personal health," Richmond said. According to the report, women smokers have from two and a half to five times greater likelihood of developing lung cancer than non-smokers. As with men, smoking also increases a woman's risk of cancers of the larynx, mouth and bladder, and doubles the chance of having a heart attack.

The report also warned of a risk that smoking poses exclusively for women—damage to their babies. Women who smoke, the report warned, have more premature or underweight infants, suffer more complications during pregnancy and have more stillbirths. Their babies also are more likely to suffer the sudden-infant-death syndrome, or crib death.

A men, but more men than women appear to have Type A personalities.

The recent trends in mortality rates for men and women confirm the importance of behavioral influences on health. Although the ratio of male to female death rates in the United States has increased steadily since 1920, there are signs that this is beginning to change. In recent years, the ratio has begun to fall for deaths from auto accidents, suicides, lung cancer, emphysema, heart disease before age fifty-four, and cirrhosis of the liver after age forty-five. However, the bad news is that these changes seem to reflect increases in female death rates associated with these causes. In other words, there is an increasing tendency for women to adopt damaging lifestyles. The movement to effect equal opportunities for women thus may be having the tragic side effect of inflicting on women the increased risk of many serious diseases associated with traditional male roles and lifestyles. Fortunately, Waldron's analysis suggests that this harmful side effect is not inevitable. Those who are working for equal opportunity must not be satisfied simply with ending sexual discrimination; they also must reform the aspects of culture, sex roles, attitudes, and lifestyles that seem so destructive to the health of both men and women.

Personal Habits and Good Health

We have seen that the behavior patterns people develop appear to be among the most powerful determinants of how long they live—and how they die.

Perhaps even more important is the fact that behavior patterns are also strongly associated with the health, vigor, and general quality of life that people experience while they are alive. A systematic study of this issue was conducted by public health scientists on a probability sample of adults in Alameda County, California (Belloc & Breslow, 1972). Nearly seven thousand adults (86 percent of the identified sample) completed questionnaires that assessed the general quality of their health as well as a variety of health-related behaviors. Information about various medical symptoms, disabilities and impairments, and their chronicity as well as general energy level was used to assign each person an overall health score on a seven-point scale ranging from severe disability to vigorous good health. Data also were obtained concerning personal habits such as smoking, eating, drinking, sleeping, and exercise. Poor health was significantly associated with each of the following seven behavior patterns:

1. Smoking (among those who inhaled more deeply and smoked longer)
2. Heavy drinking (those who imbibed five or more drinks on one occasion)
3. Frequent skipping of breakfast
4. Frequent snacking between meals
5. Being overweight (20 percent or more for men; 10 percent or more for women)
6. Infrequent participation in regular exercise
7. Unusual sleeping habits (either nine or more hours, or six or fewer hours, per night)

That these behavior patterns should be related to health is not unexpected. In fact, this is consistent with other research findings as well as with what many would regard as common sense. More surprising perhaps is the cumulative strength of the association between these personal habits and overall health, as revealed in the following findings (see also Figure 4.17):

1. The effects of health-related personal habits seemed to be cumulative. That is, the more good habits, the higher the average health rating—a relation that held true with remarkable consistency across different ages.
2. The strength of this association is impressive: persons following all seven good habits were similar in average health status to those who were thirty years younger and followed few or none of the practices.
3. With increasing age, the curves tend to fan out so that differences in average health status between those with good versus bad habits become greater at older ages.
4. The average number of good habits reported increased significantly with age, suggesting that those with poor health habits tend to die off, leaving those with good habits as an increasing percentage of the survivors.
5. The association of personal habits with health persisted even when income levels were taken into account. In fact, health status was much more strongly associated with personal habits than with income.

As with most nonexperimental data on development, we must be cautious in making inferences about cause and effect. Nonetheless, the overall pattern of data from this study suggests that personal habits have powerful and pervasive effects on physical health and vigor as well as longevity.

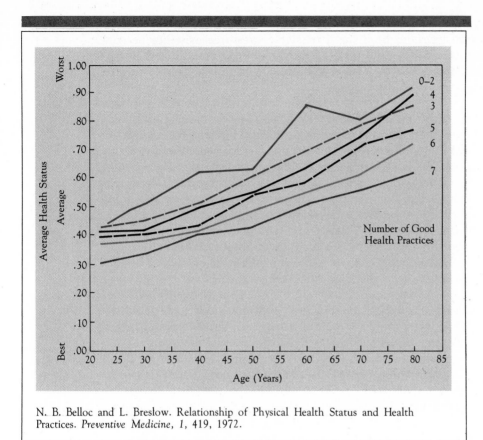

FIGURE 4.17
Average physical health status by age for groups following different numbers of health practices

N. B. Belloc and L. Breslow. Relationship of Physical Health Status and Health Practices. *Preventive Medicine, 1,* 419, 1972.

Life Events, Stress, and Illness

A growing body of research indicates that stressful life events are associated with an increased risk of developing a number of illnesses. For example, Holmes et al. (1957) found that an unusual number of social stresses tended to occur just before the onset of tuberculosis. Other studies have also found increases of other illnesses to be associated with changes in the pattern of living, such as a change in place of residence or job (Syme, Hyman, & Enterline, 1964); job loss (Kasl & Cobb, 1970); and separation from home in student nurses (Parens, McConville, & Kaplan, 1966; see also Dohrenwend, 1973).

Theorell and Rahe (1975) conducted a longitudinal study of thirty-six men and women (with a mean age of fifty-seven years) who had experienced a heart attack. Of eighteen subjects who died during the six-year follow-up period, all had experienced a significant buildup of life changes in terms of family or personal life, work, or financial situation that had reached a peak between seven and twelve months before their deaths. The eighteen patients who survived did not show this excessive buildup in life-change units over this six-year period, suggesting that stressful life events may play a significant role in coronary deaths. Apparently, stressful events producing the cardiovascular damage may occur as much as twelve months before death. Indeed, right before death the patients may appear to be living a relatively stress-free existence because they have restricted their activities to adjust to the deterioration in their cardiovascular condition. Use of a life-events scale, as in this study, can help to determine the role of prior stressful events.

Many recent studies of the effects of stress on the development of illness have used life-events scales similar to one developed by Holmes and Rahe (1967). This scale asks subjects to indicate which of over forty different life events they have experienced during a given period of time. Each event is weighted according to how much "life adjustment" it requires—as rated either by the average subject or by an individual subject. The results of many studies using this kind of approach support the view that changes in one's patterns of living produce physiological changes that stress people and render them more susceptible to various kinds of illness. These results are compatible with experimental studies of laboratory animals, which have shown that prolonged stress can severely damage health through direct physiological effects on an individual's organs and through indirect effects such as lowering one's capacity to fight infection.

Much research remains to be done, however, before we fully understand the complex relation between stress and illness. How a potentially stressful event affects a person depends on many factors, including how well the person is able to cope with the event, how much support from others is available, how the person thinks and feels about the event, how his or her body responds to stress, and the presence of other factors such as infection.

Age is one way of indexing physiological predisposition to illness. That is, older individuals tend to be less able to maintain equilibrium or physiological homeostasis; therefore, they are more likely to become ill under stress. There is some evidence that life changes occur less frequently in the middle and later years. This is understandable, as the early adult years are filled with many rapid and important changes in residence, school, work, and love relationships. What is difficult to assess, however, is the significance of such changes for people of different ages. For example, is a change in residence likely to be as stressful for a young person as it is for an older adult who may have lived in the same place for thirty or more years? Similarly, a job change for a young adult after a few years is hardly an event comparable with retirement after forty or more years of employment. Thus scaling of life changes—if it is to be used with adults of a wide age range—requires that the duration of the significant activity be taken into account and be given appropriate weight. It seems plausible to suggest that older adults are physiologically more vulnerable to stress effects. However, the changes in a single aspect of life may be more significant for older people because of their longer emotional investment and the pervasiveness of their involvement. For example, older spouses often follow their mates to the grave in a short time.

Apart from an age-related physiological vulnerability to stress—and perhaps the greater significance of some of life's changes for older adults—there remain two other characteristics that may influence the course of events: experience in handling stress, and personality or adaptive style.

Stress, Personality, and Coronary Heart Disease

"The moral flabbiness born of the exclusive worship of the bitchgoddess SUC-CESS. That—with the squalid cash interpretation put on the word success—is our national disease." So wrote William James, the great American psychologist, in a letter to H. G. Wells in 1906.

When James spoke of "disease," he had in mind primarily the moral and psychosocial consequences of this malignant materialism. Recent research on the causes of heart disease, however, suggests that James may also have been right in the physical sense of the word. A growing though still controversial body of research argues that the success-oriented American lifestyle is an important—perhaps *the* most important—contributor to our high incidence of heart disease.

The leading proponents of this view are two cardiologists, Meyer Friedman and Ray Rosenman (1978), who agree that such factors as high blood pressure, smoking, high levels of blood cholesterol, and obesity are important risk factors in heart disease. However, they also believe that perhaps the most important factor—and the one that best explains the rather steady increase in the coronary death rate in the United States since William James penned his warning about success—is stress.

As mentioned earlier, Rosenman and Friedman distinguish two archetypal personality patterns. The Type A personality is prone to heart disease because his or her attitudes toward life and consequent living habits result in great stress. By contrast, the Type B personality has a low risk of cardiac problems because he or she is able to minimize stress. The Type A individual is exceedingly and irrationally ambitious, competitive, acquisitive, and hurried. Such people are constantly driven and aggressive in their need to produce and achieve. They are impatient at any delay or frustration and are always putting themselves under time pressures. The Type B individual is free from this constant compulsion to produce, this continual fear of failure. These people are able to take the time to plan their day—and life—carefully, wisely setting goals that can be accomplished within a set period of time without unduly taxing their minds or bodies. They are able to relax without feeling guilty and to lead balanced lives that do not burden their bodily systems with a chronic load of stress.

At present, this theory remains controversial. Research evidence is mixed. From experimental research with animals, however, it seems clear that prolonged stress can have harmful effects on many systems in the body, including the coronary arteries (for example, Selye, 1978). What is perhaps less clear at this point is what exactly are the personality traits, attitudes, habits, and behavioral lifestyles in human beings that place the most harmful stress on the cardiovascular system.

Impressive research support for the general approach of Rosenman and Friedman has come from a study of rates of heart attacks in Japanese Americans. Japan has the lowest coronary heart disease rate of any industrialized country, whereas the United States has one of the highest rates. Over one million serious heart attacks occur each year in the United States. That this

How to Recognize a Heart Attack

Do you know that:

1. The great majority of people hospitalized with heart attacks survive.
2. Many who do not survive had delayed for many hours telephoning their physicians.
3. Survivors of heart attacks usually live for many years.
4. Most people who recover from heart attacks can work and lead normal lives.

But:

If you are going to take advantage of lifesaving new techniques and your doctor's ability to help you lead a normal postattack life, you must let him know immediately when you are having symptoms of an attack. Know your warning signs, and if need arises, seek prompt professional opinion. Your first impulse will be to delay. Don't! Ask a relative or neighbor to take you to a hospital emergency room immediately if you cannot reach your doctor by telephone.

   Column 1 will help you judge whether your warning signs warrant seeking professional advice. Column 2 will help keep you from becoming unnecessarily concerned with signs unrelated to a heart attack:

May Be a Heart Attack If

Prolonged heavy pain under the breastbone lasting at least 5-10 minutes. Pain is usually a severe, crushing one, but may be a slight one feeling like heartburn or indigestion.

This may or may not be accompanied by sweat-

ing and profound weakness and rarely by real breathlessness.

This chest pain may or may not spread, most often to the left arm, less frequently to the neck and jaws, and rarely to the back or abdomen.

Very Unlikely a Heart Attack If

Sharp, shooting pains last no more than a very few seconds; nor if such pains are repetitive.

Pain lasts only a very few minutes and comes with exercise or excitement and goes after stopping either. (May be a heart problem called angina pectoris. Doctor should definitely be consulted within 24 hours, but not on emergency basis.)

Pain is aggravated each time you breathe.

Pain is associated with tenderness. Painful area is tender to the touch.

Pain is a numbness or tingling sensation in fingers and toes and is accompanied by lightheadedness. (This is probably due to nervousness.)

Pain is increased by moving arms. (Is probably due to muscle strain.)

What seemed like breathlessness is really:
A feeling you can't take a deep breath.
A feeling you can't swallow easily.
(These are probably due to tension.)

Heartbeat seems to skip. (Common and seldom a cause for worry.)

Should you have the first sign listed in Column 1 rather than the signs listed in Column 2, telephone immediately for medical advice. The sign may result from a cause such as indigestion but is serious enough to warrant immediate professional opinion. Chances that you are having a heart attack increase markedly if symptoms in Column 1 increase steadily, especially if they become intolerable.

Source: This material is taken with permission of the Massachusetts General Hospital and was excerpted from its official publication, *The MGH News.*

difference may be caused largely by the greater amount of stress created by the American lifestyle is suggested by epidemiological studies at Berkeley's School of Public Health (Marmot, Syme, & Kogan, 1975). These researchers found that Japanese Americans who live in the San Francisco Bay area and who have become relatively Westernized in their lifestyles have a heart attack risk that is two and a half times greater than those who continue to lead lives according to more traditional Japanese values and customs. Japanese Americans whose lifestyles were most Westernized (as judged, for example, by the number of years spent in Japan and by schooling, religion, and ethnic backgrounds of spouses and friends) had a heart disease rate *five* times greater than that of the most traditional group. In fact, this most Westernized group had a rate as high as that for white Americans.

The difference between Japanese and American rates of heart disease had long been thought to result from dietary differences such as the greater consumption of fish and lesser consumption of meat by the Japanese, which results in lower levels of saturated fats and cholesterol. Indeed, studies by Keys (1980) have produced strong evidence that high blood pressure and high blood cholesterol levels are among the most important contributors to coronary heart disease. However, Marmot and coworkers found evidence that such factors as diet, smoking, cholesterol, blood pressure, and body weight could not explain the difference in heart disease between traditional and Americanized groups of Japanese Americans. Instead, these researchers attribute the difference to features of traditional Japanese society that protect the individual from lethal levels of stress. They note that even in modern Japanese society, there is more stability and security than in the United States. Japan has more closely knit social groups, earlier determination of vocational choices, more traditional customs to guide action in social situations, and less job mobility. There is more emphasis on the group and less pressure on the individual to compete in a constant struggle for success. Finally, for those diehard—or perhaps we should say "dieyoung"—worshippers of success, it is worth noting that Japan has had for much of the period since World War II the highest rate of economic growth of any industrialized country in the world. Therefore, reducing the heart attack rate need not necessarily mean less economic productivity (Thurow, 1977).

Because this study was not experimental, it does not provide absolute proof that differences in behavior patterns help explain why heart disease is so much worse in the United States than in Japan. Correlation does not necessarily indicate causation. Nonetheless, the evidence is highly suggestive that stress plays an important role in Americans' higher death rate from heart disease.

Conclusive proof that stress—or other factors—cause heart attacks requires long-term studies in which the suspected causal variable is experimentally manipulated. This means, first of all, recruiting a sample of thousands of people and choosing a random subsample to be an "experimental" group that gets some "treatment" expected to decrease the risk of heart attack. Factors such as smoking or diet or stressful life habits might be manipulated for this group. The remaining people in the original sample must remain as a control group. Assuming that the people in the experimental group are monitored carefully and that they faithfully maintain their experimental regimen of no smoking, low-stress lifestyle, or whatever, the experimental and control groups then must be followed for many years to see whether any difference in heart attack rates results. Such trials are controversial because they are expensive. For example, the U. S. National Heart and Lung Institute spends hundreds of millions of dollars to fund such long-term clinical trials (Kolata, 1975). But even this is a small price to pay if research can provide definitive scientific evidence of what causes cardiovascular disease.

Summary

1. The brain is composed of two basic cell types. Neurons—through their specialized processes, the dendrites and axons—receive and transmit information in the form of neural impulses. Neuroglia cells provide nutritive and structural support to neurons and form myelin sheaths to protect and insulate many axonal fibers.
2. Brain development passes through stages characterized by cell proliferation, growth, differentiation, migration, formation of synapses with other neurons, selective cell death, and elimination or stabilization of the synapses initially formed.
3. The brain grows more rapidly than other organs during human development. Maximum growth occurs from about the sixth month of gestation to one year after birth. During this period, metabolic stresses such as malnutrition are most likely to have permanent effects on brain size and composition.
4. Brain maturation, particularly myelination, continues in some areas of the brain into at least middle age. The maturation of new brain areas may account for the appearance of new cognitive abilities in adulthood as well in infancy and early adulthood.
5. Over the last several decades, children in industrialized countries have grown steadily to taller average heights and have reached them earlier. There has been a parallel trend toward earlier menarche. This accelerated maturation seems to involve better nutrition and health care as well as genetic outbreeding.
6. On average, females excel on tests of verbal ability, and males do better on tests of spatial visualization, beginning around the time of adolescence. Early maturers do relatively better on verbal tasks, while late maturers excel on spatial tasks. Differences in maturation rates were better predictors of verbal/spatial abilities than was biological sex, suggesting that average sex differences in ability patterns *may* be related in part to earlier average maturation in females.
7. Obstetrical complications can produce a continuum of reproductive casualty ranging from death to decreasing degrees of brain injury. Obstetrical complications—particularly the more serious ones, which increase the risk of asphyxic brain damage—are associated with increased risk for a number of psychological disorders, ranging from cerebral palsy to schizophrenia. Nerve cells have a high metabolic rate and are especially sensitive to oxygen deprivation, and so they may die after several minutes of total oxygen deprivation (anoxia).

8. At present, mothers at high risk for poor pregnancy outcome (for example, mothers on welfare, with four or more children, having a child out of wedlock, or in their early teens), who also need good prenatal care the most, tend to wait longest before seeking prenatal care. Social institutions could do much more to reach out to such women and promote healthful pregnancy outcome.

9. Children whose mothers received anesthetic or analgesic drugs during childbirth are at greater risk for poor prenatal development. However, it is not clear whether this is because the delivery drugs cause brain damage or because mothers who receive more delivery drugs have deliveries at higher risk for other reasons.

10. Emotional stress on a pregnant woman can increase the risk of oxygen deprivation to the fetus through several physiological mechanisms. Classes that prepare women for childbirth may help to reduce stress. Tranquilizing drugs such as barbiturates reduce the risk of infant anoxia in monkeys when the mother is under stress. Determining whether such drugs or prepared childbirth can reduce anoxia among human infants requires further study.

11. Malnutrition is one of the most important influences on development; some 300 million people living today suffered malnutrition early in life. A major factor contributing to the development of malnutrition in very young children today is the decline of breast-feeding.

12. Human and animal studies have shown that a stimulating environment and good nutrition can make up much of the behavioral deficit produced by a period of malnutrition early in development.

13. Disadvantaged children tend to be at greater risk for health hazards throughout life. Equal opportunity for learning for disadvantaged children requires health care and nutrition across the entire life span; compensatory educational programs alone cannot provide equal opportunity for learning. Poverty, poor health care, educational failure, and unemployment reinforce each other in a vicious circle that works to perpetuate poverty and poor health across generations.

14. Although the average level of intellectual ability declines markedly in old age, many elderly people maintain superior levels of intellectual functioning into their eighties and nineties. The average decline in intellectual functioning with age may arise more from increased numbers of individuals who suffer cognitive impairment as a result of specific disease processes than from declines inherent in aging.

15. Infant mortality rates tend to be several times lower in industrialized than in poor countries. However, the United States has one of the highest infant mortality rates among industrialized countries. Providing good obstetrical care to families of all income levels and ethnic backgrounds could prevent many infant deaths and neurological disorders.

16. A major proportion of pregnancies end in spontaneous abortions. Although these are not induced intentionally, many could be prevented by protecting pregnant women from poor health, emotional stress, and malnutrition.

17. Today, the leading killer of children in industrialized countries is accidents. Motor vehicle accidents are the leading cause of death for Americans under

age twenty-five. Most traffic injuries could be prevented using present knowledge (for example, some studies found that over 90 percent of small children riding in cars are totally unrestrained).

18. United States women have a life expectancy eight years longer than men. Most of the higher male mortality is caused by lung cancer, emphysema, motor vehicle and other accidents, suicide, cirrhosis of the liver, and arteriosclerotic heart disease. The excess male deaths from these diseases result largely from greater male cigarette smoking, alcohol abuse, reckless gun use and driving, and "coronary-prone" behavior patterns.

19. Poor health is associated with several behavior patterns, including smoking, heavy drinking, poor eating habits, obesity, lack of exercise, and unusual sleeping habits. People with mostly bad habits reported an average level of health and vigor that was comparable to that of people thirty years older who had good habits.

20. Stressful life changes are associated with greater risk for many illnesses. Personality differences influence how people react to potentially stressful events. Large-scale clinical experiments are needed to obtain better information about the role of stress and personality in disease.

Selected Readings

Birch, H. B., and J. D. Gussow. *Disadvantaged Children: Health, Nutrition, and School Failure.* New York: Harcourt Brace Jovanovich, 1970. Documents how poverty and poor education tend to be mutually reinforcing. The authors contend that a serious educational program to help disadvantaged children must include efforts to improve the economic, health, and nutritional status of poor families.

Boston Children's Medical Center and Richard I. Feinbloom. *Child Health Encyclopedia: The Complete Guide for Parents.* New York: Dell, 1975. (Available in paperback.) Technically accurate and highly readable book about health care and safety precautions for children; includes alphabetical listings of childhood diseases, conditions, and treatments.

Cowan, M. "The Development of the Brain." *Scientific American,* 241 (September 1979), 112-133. An excellent overview of how neurons find their proper location and make the right connections during embryonic prenatal development. The complete issue is devoted to the structure and functioning of the brain.

Eisdorfer, D., and M. P. Lawton, eds. *The Psychology of Adult Development and Aging.* Washington: American Psychological Association, 1973. A collection of articles by specialists in various aspects of aging and psychology. Of particular relevance are articles about the biological bases of aging and the role of social stress and adaptation.

Ingelman-Sundberg, A., C. Wirsen, and L. Nillson. *A Child Is Born: The Drama of Life Before Birth.* New York: Dell, 1966 (paperback). Prize-winning photographs of prenatal development illustrate text on the basics of fertilization, pregnancy, and childbirth.

Johnson, B. T., ed. *The Harvard Medical School Health Letter.* Published monthly by the Department of Continuing Education, Harvard Medical School, Boston; address inquiries to 79 Garden Street, Cambridge, Massachusetts 02138. (As of this writing, subscriptions cost $12 annually.) Brief, accurate, and up-to-date health information addressed to a lay readership.

Jones, S. *Good Things for Babies*. Boston: Houghton Mifflin Company, 1976 (paperback). A guide to safety and consumer information about a variety of toys, equipment, and clothing for children. Makes recommendations based on information from such sources as journals of pediatrics, the National Safety Council, and the U. S. Consumer Product Safety Commission.

Rugh, R., and L. B. Shettles. *From Conception to Birth: The Drama of Life's Beginnings*. New York: Harper & Row, 1971. An embryologist and obstetrician provide a detailed description of prenatal development and childbirth. This well-written book has many excellent photographs and drawings and is intended for relatively sophisticated readers.

Tanner, J. M. *Fetus into Man*. Cambridge, Mass.: Harvard University Press, 1978. A brief but authoritative overview of human physical growth from conception through puberty. Written by a leading growth researcher, this book gives special attention to the psychological and social effects of early or late maturation and discusses major disorders of growth.

Scientific American (September 1973). An entire issue devoted to aging and its various aspects. The articles are well written and illustrated and provide a good introduction to processes and issues in aging.

Winick, M. *Malnutrition and Brain Development*. New York: Oxford University Press, 1976. A brief but scholarly overview of human and animal studies involving normal cellular growth of the brain and the effects of malnutrition on brain growth, prenatal maturation, and mental development.

Chapter 5

The Biosocial Interface: Interacting Influences

Innate factors in human development, including mother-infant attachment and human emotional expression

How biological factors limit or prepare an individual for learning

The use of biofeedback to modify the biological limitations on learning

The biological foundations of language

Various developmental timetables and how they are synchronized

How the various influences on development can be distinguished

How different influences interact to shape development

Ethology and Human Development

Innate Factors in Human Development
Innate Factors in Mother-Infant Attachment
Innate Factors in Human Emotional Expression

Biological Limitations on Learning

Innate Preparedness for Learning
Innate Preparedness for Language Learning
Biosocial Interaction During Evolutionary Development
Biofeedback: Modifying Biological Constraints on Learning

Innate Channelers of Psychological Development

Biological Foundations of Language
Ecological Demands and Developmental Timetables
Synchrony in the Developmental Timetable

Distinguishing Different Influences on Psychological Development

Laboratory Studies of Behavioral Development
Field Observations of Behavioral Development

Human Nature and Development: An Evolutionary Perspective

Interactions Influencing Development

Genotype-Environment Interactions
Interactions Among Prenatal Factors
Interactions with Postnatal Experience

Introduction

This chapter is concerned with the biosocial interface—the place where various biological and psychosocial influences meet, interweave, and interact in influencing the course of psychological development. Chapters 3 and 4 have focused on particular biological and environmental influences on development. Such a division, however, is artificial. In reality, the factors shaping development are not separated so neatly. Rather, the influences on development are interwoven in complex and dynamic interrelations. This chapter examines some of the difficulties of disentangling these interrelations and some of the methods used to do so.

First we will discuss the ethological viewpoint, which offers perhaps the most comprehensive and thorough scientific effort to decipher the respective roles of environmental and innate factors in development. Then we will apply the ethological perspective to a consideration of the nature of interactions between innate and learned factors. With this approach we will try to develop a scientific understanding of the concept of human nature.

Ethology and Human Development

In 1973 the first Nobel Prize awarded to behavioral scientists was shared by three European ethologists—Karl von Frisch, Konrad Lorenz, and Nikolaas Tinbergen—for their "discoveries concerning organization and elicitation of individual and social behavior patterns." These scientists have made many important discoveries about factors influencing the development of behavior patterns in animals. Von Frisch, for example, is perhaps most famous for his classic work on the instinctual behavior by which honeybees communicate information about the distance and direction of a new food source to other bees in the hive. The information is conveyed by the bee's performance of stereotyped "dancing" movements at the hive. The orientation and vigor of the movements signal the direction and distance of the honey to other bees. Von Frisch concluded that the communicative dancing behavior of honeybees was based on innate patterns in their nervous systems that resulted from natural selection over millions of years of evolutionary development.

Lorenz and Tinbergen have studied many different species, but certain aquatic birds such as geese and herring gulls have been the target of special attention in their work. One of their more important achievements has been to show that members of a particular species of bird use stereotyped sets of ritualistic behavior patterns to communicate psychological states—such as interest in courtship or intention to defend a territory—to other members of the same species. Moreover, Lorenz (1967) and Tinbergen (1969) gathered evidence indicating that these ritualized patterns were specified in considerable part by innate factors. Closely related species tended to have similar repertoires of instinctual signaling gestures, and variations in these innate behaviors could be used to distinguish different species and to classify them according to their genetic and evolutionary relationships. Lorenz and Tinbergen thus showed that

Ethologists are concerned with the evolutionary development of the species as well as the development of individual organisms. Here Konrad Lorenz (upper left) is approached by affectionate snow geese that have imprinted on him and regard him, in effect, as their mother. Nikolaas Tinbergen (upper right) sniffs a dead tern and determines that it was killed by a fox; foxes prey on terns and mark their hunting territory with a distinctive odor. Karl von Frisch is shown observing the behavior of honeybees.

Top left: Nina Leen, Life Magazine, © 1964 Time Inc.; top right and bottom: Nina Leen, Life Magazine, Time Inc.

behavior patterns, like physiological and anatomical traits, could be used as an important technique for reconsructing the evolutionary development of species and for understanding the relationships among them.

Perhaps the most important contribution of these researchers, however, is their establishment of the basic concepts, principles, and methods of a new scientific discipline called *ethology*. Their early work focused primarily on instinctive behaviors, and ethology thus began as a biological investigation of the nature and origin of instincts. With time, however, ethologists have expanded their approach in order to provide a comprehensive biological explanation for all kinds of behavior. Ethologists emphasize that a complete understanding of the origins of behavior requires that we consider *phylogeny* (the evolutionary development of the species) as well as *ontogeny* (the development of an individual organism). Understanding a behavior thus requires knowing not only the behavior's innate and learned components and their neural basis but also why the behavior is "adaptive" for the species—that is, how it helps members to survive and reproduce in their natural environment.

Learning experiences are obviously extremely important shapers of behavioral development in most complex species, especially human beings. Chapter 11 will discuss various learning mechanisms and their effects on development at greater length. However, innate factors and the biophysical properties of an organism's external and internal (bodily) environment are also crucial. As ethologists have pointed out, some behaviors in every species are entirely innate and have no learned component whatsoever (Lorenz, 1965). By contrast, no behavior is purely learned. That is, every behavior must involve important innate components—if only because the nature of the learning mechanisms themselves is shaped by the genes and the forces of evolutionary history that have selected those genes. It follows that, for a complete understanding of psychological development, we must consider the role of innate as well as learned factors. This ethological view has provided a healthy corrective balance to the mainstream of modern psychology—especially in the United States and Russia—which in recent decades has often tended to emphasize the role of conditioning in human development, almost to the point of ignoring innate factors.

Innate Factors in Human Development

Some social scientists have argued that, with the possible exception of a newborn infant's sucking reflex, there are no instinctual behaviors in human beings. This is clearly wrong. Human beings exhibit a large number of innate behaviors, the most obvious examples being the many reflexive responses evident in young infants. As shown in Figure 5.1, some of these reflexes can be quite complex, and they are not always present at birth. McGraw (1939, 1943), for example, has shown that young infants for a time display a swimming reflex. During this period, beginning a few weeks after birth, rhythmical swimming movements of the arms and legs can be elicited by supporting the infant gently in a prone (stomach down) position in a basin of water. (This does *not* mean that infants so young can swim very far, or that it is safe to leave them alone in water.) At about four months, reflexive swimming behavior begins to disappear

FIGURE 5.1
Human reflex behav-
iors. (a) Grasping
reflex; (b) rhythmic
search for breast
(searching automatism,
sometimes called the
rooting reflex); (c)
sucking reflex; (d)
Moro, or infant
startle, reflex.

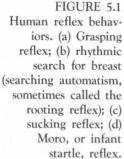

(a)   (b)

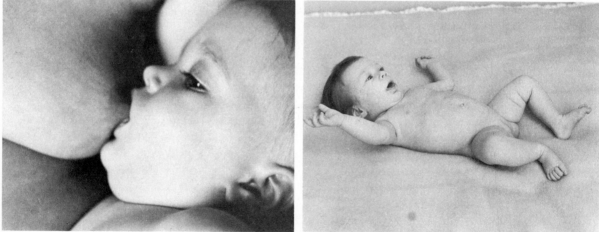

(c) Anna Kaufman Moon, Stock, Boston, Inc.   **(d)** Monkmeyer Press Photo Service

and is replaced by unrhythmical struggling movements when the infants are placed in water. Still later, at around two years of age, infants in McGraw's sample began to show purposeful and voluntary swimming movements. Even the sucking reflex is more complex than might appear at first glance. Abnormal deviations from the form and rhythm of normal sucking movements (as recorded by an electronic monitor inside a bottle's nipple) have been used to detect early signs of brain impairment in newborn infants.

Innate Factors in Mother-Infant Attachment

Innate factors also seem to help establish the affectional bonding between a mother and her infant. One such factor is the phenomenon of eye-to-eye contact, or mutual gazing of parent and infant into each other's eyes. An infant seems to be programmed from birth to search for moving objects and areas of high contrast between dark and light. The human face—particularly the eyes—possesses these properties of movement and contrast to a high degree. Moreover, some evidence suggests that an infant is programmed to "lock on" to the source of sound—the mother's face—when hearing her speak. Indeed, when congenitally blind babies are spoken to by their mothers, their eyes stop making their normal restless movements and move to the point where their gaze would meet their mother's—if they could see (Freedman, 1964).

However, social attachment is a two-way street: it does little good for an infant to become attached to the parent if the parent does not become attached to the infant. In sheep, for example, the mother becomes imprinted on the scent of her newborn lamb shortly after birth. If the lamb dies, the mother usually will not accept a substitute lamb (Scott, 1962). Some pediatricians believe that there is evidence—still controversial—for a similar phenomenon in human beings, and that a mother more readily forms an emotional bond with her infant if she can see and hold the infant shortly after birth. This is one line of research cited by those who favor drug-free or home delivery, in which the mother is alert and able to experience close contact with her baby after giving birth.

The importance of these innate shapers of social responses is often such that, if they are not functioning, the development of attachment or other crucial survival processes is disrupted completely. For example, a classic experiment by Brueckner (1933) showed that a mother hen would rescue one of her chicks in distress—even if the chick were out of sight—as long as she could hear the chick's cries of distress. However, if the chick were placed under a transparent cover so that the mother could not hear the chick's cries, she was indifferent—even though the struggles of the chick were in her full view.

Human development tends to be more flexible than this. When innate factors are involved in guiding a process such as human attachment, many different factors—experiential as well as innate—come into play. However, there is evidence that the disruption of such innate mechanisms can have serious consequences. Consider, for example, infantile autism—one of the most serious psychiatric disorders of childhood. First described by Kanner (1943) as an "inborn error of affective contact," autism involves such symptoms as withdrawal into inner fantasies indifference or aversion to others, a preoccupation with mechanical objects, and characteristic disturbances in language development. Autistic children also often show disturbances in visual attention, in particular, an indifference or aversion to eye-to-eye contact. It is possible that, as a result of hereditary or congenital brain damage, some autistic infants are born with defects in the innate mechanisms that prompt eye-to-eye contact and promote social attachment. The result may be interference with normal mother-infant attachment. As Robson (1967) points out, the infant's innate

Alienation of Affection

JAMES W. PRESCOTT

Deprived of their mothers, Harry Harlow's monkeys were at times apathetic, at times hyperactive, and given to outbursts of violence. Raised in isolation, they were socially inept; they often held themselves and rocked like autistic children.

What Harlow could not know at the time of his dramatic experiments in the late 1950s and 1960s was that these behavioral disturbances were accompanied by brain damage. More recent studies suggest that during formative periods of brain growth, certain kinds of sensory deprivation—such as lack of touching and rocking by the mother—result in incomplete or damaged development of the neuronal systems that control affection (for instance, a loss of the nerve-cell branches called dendrites). Since the same systems influence brain centers associated with violence, in a mutually inhibiting mechanism, the deprived infant may have difficulty controlling violent impulses as an adult.

If confirmed, these studies may have profound implications for human cultures that raise their infants with low levels of touching and movement. Children in these societies may be unable to experience certain kinds of pleasure—and be predisposed to apathy and violence.

The disturbance, I believe, has its origins in the somatosensory system of the cerebellum, which regulates the sense of movement and balance (vestibular system) and the sense of touch (somesthetic system). More than other senses, such as vision and hearing, touch and movement seem directly tied to emotions like affection. And this portion of the brain is one of those most susceptible to "shaping"—changes in neuronal structure—during a child's development. In numerous studies, laboratory animals deprived of tactile and movement stimulation have exhibited abnormal social and emotional behavior.

Source: Reprinted from *Psychology Today*, December 1979, p. 124. Copyright © 1980 Ziff-Davis Publishing Company.

Harlow had explained his monkeys' behavior as caused simply by social isolation and not deprivation in specific sensory, neurobiological processes. I began to suspect that the vestibular-cerebellar system was involved after a study by psychologists William Mason and Gershon Berkson, who reported that when a cloth-covered "surrogate mother" swung an infant monkey, the maternal-deprivation syndrome did not develop. To study that possibility, Robert Heath and Bernard Saltzburg at the Tulane University Medical School took electrophysiological recordings, by means of implanted electrodes, from the limbic and cerebellar regions of extremely violent, isolation-reared monkeys provided by Harlow. The bioelectrical signals from these electrodes displayed abnormal "spike" discharges, which were not seen in normal monkeys. The presence of the spikes was also detected by a unique computer analysis of scalp EEG recordings from the same monkeys' limbic and cerebellar regions. . . .

Thus, the influence of the environment seems to be imprinted on the structure of the brain, which, in turn, shapes the environment. (I call this approach to studying behavior "ecobiology," to distinguish it from sociobiology.) In addition, cross-cultural studies have established a significant relationship between the physical affection shown human infants and rates of adult physical violence. In one study of 49 primitive cultures, I found that when levels of infant affection are low—as among the Comanches and the Ashanti—levels of violence are high; where physical affection is high—as among the Maori of New Zealand and the Balinese—violence is low. I also found that restrictions on premarital sexual affection were associated with high violence.

The possible lesson for modern countries is clear. We seem to be suffering from breakdowns in affectional bonds—reflected in everything from rates of divorce to sexual crimes, alcoholism, and drug abuse. Culture is the handmaiden of our neurobiology, and without a proper environment for physical affection, a peaceful, harmonious society may not be possible.

responses to the mother—particularly eye contact and smiling—also feed back to reinforce the mother's caring behavior:

The human mother is subject to an extended, exceedingly trying and often unrewarding period of caring for her infant. Her neonate has a remarkably limited repertoire with which to sustain her. Indeed, his total helplessness, crying, elimination behavior and physical appearance frequently elicit aversive reactions. Thus, in dealing with the human species, nature has been wise in making both eye-to-eye contact and the social smile, that often releases in these early months behaviors that at this stage of development generally foster positive maternal feelings and a sense of payment for services rendered. (p. 15)

Thus an infant who fails to show such normal behaviors as eye-to-eye contact, smiling, and cuddling would reduce the mother's motivation to engage in stimulation and reciprocal play with the infant. Such activities seem to be crucial in developing an infant's early skills, which provide the foundation for subsequent social and language development.

Innate Factors in Human Emotional Expression

There is also evidence that certain patterns of motor activity, such as emotional expression in human beings, are largely innate and require no special learning experiences for their development. To demonstrate that a behavior is innate and requires no special learning experience, ethologists working with animals have devised *deprivation experiments*; that is, an animal is reared under conditions in which it has no opportunity to learn a given behavior. If the behavior still develops under these conditions, it must be unlearned.

For example, Sackett (1966) was interested in the fact that, in many species of apes and monkeys, staring by one primate at another is perceived as a threatening gesture. All adults and older juveniles of these species recognized such a glare to be a very fearful stimulus. Fear of such glares is apparently not present in the newborn, and it does not develop until some time after birth. This suggests that the behavior might be learned. On the other hand, the appearance of the behavior might be delayed because innate structures mediating it do not mature and function until some time after birth. To settle this matter, Sackett reared rhesus monkeys under laboratory conditions in which they were isolated from other monkeys. When presented for the first time with slides showing other monkeys, the isolated subjects showed fear in response to the threat-glare stimulus, but they did not do so when presented with pictures of monkeys engaged in other behaviors.

Such a deprivation experiment, of course, could not be conducted ethically on human beings. However, ethologists such as Eibl-Eibesfeldt (1970) have been clever in developing other methods to identify innate factors that underlie emotional expression. One line of evidence that suggests an innate basis for such emotional expressions as smiling in response to pleasant events or showing rage, disgust, surprise, fear, and so on is the fact that such behaviors appear to be *cultural universals*. That is, they seem to exist in basically the same form, and to be elicited by essentially the same emotional states, in every culture studied around the world, even those that have had minimal contact with other

The fact that some emotional states seem to be "cultural universals" suggests that there may be an innate basis for expressions indicating emotional states, such as sorrow, anger, surprise, fear, or joy.

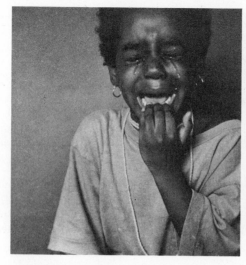

Ruth Silverman, Stock, Boston, Inc.   Elizabeth Crews, Stock, Boston, Inc.

Ira Kirschenbaum, Stock, Boston, Inc.   Richard Balzer, Stock, Boston, Inc.

societies. Of course, errors in translation can sometimes cause problems, but Ekman, Friessen, and Ellsworth (1972) designed a clever way to circumvent such possible ambiguities. They developed simple descriptions of situations that should evoke a given emotional reaction, and then they asked subjects how they would react in these situations. Similar expressions in reaction to a given description were seen in widely divergent societies. For example, when asked how they would react upon entering a hut where "a dead pig had been left for several days" (and, hence, was decomposed, giving off a putrid odor), the natives of a Stone Age culture in New Guinea displayed the same expression of disgust that was elicited in people from Western societies. To obtain candid expressions of fear, Eibl-Eibesfeldt (1970) made use of curious onlookers who often gathered around him and his crew while they were filming emotional expressions in other members of a given society. The onlookers would be handed "a small box out of which popped a cloth snake when it was opened." Eibl-Eibesfeldt then used a hidden high-speed camera to capture and record their frightened reactions for later analysis.

An even more convincing source of evidence for the innate basis of certain emotional expressions is provided by natural experiments in the form of children born blind and deaf. Such children show a number of relatively normal expressive behaviors, including laughter and crying. One deaf and blind seven-year-old girl even stomped her feet when angry. This girl was

able to distinguish strange persons from familiar ones by sniffing briefly at the presented hand. Strangers are pushed away, a gesture that is often accompanied by turning the head away. This behavior is similar, with the exception of the sniffing, to that of healthy children. In short, a whole array of even quite complex behavior patterns, which are typical for human beings, have developed also in the deaf-blind and are therefore present as phylogenetic adaptations. (p. 405)

Eibl-Eibesfeldt even claims to have found agreement "in the smallest detail in the flirting behavior of girls" among several societies around the world.

In summary, then, various lines of evidence indicate that many forms of human emotional expression (apparently including some rather complex ones) are programmed innately and are based in considerable part on information carried by the genes.

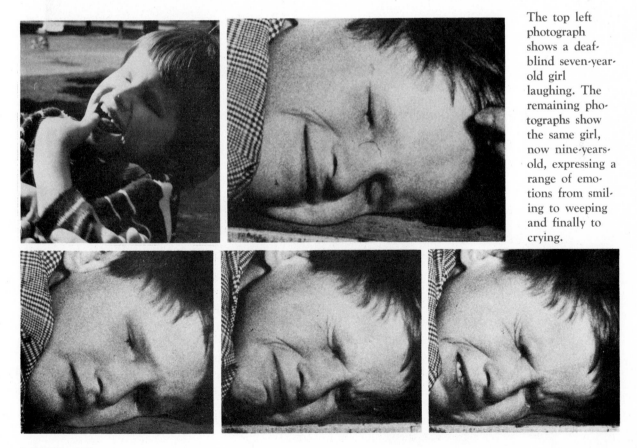

The top left photograph shows a deaf-blind seven-year-old girl laughing. The remaining photographs show the same girl, now nine-years-old, expressing a range of emotions from smiling to weeping and finally to crying.

I. Eibl-Eibesfeldt

Biological Limitations on Learning

Pioneering learning theorists such as Pavlov were so impressed with the power of conditioning to confer response-eliciting properties on apparently arbitrary stimuli that they suggested that virtually any stimulus could be made a conditioned stimulus for a response in an animal's repertoire, given appropriate reinforcement. According to this viewpoint—which Houston (1976) has aptly termed the *interchangeable-parts* conception of learning—the same learning processes apply, regardless of the nature of the particular stimulus and response being associated.

In fact, however, a good deal of research in the last two decades has demonstrated that this conception is wrong and that there are very important biological constraints on learning processes. We recognize that different species have different sensory and motor capacities. (For example, certain insects can see infrared radiation; bats can hear high-frequency sounds inaudible to the human ear; and recent research even indicates that certain species of birds can sense magnetic fields with "biological compasses" to aid their navigation over long distances.) So, too, different species vary greatly in their biological capacity for different types of learning.

Innate Preparedness for Learning

Even when different animals are capable of associating a given stimulus and response, they may differ in their readiness for learning that association. As Seligman (1970) notes, some animals seem to be primed innately to associate a certain stimulus-response combination but find other combinations very difficult, even impossible, to associate. In a classic experiment, Garcia and Koelling (1966) exposed rats to x-rays while they were drinking water flavored with saccharin. The radiation caused the rats to become sick an hour or so after drinking. Subsequently, the rats showed a strong aversion to the saccharin flavor; however, they did not show any aversion to flashes of light or noises, which also had been presented while they were drinking. Apparently, the rats were prepared innately to associate their sensations of illness with the taste of what they had eaten but not with the sights or sounds occurring at the time of food intake. By contrast, experiments showed that birds such as quail (which naturally rely strongly on visual cues in choosing food) were more likely to show aversion to the visual properties of a food that had made them sick than to its taste cues.

Another interesting feature of this research is that the rats associated the taste cue with visceral sensations of illness and gastrointestinal upset over a period of an hour or more. This contrasts with most previous research on aversive learning, in which animals learn that a previously neutral stimulus (such as a tone) precedes a painful stimulus (such as an electric shock). For most kinds of stimuli, animals typically find it difficult to learn the association if the two stimuli come more than a few seconds apart. Thus biological constraints apply not only to the types of stimuli and responses to be associated but also to the intervals between them.

An important practical application of this knowledge is the attempt, by UCLA psychologist John Garcia and his colleagues (Garcia, Hankins, & Rusiniak, 1974; Gustavson et al., 1974), to teach wild predators to stay away from pets and livestock. As reported by Burns (1977),

each spring agents of the U.S. Fish and Wildlife Service brutally slaughter coyote pups in their dens, all in the name of predator control. Their technique, referred to as "denning," is part of an annual eleven million dollar predator-control campaign. A variety of approaches are used: agents excavate dens and club pups with shovel handles; dogs dig into the dens and rip the pups apart; large hooks on steel springs are inserted into the dens, catching the pups' skins like fishhooks. (p. 4)

Many of the world's most magnificent predators are in danger of extinction—in part because they occasionally kill livestock of ranchers and farmers, who, in turn, shoot, trap, or poison the predators. In some areas such predators, particularly coyotes, also pose a considerable threat to people's pets. If such predators could somehow be "taught" to leave pets and livestock alone, it would help save the lives of pets, livestock, and the predators themselves. Predators also keep in balance the populations of rodents and other plant-eating species that pose a threat to crops and natural vegetation. Predators are thus natural allies of farmers and ranchers—if they can be taught to direct their hunting at appropriate targets.

Experiments by Garcia and his colleagues have shown that predators *can* be directed at appropriate targets under rather natural conditions. For example, if coyotes are fed lamb meat dosed with lithium chloride, they temporarily become extremely ill, but it does not kill them. After several such meals, the coyotes not only will choose rabbits over lambs but actually will run away from lambs. Subsequent experiments showed that coyotes also could be taught to eat lambs and avoid rabbits. Thus taste aversions can be conditioned quite specifically. By spreading treated samples of meat where predators roam, we may be able to protect livestock while teaching predators to restrict their hunting to natural prey.

Innate Preparedness for Language Learning

Language learning may provide an example of innate preparedness for certain kinds of learning in human beings. Students of language development have often noted that preschool children are "linguistic geniuses." With no previous language experience and without any special tutoring by language instructors, preschool children in a few years can master thousands of words and complex grammatical structures. (Chapter 12 examines language acquisition in detail.)

This remarkable facility for language learning is unique to human beings. Recent research has shown that young chimpanzees and gorillas can learn to use gestures or pictorial symbols to refer to concepts, and in some cases even seem to combine these gestures spontaneously in novel ways to create what might be called analogs of simple sentences in human speech. Moreover, chimps have used such symbols even to communicate with each other (Savage-Rumbaugh,

In recent experiments, chimpanzees and gorillas have been taught to communicate by using gestures and pictorial symbols.

Paul Fusco, Magnum Photos, Inc.

Rumbaugh, & Boysen, 1978). However, this "language" is acquired only with the most painstaking and elaborate instruction, and the amount and complexity of the "linguistic" structures pale beside those acquired by young children in the same period of time. Such cross-species comparisons suggest that there may be innate *language acquisition devices* (LADs, for short) to guide children in their attempts to understand the rules that regulate language.

Anatomical evidence points in the same direction. There are, indeed, special regions of neural circuitry in the cortex of the human brain—preferentially located in the left cerebral hemisphere in nearly all people—that are specially organized to facilitate language learning. Eric Lennenberg (1967a), a leading researcher of the biological foundations of language, points out that human beings' special facility for learning language is not simply a matter of greater brain size but also must involve a special patterning or organization of neural circuitry. For example, in certain unusual and tragic cases of nanocephalic dwarfism in human beings, a fully grown adult may be less than two feet tall and have a brain weight that barely exceeds that of a human infant. (Such individuals represent a rare and atypical kind of dwarfism; most dwarfs have an intellectual capacity within the normal range.) Although nanocephalic dwarfs usually show some mental retardation, all of them acquire language skills that are at least comparable to the skills of a normal five-year-old child—skills that are far beyond those of a chimpanzee whose brain is of comparable size.

Several lines of research have indicated that particular areas of the left hemisphere are specialized for language acquisition (for example, investigations into the effects of brain injuries and of temporary anesthesia or electrical stimulation of one side of the brain as diagnostic steps preceding surgery.) Moreover, recent studies of human infants suggest that this brain specialization is present by the time of birth. Autopsies of human infants who have died shortly after birth show that regions known to be specialized for language processing are already larger in the left hemisphere than in the right. Moreover, recording of electrical activity in the two hemispheres of the brain shows that, even in young infants, the left hemisphere is more active when the infant is attending to speech sounds, whereas the right hemisphere seems to be more involved with the processing of musical tones.

Although we still have little detailed information about hypothesized language acquisition devices, some interesting light seems to have been shed on one such device by the work of Brown University psychologist Peter Eimas (Eimas et al., 1971). Eimas's work suggests that infants know innately how to divide up the complex stream of acoustical signals in human speech into *phones,* the basic building blocks of speech. Only certain acoustical variations in speech sounds convey meaning; others are essentially noise and ordinarily are ignored by adults listening to spoken words. For example, the acoustical properties that distinguish the consonants *p* and *b* convey a meaningful difference between the words *pay* and *bay.* If one repeats the word *pay* several times and then inserts the word *bay,* an infant two or three months old will notice the difference—just as an adult would—despite the subtlety of the acoustical change. However, we can also repeat the identical pronunciation of the work *pay*—call it *pay*-1—several times (using a tape recorder and an electrical speech-synthesizing machine) and then substitute a pronunciation of *pay* that is acoustically different—call it *pay*-2. The acoustical properties distinguishing *pay*-1 and *pay*-2 may be just as great objectively as those between *pay*-1 and *bay*; yet both adults and very young infants will tend to ignore the former difference while remaining acutely sensitive to the latter. Thus infants seem to know, without any special learning, which acoustical variations in human conversation carry meaning (and should be attended to) and which are only so much noise to be ignored. It is likely that such selective processing of acoustical information is done automatically by various perceptual and attentional mechanisms, without any deliberate effort or even awareness on the infant's part.

Biosocial Interaction During Evolutionary Development

It seems likely, in the case of devices like LAD, that over the course of human evolution there was a progressive dove-tailing or interlocking of cultural and biological evolution. That is, as cultures developed languages, the speech sounds that continued to be used were those most readily distinguished by the speakers' existing psychological apparatus. Thus biological factors help shape the form of cultural institution like language. Conversely, once such a cultural invention is used widely and its acquisition conveys a significant advantage for survival and reproduction, its properties act—as do other significant aspects of the environment—as selective forces influencing the survival of particular genes and the innate developmental factors that they shape. There is thus a complex interplay between social and biological factors during the course of both *evolutionary* and *individual* psychological development.

Biofeedback: Modifying Biological Constraints on Learning

Recent psychological research has provided additional evidence of how closely interwoven are the influences of innate and learned factors in shaping the development of human behavior. Modern psychology itself has blurred the boundaries between learned and innate behaviors by innovations that enable us to transcend some of the normal biological constraints of learning. *Biofeedback* refers to methods that provide an individual with information about his or her own biological states and responses—information that individuals ordinarily would not have. Typically, biofeedback is provided via electronic equipment that can detect subtle changes in bodily functions, convert these changes into electronic signals, amplify these signals, and then convert them into auditory or visual signals that can be readily perceived by an individual.

Blood pressure, electrical activity in the brain, or blood flow in a specific area of the body are examples of particular biological responses of which we normally are unaware—and which (with the possible exception of certain highly trained specialists such as yogis) have been essentially involuntary responses beyond willful control. Until recently, such involuntary responses were thought to be susceptible primarily to classical but not to operant conditioning (which, in turn, was thought to apply primarily to the learning of behaviors under voluntary control).

Research using biofeedback, however, has eased if not removed these biological constraints on the kinds of responses persons can learn to control voluntarily. Pioneering research by psychologists such as Leo DiCara and Neal Miller (1968) showed that rats could be trained, by operant reinforcement procedures, to regulate the amount of blood flowing to particular parts of their bodies. The animals actually could increase blood flow to one ear and decrease it to the other! Miller was able to train rats to do this by providing biofeedback. A device sensitive to blood flow was attached to the animal's ear, and its measurements were converted into a stimulus, such as a tone, that the rat could perceive readily. In order to teach the rat to increase blood flow to its left ear, say, one could condition the rat operantly to increase the loudness of the tone, the volume of which is proportional to the amount of blood flow in the ear.

Now, few of us—probably not even the rat—much care whether we can learn to blush at will in one ear. However, the biofeedback method itself has aroused great interest because of its potential for treating many important medical disorders. Indeed, this potential is already being applied. For example, psychologist Gary Schwartz and his colleagues (1977) have used biofeedback techniques to treat Raynaud's disease, in which contraction of vessels supplying blood to the toes and fingers results in an insufficient supply of blood and oxygen. If the condition becomes severe enough, reduced blood supply can lead to tissue death and infection, requiring amputation of the diseased fingers or toes. Once patients are provided with immediate feedback concerning blood flow in affected digits, they can discover through trial-and-error experimentation which voluntary responses seem most effective in increasing blood flow. In essence, patients are able to use information about their own blood flow as a reinforcer to shape their responses in increasingly effective directions. Still more important potential applications of biofeedback involve such disorders as high blood pressure (Kimmel, 1967; Schwartz, 1977; Tarler-Benlolo, 1978), which, as we noted in Chapter 4, is a major contributor to cardiovascular disease, the leading killer in industrialized societies.

Tarler-Benlolo (1978) reviewed more than eighty studies on the use of biofeedback and/or relaxation techniques to treat various psychosomatic disorders, many of which seem to be related to the high levels of stress and tension that are widespread in Western societies. Tarler-Benlolo noted that caution was needed in evaluating these studies, because most did not provide follow-up data on how lasting the effects of treatment were. However, in studies that did report follow-up data, positive results seemed to be maintained over time, provided continued practice was maintained by patients. Tarler-Benlolo concluded present evidence indicates that both biofeedback and relaxation are effective in treating patients with tension and migraine headaches, in lowering blood pressure of essential [unknown-causation] hypertensives, and treating a variety of other psychosomatic disorders.

Innate Channelers of Psychological Development

Besides regulating the preparedness of an organism for certain types of learning, innate factors also help to set a developmental timetable, according to which the developing organism is maturationally ready and primed to learn crucial survival skills at the appropriate point in development.

Biological Foundations of Language

Lenneberg (1967b) has compiled several different lines of evidence that innate factors channel and schedule the development of language learning in children. For example, certain major developmental milestones in language acquisition—such as the onset of babbling, the production of the first word and the first sentence, and so on—seem to parallel the development of motor milestones (see Table 5.1). This rough synchronization seems to hold in different cultures, suggesting that the appearance of new motor and language capacities reflects not so much cultural-environmental influences as the maturation of new respective learning devices in the brain. Lenneberg also has argued that language has "a kind of self-propelling, driving quality," and he noted that it is difficult to suppress its development completely in even the most restricted environments. Lenneberg found that the amount and the onset of vowel-like cooing in the first three months was no different in infants who were reared by deaf parents (and thus heard much less adult speech) than in infants with hearing parents. (Moreover, since the deaf parents could not hear their infants' vocalizations, they could not reinforce them.) The maturation of new brain structures seems to enable the developing child to acquire new kinds of language skills. Conversely, failure of normal maturation limits the kinds of learning that can occur. Thus Lenneberg found that certain severely retarded children never combined words spontaneously to form even two-word sentences. No amount of tutoring

TABLE 5.1
Milestones in
Motor and
Language
Development

Age	Motor Development	Language Development
12 weeks	Baby supports head when in prone position; weight is on elbows; no grasp reflex	Crying has diminished; vowel-like cooing has begun and sometimes is sustained for 15–20 seconds
16 weeks	Head is self-supported, and baby can shake rattle; tonic neck reflex is subsiding	Response to human sounds is more definite; eyes seem to search for speaker; occasional chuckling sounds
20 weeks	Baby can sit with props	Consonantal sounds along with vowel-like cooing; however, all vocalizations very different from sounds of mature language
6 months	Baby bends forward and uses head for support while sitting; reaching is unilateral	Cooing is changing to babbling with resemblance to single syllables; most common sounds are *ma, mu, da, di*
8 months	Baby stands holding on and can grasp with thumb opposition	Repetitions of sounds becoming frequent; intonation patterns distinct; utterances to signal emphasis and emotions
10 months	Creeping efficient; child can take side steps holding on and can pull self to standing position	Vocalizations mixed with playlike sounds; baby attempts to imitate sounds and begins to respond differentially to words
12 months	Child walks when held by one hand, or walks on feet and hands with knees in air, and can seat self on floor	Identical sound sequences are repeated more often; words *(mamma* or *dadda)* are emerging; definite signs of understanding appear in response to commands
18 months	Grasp, prehension, and response are developed; gait is still stiff; child can crawl backwards down stairs	Word repertoire is more than three, less than fifty; understanding is progressing, but joining of words into spontaneous phrases is uncommon

Source: From Lenneberg, E. H. "The Biological Foundations of Language," *Hospital Practice*, Vol. 2, No. 12 Dec. 1967. Reproduced with permission.

seemed to teach these children to produce sentences, although it could help expand their vocabulary.

The point is not that learning experiences are unimportant—obviously they are—but that innate and maturational factors are also critical. Understanding how such factors operate and interact with environmental stimuli will help us to foster language development, especially in children whose LADs are defective for reasons of heredity, brain injury, or sensory deficits.

Ecological Demands and Developmental Timetables

Environmental demands made by the ecological niche for which a species has adapted during the course of its evolution influence the nature of innate timetables as well as the preparedness of a species' members for certain kinds of learning. For example, King (1978) has found that in tree-nesting species of mice, the young develop climbing before walking skills; in ground-dwelling species, the converse is true. Early maturation of locomotion may be less adaptive for tree-nesting species, for whom it might result in a fall from the nest. Another example is the fact that so-called precocial species such as goats or ducklings must be able to locomote and to recognize and follow the mother soon after birth. Moreover, once a young animal is able to move about over rugged terrain, it obviously must be able to perceive, to be fearful of, and to avoid cliffs or other heights from which a fall could cause serious injury or death. For such species it is essential that newly hatched or newborn animals either innately recognize and follow the mother or learn to do so quickly. This, in fact, happens, as we will see in discussing imprinting in Chapter 6. So too, when infant goats are placed on a visual cliff shortly after birth, they avoid the deep side and head for the apparent safety of the shallow portion.

When infant goats are placed on a visual cliff shortly after birth, they avoid the deep side and seek the apparent safety of the shallow side. Human infants also show fearful avoidance of such a visual cliff by the time they are able to crawl.

William Vandivert

In contrast, humans or species of birds such as ravens, which are confined to the nest for some time after being hatched, need a more extended time period for the young to learn to move about under their own power and to learn to recognize their parents. Human infants usually show fearful withdrawal from such a visual cliff by the time they are able to crawl, and will usually refuse to move out onto the glass over the deep side even when coaxed by their mothers (see Chapter 10, Figure 10.6). However, recent studies indicate that this fear of a visual cliff is not present in younger infants. Upon being moved from the shallow to the deep side of a visual cliff, young infants showed a decreased tendency to fuss or cry. Also, although their heart rates showed a noticeable change—indicating that the babies perceived the change in depth—this change was usually a deceleration (a sign of interest and attention) rather than an acceleration, as one would expect if the infants were afraid (Schwartz, Campos, Baisel, 1973). By contrast, at nine months of age, human infants showed heart-rate *acceleration* when placed on the deep side of the visual cliff, indicating a fearful response. Moreover, developmental psychologist Nancy Rader and her students at UCLA (1977) have shown that when infants too young to locomote under their own power are given mechanical aids that enable them to move about, they will blithely scoot out onto the deep side of the visual cliff.

Synchrony in the Developmental Timetable

It is not enough that the innate timetable direct an organism's learning processes so that it develops the appropriate responses and skills, associates them with the appropriate stimuli, and learns them by the necessary age. The timetable must also ensure that the development of different skills is scheduled properly. For example, if young infants develop the capacity to move about and thus encounter dangerous situations before they can perceive and be fearful of them, their chances of survival are poor. It is reasonable to suppose that other, less dramatic, failures to synchronize the development of different skills also might have maladaptive consequences for an organism. Some research data are consistent with this notion. Fish (1975), for example, found in longitudinal studies of human development into adulthood that individuals who subsequently developed schizophrenia as children or adults were likely as infants to have shown "scatter" on tests of psychological development. That is, they were more likely than other infants to be much slower than average in developing some skills but at the same time precocious in developing other skills.

Distinguishing Different Influences on Psychological Development

Charles Darwin once remarked that perhaps the most difficult task he faced as a scientist was maintaining a willingness to change his theories in light of new evidence. He noted that, with perhaps one exception, all of his hypotheses had to be modified after further investigation. In all sciences, the most important requirement is to keep an open mind and a willingness to reevaluate all theories—including one's pet hypotheses—when contrary evidence is presented.

Cradles of Eminence

VICTOR GOERTZEL AND
MILDRED GEORGE GOERTZEL

We asked several groups to listen to these descriptions of children and to predict the children's future development. In five years, we asked, would they be functioning as gifted, average-normal, psychotic, neurotic, delinquent or mentally deficient persons?

Case 1.

Girl, age sixteen, orphaned, willed to custody of grandmother by mother, who was separated from alcoholic husband, now deceased. Mother rejected the homely child, who has been proven to lie and to steal sweets. Swallowed penny to attract attention at five. Father was fond of child. Child lived in fantasy as the mistress of father's household for years. Four young uncles and aunts in household cannot be managed by the grandmother, who is widowed. Young uncle drinks; has left home without telling the grandmother his destination. Aunt, emotional over love affair, locks self in room. Grandmother resolves to be more strict with granddaughter since she fears she has failed with own children. Dresses granddaughter oddly. Refused to let her have playmates, put her in braces to keep back straight. Did not send her to grade school. Aunt on paternal side of family crippled; uncle asthmatic.

Case 2.

Boy, senior year secondary school, has obtained certificate from physician stating that nervous breakdown makes it necessary for him to leave school for six months. Boy not a good all-around student; has no friends—teachers find him a problem—spoke late—father ashamed of son's lack of athletic ability—poor adjustment to school. Boy has odd mannerisms, makes up own religion, chants hymns to himself—parents regard him as "different."

Case 3.

Boy, age six; head large at birth. Thought to have had brain fever. Three siblings died before his birth. Mother does not agree with relatives and neighbors that child is probably abnormal. Child sent to school—diagnosed as mentally ill by teacher. Mother is angry—withdraws child from school, says she will teach him herself.

When Eleanor Roosevelt, Albert Einstein, and Thomas Edison had been categorized by our audience as delinquent, mentally ill and retarded, respectively, we then spoke of the danger of making snap decisions on superficial, incomplete evidence and emphasized the need for objective examination and adequate case study in making proper judgments. . . .

We have ourselves seen a number of intellectually gifted youngsters grow up and fit themselves competently into suitable and remunerative positions which offer them little intellectual stimulation or deep satisfaction. These same children had financial and emotional security in their childhood homes and received the best of schooling. When we turn to biographies and autobiographies, we find exciting, experimental, creative men and women who in their childhood experienced trauma, deprivations, frustrations and conflicts of the kind commonly thought to predispose one to mental illness or delinquency.

The inexplicable difference between the bright child in the classroom who becomes the competent, unimaginative adult and the academically unsuccessful child who later makes his impact felt on a whole generation continues to challenge our attention with increasing force and persistence.

Source: Adapted from *Cradles of Eminence* by Victor Goertzel and Mildred George Goertzel. Copyright © 1962 by Victor Goertzel and Mildred George Goertzel. Reprinted by permission of Little, Brown and Company.

Scientists, like other people, are not immune to prejudices, intellectual or otherwise. But in trying to understand scientific phenomena, it is crucial that we not let personal, academic, political, or other preconceptions distort our perception of the truth.

Keeping an open mind is especially important in the case of developmental psychology because the subject matter so often involves deeply held moral or political values likely to cause us to prejudge the facts and because so many different factors potentially are involved as causes of behaviors (making it easy to overlook the crucial factors). Too often, for reasons of either ideology or academic training, we focus on one class of causal factors in trying to explain individual or group differences in behavioral development and ignore other possible causes. To take familiar examples, people who are trained in the biological sciences or whose political sympathies lean toward the right usually (though, of course, not invariably) seem more ready to look for innate causes of behavior. Those who are trained in the social sciences or whose political leanings are toward the left, on the other hand, are usually more likely to emphasize the role of social conditions and learning in development.

To illustrate the importance of keeping an open mind and considering all possible kinds of influences on psychological development, we will consider two examples of research. The first involves laboratory experimentation; the second is based on natural observation in the field.

Laboratory Studies of Behavioral Development

Lorenz (1965) cited a study of the motor patterns with which shrikes (sometimes popularly called "butcherbirds") impale their prey on thorns in order to store them. To determine whether this impaling behavior reflected innate factors or was dependent on the birds' learning through experience or modeling of other birds, a deprivation experiment was performed in which young shrikes reared in the laboratory were deprived of any opportunity to practice or imitate impaling behavior. Upon being presented with prey and artificial "thorns" in the form of nails driven through their perch, the shrikes failed to show an innate tendency to impale their prey; they discovered the impaling behavior only through a process of trial and error. At first it would seem that this study had demonstrated the importance of learning experiences in the development of behavior. Another study, however, showed that the failure of the birds to show impaling behavior when first presented with thorns was the result not of learning deprivation but of nutritional deprivation. When another brood of shrikes was reared with an adequate diet, the "birds did not need any trial-and-error behavior to condition them to the thorn. They immediately went for the thorn when it was first offered. When offered a rubber dummy of equal shape, they persisted in directing their impaling movement at that unsuitable object. Lack of success was unable to effect a negative conditioning" (Lorenz, 1965, p. 94). Thus if the ethologists had focused only on innate and learning influences and had not considered the possibility of a third factor, nutritional deprivation, they would have drawn the wrong conclusion. Similar failures are not uncommon in research involving human beings. For example, in discussing the results of adoption studies, researchers have sometimes concluded that a disease is largely hereditary if it is found to be unusually prevalent in the biological but not the adoptive relatives of adoptees. The evidence does not permit this conclusion, of course, because the biological parents supply both the prenatal and the perinatal environment for the adoptee, as well as his or her genes.

Such examples show how difficult it is to determine the causes of behavior, even in the laboratory. It is expecially difficult to do so in studies of human beings in their natural environments, where it often is unfeasible or unethical to manipulate the relevant variables experimentally.

Field Observations of Behavioral Development

Disentangling the roles of maturation and learning in human development can be tricky, even for something as seemingly simple as how a person carries a load of books. Readers are invited to do their own observational research on this phenomenon: how do most male and female students carry their school books? Actually, several studies of this behavior have been made by human ethologists (for example, Hanaway & Burghardt, 1976). These studies show that male high school and college students in the United States usually carry their books at their sides, whereas females carry their books in front. It seems reasonable to think that these sex differences in preferred carrying styles reflect sex differences in physique; that is, the relatively longer and stronger arms of males, their stronger handgrips and their narrower pelvises and hips, make it more comfortable for them to carry objects at their sides, whereas the converse is true for females.

At first glance, observations of how sex differences in carrying styles change with increasing age also seem to support the idea that how a child carries a book is simply a function of anatomy at that point in time. With increasing age from kindergarten through college, there is increasingly greater differentiation between male and female students in how they carry their books—a difference that corresponds to the marked differences in sexual anatomy and secondary sexual characteristics that develop during this time. However, definite sex differences in carrying styles also appear in the early elementary grades, even before any significant differences in physique are relevant to the comfort of carrying books. It appears that these behavioral differences are not simply a function of differences in anatomy. It seems that for elementary schoolchildren, how books are carried is basically a sex-typed behavior, determined not by physical maturation but by such learning processes as modeling of older members of the same sex and pressure ("social reinforcement") from peers and others. A child wants to carry books in a manner thought to be appropriate to his or her sex. The result can sometimes be ludicrous, as when a young schoolboy, trying to carry his heavy load of books "like a man," assumes a style that is, in fact, inappropriate and uncomfortable for his physique at that point in development.

In sum, if we ask whether sex differences in the way students carry their school books result from learning or maturation, the answer would seem to be learning—at least at first, in the elementary grades. Ultimately, however, this sex difference in behavior is basically a result of what is for adults a practical adjustment to anatomical sex differences. But even this is somewhat of an oversimplification. In fact, it seems likely that the sex differences in *anatomy* were themselves shaped during the course of human evolution by the selection pressures that reflected the requirements of sex differences in survival *behaviors* engaged in by men and women (for example, carrying weapons such as spears for hunting, or delivering and nursing infants). During both human ontogeny and phylogeny, therefore, it appears that even so simple a matter as a sex difference in how objects are carried reflects a complex interweaving of learning and maturation, of anatomy and behavior. The complexity of the factors underlying sex differences in even this simple behavior should warn us not to expect simple explanations for individual and group differences in other, more complex, behaviors.

As developmental psychologists Eleanor Maccoby and Carol Jacklin (1974) concluded in their review of the development of sex differences in human beings:

it is tempting to try to classify the differential behaviors as being either innate or learned, but we have seen that this is a distinction that does not bear close scrutiny. We have noted a genetically controlled characteristic may take the form of a greater readiness to learn a particular kind of behavior, and hence is not distinct from learned behavior. Furthermore, if one sex is more biologically predisposed than the other to perform certain actions, it would be reasonable to expect that this fact would be reflected in popular beliefs about the sexes, so that innate tendencies help to produce the cultural lore that the child learns. Thus he adapts himself, through learning, to a social stereotype that has a basis in biological reality. (Of course, not all social stereotypes about the sexes have such a basis.) It is reasonable, then, to talk about the process of acquisition of sex-typed behavior—the learning of sex-typed behavior—as a process built upon biological foundations that are sex-differentiated to some degree. (pp. 363-364)

Human Nature and Development: An Evolutionary Perspective

Most of us probably have used, at one time or another, some expression like "It just came naturally" or "It was just a matter of human nature," or we may have described someone's behavior as "unnatural." We tend to say such things when we are really expressing only a personal egocentric or ethnocentric preference. That is, we are really saying, in effect, "This is the way I do it, and I think everyone should do it my way"; or, "this is the way my culture does it, and any other way is bad, perverted, immoral, and so on." The concept of human nature certainly is to be avoided if it represents this kind of egocentric or ethnocentric ignorance and arrogance—if it denies the importance of recognizing that different individuals and cultures may find different behavioral patterns more suitable to their individual biological needs or to the particular environmental demands on their culture.

Still, the concept of human nature, if understood in the right way, can express an important and scientifically valid idea. This idea is that the basic genetic makeup of human beings—and the psychological needs, response tendencies, and patterns of development influenced by that genetic constitution—was shaped by natural selection because it was adapted to environmental conditions that are in many ways radically different from those in which most human beings live today. Our ancestors have lived in cities for only several thousand years, at most, and even stable villages based on agriculture date back, to be generous, only twenty thousand years (Braidwood, 1960). For over 99 percent of the millions of years of our evolution, human beings and our humanlike ancestors lived as small nomadic bands, subsisting through hunting and the gathering of edible fruits and herbs.

Present-day hunting and gathering peoples, such as the Australian Aborigines or the Bushmen of the Kalahari Desert and their Stone Age counterparts, are often thought to lead, in the words of the political philosopher Thomas Hobbes (1651), lives that are "solitary, poor, nasty, brutish and short." In fact, however, as biologist René Dubos points out, many contemporary "primitive" societies are "compatible with longevity, health, and *joie de vivre*. Disease and a very short life span, as well as miserable social habit, are expressions not of primitive life per se, but of disturbances in the traditional ways of tribal existence during the first phases of contact with Western civilization" (1972, p. 258). Dubos notes also that

the legend of a Golden Age is so universal and so ancient that it must have a base of truth, as do most prehistoric legends.... [It] may thus be the remembrance, poetized by time and by imaginative embellishments, of a very distant past when certain groups of people had achieved biological fitness to their environment. To a large extent, the fitness of primitive people was a product of Darwinian evolution, very similar to the fitness achieved by animals that live in the wild and are well adapted to the environments in which they have evolved. Biological memories long persist as a component of culture when they are transmitted orally in the form of myths or legends. (pp. 256-259)[1]

Of course, the environments for which human beings *have* evolved a biological fitness have changed dramatically during the past several thousands of years, and particularly so in recent centuries. The pace of technological change has been accelerating, so that the environments in which human beings now grow and develop are increasingly different from those of our prehistoric forebears.

Social scientists have long talked about the problem of "cultural lag"—the difficulties a society and its members face when the pace of scientific and technological advance outstrips the capacity of the society to develop new customs, attitudes, and social institutions to deal with these technological innovations and the changes they bring about. A less studied but perhaps even more difficult problem is a kind of psychological and "biological-evolutionary lag." Major biological-evolutionary changes usually take place over extremely long periods of time, and it well may prove even more difficult to adjust our biologi-

---

1. From *A God Within* by Rene Dubos. Copyright © 1972 by Rene Dubos. Reprinted by permission of Charles Scribner's Sons.

cal patterns of development than to change our societal patterns. As Tinbergen (1969) puts it,

> paradoxically . . . the unprecedented degree of power over natural events which we have achieved carries in its wake a dangerous consequence; we have broken out of our ecological niche into the niches of almost all other species, and have thus changed our environment (including our social environment) out of all recognition. As a result, our behavioral organization is no longer faced with the environment in which this organization was molded and, as a consequence, misfires. These disruptive consequences of our behavior now threaten the very existence of our species: pollution and depletion of our natural resources, our population explosion, our stressful social environment, the threat of nuclear war are all consequences of misfiring of our behavior. An increasing but still far too small number of people begin to realize that we are caught in a vicious circle: the very success of our behavior has led to a situation from which only a better understanding and controlled change of our behavior can extract us. (p. x)

Alvin Toffler (1970) has coined the term *future shock* for the psychological effects of accelerating technological change. He notes, for example, that a child reaching adolescence today is quite "literally surrounded by twice as much of everything newly man-made as his parents were at the time he was an infant" (p. 24). This, combined with the increasing mobility of families and individuals in technologically advanced societies, means there is less permanence in our relationships to both things and, more important, people. Few children today grow up in an extended family composed of grandparents or family members besides parents and siblings. Indeed, with the increasing rates of divorce and children born out of wedlock, even the nuclear family shows signs of breaking down.

Dubos notes that studies of skeletal remains indicate that the average life span of hunters of the Old Stone Age was actually longer than that of the New Stone Age farming peoples. Indeed, contemporary anthropological studies suggest that the health of hunting and gathering people may be superior in some respects to the health of people living in technologically more advanced societies. Some studies, for example, suggest that children growing up in some so-called primitive societies—eating and chewing tough, unprocessed meat and other natural foods—may have fewer dental problems than "privileged" children in more "advanced" societies, who eat a diet of processed foods that are unnaturally softened and sweetened. Research similarly indicates that atherosclerosis—the arterial disease that is primarily responsible for strokes and heart attacks, our leading killers—is a rarity in many primitive societies. Furthermore, the absence of sufficient natural roughage in our diets may contribute to our higher incidence of cancer of the colon.

A particularly striking example of the pathological effects on development of shifting to a lifestyle to which human populations are not naturally adapted comes from studies of the development of *myopia,* or "nearsightedness." Research on the incidence of myopia in individuals of different ages in Eskimo villages has found that although virtually none of the elderly villagers have myopia, the majority of the youngest schoolchildren do. The incidence of myopia increases progressively among groups who were born at successively later dates, thus corresponding closely with the Eskimos' degree of exposure to

The pollution and depletion of our natural resources have created a social environment that imposes unnatural demands on our psychological development.

Bill Saidel, Stock, Boston, Inc.

Western lifestyles, including indoor lighting with the many hours spent using the eyes for reading and other close work. Experimental studies have demonstrated that prolonged use of the eyes at close distances and under poor lighting conditions could produce myopia in laboratory monkeys.

It is interesting to note that many previous researchers had neglected the role of eyestrain in the development of myopia because twin studies had suggested that myopia was primarily a hereditary trait. It was usually assumed that the genetic factors responsible for myopia acted rather directly on the maturation of the eye to produce the abnormal shape of the lens and eyeball that are responsible for myopia. New research findings, however, suggest that the pathway of genetic influence may be more subtle. For example, perhaps the genes conducive to myopia are concerned not exclusively with the physical properties of the eye as such but also with psychological traits (such as intellectual interest, aptitudes, or temperament) that lead a person to engage in intensive reading or other close work; hence the genes typically may lead indirectly to myopia.

Obesity may be another example of a health problem that is often the result of a mismatch between an individual's psychological makeup and an unnatural environment. Nutritional research suggests that the appetite-regulating mechanisms in the brain operate properly only within a certain range of daily caloric intake. However, many individuals in technologically advanced societies today exercise so little that the amount of calories they burn falls below the level at which their appestatic mechanism was "designed" by evolutionary selection to operate properly. In other words, the level of calorie expenditure has fallen so far below that which was normal for our prehistoric ancestors (or even for our grandparents' generation) that it makes "unnatural" demands on the operating characteristics of this appetite-control mechanism. In this sense such a lifestyle, with its low level of exercise, really does represent a violation of human nature.

Dubos suggests that modern technological societies similarly impose unnatural demands on other areas of our psychological development. If our society is to survive, he argues, we must learn to live in greater harmony with our natural environment. Dubos is not advocating a return to primitivism (for example, that we all pack our bags and head for the backwoods to scratch a life out of the land on communes). By comparison with the lifestyle of Stone Age hunters and gatherers, even life in a simple farming village is a major change toward a new and more "artificial" way of life. Rather, Dubos urges a saner use of modern technology, one that respects the psychological needs of human beings as well as the integrity of the ecosystems in which we live:

It is a distressing fact that the Faustus legend is the only important one created by Western civilization. . . . the learned and dynamic Dr. Faustus . . . was willing to sell his soul to the devil for the sake of worldly pleasures and his own selfish ambitions, just as modern Faustian man does not hesitate to jeopardize the future of mankind in the pursuit of his goals. . . .

A problem of . . . potential danger is being created all over the world by the development of huge breeder nuclear reactors which will produce large amounts of plutonium—an incredibly dangerous substance. . . . Even if we had all the technological and ecological know-how for the planning and management of these complexes (and what a big if!), it is likely that they would create social environments in which life would have to be highly regimented and would soon create the feeling of alienation. Modern man does not ask the help of the devil in the pursuit of his ambitions; instead he uses and misuses science and technology with little concern for the future. (Dubos, *A God Within*, 1972, p. 264)

Fortunately, Dubos points out, the general public as well as the scientific community has increasingly come to recognize the ecological dangers posed by irresponsible technological and industrial expansion. But much less attention has been given to the "deterioration of the psychological environment," which is "as dangerous as environmental pollution but less well understood" (pp. 281-282).

To cite but one example, Dubos notes the loneliness and alienation that are the increasing curses of modern urban life:

Modern cities are unfavorable to human relationships probably because they are almost incompatible in their present form with needs created during social

Paul Fusco, Magnum Photos, Inc.

evolution. Early man probably lived in bands of a fairly uniform size. The hunt for big game was a collective enterprise which demanded that the group be fairly large, and this generated complex social relationships. But the ecological limitations imposed by the hunter-gatherer way of life kept the group within a size determined by the availability of natural resources. . . .

Because he evolved as a social animal, man has a biological need to be a part of a group and even perhaps to be identified with a place. He is likely to suffer from loneliness not only when he does not belong but also when the society or the place in which he functions is too large for his comprehension. Transient therapeutic experiences in encounter groups cannot satisfy the biological need to be a functioning part of a normal human community, a true supraorganism. Encounter groups, like technological fixes, at best alleviate or mask for a time the effects of a pathological state; they do not really correct it and they commonly generate new problems of their own.

Modern societies will have to find some way to reverse the trend toward larger and larger agglomerations and to recreate units compatible with the limits of man's comprehension—in other words, small enough that they can develop a social identity and a spirit of place. (Dubos, *A God Within*, 1972, pp. 282-286)

Interactions Influencing Development

Other chapters consider a number of factors in the prenatal and postnatal environments that can strongly influence the development of an individual exposed to them. But these factors do not always produce significant effects. For example, not all women who smoke or use drugs heavily during pregnancy have serious problems. How can we explain the fact that such prenatal factors seem to affect some pregnancies more than others? Two factors seem especially important: (1) the interaction of the prenatal environment with the genetic makeup of the developing organism, and (2) interactions of different prenatal factors with each other and with postnatal experiences.

Genotype-Environment Interactions

We know from experiments with genetically inbred strains of animals that the effect of particular prenatal environments is often critically dependent on the genetic makeup of the individual exposed to that environment. For example, the chemical 5-fluorouracil produces birth defects in a genetically susceptible strain of mouse, but not in a strain that possesses a gene for manufacturing a liver enzyme that can effectively break down the 5-fluorouracil and render it harmless (Runner, 1967). A number of other prenatal factors have been shown similarly to interact with genetic factors in experiments with animals. It is likely that such interactions also occur in human beings.

Mednick (1970) has hypothesized that such an interaction might play an important role in causing schizophrenia, perhaps the most serious form of mental illness. Experiments with mice have shown that the extent to which exposing a pregnant mouse to partial asphyxia produces congenital defects in her offspring depends critically on the genetic makeup of the mouse and her offspring. Mednick and his colleague Schulsinger suggest that, analogously, schizophrenia might result from an asphyxia-producing obstetrical complication acting on a genetically vulnerable fetus. Evidence for this hypothesis comes from a prospective study comparing the development of children who are at high genetic risk for schizophrenia—by virtue of having a schizophrenic mother—with those who are at low risk because their parents are not schizophrenic. (Other evidence, also suggests a major genetic contribution to schizophrenia; children with a schizophrenic mother are much more likely than children with normal parents to have inherited genes predisposing them to schizophrenia.) Mednick and Schulsinger found that, whereas all of the low-risk children were well adjusted by late adolescence, about half of the high-risk children were showing signs of psychiatric problems. Among the high-risk children, the psychologically healthy groups seem to differ markedly in the incidence of pregnancy and delivery complications that might have produced asphyxia and resulting brain damage to the fetus: 70 percent of the disturbed high-risk children had suffered such complications, compared with 15 percent of the healthy high-risk group and 33 percent of the low-risk, control group. The results thus suggest that a combination of genetic risk and obstetrical complications might be especially conducive to schizophrenia. Moreover, the obstetrical complications were associated with an abnormal responsivity of the autonomic nervous system. Mednick (1970) believes this means that the pregnancy and birth complications (PBCs) "trigger some characteristic which may be genetically predisposed. The PBC's seem to damage the modulatory control of the body's stress-response mechanisms" (p. 56). Although it is still too early to be certain how valid this theory of schizophrenia is, the bulk of subsequent research supports the view that obstetrical complications contribute causally to schizophrenia, in interaction with genetic influences (McNeil & Kaij, 1978; Jacobsen & Kinney, 1981).

Interactions Among Prenatal Factors

Animal experiments show that the *teratogenic* (congenital-deformity-producing) effects of one prenatal factor may be influenced crucially by the presence or absence of other such factors—which, depending on the nature of the factor, may antagonize, simply add to, or even potentiate the effects of the first agent. When two teratogenic agents interfere with the same step in a metabolic pathway, they are likely to act synergistically—that is, the combined effects of the two acting together are greater than one would expect from simply adding up their individual effects. Although this kind of synergistic interaction has been reported most often in the literature concerning experimental research with animals, there is some research suggesting that adverse prenatal factors may tend to act synergistically in human beings as well. Pasamanick and Knobloch (1966), for example, report that smoking during pregnancy is associated with obstetrical problems more in women of lower socioeconomic status than in affluent women. Perhaps this is because a pregnant woman is often physiologically resilient enough to handle one physical stressor such as smoking. But when smoking is imposed on other adverse factors such as poor nutrition or medical care (or other factors more prevalent in women with less income and education), the fetus can no longer be protected from harmful effects. If, as seems likely, such synergistic effects do, indeed, exist in human pregnancies, it is vital that we learn more about them. Then we might identify high-risk pregnancies that may be unusually vulnerable to certain factors. For example, exposure to a certain level of air pollutants such as carbon monoxide (as from living near a heavily trafficked street) might have little effect on the average pregnancy but could have serious consequences for the pregnancy of a woman who smoked heavily or had anemia, emphysema, or an already impaired respiratory capacity.

Interactions with Postnatal Experience

Although the research we have discussed indicates that adverse prenatal factors are likely to contribute to the development of many psychological problems such as schizophrenia, this does not mean that the postnatal environment is unimportant. Fish (1975), in reporting the findings of her longitudinal research on infants at high risk for schizophrenia, states that even when those infants suffered neurological damage, the quality of postnatal care provided by parental figures often played a critical role in determining the psychiatric outcome of the children. Research on intellectual development also indicates that the quality of postnatal care may be most important for precisely those infants at highest risk for congenital brain damage. Data from several studies point to a synergistic interaction between the biological integrity of an infant's nervous system and the quality of parenting he or she receives after birth. The social class of the rearing parents is correlated more highly with later IQ for children who are at high risk than for those at low risk for neurological damage. This is true whether the children are at high risk because they are premature (Drillien, 1964); have been exposed to serious delivery complications (Werner, Bierman, & French, 1971); or show particularly slow mental and motor development eight months after birth (Willerman, Broman, & Fiedler, 1970).

As Willerman (1972) notes, these findings imply that unstimulating postnatal environments are likely to be particularly damaging for brain-injured babies. Conversely, there often may be cause for optimism with regard to the intellectual development of brain-damaged infants, given a stimulating environment. Understanding how parental rearing practices interact with constitutional vulnerabilities is particularly important if, as Fish suggests, such interactions are rather specific, that is, if the parental practice that is best for one infant is neutral or even harmful for another.

Summary

1. Factors influencing psychological development are interwoven in complex and dynamic patterns of interrelations. Ethology provides a comprehensive approach to the roles of early experience, learning, and innate factors in development. Ethologists strive for a complete biological understanding of the nature and origins of behavior, including not only how a behavior develops during the course of an individual's life span but also how it developed during the evolution of the species. Another concern is how the behavior has helped members of the species to survive and reproduce in their natural environment or ecological niche.

2. Ethologists point out that some behaviors in every species are innate and that every behavior has some important innate components, since the nature of the learning mechanisms themselves is shaped by the genes and the evolutionary history that selected those genes. Many innate reflexes are present in the human infant at or shortly after birth; examples include the rooting, Moro (startle), and swimming reflexes.

3. Innate factors also seem to be involved in shaping human social development. For example, eye-to-eye contact between parents and child seems to be one process that helps to establish mutual attachment, and studies of congenitally blind individuals suggest that infants may be programmed innately to search for and lock onto parents' eyes. Infantile autism may result in part from congenital defects in innate mechanisms that normally help to promote social attachment.

4. Some emotional expression in human beings is innate. Evidence for innateness in animals appears in deprivation experiments in which animals are reared under conditions that give no opportunity to learn a given behavior. If that behavior still develops, it must have an innate basis. Children born deaf and blind can show many relatively normal expressive behaviors, including smiling, laughing, and crying. In addition, many expressive behaviors also appear to be cultural universals.

5. Learning processes themselves have biological constraints. For example, species differ in their innate preparedness to associate particular stimuli and responses. Human beings have innate language acquisition devices, with the left hemisphere of the brain being specialized for language learning in most people.

6. Biofeedback procedures provide individuals with information about their biological states, such as blood pressure or brain waves, of which they would normally be unaware. Given such biofeedback, people can see how their behavior influences such states and can learn operant control of states that normally would be subject only to classical conditioning.

7. Innate factors also establish a developmental timetable so that an individual is maturationally ready to learn crucial survival skills at adaptive times during development. In language learning, major developmental milestones (such as the onset of babbling or the first word) roughly parallel the development of motor skills. The amount and onset of vowel-like cooing sounds in the first three months are no different in children reared by deaf parents. Experience is crucial for language development, but maturation sets key constraints; new brain structures must mature before a developing child can advance to higher stages of language development.

8. To meet the environmental demands of the ecological niche for which a species is adapted, different skills must mature not only at the right time but in the right order. If placed on a visual cliff, young individuals of species that must move about on their own shortly after birth *avoid* the deep side, whereas human infants show curiosity rather than fear for several months after birth—long after they can perceive depth.

9. Understanding the factors that shape development is difficult, even when it involves something as ordinary as how students carry school books. Sex differences in how older students carry books are consistent with differences in anatomy, but in younger children the differences seem to reflect social learning.

10. The importance of genotype-environment interactions for development is shown in many studies. Whether prenatal exposure to certain chemicals produces birth defects in mice depends on whether the mice are genetically susceptible. Some research suggests that some cases of schizophrenia may result from a combination of obstetrical complications and a special genetic vulnerability. Whether a pregnancy hazard has harmful consequences for an infant may depend on whether the pregnant woman is vulnerable because of exposure to other stressful influences.

11. Even if an infant has suffered brain damage because of adverse prenatal influences, the long-term effects on development may depend crucially on the postnatal environment. Studies of cognitive development in children born at high or low risk for brain injury suggest an interaction with the postnatal environment. That is, differences in the quality of the rearing home usually seemed to have an even greater impact on brain-injured than on healthy babies. Unfortunately, parents with children at high risk for brain injury because of adverse pregnancy and delivery factors also tend to be least able to provide a favorable postnatal environment for intellectual development.

12. The concept of human nature can express an important and scientifically valid idea. The genetic constitution of human beings and the patterns of development influenced by that constitution were shaped by natural selection so that the species was adapted to environmental conditions that often differ greatly from those in which most people live today. The acceleration of technological development means that the environments in which human beings develop increasingly differ from those of our prehistoric forebears. Cross-cultural studies suggest that many ailments of modern societies partly result from "unnatural" environments. That is, the environments we encounter, and the behavioral patterns we develop with age, place the developing body and brain under environmental stresses for which they are not adapted naturally. Biologists argue that if our civilization is to survive, we must develop a better scientific understanding of human nature and must design physical and social environments that are better suited for human development.

Selected Readings

Dubos, R. *A God Within*. New York: Charles Scribner's Sons, 1972. (Available in paperback.) A collection of essays about human nature, evolution, development, and the relation of human behavior to the natural environment.

Eibl-Eibesfeldt, I. I. *Ethology, the Biology of Behavior*. 2nd ed. New York: Holt, Rinehart, and Winston, 1972. Describes the ethological approach to understanding behavior. It includes many fascinating photographs and anecdotes as well as a stimulating, though speculative, chapter about ethology and human behavior.

Fishbein, H. D. *Evolution, Development, and Children's Learning*. Pacific Palisades, Calif.: Goodyear, 1976. Reviews present knowledge about human evolution and brain development and relates that knowledge to the development of psychological processes in children, with separate chapters on the development of motor skills, language, attention, spatial relations, and moral judgments.

Tinbergen, N. *The Study of Instinct*. New York: Oxford University Press, 1969. (Available in paperback.) A classic presentation of basic concepts, methods, and principles of the ethological approach, written in elegant and sometimes moving prose by the Nobel Prize-winning ethologist.

III SOCIAL AND ENVIRONMENTAL INFLUENCES

To understand how we develop we need to grasp not only the nature of biological influences but also the effects of the social environments in which we develop. The chapters in Part III add information on effects of the environment to our earlier discussion of genetics, maturation, and health. Chapter 6 discusses the effect of early experience on shaping the individual life. Much of early experience is provided first in the family, so it is logical that Chapter 7 next presents information about the effects of the family upon development. The family in turn is shaped by broader social influences, and Chapter 8 describes these. Finally in this part we come to the role of culture as presented in Chapter 9. Culture is the humanly created part of the environment that is passed on with modifications from generation to generation. Dietary habits, religious customs, language, dress, and other aspects of behavior show the influence of culture not only in shaping our behavior during childhood but also in determining what kinds of persons we will be in later life.

Chapter 6

Early Experience
and Developmental Effects

The effects of the prenatal environment on human development, including drugs and smoking during pregnancy, infectious diseases, radiation, and the mother's emotional states

The risks and consequences of prematurity, low birthweight, and short gestation

How early perceptual and learning experiences affect development

Imprinting and critical periods for learning, along with the "sleeper" effects of early experiences

The effects of early social deprivation

Prenatal Influences on Human Development

Drugs During Pregnancy
Smoking During Pregnancy
Infectious Diseases
Radiation
Emotional Stress During Pregnancy
Prematurity, Low Birthweight, and Short Gestation

Effects of Early Perceptual and Learning Experiences

Imprinting and Critical Periods for Learning
Sleeper Effects of Early Experience
Effects of Social Deprivation
Effects of Early Experience on Brain Development
Effects of Early Experience on Human Development: Early and
Varied

Introduction

This chapter describes the effects on development of early experience, including variations in the quality of the prenatal environment as well as early postnatal sensory and learning experiences. The earliest and often most important experiences take place even before birth. We therefore will begin this chapter by reviewing research on some important ways in which the quality of the intrauterine environment can affect development. In doing this we will consider the steps that prospective parents and society as a whole can take to promote healthy pregnancies. Then we will discuss the effects of early postnatal sensory and learning experiences on development, including the concepts of critical periods and sleeper effects on later development. We will examine the developmental effects of different kinds of experience after birth, including social, perceptual, and linguistic deprivation. We will see that such effects can often be surprisingly powerful and can influence not only psychological processes but also brain maturation, body growth, and even survival itself.

Prenatal Influences on Human Development

A great variety of factors can influence the quality of the prenatal environment and thus can shape development even before birth. This chapter focuses on several of the more important classes of prenatal influences, including (1) drug and tobacco use during pregnancy, (2) infectious diseases, (3) exposure to radiation, (4) premature delivery, and (5) the emotional state of the expectant mother. These classes of prenatal influences warrant special attention first of all because they can have such serious—even fatal—consequences for the developing individual. Second, the prenatal hazards we will consider tend to be widespread in the United States and other industrialized countries. Many of them jeopardize the development of literally millions of infants each year. Finally, the factors we will focus on are particularly important because the harm they cause is largely preventable. Nearly all these prenatal hazards can be avoided, if only expectant mothers and those close to them take the time to learn about these hazards and then take simple precautions to minimize the risks involved.

Drugs During Pregnancy

The possibility of having a child with birth defects strikes fear into the heart of every prospective parent, and with good reason. It is estimated that 2 percent of all infants born alive have major defects, and that fetal defects usually are responsible for the more than 20 percent of all pregnancies that end in spontaneous abortions (Marx, 1973). Moreover, nearly all of us were born with at least some minor defects that may cause us varying degress of trouble. For example, most "normal" individuals have been found to have at least two of eighteen minor physical defects associated with Down's syndrome (such as malformed ears or a furrowed tongue). Having many such minor defects has been reported to be associated with problems in psychological development, including hyperactivity (Waldrop, Bell, & Goering, 1976).

The dangers of taking drugs during pregnancy were illustrated when thalidomide caused a tragic epidemic of congenital defects in Western Europe in the 1960s.

Anestis Diakopoulos, Stock, Boston, Inc.

A number of factors, including genetic ones, can play a role in causing developmental defects. In recent years, however, an increasing array of evidence has pointed to the important role that drugs may play in causing such defects. The dangers of taking drugs during pregnancy were illustrated in Western Europe in the 1960s by a tragic epidemic of congenital defects caused by the drug thalidomide. A look at that situation will help us to understand several important points about the effects and dangers of taking drugs during pregnancy.

The Thalidomide Tragedy   The effects of the tranquilizer thalidomide on the developing human fetus graphically illustrate the embryological concept of a *critical period*—that crucial stage in the development of an organ or system during which it is particularly sensitive to the effects of a given environmental agent. The period is said to be critical because the environmental influence must occur during that particular time in order to exert its effect. If the environmental factor occurs before or after the critical period, it will have little or no effect.

Table 6.1 lists the critical periods of human fetal development during which different organs are sensitive to the effects of thalidomide. Note how specific the critical periods can be. For example, the characteristic of *phocomelia*, in which the limbs are reduced and deformed so as to resemble the flippers of a seal, occurred only if the fetus was exposed to thalidomide from thirty-nine to forty-four days after the pregnant women's last menstruation. If the woman took thalidomide only a few days earlier or later, the child's limbs would be normal, but there would be defects of the outer ear, the fingers, or the cranial

TABLE 6.1
Thalidomide:
Period of
Sensitivity and
Risks Involved

Days After Last Menstruation that Thalidomide Was Administered	Child's Organ in Which Malfunctions Occurred
34–38	thumbs (extra), cranial nerves, external ear (pinna)
39–44	upper limbs
40–45	heart, gall bladder, duodenum
42–45	lower limbs
44–48	femur or tibia (large bones of thigh and calf)
50	rectum

Source: Based on W. Lenz, in *Proceedings of the Second International Conference on Congenital Malformations.* London: International Medical Congress, Ltd., 1964, p. 270.

nerves (Lenz, 1964, 1965; Runner, 1967). Thus critical periods may vary, depending both on the drug or environmental agent involved and on the particular organ being considered. In general, developing systems tend to be most vulnerable when they are growing most rapidly.

Thalidomide is an unusually powerful *teratogen,* an agent that produces congenital defects (the term is derived from the Greek word *teratos,* meaning "wonder" or "monster"). For example, one thalidomide specialist was unable to find a single record of a woman whose baby did not suffer malformed limbs if she had taken thalidomide during the critical period (Lenz, 1965). Because of its powerful teratogenicity, and because it gained popularity and widespread use rather quickly for a new drug, thalidomide produced an epidemic of literally tens of thousands of congenital defects around the world, including many defects that are otherwise quite rare.

Even with these strong clues, however, it was difficult for scientists to establish that thalidomide was indeed the culprit. After all, pregnant women are exposed to thousands of chemicals, including many artificial ones that have been invented only recently. Moreover, congenital defects can be caused by many factors other than drugs. The phocomelia produced by thalidomide was in many cases an almost perfect *phenocopy,* or environmentally induced mimic, of a typically hereditary defect. The identification of thalidomide as the teratogen responsible for this particular epidemic of birth defects was thus a difficult task. It was achieved only after months of exhaustive investigation in which questionnaires were administered to mothers who had given birth to infants with phocomelia. Every reasonable possibility was checked out—from detergents and cosmetics to nuclear fallout—until it finally became apparent that thalidomide was the common factor among all the women (Levy, 1968).

If it was so difficult to identify thalidomide as the culprit in this epidemic, imagine how much harder the task is in the case of a drug that has more subtle or more variable teratogenic effects. We know from animal experiments, for example, that the teratogenic effects of an external agent can vary greatly and may affect only a fraction of exposed pregnancies, depending on such factors as the animal's specific genetic constitution and other drugs or agents to which it is exposed at the same time (Runner, 1967).

Heroism in the Face of Tragedy   The thalidomide incident was at once a tragic lesson and a fascinating case of scientific detective work. But it also was a story of remarkable personal heroism. It is worth considering this example of how individual effort, dedication, and personal courage can make an enormous difference—in this case, by saving thousands of children from the tragic effects of thalidomide.

When their son Jan was born with deformed limbs, Karl and Linde Schulte-Hillen, a West German couple, were advised by a gynecologist that the problem was hereditary and that they would do best to keep it a secret and not have any more children. Skeptical of this advice because a friend's wife and his sister had also had infants with the same deformed limbs at about the same time, Karl Schulte-Hillen began to investigate the problem. Although he was rebuffed by a number of doctors, his persistence eventually paid off: he was able to interest pediatric specialist Widukind Lenz in the problem. Together they tracked down thalidomide as the culprit.

However, Schulte-Hillen did not stop there. Next he helped lead a successful public effort to get the giant drug company that manufactured thalidomide to withdraw the drug entirely, so that women could not take it by mistake when they were unaware that they were pregnant. He also allowed his own family to be exposed to the glare of publicity to help erase the stigma that led many parents to hide their thalidomide babies. And he hired—at his own expense, at first—seven physical therapists to roam all over West Germany and contact 1,800 parents of thalidomide babies, whom he helped organize to lobby for special educational treatment facilities for thalidomide infants. Finally, ignoring warnings that he should not speak out against the powerful drug company that manufactured thalidomide, Schulte-Hillen helped lead the legal battle to sue the company for compensation for the victims and to bring criminal negligence indictments against company officials (Levy, 1968).

Although thousands of European infants were exposed to thalidomide, all but a few American infants were spared, thanks to the courage and intelligence of Dr. Frances Kelsey, whose job at the U.S. Food and Drug Administration involved certifying the safety of drugs such as thalidomide. Thalidomide had proved extremely popular—and profitable—in Europe, and American drug companies put enormous pressure on Kelsey to allow them to distribute the drug in the United States. Fortunately, Kelsey recognized that there was insufficient evidence for the safety of thalidomide. She had the courage to insist on further testing, and she resisted the pressures until the work begun by Schulte-Hillen showed how dangerous thalidomide really was.

The success of Kelsey and Schulte-Hillen in forcing government and industry to act more responsibly is worth emphasizing, for thalidomide is just one of thousands of new chemicals being produced each year, many of which may well interfere with fetal development. To cite just one example, women suffer twice the normal miscarriage rate during the time their husbands work at plants producing the chemical vinyl chloride—probably because vinyl chloride damages genetic material in the sperm cells of these men.

An even more important battle must be waged to educate prospective parents about the dangers of using alcohol, tobacco, marijuana, amphetamines, and other drugs during pregnancy. Even though these drugs may not be as potent teratogens as thalidomide, they are used on such a massive scale around the world that the total damage they cause in terms of fetal deaths and congenital malformations dwarfs even the tragic consequences of thalidomide use. Moreover, we have seen the difficulty that Kelsey, Schulte-Hillen, and others had in getting the pharmaceutical industry to stop producing thalidomide. Yet the economic powers and vested interests that Kelsey and Schulte-Hillen had to fight pale beside the economic colossus represented by the tobacco or alcohol industries—to say nothing of the billions of dollars that organized crime syndicates and others make from illicit drugs ranging from marijuana to heroin. To date, these vested interests have shown no more concern about the effects of their products on unborn children than did the pharmaceutical industry. For example, the alcohol lobby has fought even the modest step of placing labels on alcoholic beverages to warn pregnant women about the hazards involved. To overcome these powerful economic interests will require the kind of courage and dedication displayed by Kelsey and Schulte-Hillen. It is hoped that their example will encourage readers to become involved in working for measures—such as better education of the public and stricter screening for teratogenic and mutagenic chemicals—to protect the rights of future generations who cannot speak for themselves.

Avoid All Drugs During Pregnancy　The difficulty of knowing the effects of drugs taken during pregnancy has caused great medical concern, particularly in view of the widespread use of drugs by pregnant women. A survey in Scotland, for example, found that 82 percent of pregnant women took prescribed medicine, and 65 percent took drugs that had not even been prescribed. In addition, 57 percent smoked, and 85 percent imbibed alcohol while pregnant (Marx, 1973).

Medical concern about taking drugs during pregnancy has also increased because of a growing recognition that the placental barrier does not protect the fetus from toxic chemicals—at least not to the extent that was once believed. Although the placenta normally does act to screen out certain chemicals and to detoxify others, it is an imperfect filter. Many potentially harmful chemicals can pass readily from the mother's blood stream into that of the fetus.

In recent years, therefore, biomedical experts increasingly have advised pregnant women to avoid *all* drugs, even those previously prescribed by a doctor (Marx, 1973). Of course, in certain cases some drugs may prove beneficial to a pregnancy or may even be essential for the survival of mother or fetus. But unless they have been prescribed specifically by the woman's physician, who *knows* that she is pregnant and has weighed the risks and benefits carefully, all drugs should be avoided. Even substances that are normally innocuous for adults that we often take routinely, almost without a second thought, should be avoided during pregnancy. This includes pain relievers such as aspirin; antihistamines (as in cold and hay fever tablets); antibiotics such as penicillin; amphetamines and barbiturates as in diet and sleeping pills; high doses of vitamins that are not prescribed by a doctor; caffeine-containing beverages such as coffee, tea, and colas; and nicotine, alcohol, and marijuana. For some fetuses it is possible that those "tiny time pills" may become tragic time bombs.

This prudent advice to avoid all drugs is based on the recent discovery that drugs once thought to be perfectly safe for adults are, in fact, terribly dangerous for unborn children. Indeed, one reason that thalidomide affected tens of thousands of babies around the world was because it *was* so popular with mothers and obstetricians. And it was popular precisely because it was an effective tranquilizer that seemed to have no harmful side effects. However, a fetus is quite different, physiologically, from an adult. Certain enzymes that an adult uses to break down and detoxify potentially harmful chemicals are not yet present in the human fetus. This "enzymatic immaturity" makes the fetus vulnerable to many drugs that cause little or no harm to most adults (Bowes, 1970; Marx, 1973). Table 6.2 lists drugs that surveys have found to have been taken more frequently than normal by women who had children with congenital defects.

Avoid Drugs Even When at Risk of Pregnancy   The critical period of vulnerability to many agents occurs during the early weeks of an embryo's development, when the basic structural foundations of many organs are being laid down. Thus a teratogenic agent may have damaged the fetus even before a woman has missed her period and realizes she is pregnant. In fact, many women took thalidomide, with its tragic effects, before they even knew they were pregnant; some had taken only one or two pills. As one parent put it, "Two little white pills taken one evening and never again. Two little white pills—and in payment, two childish arms . . ." (Levy, 1968). It is best, therefore, to avoid drugs even when at risk of becoming pregnant.

Dangers of Hallucinogens, Alcohol, and Caffeine   Western societies have seen a striking recent increase in the number of people—especially adolescents and young adults—who (1) are trying a variey of psychotropic drugs, ranging from marijuana and alcohol to amphetamines and LSD, and (2) are engaging in reckless sexual activity, often without any planning or precautions whatsoever. The result is an increasing number of young parents who not only are risking their own health but at the same time are unwittingly exposing their children to drugs while they are still in the womb. Because pregnant women who use one drug often may use others as well and because investigators cannot ethically give pregnant women drugs suspected of being harmful, it is difficult to prove conclusively that a particular drug damages the fetus. However, research has established clearly that women who have experimented with various drugs are much more likely to have miscarriages or to give birth to children with major congenital defects—ten times more likely than normal, in one large sample (Jacobson & Berlin, 1972).

TABLE 6.2
Fetotoxic Drugs

Maternal Medication	Fetal or Neonatal Effect
Established teratogenic drugs	
Thalidomide	Fetal death or phocomelia, deafness; cardiovascular, gastrointestinal, or genitourinary anomalies
Organic mercury	Cerebral palsy
Sex hormones	
Androgens, progestogens, estrogens	Masculinization, advanced bone age
DES (diethylstilbestrol)	Carcinoma (cancer) of the cervix or vagina, usually in adolescence
Antineoplastic agents	
Antimetabolites: methotrexate, flourouracil, 6-azauridine	Multiple anomalies, abortion
Alkylating agents: cyclophosphamide	
Antibiotics: amphotericin B, mitomycin, DON	
Possible teratogenic drugs	
Vitamin D (large doses)	Multiple anomalies and fetotoxic effects have been ascribed to these drugs but etiologic relationships are uncertain and questionable
Antihistamines	
Hallucinogens	
LSD, mescaline, etc.	
Antidiabetes drugs	
Sulfonylurea derivatives	
Corticosterioids	
Insulin (shock or hypoglycemia)	
Antithyroid drugs	
Thiouracils, inorganic iodides	
Human fetotoxic agents	
Analgesics	
Narcotic drugs: heroin, morphine, meperidine	Neonatal depression, convulsions, tremors, or death.
Aspirin and other salicylates (excessive)	Neonatal bleeding
Anesthetic agents	
Inhalational anesthetics (excessive): nitrous oxide, cyclopropane	Neonatal depression or death
Regional anesthetics (especially the amides), lidocaine, prilocaine	Neonatal depression, methemoglobinemia, or death
Intravenous anesthetics	Neonatal depression or death
Anticoagulant drugs	Fetal death or hemorrhage
Anti-eclampsia drugs	
Magnesium sulfate	Flaccidity, lethargy, and neonatal depression

(continued)

Maternal Medication	Fetal or Neonatal Effect
Anti-infective drugs	
Chloroquine	Death or deafness or retinal hemorrhage
Erythromycin	Hepatic injury
Nitrofurantoin	Hemolytic reactions
Novobiocin	Hyperbilirubinemia
Quinine, quinidine	Nerve deafness, thrombocytopenia
Streptomycin	Nerve deafness
Sulfonamides (Kynex®, Midicel®)	Kernicterus
Tetracyclines	Hemolysis, hepatotoxicity, inhibition of bone growth, discolored teeth
Sedatives, hynotics, tranquilizers	
Barbiturates (short- and medium-acting): secobarbital, amybarbital	Neonatal depression
Benzodiazepines: chlordiazepoxide, diazepam	Neonatal depression
Meprobamate	Retarded development
Phenobarbital (excessive)	Neonatal bleeding
Phenothiazines	Hyperbilirubinemia, neonatal depression
Tobacco smoking	Undersized babies
Vaccines	Routine immunization with live virus vaccines should be avoided during pregnancy, except when required for rabies and cholera. The possibility of existing pregnancy should be considered before administering smallpox, mumps, measles, rubella, polio, and yellow fever vaccines
Vitamin C (excessive)	Acidosis, abortion
Vitamin K (excessive)	Hyperbilirubinemia

Source: R. C. Benson. *Handbook of Obstetrics and Gynecology.* Los Altos, Calif.: Lange Medical Publications, 1974, pp. 82–83.

In addition, researchers found that mothers who drank heavily throughout their pregnancies had infants whose growth was stunted and who had an unusually high number of serious congenital defects (Jones et al., 1973). This has distressing implications, given the large number of women of childbearing age who drink, including an estimated one million alcoholics. A review of research by Streissguth et al. (1980) concluded that in "humans exposed to alcohol during gestation the effects can range from fetal alcohol syndrome in some offspring of chronic alcoholic women to reduced average birth weight in offspring of women reporting an average consumption of two to three drinks or more per day. The behavioral effects of such exposure may range from mental retardation in children with fetal alcohol syndrome to milder developmental and behavioral effects in infants born to social drinkers" (p. 354). Other experiments show that caffeine causes congenital defects such as cleft palate when given to pregnant animals in levels equivalent to eleven cups of coffee per day. Pregnant women are therefore urged to minimize consumption of caffeine-containing beverages such as coffee, tea, and colas (Jacobsen, 1976).

Smoking During Pregnancy

The risk that smoking parents pose for their child is most evident during pregnancy. Cigarette smoke inhaled by a pregnant smoker contains carbon monoxide, nicotine, and various cancer-producing agents—all of which can pass into the fetal blood stream. A number of studies have found significantly higher rates of stillbirth and prematurity among infants whose mothers smoke (see Figure 6.1). The U.S. Surgeon General (Office on Smoking and Health, 1979) estimates that smoking by pregnant women is responsible for 4,000 stillbirths each year in the United States. Smoking by fathers can also be harmful to children, for pregnant women and children can become involuntary or "passive" smokers whose health can be damaged by breathing cigarette smoke around them. A study of more then two thousand adults found that those who were long-term passive smokers actually showed a degree of impaired respiratory function comparable to that of light active smokers and heavy smokers who did not inhale (White & Froeb, 1980). Moreover, the incidence of respiratory infection in the first year of life is increased in infants whose parents smoke (Office on Smoking and Health, 1979). Indeed, an editorial in *Science*

FIGURE 6.1
Fetal and infant deaths per 1,000 births in smoking and nonsmoking women.

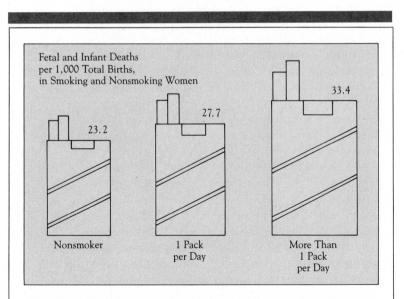

Fetal and Infant Deaths per 1,000 Total Births, in Smoking and Nonsmoking Women

Nonsmoker	1 Pack per Day	More Than 1 Pack per Day
23.2	27.7	33.4

Data from "The Second Report of a Perinatal Study in Ten University Teaching Hospitals, Ontario, 1967," a publication of the Ontario Ministry of Health.

magazine points out that cigarette smoke may well be a more serious form of air pollution than automobile emissions—even for nonsmokers. One of the more harmful auto emissions, for example, is carbon monoxide. Exposure for only one hour to a concentration of 120 parts per million (ppm) of carbon monoxide commonly causes such symptoms as headaches and dizziness. Concentrations of 100 ppm can occur in garages or tunnels, but such concentrations are dwarfed by the 42,000 ppm found in cigarette smoke. A smoker can survive these high concentrations because most of the time he or she is breathing air that is not so heavily polluted. "However, in a poorly ventilated, smoke-filled room, concentrations of carbon monoxide can easily reach several hundred parts per million, thus exposing smokers and nonsmokers present to a toxic hazard" (Abelson, 1967).

Moreover, even when drugs other than tobacco are involved, a father can affect his child's exposure to drugs because his own attitudes and the example he sets in the usage of drugs can strongly influence his mate's. For fathers as well as mothers, then, the moral responsibility is clear: when they risk their own health through drugs, they also make their own children unwilling targets for injury and even death.

Infectious Diseases

Rubella and Other Viral Diseases As is the case with drugs, infectious diseases that usually produce no serious symptoms in an adult can have very serious, even lethal, effects on a fetus. *Rubella,* popularly known as German or three-day measles, is perhaps the most serious viral threat to the human fetus and can cause a number of congenital defects including blindness, deafness, and heart defects as well as fetal death. Moreover, research (Chess, Korn, & Fernandez, 1971) has shown an unusually high percentage of children with infantile autism whose mothers were exposed to rubella during pregnancy, suggesting that the virus may also cause many cases of that tragic childhood psychosis. Rubella is a textbook example of a critical period of vulnerability during pregnancy: if a woman contracts it during the first month of her pregnancy, there is an estimated 50 percent chance of a major congenital defect; by the third month the risk is about 17 percent, and there is a much smaller risk of congenital defects if exposure occurs after the third month.

Fortunately, there are now techniques for determining whether a woman is immune to rubella *before* she becomes pregnant. This involves testing the woman's blood for antibodies to rubella. The test can be done during a regular checkup or at the time of the marital examination legally required in most jurisdictions (when the blood is also sampled to test for the presence of syphilis). A history of having had rubella is not considered reliable evidence of immunity, and it is not an adequate substitute for laboratory diagnosis. If a woman is found through testing to be immune, she has the satisfaction of knowing her baby is safe from rubella; if she is not immune, she can then be given a vaccine to provide immunity. However, because the rubella vaccine uses live, though "weakened," viruses, the vaccine itself can damage the fetus if it is given when the woman is pregnant. For this reason women are given the vaccine only if they can be certain not to become pregnant for at least two months after vaccination (Benson, 1974; Boston Children's Medical Center, 1971). It is probably best, therefore, for a woman to consult a gynecologist before being vaccinated. Once pregnant, it is too late to be vaccinated, which is why it is so important during pregnancy to avoid exposure to anyone known to have rubella. Young schoolchildren are particularly likely to be carriers of viral infections, and so campaigns to immunize against rubella have emphasized the vaccination of schoolchildren.

Other viral infections during pregnancy appear to pose less of a threat to the fetus than rubella does. However, there is some evidence that viral infections such as mumps, measles (rubeola), or chicken pox during pregnancy may be associated with slightly higher rates of spontaneous abortion (Benson, 1974). It thus seems prudent during pregnancy to avoid persons carrying these diseases as well.

Toxoplasmosis   *Toxoplasmosis* is a disease caused by Toxoplasma, a microscopic protozoan parasite. Its principal host is the cat, but it also commonly infects many other animals, including cattle, swine, sheep—and human beings. Although many, perhaps most, people are infected sometime during their lifetime, toxoplasmosis in adults does not usually produce serious symptoms and is not considered a major public health menace. However, if a woman without prior immunity is infected by Toxoplasma while she is pregnant, there is a sizable risk that the infection will spread across the placenta to the fetus, where it often causes blindness, brain damage, or death. It is estimated that each year in the United States toxoplasmosis kills or causes serious damage to at least one thousand babies.

Although on the average only about one in three hundred women will become infected during a given pregnancy, the serious consequences for the fetus make it well worth taking a few simple precautions that can largely eliminate the risk to the fetus. Human beings are usually infected either by eating raw or uncooked meat or by contact with domestic cats—particularly with soil or sand that has been contaminated with the cats' feces. Therefore, pregnant women and young children should avoid all rare meat, including steak and hamburger as well as pork and mutton. Pregnant women should also use special caution in handling raw meat or soil (for example, when gardening) that may be contaminated with cat feces. They should use gloves; avoid contact with mouth, eyes, or cuts; and wash hands with special care when through. Pet cats should be prevented from hunting and should be fed only meat that is dry, canned, or well cooked. Pregnant women should avoid contact with cats who roam outside, and they should delegate the cleaning of cat litter to others (or use disposable gloves when this is not possible). Similar precautions apply to young children, and it is wise to cover children's sandboxes when they are not in use (Frenkel, 1973).

Venereal Disease   *Venereal disease (VD)* includes a number of disorders that are transmitted primarily through sexual contact. The most serious of these are *gonorrhea* and *syphilis*, which now rank first and third among reportable com-

FIGURE 6.2
Reported cases of
communicable diseases
(in thousands, United
States, 1977)

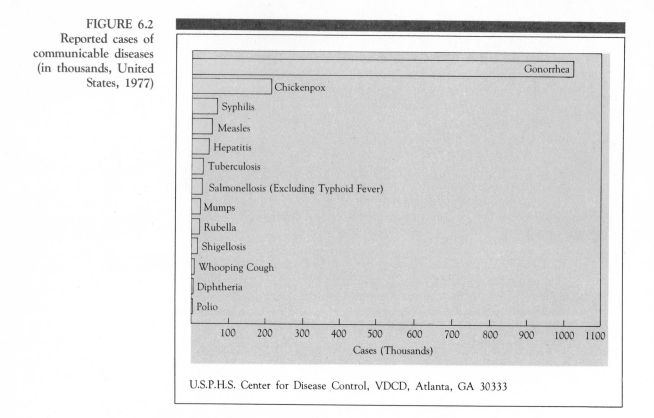

U.S.P.H.S. Center for Disease Control, VDCD, Atlanta, GA 30333

municable diseases in the United States. Even more distressing is the rate at which VD is increasing. Several million new cases of gonorrhea occur each year in the United States, along with tens of thousands of new cases of syphilis. Indeed, more cases of gonorrhea are reported each year than cases of *all* other reportable communicable diseases combined, including mumps, measles, rubella, chicken pox, tuberculosis, and hepatitis. There are nearly half a million persons in need of treatment for syphilis at this time (U.S. Department of Health, Education, and Welfare, 1979, pp. 250–251; Kolata, 1976). Figure 6.2 lists the major communicable diseases and their incidence.

Gonorrhea and syphilis are both caused by bacteria that require moisture for their survival and transmission. They die quickly outside the human body, and they are quite susceptible to drying, antiseptics, and soap and water. Transmission nearly always occurs during sexual contact with an infected partner.

In both sexes, the symptoms of *gonorrhea* begin to appear after an incubation period of from two to twenty-one days following infection. Most men have obvious symptoms, such as a burning sensation during urination and the discharge of yellow pus from the urethra. In women, there may be discomfort or pain during urination, or slightly increased vaginal discharge, but usually in the initial stages there are *no symptoms at all*. If the disease progresses, a woman may have other symptoms, such as abdominal or lower back pain, disturbed menstruation, or pain on intercourse.

If untreated, gonorrhea can cause sterility in both men and women. Indeed, scarring of the Fallopian tubes by gonorrhea is a major cause of infertility among American women. Eventually the gonococci can spread throughout the body to cause other problems such as arthritis (of which it is the leading infectious cause in the United States) or fatal heart and brain inflammations (Handsfield, 1975).

A mother with gonorrhea also can infect her *newborn infant*. Infection of the infant's eyes—usually transmitted during passage through the cervical canal—was a leading cause of infant blindness early in this century. For this reason, the eyes of newborn infants in most countries today are swabbed routinely with a preventative solution (usually of silver nitrate). Pregnant women with gonorrhea are also more likely to have obstetrical problems such as a premature delivery (Handsfield, Hodson, & Holmes, 1973).

The first, or primary, stage of *syphilis* begins from two to twelve weeks after initial contact with the germ. It usually takes the form of a sore or ulcer. These primary sores are usually hard but not painful. However, because they can vary in size and appearance, any genital sore should receive prompt medical attention. In many patients, especially women, the sores may be internal and may go unnoticed. If untreated, syphilis invades the blood stream and organs of the body. Symptoms during this secondary stage can vary, and include brownish-red skin rashes, headaches, malaise, paleness, and weight loss. Even if untreated, these primary and secondary symptoms eventually heal, but the victim is *not* necessarily cured. The disease may remain latent for years, eventually breaking out to attack the spinal cord, brain, or arteries and cause paralysis, insanity, and death. Moreover, even during the latent stage, a pregnant woman who has syphilis can infect her unborn child, for whom it can mean blindness, retardation, or spontaneous abortion (Morton, 1972; *Newsweek*, 1972).

VD bacteria are becoming more resistant to antibiotics. Indeed, one new strain of gonorrhea is totally resistant to penicillin (Culliton, 1976). Still, other antibiotics can be used, and VD can almost always be cured, provided the patient cooperates with the physician and returns for repeated testing and treatment to ensure against relapse. Given that syphilis and gonorrhea can be cured readily with antibiotics, why are Western countries undergoing an epidemic of these diseases? There appear to be several reasons. First, birth control pills and the IUD have increased sexual experimentation and promiscuity. Moreover, unlike the condom, these devices provide no protection against VD. Second, some individuals who suspect they have VD may avoid seeking medical help for fear that their covert sexual activities will be revealed. Teen-agers especially might be concerned about this. Many clinics therefore now provide complete confidentiality, even to minors, and may provide free treatment as well, thus encouraging VD victims to seek medical help.

A third contributor to skyrocketing VD rates is misinformation—for example, that one is likely to contract VD only from the poor or from those who are promiscuous or are prostitutes. In fact, VD respects neither economic nor social-class barriers. Studies of college students indicate that most of them contract the disease from "nice" people—such as good friends, steady dates, or fiancés and spouses.

A fourth factor is the insidious nature of VD symptoms, which may disappear in their more obvious forms. A patient may be misled into thinking that he or she has been "cured" when, in fact, the disease has taken on a less obvious but more dangerous form. The patient then may fail to seek treatment or may stop it prematurely—until irreparable damage has been done. Even the initial symptoms of VD may go unnoticed, particularly in women. Indeed, most women with the early, uncomplicated forms of gonorrhea have no symptoms at all (Morton, 1972). Millions of symptomless women around the world form a great reservoir of infection, unknowingly carrying the disease and transmitting it to their sexual partners.

Ultimately, stemming the VD epidemic may depend on the development of vaccines against gonorrhea and syphilis. Some progress toward a gonorrhea vaccine is being made (Clark, Gosnell, & Coppola, 1979). If an accurate diagnostic blood test were available for gonorrhea, as it now is for syphilis, then it would be easier to identify and treat those with gonorrhea.

While medical research proceeds, there is an urgent need for greater efforts to inform the public and to identify infected persons. In recent years, Chicago health officials have routinely screened persons coming to city medical facilities for reasons *other* than VD. In a recent year, 9 percent were found to have gonorrhea. At some colleges, students have lobbied to make VD screening part of physical exams for all students. Education efforts must also be expanded. Many VD experts contend that education should be begun before puberty, for each year in the United States there are more than seven thousand cases among children fourteen and younger, two thousand of these involving children under nine (U.S. Department of Health, Education, and Welfare, 1979; *Newsweek*, 1972). Above all, we must strip away the shame, apathy, and ignorance that have surrounded VD, replacing them with the honesty needed to face unpleasant facts. These diseases can be eliminated through the kind of concern and commitment with which societies have successfully battled such diseases as smallpox and polio.

Radiation

There is no question that radiation from a variety of sources such as x rays or nuclear fallout can cause damage to a fetus. The damage can result either from direct exposure of the fetus during pregnancy or from radiation exposure of the parents' reproductive cells before conception, which may cause the fetus to inherit defective genes. Many animal experiments have proved the mutagenic and teratogenic power of radiation (for example, Runner, 1967). Indeed, radiation has been used as a scientific tool by geneticists who wished to produce deliberate genetic mutations for study.

Microcephaly Women whose uteruses have been subjected unavoidably to heavy radiation during pregnancy (for example, by x ray treatment of cancer in the pelvic region) give birth to infants with an unusually high percentage of congenital defects. One such defect is *microcephaly*, a congenital deformity involving the central nervous system. This form of severe mental retardation, resulting from a developmental aberration in which the skull and brain are abnormally small, either can occur as the result of a recessive gene or can be a phenocopy caused by a prenatal factor such as maternal infection or x-radiation (Grosch & Hopwood, 1979; Robinson & Robinson, 1965).

Dangers of Diagnostic X Rays Because the risk of damage to a fetus or to the genetic material of a prospective parent is proportional to the amount of radiation received, the probability of genetic or fetal damage from exposure to diagnostic x rays (such as those administered by a dentist, an orthopedic surgeon, or an obstetrician) is rather small in a given case. However, the danger is still real. Exposure to x rays, therefore, should not be treated casually. For example, dentists and physicians should routinely provide patients with lead aprons to protect the pelvic area during x rays.

In their text on the biological effects of radiation, Grosch and Hopwood (1979) conclude:

The majority of deaths and abnormalities from radiation occur during the first six weeks in women not aware of their pregnant condition. Therefore the use of diagnostic radiation procedures should be delayed when possible if pregnancy cannot be ruled out. Many hospitals have instituted a form that includes a checklist of factors which may eliminate the potential of pregnancy: birth control, menopause, tubal ligation, menstrual period less than 14 days previous. (p. 185)

Ultrasonic Monitoring of Pregnancy During pregnancy, of course, the need for an obstetrician to obtain information about the fetus or the mother's pelvic structure may outweigh the risk of x rays to the fetus. Still, obstetricians have been concerned with minimizing the exposure of pregnant women to x rays, especially during the early stages of gestation. It is, therefore, encouraging that a new diagnostic tool has been developed that uses a kind of sonar system like that used by bats and submarines. Ultrasonic sound waves are beamed at the fetus, and the echoes from various surfaces are recorded and translated electronically into a visual image on a television screen (*Newsweek,* Nov. 15, 1976).

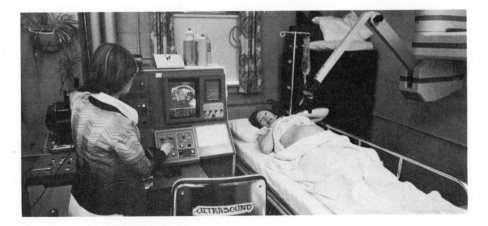

To avoid x ray exposure of pregnant women, obstetricians have turned to ultrasound monitoring of the fetus.

James Holland, Stock, Boston, Inc.

Testing Fetuses: A Checkup in the Womb

Is the unborn baby healthy, or does a defect destine it to an early death or a life of debilitating illness? In many cases the answers to these worrisome questions can be found in laboratory analysis of a small sample of the amniotic fluid drawn from the sac surrounding the baby in the womb. Using amniocentesis, as the technique is called, doctors can accurately predict serious disorders like Down's syndrome (mongolism) and Gaucher's disease (a metabolic disorder); faced with a grim certainty, prospective parents can opt for abortion. But amniocentesis has its limitations; it cannot foretell all defects. Now comes fetoscopy, a technique that takes over where amniocentesis leaves off by allowing direct examination of the fetus.

Using fetoscopy, physicians can actually see the fetus in the uterus and spot certain physical defects. Says Dr. Thomas Gindhart, of the National Cancer Institute: "You can look right at the parts of the fetus as it floats by. You can count the number of fingers." That alone can reveal much about the condition of the fetus. A six-fingered hand, for example, may accompany some forms of retardation. Also discernible are such features as eyes, ears, mouth and genitals. Even more important, the technique enables doctors to take blood and tissue from the fetus. From these samples they can diagnose a severe skin disease known as epidermolytic hyperkeratosis and such blood disorders as hemophilia and thalassemia, and the 40% of sickle cell anemia cases that amniocentesis misses.

The exceptionally delicate procedure, performed some 15 to 20 weeks into the pregnancy, is done under a local anesthetic. Doctors scan the woman with pulsed sound waves to locate the fetus, the umbilical cord and the placenta. After making a small incision in the abdomen, they insert into the uterus and the amniotic sac a pencil-lead-thin tube containing an endoscope with fiber-optic bundles that transmit light. This enables the physicians to see tiny areas of the fetus. By inserting biopsy forceps into the tube, doctors can take a 1-mm (.04 in.) skin sample from the fetus. They prefer to excise it from the head, where there are no major blood vessels or nerves and the skull provides a firm surface for their work. To draw a blood sample, the doctor inserts a needle through the tube and punctures one of the fetal blood vessels lying on the surface of the placenta. Says Dr. Mitchell Golbus, a fetoscopy expert and director of the prenatal detection program at the University of California at San Francisco: "It has to be done with a great deal of care and skill because we want the pregnancy to continue unharmed if the test comes back normal."

At the Yale-New Haven Hospital, doctors have been performing fetoscopies on women who fear (usually because of family histories) that their children will be defective. In many cases the test can reassure patients that their babies will be normal. Says Yale obstetrician John Hobbins, who with Maurice Mahoney, a pediatrician and geneticist, pioneered fetoscopy: "Its benefit is that we can salvage 75% of the fetuses that would otherwise be aborted." But Hobbins and other doctors stress that the technique is still highly experimental. It induces miscarriage in about 5% of the cases (the rate for amniocentesis is less than 1%), and has been tried on only a few hundred women, most of them at Yale and the University of California at San Francisco.

Though the disorders that fetoscopy now helps diagnose are few, and quite rare, researchers expect to use it eventually to detect such maladies as albinism (lack of pigment) and muscular dystrophy. Refinements in blood analysis may also make it possible to discern in the fetus levels of any toxic substances the mother has been exposed to. Some doctors foresee a more startling prospect using fetoscopy to administer medicine directly to fetuses and perhaps even perform minor surgery on them while they are still in the womb.

Nuclear Fallout   An even greater radiation threat is posed by radiation from nuclear explosions and their fallout. Women less than five months pregnant and living within a half mile of the epicenter of the atomic bomb explosion in Hiroshima suffered a greatly increased incidence of stillbirths and children with congenital defects such as microcephaly (Lifton, 1967; Plummer, 1952). One of the most dangerous aspects of such radiation damage is its insidious nature. The deaths caused by the radiation—through cancer, stillbirths, and genetic mutations that will have lethal effects in future generations—may be delayed years or even centuries after the time of the explosion. Because the deaths can be so distant in time and space from the actual human decisions that caused them, we are less likely to hold the people who made those decisions accountable. For example, if one country through some military action such as shelling killed hundreds of people in another country, it would prompt the greatest outrage if not outright war. Yet thousands of people have died and will die in the future as a result of radioactive fallout from nuclear bomb tests that rarely have evoked strong protest by the governments of the people who will die as a result. Most frightening of all, the effects of radiation are so insidious that they have even been overlooked by some strategic arms specialists in the armed services and defense departments, who have underestimated by tens of millions the number of lives that would be lost from radioactive fallout in a nuclear war.

For example, some nuclear planners have argued that a nuclear war in which nuclear bombs were aimed primarily at the other side's missiles and other weaponry remote from major population centers would result in "only" a few million casualties—a level that ruthless or desperate leaders might consider an acceptable loss to achieve their political ends. These calculations, however, overlook the effects of radiation from nuclear explosions. For example, an all-out attack on just one of the missile installations in Missouri would produce an enormous cloud of deadly fallout that, during a period of strong winds, could stretch across half the continent, all the way to Washington, D.C. (Drell & von Hippel, 1976).

In summary, because the effects of radiation can be so insidious, we need to take additional steps to reduce human exposure to radiation from all sources—whether from diagnostic x rays, nuclear power plant wastes, or fallout from nuclear weapons. Above all, special precautions are needed to minimize the exposure of pregnant women to such radiation.

Emotional Stress During Pregnancy

Is a mother's psychological as well as physical environment important during pregnancy? Interest in how the emotional state of a pregnant woman may affect the child she carries is at least as old as the Hippocratic writings and the Vedas dating back to 400 and 500 B.C. (Ferreira, 1965). A number of empirical studies have linked psychological stress to poor pregnancy outcome. Berle and Javert (1954), for example, note that the occurrence of spontaneous abortions was frequently related to periods of emotional turmoil in the lives of their patients. They also found that psychotherapy helped to relieve anxiety and achieve successful deliveries in women who had had repeated spontaneous abortions.

Other researchers have found that a high proportion of women with pre-eclamptic toxemia had experienced emotionally upsetting events during their pregnancies (Coppen, 1958) and that psychological factors were associated with prolonged labor (Kapp, Hornstein, & Graham, 1963) and vomiting (Hetzel, Bruer, & Poidevin, 1961).

As with drugs and other factors suspected of having an adverse influence on pregnancy outcome, it is difficult to prove that emotional stresses—although correlated with obstetrical problems—have actually caused the problems. However, the idea of a causal link is supported by several lines of evidence, including some studies that used standardized questionnaire measures of anxiety. Davids, Spencer, and Talmadge (1961) gave the Manifest Anxiety Scale to forty-eight women before and after they had delivered. Problems in pregnancy and delivery were correlated with high anxiety during pregnancy but not after it, suggesting that anxiety probably was the cause rather than the effect of these women's problems. McDonald, Gynther, and Christakos (1963) found that pregnant women who were to have obstetrical complications or to deliver children with congenital abnormalities had higher anxiety scores during pregnancy than did women without such problems.

Still more convincing are studies that report that stress or anxiety imposed on a pregnant woman by external events may be related to increased obstetrical problems. One study asked women to indicate (1) the number of stressful life events they had experienced during pregnancy, such as financial or marital problems or a death in the family; and (2) the social resources they had for coping with such stressors, such as help from family, neighbors, and friends. Women who had both high scores for stressful life events and few resources to help in coping with these stresses had significantly more obstetrical complications (Nuckolls, Cassel, & Kaplan, 1972).

Interpersonal Tension   A prospective study of the relation between pregnancy stress and early childhood development was conducted in Great Britain by Stott (1973), who interviewed a cross-section of 153 women within a month after they had delivered their infants, after which public health nurses followed the development of these infants over the next four years. The children were rated at regular intervals for the presence of various physical and mental problems that might be related to prenatal stress, including failure to gain weight, neurological symptoms such as convulsions, somatic abnormalities such as obesity or pallor, congenital malformations, retardation in the development of skills such as walking and speech, and behavior problems such as overactivity. Children who suffered greatly from such problems were much more likely than those with few problems to have had a mother who experienced prolonged interpersonal tension during her pregnancy (caused by factors such as repeated and severe quarreling with a husband, mother-in-law, or hostile neighbor). Stott believes that such interpersonal tensions for the mothers were an important cause of the illnesses seen in the children after birth. First, he notes, prolonged interpersonal tension and anxiety during pregnancy were associated strongly with the children's problems. On the other hand, brief periods of fright or depression were *not* correlated with the children's illnesses. Second, although many mothers of children with problems lived in wretched slum conditions, other women living in these same conditions had healthy children. Third, if one excluded the women with severe tension during their pregnancies, the significant correlation between poverty and children's development problems disappeared. Stott suggests that the adverse effects of poverty on children's health and development are caused primarily by the increased interpersonal tension that their mothers experience during pregnancy.

We must view Stott's conclusion with caution, however, for his findings might be explained in other ways. For example, women who experience prolonged interpersonal conflict during their pregnancy may—either because of their circumstances or their own personalities—be disturbed or inadequate mothers once their children are born. Stott's results need to be replicated using more conclusive methods (for example, through adoptive samples in which the effects of prenatal and postnatal environments can be separated or through experiments in which pregnant women already suffering from severe interpersonal stress are offered help to relieve their distress). Still, Stott's findings are in line with other research suggesting that more should be done to protect pregnant women from prolonged emotional as well as physical distress. This conclusion is also supported by our growing knowledge of physiological mechanisms that may mediate the effects of a mother's emotional state on her pregnancy.

Maternal Stress and the Fetus   Although it seems unlikely that even a near-term fetus is aware of its mother's emotional states, those maternal states can have a powerful effect on the developing child by means of physiological pathways. Distressing events can produce tremendous physiological changes in the body, including the release of various hormones such as epinephrine (adrenalin) and changes in the distribution of blood flow and activity in various organs such as the nervous system. Such changes in body chemistry and function are usually adaptive, in that they prepare the organism to cope with danger—for example, to flee from or fight an adversary. This general stress response, however, is also a strain on the body's resources. It interferes with the general growth and body maintenance functions, and, if maintained for too long, can actually kill an animal (Selye, 1978). Experiments with animals show that stressing a pregnant animal can strongly affect the behavior of its offspring (see Joffe, 1969) and that injecting the pregnant animal with hormones released by stress produces similar effects.

In the case of human beings, it is clear that a fetus can respond rather directly and quickly to emotional arousal in the mother. Fetuses have been found to be several times more active in their bodily movements when their mothers were under stress. Even trivial changes in the mother's environment can affect the fetus. If a pregnant woman lies quietly listening to music, simply switching from soothing to emotionally stirring music can increase the mother's heart rate—and, within a few seconds, that of the infant as well (Sontag, 1941, 1944). Although available evidence does not indicate that momentary emotional changes of this kind are likely to interfere with fetal development, prolonged and severe stress may well do so. There is evidence, for example, that maternal stress may produce a congenital defect known as *infantile pyloric stenosis*, in which the infant suffers from an excessive development of a valvelike muscle in the stomach, which can cause projectile vomiting beginning a few weeks after birth (Dodge, 1972).

Prematurity, Low Birthweight, and Short Gestation

As Tanner (1970) notes, until rather recently babies weighing less than 2,500 grams (5½ pounds) at birth were called *premature*. However, this term is now being replaced in scientific usage by a more useful distinction. According to a definition established by the World Health Organization, infants weighing less than 2,500 grams at birth (Tanner feels it should be 2,000 grams) are termed *low birthweight*. By contrast, infants who stay less than the normal time in the uterus are referred to as *short-gestation* babies. The distinction between low birthweight and short gestation is important, not only because these terms refer to two different processes but because the consequences for the infant tend to be different. As Tanner notes, "Clearly the prognosis for a small child born after the normal length of gestation and an equally small child born after a shortened gestation may be very different. Leaving the uterus early is not in itself necessarily deleterious, whereas growing less than normally during a full uterine stay implies pathology of fetus, placenta, or mother" (p. 92).

Low-birthweight infants tend to grow more rapidly than others during the first two years; but even so, it appears that they never completely catch up, on the average, with normal-birthweight infants. The same seems to be true of scores on mental ability tests. However, the size of the average mental and physical deficit associated with low birthweight depends critically on how much the birthweight falls below normal. Infants with birthweights between 2,000 and 2,500 grams show only slight average deficits in physical size and mental ability. But the risk of mental and physical defects is significantly increased in infants weighing less than 2,000 grams at birth. As Tanner suggests, it appears that many or most of the newborns weighing between 2,000 and 2,500 grams are simply infants who are small because of their genetic constitution; they have developed normally during a normal period of gestation. By contrast, most newborns weighing less than 2,000 grams seem to have suffered from some problem in prenatal development.

As birthweight decreases, rates of infant mortality, congenital defects, and serious developmental delay all increase in accelerating fashion. However, it should be noted that today most low-birthweight or short-gestation infants can develop normally, given good care. A recent study in the United States of over five thousand infants seen at one year of age found that even among infants with the very low birthweights of 1,500 grams or less, 43 percent seemed to be developing well. Conversely, among infants of normal birthweight—5 pounds, 8 ounces (2,500 grams) or more—nearly 30 percent had a significant health problem (Karel, 1978).

The risk of low birthweight is greater in families with low incomes and little education than in those with adequate incomes and more years of education.

Women receiving no prenatal care were at especially high risk (23 percent, or four to five times that of women who did receive prenatal care; U.S. Department of Health, Education, and Welfare, 1979, p. 258).

Effects of Early Perceptual and Learning Experiences

Having considered some of the more important ways in which the prenatal physiological environment can shape development, let us now turn to the role of early perceptual and learning experiences. These occur primarily though not exclusively after birth. From the now large body of research literature, we have selected for discussion several of the more important studies to illustrate how early experience can critically affect social, language, and intellectual development, as well as brain and body maturation.

Imprinting and Critical Periods for Learning

The term *imprinting* was first used by Austrian ethologist Konrad Lorenz (1952, 1965) to describe the process by which young goslings tend to follow and become attached to the first moving objects they see during a critical period shortly after birth. In his pioneering studies, Lorenz took eggs from the same clutch laid by a greylag goose and divided them into two groups. One group was reared by the mother, and the other was raised by Lorenz in an incubator. Goslings that were hatched by their mother showed the natural behavior of following her about soon after birth. For the incubated goslings, however, Lorenz was the first moving object with which they had regular contact, and soon after birth they followed him around. If the incubated and normally reared goslings were marked so that they could be told apart and then were mixed together under a large box, when the box was lifted each group would run to the respective object on which it had imprinted—with the incubated goslings rushing to "Mother Goose" Lorenz.

Lorenz noted that the goslings appeared to imprint most readily during a critical period lasting only a day or two after birth, and this hypothesis was subsequently confirmed by experimental laboratory studies. Hess (1967) and his colleagues, for example, studied the imprinting of newly hatched ducklings under standardized laboratory conditions. The ducklings were kept in individual boxes with no visual experience until they were exposed to the imprinting apparatus, which consisted of a circular track on which a painted wooden model of an adult duck could be pulled mechanically ahead of the ducklings. The decoy also was wired so that it could emit a tape-recorded sound (a human voice saying "gock, gock, gock") while moving around the track.

By experimentally manipulating various conditions of this experimental test situation, Hess and his colleagues were able to show that, indeed, there seemed to be a critical period lasting about thirty hours after birth during which the ducklings were imprinted most readily. The readiness for imprinting seemed to

Konrad Lorenz play-
ing "Mother Goose"
to a hatch of goslings
that have imprinted
on him.

Thomas McAvoy, Life Magazine, © 1955, Time, Inc.

reach a peak for these ducklings at about sixteen hours after birth (see Figure 6.3). The investigators also found that they could imprint ducklings by using only a silent moving object, and even by using sound alone. Thus ducklings seemed ready to imprint on both visual and auditory cues associated with the mother. It also was found that the imprinting followed a *law of effort*; that is, the strength of imprinting was affected greatly by the amount of effort the ducklings exerted in following the object on which they imprinted. Ducklings were imprinted more strongly, for example, if they had to climb over obstacles or walk a longer distance to keep up with the moving model. This was not simply a matter of being exposed to the model for a longer period of time, because longer exposure did not increase the strength of imprinting if the amount of effort was held constant.

Other research has shown that in some species, at least, the imprinting process begins even before young birds hatch out. Controlled studies have shown that in these species the young birds can hear their mother's vocalizations through their shells, and they become imprinted on these auditory cues. This helps them to direct their following behavior to the appropriate visual target of the mother after they hatch (Gottlieb, 1977). Indeed, experimental studies conducted by Hess (1973) in natural field settings with mallards have revealed that there is an intricate ballet of reciprocal influence—even before hatching—of calls made by ducklings and their mother. In the wild, a brooding female mallard gives maternal clucks to her unhatched clutch of eggs during the latter part of the incubation period. The maternal clucks influence the hatching behavior of the ducklings and help to ensure that all hatch out at about the same time. Conversely, the mother is stimulated to make her maternal vocalizations by the sounds made by the ducklings from inside the eggs.

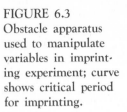

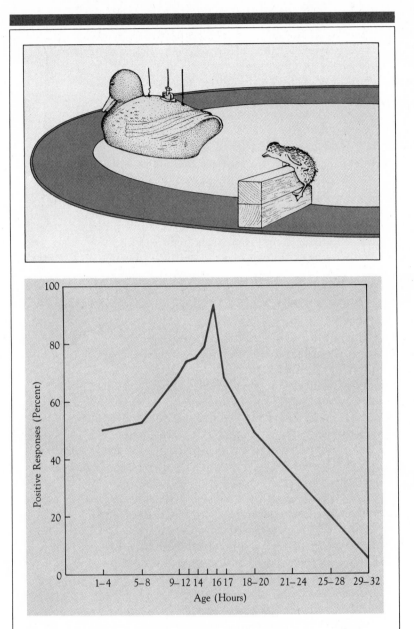

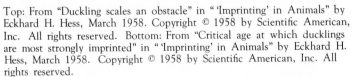

Top: From "Duckling scales an obstacle" in " 'Imprinting' in Animals" by
Eckhard H. Hess, March 1958. Copyright © 1958 by Scientific American,
Inc. All rights reserved. Bottom: From "Critical age at which ducklings
are most strongly imprinted" in " 'Imprinting' in Animals" by Eckhard H.
Hess, March 1958. Copyright © 1958 by Scientific American, Inc. All
rights reserved.

Related Factors in Human Development   There does not appear to be anything in human development exactly like the imprinting of young ducklings and geese. For one thing, the formation of social attachments of the young to their mother must occur much more quickly in these species of birds than in human beings, for whom there is a prolonged period of infantile dependency. This prolonged period of dependency (a point to which we will return later) permits attachment to be established over a much longer period of time, and at a more leisurely pace. However, developmental phenomena and principles similar to those illustrated by imprinting in ducklings do appear in human development.

Developmental psychologists such as Bowlby (1969) have pointed out that a number of behaviors in human infants make greater sense if viewed in terms of their evolutionary adaptiveness. For example, an infant's fear and crying in the presence of strangers or upon separation from the parents in a strange place may be a nuisance when the parents want the baby to smile at his namesake, rich old uncle Ezra, or when the parents are unable to enjoy the gala night out because the baby is terrified of the new babysitter. But during most of human evolution, stranger and separation anxiety are likely to have increased significantly an infant's chances of survival, for these behaviors seem to be present in nearly all infants, and their maturation is under a high degree of genetic control.

Prenatal Imprinting in the Human Fetus?   If small microphones are inserted into the uterus beside a human fetus's head, recordings indicate that the fetus is exposed continuously to loud noises. Besides occasional rumbles from the mother's stomach, the fetus constantly hears the rhythmical rushing noise produced by blood passing through the mother's uterus in tempo with the mother's heartbeats (Grimwade, 1971; MacFarlane, 1977; Walker, Grimwade, & Wood, 1971). Most sounds coming from outside the mother's body are diminished greatly before they reach the fetus, and only extremely loud external sounds are likely to be perceived through the background of intrauterine noises.

Pediatrician Lee Salk has suggested that the human fetus might imprint on this rhythmical sound and might be comforted by similar sounds after birth. Salk conducted an experiment in which newborn infants were assigned either to an experimental group that heard tape recordings of an adult heart beating eighty times per minute or to a control group not exposed to heartbeat sounds. After a period of four days, the newborns exposed to the sound of the heartbeats were found to have cried less and to have gained more weight than did the controls (Salk, 1973; MacFarlane, 1977). A second experimental group, which listened to heartbeats with a rate of 120 beats per minute, seemed to become distressed rather than soothed. Salk also pointed out that mothers tend to hold their babies so that the baby's head is on the left side of her body, closer to her heart and the presumably comforting sound of her heartbeat. Salk found that this seemed to be true regardless of whether the mother was right- or left-handed, and a survey of historical paintings showed that in most of them the baby's head was, indeed, held on the left. Perhaps mothers themselves become conditioned to hold the baby on the left side because they discover (not necessarily at the level of verbal awareness) that this is more likely to comfort the infant. Salk's hypothesis is still controversial (for example, it is possible that other sounds may also be comforting to the newborn), but at the least it has spurred new research into the intriguing possibility of prenatal conditioning in infants.

A Critical Period for Language Acquisition?   The example of critical periods in the development of other vertebrates has sparked interest in whether there might also be critical periods in human psychological development. Special attention has been focused on the possibility that such a period might exist for the acquisition of language (see Chapter 12). One specialist in language development, Eric Lenneberg, has proposed that there is such a critical period between late infancy and puberty. He proposed that if a youngster were not exposed to language during this period, the child would be unable to acquire language later.

One line of evidence supporting this idea might humorously be termed the *Henry Kissinger phenomenon,* after the former secretary of state, who, despite his excellent understanding of the English language, seems unable to speak English without a thick German accent. Kissinger did not come to the United States and begin to speak English until he was a teen-ager, and his case illustrates a remarkably general phenomenon. That is, most people seem to find it quite difficult to speak a new language without an accent or with the same fluency as a native speaker if they first learn the language after puberty.

A given language uses certain phonemic distinctions that are not used in other languages, and if an individual does not use these distinctions, the childhood capacity to perceive the phonemic boundary is lost. For this reason, native speakers of Japanese, for example, have difficulty in distinguishing the English consonants *r* and *l*. Eimas (1975) notes that the problem appears to be not an inability to produce well-formed *r*'s and *l*'s but rather an inability to any longer hear the difference. The difficulty is, of course, reciprocal; adult speakers of English are likely to be equally bewildered by unfamiliar phonemic distinctions in Japanese.

Indeed, learning to speak a new language without an accent as an adult is so difficult that it has inspired such popular works of art as G. B. Shaw's *Pygmalion,* later adapted into the musical *My Fair Lady.* By contrast, children who learn a second language before puberty are often able to speak it with native fluency and are likely to acquire conversational skills much more readily than adults. This sometimes is a source of chagrin for parents who move to a foreign country and find their young children conversing fluently while they themselves must struggle with the new language. A more important implication, however, is the value of teaching conversational skills in foreign languages at the primary school level, rather than waiting until high school or college, as is still a widespread practice in the United States.

A second line of evidence supporting a critical period for language acquisition (and the value of teaching second languages before puberty) comes from research concerning the effects of brain injuries and diseases at different ages (for example, bullet wounds, accidents, strokes, and surgical removal of brain tissue containing tumors or sites causing epileptic seizures; see Penfield & Roberts, 1959). These and other findings indicate that, for most people, the left hemisphere of the brain plays the dominant role in language functions. If the language centers of the left hemisphere are damaged severely or removed *after* puberty, most people find it extremely difficult to learn to speak again. But if the damage occurs *before* puberty, the chances of recovering normal language functions are greatly improved. In general, the earlier the brain injury occurs before puberty, the better the chances of language recovery. Brain development seems to be more flexible—more "plastic"—earlier in development, when regions of the right hemisphere are more able to take over the functions that would normally be handled by the left side of the brain.

The most clear-cut test of Lenneberg's hypothesis regarding a critical period for language acquisition would be to rear a child from birth without any exposure to language until after he or she had passed puberty—at which time an attempt would be made to teach the child language. Such a research project would obviously be unethical. Sometimes, however, tragic cases of children who have suffered extreme parental neglect constitute natural experiments that can yield much the same information. One such case involves Genie, a girl whose childhood was as tragic in human terms as it was fascinating to researchers probing the secrets of language development (Curtis et al., 1975; Fromkin et al., 1974).

Genie's father had severe emotional problems, which led him, among other things, to conclude mistakenly that his infant daughter was mentally retarded and should be confined to a back room of his house. For the first fourteen years of her life Genie was kept under conditions of extreme deprivation. Because the father had a phobia about loud conversation and insisted that everyone speak in whispers, Genie was exposed to virtually no language until she was rescued. Eventually, Genie came to the attention of welfare authorities and was placed with foster parents. Genie also became the subject of perhaps the most intensive study and therapy ever given to one person by behavioral scientists.

By the time Genie was rescued and began to receive exposure to language, she had already passed puberty, the point that Lenneberg had hypothesized to be the upper boundary of the critical period for language acquisition. In fact, Genie was able with instruction to learn a considerable amount of language. By age eighteen, for example, she was able to produce simple sentences. This case, therefore, seems to disprove the strong version of Lenneberg's hypothesis; it appears that it *is* possible for a person to learn language even if not exposed to it until after puberty. However, Genie does appear to provide some support for a weaker version of the hypothesis. Whereas evidence to date indicates that in most normal people language learning and processing is mediated increasingly with age by structures in the left hemisphere, in Genie all language processing seems to be performed by the *right* hemisphere. It is as though the areas in the left hemisphere that normally would be involved in processing language either atrophied or were recruited for other functions.

Sleeper Effects of Early Experience

The "sleeper" effect, in which the impact of an early experience does not manifest itself until later in development, is well known in the case of anatomical development. One example that has caused much recent concern involves diethylstilbesterol (DES), a synthetic estrogen or female sex hormone that was administered in the past to pregnant women with a history of miscarriages. Recently, evidence has come to light indicating that, when given during pregnancy, DES may have a tragic sleeper effect on female offspring, increasing their risk of subsequently developing vaginal cancer as adults. Moreover, when they themselves become pregnant as adults, these young women seem to be at somewhat greater risk of having an unfavorable pregnancy outcome, such as a miscarriage or premature delivery (Barnes et al., 1980). Thus the exposure of these women to DES even before birth produced changes leading in some cases to the development of reproductive problems or cancer two or three decades later.

Another example of the sleeper effects of early learning experiences on later behavior is seen in the legendary homing behavior of salmon, which, after as many as five years at sea, return to the exact stream where they were born in order to spawn and produce a new generation. As two scientists who have studied this instinctual behavior note, "No one who has seen a 100-pound Chinook salmon fling itself into the air again and again until it is exhausted in a vain effort to surmount a waterfall can fail to marvel at the strength of the instinct that draws the salmon upriver to the stream where it was born" (Hasler & Larsen, 1967, p. 20). Perhaps even more remarkable than the strength of this homing behavior is its accuracy. Canadian researchers who marked nearly half a million young salmon born in a tributary of the Fraser River later recovered over ten thousand of these fish in the same stream—after they had migrated to the ocean and returned; yet not a single marked fish was ever found to have returned to any other stream.

How can salmon so unerringly find their way back to their home stream, which may be up to a thousand miles from the ocean? Research (Hasler & Larsen, 1967; Schol et al., 1976) indicates that the secret to the mysterious homing behavior of salmon lies in their sensitive sense of smell, which allows them to detect certain chemicals in water in concentrations as low as one part per million. Newly hatched salmon imprint on the distinctive odor of organic materials in the stream where they are born. During their return migration to spawn, they apparently smell their way to their birthplace, drawn by the scent of the distinctive odors on which they imprinted. This research has important implications, both for the survival of salmon species and for the multimillion dollar fishing industry and its workers. Knowledge of the imprinting basis of migratory behavior should help to save the salmon by guiding them to breeding streams that are not obstructed by dams or fouled by pollution.

Effects of Social Deprivation

Perhaps the most famous and influential research on the effects of social deprivation on psychological development is that of psychologist Harry Harlow and his colleagues (including his wife Margaret) at the University of Wisconsin Primate Laboratory. Since the 1930s, Harlow has conducted research on the development of learning abilities in rhesus monkeys and on social factors influencing that development.

One major line of Harlow's research concerned the manner in which infant primates become attached to their parents. Before Harlow's research, a major school of scientific thought had contended that an infant's attachment to the mother developed largely as a result of the infant's associating the mother with the satisfaction of basic physical needs such as hunger and thirst. In the terminology of learning theory, the mother became an acquired or conditioned reinforcer by virtue of having been associated with more primary reinforcers such as food provided during nursing. Other workers, by contrast, suggested that attachment was influenced by a wider range of interactions with the parents, including cuddling, clinging, mutual staring, and vocalization.

Because it would be difficult both practically and ethically to conduct human experiments on this subject, Harlow (1973a) began an investigation using infant rhesus monkeys. Actually, his research on this topic was initiated by a serendipitous discovery. To reduce the incidence of infection, Harlow had originally adopted the practice of rearing young monkeys in isolation from their mothers, feeding them from a bottle and providing a soft gauze diaper on the floor of the cage for comfort. The infant monkeys quickly soiled their diapers, which were changed daily. However, it soon became apparent that the infants had formed strong attachments to the diapers, much like the legendary attachment of Linus (in the *Peanuts* comic strip) to his blanket.

Experiments with Surrogate Mothers   Spurred by this observation, Harlow set out to compare the relative importance of bodily contact and nursing in the development of the infant's attachment to its mother. To do so, he constructed artificial, or *surrogate*, mothers. In early experiments, two such mothers were used: one with a welded wire surface, the other a soft terry-cloth material to which the infant rhesus could cling readily. A wire and a terry-cloth mother were placed with each infant, but in half the cages (chosen at random) the nursing bottle was attached to the wire mother, and in the other half it was attached to the terry-cloth mother. Subsequent observation indicated that, regardless of which surrogate mother contained the source of food, the infant monkeys became "attached" to the terry-cloth mother, who provided greater "contact comfort." Even when the floor of the cage was warmed with an electric blanket, as soon as the infants were able to climb, they spent much more time clinging to the terry-cloth mother and were much more likely to go to her for comfort when confronted with a strange and fearful object (for example, a mechanical teddy bear beating a toy drum). Finally, infants who rushed to the cloth mother did, indeed, tend to be comforted by her. Once emboldened by the reassurance of clinging to her surface, they would show much greater readiness to observe and even explore novel and initially frightening objects. For example, if placed in a large room filled with strange objects, the infant without its cloth mother present typically would huddle in terror in one corner of the room; but with the mother present, the infant rhesus was much more likely to explore the room and interact with the objects.

In sum, Harlow's research indicates that the comfort provided by bodily contact plays a major role in the development of the infant's attachments for its mother, whereas nursing plays little if any role. Other research indicates that

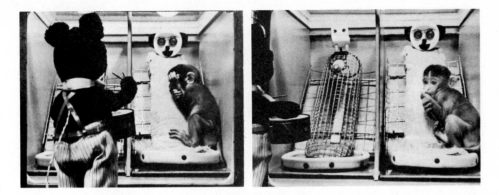

Given a choice between a wire and a terry-cloth mother surrogate, infant monkeys when frightened are much more likely to seek the contact comfort of the cloth than the wire mother, even though the wire mother has provided their food.

University of Wisconsin

clinging, bodily warmth, and movement of the mother are also characteristics that help to cement attachment of the infant rhesus to its mother, although the basic factor of bodily contact seems especially crucial.

Harlow's conclusions are largely supported by other lines of research. For example, studies of rhesus monkeys in their natural environment reveal the adaptive value of their innate tendency to seek out and cling to the warm pliable bodies of their mothers. If infants are to survive in the wild, they must stay close to their mothers, seeking them out in situations of danger and quickly learning to cling to their furry coats as the mothers move about or make a quick escape through the trees. Indeed, not long after birth, the young rhesus rides jockey-style astride the mother's back as she moves about. It appears that the factors that Harlow found to help establish attachment in the laboratory have rather obvious adaptive value in the wild. Indeed, they have been selected during evolutionary development for that reason.

Related Phenomena in Human Development   Analogous results regarding factors involved in attachment have been found in research with human infants. For example, studies in several countries have found that attachment of young infants to people around them was related most strongly to how readily the parents or other caretakers responded to the infants' cries for help or spontaneously initiated cuddling, vocalizing, and other kinds of social interaction with the infants. Who fed the baby and cared for an infant's basic physical needs seemed to be less important (Bowlby, 1969; Schaffer & Emerson, 1964). For example, in families in which the mother fed the baby but the father spent more time in other forms of social interaction with the infant, the baby tended to be more attached to the father. Other studies have shown that even newborns only a few days old are comforted by rocking and having a soft blanket they can cling to. Moreover, when confronted with a strange room filled with novel toys, human infants seek out bodily contact with the mother or other familiar caretaker as a source of emotional reassurance, using that person as a kind of "home base" for exploration. A strange room filled with novel toys typically provoked anxiety and crying when the parent was absent, but children enjoyed playful exploration when the parent was present—just as was true with rhesus infants.

Long-Term Effects of Deprivation   In later studies (Harlow & Harlow, 1973b; Harlow, Harlow, & Suomi, 1977), Harlow and his colleagues studied the long-term effects of social deprivation on cognitive and social development. The effects of deprivation of social contact with real mothers, with other juveniles of similar age, and even with father monkeys were studied systematically. The effects of being reared in even total isolation from other monkeys seemed to have little consequence in terms of the capacity to learn nonsocial tasks such as learning "sets." In acquiring a new learning set, a monkey must learn that a similar concept or strategy is involved in an entire succession of individual problems. For example, in one type of learning-set problem, the monkey's task might be to learn that, for a given set of problems—if presented with three objects, two similar and one different—the correct choice is always the "odd" or different item. Social deprivation seemed to affect performance adversely only on the most difficult and complex nonsocial learning tasks.

By contrast, the social effects of deprivation—especially if prolonged and involving isolation from all kinds of social contact—were devastating. As adults,

The effects of social deprivation—especially if prolonged and involving complete isolation—are devastating, particularly during infancy and the juvenile period.

University of Wisconsin

such male monkeys were unsuccessful in attempts at mating; females who had been impregnated rejected their infants; and social play and defense behaviors were severely disturbed. Other striking behavioral disturbances are described by Harlow and Harlow (1973b):

> As a group they exhibit abnormalities of behavior rarely seen in animals born in the wild and brought to the laboratory as preadolescents or adolescents. . . . [The isolate-reared monkeys] sit in their cages and stare fixedly into space, circle their cages in a repetitive stereotyped manner and clasp their heads in their hands or arms and rock for long periods of time. . . . Occasionally such behavior may become punitive and the animal may chew and tear at its body until it bleeds. . . . Similar symptoms of emotional pathology are observed in deprived children in orphanages and withdrawn adolescents and adults in mental hospitals. (p. 110)

Although the effects of social deprivation on the social development of rhesus monkeys are rather complex, depending on the particular social skill measured, Harlow's general finding is that peer interaction is, if anything, more important than maternal care for normal social development. Interaction with peers can compensate to a considerable extent for disturbances in social development that result from being reared without a real mother. The length of social isolation is also a crucial variable; longer periods of isolation during infancy and the juvenile period produce increasingly abnormal development.

Effects of Early Experience on Brain Development

Remarkably enough, early perceptual and learning experiences have been shown to affect not only behavior but also the development of the physical properties of the brain itself. In a classic research program carried out over the last two decades at the University of California in Berkeley, Rosenzweig, Bennet, and Diamond (1973) as well as other investigators have studied how various aspects of brain development in rodents are affected by the rodents being reared in different environments. Their typical research design uses many litters of rats. Three male rats from each litter are assigned randomly. One member remains in a standard laboratory cage, the second rat is placed in a more experientially "impoverished" condition, and the third littermate is put in a more stimulating or "enriched" environment (see Figure 6.4). The standard laboratory cage (Figure 6.4a) houses a few rats along with plenty of food and water in all experimental conditions. In the enriched condition (Figure 6.4c), each rat shares a large cage with several other rats and is exposed to a variety of "toys" (such as ladders, swings, children's toys); the toys are changed daily so that the rats are exposed constantly to novel stimuli. Finally, in the impoverished condition (Figure 6.4b), rats are housed alone in cages with neither toys nor other rats with which to interact. After a period of time (ranging from 25 to 105 days in various experiments), the rats were sacrificed, and various characteristics of their brains were examined. Rearing conditions had significant effects on a number of characteristics. For example, compared with rats reared in the impoverished condition, those raised in the enriched condition developed slightly heavier brains, with the weight gain being concentrated in the cortex, especially

FIGURE 6.4
Three experimental
environments: (a)
standard, (b) impover-
ished, and (c)
enriched; rearing con-
ditions had significant
effects on brain
weight, development
of glial cells, and
metabolic activity.

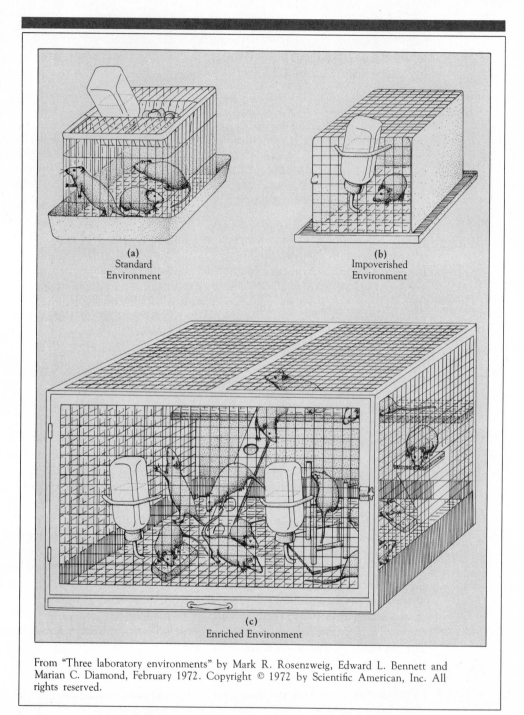

(a)
Standard
Environment

(b)
Impoverished
Environment

(c)
Enriched Environment

From "Three laboratory environments" by Mark R. Rosenzweig, Edward L. Bennett and
Marian C. Diamond, February 1972. Copyright © 1972 by Scientific American, Inc. All
rights reserved.

in certain regions such as the occipital area. (The gains in weight were moderate—between 5 and 10 percent in various studies—but they were nonetheless
real and were replicated rather consistently in over a dozen different experi-

ments.) Rats from the enriched condition also developed more glial cells (which help to insulate the impulse-conducting fibers of neurons and to transport materials between neurons and capillaries) and showed greater metabolic activity in their brains.

Complementary studies at the University of Illinois (Greenough, 1977) have shown that environmental enrichment increased the subsequent ability of mice to learn a maze, as well as increasing the number of synapses between different neurons. (*Synapses,* as described in Chapter 4, are the junctions between different neurons, across which the neurons communicate by releasing molecules of chemical neurotransmitters.) The great Spanish neuroanatomist Ramon y Cajal picturesquely but aptly described synapses as "protoplasmic kisses" between neurons. The increased number of synaptic connections produced by environmental enrichment appears to affect different regions differentially, depending on the specific functions of the brain region examined and the nature of the enrichment stimulation provided. In the standard enrichment condition, cortical areas concerned with processing of visual information show the greatest increases in the number of synapses. This probably reflects the fact that the enrichment procedures emphasized visual stimulation. As Greenough notes, the increased number of synapses resulting from enrichment is what one would expect if "the organizing information imparted by the environment during development were stored by the brain through the formation of new connections between nerve cells" (p. 88).

Rosenzweig and associates (1973) note that environmental enrichment can produce just as great an increase in brain weight in fully mature rats as it does in young ones, although a longer period of enrichment is required to produce a maximum effect in adults. Other studies by Rosenzweig and coworkers suggest that the changes in brain structure associated with enriched environments do not result from such nonspecific influences as stress or handling and thus probably reflect the actual effects of more extensive learning experiences. However, there is still need for some caution on this point. Rosenzweig has also shown that even the so-called enriched laboratory environment is itself a condition of experiential deprivation compared with the kind of natural environment rats might encounter in the wild. For example, rats reared in a seminatural environment composed of an outdoor enclosure 30-feet square with a screen top and a concrete base covered with soil reverted to burrowing—"something their ancestors, which had lived in laboratory cages, had not done for more than 100 generations" (p. 119). Rats kept in this seminatural enclosure for a month showed greater brain growth than did those in the enriched laboratory condition, indicating that even the enriched condition is still relatively impoverished when compared with the natural environment.

Rosenzweig and associates (1973) properly urge caution in extrapolating the results of their research to human development. It is, of course, always risky to generalize from one species to another. Still, they note that as far back as 1892 a report was published on the post-mortem study of the brain of a deaf-mute woman named Laura Bridgeman. In her brain, the regions of the cortex that normally process visual and auditory information were abnormally thin and lacking in the normal patterns of convolution, or folding. By contrast, other areas of her cortex seemed to have developed normally, including areas specialized for processing the sensation of touch (which typically is developed to a normal or even superior degree in deaf-mutes). These investigators suggested that more careful and large-scale studies of this kind might help to determine whether "heightened employment of a sense leads to supranormal development of the associated brain region. Would musicians as a group, for example, show an enhanced development of the auditory cortex?" (p. 124). Perhaps an even more crucial question would be whether early sensory deprivation may produce an irreversible stunting in brain growth. Studies of the brains of infants and young children who were exposed to varying conditions of sensory stimulation and had died at varying ages for other reasons such as accidents might yield information on the magnitude and permanence of the effects of early sensory stimulation on brain development.

An interesting study carried out by Kagan and Klein (1973) in rural villages of Guatemala suggests that development of the human infant may be more resilient to the effects of early deprivation than many scientists had feared. They found that infants in poor Indian families in many of these villages were normally reared under conditions that by Western standards constituted extreme deprivation. For example, infants routinely were kept inside small shacks for most of the day. The shacks were typically dimly lit (having no electrical lighting). Moreover, families were too poor to afford any toys, and the mothers (typically lacking knowledge of birth control) often were occupied with caring for older siblings and had little time to stimulate their infants. Not surprisingly, these infants typically scored months behind Western babies of the same age on standardized tests of mental development. Yet when the older, school-age, children in these same villages (who *presumably* had grown up as infants under similar conditions) were tested, their development was no longer as retarded as that of the infants, and their test performance approached that of American children on comparable tests of cognitive abilities (though average performance still lagged somewhat behind that of American children of the same age). These results and others suggest that, while the effects of early experience are important, early retardation of development resulting from deprivation can be reversed considerably. Children who get off to a slow start because of an unstimulating environment can catch up in large part, so long as they are subsequently given stimulating environments rather than being neglected because they have been stigmatized as hopelessly retarded.

A second and even clearer implication of such research concerns the way in which most Western societies treat other animals—particularly members of wild species. Most existing zoo environments, including even the relatively more enlightened wild animal parks and aquariums where animals have considerable territory in which to move about rather than being confined in a small cage, constitute cruel forms of environmental deprivation. As Lorenz (1965) notes, a gruesome but rather typical effect of this kind of ignorant rearing of wild animals is "the disintegration of social inhibitions. It is known all too well by all animal breeders and zoo men that carnivorous and omnivorous animals, when breeding in captivity, are prone to eat their own young. Saying that they do so 'as often as not' is hardly an overstatement" (p. 94).

Most zoos are a cruel form of environmental deprivation that may even endanger the ability of some species to survive.

Julie O'Neil

It follows that the people who run such zoos and parks—and the people who visit and support them, however well intentioned—are really guilty partners in the ignorant, cruel, and inhumane exploitation of other creatures. Worse, in many cases they are endangering the very existence of species. Even if one regards the other species as having no intrinsic value of their own, these wild species are the product of hundreds of millions of years of evolutionary adaptations to varying ecological conditions. These biochemical, anatomical, and behavioral adaptations—and the scientific information and potential economic and aesthetic benefits they contain—are literally priceless treasures for all the world's people, including countless future generations. It would be a great tragedy to continue to permit these treasures to be squandered, now that we have the knowledge to prevent it.

One solution would be to replace present zoos with true wild animal preserves. New lands could be purchased and converted into wilderness areas where wild species' natural habitats could be preserved and protected from destruction by commerical development and animals could be permitted to develop normally in their natural environments. If designed in collaboration with ethologists and other specialists in animal development, such parks can provide the opportunity for scientists to study—and laypeople to observe—wild species' development in natural surroundings, rather than ignorantly gawking at imprisoned creatures whose physical and psychological development is grossly disturbed by conditions of environmental deprivation.

Effects of Early Experience on Human Development: Early and Varied

The quality and quantity of sensory stimulation and opportunities for learning affect many major areas of behavioral and even anatomical development in human beings. Some important lines of research illustrating the effects on children of variations in parental care are described at greater length in Chapter 7. However, two points should be emphasized here. First, the effects of perceptual stimulation on development begin at a very young age. For example, a number of researchers have shown that providing additional sensory stimulation (such as gentle rocking or colorful visual patterns and mobiles suspended within range of the infants' maximum visual acuity) to premature infants still in their incubators can accelerate sensorimotor development significantly (Cornell & Gottfried, 1976). Second, social deprivation can affect not only the behavioral development of young children but also their physical growth and even survival itself.

Perhaps the most amazing effects of social deprivation are on physical growth. Gardner (1973) notes that pediatricians have long suspected that the deprivation of affection and stimulation experienced by infants in orphanages and foundling homes might be responsible in large part for the terribly high mortality rates that historically have been found in many of them. As early as 1915 a Baltimore physician found that, despite apparently adequate physical care, 90 percent of the infants in foundling homes were dying within one year of admission. Although poor care before reaching the homes and greater exposure to disease may have contributed to these high mortality rates, the fact that the infants died despite adequate physical care seemed to implicate emotional deprivation.

Research during and after World War II provided additional evidence that infants deprived of adult love and attention might suffer from a stunting of physical growth—what Gardner (1973) and others have termed *deprivation dwarfism*. For example, it was found that when infants were separated from their mothers, they often became depressed, apathetic, and lethargic. In addition, such infants were unusually likely to show signs of physiological distress, such as diarrhea, failure to gain weight normally, and persistent respiratory diseases of unknown cause. (A not uncommon reason for such early separation of an infant from the parents arises when the child must undergo surgery or other medical treatment requiring hospitalization. Traditionally, this has meant the infant would be separated from the parents during most of the time spent in the hospital. However, with increasing recognition of the possible psychological and psychosomatic effects of such separation, progressive hospital administrators are beginning to experiment with arrangements that allow the parents to "room in" with their infants or young children during the period of hospitalization.)

Lack of adult affection and attention can jeopardize not only a child's behavioral development, but even physical growth and survival itself.

Erika Stone, Peter Arnold, Inc.

Particularly influential was the report by René Spitz and Katherine Wolf (Spitz, 1946; Spitz & Wolf, 1946), who examined the development of ninety-one infants from foundling homes in the United States and Canada. They found that these infants rather consistently displayed not only signs of emotional distress and depression but also sleep disturbances and poor weight gain. Most shocking, however, was the fact that thirty-four of the infants actually died—despite the fact that, so far as Spitz and Wolf could determine, they had received excellent nutrition and medical care. Even those infants who managed to live past the first year almost always suffered severe physical retardation.

Many physiologists and psychologists have been skeptical that deprivation of parental care and affection could impair physical growth and threaten survival because they could not see what causal mechanisms might mediate such an effect. However, research over the last two or three decades has provided evidence for physiological processes by which emotional and sensory deprivation in infants could disturb their physical growth and resistance to disease. One such process may involve the depression produced by separation from the parent to whom the infant is attached, and by the general lack of sensory stimulation normally provided by parents. These emotional states, in turn, disrupt normal digestion. A dramatic illustration of this is provided by the case of a fifteen-month-old girl who had been born with a defective esophagus. To make adequate feeding possible, a surgical opening had been made in the baby's stomach through which a feeding tube was inserted so that the mother could supply a nutrient formula by means of a syringe. Although the mother had apparently been very careful to follow the prescribed feeding schedule, her anxiety about disturbing the feeding tube had led her to avoid handling the child. As a result, by fifteen months, the infant showed signs of physical and mental retardation, sleep disturbances, and apathetic withdrawal. Moreover, her stomach was secreting abnormally low levels of hydrochloric acid and the enzyme pepsin, which are important for normal digestion. After being brought to the hospital and receiving increased attention and stimulation, the infant showed remarkable improvement in both emotional states and physical growth, despite the fact that there was no apparent change in the amount of food consumed by the child. In addition, the presence of the feeding tube made it possible to examine the immediate effects of changes in emotional state on stomach secretions. Depression and withdrawal in the infant reduced her hydrochloric acid production, while more active and positive states increased it. These results were consistent with other findings.

Other studies have been conducted on children who were both abnormally short and thin for their age, and in whose cases no clear medical causes could be found (such as lesions of those endocrine glands involved in secretion of growth-regulating hormones). Such children were likely to have a family history of emotional disturbances and rejection by at least one of the parents. Moreover, Gardner (1973) notes that studies of such infants reveal that even the growth of bone tissue can be retarded markedly—a result consistent with the earlier experimental findings that chimpanzees reared in the dark for long periods showed retardation of bone growth as well as disturbances of visual development.

A disturbance in sleep patterns may also play a significant role in producing deprivation dwarfism. Gardner notes that recent research has shown that in normal children and adults the greatest secretion of the growth hormone somatotrophin occurs during the first hour or two of sleep. Moreover, disturbances of both hormone secretion and sleep patterns have been found repeatedly in infants suffering from the deprivation dwarfism syndrome. Finally, it is well established that physiological pathways exist whereby sensory stimuli can affect the secretion of various hormones. The hypothalamic centers of the brain lie in very close proximity to the pituitary gland—the "master" endocrine gland whose trophic hormones help regulate the amount of hormones secreted into the blood stream by other endocrine glands. In turn, the amount of such trophic hormones secreted by the pituitary is influenced by "releasing factors" produced by the hypothalamus and carried from it via a special set of blood vessels to the adjacent pituitary. Experimental evidence in support of this view comes from studies of laboratory rats. Maternal deprivation caused a reduction of growth hormone levels, which was reversed rapidly when the rat pups were returned to their mothers (Kuhn, Butler, & Schanberg, 1978).

In sum, there is persuasive if not conclusive evidence implicating emotional deprivation and resulting sleep disturbance as causal contributors to the syndrome of deprivation dwarfism. In any case, as Gardner notes, it seems clear that deprivation dwarfism presents "a concrete example—an 'experiment of nature' so to speak—that demonstrates the delicacy, complexity, and crucial importance of infant-parent interaction" (p. 107)

Summary

1. The quality of the prenatal environment is one of the most important influences on development. Of particular importance are the many agents that are *teratogenic*, that is, that produce congenital deformities. There is often a critical period during which a developing system is vulnerable to a particular teratogenic agent. Developing systems tend to be most vulnerable when they are growing most rapidly.

2. Most biomedical experts advise pregnant women to avoid *all* drugs when they are pregnant. This includes even drugs that normally do not have serious side effects or that have been prescribed by a physician. One reason thalidomide maimed so many children was precisely because it was thought to be so safe and to have so few side effects on adults. The safest course during pregnancy is to avoid all drugs, including alcohol, tobacco, caffeine, and marijuana except for overriding medical reasons.

3. The critical period of vulnerability to many agents occurs during the early weeks of embryological development, when the basic structural foundations of many organs are being formed. A teratogenic agent may thus damage a fetus even before a woman has missed her period and realizes she is pregnant; therefore, women should avoid taking drugs even when they are at risk of becoming pregnant.

4. Mothers who smoke have a higher risk of having stillbirths and low-birth-weight infants. Because cigarette smoke contains high concentrations of carbon monoxide and cancer-producing agents, smoking by fathers as well as by mothers may be harmful to their children. The incidence of respiratory infection in infants has been found to be higher if their parents smoke.

5. Many infectious diseases can have harmful effects on the fetus. Among the most teratogenic is *rubella*, or German measles, which is especially harmful if contracted during the first three months of pregnancy. Prospective mothers should be tested to determine whether they are immune to rubella. If they are not immune, they should see a gynecologist about being vaccinated. Once a woman has become pregnant, it is too late to be vaccinated. It is prudent for pregnant women to avoid exposure to people who are known to have rubella or other viral infections.

6. *Toxoplasmosis*, a disease caused by a protozoan parasite, is a serious threat to the fetus if contracted by the mother during pregnancy. Pregnant women and young children should avoid eating rare or poorly cooked meat and should avoid handling raw meat or soil—particularly soil that may be contaminated by cat feces.

7. Western countries are undergoing a serious epidemic of venereal diseases, particularly gonorrhea and syphilis. These diseases are important causes of many illnesses, including blindness, retardation, and other defects in offspring infected during pregnancy. Although most cases of gonorrhea and syphilis can be controlled readily with antibiotics, these diseases rank first and third among reportable communicable diseases in the United States. Important reasons for this are widespread ignorance and myths about VD, as well as the insidious nature of VD symptoms.

8. The risk of damage to a fetus or to the genetic material of a prospective parent seems to be proportional to the amount of radiation received. Any amount of radiation therefore carries some risk, making it important to avoid any unnecessary exposure, whether the source be nuclear fallout or diagnostic x rays.

9. Emotional stress in pregnant women—particularly prolonged interpersonal conflict—may increase the risk of obstetrical complications and poor development after birth. The effects of maternal stress on the fetus may be mediated by hormones that pass across the placenta, and by a reduction in the supply of blood and oxygen to the fetus.

10. Infants of very low birthweight (less than 2,000 grams) seem to be at great risk for poor development after birth. Low birthweight and short gestation may have different effects on development.

11. *Imprinting* is the process by which young animals tend to follow and become attached to a parental figure during a critical period shortly after birth. Ducklings imprint on the sound of the mother's voice even before they hatch out. A human fetus may imprint on the rhythmical sound of blood pulsing through the uterus, but further research is needed to confirm this.

12. Several lines of evidence suggest that in human development there may be a critical period, lasting roughly from infancy to puberty, during which a new language can be learned most readily.

13. Early experiences can have long-delayed, or sleeper, effects on later development. Examples of sleeper effects include the increased risk of vaginal cancer in women whose mothers took the drugs DES during pregnancy and the ability of adult salmon to return to the stream where they were born by following its distinctive scent, on which they were imprinted.

14. Experiments in which infant monkeys were reared with artificial mothers show the importance of contact comfort in the development of infants' attachment to their mothers. Maternal deprivation produces severe disturbances in social development, and deprivation of peer contact has even more serious effects.

15. Rearing rats under conditions of perceptual enrichment or deprivation affects not only subsequent learning ability but the size of the brain and the number of synaptic connections. Such research indicates that zoos, which subject animals to social and perceptual deprivation, should be replaced with wilderness preserves in which species can develop under natural conditions.

16. The effects of perceptual stimulation in human beings begin at a very young age. Providing additional stimulation to premature infants enhances their sensorimotor development.

17. Cross-cultural studies suggest that many children whose early development has been retarded because of an unstimulating environment may be able to in large part catch up, provided they subsequently are given stimulating environments.

18. Infants deprived of adult love and attention may suffer from a stunting of physical growth termed *deprivation dwarfism*. Deprived infants, even when

receiving adequate nutrition and physical care, also show increased susceptibility to infection and death—effects related to emotional distress that
disrupts normal patterns of sleep and growth hormone secretion.

Selected Readings

The Boston Children's Medical Center Staff. *Pregnancy, Birth and the New Born Baby: A
Complete Guide for Parents and Parents-to-Be.* Boston: Delacorte Press/Seymour
Lawrence, 1972. (Available in paperback.) This book provides a comprehensive
guide to pregnancy, childbirth, and the first six weeks of an infant's life, distilling the
collective wisdom of specialists in obstetrics, gynecology, pediatrics, psychiatry, genetics, sociology, and developmental psychology.

Greenough, W. T., ed. *The Nature and Nurture of Behavior: Developmental Psychobiology.* San Francisco: W. H. Freeman, 1973. A paperback collecton of reprinted
articles from *Scientific American* that provide authoritative yet highly readable reviews of research in a variety of topics related to early learning and experience.
These articles provide greater coverage of a number of topics discussed in this chapter, such as deprivation dwarfism, social deprivation in monkeys, and the effects of
sensory deprivation or enrichment on brain development.

Levy, A. "The Thalidomide Generation." *Life* (July 26, 1968), 42–62. A fascinating
report about several children born with congenital defects because their mothers took
thalidomide during pregnancy.

Lorenz, K. *King Solomon's Ring.* New York: Thomas Y. Crowell, 1952. A best-selling
book by the Nobel Prize-winning ethologist in which he describes the development of
behavior in a variety of species of animals, many of which he has reared in his own
home. Lorenz makes many important points about the effects of early experience and
learning on development. Above all, this book is *fun* to read, as Lorenz describes
some of the most fascinating and humorous anecdotes from a lifetime of work with
animals.

Streissguth, A. P., S. Landesman-Dwyer, J. C. Martin, and D. W. Smith. "Teratogenic
Effects of Alcohol in Humans and Laboratory Animals. *Science, 209*: 353–361, 1980.
A scholarly review of human and animal research on the effects of alcohol during
pregnancy. Of particular interest is research indicating that even moderate social
drinking—not just heavy alcohol use—may be harmful to the fetus and should be
avoided by pregnant women.

Chapter 7

Family Influences

The patterns and roles of American family life and how they are changing

The relationships between parents and children—and between grandparents and children—and how they contribute to attachment, dependency, competence, self-reliance, and aggression

How an individual is affected by family composition, including birth order, the number and sex of siblings, whether parents are single or divorced, and family dynamics

Alternatives to the traditional family, such as childless marriages, multiple marriages, and collectives and communes

How relations between the generations can be improved and how communities can be structured to provide the best opportunities for all ages.

The Changing Family

Changing Patterns of Family Life
Changing Role of the Family in Society
Changing Patterns of Child Rearing

Parent-Child Interactions

Paternal and Maternal Influences
Attachment
Dependency
Competence and Self-Reliance
Aggression
Grandparent-Child Interactions

Family Composition

Birth Order
Number and Sex of Siblings
Single and Divorced Parents
Family Dynamics

Alternatives to the Traditional Family

Childless Marriages
Multiple Marriages
Collectives and Communes

Age Integration and Age Segregation

Intergenerational Relations
Retirement Communities
Age-Integrated Living Arrangements
Options for All Ages

Introduction

Individuals do not develop in isolation, for it is the nuclear family and the extended family that provide the most immediate context within which a child acquires the skills to cope with the environment. The models offered by particular family patterns and their demographic characteristics may differ widely. Opportunities, intensiveness of experience, and model credibility are much affected by a number of family characteristics. But the interaction among these characteristics and their impact on human development is not fixed either; rather, it is deeply embedded in the context of the larger society. Our consideration of family influences, therefore, must begin by examining the changing role and characteristics of the modal family in our society. We are concerned not only with changing patterns of family life but also with whether an individual develops differently within a nuclear family or a multigenerational one. We also must examine the cycle of differential patterns of child rearing.

Parent-child interactions need to be differentiated into father-child, mother-child, and grandparent-child components. In addition, attention must be given to such factors as attachment, dependency, aggression, competence, and self-reliance. Of course, familial influences are also affected by family composition, which has impact both on patterns of child rearing and on intergenerational relations.

It is apparent that there are both successful and unsuccessful families. To understand what differentiates them, we need to look at family tempos and rhythms, at patterns of successful family development, and at the crises that—if unresolved—may lead to separation, divorce, and family dissolution. Moreover, some current modes of crisis resolution require that we understand several alternatives to the traditional family.

Finally, as life-span developmentalists, we must explore how age integration and age segregation affect family life. Family influences are obviously important during the early stages of human development, but we must recognize that they persist and nourish or defeat our progress throughout life.

The Changing Family

To see how family life has changed over the past century, we will examine the basic patterns of family life, the role of the family in society, and patterns of child rearing.

Changing Patterns of Family Life

One by-product of the rapid sociocultural changes that have characterized Western societies during the past century is a dramatic change in patterns of family living. This affects the family roles of both sexes, the relationships between men and women, the nature of the interaction between parents and children, and the function of the extended family. Although there is no simple way to trace the specific causes of changes in family patterns, at least three

273

developments seem to be important antecedents: (1) changes in life expectancy, (2) changes in living arrangements, and (3) economic changes. How have such factors influenced our lives at home?

Changes in Life Expectancy The dramatic lengthening of life expectancy implies that, for almost everyone, there will be an adult-centered stage of life as well as the child-centered stage. A remarkable change in philosophy regarding the child's status in the family has resulted in a shift from the adult-oriented family of the past to the child-centered family of the present. However, this trend is a direct result of the family's expectation that the child-centered phase will, indeed, be followed by an extended period of life when adult concerns can again come to the fore. The effect of changes in life expectancy on the different phases of the family cycle is shown in Figure 7.1. Notice the progression from the past situation—in which children were present in the family setting throughout the parents' lives—to one in which an extensive postparental period prevails.

Related to the development of these distinct phases has been the shift from authoritarian to more permissive methods of child rearing. The child-centered

FIGURE 7.1
Shifts in median age
of husband and wife
at various stages of
the family cycle.

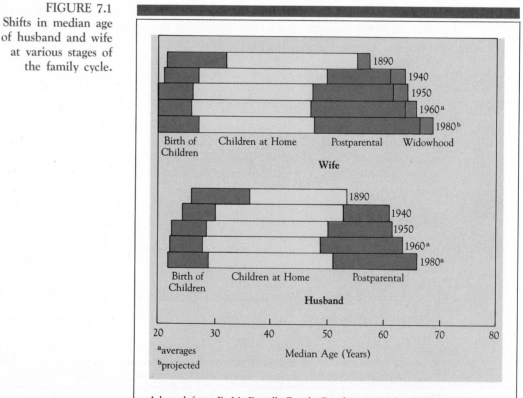

Adapted from E. M. Duvall, *Family Development*, 4th ed. Philadelphia: Lippincott, 1971. Reprinted with permission of J. B. Lippincott Company, Copyright © 1971.

family is willing to give children greater responsibility for their own behavior rather than insisting on the authoritarian adult controls characteristic of more traditional family settings.

Increased life expectancy has also led to an increase in the number of people who marry. This means further that the proportion of married older people will increase, so that there will be a substantial increment of married couples between sixty-five and seventy-five. Above that age—because of the differential life expectancy between men and women (sixty-nine years for men and seventy-seven years for women)—we would expect an increase in the number of widows (Atchley, 1977).

Other changes in family patterns that may be attributed indirectly to the realization of longer life expectancy include the increasing frequency of divorce, separation, and remarriage. In addition, ties with relatives have weakened as the nuclear family unit moves from one extended family setting to another (Brody, 1963).

Changes in Living Arrangements   The traditional *extended family* frequently involved a three-generation pattern within a single household, consisting of grandparents (who might no longer be working) and several young to middle-aged couples, each with one or more children of their own. By contrast, most families in contemporary society are *nuclear families* consisting of father, mother, and children. One result is that housing arrangements have changed to accommodate these patterns. While such changes may have increased the incidence of individually owned material objects, they have also increased individual responsibilities for housekeeping chores and child-rearing activities. In the extended family, for example, child-rearing activities were often preempted by a nonworking grandparent, whereas in the nuclear family fathers play a greater role, particularly when the mother works outside the home.

Nevertheless, many ties of the traditional extended family are maintained today by nuclear families. Frequently, family networks provide both economic help and support to each family unit. Such a network—sometimes called a *modified extended family* (Sussman & Burchinal, 1962)—has some of the characteristics of the traditional extended family in that it maintains relations among siblings and across generations. At the same time, this arrangement maintains the autonomy and mobility of the nuclear family. Surprisingly enough, it is frequently the younger generation that feels the greater responsibility for maintaining the intergenerational network (Hill, 1971).

Of particular interest for more and more individuals are the changes in living arrangements that result from divorce and remarriage. For example, some members of two previous nuclear families live during the week or most of the year as a single family unit, but on weekends and vacations the arrangements shift; children then visit the reconstructions of their earlier nuclear families or the extended families associated with earlier marital combinations.

Needless to say, a much more radical shift is made by family units that join communal living arrangements. Examples include the Oneida commune in upstate New York (Kanter, 1970) and the more familiar Israeli collective settlements, or *kibbutzim* (Rabkin & Rabkin, 1961). Although most communal arrangements reduce the primary family roles normally represented by the

Even in communes, which reduce the primary roles associated with parenthood, the family remains the basic source of intimacy.

Paul S. Conklin

parents, the family unit remains the primary source of intimacy for both parents and children.

A number of other changes that affect the quality of living arrangements should be noted. Most of these seem to be direct corollaries not only of the trend toward the nuclear family unit but also of the fact that such units have become smaller. This change has focused greater attention on the material quality of the home. In addition, the home no longer plays a major role as a work site. Finally, major recreational activities have shifted out of the home, and now the remaining family recreation often is restricted to television watching.

Economic Changes   Changes affecting family patterns are specifically related to the differential distribution between work and leisure, to greater job mobility, and to the dramatic increase in women's participation in the work force.

Marked social-class differences prevail in how work and leisure are valued. Moreover, these values themselves have changed during the past half century.

The privileged group that earlier was identified as the "leisure class" is now characterized much more by intensive occupational involvement (Maddox, 1966). It is typically those who have little chance to express themselves in their jobs—such as urban working-class blacks or those who live in remote rural environments like the Ozarks—who tend to define their major satisfaction through leisure rather than work-related activities (Hearn, 1971; Oliver, 1971). However, we should not assume that the increase in available leisure time necessarily means that more time is actually devoted to family-oriented leisure activities. The reduced average time for work-related activity may lead simply to a second work role, or it may make it possible for women who have child-rearing duties to take a time-consuming job.

Although the increase in the proportion of women in the work force has been dramatic at all ages, its impact on family development is particularly impressive for women with young children. Figure 7.2 shows a significant increase in the incidence of working mothers with preschool children over the quarter century from 1948 to 1967, as well as an increase in the incidence of working mothers with school-aged children. These figures have increased since 1967 to

FIGURE 7.2
Participation in the work force by mothers with children.

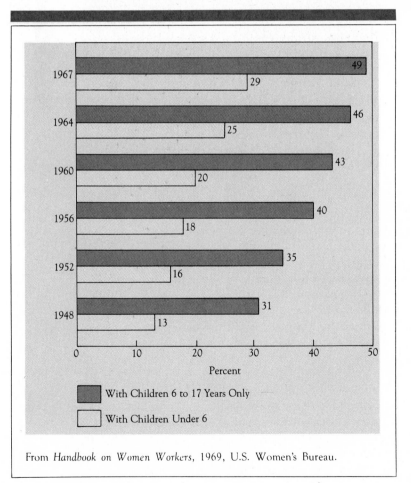

From *Handbook on Women Workers*, 1969, U.S. Women's Bureau.

the point where, by 1974, every second such mother was employed outside the home (Bronfenbrenner, 1975).

Other economic changes that have affected family patterns include the gradual shift from a rural to an urban economy, the movement from self-employment or employment in small business units to corporate employment, and increasing employment mobility. The trend toward people having multiple careers over a lifetime has the additional effect of creating new periods of economic stress for the family unit while husband and wife undertake the retraining or additional education for a second or third career (Troll, 1971).

Having examined how the basic patterns of family life have changed during this century, we are ready to explore the changing role of the family within society.

Changing Role of the Family in Society

Traditionally, the role of the family has been viewed primarily as society's vehicle to provide for procreation and socialization of the next generation. When examined in the life-span context, however, socialization is a lifelong process (Brim & Wheeler, 1966). The role of the family as a source of maintenance, placement, and affection remains throughout life (Streib & Thompson, 1960).

Although procreation is generally reserved for the young adult stage of the family cycle, we are beginning to see a greater incidence of reproduction involving older males married to younger females, since males are capable of reproducing well into their seventies. And the frequency of repetitive marriage (and family) cycles is also increasing. Moreover, important pressures on young married couples to have children frequently come from their parents, who would like to have grandchildren to have fun with or to carry on the family name (Atchley, 1977).

The change from an extended to a nuclear family setting has caused a child's parents to become the principal socialization agents within the family; grandparents now serve that function only rarely. But older persons play a continuing role in the socialization of their adult children. Modeling may be quite important in this regard, whether the parental model is accepted or rejected.

The family continues to have socializing functions long after young children have grown up. For example, the family setting must help the older woman to restructure her life when children marry and leave home, and both husbands and working wives require resocialization by means of their family setting upon retirement, when they must make the transition from a work orientation to a leisure one.

The maintenance function of the family involves the provision of economic support. This role is obvious during the child-rearing stage, but it continues in subtle but changing ways throughout life. For example, most young adults expect their parents to provide for college and sometimes for professional education. On the other hand, it is expected that older parents should look at least in part toward their often more affluent middle-aged children for support. But not all children are in a position to support their parents, and it is not uncommon for even part of a meager retirement income to be used to provide some support to adult children. Ability and willingness to contribute toward the maintenance of one's parents or children may influence family dynamics in many ways and may create stress when the traditional maintenance relationship cannot be upheld.

The social position of children is involved in the family's placement role. In a rapidly changing society, we almost expect that children will be upwardly mobile and that this may involve stresses to parent-child relationships once children reach adulthood. In contrast to traditional societies, in which children's societal roles are transmitted largely through their parents, this upward social mobility may lead children to become ashamed of their parents and consequently to seek minimal interaction with them.

Finally, the family's function is that of providing affective or emotional support. Although this role is exerted primarily on parents in terms of providing emotional support to their children early in life, once the children become adults, the affective role becomes centered on the relationship between husband and wife. We will return to that relationship later in the chapter. First, let us look more closely at the relationship between children and parents.

Changing Patterns of Child Rearing

Changes in Ways of Thinking About Children   Bronfenbrenner (1961) succinctly asked the question, "Has the changing American parent produced a changing American child?" It appears that, indeed, over the past half century remarkable changes in child-rearing patterns have occurred. Moreover, the earlier marked gaps between different social classes and ethnic groups have narrowed, with white middle-class values increasingly becoming accepted as the norm. In addition, prestigious professional figures and widely read popular volumes on child care (such as Dr. Spock's *Baby and Child Care*) have hastened the dissemination and acceptance of such values.

What is at issue here is a change in attitude. There has been a shift from an authoritarian pattern of child rearing (which assumed that ignorant and willful children had to be socialized and prepared for a hard life) to the notion that children should be permitted to develop their own personalities and modes of coping in what was expected to be an increasingly supportive and satisfying society. The first view, of course, sees children as chaotic, unformed, and impulse-ridden individuals who must be indoctrinated with values that will lead to strength of purpose and prepare them to succeed in a harsh, suppressive society of scarcity and competition. In the latter view, children are seen as emerging creative persons who should be enabled to develop individual behavior patterns that will prepare them for socially enhancing self-expression in an affluent and permissive society.

Changes in Discipline   Changes in thinking about children also led to the rejection of authoritarian methods of child rearing, which required subduing the will of the child for his or her own good. Many childhood educators—in response to the widespread influence of Freudian psychology and the reduced impact of organized religion—successfully taught middle-class parents to question the methods of their own authoritarian parents. Thus during the 1940s and 1950s many middle-class families were willing to give unlimited acceptance to their young children's impulses and to allow their children maximum freedom of choice and self-expression. But by the late 1950s some people began to recognize that unrestricted permissiveness was getting more parents in trouble than restrictive behavior ever had (see also Spock, 1957).

The problem with permissive child-rearing techniques is that some of their assumptions have turned out *not* to warrant scientific support. The first assumption made is that scheduled feeding and insistent toilet training result in adult neuroses. But unless the demands made on infants exceed their physical limitations, there has been no evidence that feeding schedules and firm toilet training are harmful to normally developing children. The second major assumption has been that punishment is harmful and not effective. Research evidence suggests that brutal punishment and threats of punishment that are not carried out are, indeed, harmful. However, properly administered punishment that provides children with information about what their parents want and that teaches children the consequences of not conforming to an authority's demands has been shown to be effective in controlling behavior. The goal, of course, is to help young children control their own behavior. Toward that end, effective punishment must include the use of reason to define for the child what the parents conceive as being right or wrong conduct.

A third fallacious assumption of permissive child-rearing techniques is that a child benefits from the unconditional love of the parents. This may be the crux of the failure of permissive child-rearing techniques. It is harmful rather than helpful for parents to accept obnoxious and manipulative behavior, because then the child does not learn the skills needed to cope in situations where there is no one to provide unconditional love. Children who are accustomed to immediate gratification necessarily will suffer greater deprivation when gratification is impossible than will children who have learned to associate love with appropriate discipline.

The above considerations have fostered a trend away from permissive child rearing in recent years. This does not signal a return to authoritarian control but rather to a model that Baumrind (1972) has described as *authoritative parent* control. By that term Baumrind means that the parent in relation to the child should be someone whose expertness makes it possible to tell another person what to do when the behavioral alternatives are known to both. Moreover, an authoritative person is someone who does not have to exercise control but who is recognized to be fit to exercise authority. According to Baumrind, authoritative parents must be expert with respect to matters that pertain to the young people placed in their charge. They must be willing and able to behave rationally, as well as to explain the rationale for their values and norms. Finally, authoritative parents must value self-assertion and willfulness in their children.

Figure 7.3 characterizes parental behavior within a two-dimensional model involving the dimensions from love to hostility and from autonomy to control (Schaefer, 1959). In this view, the authoritarian parent is engaged in hostility-controlling behavior, whereas the permissive parent vacillates between con-

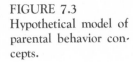

FIGURE 7.3
Hypothetical model of parental behavior concepts.

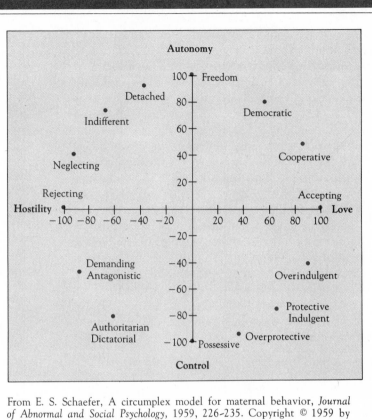

From E. S. Schaefer, A circumplex model for maternal behavior, *Journal of Abnormal and Social Psychology*, 1959, 226-235. Copyright © 1959 by the American Psychological Association.

trolled love and hostile autonomy. In contrast to both, the authoritative parent, as the child develops, proceeds from loving control to loving autonomy.

Parent-Child Interactions

The many changes in family role and patterns described so far do not undercut the fact that the family remains the child's most significant interactional network. Not all family members interact equally, however, and the quality of their interaction may differ markedly (Clark & Van Sommers, 1961). For example, the intensity of the parent-child relationship may be affected by the amount of time father and mother spend at home, by whether there are siblings sharing the same relationship, and by whether grandparents are an integral part of the family setting. Parent-child interactions may also differ with respect to such critical processes as the development of attachment, dependency, competence and self-reliance, and aggression. The following sections examine these ideas in greater detail.

Paternal and Maternal Influences

In most American families mothers spend more time with their children than fathers do, and they are also likely to show affection to their children more openly. When a family includes several children, there is often a division of responsibilities; the father may take greater interest in the older children, whereas the mother may be associated more closely with the younger ones (Sears, Maccoby, & Levin, 1957). In both authoritarian and permissive child-rearing patterns, greater roles are assigned to the mother. This is so in the former case because the paternal role is primarily that of laying down rules, which leaves enforcement to the mother. In the latter case it is the mother who allows the child to engage in self-initiated behavior, whether it is constructive or not.

Some sociologists feel that Western industrial society can be described as "mother-centered" in its philosophy of child care (Nash, 1965). This focus is attributed to the role of the father as principal economic support of the family, which, in turn, requires delegation of child-rearing activities to the mother. The resulting cultural norm of child care is often accepted uncritically as being the most desirable pattern. Consequently, many psychologists pay little or no attention to the role of the father as a major influence on the children.

The assumption that child rearing is a specifically feminine duty is fraught with potential hazards for the mental health and adjustment of children. Indeed, some studies of early paternal deprivation indicate that a warm relationship with a father figure during the period from weaning to the early school years is essential to the establishment of an effective masculine role identification, even though later intermittent absence of the father may be less important (Crain & Stamm, 1965). By contrast, psychosexual difficulties, including homosexuality, may result when children identify predominantly with the opposite-sex parent (Hetherington, 1965). While this may seem particularly important for boys, father-daughter relationships are also important in permitting the girl to acquire a model for eventual adult heterosexual relationships.

Young children typically think of mother as the individual who does things for them, tolerates their misbehavior, takes care of their physical needs, and comes to their aid when difficulties occur. Although young children see their mother as exercising stronger authority than their father, older children begin to recognize that her power and prestige may be less than that of their father (Stoodley, 1952).

By contrast, the father is often seen as someone who teaches by example, even though he also may be seen as the children's adult companion who is doing things for and with them. In differentiating the roles of father and mother, children often picture the father as being away from home more than mother is, as being important because he earns money, as knowing more than mother does, and as being more powerful but also more punitive than mother (Hurlock, 1972). Of course, these concepts change markedly as the role of women shifts from being primarily domestic to being work oriented. Indeed, these role shifts may be leading to the increasing abandonment of both authoritarian and permissive child-rearing modes in favor of the authoritative mode.

Whether the child-rearing pattern of a family is authoritarian or permissive, the mother is assigned greater roles.

Jean-Claude Lejeune, Stock, Boston, Inc.

Attachment

The manner in which a young child develops emotional relationships with the parents or other caretaking figures is sometimes described as the process of *attachment*. Three different bits of evidence indicate whether attachment to a specific person has occurred. First, the infant seeks out contact with the person involved (Ainsworth, 1973). Second, there are signs of distress when that person is absent (Schaffer & Emerson, 1964). Third, the infant shows signs of relaxation and comfort in the presence of the person to whom attachment obtains, but is less relaxed or anxious in the presence of others (Bronson, 1973).

An infant's establishment of attachment goes through several stages. It begins during the first months of life, when the infant simply emits positive responses in the presence of the primary caretaker and then seeks physical closeness. During the first few years of life, children engage in various manipulations to control the behavior of the object of attachment and to satisfy the need for being close to that object. It has been argued that the attachment process during infancy provides the prototype for the development of later successful interpersonal relationships. That is, successful early attachment proves to a child that he or she is capable of loving and receiving love from others—an experience without which later experiences of trust and closeness might be difficult to obtain (Newman & Newman, 1975).

Dependency

Besides providing a prototype for interpersonal relations, the attachment process also results in the establishment of a dependency relationship with another person. Specifically, *dependency* is the tendency of an individual to seek support and affection from others. Early life dependency is typically expressed in a child's relationship with the primary caregiver, most often the mother. But the pattern that is established during early childhood may be transferred later on to other adults, such as teachers. Of course, a pattern of dependency is expected for a young child, but an important part of adequate child rearing is to encourage increasing independence.

Overdependent children have been found to be nonaggressive and noncompetitive, submissive to peers, socially withdrawn, relatively inactive, and obedient to adult demands (Longstreth, 1968). When such children reach maturity, they continue to be dependent on their parents and then transfer such dependency to their spouses. They tend to withdraw from stressful situations, to avoid career risks, and to be much concerned with financial security (Kagan & Moss, 1962). Seeking to avoid such consequences, most parents tend to reinforce their children's initiative and expect them gradually to assume control over their own decisions as they grow up. This is all to the good in creating effective adults.

However, there is an opposite side to this coin as well. Because society disapproves of dependent behavior, one of the most difficult role changes facing the elderly is often the necessary shift from an independent adult role to that of dependence on others (Clark & Anderson, 1967; Kalish, 1969a). Paradoxically, then, individuals who have had dependent relationships throughout life may suffer least from what—for most successful adults—is perceived as a painful role reversal.

Competence and Self-Reliance

While the parents' major roles are to serve as objects for the child's attachment and as caregivers, an equally important function consists of their conscious activity in providing role models and incentives for the child's development of increasing competence and self-reliance. Competence implies action, which involves both adapting to the environment and attempting to change the environment (Connolly & Bruner, 1974). Children who lack confidence in their ability to cope have been found to seek immediate rewards and to be unwilling to take the risks involved in waiting for future gains (Mischel, 1961).

Several detailed analyses of the manner in which children acquire competence clearly implicate the role of the primary caregiver, usually the mother. A most important variable—related typically to the socioeconomic status of the mother—is whether the mother sees herself as a competent, coping individual (Hess & Shipman, 1965). However, more specific maternal skills and attitudes basic to the mother's teaching role may be equally important. These include basic language skills, skills in considering alternatives and integrating multiple facets of a problem, and personality factors such as a sense of efficiency, goal setting, and the ability to delay gratification (Carey, 1974).

Child-rearing patterns that result in the development of competence and self-reliance seem to include early achievement-oriented training involving setting standards of excellence and reflecting approval after success. Some differences in this respect have been found between mothers and fathers. Mothers tend to both encourage and punish, depending on the quality of their child's performance; fathers, however, allow (at least for their sons) greater independence and self-reliance while the child is achieving mastery (Rosen & D'Andrade, 1959).

Aggression

Aggression in children may be expressed by a number of different behaviors. The most prominent of these are physical aggression to peers; indirect aggression to peers (such as teasing or destroying a playmate's belongings); dominance of peers; behavioral disorganization (such as might be displayed by outbursts of anger or temper tantrums); and competitiveness (Kagan & Moss, 1962). How is such aggressive behavior formed?

There is by now a substantial amount of evidence that parents of aggressive children tend to use power-assertive techniques (Chwast, 1972). It has been hypothesized that physical punishment frustrates children and reinforces their aggressive impulses. In addition, parents who use physical punishment thereby offer a model of aggressive behavior. Finally, some parents who punish their children's aggressive behavior toward themselves also tend to encourage such behavior toward others.

By contrast, the authoritative discipline described earlier reduces aggression by teaching a child concern for others and by pointing out the consequences of aggressive behavior. In this case aggression is controlled by a warm communicative atmosphere coupled with concern and consideration of others, as well as by a firm setting of standards appropriate to the developmental level of the child (Baumrind, 1971; Odom, Seeman, & Newbrough, 1971).

Grandparent-Child Interactions

Parent-child interactions become more complicated in the extended family setting. For example, if the mother pursues a career and is out of the home during much of a child's early infancy, the child's grandmother may become the primary caregiver. Thus the mother-child interactions described earlier may be generalized to the grandmother-child interaction. Complications arise under these circumstances, however, because the mother rarely will give up her primary role entirely but instead may share it with the grandmother. In fact, the particular role played by the grandparents will determine the nature of their interaction with their grandchildren.

Neugarten and Weinstein (1964) described at least five different common roles played by grandparents in the modern family setting:

1. In the *formal role,* the grandparents give special treats and gifts to the grandchildren but otherwise take a "hands-off" policy in child training.
2. The *fun-seeking role* is characterized by an informal relationship in which grandparents see their grandchildren as companions in mutually enjoyable play activity.

The extended family setting may complicate child-rearing patterns, and a grandparent may become the primary caregiver.

Susan Lapides

3. The *surrogate-parent role* is played mostly by grandparents, who assume responsibility for care and discipline.
4. The *reservoir-of-family-wisdom* role—exercised often by grandfathers—involves teaching the child special skills and knowledge rather than attempting to control the child's behavior.
5. In the *distant-figure role*, the grandparents make only infrequent and formal contacts with their grandchildren.

Children's interactions with grandparents change as they mature. Preschool children welcome the grandparent's attention, but later on their responses may depend on their perception of whether the grandparents exert authority over them or are simply another source of indulgent emotional support (Hickey, Hickey, & Kalish, 1968; Kahana & Kahana, 1970).

Although the grandparents' role is often supportive and helpful, it can also introduce less favorable elements into the family interaction. For example, the presence of a maternal grandmother in the home may cause the father to withdraw from many family activities, and children may suffer from contradictory demands made by the mother and the grandmother (Hurlock, 1972).

Family Composition

We have noted already that familial influences and patterns of child rearing are affected by certain aspects of family composition. The most obvious of these are a child's birth order and the number and sex of siblings. Another important variable relates to the question of whether a child develops in a nuclear family setting or is raised by a divorced or single parent. Finally, we should investigate variables of family dynamics, such as might be explored through interactional analysis of the parent-child relationship and of intergenerational relations.

Birth Order

Birth order refers to an individual's sequential position among brothers and sisters. Many developmentalists have studied this variable and have found it to be related significantly to the development of various personality traits as well as to cognitive capability and adjustment (for example, Adams, 1972; Kellaghan & MacNamara, 1972). There is an obvious environmental difference for first-born and later children (as well as for only children throughout their development) in that a period early in life is free from competition with other siblings.

Firstborn children tend to assume dominant roles and have the additional advantage of teaching younger children.

Erika Stone, Peter Arnold, Inc.

TABLE 7.1
Birth Order and
Average
Personality
Tendencies

The Firstborn Child

Uncertainty, mistrustfulness, insecurity, shrewdness, stinginess, dependency, responsibility, authoritarianism, jealousy, conservatism, lack of dominance and aggressiveness, suggestibility, excitability, sensitiveness, timidity, introversion, strong achievement drive, need for affiliation, petulant, spoiled, and prone to behavior disorders

The Second Child

Independence, aggressiveness, extroversion, fun-loving, gregarious, adventuresome, dependable, well adjusted

The Middle Child

Aggressiveness, easily distracted, craves demonstrations of affection, jealousy, plagued by feelings of parental neglect, inferiority, and inadequacy, and prone to behavior disorders

The Last Child

Secure, confident, spontaneous, good-natured, generous, spoiled, immature, extroverted, ability to empathize, feelings of inadequacy and inferiority, resentments against older siblings, envy and jealousy, irresponsible, and happy

Source: From *Child Development*, 5th, ed., by E. B. Hurlock. Copyright © 1972 by McGraw-Hill Book Company. Used with the permission of McGraw-Hill Book Company.

Firstborns also tend to assume dominant roles toward their younger siblings (Sutton-Smith & Rosenberg, 1966). They frequently employ high-power persuasive techniques on younger children. It is not clear, however, whether this is a function of their ordinal position in the family or whether it is simply the outcome of their being older (Bragg, Ostrowski, & Finley, 1973).

Zajonc (1976) proposes cogently that the oldest child typically has the advantage of sharing the home with two adults, so that the average level of intellectual stimulation is geared to the adult level. When other children arrive, the average intellectual level of the family is lowered, bringing it closer to the level of the child. Thus smaller families and those in which children are widely spaced are thought to produce more intelligent children. Firstborn children have the additional advantage of benefiting from their roles as teachers of the younger children—which explains why firstborns who have siblings are frequently shown to perform above the level of only children.

On the negative side are the findings that mothers are generally more relaxed with their later children than with their firstborn (Warren, 1966) and that only children and firstborn boys with sisters tend to identify with their mother. Such identification may be disadvantageous, because good adolescent adjustment has been related to boys' associating with more masculine fathers and girls' associating with more masculine mothers (Heilbrun & Fromme, 1965). Table 7.1 gives capsule descriptions of children in different birth-order positions and conveys the flavor of some of the many attributes that researchers have related to this variable.

Number and Sex of Siblings

It seems obvious that children should be affected by the family composition in terms of the number of children and their sex. Yet research literature on this subject is confusing. An older longitudinal study of sibling pairs (Schoonover, 1959) reports that both boys and girls did significantly better if they had a brother than if they had a female sibling. This finding was explained by noting that the male sibling provided a model of aggressive and competitive behavior. A later study by Sampson and Hancock (1967), in which a variety of personality variables were investigated, concluded to the contrary that having a younger sister or an older brother is more conducive to the development of high achievement than having either a younger brother or an older sister. The effects of birth order described earlier have been found to be greater in large families, with differences between firstborn and lastborn decreasing with family size (Oberlander, Jenkins, Houlihan, & Jackson, 1970).

Family size, however, has been declining steadily. For example, in 1910 the average family included 4.5 children, but by 1970 this number had declined to 2.4. This shift not only has significant consequences for early development but also affects the likelihood of an available kin network during adulthood. Most older people today have brothers and sisters (Streib & Thompson, 1960), but the trends imply that older persons in the future will have fewer siblings and, therefore, even less of an extended family support system.

Several variables may be implicated in the importance of family size in determining many aspects of family relationships. First of all, family size determines the number of different interactions each member is involved in. If the number of such interactions is large, conflict may result, and parents may tend to resort to authoritarian child-training methods more frequently than would be the case in smaller families (Bossard & Boll, 1966). Second, parental attitudes about family size may be important. Parents expecting large families may generate a warm and accepting climate, whereas those who looked forward to a small family may respond resentfully to the burden of a large family.

Sex composition is a third family variable that is likely to be important. In spite of many role changes, females still tend to be in the home more extensively than males, and thus a greater ratio of female to male children is thought to result in greater friction. Finally, the spacing of children affects parental attitudes, depending on whether children arrive at a planned time, or interrupt the mother's career, or introduce an excessive financial burden at an inopportune time for optimal family development (Freedman & Coombs, 1966).

The manner in which boys and girls react to their brothers and sisters also depends often on who is older and younger. Generally, however, male sibling and male-female sibling pairs tend to get along better than female siblings do. On the other hand, boys fight more with their brothers than with their sisters, because parents are more likely to restrict aggressive behavior of boys against girls.

Single and Divorced Parents

Some adults do not marry, and others do not remain married. Nevertheless, such individuals sometimes do raise families, with their normal problems as well as special ones that arise out of the parent's single status. Although there is an increasing incidence of divorced fathers raising children, the cultural norm is still that of a single, divorced, or widowed woman raising her children. Thus available research data are restricted to that particular circumstance.

Much attention has been given to the possible psychological damage to children, particularly males, who are raised in a fatherless family. Biller (1971), in a summary of available data, concludes that it is the nature of the mother-son relationship that determines whether the lack of a stable father figure has a positive or negative effect on the boy's sex-role and personality development. It appears that in matriarchal families—in which there is no father or the father is relatively ineffective—maternal overprotection results in undermining the boy's feeling of masculine adequacy. Father absence may be less serious if the mother has a positive attitude toward males and generally expects and encourages masculine behavior in her son. There is also some evidence that father absence before age five has greater effects on sex-role development than if the absence occurs later. And, generally, the significance of father absence may be affected by the extent of peer-group interaction, by the family's sociocultural background, and by the length and timing of father absence.

Sociocultural factors are important, first, because there may be less of a stigma attached to father absence in lower-class families and also because there may be a lower frequency of overprotection since the mother is more likely to be engaged in a full-time job. However, the latter fact may also lead to maternal rejection, since lower-class mothers without husbands may be more concerned about their own needs and about the economic demands forced upon them. In such instances boys are rejected more often than girls (Bronfenbrenner, 1967). In fact, girls seem to fare better in the single-parent family, even though their ability to establish appropriate heterosexual interpersonal relations may be affected by the absence of an early male adult model (Biller & Weiss, 1970). To be fair, however, we should note that the father-absent home does not necessarily pose unusual risks to the normal development of children, particularly if the father absence occurs after the age of five and if the mother can assume the essential function of sex-role differentiation.

Family Dynamics

The number of interactional systems in a given family is, of course, a function of family size. Figure 7.4 gives graphic examples of the systems in one-, two-, and three-children families. In a one-child family, there are only three interactional systems available; but the number of such systems increases rapidly with the addition of more children or with the inclusion of grandparents or other kin.

The most systematic study of interactional systems in early childhood has been devoted to a formal analysis of dyadic (two-person) relationships between

California's Children of Divorce

JUDITH S. WALLERSTEIN
AND JOAN B. KELLY

The conventional wisdom used to be that un-happily married people should remain married "for the good of the children." Today's conventional wisdom holds, with equal vigor, that an unhappy couple might well *divorce* for the good of the children; that an unhappy marriage for the adults is unhappy also for the children; and that divorce that promotes the happiness of the adults will benefit the children as well.

Testing the new dogma was among our goals in 1971 when we started what became known as the Children of Divorce Project. We interviewed all the members of 60 families with children that had recently gone through divorce, and reinterviewed them 18 months later. Recently, we saw them again, after a lapse of five years.... Our study has no counterpart in the United States or in Europe in the span of years it covers, in the participation of so many children of different ages, and in the kinds of questions that were posed....

What made the biggest difference for the children was not the divorce itself, but the factors that make for good adjustments and satisfaction in intact families: psychologically healthy parents and children who are involved with one another in appropriate ways. Yet providing these optimal conditions is difficult in the post-divorce family, with its characteristic climate of anger, rejection, and attempts to exclude the absent parent....

Perhaps the most crucial factor influencing a good readjustment was a stable, loving relation-ship with both parents, between whom friction had largely dissipated, leaving regular, dependable visiting patterns that the parent with custody encouraged....

Even though the majority of fathers and children continued to see each other fairly often, by the five-year mark three-quarters of these relationships offered the children little in fully addressing the complex tasks of growing up. Yet, paradoxically, by his absence a father continued to influence the thoughts and feelings of his children; most particularly, the disinterested father left behind a legacy of depression and damaged self-esteem.

Except in extreme cases in which a father was clearly abusing children or seriously disturbed, some contact seemed better than none at all. The father's presence kept the child from a worrisome concern with abandonment and total rejection and from the nagging self-doubts that follow such worry. The father's presence, however limited, also diminished the child's vulnerability and aloneness and total dependency on the one parent.

A few other factors that we had expected to be significant in helping children adjust turned out not to be. Children were incapable of using friends to make up for troubled conditions at home; rather, those with comparatively stable homes were the ones most likely to have friends outside.... Most children did not seem to be influenced either for good or ill if their mother worked, although some of the youngest boys appeared to do significantly better in school and in their overall adjustment when the mother did not work full time....

It seems that a divorced family per se is neither more nor less beneficial for children than an unhappy marriage. Unfortunately, neither unhappy marriage nor divorce is especially congenial for children. Each imposes its own set of differing stresses.

Our other major finding about how important it is for a child to keep a relationship with both original parents points to the need for a concept of greater shared parental responsibility after divorce.

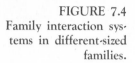

FIGURE 7.4
Family interaction sys-
tems in different-sized
families.

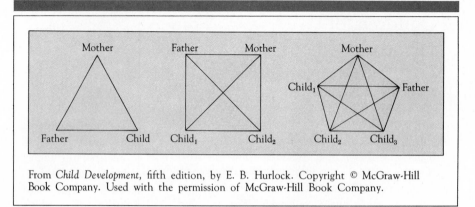

From *Child Development*, fifth edition, by E. B. Hurlock. Copyright © McGraw-Hill Book Company. Used with the permission of McGraw-Hill Book Company.

parent and child. It often has been thought that attachment begins with the model infant-mother relationship described earlier in this chapter, but current thinking suggests that this relationship is not a one-way street at all. Rather, it represents a complex interactional system in which the mother's behavior is cued by the young infant and the infant's behavior is elicited by maternal stimulation (Hartup & Lempers, 1973). In this view, then, family dynamics—including attachment—are regarded not as the characteristics of any particular family members but rather as the structural property of the particular interaction (Parsons & Bales, 1955). Thus from the very beginning, the mother-child interaction along with all other family interactions can be viewed as small social systems.

One way of studying family interactions is to fit together the behavior profiles of two or more family members to form a group profile. Development in relationships could then be inferred from changes in individual behavior profiles relative to the group profile. For example, an infant beginning to walk becomes the more frequent initiator of closeness to the mother, whereas previously proximity would have been instigated more frequently by the mother (Lusk & Lewis, 1972). However, this change may induce other changes in the mother's behavior. For instance, instead of approaching her child physically, she now may engage more frequently in vocalized approaches.

Other ways in which interactions may be measured include the consideration of spatial distance, dyadic gazing, and dyadic mimicry. For example, experiments have assessed how far a child will move away from the mother when she is not initiating any interaction (Maccoby & Feldman, 1972). Similarly, interaction has been measured by observing the incidence of mutual visual regard between mothers and their young infants (Robson, 1967); and both immediate and deferred imitations have been looked at as evidence of mother-child interaction (Uzgiris, 1972).

Although most studies of family interaction in early childhood have involved mother-child interactions, there is some work on interaction between father and infants. As might be expected, this work suggests that father-infant interactions occur primarily during morning and evening hours. Interestingly, one study suggests that—in contrast to mother-child interactions—fathers tend to reduce the amount of time spent vocalizing to their infants from the first to the third month of the infant's life. Moreover, fathers tend to interact more verbally with their daughters and more physically with their sons (Rebelsky & Hanks, 1972).

Family interactions are of interest throughout the life span. Their detailed analysis is helpful in understanding developmental transitions at many points in the life cycle, including courtship, different stages of the marital relationship, sibling relationships in adulthood, the "empty-nest" phase, and role changes at retirement. But very different measures would be needed to analyze these interactions. Troll (1971) suggests that appropriate interaction measures would include geographical distance between family members, frequency of face-to-face contacts, patterns of mutual aid, affective attributes of the family relationship, and various indicators of family solidarity. Again, it should be stressed that the interaction pattern is never a one-way street. For example, when considering the direction of help given within an adult parent-child dyad, it has been found that the proportion of older persons who help their children exceeds the proportion who obtain help from their children (Shanas et al., 1968).

Alternatives to the Traditional Family

Our discussion of family influences on individual development has been mostly within the context of the contemporary Western family pattern. This is not the only possible pattern, of course. Of the many alternatives, three deserve special attention because they are beginning to affect increasing numbers of individuals in Western society: (1) the planned childless marriage, (2) multiple marriages (sometimes jokingly called sequential polygamy), and (3) the collective and commune as a modern substitute for the extended family.

Childless Marriages

With more effective means of fertility control and increasing population pressures, more and more married couples consciously decide to forgo their reproductive role. These people who for physiological reasons cannot have children but do not wish to acquire children by adoption might develop in a somewhat different manner than the traditional family, since they will remain essentially a dyad throughout their adult lives. Their developmental changes and crises will relate primarily to their own career and life changes rather than being influenced by developmental changes occurring in the lives of their offspring.

Although we have almost no adequate empirical data, there has been discussion about whether or not childless marriages are particularly difficult (see also Bischoff, 1969). For one, traditional attitudes tend to deprecate women who do not have children. On the other hand, many marriages break up at an early stage because couples cannot adjust to the intrusion of children into their relationship. Questionnaire studies of marital satisfaction often show most favorable responses from childless couples (for example Renne, 1970).

Advantages and Disadvantages of Having Children

The most common disadvantage of having children is the loss of freedom, according to American parents questioned in a University of Michigan study. The advantages most frequently mentioned are "love and affection and the feeling of being a family," "stimulation and fun," and "expansion of self" or "having someone to carry on after you have gone." The findings were reported by Lois Hoffman and Jean Manis, researchers with Survey Research Center, a unit of the university's Institute for Social Research. They interviewed some 1,569 married women between the ages of 15 and 39, and the husbands of about one-third of the women, to learn more about the psychological satisfactions of having children. Similar studies were carried out in Korea, Indonesia, the Philippines, Singapore, Taiwan, Thailand, Turkey, and West Germany.

Economics and women's careers can have an important effect on desired family size. . . . The most common reason given for not wanting children, they found, is financial burden. . . . However, in answer to a general question about the disadvantages of having children, the women who wanted smaller families—one or two children, or no children at all—were far more apt to mention the loss of freedom associated with having children than they were to cite financial problems.

More than half of the women in the survey were employed and 49% of the women with children were working. "The women who are not working now and who do not anticipate working in the future expect to have larger families and they are more apt than other

women to feel that large families are desirable." Since four-fifths of the women who were not working said that they would like to work in the future, the implication is likely to be smaller families. . . .

The primary advantage of children for the adults questioned was associated with the desire for love and affection and the feeling of being a family. Among parents, 66% of women and 60% of men gave this type of answer. With nonparents, 64% of women and 51% of men made that reply.

A close second in importance was the value "stimulation and fun." This included statements such as "there is always something going on," or "children bring liveliness to your life," or "we love playing with them." Couples with children were more likely to mention this advantage than those without children.

About one-third of respondents mentioned values related to "expansion of self"—answers such as "having someone to carry on after you have gone" or "having new growth and learning experiences." . . .

The most common disadvantage of children is the loss of freedom, according to American parents questioned. This response was mentioned by 53% of the mothers and 49% of the fathers. Among women without children, this was also the most frequently cited disadvantage. Among men who were not parents, the financial cost of having children was seen as the biggest disadvantage.

The researchers explain that one purpose of the study was to see whether having alternative ways of satisfying the psychological needs that might be met by having children would affect the values attributed to children. They report that several findings support this "alternatives" hypothesis. . . . "Nonparents are less likely to see children as essential to achieving satisfactory adult status, and they are more concerned about the economic costs associated with having a family."

Source: *USA Today*, August 1979, p. 7.

The relationship of couples who for physiological or personal reasons do not have children may develop in a different manner than the traditional family.

Ellis Herwig, Stock, Boston, Inc.

Childless middle-aged couples often have a very close, affectionate relationship. Because there are no children to rear, it is possible to pay greater attention to the spouse. It is also easier to come to mutually supportive career arrangements. Childless couples have greater financial resources and thus frequently are able to become involved in societal causes, whereas families with children might have to make choices that are disadvantageous to their own children. Finally, it is much easier for late-middle-aged and elderly couples to experiment with unconventional innovations to their marriage arrangement, for they do not need to feel concern about their children's responses to their nonconformity (Cavan, 1973).

The most disadvantageous effect of a childless marriage typically appears upon the death of the spouse, at which time the remaining partner does not have the economic and psychological support of adult children. Even so, alternative kin and friendship networks may compensate (see also Troll, 1971).

Multiple Marriages

With the increasing acceptance of divorce and the high probability that divorced parents with young children will remarry (Hunt, 1966), we are seeing a large number of children who grow up under circumstances in which they experience successive different sets of nuclear families. They are often part of a semiextended family that includes the successive spouses and other offspring of their biological parents.

Remarriage of the parent who has custody of the children may have the positive effect of reestablishing what is considered a normal family pattern, and it may resolve the economic problems of the one-parent home. On the other hand, interpersonal problems may result for the children, because the new parental family member may set standards and have values that conflict with those introduced by the departed parent.

Table 7.2 lists some factors that contribute to the establishment and tone of relationships between children and stepparents (Hurlock, 1972). It should be noted that conflict between children and the new parent also may have adverse effects on the new marital relationship. Interestingly, stepfathers tend to get along better with their new children than do stepmothers. This is because in

TABLE 7.2
Factors
Contributing to
Stepparent-Child
Relationships

Child's Contributions	Stepparent's Contributions
Memories of own parent, if dead	Reason the stepparent had for assuming role—whether love for child or wanting to marry
Occasional contacts with real parent, if living	
How well the child knows the stepparent before he or she assumes the role	Stepparent's interest in and concern for the child
How radically child training differs from what the child is accustomed to	Resentment of child's interest in absent real parent, as shown by talking about dead parent or wanting to be with real parent, if alive
How much affection the child has for and shows the stepparent	
Attitude of the peer group toward the child because he or she has a stepparent	Resentment of the child's lack of appreciation for what the stepparent does or the sacrifices he or she makes
Acceptance of the stereotype that *all* stepparents are "wicked"	Favoritism for own child
	Effect of stepchild on marital relationships

Source: From *Child Development,* 5th ed. by E. B. Hurlock. Copyright © 1972 by McGraw-Hill Book Company. Used with the permission of McGraw-Hill Book Company.

traditional families the stepmother soon assumes disciplinary and child-rearing functions, whereas the stepfather often assumes less supervisory responsibility for the newly adopted children than for his biological children.

There are obvious possibilities of conflict for children when they have to operate within the context of a social network made up of two or more families with different values and lifestyles. And the likelihood that such differences exist may be particularly great in successive marriages, when a partner has been exchanged precisely because of incompatible lifestyles. Nevertheless, children seem to handle these situations well as long as they perceive that they are accepted warmly and are made welcome in both families; however, they react strongly when they are made pawns in a continuing interpersonal struggle.

Lest it be thought that multiple marriage occurs only in situations involving young children, we should note that there is a substantial increase in remarriage among the elderly, frequently in response to the death of a spouse (78 percent of older brides and grooms are widowed). Nevertheless, the remarriage rate among the aged is still quite low because of frequent obstacles related to cultural stereotypes (Treas & VanHilst, 1976), even though questionnaire studies suggest that as many as 81 percent of widows express a wish for remarriage (Lopata, 1973).

Collectives and Communes

Current family patterns are thought by some to perpetuate such psychological problems as isolation, lack of interdependence, limited adult models for children, and overdependence on one other person (in the case of traditional marriage). It is also held that ecological problems can never be solved if everyone in our society is encouraged to seek the middle-class patterns of housing and consumer affluence that are required by the retention of the nuclear family as the model unit. In addition, the almost total separation of work place from family living place is a pattern that may have to be challenged—if only because of the excess energy expenditure and the psychological problems occasioned by the artificial separation of work and nonwork environments.

There are at least five different types of experimental communities, each of which may have different impact on their members and their children. These are (1) religious communities, (2) utopian communities, (3) planned communities, (4) Israeli kibbutzim, and (5) communes.

Religious communities were the earliest form of alternative lifestyle based on interdependence beyond the nuclear family units. They were inspired particularly by the early Christian attempts at seeking greater fellowship among believers, and they are represented in America today by such communities as the Amish in Iowa and by other descendents of the Hutterite movement. In these cases, interpersonal relationships and attitudes toward family structures are governed primarily by sets of religious principles.

In the same manner, *utopian communities* are formed along the lines of shared philosophical principles about ideal lifestyles that are not possible in our society at large. One prominent example of such attempts that has been well studied is the Oneida community of upstate New York (Kanter, 1970). A major principle of this community was that children should be socialized in terms of community rather than family values. As a consequence, children were raised outside the parental homes, although they visited their parents frequently.

Planned communities are organized more loosely and may serve to integrate members of different socioeconomic classes, to break intergenerational barriers, or to permit maximal planning for physical settings to satisfy human needs, often with particular emphasis on reducing the ecological misfit and resource waste of conventional communities (see Margolies, 1971, for an extensive discussion).

Although the primary function of the *Israeli kibbutz* was to occupy territory and to act as an outpost settlement to serve national goals, the kibbutz movement has also served as a major lifestyle experiment. In contrast with the values of urban middle-class homes, communal child-rearing practices of the kibbutz tend to prepare children from an early age to cooperate and work as a group. Formal teaching methods have minimal emphasis on competitive goals or approaches to problem solving. As a result, children do not accept competition as a socially desirable norm, and they dislike those who excel (Shapira & Madsen, 1969). In the development of kibbutz children, the peer group takes the place of the sibling group, and the child's primary caretaker may take on many attributes of the maternal role.

Perhaps the most revolutionary contemporary form of experimental community is the commune. *Communes* are small groups of people who wish to experiment with alternate family concepts, including the sharing of family responsibilities. Some of these endeavors reject the urban environment and set up rural settings in which members of the commune try to raise their own food and satisfy their other needs. Recent communes often have had short life spans, especially when their organization was haphazard and little thought was given to the division of labor necessary even with a communal living arrangement (Howard & Howard, 1973).

Child-rearing practices in communes are often quite deliberate because the communards have rejected much of their own upbringing and are seeking to raise children whose socialization will differ from their own. Although there is the general goal of raising children within an extended family setting, most communes actually have well-recognized nuclear units within them. Much ambiguity is shown with respect to discipline. Although the dominant ideology calls for children to do their "own thing," there are counterpressures on parents to push their children toward the communal goals, which may be oriented toward self-discipline (through yoga or other meditation-based principles) rather than toward self-gratification. As in the kibbutz, children are seen much more as the common responsibility and joy of the group than of the biological parents (Berger et al., 1972).

Age Integration and Age Segregation

Most of this chapter has been concerned with the impact of the family on early development, but, as we have noted in passing, family influences continue to be important throughout life. These influences in the life of adults are multidirectional in nature, but they often relate to the central issue of whether there are effective intergenerational communications. That is, is the older generation involved in transmitting culturally and psychologically desirable values and skills to the succeeding generation? In turn, is the younger generation successful in transforming such transmissions to the needs of a changing society? At the same time, the question arises of whether the younger generation can establish mutually acceptable interdependence with their elders, so that positive cultural change can also be reflected in a higher quality of life for the older generations.

Now we will try to indicate current opinions regarding the possibilities and difficulties of integrating people across generations and to sketch what happens when age segregation is prescribed or selected arbitrarily.

Intergenerational Relations

Relations between generations have been described as "continuous bilateral negotiations in which the young and old exchange information and influences from their respective position in developmental and historical time" (Bengtson & Black, 1973, p. 207). These authors also suggest that there are inevitable differences between generations because of age differentials in social position; because the young and the old have different types of contacts with cultural institutions; and—not least of all—because there is considerable intergenerational solidarity among life-stage groups who have had common historical experiences not shared with successive generations (such as the Great Depression). But there are also clear intergenerational similarities. These arise because there is considerable interdependence across generations and because parents and society at large engage in many explicit efforts at information transmission, while children try to modify that process and move toward cultural change.

One major factor in intergenerational conflict is that young people and old people do not always share the same perception of reality (Ahammer & Baltes, 1972; Nardi, 1973). The young often identify cultural inconsistencies and seek novel forms of behavior that they think are likely to lead to the resolution of such inconsistencies. The selected behavior, however, may be quite incomprehensible or even reprehensible to the older generation, which does not accept the social reality of the inconsistencies identified by the young. What is at stake may be the relative position of young and old with respect to the finite life span. The limitless future perceived by the young is not part of the social reality of the old (also see Bortner & Hultsch, 1972). The frustration of both the young and the old is increased by their perceived powerlessness as compared with the middle-aged (Martin, Bengtson, & Acock, 1974).

Contributing to the differences between generations that may lead to age segregation are conditions that foster intragenerational solidarity. These may involve a common location with respect to developmental phenomena, as well as common historical experiences. Kalish (1969b) has argued that the same conditions that give rise to generational consciousness for the young might also operate for the old. These could cause older people to form a distinct subculture that could develop its own class consciousness (Palmore & Whittington, 1971).

Nonetheless, successive generations do have a common culture and, while differing in age, share an overlapping period in historical time. Thus the ideas of youth movements are always related to the ideas that dominate contemporary culture (Goetzel, 1972). That is, the attempts of the younger generation to change society are obviously related to the problems that are current and involve all other present generations. Even in times of rapid technological and cultural change, many cultural features remain constant and are shared by all generations. Moreover, the developing individual—particularly in childhood—shares many common experiences with all other family members. It is not surprising that most young people share standards of morality, religious participation, and other behaviors with their family and, consequently, that there are greater attitudinal similarities within families from one generation to the next than between families (Thomas, 1971).

Retirement Communities

With the increasing numbers of relatively healthy and independent older people, there has been an increasing emphasis on intergenerational differences as a major argument for devising separate living environments for the elderly. Just as there are communities that cater to the unmarried and to young families, it has been argued that there ought to be communities that give priority to the needs of the elderly. What characteristics would make for a desirable retirement community, and what are the major obstacles?

Considering the diversity among our elderly, it is unlikely that there will ever be a single most desirable type of retirement community. In addition, there are at least two major subgroups of individuals who seek age-segregated retirement housing. The first group is looking for a sedentary, low-stress, and uneventful environment—essentially seeking protection from the noise and bustle and crime and insecurity of modern cities. But another group wants to supplement such security arrangements with an intensive program of activities (see also Jacobs, 1974).

Because of the heterogeneity among individuals, successful retirement communities must attempt to satisfy a wide range of needs for people from many different backgrounds. However, most communities try to avoid such flexibility by seeking to have fairly homogeneous residents (often implicitly restricted to white middle-class individuals). Such a setting may produce peace and quiet for the residents but at the price of considerable social isolation. Furthermore, even near-adequate retirement communities have never been available in the United States for persons of moderate income or for disadvantaged minority groups.

Age-Integrated Living Arrangements

As has been implied in the preceding section, age-segregated homogeneous retirement communities are not likely to be the answer to the problems of finding successful living arrangements for the elderly. Nevertheless, since a large proportion of the elderly live by themselves (see Table 7.3), the opportunities for

TABLE 7.3
Family Living
Arrangements of
Older People,
United States,
1963

Living Arrangements	People with Living Children	
	Married	Divorced, Widowed, Single
Total	100.0	100.0
Living alone	0	46.5
Living with:		
Spouse only	77.9	0
Married daughter	1.0	4.5
Married son	11.1	4.1
Unmarried child	14.6	24.1
Sibling	1.3	2.5
Grandchild	2.3	2.2
Other relative	0.8	1.4
Nonrelative only	1.0	4.6

Source: From M. W. Riley and A. Foner. *Aging and Society: An Inventory of Research Findings.* New York: Russell Sage Foundation, 1968. Reprinted by permission of Basic Books, Inc.

TABLE 7.4
Comparison of
Help Received
and Given
Across
Generations
(Percent)

	Type of Crisis									
	Economic		Emotional Gratification		Household Management		Child Care		Illness	
	Gave/Received		Gave/Received		Gave/Received		Gave/Received		Gave/Received	
Total	100	100	100	100	100	100	100	100	100	100
Grandparents	26	34	23	42	21	52	16	0	32	61
Parents	41	17	47	37	47	23	50	23	21	21
Married Children	34	49	31	21	33	25	34	78	47	18

Source: From R. Hill. "Decision Making and the Family Life Cycle." In Ethel Shanas, Gordon F. Streib, *Social Structure and the Family: Generational Relations* © 1965, p. 125. Reprinted by permission of Prentice-Hall, Inc., Englewood Cliffs, N.J.

more effective housing arrangements are an urgent priority for most American communities. As was indicated by the White House Conference on Aging (1973), which reported on youth and the elderly, there are many possible symbiotic interactions between the young and the elderly, and the interchange of economic and emotional support between the generations is substantial. Table 7.4 indicates the extent of intergenerational support covering economics, emotional gratification, household management, child care, and help in time of illness (Hill, 1965).

Age-integrated living arrangements provide many possible interactions between the young and the elderly.

Paul Sequeira, Photo Researchers, Inc.

Communities need to be structured so that they can maximize constructive intergenerational contact but reduce its annoying features. For example, it is quite possible to arrange apartment buildings that set aside different floors for families with or without young children. It is quite clear that social isolation is much more disadvantageous for the elderly than is a modest amount of annoyance and conflict. There is now convincing evidence that much of the perceived difficulties of the elderly can be attributed to cultural obsolescence rather than to individual decrement (see also Schaie, 1974). Such obsolescence can be countered effectively only by maintaining the elderly within familiar urban settings that maximize intergenerational contact and continued exposure to both the hazards and the advantages of a rapidly changing society.

Options for All Ages

Intergenerational influences can be both positive and negative, and their effects on the psychosocial aspects of human aging have been well demonstrated. To the extent that such influences mandate ecological decisions with respect to the opportunities for self-expression and resources, they may make all the difference between a generation of happy and well-adjusted or thoroughly disgruntled elders (Beattie, 1970; Bruhn, 1971).

It has been argued frequently that society's acceptance of people of all ages depends on modifying the behavior of the elderly as a deviant population group within a youth-oriented culture (see also Birren & Gribbin, 1973). We would like to argue instead that the target is misperceived. What needs to be done is to maximize opportunities for all ages—and that will require a major effort at abandoning the age-graded society. However, our cultural myths and stereotypes are strong, and age-grading is a social reality (Neugarten & Datan, 1973).

Table 7.5 lists a series of basic assumptions that would be required for a society in which age-graded disabilities are to be minimized (Schaie, 1973).

TABLE 7.5
New Assumptions for a Society That Offers Options to All Ages

New Assumption I

Adult psychological and physiological functions required to sustain socially significant behaviors are not subject to normal age decrement.

Corollary Ia: Minor age changes in speed of reaction and energy level occur as a function of incompletely controlled cumulative environmental insult, but the effects of such changes on significant social behavior can be eliminated by minor adjustments of life support systems suitable for adults at any age.

Corollary Ib: Psychological and physiological functions required to sustain socially significant behavior are impaired by traumatic events at all ages. The possibility of reversing such impairment and the treatment required for such reversal is a function of the nature of the impairment and not of the age of the impaired person.

Corollary Ic: A major share of presently observed behavior decrements in the elderly is due to perceived age-graded role expectations. Such phenomena will fail to occur when role expectations are shifted to criteria other than age.

New Assumption II

A mature and civilized society, which intends to stabilize its population at an optimum level, does not need to discriminate against any age group in the allocation of its resources, economic rewards, and social roles.

Corollary IIa: Economic rewards and societal roles are assigned primarily as a function of the present contribution of the individual regardless of his age and not as a reward for past performance or future expectation of performance.

Corollary IIb: Compulsory retirement on account of age is abandoned as not in the interest of society. Temporary or permanent retirement on account of disability is available for individuals at any age and is mandatory when in the public interest.

Corollary IIc: Adequate opportunities for leisure-time pursuits are provided to all age groups as necessary aspects of a civilized society. Such opportunities are neither the special privilege of the young nor the old.

New Assumption III

A highly developed society does not expect a given role or career to continue indefinitely for any individual. It does not view the initiation or maintenance of a particular role as being restricted to a specific age level.

Corollary IIIa: Educational opportunities related to career entry patterns are not restricted to particular age levels. Modifications of conventional training patterns are, of course, required for in-

(continued)

dividuals entering second or subsequent careers.

Corollary IIIb: Public and private recreational and educational facilities are organized in terms of functional objectives. Their clientele is selected not on the basis of age, but on the basis of common interests and objectives.

New Assumption IV

Sexual and related behaviors and attitudes appropriate for all normally functioning human beings regardless of age.

Corollary IVa: Whenever reproduction is a desired element of the sexual relationship, assortative mating by age may occur.

Corollary IVb: Social institutions facilitating or encouraging sexual or related behaviors are differentiated not on the basis of age but on dimensions reflecting interest and behavior patterns.

Corollary IVc: Whenever reproduction is not a desired element, assortative mating will occur as a function of variables such as physical attractiveness, shared interests and common behavior patterns. But common past experiences may nevertheless lead to assortative mating by age for reasons of shared experiences rather than common age.

Source: From Schaie, K. W. Reflections on papers by Looft, Peterson and Sparks: Intervention toward an ageless society. *Gerontologists*, 1973, *13*, 31-35.

These assumptions would be accepted by most of the old, but much education would be required before the young and the middle-aged would accept them. Nevertheless, it is only such attitude change that will permit a significant increase in the quality of life for our elderly—an increase that would, we believe, have a general impact on the quality and dignity of all human existence.

Summary

1. The lengthening of life expectancy implies that almost everyone will experience an adult-centered stage of life in addition to a child-centered one. One result has been a shift from the three-generation extended family to the nuclear family. Because of the ease of modern communications, there is a contrary trend toward maintaining a family network sometimes called the modified extended family. Shifts from the traditional nuclear family arrangement occur because of divorce and remarriage. More radical family alternatives are provided by experimental communities.
2. Economic factors that have changed family patterns include greater job mobility, an increase in women's participation in the work force during and after the child-rearing years, and the differential distribution between time spent on work and on leisure.
3. The roles of the family include procreation, socialization (both in childhood and adulthood), provision of economic support, placement in a social position, and affective and emotional support.
4. Our view of children has changed from one of chaotic and impulse-ridden creatures, who must be controlled and civilized to ensure their survival, to

that of emerging creative persons whose individualized unfolding and development should be encouraged and facilitated. As a result, our approach to child discipline has changed from an authoritarian, repressive, and punitive pattern; through a permissive but basically irresponsible pattern; to a warm, guiding, and modeling authoritative pattern.

5. In American families, mothers spend more time with their children than do fathers. But paternal participation in child-rearing activities is increasing rapidly. A warm relationship with a father figure is important during the early school years, and psychosexual difficulties may occur when children identify predominantly with the opposite-sexed parent.

6. The manner in which young children develop emotional relationships is important for the development of later experiences of trust and closeness. The attachment process also results in the establishment of *dependency*, the tendency to seek support and affection from others. Adequate child-rearing techniques encourage increasing independence by reinforcing children's initiatives and allowing them gradually to assume control over their own decisions. Competence and self-reliance are fostered by providing adequate role models as well as early standards of excellence and expressions of approval for a child's successful performance.

7. Aggression in children is thought to be caused by parents who use power-assertive techniques and who frustrate their children by the use of physical punishment, offering them a model of aggressive behavior that is then displaced toward others. By contrast, authoritative child-rearing practices are thought to reduce aggression by teaching children concern and respect for others.

8. Five different roles are played by grandparents: formal, fun-seeking, surrogate-parent, reservoir-of-family-wisdom, and distant-figure. The particular role exercised may be determined by the children's age and by the grandparents socioeconomic status.

9. *Birth order* refers to the sequential position of an individual in terms of brothers and sisters. Firstborn or only children are often brighter and have competitive advantages over younger siblings. Birth-order effects are most important in large families. Family size determines the number of different interactions each family member is involved in. Larger families may lead to more interpersonal friction and may require parents to resort to authoritarian child-rearing methods.

10. Children of single and divorced parents are usually raised by their mothers. Possible psychological damage to male children in fatherless families depends primarily on the nature of the mother-son relationship and on the age when the father figure became unavailable.

11. Family dynamics, including the initial mother-child interaction, can be viewed as small social systems. As such, they can be studied by observing spatial distance, dyadic gazing, and vocal approaches; by comparing individual family-to-family group profiles; and (in adulthood) by measuring such factors as geographic distance between family members, patterns of mutual aid, face-to-face contacts, and other indexes of family solidarity.

12. Contrary to common stereotypes, childless couples report greater satisfac-

tion with their marriages than do couples with children. The most disadvantageous effect of a childless marriage is the lack of support from adult children upon the death of a spouse.

13. Increasingly common alternatives to the traditional nuclear family are provided by childless marriages, multiple marriages, and collectives and communes. Multiple marriages may result in conflict for children, who must meet the expectations of two families that may differ in values. In return, however, children may be provided with the advantages of an extended family network.

14. Experimental communities typically view children as the common responsibility of the group. Five types of experimental communities are the religious community, the utopian community, the planned community, the Israeli kibbutz, and communes.

15. Family influences remain important throughout life. Relations between generations represent "continuous bilateral negotiations in which the young and old exchange information and influence." Conflict between generations is often caused less by actual differences than by the fact that old and young people do not always share the same perception of reality. Common historical experiences may lead to the development of intragenerational solidarity, which can result in differences between generations and can contribute to the tendency toward segregation.

16. The increasing number of relatively healthy and independent older people has led to the establishment of retirement communities. Because of great diversity among the elderly, it is unlikely that there can be a single most desirable type of such a community or that these communities can serve the needs of most elderly. Communities can be structured to provide age-integrated living arrangements that foster constructive contacts between generations while reducing the annoying features of such contacts, which in the past have led to the establishment of age-segregated communities.

17. Society's acceptance of people of all ages may depend on the modification of stereotypes held by the middle-aged about persons at other life stages. Acceptance of relevant and benevolent basic assumptions would minimize age-graded disabilities and improve the quality of life for all.

Selected Readings

Baumrind, D. "Some Thoughts About Child Rearing." In *Influences on Human Development*. (Ed.) U. Bronfenbrenner. Hinsdale, Ill.: Dryden, 1972. A very readable account of a major research program and its implications for different models of child rearing. Particulary useful in clarifying the important distinctions among authoritarian, permissive, and authoritative child-rearing approaches.

Goldberg, S. R., and F. Deutsch. *Life-Span Individual and Family Development*. Monterey, Calif.: Brooks/Cole, 1977. Parts 1, 2, and 4 expand on many of the themes treated in this chapter in language suitable for nonpsychologists and nontechnical readers.

Lynn, D. R. *The Father: His Role in Child Development*. Monterey, Calif: Brooks/Cole, 1974. The author treats this widely neglected yet most important topic in depth.

Examples of different types of father-child interaction are provided, and the impact of parental influence is analyzed carefully. There is also a thorough discussion of the effects of father absence on children's personality development and mental health.

Sussman, M. B. *"The Family Life of Older People."* In *Handbook of Aging and the Social Sciences.* (Eds.) R. H. Binstock and E. Shanas. New York: Van Nostrand Reinhold, 1976. The most recent authoritative update on the literature on the family life of the elderly. Contains discussions of theoretical models as well as a full review of recent empirical data on the family in old age.

Troll, I. E. "The Family of Later Life: A Decade Review." *Journal of Marriage and the Family,* 33 (1971), 263-390. The sparse literature on family development beyond the child-oriented life stage is reviewed fully, including sociological, anthropological, and psychological sources. Emphasis is on the establishment and maintenance of family networks as well as on intergenerational exchange of support.

Chapter 8

Social Influences

How social learning and modeling help children to understand what behaviors are acceptable or unacceptable

The effects of social deprivation, institutionalization, and social disadvantage

Socialization over the life span, including role learning and the transmission of norms

How social class influences an individual's behavior, family life, and physical and mental health

Peer relations, group influences, and leadership

The school as a socializing force, including the effects of teachers' attitudes and classroom atmosphere

Religious influences on behavior throughout the life span

Identification
  Modeling
  Social Learning

Social Deprivation
  Animal Studies
  Effects of Institutionalization
  Social Disadvantage

Socialization over the Life Span
  Social Aspects of Individuals
  Role Learning
  Transmission of Norms

Social Class
  Interpersonal Behavior
  Intrafamily Operations
  Physical and Mental Health

Peer Relations and Influences
  Patterns of Interaction
  Friendship
  Group Influences
  Leadership
  Peer Versus Adult Influences

The School as a Socializing Force
  Values of Teachers and Administrators
  Effects of Teachers' Characteristics
  Effects of Classroom Atmosphere

Religious Influences
  Development of Values
  Sense of Community
  Sense of Identity
  Development of Esthetic Appreciation
  Ethnocultural Traditions
  Religious Influences in Adulthood and Old Age

Introduction

Chapter 7 dealt with family influences on human development, the ways in which parents and other kin affect our development. Although such influences have enormous impact on early development and remain striking throughout life, they are soon joined by input from outside the family. Children learn early that human beings are a highly social species and that there are many sources within the community and society at large that may influence and shape their behavior and development. In Chapter 7 we identified the concepts of attachment and dependency as basic mechanisms by which family influences are exerted. This chapter points first to the mechanism of identification as the basic process by which social influences are exerted, both through modeling and through social learning. Then we will consider the effects of social deprivation, as based on animal studies and as observed in certain forms of institutionalization. The process of socialization will be traced throughout the life span, and a number of specific social forces that tend to affect it will be examined. Such forces include the effects of social-class membership, peer relations and influences, the school environment, and religion.

Identification

The manner in which much early learning occurs may discomfort parents who believe in the adage that their children "should do as we say, not as we do." Extensive research on imitation and modeling processes suggests that, once a child has identified a role model, it is highly probable that he or she will imitate both socially desirable and socially undesirable behaviors (see also Bandura & Walters, 1963). Parental models may play a central role in the development of children's behavior, since many opportunities exist to observe and imitate parental behavior. Moreover, identification seems to occur specifically when

As models, parents play a central role in their children's behavioral development.

Phoebe Dunn, Design Photographers International, Inc.

311

children can identify similarities between themselves and a role model (Mussen, Conger, & Kagan, 1974). Nevertheless, many aspects of both interpersonal skills and negative behaviors are established by the imitation of other significant children and adults. Imaginary models provided by television programs as well as real-life interactions on the playground or in school may contribute to the development of such behaviors as aggression (Stein & Friedrich, 1975).

Modeling

It has been suggested that learning by imitation, or *modeling*—unlike the otherwise slow process of trial and error in instrumental learning—is an effective way of rapidly acquiring large segments of behavior. For example, observation of children's play may show that characteristic parental role behaviors are reproduced in their entirety (Bandura, 1962). That such modeling is not confined simply to the direct observation of real-life models is illustrated by an interesting experiment on the transmission of aggression through modeling (Bandura, Ross, & Ross, 1963).

In this experiment, some children were shown a film that depicted aggressive acts by adults whom other children had seen earlier engaging in aggressive acts toward an inflated doll. A third group of children saw a film in which a model disguised to look like a cartoon cat engaged in aggressive acts toward a doll. After the modeling session, all experimental groups and control groups that either had no model or had a nonaggressive model were tested for the amount of imitative aggression in response to mild frustration. Figure 8.1 (Bandura, 1967) shows clearly that direct observation of aggressive models as well as of surrogate models resulted in increased aggressiveness in response to frustration. Of equal importance was the finding that children who observed the nonaggressive model displayed the behavior of that model to the extent of showing significantly *less* aggression than did the control group without a model.

Social Learning

Modeling may be the principal mechanism that mediates the identification process required for social influences to make an impact on individual behavior. But the concept of *social learning* is considerably broader, for it includes the manner in which social behavior is formed from the stimuli provided by others (Gewirtz, 1969). Such stimuli are not necessarily presented solely by other people. For example, certain physical events such as crowding can be important, and manipulation of the physical environment can be used to determine the expression of social behavior (Freedman, Klevansky, & Ehrlich, 1971).

Indeed, it is the characteristics of the immediate environment that tend to determine a person's observable behavior patterns, regardless of the more stable characteristics of the individual. The latter—and in particular genetically determined predispositions—provide the limits within which behavior can occur; but it is the immediate environment that controls the behavior expression. Gelfand (1975, pp. 1–2) provides the example of a child who has a highly favorable genetic background but nevertheless fails to obtain a high IQ score if he or she

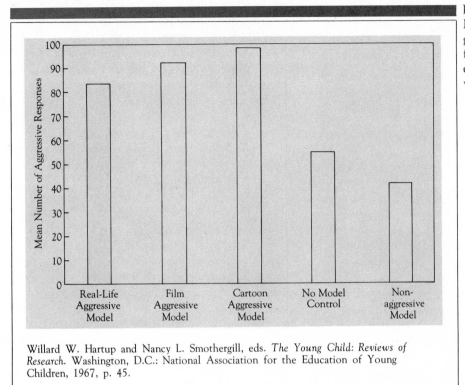

FIGURE 8.1
Mean number of aggressive responses performed by children in each of five groups with different models.

Willard W. Hartup and Nancy L. Smothergill, eds. *The Young Child: Reviews of Research*. Washington, D.C.: National Association for the Education of Young Children, 1967, p. 45.

belongs to a population group whose standard environment differs markedly from that upon which the intelligence test was developed. For example, such a child might never have been made aware of the importance of speed, and thus may respond accurately but at a slower rate than children of comparable genetic background who had been socialized in the culture for which the test was designed. The major point is that the socialization pattern of a person's environment tends to interact with inherited and physical characteristics, as well as with specific socialization patterns within a child's primary family unit.

Of course, social learning is not confined to early childhood. Peer groups become increasingly important as socializing agents and role models, and for a large segment of the population, undergraduate education provides exposure to a diversity of value orientations. In particular, undergraduate education may expose young adults to expressions by their teachers of cultural rather than material or political values, thus providing opportunities for identification with more humanistic models than might be posed in the average home (Parsons & Platt, 1973). Even throughout adulthood, our perceptions of significant others in the environment will affect our self-concepts and shape behavioral expression, whether positively or negatively. We will examine these issues in more detail later in the chapter. But first we need to consider some of the consequences of *social deprivation*, when opportunities for social influences are denied to a developing individual.

The Hazards of Family Viewing

WAYNE SAGE

The medium that gave us *Ozzie and Harriet* and *Make Room for Daddy* today stands accused of doing violence to American life in a string of bizarre trials.

In San Francisco, the mother of a young girl raped with a Coke bottle sued NBC for broadcasting an incident which the mother claims incited the attack on her daughter. In Miami, a teenage murderer pleaded innocent on the grounds that watching televised violence had predisposed him to homicide. In yet another incident, young boys drenched an old man in gasoline and set him on fire, just as the act had been portrayed on television the night before.

By judging from the results of research at UCLA, the repetition of heinous acts by predisposed individuals, however appalling and regrettable, may not be nearly so dangerous in the long run as a more subtle eroding of the environment of the home. And perhaps just as importantly, television seems to have the potential to influence its audience to treat one another more humanely.

Evidence that television can adversely affect children has long been mounting. That adults may be affected by the police stories and sitcoms beamed into our homes is demonstrated by the work of psychologist David Loye, psychiatrist Roderic Gorney, and research coordinator Gary Steele, who selected 183 married couples and for one week subjected each of the husbands to one of five different viewing schedules.

Some of the men watched *Kojak* and the detectives of *Hawaii Five-O* chase criminals and slug punks on high-violence shows. Others saw only "pro-social" shows, such as *The Waltons,* which stress helpful behavior. A third group of husbands sat through yet another rerun of *I Love Lucy* and other neutral or light entertainment. For further comparison, yet another group was left free to watch or not watch whatever they chose.

Unbenownst to the men, the wives kept tabs on their husbands during the week, recording each instance of hurtful behavior, such as a father losing his temper and kicking a kid's tricycle out of the driveway. The women also noted helpful behaviors, such as volunteering to take a child for a walk while the wife rested. The wives did not watch television during the test week and did not know what sort of programs their husbands were scheduled to watch.

By the end of the week, the men who viewed the violent shows had racked up a greater incidence of hurtful behaviors around the home, according to their wives' tallies, while the husbands who saw the pro-social shows committed the least number of hurtful acts of any group in the study. Also, psychological tests administered throughout the week indicated an increase in aggressive mood for the men watching the violent shows but a decrease in aggressive mood for those who watched the pro-social programs.

Thus it would seem that at least to some extent, we are what we watch. The nation's current video diet, Gorney believes, is psychological junk food, and may be more insidiously hazardous than we realize. . . .

Explains Gorney: "For relationships in society, the human organism depends on a whole series of behaviors such as patience, treating people as individuals, and willingness to admit one is wrong and to think things over and to persevere in solving problems. What television does to all these aspects of a personality may be extremely important.

"If we produce a generation of children who feel embarrassed to have a problem that cannot be solved in an hour, who judge others through stereotypes, or who denigrate a man who thinks before doubling up his fists to punch somebody, we may change the nature of our society in ways that are more important than these regrettable events where specific violent acts are replicated."

Source: *UCLA Monthly,* September-October, 1978, pp. 1-2. Reprinted by permission of the UCLA Alumni Association.

Social Deprivation

Evidence for the effects of social deprivation comes from three different sources. The first uses animal models to show that, indeed, there are critical periods in behavioral development and that such periods have profound effects (see also Scott, 1968). A second source of information about social deprivation comes from studies of the effects of institutionalization, where restricted environments typically involve below-normal social stimulation (Casler, 1961). A third source of information comes from studies of the early experiences of socially disadvantaged children (for example, Birch, 1968). We have considered some of these matters already, in Chapter 6.

Animal Studies

Critical periods for socialization have been reported for many animal species. For example, King and Eleftheriou (1964), in summarizing work with laboratory rats, concluded that systematically handled rats have faster growth rates and as adults respond better to stress and learn faster than do unhandled rats. Songbirds reared in isolation will not later produce songs of a quality comparable with those produced by birds reared normally (Thorpe, 1958). And monkeys reared in isolation when placed in a normal monkey colony at two years of age were almost unable to engage in typical social grooming and play behavior (Harlow & Harlow, 1962).

It appears that socialization experiences must occur during a brief period in the early life of organisms, when fear of strangers has not yet developed (Hess, 1970; Scott, 1962). The specific period depends on the pattern of social behavior in a given species. Thus for lower mammals it may depend entirely on sensory and motor development, since social behavior requires that a young animal follow other animals. The socialization of infants, however, may begin through visual exploration even before the development of more mature motor patterns (Caldwell, 1961).

Effects of Institutionalization

It has long been known that children growing up in institutional environments experience social deprivation that damages their later adaptive functioning. Perhaps the best-known early study of institutional effects is a comparison of children raised in a foundling home with those raised in the nursery ward of a prison for women (Spitz, 1945). The children in the prison nursery were often cared for by their mothers and were frequently out of their cribs, whereas the activities of the children in the foundling home were restricted severely. Spitz found drastic differences between the two groups by age two, among them that a third of the institutionalized children had died of a variety of diseases, whereas all comparison children were still alive.

It has been argued that the critical developmental period is the first half-year of life (Scott, 1968) and that, in restrictive institutional environments, the lack of care or early mistreatment may prevent children from acquiring such social behaviors as smiling, approaching, and communicating with others. These skills are essential for eventually establishing adult modes of love, friendship, and marriage relationships. When such models are absent, significant emotional retardation can result (Bijou, 1968).

Before readers assume that such effects are irreversible, we should point out that withdrawal and fear behaviors that are established by children severely deprived in early childhood can be remediated to some extent. Modern behavior modification techniques have shown some success (for example, Lovaas et al., 1973), and rehabilitative experiences also can reverse some of the negative effects of early deprivation (Kagan & Klein, 1973).

Social Disadvantage

The deprivation effects that occur in groups of socially disadvantaged children may be a function of very complex patterns. For example, one major cause may be poor nutrition, which may lead in subtle ways to a reduction of a child's ability and likelihood to take advantage of social stimulation. Although conditions of poor health may directly affect the development of the nervous system, the role of poor nutrition—found so commonly in groups that are disadvantaged economically and socially—may have a much more indirect effect on behavioral development. Thus undernourished children are likely to be less responsive to their environment and therefore will not respond to the same amount of stimulation during critical periods as would properly nourished children (Cravioto, DiLicardie, & Birch, 1966). Indeed, it has been shown that malnutrition occurring before six months of age may lead to learning deficits that are not overcome later precisely because of the critical period, during which the infant was insufficiently available to social stimulation (Cravioto & Robles, 1965). Even more complex is the interaction between a mother's response in stimulating her child and the child's reactivity to the stimulation. That is, apathetic children fail to reinforce their parents for providing social stimulation (Hartup & Lempers, 1973).

As a disadvantaged minority group, the elderly are also prone to the harmful effects of social deprivation, both directly and indirectly. Direct social isolation is a particular risk for older people, since as many as 28 percent of community-dwelling adults over age sixty-five live alone (Pfeiffer, 1973). And studies of cognitive deficits in the elderly suggest strongly that individuals who are social isolates suffer the greatest disadvantage (Schaie & Gribbin, 1975, Gribbin, Schaie, & Parham, 1980).

Socialization over the Life Span

Social Aspects of Individuals

Social development has been characterized as the process by which an individual is led to adopt behaviors within a range that is customary and acceptable by the standards of his or her reference groups (Child, 1954). Three related processes seem intimately involved with such social development. First, it is recognized that every social group has expectations of its members by situation, sex role, and life stage. Children must learn the expected social roles under all of these circumstances. Second, within each of these roles, it is necessary to learn the range of approved behaviors accepted as relevant by one's reference group. The third requirement is the development of appropriate attitudes toward one's reference group, which permits interaction in social settings and creates opportunities for social reinforcement. The last process often involves learning to like social interactions and to become a friendly person. Although few individuals adopt all the expectations of their group (which would be total conformity), social approval nevertheless requires most people to reconcile their needs with group expectations. A well-socialized superior individual eventually will become skilled at knowing how far ahead of the group one can be and yet be perceived as a leader and a fashion setter rather than a social deviant.

There is sometimes confusion about how we use the term *social*. A *social* person is one who has mastered the three processes described above; a *nonsocial* person has not done so; and a *gregarious* person is one who has mastered the social aspects and also has received much reinforcement from (and thus seeks contact with) others. On the other hand, an *unsocial* person is someone who has not achieved mastery of the social processes and therefore is forced to spend much time alone. Finally, an *antisocial* person is aware of the group's expectations but has developed an antagonistic stance toward the reference group (Hurlock, 1972, p. 221).

Many traits developed by children as part of the socialization process remain quite stable throughout life (see Chapter 16), but social norms and expectations do change in response to the pressures and role changes of adult life (Neugarten & Datan, 1973). It is not unusual, therefore, to find that an individual's coping style—which has provided successful social behavior throughout much of the life span—may require adjustment in old age. Such change may result in part from the stereotypes of what is age-appropriate behavior, often imposed on the elderly by the middle-aged (Schaie, 1973). But there also are changing demands made upon the elderly that, while acceptable to some, may result in disengagement and breakdown of adaptive social responses in others (Maas & Kuypers, 1974).

Role Learning

The development of social roles begins early in life. Obviously, young children cannot directly assume a variety of roles appropriate to older children or adults. Therefore, initial development of roles often takes the form of *role-playing activities*, rehearsal devices that eventually will aid role enactment. Children who have superior verbal skills will be most at ease in role-playing activities (Bowers & London, 1965). Not only do young children rehearse later roles, but they also begin quite early to ascribe roles to their peers. For example, even at the kindergarten level, children describe others as crybabies, or hitters, or talkers; and the stereotypes that children develop about the roles played by others begin to firm up as they get older (Radke-Yarrow, Trager, & Davis, 1970).

Within the home, children soon differentiate the roles of father and mother, which leads to the adoption of specific sex roles. Indeed, a large proportion of sex differences in behavior may be related to this early role learning. Also, the ascription of stereotyped roles to others is often a function of observing parental role assumption with respect to people of different sex, ethnic group, or social class (Maccoby & Jacklin, 1974). Of course, roles learned in the home are modified as children move through nursery school and the formal school system. Frequently, however, later experiences are judged by or are discounted in terms of the modeling that influenced the earlier experience.

A number of major role identities tend to structure an individual's connection with and orientation to crucial aspects of social life. Many different roles could be listed, but at least five seem most noteworthy (Gordon, 1976). The most pervasive and consistently reinforced of these is, of course, *sexual identity* (Money & Ehrhardt, 1972). Besides the initial identification, there are other, related role attributes, such as being identified as a "virgin," a "prude," or a "dirty old man." Almost as important is one's *ethnic identity*. Personal values, association patterns, and potential marriage partners will depend on whether an individual develops a particular ethnic identification, which furthermore is so labeled and recognized by others (Rose, 1974). *Occupational identity* requires that an adult individual develop an identity concerning work that is different from the role displayed in the home. *Membership identity* forges the link between an individual and the formal and informal organizational life of the community. And, relatively late in life, *political identity* is described in terms of membership in a political party as well as one's identification as a liberal or conservative or as a leader, loser, or peacemaker.

Role-playing activities help children rehearse; many sex differences in behavior may be related to early role learning.

Eileen Christelow, Jeroboam, Inc.

Acting One's Age: New Rules for Old

BERNICE NEUGARTEN
INTERVIEWED BY ELIZABETH HALL

A professor at the University of Chicago, Bernice Neugarten is one of the major authorities in this country on the psychology and sociology of aging. She is also known for her maverick views on some of the issues. Neugarten argues, for example, that the family is not falling apart, that menopause is neither frightening nor terrible, that women welcome the "empty-nest" syndrome rather than fear it, that old age does not mean poverty, isolation, and sickness, and that far from being placid inhabitants of rocking chairs, grandparents can be the shakers and movers of society.

Elizabeth Hall Dr. Neugarten, you've said on several occasions that the United States is becoming an age-irrelevant society. Just what do you mean by that?

Bernice Neugarten Simply that chronological age is becoming a poorer and poorer predictor of the way people live. An adult's age no longer tells you anything about that person's economic or marital status, style of life, or health. Somewhere after the first 20 years, age falls away as a predictor.

Hall Does that mean we are becoming a less rigid society?

Neugarten Yes, I think so. Lives are more fluid. There's no longer a particular year—or even a particular decade—in which one marries or enters the labor market or goes to school or has children. The whole internal clock I used to write about that kept us on time, the clock that tells us whether we're too young or too

old to be marrying or going to school or getting a job or retiring, is no longer as powerful or as compelling as it used to be. It no longer surprises us to hear of a 22-year-old mayor or a 29-year-old university president—or a 35-year-old grandmother or a retiree of 50. No one blinks at a 70-year-old college student or at the 55-year-old man who becomes a father for the first time—or who starts a second family.... A man can become a father again at the same time he becomes a grandfather.

Hall So we may see some great changes in what we think about the way people function. The irrelevancy of age to life in this society must have implications for public policy....

Neugarten The primary message is to stop legislating on the basis of age and start providing services only on the basis of need. It's the needs of the old-old that concern us. But if programs meant to assist them are drawn up in terms of age, then society may become so burdened by similar benefits going to the young-old—who don't need them—that adequate programs can't be funded. For example, no more than 15 percent of people over 65 need special health or social services—and they should have them. But, in a time of inflation, a program that offers those services to everyone over 65 is an easy target for budget-trimmers.

Hall You're suggesting we provide those services for people who need them—no matter what their age.

Neugarten That's right.... Some people have tried to help the old by pressing for special benefit programs. I happen to believe that it's far better to integrate old people into society. Let's make this a truly age-irrelevant society and just ignore age differences whenever we can. Let's worry about the poor, the disabled, and the isolated. If we meet their needs, we'll also have met the needs of the old-old.

Source: Reprinted from *Psychology Today*, April 1980, pp. 66–80. Copyright © 1980 Ziff-Davis Publishing Company.

One concern of many healthy elderly people is that they are expected gradually to give up their occupational and membership identities. It sometimes is argued that this "rolelessness" of the elderly is a peculiar attribute of Western culture. But this contention may reflect more the myths regarding the status of the elderly than the actual roles permitted them. For example, a study of three traditional villages in India showed that there was a wide gap between the ideal norms and the actual situation with respect to the status of the elderly. In these villages very few people after midlife played leadership roles, controlled family affairs, or participated actively in community affairs (Neugarten, 1966).

In their studies of disengagement (see Chapter 16), Cumming and Henry (1961) report massive reduction in roles during the later half of life. Such findings, however, may be quite specific and moreover may relate to changing opportunities for role involvement (Roman & Taietz, 1967), as well as to opportunities and desire for continued involvement (Carp, 1968). Table 8.1 summarizes age and sex differences in active role participation for a variety of roles after age fifty. A more extensive discussion of role change over the life span may be found in Rose (1974).

TABLE 8.1
Proportion of Men and Women with Active Roles at Various Ages

Age and Sex	N	Spouse	House-hold	Kin	Friend	Neigh-bor	Worker	Organ-ization
Males	107							
50-54	19	89.5	100.0	68.4	73.7	68.4	94.7	36.8
55-59	18	88.9	94.4	61.1	50.0	66.7	100.0	55.6
60-64	19	84.2	84.2	63.2	73.7	47.4	78.9	21.1
65-69	12	91.7	100.0	83.3	83.3	66.7	33.3	33.3
70-74	25	64.0	76.0	76.0	72.0	48.0	24.0	20.0
75 and over	14	78.6	85.7	71.4	71.4	35.7	21.4	7.1
Females	104							
50-54	17	82.4	82.4	64.7	70.5	58.8	82.4	35.3
55-59	16	62.5	87.5	87.5	75.0	75.0	31.3	43.8
60-64	15	60.0	86.7	80.0	66.7	73.3	53.6	53.3
65-69	19	36.8	57.9	52.6	63.2	57.9	26.3	36.8
70-74	25	28.0	52.0	56.0	60.0	52.0	16.0	32.0
75 and over	12	16.7	50.0	50.0	83.3	50.0	16.7	25.0

Source: From *The Social Forces in Later Life: An Introduction to Social Gerontology*, Second Edition, by Robert C. Atchley. © 1977 by Wadsworth Publishing Company, Inc., Belmont, California 94002. Reprinted by permission of the publisher.

Transmission of Norms

In spite of all the popular talk about the so-called generation gap, research suggests that cultural and behavioral norms continue to be transmitted from one generation to the other. Indeed, the same studies that show reported stereotypes of perceived generational differences in society as a whole also show quite small differences among members of the same family belonging to different generations (Bengtson, 1971; Bengtson & Black, 1973; Bengtson & Cutler, 1976).

Sociologists describe the transmission mechanisms via the concept of *intergenerational solidarity*, which can be subdefined into three elements: *association*, or objective interaction between generations; *affect*, or the degree of sentiment among family members; and *consensus*, or agreement of values and opinions (Bengtson, Olander, & Haddad, 1976). Obviously, transmission of norms can occur only if there is continuous closeness among generations at many life stages. And despite our apparent great mobility, such propinquity does occur, both for most young people and their parents and also for elderly parents. Thus Shanas et al. (1968) report that at least 84 percent of elderly parents in three industrial societies lived within an hour's travel time from at least one

Despite the generation gap, cultural and behavioral norms continue to be transmitted from one generation to the next.

Jan Lukas, Photo Researchers, Inc.

child, and 85 percent of these individuals had seen one of their children during the week before the survey. Evidence concerning the presence of affective solidarity is provided by a study of three-generation families (Bengtson, 1975). However, older members report higher levels of affection than do their middle-aged children, who report more involvement in giving and receiving help across generations.

Perhaps the most important evidence for the transmission of norms across generations are the findings concerning real and attributed contrasts in attitudes within families. First, in contrasting parents and children, we find that there is marked similarity in some instances (for example, the values regarding fatalism and optimism or collectivism versus individualism; Bengtson, 1975; Hill et al., 1970). On other variables, such as general orientation toward materialism versus humanism, there seem to be marked contrasts. More surprising, however, is the even greater similarity among nonadjacent generations. That is, young people and their parents tend to agree on norms concerning expressive behavior (Kalish & Johnson, 1972) as well as on values toward humanism or materialism (Bengtson, 1975). The continuity of norms within families becomes even more apparent when a younger individual moves into adult status and encounters life transitions already experienced by an older role model. We find then a continuation of norms, with intergenerational similarities occurring even in spite of ideological differences arising from the younger generation's peer interactions (Hill & Aldous, 1969).

Social Class

The social class or socioeconomic status of a child's parents has an important bearing on the course of the child's social development. In fact, many of the developmental aspects described in Chapter 7 are frequently confounded by variables of social status. In an upwardly mobile society like ours, we would expect shifts in social status over the life span. But early social-class expectations may well influence behavior throughout life, particularly with respect to interpersonal behavior and family life. On the other hand, the social status of an adult is likely to relate to such issues as life expectancy, physical and mental health, and role maintenance into old age.

Interpersonal Behavior

A number of personality traits have been studied in early childhood with year-old children divided into middle and lower economic status. McKee and Leader (1955) find higher levels of competitiveness and aggression in the lower-class children. In a study of nursery school children (Estvan, 1965), low-status children were less aware of their social status than were high-status children. However, some of the widespread behavioral effects of social class occur as a result of the high relationship between intellectual function and social-class membership. That is, children who are intellectually advantaged are also better

TABLE 8.2
Wolf's Thirteen
Hypothesized
Characteristics of
High Socioeco-
nomic Families
that Produce
Highly Intelli-
gent Children

A. Press for Achievement Motivation

1. Nature of intellectual expectations of child
2. Nature of intellectual aspirations for child
3. Amount of information about child's intellectual development
4. Nature of rewards for intellectual development

B. Press for Language Development

5. Emphasis on use of language in a variety of situations
6. Opportunities provided for enlarging vocabulary
7. Emphasis on correctness of usage
8. Quality of language models available

C. Provisions for General Learning

9. Opportunities provided for learning in the home
10. Opportunities provided for learning outside the home (excluding school)
11. Availability of learning supplies
12. Availability of books (including reference works), periodicals, and library facilities
13. Nature and amount of assistance provided to facilitate learning in a variety of situations

Source: Adapted from B. S. Bloom. *Stability and Change in Human Characteristics.* New York: Wiley, 1964.

problem solvers, more sensitive to the demands of their interpersonal environment, and more effective in their interpersonal interactions. Thus it is most important to ask what some of the factors might be that make social class such a potent predictor of intellectual ability.

A study by Wolf (1964) provides some clues. Thirteen characteristics of home environment that were thought to be related to high intelligence were identified (see Table 8.2). Wolf then interviewed the mothers of sixty fifth-grade children and scored how closely the home environment matched these characteristics. Correlating IQ scores with the scores for environmental characteristics produced a value of .76, suggesting a quite strong effect.

Social-class differences become even more apparent during adolescence, since lower-class children often may be treated as second-class citizens in school settings, in clashes with police, and in contacts with welfare and other public agencies. Most activities open to adolescents are so dominated by middle-class values that lower-class youngsters may find little meaning in them and may see themselves as out of place. Unless—because of some specific gift such as athletic skill or a high level of scholastic ability—an adolescent effectively shifts to a middle-class lifestyle, there will be a self-fulfilling prophecy in the sense that patterns will be adopted that lead to rejection by middle-class individuals. On the other hand, there may be less pressure on lower-class adolescents toward achievement-oriented activities, and in some subcultures a higher degree of sexual permissiveness is allowed to lower-class adolescents than those of higher social status (Friedenberg, 1959).

Turning to effects on adult behavior, a national survey of employed men found that the higher a man's social-class position, the more likely he was to value self-direction, to have greater self-confidence, to be more openminded and more personally responsible, to be more trustful and more receptive to innovation and change, and to show greater intellectual flexibility (Segal, Boomer, & Bouthillet, 1975).

Social-class effects have also been noted in the development of adult role differentiation. Well-educated adults expect to play many roles, both within the family and without, whereas lower-class individuals tend to expect a great deal of role differentiation (Troll, 1975). Substantial class differences have also been found in patterns of friendship. Lower-class individuals have fewer "family friends" than middle-class couples do, and more working-class interactions are segregated by sex; women associate primarily with relatives and neighbors, whereas men associate with their coworkers (Adams & Butler, 1967; Babchuck & Bates, 1963). Similar patterns prevail among the elderly. Older middle-class individuals actually may be at a disadvantage because family friends who were acquired as couples frequently do not survive marital difficulties or the death of a spouse (Lopata, 1973).

Intrafamily Operations

Some effects of class differences on interpersonal interactions may be traced back to class differences that are apparent in intrafamily operations. For example, it appears that among nursery school children, those from the higher classes are more conscious of boys, but those from the lower classes are more conscious of girls. This reflects class differences regarding the role of the male within the family structure (Estvan, 1965). More important, social class often affects family roles. Thus lower-class husbands frequently are not expected to be much involved in family affairs as long as they take on the role of provider. But college-educated men have a more ambivalent role and resulting conflicts, in that they are expected to share in housework and child-rearing activities (Veroff & Feld, 1970). Similarly, whether or not a woman works and thus needs to share child-rearing activities is often related to social-class level. That is, educated women tend to seek employment outside the home while children are young—even when financial considerations are secondary. Again, with increasing social status there is less interest and satisfaction with housework and child-care activities (Bernard, 1973).

Class differences tend to affect both maternal and paternal behavior. Lower-class mothers frequently have negative feelings toward their maternal role, particularly since they are more likely to have unwanted pregnancies and more often tend to raise children without a husband. But middle-class mothers are often handicapped by the expectation that they must be "good" mothers; their children's failures are thought to reflect on the mother's capability (Veroff & Feld, 1970). We have already noted that lower-class fathers are found to be less

TABLE 8.3
Relationship of
Family Income
and Chronic
Health
Conditions for
Different Age
Groups

Age Group and Family Income	Percentage of Total Population with Chronic Conditions that Limit Major Activity
Under 45 years	3.0
Under $3,000	5.6
$7,000 or over	2.0
44 to 64 years	14.4
Under $3,000	30.1
$7,000 or over	7.7
65 years and over	41.5
Under $3,000	47.0
$7,000 or over	32.6

Source: From *Age Patterns in Medical Care, Illness and Disability, U.S. July 1963–June 1965.* National Center for Health Statistics, Series 10, No. 32, data shown computed from Table 22.

involved with their families (Bowerman & Elder, 1964). In addition, they tend to communicate less with their children (Walters & Stinnett, 1971) and to use physical punishment rather than reasoning, which is more characteristic of middle-class fathers (Rosen, 1964).

Physical and Mental Health

Social class also acts as a determiner of physical and mental health variables. In earlier chapters we have noted the effects of deprived environments on early development. What is often less well known is the substantial relation between social status and physical and mental health with advancing age. Data from the National Health Survey, for example, document the substantial relationship between family income and the incidence of chronic disease (see Table 8.3), a relationship that favors the economically better off. This relationship is particularly true in midlife—but remains strong into old age.

Studies of environmental factors relating to decline in intellectual functions strongly implicate social status (Schaie, 1979; Gribbin, Schaie, & Parham, 1980). Individuals having high social status tend to be in good health and to be engaged substantially in a supportive environment; they thus tend to maintain intellectual competence. Those who show decline typically are of low status and suffer from relative social isolation.

Numerous studies have shown a strong relationship between the incidence of certain mental disorders and social class. Schizophrenia appears to be much more frequent in the lowest levels of urban societies, although it is now felt that this may result from the strong interaction among genetic factors, social class, and stress. Once mental health problems occur, social class is again important in determining the kind of treatment received. Thus lower-class patients tend to be treated with drugs and electroconvulsive therapy, whereas middle- and upper-class patients are typically candidates for psychotherapy (Segal, Boomer, & Bouthillet, 1975).

Peer Relations and Influences

The effects of peers begin to be important during the nursery school years and remain important throughout life. The major developmental impact of peers, however—both in developing a lifelong prototype and in affecting immediate behavior—occurs during adolescence. We therefore will emphasize that life stage in our discussion. A number of variables are important in understanding how peer influences affect development. First we will consider patterns of peer interaction. Then we will turn to the establishment of friendships, the nature of group influences, and the development of leadership characteristics. Finally we will consider the effects of peers as opposed to adult influences during adolescence.

Patterns of Interaction

The origin of peer groups is often found in informal aggregations of preadolescent youngsters living near each other who play together (Wattenberg, 1973). Later on, informal groups develop around favorite sets of activities. As children begin to move away from emotional ties that are exclusive to the home, they begin to form friendships with children close in age in their neighborhood and in school. These age-mates are likely to have similar needs and problems; they soon may become more reasonable role models for the behavior of children and adolescents than are the adults in the home.

During adolescence, peer influences have major developmental impact.

Joel Gordon, Design Photographers International, Inc.

It has been argued that in our culture boys are more likely to relate to peers in small groups, whereas girls seem to rely primarily on close personal friendships in dyads or at most quite small groupings. A study by Douvan and Adelson (1966) suggests that boys' behavior in groups is dominated by needs for achievement and independence, whereas that of girls is more concerned with the development of interpersonal skills and the need for shared feelings of love and security.

Maccoby (1961) suggests that children's social interactions with peers employ similar behaviors to those their parents have used in comparable situations. This study shows that boys who were raised by strict parents tended to accept rule enforcement from peers, whereas girls who insisted on rule enforcement, in turn, had parents who used relatively punitive child-rearing strategies during early childhood.

By contrast to the informal aggregation of adolescents, organized youth groups most frequently are established under adult auspices. Such groups are quite attractive to children who want to be part of a peer group but who also seek their parents' approval, which might not occur if they participated in a street gang. Although group values are most frequently set by adults, youngsters will often develop codes and hidden agendas of their own. In fact, organized groups tend to have substantial membership turnover, because their principal function may well be to provide an environment in which preadolescents and adolescents can practice social skills or make contact with members of the opposite sex in a socially approved climate. In cases where membership remains stable, it is often a function of the organized groups' serving as a convenient meeting place for previously established informal aggregations of youngsters.

Outside the orbit of adult programming are the adolescent street gangs. They may simply represent a well-structured form of the earlier informal play and interest groups. Depending on the values of their members, they may be no more than elitist cliques or adolescent social clubs, or they may serve as a mechanism to generate greater freedom from parental control; in environmentally unfavorable circumstances, they may develop organized delinquent and antisocial activity patterns. Individual members of such gangs may find security from belonging to a prestigious or feared group, and they may exercise leadership potential by acquiring positions of influence and power within the group structure.

It should be noted that many teen-age formal and informal groupings merely replicate culturally accepted or tolerated adult groups. They prepare youngsters for eventual participation in adult structures such as college fraternities, lodges, professional associations, or even organized crime.

Friendship

The origin of friendship in childhood occurs as playmates take on the role of confidants who can communicate with each other, seek advice, and tolerate criticism. During childhood friends are most frequently chosen from children of similar age, sex, and level of maturity. But middle-class children soon learn

Although many
friendships are long
lasting, older persons
often lose friends
through death and
changing circum-
stances.

Bill Price, Design Photographers International, Inc.

through parental approval or disapproval that it is more rewarding to have friends from their own social class and ethnic group (Hartup, Glazer & Charlesworth, 1967; Smith, Williams, & Willis, 1967).

In every social class, however, the preferred friends are those who have social prestige in their group—whether through athletic prowess or other desirable attributes—if only because one's own prestige seemingly is increased by the caliber of one's friends (Lott, Lott, & Matthews, 1969). As children grow older, however, the importance of personality traits increases (Griffitt, 1969). Friends are increasingly chosen in terms of similarity of interests, shared values, and the fact that the chosen friend is willing to express interest and affection.

There appears to be a peak in the number of dyadic friendship relationships in young adulthood, followed by a falling off. Many studies of the maintenance of friendship throughout life report that while friendships often last, there is a decrease because friends die and move away, and older persons who are not in good health have difficulty making new friends (Lowenthal & Robinson, 1976; Riley & Foner, 1968). But there are many different patterns. Thus Maas and Kuypers (1974) found that older persons who are highly involved with spouses and family also have enduring relations with their own friends. In old age as in childhood, there tends to be considerable age homogeneity, particulary among the working-class elderly (Rosow, 1964). Friendship networks seem to be particularly fragile if they depend on work associations or are formed between couples rather than individuals. In either case, retirement, divorce, or widowhood is likely to lead to the loss of friendship relations (Blau, 1973). When friendships are maintained, however, they have important functions until late in life. There is strong evidence that the presence of a confidant reduces stress and leads to greater morale in otherwise isolated elderly individuals (Lowenthal & Haven, 1968).

In a study of the life course of friendship, Lowenthal, Thurnher, and Chiriboga (1975) found that women consistently have a greater number of friends than men and that four-fifths or more at each stage reported their closest friends to be near their own age. Again, when asked about the characteristics of friends, they judged similarity as expressed by shared experience as most important, with reciprocity of relationship and compatibility being next most important. One interesting developmental aspect of this study was the finding that friendship patterns were quite complex in young adulthood, became simpler and less important in midlife, but reached maximum individuation and richness in old age.

Group Influences

Although friends are important for individuals to experience feelings of love and security, it is the social group that tends to be next in importance to the parents in providing models for social interaction and the adoption of values. Such values may be positive if they are exerted by constructive religious and other responsible social groups, or they may be largely negative when espoused by gangs and associations formed to protect the interests and social isolation of narrow-minded and self-interested groups. Peer influence exerted through groups during middle childhood is frequently more important than that of either family or teachers (Utech & Hoving, 1969).

Groups influence social development in three particular areas of functioning. These relate to the establishment of achievement motivation, to the motivation to conform, and to the development of a self-concept. One basic need of adolescents is to establish a separate identity from parents, and this can be done primarily by independent patterns of achievement. Through identification with a peer group, adolescents can, with greater security, learn to think independently and to try out values not necessarily acceptable to their families, while receiving some reinforcement from the group (Douvan & Adelson, 1966).

The development of some degree of conforming behavior is essential for social survival. It is the peer group that sets some public bounds that are recognized to be different from the conceivably arbitrary limits set by parents. Indeed, discrepancy between home and peer group may teach some individuals to learn that one may be able to conform in public but not in other circumstances (Collins & Thomas, 1972; Salmon, 1969). The third important socializing function of the group is in the development of a positive self-concept. Children know what their parents or friends accept through love and emotional involvement, but it is the peer group whose acceptance reassures a child that the acceptance has been earned rather than granted (Coleman, 1961).

Adult social groups tend to be organized primarily around work-related and leisure-interest activities. Yet they continue to have an important role in permitting continued growth of feelings of personal identity and recognition of worth. They can also serve as a guilt-reducing mechanism when an individual participates in groups that endorse attitudes and values that are seen as being rationally unacceptable but that have much emotional appeal. Thus it is much easier for most persons to express bigoted attitudes and behaviors in social groups that reinforce such behavior than in specific small-group contacts.

Groups such as senior-citizen clubs or congregate housing communities may offer considerable support to the role loss incurred by the elderly at retirement or loss of a spouse (Back, 1976; Kleemeier, 1961). However, some have argued that the major role of social groups for the elderly may merely be rather temporary surrogates for lost work roles and family settings, rather than serving the more innate functions characteristic of earlier associational groupings (Lowenthal & Haven, 1968).

Leadership

Another major influence of peer groups is the opportunity for an individual to try out and develop leadership roles. Whether this can be accomplished depends both on the personal attributes of the individual and on the characteristics of the group, since leaders usually represent the group's concept of an ideal group member. Perhaps more important, however, is that a prospective leader must be able to stir the group to action in a goal-directed fashion (Katz et al., 1957). It has been argued that successful leaders, whether they use an authoritarian or a democratic approach, have many of the attributes of their followers but are ahead of them somewhat (but not too much).

Studies of leadership characteristics suggest that peers accepted as leaders often have a better appearance than the group average, are not necessarily popular but are respected, have a sense of security and high personal adjustment, are more mature than other group members, are highly motivated and somewhat extroverted, and conform closely to the group ideal (Nelson, 1964). Leadership characteristics are often acquired through early childhood training and may be related to family position. Thus only children and oldest children tend to develop leadership characteristics more often than younger children. This is because only children have more interaction with mature adults, whereas older children are given early family responsibilities (Bossard & Boll, 1966).

Although the early display of leadership characteristics may often predict the persistence of leadership behavior, a number of other characteristics determine whether leadership is maintained or abandoned. For example, it is easier to display leadership in a stable group than in one where membership is more transient. Also, it is much more likely that a peer group will maintain a leader selected by its own appraisal of that person's qualities than a leader who is imposed by teachers, adults, or some other superior authority. Leaders who are adaptable will be able to move from one age grouping to the next without losing leadership attributes. But some degree of altruism is always required to maintain leadership, since the needs of the group often require some subordination of the leader's personal goals to those of the group.

Peer Versus Adult Influences

We indicated earlier that there may be a transition from family and adult influences to the greater impact of peers on role modeling during middle childhood and adolescence. This transition has been documented by a number of researchers. For example, a study of the relative influence of peers and parents during middle childhood found that when advice of parents and peers differ, children are more likely to be influenced by peers than by parents as they get older (Torrance, 1969). In a study of sixty eighth-grade and sixty twelfth-grade students, Lassigne (1963) found that these adolescents were more influenced in their attitudes by their peers than by adults. This study also noted that lower-class students and girls were more subject to peer influence than were boys.

Why does influence shift from the family to the peer group? One explanation that has been offered relates simply to the amount of waking time children from school age on spend in their home as compared to peer settings. Another explanation is the increasing need for children to have their perceptions validated by peers, who are increasingly important to them (Vogler, Masters, & Merrill, 1970). But peer pressure does not necessarily contradict parental values. In fact, peer groups may provide a useful transition from dependency to autonomy, and peers are often prescribers of values that are shared by parents and teachers (Brim, 1965). It has also been found that, although peer groups develop norms and values that reflect but do not duplicate parental values, it is the parents who have major impact on an adolescent's future planning (Kandel & Lesser, 1969). In many ways, then, peer groups turn out to perpetuate values reflected by parental attitudes and membership in ethnic and social-class groupings.

The School as a Socializing Force

Although the primary purpose of the school system may be described as the societal mechanism to teach children skills needed to function in a complex society, it also serves as an important mechanism for the transmission of cultural values and as a socializing agent. Many value patterns that are laid down in the home early in life may be modified significantly by school experiences. Of particular importance are the personal characteristics of teachers and the emotional climate in the classroom. But other matters of concern are the way in which discipline is used, the emphasis on academic versus social achievement, and the extent to which the school seeks to transmit and enforce the value system of the majority culture.

Values of Teachers and Administrators

Besides the peer influences previously discussed, the school exposes children directly to the influence of teachers and administrators and indirectly to the policy-making roles of school boards. Although teachers and administrators set up expectations and norms for discipline, academic performance, and social interactions, these expectations may be influenced by a number of variables that influence the decision maker's stereotypes. For example, expectations may be set by a teacher's experience with an older sibling (Seaver, 1973) or by a teacher's identification of a student as being an underachiever on the basis of comparing performance on intelligence tests with classroom behavior (Rosenthal & Jacobson, 1968).

There may have been some shift away from the tendency of teachers and administrators to foster the values of the white Anglo-Saxon Protestant majority culture in children regardless of their socioeconomic status or ethnic heritage (Medinnus, 1962). Yet there still is usually a wide discrepancy between the social characteristics of teachers and their students. We know, for example, that most school boards are dominated by professionals with an upper-class background (Dejnozka, 1963). Although the majority of teachers generally are perceived by society as having high status, typically just below professionals, they are an upwardly mobile group; thus even the increasing numbers of teachers from a working-class background tend to represent middle-class attitudes and values (Campbell, 1967).

Effects of Teachers' Characteristics

Much evidence has been gathered concerning the effects of teachers' personalities on the social development of students (Solomon, Bezdet, & Rosenberg, 1964). Well-adjusted teachers express positive and accepting attitudes and thereby motivate children to conform to the school's expectations. Teachers with a positive self-concept, in turn, are reasonable in their expectations and will facilitate opportunities for successful experiences, thus developing favorable self-concepts in their students. On the other hand, teachers with emotional problems set up conditions of confrontation and arbitrary interactions, thus providing a model that children may imitate to disadvantage. Such behavior models teach children to develop feelings of inadequacy and hostility toward authority figures in general.

An interesting study by Ryans (1961) investigated the relationship between teacher characteristics and student behavior. Teachers were rated on the three dimensions of (1) kind and understanding versus aloof but objective, (2) responsible versus evasive and planless, and (3) stimulating versus dull and routine. In turn, students were rated on seven characteristics: (1) disinterested versus alert, (2) obstructive versus constructive, (3) restrained versus participative, (4) rude versus self-controlled, (5) apathetic versus initiating, (6) dependent versus responsible, and (7) uncertain versus confident. These ratings were combined to yield a measure of the "goodness" of student behaviors. Correlations between teacher and student characteristics are given in Table 8.4. Note the strong relation for elementary school classes, with low positive relations for high school. This study suggests that teachers' personal characteristics most likely are implicated in the socialization of young children, whereas teachers' skills may be more important at the secondary level (Longstreth, 1968).

Groups	r_1	r_2	r_3
Elementary school classes			
834 classes, grades 1–6	.82	.80	.75
144 classes, grades 1–6	.83	.78	.80
Secondary school classes			
497 classes, mathematics and science	.20	.18	.21
568 classes, English and social studies	.18	.21	.26
114 classes, mathematics, science, English, and social studies	.17	.11	.14

r_1: correlation between student behavior and teacher ratings on *kindly, understanding* versus *aloof and objective.*

r_2: correlation between student behavior and teacher ratings on *responsible and businesslike* versus *evasive and planless.*

r_3: correlation between student behavior and teacher ratings on *stimulating and imaginative* versus *dull and routine.*

Source: From L. E. Longstreth. *Psychological Development of the Child.* New York: Ronald, 1968. Adapted from Ryans, 1961.

TABLE 8.4 Correlations Between Student "Good" Behavior Scores and Scores on Three Dimensions of Teacher Behavior

Effects of Classroom Atmosphere

Besides specific teacher characteristics, the atmosphere of a classroom may have an important impact on children's socialization and personality formation. This atmosphere may be set by administrative requirements (such as the imposition of formats like fundamental school, open classroom, self-paced individualized schedules, and so on). But it may also be set by the teacher's attitudes in determining whether he or she wishes to run an *autocratic classroom* (in which the teacher announces what is to be done), a *permissive classroom* (in which children initiate activities under the guidance of the teacher), or a *democratic classroom* (in which students and teachers jointly decide in what specific ways learning activities are to be implemented).

The issue of classroom atmosphere was investigated in a classic study by Lewin, Lippitt, and White (1939). In this study, groups of ten-year-old children participated in recreational activities led by instructors who took on authoritarian, democratic, or permissive roles. It was found that authoritarian leadership seemed to produce hostility toward fellow group members and a lack of constructive behavior when the leader was absent. The permissive leader produced boredom, lack of productivity, and —in some members—hostility as well. The democratic group yielded good interaction and productivity whether the leader was present or not, as well as much less hostility. Although this study is cited widely as an example of the superiority of a democratic atmosphere, there are a number of flaws. Critics feel that the real issue was the warmth displayed by the teacher. Since the participants in the study were all committed liberals, they likely were most sympathetic with the democratic role and more cold toward the authoritarian role (Longstreth, 1968; Sechrest, 1964). Other studies suggest that it is warm, authoritative teachers who may be most successful in socializing their students (McCandless, 1961).

Religious Influences

Although ours is a secular society, a large majority of the population feels allegiance to some set of religious beliefs or formal religious community, and a large plurality are active churchgoers and participants in programs sponsored by religious groups. It is not unreasonable to suppose, therefore, that next to the home, school, and informal peer groups, it is the formal and informal religious context that makes a major impact on the formation and maintenance of many attitudes and behaviors. This section briefly discusses the impact of religion on five areas of individual development: (1) values, (2) feelings of relatedness outside the immediate family, (3) the establishment of a sense of identity, (4) early reinforcement of esthetic appreciation, and (5) fostering of the relation of an individual to ethnic and cultural traditions. We will also comment briefly on the role of religious associations as a source of meaning and roles in old age.

Development of Values

One major contribution of all religious belief systems is a position regarding the role of the individual. Children growing up in families who relate to liberal religious traditions would be exposed to a set of values that describe persons as positive constructive agents, oriented toward self-actualization, whose life goal is seen as self-development in the service of the community and humanity in general. Such values can develop positive self-concepts and produce adults who are socially responsible and active.

Other religious belief systems, however, hold a much different version of humanity, seeing people as potentially evil sinners who must be protected from their own impulses. To the extent that religious groups see persons as potentially destructive or as obstacles to the working out of a deistic plan, then such belief systems can be instrumental in fostering negative self-concepts and feelings of guilt, as well as influencing individuals to be critical and nonaccepting of others who do not believe in or conform to their own concepts of morality.

A third effect of religious groups on the development of values is posed by belief systems that encourage withdrawal from active participation in society. In this case, reinforced values relate to the attainment of inner peace. Such a belief system may see participation in society to be irrelevant; it even may foster the attitude that other individuals are irrelevant to the psychological development of the believer.

Sense of Community

An important influence exerted by most organized religious groups is their programmed effort to develop feelings of relatedness and experiences of shared values in their members. As a result, children participating in religious groups soon learn about concerns that extend beyond their immediate family. Again, different traditions govern the extent to which such concerns may be expressed. Some traditions teach that only a very narrow range of beliefs and behaviors is permissible. When such a restriction is accepted, social growth and exploration are limited, and the believer will experience intense conflict when confronted with other belief systems or lifestyles. Such confrontation, however, is then likely to create either intensified dependency on the narrowly defined religious community or, often, complete dissociation from that community.

Modern liberal religious communities, however, encourage their members to value differences in feelings and insight that persons with different backgrounds can bring to religious understanding and experience. Such a point of view encourages the working out of individualized belief systems. It also encourages exposure to a wide variety of experiential possibilities and leads individuals to express greater tolerance. On the other hand, religious liberals inevitably will draw heavy criticism from individuals coming from a more limited and narrow tradition.

Sense of Identity

Members of religious groups often gain much strength from being able to identify with a cause, a moral position, and a belief system that creates feelings of relatedness to the world at large. Thus positive religious growth experiences should contribute to the kind of ego development posited by such writers as Eric Erikson (see Chapter 16). In particular, religious influences would seem to foster development toward Erikson's stage of identity achievement, or what Kohlberg (1964) describes as *principled morality*. That is, religious traditions tend to emphasize the development of moral thinking from a hedonistic or punishment-obedience orientation, through an orientation to interpersonal mature behavior, to a higher law and conscience orientation. But beyond that level, which may be attained by any rational or humanistic value system, liberal religious tradition seeks to develop people further, to the attainment of universal ethical principles (Kohlberg, 1973).

Development of Esthetic Appreciation

If cognitive complexity in childhood is indeed important for reaching one's greatest potential (see Chapter 13), then religious experiences may provide a further dimension beyond what occurs in the home. Most religious traditions make use of music and art objects as part of their services and houses of worship. Church ritual introduces pageantry and identification of life themes with the seasons, and it interweaves the dimensions of emotional and cognitive experience. Children from otherwise unstimulating home environments may thus acquire some appreciation for the intangible aspects that not only enrich life but are likely to be helpful to the upward mobility of a bright child coming from an impoverished environment.

Ethnocultural Traditions

In a pluralistic society with many different cultural roots, it often has been religious groups that have helped to form the continuity among traditions of other countries and cultures. Religious groups preserve what is valuable in a multicultural society and bridge the perceived gap between a developing individual's ethnic group and the expectations of the majority culture. It is the synagogue and the ethnic church that help perpetuate the cultural tradition and separate it from nationalistic concerns that might clash with the expectations of a secular culture. No other societal group seems to have as far-reaching a role as do religious groups in dealing with the peculiar demands and expectations of a multicultural society like ours.

Religious Influences in Adulthood and Old Age

Concern with religious belief, interest in participation in religious communities, and church attendance appear to remain fairly stable from early to late adulthood. For example, in the longitudinal study of Terman's advantaged children, a slight rise of interest in religion was found over their adult years (Terman & Oden, 1959). We must remember, however, that such findings may not appear consistently in cross-sectional studies. It is important to note that there is much continuity between adjacent generations in terms of involvement in religious groups and acceptance of religious values (Kalish & Johnson, 1972).

To the extent that older people become more isolated and have to depend on passive ways of interacting with society, certain religious influences tend to

Religious influences become more important to older people who are isolated or limited in social interaction.

Michael Serino, The Picture Cube

become increasingly important. Survey findings, however, suggest that while church membership is more frequent among the elderly than at any other life stage, active church involvement tends to decrease. On the other hand, such activities as listening to church services on television, private prayer, Bible reading, and meditation all become more frequent (Moberg, 1971).

Religious groups have become increasingly aware of their responsibilities toward their aging members. A number of denominations have active programs designed to maintain older persons in the community through such devices as religiously sponsored group homes or congregate housing arrangements. In addition, the more liberal denominations tend to direct older persons toward finding meaning in their life by involving them in socially constructive activities rather than providing the more traditional preparation for coming to grips with the end of their lives (Ailor, 1969).

Summary

1. Once a child has identified a role model, it is highly probable that he or she will imitate both desirable and undesirable behaviors of the model. Imitation, or modeling, is effective in the rapid acquisition of large segments of behavior. Direct observation of aggressive models results in aggressiveness in response to subsequent frustration.
2. Social learning involves the manner in which social behavior is formed from the stimuli provided by others. Within the limits of inherited predispositions, it is the immediate environment that determines observable behavior patterns.
3. Critical periods for socialization have been observed early in life in many species. To be successful, socialization experiences must occur during a brief period early in life, before fear of strangers has developed.
4. Children growing up in institutionalized environments have been found to experience social deprivation that damages their later adaptive functioning. Socially disadvantaged children who are undernourished may be less responsive to environmental stimulation during critical learning periods. Some elderly persons also suffer the effects of social deprivation, including cognitive deficits, because of social isolation.
5. Social development is the process by which individuals adopt behaviors that are within the customary and acceptable standards of their reference group. Young children learn later life roles by means of role-playing activities. Children's differentiation of the roles of father and mother lead to the adoption of specific sex roles.
6. Five of the most important life roles are sexual identity, ethnic identity, occupational identity, membership identity, and political identity. The often reported "rolelessness" of the elderly may be cohort specific and may relate more to changing opportunities for role involvement than to a desire to give up occupational and membership identities.
7. Intergenerational solidarity involves *association* between generations, *affect* or sentiment among family members, and *consensus* of values and opinions.

There is much greater agreement about social norms among members of different generations within the same family than among members of the same generation who belong to different families.

8. Early social-class expectations influence interpersonal behavior and intrafamily operations, but adult social status affects life expectancy, physical and mental health, and role maintenance into old age.

9. Social status characteristics expressed through the home environment are related to levels of intellectual functioning in early childhood and to social participation in adolescence. High-status children are found to be more intelligent and more likely to participate.

10. High-social-status adults expect to play many life roles within and without the family, while low-status adults expect to play only highly differentiated roles. Lower-class husbands frequently are not expected to be much involved in family affairs, whereas well-educated men are expected to share in housework and child-rearing activities besides being good providers. Educated women are more likely to seek employment outside the home while children are young, even when financial considerations are secondary.

11. There is a substantial relationship between high social status and the maintenance of good physical and mental health with advancing age.

12. In American culture, boys are more likely to relate to peers in small groups, whereas girls rely primarily on dyadic friendships. Organized youth groups, most often established under adult auspices, are most attractive to children who want to be part of a peer group that meets with their parents' approval. Adolescent street gangs, depending on the values of their members, may simply be social clubs that serve to generate more freedom from parental control or, in unfavorable circumstances, may be instrumental in the development of delinquent and antisocial behaviors.

13. In every social class, preferred friends are those who have social prestige in their group. As children grow older, friends are chosen increasingly in terms of shared interests and values. The number of friends people have peaks in young adulthood, followed by substantial attrition. Women have more friends than men, and closest friends tend to be near one's own age.

14. Peer influence during middle childhood may be more important than that of either family or teachers. Groups influence social development in particular with respect to achievement motivation, motivation to conform, and self-concept development.

15. Adult groups permit continued growth of feelings of personal identity and recognition of worth; groups of the elderly provide support for the role loss suffered upon retirement or the loss of a spouse.

16. Peer groups provide opportunities to try out and to develop leadership roles. Successful leaders are more personable, more mature, and more highly motivated than the average members of their groups. Peer groups also provide useful transitions from dependency on parents to autonomy. Such groups often prescribe values that reflect but do not duplicate parental values.

17. Besides the teaching of skills, schools also serve as an important mechanism for the transmission of cultural values and as a socializing agent. However,

teachers tend to represent middle-class attitudes and values. Teachers with positive self-concepts tend to be reasonable in their expectations and to facilitate opportunities for successful learning and socialization experiences; teachers with emotional problems often create conditions of confrontation and arbitrary interaction.

18. Classroom atmospheres have been described as being autocratic, permissive, or democratic. Some studies suggest that the democratic classroom is the most productive, whereas others indicate that warm but authoritative teachers are most effective.

19. Religious influences are important in the development of values and feelings of relatedness to the larger community outside the immediate family. Members of religious groups are often able to gain strength by identifying with a belief system or moral position. Religious influences are important also in the development of esthetic appreciation and in maintaining ethno-cultural traditions in a pluralistic society.

20. Religious influences increase in importance in old age. Supportive religious groups aid their older members by encouraging socially constructive activities as well as by helping them to come to grips with the impending end of life.

Selected Readings

Atchley, R. C. *The Social Forces in Later Life.* 3rd ed. Belmont, Calif.: Wadsworth, 1980. A very readable introduction to social gerontology covering a broad range of societal influences on aging individuals, as well as extensive discussions of societal stereotypes that affect the lives of older people.

Bengtson, V. L., P. L. Kasschau, and P. K. Ragan. "The Impact of Social Structure on Aging Individuals." In *Handbook of the Psychology of Aging.* Eds. J. E. Birren and K. W. Schaie. New York: Van Nostrand Reinhold, 1977, pp. 327-354. An up-to-date and scholarly review of the research literature on the effects of societal forces on older persons. Includes discussion of social definitions of time and aging, group variations in patterns of aging, and the effect of social change.

Gelfand, D., ed. *Social Learning in Childhood.* Belmont, Calif.: Brooks-Cole, 1975. A carefully selected anthology of research articles covering a wide array of topics related to children's acquisition of social behavior. Sections are preceded by introductions designed to focus the readers' attention to the points to be illustrated by the research papers.

Newman, B. M., and P. R. Newman. "Children and Schools." Chapter 11 in *Infancy and Childhood: Development and Its Context.* B. M. Newman & P. R. Newman. New York: Wiley, 1978, pp. 447-501. A discussion of the school as the context for development in middle childhood. Covers aspects such as the physical setting, school curriculum, methods of instruction, classroom characteristics, adaptation to the school setting, and an ecological analysis of the school's influence on development.

Shantz, C. W. "The Development of Social Cognition." In *Review of Child Development Research,* Ed. E. M. Hetherington. 5 (1975), 257-323. A good discussion and review of research concerning how children learn to make social inferences and develop social understanding, including sections on how children learn to infer what other persons see, feel, think, intend, and like.

Chapter 9

Cultural Influences

The major characteristics of the concept of culture

Ways to study cultural influences

How culture influences motor and physical development

Cross-cultural practices regarding pregnancy and childbirth, early and formal training of children, initiation into adulthood, sexual and family behavior, and aging

The Concept of Culture

Methods for Studying Cultural Influences
- Participant Observation
- Informal Interviewing
- Sampling and Quantification
- Objectivity in Cross-Cultural Research

Cultural Influences on Behavioral Development
- Motor Development
- Perceptual Development

Development in Different Cultures
- Pregnancy and Childbirth
- Infant Care
- Early Training
- Formal Training
- Initiation to Adulthood
- Sexual Behavior
- Family
- Age Grading
- Status of the Aged

Introduction

From the material presented in Chapters 7 and 8 about family and social influences on behavioral development, it should be clear that maturational and aging processes do not express themselves in a vacuum. The environment to which a developing individual is exposed has a tremendous impact on the manner in which behavior is expressed. While we are often aware of many social and family influences on our thoughts and actions, cultural influences on behavior are so widespread that they are frequently overlooked. So familiar are we with the typical patterns of development in our own culture that we tend to assume that development occurs in a similar manner for all members of the human species.

Although many maturational and aging patterns are common throughout humanity, it is a mistake to assume that development is similar across cultures.

Jan Lukas, Photo Researchers, Inc.

Klaus D. Franke, Peter Arnold, Inc.

Indeed, many maturational and aging patterns are common to all humanity. For example, certain sensorimotor behaviors generally appear at around the same age in children who have experienced vastly different child-rearing patterns; indeed, investigators have used these cross-cultural data to support the universality of their theories. For example, Piaget used such data to support his theory about the nature of cognitive development. Chomsky also supported his notions about language acquisition with cross-cultural data. And Whiting and Child (1953), who were among the first to undertake cross-cultural comparisons of child-training practices, found important similarities in parent-child interactions throughout the world.

Although universals have been identified across cultures, cross-cultural work has emphasized variation (LeVine, 1970). Human beings develop in environments that foster different ideas about child-bearing practices, mother-infant contact, severity and age of weaning and toilet training, status of the aged, and countless other aspects of human life. So numerous are the differences in human environments that it is challenging to isolate those critical variables that lead to differences in behavioral development.

Thus when we examine behavioral development cross-culturally, we have at least three goals in mind. First, we can begin to see how our own culture has influenced the way we act and the manner in which we view the world, recognizing that North American patterns are neither unique nor universal. Second, we can come to a clearer understanding of those aspects of development over the life span that we all share as members of the human species. Third, a cross-cultural perspective leads us to consider the vast range of human potential and the variety of forms that human development can take.

To examine cultural influences on behavioral development, we must compare development in different cultures. Typically, such cross-cultural comparisons have constituted the research strategy of cultural anthropologists, and their focus has been on group performances and group products as they relate to outside factors or social conditions such as climate, geography, or history. Eckensberger (1973) distinguishes cross-cultural psychology from cultural anthropology by noting that psychological investigation is concerned with the *individual* living organism (as opposed to the group orientation of anthropologists). In undertaking cross-cultural studies of development, psychologists aim to determine the different expressions of behavior that occur as an interaction between a developing individual and the cultural environment.

Cross-cultural research involves the systematic comparison of psychological measures obtained under different cultural conditions. This strategy of research is a means of maximizing environmental variation. It represents an attempt to examine the extremes of variability that human development can encompass as well as the basic similarities in human growth and change.

The Concept of Culture

The term *culture* was first used over a hundred years ago by a British anthropologist named Edward B. Tylor. Tylor defined *culture* as that "complex whole which includes knowledge, belief, art, morals, law and any other capabilities and habits acquired by man as a member of society" (Tylor, 1871, p. 1). This definition of culture is still accepted in principle, even though a century has elapsed since that time. An analysis of Tylor's definition of culture leads to the identification of the following four major characteristics:

1. Culture involves acquired capabilities, as opposed to capacities that are inherited genetically.
2. Culture involves behavior that is learned, but not all learned behavior can be characterized as culture. For example, many behaviors characteristic of all people, such as walking and talking, involve learning, but they will occur regardless of the culture.
3. Culture cannot exist outside of society. This means that individuals learn culture as members of a society.
4. Culture is not haphazard. It has a system or a pattern and therefore is referred to by Tylor as a "systematic whole." Culture is composed of several interrelated parts; no single part can be understood without having adequate understanding of other parts.

Different parts of a culture or the cultural content of a group can be divided into material and nonmaterial components. Although controversy exists regarding the validity of including material objects as parts of culture, no one denies that the knowledge and skill needed to make and use the artifacts is definitely a part of culture. In other words, a particular item of food is not culture, but the theory that distinguishes food from nonfood—and the beliefs associated with it—is definitely part of culture.

Whereas material aspects of culture such as technology, food preferences, and eating habits can be observed, the nonmaterial aspects of culture—beliefs and values—must be discerned from observable behavior. Values (the attributes desired by a cultural group) are manifested in the behavior of individual members of a culture. Although no individual manifests all desired values, everyone has knowledge about the values characteristic of his or her group.

Newborn children have no value orientation, but as they start to mature, the values peculiar to their group are imparted. As children mature biologically, they go through a continuous learning process. Upon birth they are exposed to a barrage of objects, ideas, beliefs, and norms characteristic of their own cultural group. Typically, children are exposed to only one culture and know the patterns of only that culture. Indeed, most human beings spend their entire lives in one culture and conceive of human nature within the confines of their own cultural experience. The very concept of culture was identified by Tylor only a century ago, and it is only in relatively recent times that communications and transportation systems have advanced to the point that average individuals in one culture are aware of the existence and practices of other cultures. Even today, individuals in some isolated areas have no awareness of human behavior beyond that which they have observed in their own society and culture.

Although the culture aims at molding people according to its prescribed norms, an individual does not always choose to respond to cultural demands. Nevertheless, individuals and culture are not always at odds. Culture does

Most people spend
their entire lives in
one culture and thus
view human nature
within its confines.

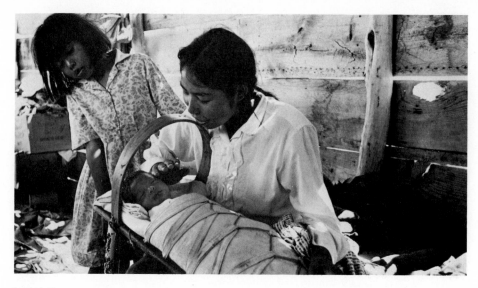

Michal Heron

provide individuals with the knowledge necessary to cope with the environment. In attaining this knowledge, human beings behave as active rather than
passive agents. Thus they are not only the carriers but also the architects of
culture.

Only members of the human species are born with the capacities that lead to
the development of culture (Schusky & Weiss, 1973). Indeed, the origin and
perpetuation of culture are based on our human ability to develop linguistic
symbols. Although some higher primates may be taught to respond to certain
symbols, no animal appears capable of spontaneously bestowing meaning on any
symbol. It is this capacity to develop symbols and to use such symbols that
makes culture uniquely human. The ability to symbolize enables us to store
knowledge, and thus human learning becomes continuous and cumulative.
Differences in cultural patterns can explain in part the variety in human behavior, but the capacity to develop and maintain culture is a trait universal in
human beings and unique to us as a species.

Methods for Studying Cultural Influences

The *cross-cultural perspective* involves comparisons among different cultural
groups as well as in-depth work within one culture. In attempting to answer
questions about development in various cultures, psychologists often borrow
techniques and data from cultural anthropologists and sociologists. The totality
of human behavior within various cultural patterns is the domain of cultural
anthropologists, who report on a whole community; from these observations,
psychologists can extract information about individuals and their development.

It is mainly through close, direct, and long-lasting contact that anthropologists
try to learn about the behavior and customs of other people. Obtaining data

Field work involves close, direct, and long-lasting contact that aims to learn about the behavior and customs of other people.

Yoram Kahana, Peter Arnold, Inc.

firsthand by living with the group under study is generally known as *field work*. It provides experience and knowledge that is otherwise unattainable. To interpret behavior patterns in different cultures appropriately, it is essential to get an in-depth perspective of the people through field work.

Participant Observation

A central practice of anthropological field work is to collect data through participant observation. The role of a participant observer entails great responsibilities. A researcher is expected to know the native language and to spend usually a year or more living with the members of the community. Data gathered through participant observation provide researchers with insights that are impossible to obtain through other methods. Subtle and covert customs can be inferred only through long and continuous participation in the native culture.

To assume the role of a participant observer is not an easy task. When a scientist enters a community with the purpose of carrying out field work, the feeling of being an intruder is typical. In trying to establish and maintain rapport, the researcher tries to adopt some of the customs and habits of the alien culture. Practices and habits that meet with disapproval from the people in the community may even be concealed. Though total immersion in the other culture is the goal, it is not really possible for a researcher to go totally "native." Being an adult member of one's own society, a researcher cannot easily be rid of the values and habits attained in that culture. Nevertheless, despite the problems associated with participant observation, it is considered a basic tool in cross-cultural research. Data gathered in this way are often supplemented with data gathered by other techniques, such as informal interviewing, sampling, and quantification.

Informal Interviewing

Participant observation is always accompanied by informal interviewing. The informants are individuals native to the culture being studied who are paid to tell about their culture or who voluntarily give information. The use of informants is indispensable when a researcher's interest lies in recovering information about ways of living that no longer exist. The use of multiple informants of various ages, both sexes, and different religious groups makes it possible to check and evaluate data closely. It has been noticed that informants—in trying to project a good image of their community—reveal only the ideal patterns of behavior. Thus a distinction must be drawn between ideal and actual behavior patterns. This can be done only by integrating participant observation with informal interviewing. Relying on the interviewing technique alone cannot give the kind of insight gained through living in a culture as a participant observer.

Sampling and Quantification

Although sampling and quantification of data recently have become more common in anthropological research, the importance of using such techniques was recognized and advocated years ago by Malinowski, the pioneer of modern field work in anthropology (Beals & Hoiger, 1971). Examples of numerical data in anthropological writings were not completely absent from earlier work, though they were fewer in instance. However, the numerical descriptions of earlier reports did not follow standard procedures of statistical analysis. Moreover, even when samples were gathered, they did not meet the criteria of true random sampling. What was considered as random sampling was often haphazard sampling.

There are a number of reasons why random sampling is difficult in cross-cultural research. To obtain a random sample, a researcher has to assign numbers to each individual in the population and then select them randomly by number. This is possible only in a community where the size of the population is small. Even then, the researcher may not be able to get the cooperation of all individuals selected. Moreover, in many communities—particularly those in which women are secluded—male researchers are unable to interview and obtain data about female members of the community. This difficulty can be overcome by having a woman member of the research team. Husband-wife teams in cross-cultural research are not uncommon (but they have not necessarily been engaged in collecting data through random sampling).

When working in a community composed of various subgroups, anthropologists attempt to have representative samples from every subgroup, thereby getting a good cross-section of the whole community. Stratification of samples by various ethnic groups may be useful in making a comparative study within a single community. This means that the number of individuals in a given ethnic group included in the sample will be proportionate to the size of the subgroup in the total population.

Besides the techniques mentioned above, some cross-cultural research projects involve the use of psychological tests. The Rorschach Inkblot Test and the

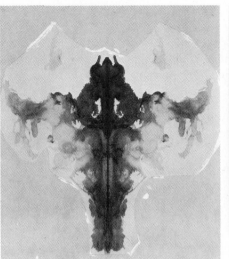 

Some cross-cultural research involves such projective techniques as the Rorschach test and the Thematic Apperception Test.

Right: *Apperception Test*, Harvard University Press, © 1943, 1971. All Rights Reserved.

Thematic Apperception Test (TAT) were used in early cross-cultural studies to uncover certain covert aspects of behavior.[1] More recently, a number of psychological approaches have been used, and we will examine the results of some of these studies later in this chapter. However, there is still some disagreement about the value and effectiveness of psychological tests in cross-cultural studies. Because most tests were developed by Western scientists in their own environment, their application in non-Western environments poses a number of difficulties. For example, even the colors of stimulus material can produce a bias, since different cultures place varying interpretations on different colors. Some colors even have special supernatural meanings. Under such conditions, the interpretation of such tests as the Rorschach (which uses color as one of the pattern parameters) becomes all the more difficult. Hence it is extremely important for cross-cultural researchers to have an in-depth knowledge of the group they are studying so they can interpret more accurately the patterns of behavior they observe.

Objectivity in Cross-Cultural Research

Traditionally, anthropologists in the field have been expected to become involved in the community and to be objective at the same time. It often is forgotten that a social scientist is a human being engaged in the collection of human data, not an automatic collector of information. Cross-cultural researchers have become aware that total objectivity is an impossible goal. An observer's training, background, personality, and biases cannot be without influence on the study. Bennett (1960) rightly points out that "the good field

1. The Rorschach and TAT are called projective tests. The testee is asked to tell a story about the TAT picture or to describe what he or she sees in the Rorschach inkblot.

worker must work with and through his biases, become aware of them, control them and use them" (p. 431).

Having reviewed some of the methods and some of the difficulties of collecting objective cross-cultural data, we are ready to examine cultural influences on psychological development and some developmental patterns in different cultures.

Cultural Influences on Behavioral Development

Environmental influences have widespread effects on the development of behavior. So extensive is the impact of cultural and environmental contexts on behavior that some developmentalists have been led to wonder whether any universal patterns can be identified (Nesselroade & Baltes, 1974). The suggestion that the human organism is so plastic as to express behavioral development in divergent patterns depending on the cultural context leads us to examine several behavioral processes in terms of cultural influences. In this section we will look at two basic behavioral processes: motor development and perceptual development.

Motor Development

Among the most basic and presumably universal features of development in infancy is the progression of an organism's *motor development,* the ability to move about in the environment. The work of Arnold Gesell (1928) demonstrated that an infant's motor capacities are gained in a sequence—from being able to raise the head and hold it erect, to being able to crawl, to being able to stand, and then to being able to walk. This sequence was illustrated in Chapter 4 (see Figure 4.10). Gesell was impressed with the regularities in patterns of motor development. This led him to theorize that motor skills emerged as a function of maturation. Although individuals differed in their *rates* of attaining the various motor skills, the *sequence* of those skills appeared similar in American babies. Moreover, Gesell believed that experience and practice were not very effective in altering the timing and sequence of motor abilities. Gesell worked with identical twins. One twin was given practice in motor tasks while the other was allowed to develop the skills at his own rate. Practice did not greatly accelerate the development of the trained twin, which supported Gesell's notion that motor capacities are attained as a function of genetic programming.

Another test of Gesell's notions is to look at motor development in various cultures that differ with regard to how infants are handled and treated. Does a baby's being carried in a cradleboard affect the rate at which motor tasks are attained? Are there some cultures in which motor development is accelerated? Such are the questions cross-cultural researchers seek to answer.

Most early cross-cultural studies suggested that the general stages of motor development and the timing of these stages are fairly uniform across diverse cultural groups, although some groups show variant patterns (DeVos & Hippler, 1969; LeVine, 1970). American Indian children—who are more restricted as infants than are white American children—walk alone at a later age (Dennis, 1963). Because the gene pools of American Indians and white people are also different, these data do not tell us whether Indian children walk later as a result of restrictions on their movement during infancy (imposed by such practices as keeping the infant in a cradleboard) or as a function of their genetic background.

Genetic as well as environmental factors have been used to explain differences in motor development between African and European infants. LeVine (1970) asserts that the possibility that there are gross differences across populations in the timing of motor development was raised by the studies of African infants. This research was conducted primarily by Falade (1955), who worked in Dakar, Senegal; and by Geber and Dean (1957a, 1957b) and Ainsworth (1967), who worked with the Ganda people in and around Kampala, Uganda. African infants appear to be extremely precocious, especially during the first year of life. They sit, crawl, stand, and walk much earlier than Western babies. For example, Ainsworth reported that babies in Ganda society crawled about 2½ months earlier and crept about 3½ months earlier than Western infants. After the second year, however, this precocity declines so sharply that, by around age three, African children perform below American and European norms.

Geber and Ainsworth believe that differences in the environment lead to the acceleration of early development in African babies. Geber attributes the difference to the way Gandan mothers treat their infants. Mothers are continually available. They maintain physical closeness to their infants (carrying them much of the time), and they provide much nurturance. At the age of two the infants are weaned, and Geber feels that the decline in motor development after the second year can be accounted for by the "emotional rejection" of weaning. Ainsworth places less emphasis on the emotional aspects of Ganda mother-child interactions, instead stressing the absence of infant confinement, the freedom to move about and interact with others, and the "postural adjustments to being held and carried during the earliest months" (Ainsworth, 1967, p. 328). Although the environmental position found support when Geber and Dean (1957a) reported lack of precocity in Gandan infants who were treated like European infants, it is challenged by other data. When Geber and Dean (1957b) examined newborn Gandan infants, they found a high degree of precocity present at birth. Such precocity in the absence of experience in the environment would have to be attributed to genetic or other prenatal factors. The fact that black American infants also attain landmarks in motor development somewhat earlier than white infants further suggests that genetic rather than cultural factors account for the observed differences in the rate of motor development.

LeVine (1970) points out that differences in motor behavior exist between groups other than Africans and Europeans and Americans. Comparing middle-class American with Japanese infants in a longitudinal study, Caudill and Weinstein (1966) report large differences in activity level between the two groups when the infants were three to four months old. American infants were so much more active than Japanese infants that there was almost no overlap between the two groups. Caudill and Weinstein attributed the differences to the different maternal styles in the two cultures, as well as to the different infant living conditions. Japanese mothers are much less verbal than their American counterparts in interacting with their infants. Soothing and quieting the baby through nonverbal means such as rocking is a behavior engaged in much more frequently by Japanese mothers, while talking to the baby and offering verbal stimulation is the typical mode of American mothers. Additionally, in Japanese households children rarely sleep alone. About half of the children sleep with at least one parent until the age of fifteen. Even if a child sleeps in a room apart from the parents, he or she is likely to be with other siblings (Caudill & Plath, 1966). Thus the experience of Japanese infants and children is dramatically different from that of American children. One result of this may be the degree to which an infant engages in gross repetitive bodily movements of the arms and legs.

Even though mother-infant interaction varies tremendously between Japanese and American cultures, it is important to note that the gene pools of these two groups also differ. Thus the different motor behaviors may result from genetic difference. LeVine (1970) points out that regardless of whether the differences are of environmental or genetic origin, such major differences in gross activity level at three to four months must be considered when attempting to assess the impact of later child-rearing practices. Moreover, if middle-class Japanese and American infants are already behaviorally dissimilar at three months, it is highly unlikely that any other pair of populations of diverse origins can be assumed to be similar even early in life. Such divergence on even simple motor behavior suggests the vast range of behavioral divergence that potentially exists between individuals born of various gene pools and developing in a variety of cultures.

Perceptual Development

Another basic behavioral process examined by developmentalists is perception. As in the case of motor development, it is argued that simple perceptual processes—seeing, hearing, smelling, touching, tasting—are innate, biologically mediated capacities and hence are more universal in patterns of development than are behaviors that must be learned. Although there is impressive evidence for this nativist perspective of perceptual development (see Chapter 10), it is also clear that even on a perceptual level behavior is influenced by cultural and ecological factors.

One matter that has intrigued biological, behavioral, and social scientists for over a century involves the perception of color. When we look at a rainbow, we tend to see pure colors separated by transition areas that appear to consist of mixed colors. We might have little difficulty in designating the "pure" colors as red, yellow, green, and blue, and the "mixed" colors as orange, yellow-green, and blue-green. To Western observers, these distinctions seem natural. Thus it may be a great surprise (as it was to those who first noted this cultural discrepancy) to learn that our classification of the spectrum into the colors red, orange, yellow, green, blue, and violet is culturally arbitrary. Members of other cultures divide the spectrum quite differently.

Is the ability to distinguish among hues mediated by cultural influences? This issue of color perception and the vocabulary for colors is the oldest debate concerning culture and perception, and scholars have yet to resolve the question of whether genuine differences in perceptual capacity have been demonstrated or whether the observed differences merely result from differences in color vocabulary.

In the initial phase of this research it was believed that primitive people like the ancient Greeks lacked the capacity to distinguish between blue and green. This conclusion resulted from Gladstone's (1858) analysis of the writings of Homer, in which the same word was used for blue, gray, and dark colors generally. Other classics scholars analyzed a variety of ancient documents and found them generally lacking in color vocabulary for blue, and sometimes for green. Besides analyzing written works, Magnus (cited in Segall, Campbell, & Herskowits, 1966) sent questionnaires and color samples to traders and missionaries and concluded that most non-Europeans possessed a "defective" color vocabulary.

Rather than assuming mere vocabulary differences, Magnus and other scholars in the late nineteenth century interpreted the data to indicate differences in color perception. Influenced by Darwinian notions of evolution, they concluded that the human color sense had evolved to its present form in European societies over the three-thousand-year period since the Homeric Greeks.

Allen (1879) made the most prominent challenge of this view, and his extensive research and careful interpretations essentially agree with current views. Like Magnus, Allen used questionnaires to collect systematic data from divergent cultures. His questions were carefully phrased to distinguish between color naming and color perception. For example, Allen asked whether people in various cultures could distinguish between colors x and y and whether they had names for those individual colors. He found that while languages in many cultures did not include words for some colors, respondents always could distinguish between those colors. Allen concluded that the color sense is universal and identical in all members of the human race.

Substituting a sociocultural theory for the biological, evolutionary explanation of Magnus, Allen argued that color terms develop in a language only when they are needed to distinguish among objects that are otherwise similar. In instances where color and objects are systematically related, no color name is necessary, and the object name suffices. When pigments and dyes are available in a culture, it becomes necessary to invent more color names. Hence the existence of pigments and dyes increases the need for additional color words— words that identify the color regardless of the object on which it is found. From this perspective, color names evolve in a language as a result of cultural and ecological influences, not as an indication of the biological capacity of members of a given society to perceive color.

Allen's interpretation of the color perception issue did not satisfy Rivers (1901), who rejected the notion that color sense had evolved and instead interpreted observations of differences in color naming as being evidence for perceptual differences. Rivers observed different incidences of color blindness known to be genetically mediated, in different societies, and he also conducted extensive perceptual tests on the Murray Islanders. This work led him to conclude: "We have, in fact, a case in which deficiency in color language is associated with a corresponding defect in color sense" (1901, p. 52). The "deficiency" observed by Rivers involved the discrimination of blues.

A more recent proponent of the proposition that perceptual differences among cultures reflect genetically mediated biological differences among races is Pollack (1972), who has identified varying levels of retinal pigmentation in different cultural (and hence different racial) groups. The pigmentation factor operates on short wavelengths (the blue end of the spectrum) to a greater degree than on long wavelengths (the red end). In support of Pollack, Jahoda (1971) noted that topological maps used red-related colors for land areas and blue-related colors for water areas, and he found that members of the Malawi tribe (with greater retinal pigmentation than Europeans) made more errors in discriminating water than land areas. Scottish subjects distinguished differences in land and water areas about equally. Although Pollack's and Jahoda's data are not without inconsistencies, they provide good evidence for a biological interpretation of some of the cultural differences in color perception data.

For the most part, proponents of the argument against color perception differences have predominated. Several prominent American experimental psychologists—including R. S. Woodworth and, later, E. B. Titchener—joined the debate on the side of Allen and disputed Rivers's arguments in favor of color perception differences. These psychologists provided evidence that higher cognitive processes, rather than mere perceptual ability, are involved in naming and identifying colors. Colors with names appear to be identified more readily than colors that are not named. This does not necessarily mean that the named colors are perceived better; it could be that a clear-cut label mediates the color recognition (Brown & Lenneberg, 1954). Triandis (1964) points out that human beings can discriminate as many as 7½ million colors, and no language has words for more than a small percentage of these. Hence the ability to discriminate is not determined by language and culture, though language may cause some colors to be distinguished more readily. Clearly, we are dealing with cognitive as well as perceptual aspects of behavioral development, even as we observe behavior at the level of the perception of color.

Although the argument for and against differences in color perception still remains unresolved, the fact that perception of color is influenced partially by cultural factors is no longer debated. The absence of native words for certain colors cannot be taken as an indicator of people's color sense, though it may be an indication of their preferences and of colors that are not attended to in the environment. Even in societies where there exist no words for blue, green, or violet, children develop with the capacity to discriminate among these colors. Although the physical ability to perceive colors may not be affected by culture, various societies place different emphases on the frequency bands of the color spectrum, leading infants and children in those cultures to pay more attention to selective spectral inputs.

The data indicate that development in a given culture leads a person to organize the world in a specific manner. Cultural forces appear to be more important than intrinsic biological structure in shaping how perceptions are organized. Thus the biological program for perceptual development is read out and organized as a function of cultural influences.

Development in Different Cultures

The experience of human development and aging can vary widely, both within a given culture and among individuals in different cultures. Using data that have been gathered by cross-cultural psychologists and cultural anthropologists, we will trace development as it passes through various phases of the life span, examining some of the different ways in which individuals experience characteristic life periods.

Clearly, even the periods and the number of phases into which different peoples divide the life span vary. Whereas we in Western cultures progress through a rather rigidly age-graded system composed of graded educational levels and occupational hierarchies that end in retirement, some agrarian societies initiate young children into patterns of tasks that they continue to perform throughout their lives. In some societies there may be many roles and role transitions, and in other cultures status and role can remain relatively stable throughout life. Finally, transitions from one stage to another can be clear and marked by elaborate ceremonies, or they can be subtle and lacking in demarcation.

To clarify more fully the amazing range of human capacity and experience, we will begin by examining the manner in which babies are born and the attitudes and beliefs that parents in some cultures have about childbirth and child rearing. After looking at the experience of childhood in various cultures, we will see how clearly passage into adulthood status is marked. Then we will investigate various approaches to sexual behavior and family life. Our discussion will end with considerations of age grading in societies and the manner in which aging and the aged are viewed.

Pregnancy and Childbirth

How life begins in the womb has been a matter of concern for people of all cultures. Although most groups recognize a connection between pregnancy and sexual intercourse, the lack of scientific understanding of the process of conception often leads to the belief that conception results from a combination of sexual intercourse and supernatural act. Relating conception to a supernatural act is not totally illogical. Not all sexual unions result in pregnancy, so it is reasonable to assume that there must be some other reason for the beginning of life in a woman's womb. Such notions in the minds of adults clearly stand in tremendous contrast to those of middle-class parents in the United States, many of whom are explaining in great physiological detail the technicalities of intercourse and conception to their preschool children (Bernstein, 1976).

In contrast to the young child in contemporary Western society who has read a best-selling book explaining where babies come from, consider the adult Hopi (if he or she has remained isolated from the dominant stream of American culture). This person has a very different notion about conception. Hopi Indians know that pregnancy cannot begin without intercourse, but this biological explanation is supplemented by other beliefs. For example, the Hopis of the Third Mesa believe that a child who dies before initiation enters into the womb of a female member of the matrilineal household. Similarly, Hidasta Indians of western North Dakota attribute conception partially to intercourse but primarily to the entering of a spirit from the nearby hills. The spirits of the babies are believed to reside in the hills and to leave their place of residence when they wish to be born.

Where knowledge of the necessity of sexual intercourse exists, the role of each partner is conceived differently in different cultures. The people of Tikopia, a small island community of Polynesia, know that pregnancy cannot occur without intercourse. However, according to their belief it is only within the man that the germ of the new life exists. During sexual intercourse, the germ is placed in the woman's body; therefore, her contribution is limited to providing a suitable place for the fetus to grow.

The belief of the Trobriand Islanders of Melanasia regarding pregnancy is in direct contrast to that of the Tikopians. Not only do Trobriand Islanders deprive the husband of the role of "pater" (the socially recognized father), but they do not even consider him "genitor" (the biological father). They have been reported to have no knowledge of the relationship between pregnancy and sexual intercourse. According to them, the sexual act is necessary only to facilitate the opening of the vagina, through which the spirit of the dead ancestor enters the female's womb. Many ethnographers are questioning whether the Trobrianders are totally ignorant of the role of sexual intercourse in conception. Their belief of the role of spirit in the beginning of life is similar to that of other primitive groups. But while Tikopians and others attribute pregnancy explicitly to a combination of sexual and supernatural acts, Trobrianders make no such explicit statement. For this reason they probably have been misunderstood. Since Trobrianders live in a matrilineal society, they have been accustomed to deemphasizing the role of males. It may be for this reason that the father's role in conception has not been explicated.

Like the Trobrianders, the Australian Aborigines also rule out the male's role in conception. They believe that a woman becomes pregnant after an ancestral soul enters her body when she passes by the residing place of the dead ancestors. The Arapesh of New Guinea, on the other hand, give equal credit to women and men for the beginning of a new life, but believe that men play an important role in the continuing development of the fetus by depositing semen regularly throughout pregnancy (Mead, 1928). Whereas the Arapesh consider the sexual act as being conducive to the developing fetus, the rural Chinese regard intercourse during pregnancy as harmful.

Taboos Associated with Pregnancy   People throughout the world are concerned about the health of the mother and the unborn child. To ensure the birth of a healthy and normal child, pregnant women observe various taboos. Food taboos seem the most common. For example, Trobriand women avoid most fruits after the fifth month of pregnancy because fruits are considered harmful to the health of the baby. They are also prohibited from eating any fish that live in a hole (because of the belief that the baby's delivery might be as difficult as pulling the fish from the hole). The fear of having a deformed child leads rural Japanese women to avoid eating shrimp, octopus, and malformed vegetables and fruits. But it is not only mothers who observe taboos. In some societies fathers are also put under certain restrictions. Among the Hopis, for instance, the father of a baby has to avoid injuring any living creatures. Many societies also have prohibitions against intercourse during pregnancy—and sometimes long after it.

Childbirth The techniques and positions used by a woman at the time of delivery vary from one society to another. The reclining positions characteristic of Western and peasant societies are considered unusual in many tribal societies. A Trobriand mother sits on the ground, legs apart, with her hands pressing on the ground to aid delivery. Squatting is the usual delivery position among the Baska and the Hopi. The Todas of the Nilgiri Hills in southern India make the mother kneel by putting her head on the husband's chest. The presence of the husband during the birth of the child, as practiced among the Todas, may be considered unusual in most societies and can be compared with the Western custom of having the husband attend delivery. In most societies, however, husbands are banished from the place of delivery, along with small, young members of the family.

It is interesting to note that biological realities such as conception, pregnancy, and childbirth are viewed and experienced by various peoples as a function of their beliefs and values. The roles males and females are thought to play in conception and delivery depend to some extent on their status in society. Surely the notion that a child reflects the union of mother and father must lead to a different perspective on parental roles than the idea that the fetus represents the lodging in the mother's womb of a spirit from the hills. Thus the way an infant will be treated is affected dramatically by the attitudes and beliefs in a given culture, as well as by the values of individual parents.

Infant Care

Human infants are helpless at birth and need the care of adults to survive. Although the way infants are reared varies from one culture to another, within this diversity a general pattern of similarities can be discerned. For example, young infants of all societies thrive on milk and other liquids, and then they are gradually introduced to culturally prescribed solid foods (which are more varied than the first liquid diet). In most societies the responsibility of feeding and caring for the baby lies mainly with the mother. Among the Todas of the Nilgiri Hills in India, the mother and child are secluded in a separate hut; for the first three months, the baby's face is concealed from all persons except the mother. The Alorese mother, on the other hand, spends only a week to ten days with her baby before she comes out of the house to work in the fields, at which time the baby is cared for by older siblings and grandparents. Because of the mother's absence, the Alorese baby is deprived of nursing during the work-

Children placed in day-care settings show that mother absence need not result in abnormal personality development.

Erika Stone, Peter Arnold, Inc.

ing hours and therefore is introduced at a very early age to solids like premasticated bananas or gruel.

What kind of impact does mother absence have on the social and emotional development of an infant? Many have feared that mother absence could have severe consequences for a child's ability to become attached to others, and the data on infants who have spent their first years in impersonal institutions certainly present a picture of apathy and poor emotional development in the absence of human warmth and stimulation. Freudian notions about the tremendous impact of early experience with parents are reflected in the value judgments some social scientists have made regarding the Alorese method of infant care. Alorese infants were viewed as growing up in an atmosphere of neglect, with erratic and unusual feeding patterns. Anthropologists working with the Alorese believed that growing up in such surroundings contributed to the development of a suspicious, resentful, and confused personality. However, it seems erroneous to conclude that a whole group of people share personality characteristics. Additionally, this view unduly emphasizes early training and child care and ignores the range of variables contributing to and expressed in personality patterns within a given culture. Indeed, studies of Kibbutz-reared children in Israel—who in some cases have experienced infant care similar to that of the Alorese—suggest that the children may be more stable and confident by the age of ten than home-reared children are (Bee, 1974). Research on children reared in day-care settings also suggests that abnormal personality need not be a consequence of mother absence. Interestingly, in a period when almost half the mothers of young children in the United States are in the work force, the pattern of infant care practiced by the Alorese can serve as a model and natural laboratory in which to examine infant development in a society where working is the norm for mothers.

Early Training

Learning occurs from birth on (and even before) and continues throughout the life span. Just as learning begins in the earliest phases of life, so do parents, siblings, and others in close interaction with infants begin to shape their behavior. This shaping may be subtle and may be expressed nonverbally as well as verbally. It begins in a more or less concrete manner, depending on the infant's readiness and the prescriptions of the culture. Early training involves weaning, toilet training, and teaching the child to stay away from harmful objects.

In most primitive and rural peasant communities, weaning does not start before the age of two. Several reasons account for what, by Western standards, would be considered late weaning. Nursing serves as a natural contraceptive, thus helping to widen the space between children, and ensures a steady supply of milk for the baby, whose family is often unable to purchase it. Also, in many cultures breast milk is considered the ideal food for babies. In traditional Chinese and Japanese societies no other milk, such as animals' milk, has been

Nursing serves as a natural, though unreliable, contraceptive and ensures a steady supply of milk, an ideal food for babies.

Jim Harrison, Stock, Boston, Inc.

considered fit for human consumption. Before their contact with Europeans, the people of the Far East had traditionally thought cow's milk to be as dirty as urine. The Hindus of India, on the other hand, consider the cow sacred—mainly because it helps to keep babies alive by providing milk. (For this reason cows are equated with motherhood and often are addressed as *gomata*, or "mother cow.") Ironically, most children in India are deprived of additional sources of milk because families are too poor to afford it. In affluent countries like the United States and industrialized countries of Western Europe, most mothers do not give breast milk, so babies are introduced to the bottle right after birth. Therefore, weaning is not part of the early training process.

Though techniques for weaning vary, they usually follow a general pattern. The mother pushes the child gently away from the breast or distracts the child either by putting something bitter on the nipple or by attracting the child to other activities. The pressure to wean a child increases when the mother becomes pregnant again. In societies where the mother is expected to abstain from sexual intercourse during the nursing period, there is a desire to wean the child at a relatively early age.

Like weaning, the time for beginning toilet training varies, but it cannot be successful before a child is able to detect and control bowel and bladder sensations. Thus the onset of toilet training is less variable than weaning, since there are some biological limitations on the earliest point at which a child can attain control.

Formal Training

In all societies children need to be trained to develop appropriate attitudes, values, and skills. This training most often begins within the circle of close kinspeople. Unlike modern industrialized societies—in which formal training is provided by schools—children in less modernized societies acquire the necessary skills mainly from kinspeople and the peer group. In all societies, however, a large part of education during early childhood occurs through emulation of adult behavior. In some less Westernized societies, children are disciplined and taught values and attitudes solely through explicit instruction, storytelling, and modeled behavior. Children are made to conform to the cultural patterns of their group, and they are trained to internalize the basic value patterns.

Up to the age of four or five, children in most cultures are reared in a highly permissive atmosphere. In the rural communities of Egypt, infants and young children go through a period of indulgence, after which they gradually enter the strict disciplinary period of training. The process of education remains mostly informal, though there is a deliberate attempt to instill in children the two most important values of the society: respect for the elders and work. Although children are expected to be obedient to adults, any kind of submissive behavior toward one's age-mates is considered contemptible and is punished. In Egyptian society children must not display docile behavior toward their peers.

Hopi children also go through an early permissive period followed by a strict disciplinary period of training. Like the Egyptians, the Hopis put great emphasis on respect for elders. In addition to learning obedience and respect, children learn to live in cooperation and harmony and to adapt to nature. Hopi children are not punished physically by their parents, nor are they deprived of affection and favors. The usual form of punishment is to invoke the feared *Katchinas*—the spirits of the ancestors—who mete out harsh punishments when children break the rules of the society. Thompson and Joseph (1945) suggest that the projection of fear to the supernatural *Katchina* figure is believed to help maintain healthy relations between children and their elders:

> If Hopi beliefs and training methods have succeeded in imbuing the children with great fear, they have apparently also succeeded in concentrating and directing the fear into the supernatural sphere, a fact which implicitly will accentuate the security represented by the mother's lap, the familiar house, the laws and rules and finally the group itself. (p. 105)

The Hopi way of threatening children with supernatural punishment is not a unique phenomenon. In many societies a supernatural threat is accomplished by other forms of punishment. Many Muslim parents introduce the concept of heaven and hell to their children and say that they will be rewarded in heaven for appropriate behavior and punished in hell for failing to behave properly. Thus not only do societies instill different values in children, but they also use different means of instilling those values.

Initiation to Adulthood

With the onset of puberty, children enter a period during which they are expected to assume the roles of adulthood. Societies vary in the length of the transition period from childhood or adolescence to adulthood and also in terms of the clarity with which adult status is marked. Since the transition from childhood to adulthood involves a change of social status, many societies find it necessary to recognize this change through elaborate rituals known as *initiation rites*. The primary function of these rituals is to make young people aware of their new status and its related duties and obligations. Although both boys and girls go through initiation rites, in many societies the boys' rites are directed more toward the development of the skills, attitudes, and values that are demanded by the careers they are expected to pursue within society.

Initiation rites for boys do not necessarily coincide with signs of physical puberty. In most societies rites are held after the appearance of pubic hair or beard growth, and in some groups rites may be delayed until well after puberty. Among the Sekei of Uganda, East Africa, boys do not go through the initiation experience until they are eighteen or twenty.

Girls' initiation ceremonies are usually held after the onset of menstruation. These rites prepare girls to assume the roles of womanhood by instructing them in societal values and by helping them cope with physiological changes. In some societies, however, the initiation rite takes place before a girl reaches puberty. Although there is no elaborate initiation ceremony for girls among the Todas of southern India, an important ritual that may be considered similar to the initiation rite is the "deflowering" ceremony, without which a girl is considered unfit for marriage. In the first part of the ceremony, the girl lies beside a man for a few minutes; the man belongs to a clan different from the girl's. Two weeks later, another man from any clan other than the girl's joins her for a night and then has intercourse with (or "deflowers") her. Only after this part of the ceremony is a girl considered eligible for marriage.

In most societies menstrual blood is considered harmful and dangerous. During menstruation girls are expected to stay away from males and are not allowed to participate in any religious ceremony. The Brahmins of India do not allow a menstruating woman to cook for the first three days of her period; she is also prohibited from touching any cooking utensils. The Muslims do not look upon menstrual blood as dangerous, but they do consider women to be unclean during this time. Menstruating women may attend a religious ceremony, but they may not touch any objects connected with the ritual. There are no restrictions on daily chores such as cooking.

Initiation Among Sekei Boys The initiation rite is a highly important social event for Sekei boys of East Africa. The Sekei are traditionally a pastoral people, and a male's status and prestige are determined by the size of his cattle herd. Although training for the role of a cattle herder begins in early childhood, it is during initiation that boys become aware of the need for unity and collaborative action as well as for the bravery and strength required by such a career. All boys of the same age group go through the initiation rite at the same time, and they are then inducted into the same age set, to which they will belong for the rest of their lives. The age set of the Sekei is an institutional device designed to meet the needs of a pastoral group. The members of the age set act together to protect the cattle from enemy attack and also carry out raids to increase the size of their cattle herds. The members of the age set develop a strong sense of identification and a long-lasting bond among themselves.

Besides strengthening the unity among members of the age group, which is so essential for the Sekei career, the initiation ceremony also focuses on other career demands. The circumcision ritual—the dramatic point of the whole ceremony—tests the endurance and bravery of each boy and creates a strong sense of individualism. The emphasis on circumcision is so great that until a boy goes through the ceremony he is not considered a man. The initiation rite also involves fasting and hazing, both of which are designed to test endurance.

In many non-Western societies, the assumption of adult status is clearly marked and occurs relatively early in the life span. Adolescence does not exist in many societies where the onset of puberty is accompanied by a ritual leading to adult status. Freudians consider the stress experienced by many teen-age individuals to reflect a universal stage of difficult transition. According to psychoanalytic theory (see Chapter 2), the major source of difficulty is the transition from the *latency period*, in which sexual desires have been repressed, to the *genital phase*, in which heterosexual activity is achieved. Cultural anthropologists suggest that the "storm and stress" of adolescence is a phenomenon of Western society—in which there is no demarcation between childhood and adult status and in which adult heterosexual activity is not sanctioned formally until after marriage—which typically occurs after the teen-age years. Without ritual landmarks (except for such standards as the legal ages for drinking and voting),

The biological, maturational changes of puberty often lead to a more or less "psychological crisis," depending on the culture involved.

George W. Gardner

individuals experience greater uncertainty and difficulty in assuming adult roles. Thus the major crisis of the teen-age period—identified by Erik Erikson (1950) as the identity crisis—has as one of its components the biological maturational changes of puberty. These changes lead to a kind of psychological crisis, depending on the culture of which the individual is a part.

Sexual Behavior

Sexual urges stem from a physiologically determined drive that human beings share not only with members of their own species but also with other animals. However, continued sexual readiness and the receptivity associated with the onset of puberty are not characteristic features of other primates. Moreover, human beings are the only primates who have tried to regulate sexual behavior. To maintain a stable family organization and to reduce competition and conflict among the members of close kin groups, societies everywhere have found it necessary to regulate incest. While incest laws vary, they have a universal, general pattern that forbids father-daughter, mother-son, and brother-sister matings (although in rare cases—as among the nobilities of Peru and ancient kingdoms of Egypt and Hawaii—marriage between siblings was encouraged). Father-daughter matings are prohibited in all societies, but evidence of their occurrence does exist. On the other hand, violations of the mother-son taboo have rarely been reported by social scientists.

Cross-cultural studies of sexual behavior have traditionally been concerned with the incest laws, both universal and particular. The importance of studying sexual behavior in different societies has been recognized by only a few scientists, and they have had difficulties in undertaking research. The participant-observer technique of cultural anthropologists has proved inadequate for the study of sexual behavior, which usually occurs in private. Thus social scientists have had to rely on various cues and on reports of individuals in describing sexual behavior in various cultures.

Although every culture has standards for sexual behavior, variations from the norm as a result of individual differences are always evident. Kinsey, Pomeroy, and Martin (1948) first pointed out a vast range of variation in sexual behavior in the United States, and it is clear that any homogeneous picture of sexual behavior is inaccurate. Nevertheless, there are cultural differences in sexual norms and these varying norms dictate the appropriate sexual attitudes and attempt to regulate the physiological drive for sexual satisfaction.

In the rural communities of Ireland the subject of sex is taboo and is never discussed in front of children. Boys and girls are separated from early childhood on, and elders try to teach the children to avoid premarital sex. Any form of sexual expression is likely to be punished. Catholic religious sanctions, which insist that sex be experienced only for the purpose of procreation, also act to perpetuate a prohibitive attitude toward sex. In some small islands off the Irish coast, sexual repression is carried to an extreme, and even breast-feeding is uncommon because of its sexual connotation.

Sexual repression is also characteristic of many Arab-Muslim societies. Islam religion acknowledges the necessity of satisfying sexual urges, but it prohibits premarital and extramarital sexual union. Sex outside of marriage is considered a sin. Therefore, a great effort is made to repress sexual urges before marriage. In conservative Muslim families of the Arab world, girls, after reaching puberty, are not encouraged to look attractive in public because of the underlying fear that males may be tempted by their appearance. From the age of twelve, girls and boys are separated. Since chastity is both a moral and a religious imperative, many precautions are taken to ensure that no sexual infidelity occurs. Although stringent sex rules theoretically apply to both boys and girls, loss of virginity for a girl brings greater shame and, in turn, negatively affects her kinspeople's honor and prestige. Muslims believe that a girl's loss of honor through sexual immodesty—unlike a boy's—cannot be retrieved; hence they attach more importance to a girl's chastity (Antown, 1972).

A contrast to the Irish and rural Arab-Muslim sexual attitudes can be found among the inhabitants of Mangaya, located in the South Pacific on Cook Island in central Polynesia. Despite the segregation of sexes in public, Mangayan boys and girls go through a period of sexual adventure before they are married legally. Both boys and girls engage in premarital sexual activity, which is approved tacitly by the family and community. The first sexual act usually occurs outside the home, but as a girl reaches maturity, her sexual partner enjoys the privilege of mating with her in his or her house. The parents of the girl expect her to engage in premarital sexual relations with a number of boys because it is believed that this experience will help her to select the right man.

Clandestine sexual activity is also permitted in Samoa, and virginity is required only of the chief's daughters. In both Mangayan and Samoan societies, extramarital relations are disapproved. However, in both cultures it is acceptable for a man to have another sexual partner when he has to be away from his wife. This same attitude does not exist for married women. The double standard is based on the Polynesian belief that a normal human being must satisfy the sexual urges but that the urges are greater in men because they are the aggressive partner (Mead, 1928).

Among many Bantu tribes of East Africa, sexual foreplay—short of actual penetration—is widely permitted. Among these people the main concern lies with "deflowering"; it is disgraceful for a girl to have intercourse before marriage. To ensure that this does not happen, girls are periodically questioned by their kin members, and young unmarried couples are placed under limited supervision.

Members of the new religious group called the International Society of Krishna Consciousness not only believe in sexual chastity before marriage but also restrict the amount of sexual intercourse for married couples to once a month—during the optimal time for conception. Married couples are taught that sexual activity is not for pleasure but for procreation. To curb natural sexual desire, members of the group, including the youngest kindergartner, are required to take two cold showers a day.

Family

Our interest in the human developmental process in various cultures leads to the study of families. In most cultures it is within the family unit that the physiological and emotional needs of helpless newborn infants are met. While providing for a child's needs, the family also indoctrinates the child into the mores of the society. The enculturation or socialization process typically begins within the boundaries of the family unit. There is an interrelationship between the societal family structure and the individual. Indeed, the survival of a society often depends on the continuation of the family, whose members become new recruits carrying out the cultural tradition of the society and transmitting it to the next generation.

What constitutes a family has been a topic of discussion among social scientists. Although social scientists do not completely agree on this question, they do seem to agree on the primary functions of the family. These universally include procreation; care, nurturance, and protection of human infants; socialization of children; and satisfaction of the group's emotional and economic needs. These functions can be met by a variety of family structures. The basic family unit consisting of father, mother, and offspring is characteristic of American and other Western societies and is called the *nuclear family*. This basic unit is often obscured and at times may be unrecognizable in societies where several primary or nuclear families reside, eat, and work together in a large household. Such an *extended family* is held together by a rule of descent that can be traced through the father or mother or both.

In most peasant societies in which farming is carried out by male members of the group, the patrilineal and patrilocal extended family patterns are characteristic.[2] Examples include the traditional Chinese family, the Hindu and Muslim families of India, and the Muslim families of Arab countries. In such families a woman lives with her husband's family. This means that many individuals live together as one family unit. Except for procreation, all functions (such as care of children, socialization, emotional gratification, and economic activities) are performed cooperatively. Growing up in such a family represents an experience of development different from that in the typical American pattern, the nuclear family. In an extended family, children grow up in surroundings that include many sources of love and affection as well as hostility, conflict, and tension. Although these features are not unique to the extended family, the intense emotions typical of close human relationships are increased when a family includes more than one nuclear unit.

2. A *patrilineal* family is based on the male's line of descent; a *patrilocal* family is based on the home territory of a male's family or tribe.

In an extended family, children face many sources of love and affection as well as conflict.

Rene Burri, Magnum Photos, Inc.

Breaking the Age
Barrier to Friendship

ZICK RUBIN

The assumption that children should associate largely with their age-mates grew out of the age-segregated educational system that was introduced in the mid-19th century. It has, in recent times, filtered down from elementary school to even younger children; most day-care and other pre-school programs are age segregated, with three-year-olds in one group and four-year-olds in another. . . .

By the middle and later years of childhood, age-consciousness can be intense. One 13-year-old who transferred to a new school in which she was one of the oldest in her class sent her teacher an impassioned complaint: "The kids are really irritating me. Before vacation I had sort of gotten on their level and I could talk to them and have a great time, sort of. Now, after a whole vacation of being with my *friends,* I can't stand these kids. I feel like I'm in sixth grade again—what a pain—I wish to God there was someone my age here."

No one would deny the importance of same-age relationships to children. The potential for intimacy—for becoming real chums—seems likely to be greatest among children who can regard one another as equals, facing common challenges and concerns. Even young children are apparently aware of this special potential. Within mixed-age day-care centers and nursery schools, which are increasingly common, children remain likely to establish their closest ties with those who are their age-mates.

Source: Reprinted from *Psychology Today*, March 1980, pp. 96–99. Copyright © 1980 Ziff-Davis Publishing Company.

But relationships that cross age lines can supplement same-age contacts in beneficial ways. For one thing, as preschool educator Helene Rand points out, children who are "equals" in a particular domain—whether in physical size or verbal fluency or athletic skills—are not always of the same age. For three-year-old Suzanne, who is large for her age and sometimes frightens off other three-year-olds, association with four-year-olds may prove to be more rewarding. For five-year-old Pedro, a newcomer to the United States who has never before spoken English, interaction with three-year-olds—themselves fluent in English—may be the best way to gain entry into the group. Mixed-age settings allow children like Suzanne and Pedro greater flexibility in finding their peers.

Even when children of different ages are not "peers," they can establish rewarding relationships. Same-age groups often seem to breed competition and aggressiveness, as individual children strive to be the strongest or most successful among their peers. Interaction across age lines may help to diffuse this competition. . . .

Similar benefits are likely to accrue from experiments that have been set up in many schools with cross-age or ungraded classrooms, and from programs in which older children volunteer to tutor younger ones in school subjects. Mixed-age day-care and nursery school programs, clubs, and teams can all give children the chance to make social contacts that cross age lines. Such activities help to instill a new attitude in the kids: that their friendships in childhood—and later life—need not be rigidly segregated.

Of course, cross-age friendships can have a negative as well as a positive side. Such alliances may sometimes lead to the bullying of a younger child by an older one or to the rejection of an older child by his or her peers.

(continued)

Parents or teachers may sometimes fear that cross-age friendships lead younger children to engage in activities that they are not ready for, or that cause older children to "regress" to an immature style of behavior. There may be cases in which a child's exclusive preference for older or younger friends really is a psychological danger signal that adults should attend to.

But the dangers of cross-age friendships are . . . outweighed by the potential advantages. Anthropologist Beatrice Whiting has placed these benefits in their broadest perspective. In societies in which mixed-age interaction is the norm, she notes, children come to be less dependent and demanding of their parents, less individualistic and competitive, and more concerned with the welfare of their community than do children in Western societies. Mixed-age interaction, she believes, has the effect of extending children's sense of communal involvement and responsibility. By giving children the opportunities and encouragement needed to make friends across age lines, we may be not only expanding their individual social worlds but also increasing the level of social concern and fellowship in society.

The conflict between the mother-in-law and the daughter-in-law in a traditional Chinese extended family (in which the woman joins her husband's parents' household) has been the subject of discussion among scholars of many different fields. Although tension exists, it would be wrong to assume that the relationship between the two is based solely on hostility and hatred. As a newcomer to the family, the daughter-in-law is made to conform to its standards and to yield to the demands of familial cohesion. As she becomes acculturated to the ways of her husband's household, the daughter-in-law begins to enjoy more privileges and to establish affectionate bonds with the members of the household, including her mother-in-law. As children, Chinese women raised in the traditional manner learn to be obedient and respectful to elders and to curb "selfish" desires. The repeated emphasis on these values helps a woman cope with the demands of her husband's family.

It often has been mentioned that a person growing up in a traditional Chinese family—or any patrilineal extended family—ceases to be an individual. Subordination of the individual to the welfare of the family has never been complete; had it been so, conflict and tension would not arise. Moreover, subordination does not mean that the individual is insignificant. Rather, the family regards each individual as a valuable member of the group, whose achievement, success, and good conduct determine the status and position of the family in society.

Matrilineal and matrilocal families (whose members are united through the mother's line or home territory) are found less frequently. An extreme example of this type of family organization exists among the Nayars in Malabar, India. A Nayar family consists of mother, children, and relatives of the mother. Unlike other matrilineal units in which a husband joins the household of his wife, a Nayar man and woman do not set up a permanent household. A woman in Nayar society participates in a ceremonial wedding, at which time a man from another lineage puts a neckband on her to mark the union. This first ceremonial wedding rite is not necessarily followed by the sexual act. Its purpose is to confirm on a girl the status of adulthood and indicate her readiness to receive other mates. A Nayar woman usually has several sexual partners. However, when she becomes pregnant, the father is expected to recognize his paternity by paying the midwife's fees. Apart from this payment, the father has no further obligation to the mother or child. Since Nayar men must participate in war, the continuation of such an extreme form of maternal family may be an adaptation to the lengthy absences and deaths of men in this society.

Authority and Deference In all patrilineal societies, adult male members of the family have final authority in important and crucial matters. Although authority in a joint family is technically vested in its senior male members, women of the household exercise control and power in certain areas. Managing the household budget is usually the women's responsibility, and they also have authority over the younger children. As the children grow older, the authority of the father often prevails. Women treat the children with greater leniency and often identify with the children's interests. In important decisions, such as arranging a child's marriage, husband and wife consult with each other.

Children of patrilineal families are expected to behave with the father in accordance with the norm of the group. In the traditional Chinese family, the father plays with the young children; but as the children grow older, a certain amount of formality is observed. In the patrilineal Dinka society, authority and responsibility always lie with the father. He may allow his kinsmen to sleep with his wife, but a kinsman who is the genitor does not have any authority over the child.

In matrilineal societies authority is not vested in the father. Among the Trobriand Islanders, for example, a father does not act as disciplinarian and is not recognized as guardian. A similar pattern is apparent in the matrilineal society of Igaliva in the French Congo in Africa. Among these people authority lies with the mother's brother, who is recognized as legal guardian of the children. Property is inherited through him, and if the mother dies, it is he—not the father—who is responsible for rearing the children.

In sophisticated urban families in which there is no rigid division of labor between husband and wife, no one member enjoys complete authority over the children. Both parents may have equal authority. It is to be remembered, however, that these are the ideal norms of the society. Depending on the personalities of individuals and on their family backgrounds, some variation is always present.

Division of Labor Even in the most simple societies, tasks are divided according to age and sex. Very young and very old individuals are usually relieved from productive and laborious tasks, although more work may be expected of children and old people than is traditional in the United States. For example, the Abkasians of Russia, who farm throughout their lives, begin as young four- or five-year-old children with simple chores and work on the land in some capacity until they die—usually at a very old age. Retirement is unknown in such a society.

Although there may be no biological basis for the allotment of tasks such as cooking and caring for children, in most societies of the world women take greater responsibility for these tasks. In traditional male-oriented societies, it is considered below the dignity of males to take part in or assist females in household work. The shift from the traditional extended household to the nuclear family has often blurred the boundary between the tasks of men and women. In an urban nuclear family, both husband and wife may act as breadwinners and often assist each other in performing household tasks.

In societies where cooking demands elaborate work, skilled hands, and several years of training, males often find it difficult to prepare the food. Among the Mixe Indians of Mexico, where divisions of labor between sexes are rigidly enforced, males lack the knowledge to process the maize and prepare the tortilla. Similarly, male members of an Indian family—lacking the training needed to prepare the traditional unleavened bread called *chapah*—initially find this task difficult and cumbersome.

Age Grading

Societies also vary in the significance they attach to an individual's age and the degree to which they formalize roles and tasks around certain age groups. In some societies members of each age set go through different age grades and are assigned different tasks as they move through these age categories. Among the Sekei the new initiates perform the functions of warriors. With increasing age they reach the grade of junior elder, and after reaching the grade of elder they are relieved from military duties. A distinction must be drawn between the terms *age set* and *age grade*. *Age set* refers to an institution into which one is admitted by an initiation ceremony. The members of the same age set pass through different *age grades*, which are applied to categories or divisions based on age. In many tribal and peasant communities, age grading appears in either explicit or implicit form.

In Japan, where age has always been significant, age grading has existed in the past and still exists in many rural communities. Although formalized age grading has virtually disappeared from urban communities, the remnants of this practice can still be discerned from behavioral patterns. Traditionally in Japan, four major classes based on age were recognized. Preadolescent children belonged to one major class, which was subdivided into two groups. Children younger than age seven formed one group. At age seven, considered the transitional phase between early childhood and boyhood or girlhood, they underwent important ritual observances. These ceremonies were believed to perform several functions. A visit to a Shinto shrine ensured the blessings of the community god for a safe transition from one period to another. Purification ceremonies also were held at this time to remove the impurity that children were believed to have incurred at birth. After age seven, children formally became members of the family and community, and they began participating in the rituals of Shintoism. Although purification ceremonies no longer are practiced, the visit to a Shinto shrine at the age of seven still persists among both rural and urban Japanese.

Admittance into the age grade of young men and women took place after puberty and was usually marked by initiation rites. Male members of this second age class were expected to do work requiring physical strength. They were also responsible for organizing recreational activities within the community. The upper age limit of this grade was not fixed, and it sometimes included members as old as forty.

Men were usually considered to be of the middle age group when their sons reached marriageable age. These men were recognized as leading members of the community, and were responsible for funeral activities. Young adults and children were expected to observe the taboo against attending funerals of members of the same age group. Therefore, it became the duty of the members of the middle age group to attend and perform the necessary activities associated with the funeral. Although the taboo against attending funerals of the same age group applied to everyone, younger members and children were believed to be more affected by the misfortune; therefore, the taboo applied especially to them. Some communities, like that on the island of Talami in the Indian Sea, symbolically stop the news of a child's death from reaching other children by blocking their ears momentarily with the lids of cooking pans.

In Japan, people over the age of sixty-one (the retirement age) belong to the age grade of "old age." Traditionally, people belonging to this fourth age grade did religious work. Although such work is no longer believed to be the only work for the aged, traces of traditional custom still linger. Even now, it is customary for the oldest member of the house to be in charge of rituals and major ceremonies. After reaching the old age of sixty-one, men and women can wear colorful clothing if they wish to do so.

Status of the Aged

The way aged people are viewed and treated in a society reflects the values and emphasis that society places upon age. Unlike the American culture—in which many elderly live a segregated life and are less valued by younger members of society—the aged of most primitive and peasant societies enjoy a privileged position in the community. They are given status and privilege for a variety of reasons. Senior members of society are believed to be more experienced, more knowledgeable, and more skilled in magic and rituals. Also, in societies in which ancestor worship is practiced, a son feels obligated to respect and obey his father. This respect for one's parents is extended to all senior members of the community. In China, the concept of filial piety is so deeply ingrained in the social structure that even the Communist regime has found it convenient to utilize this Confucian value in the interest of promoting the welfare of the state. Since the Chinese have traditionally been accustomed to paying respect and homage to the family and community elders, the idea of paying respect to Communist party officials is not totally foreign to them. The presence of so many elderly people in key positions of the government and Communist party reveals that the Chinese still adhere to the belief that the elderly are especially competent, skilled, and learned. Respect for elders is also emphasized in Muslim families, because it is believed that blessings of the elders—whether dead or

In Chinese families the elderly are still revered as being especially competent, skilled, and learned.

George W. Gardner

alive—are necessary to avert misfortune. In societies where extended families still persist, the elderly participate in child rearing and thereby help give children a glimpse from the living past.

In most primitive societies the aged continue to occupy prestigious and secure positions in the community even after they retire from the tasks of subsistence. In contrast to industrialized societies, a person's worth is not measured in terms of input into the productive machinery. Among primitives, the prestige of a person is enhanced with increasing age. This is reflected in many tribal legends and myths. Since the transfer of knowledge in primitive societies occurs through an oral tradition and the elderly often assume the role of great teacher and narrator, the legends and myths glorifying the aged perpetuate the belief that they have special skills and knowledge. Polar Eskimos believe that the source of magical formula may be traced back to the great-grandparents. The Greeks believed that the power to heal the sick and injured was revealed to the old men. The magical powers of the old, however, are not always viewed as beneficial. Hopi legends and folk tales allude to evil-minded old people who are to be feared for their magical powers. Among a nomadic tribal group of North Africa, legends tell of wicked people who atoned for their sins by providing services for the aged and poor.

Such legends help to maintain the long-lasting traditions of respect and care for the aged. These traditions may be said to have stemmed from beliefs in tribal legends and myths. Whether for their magical powers, their role as mediator between the dead and the living, their possession of supernatural favor, or their experience in performing rituals, the aged have continued to enjoy high status in the community.

So far, we have made no reference to sexual differences in the status of the aged because of the scarcity of data concerning women. However, it is possible to make a few generalizations. In societies that consider menstruation polluting and harmful, premenopausal women are not allowed to assume the role of medicine woman and are often barred from joining secret societies. For women, the attainment of old age often means the opening of new, prestigious positions. Eskimo women are allowed to become shamans after reaching menopause, and the Kwakiutl of the northwest coast of British Columbia allow women to join secret societies after they stop menstruating. The Dahomeans of

West Africa allow women to gather indigo only after they reach menopause. This practice stems from a tribal custom that says that a woman may not refuse a man when he desires "connections" with her. Because indigo is used for sacred and medicinal purposes, the reasons for prohibiting young women from gathering indigo become quite apparent.

In general, an aged woman's position has been more secure and prestigious in matrilineal family organizations, although some patrilineal societies have accorded prestige to women with advancing age. In peasant patrilineal societies of Asia, a woman is held in high regard after her children reach maturity, although exercises of her power may be confined to her extended household.

In societies where tradition imposes a great number of restrictions on young men and women, the attainment of old age can signal a new freedom. The "privilege of old age" allows the aged to use obscenities in speech and to make sexual jokes. This should not be construed to mean that only the elderly or that all elderly engage in such behavior. Obscene language is used, and sexual jokes are told, when younger individuals are not around.

Primitive societies place great emphasis on age, probably because so few members of such groups survive to old age. Indeed, to attain old age in cultures where modern medical practices are nonexistent is an accomplishment to be respected. In industrialized nations with modern technologies, more people live to old age and age is not regarded with respect. Rather than being the repositories of knowledge and culture, the elderly in rapidly changing industrial societies are obsolete in terms of their education and background, and they lose rather than gain status in their old age.

Summary

1. Culture is characterized by the fact that it involves acquired capabilities; it is learned; it exists within the framework of a society; and it has a system or pattern rather than being haphazard. Usually a child is exposed to one culture and knows only the patterns of that culture.

2. Cross-cultural research involves comparisons among different cultural groups as well as in-depth work within one culture. Participant observation is the technique of living within a culture and observing it, often through informal interviews. Cross-cultural research is useful in establishing the universals in human development over the life span, but its emphasis is usually on variation in behavior.

3. Motor development has been studied cross-culturally and has been found to vary in terms of the age of onset of certain behaviors. Although it has been argued that cultural differences in mother-infant interaction might account for these differences, the fact that the different groups come from different gene pools adds the possibility of a genetic cause.

4. The ability to perceive and name colors has been compared across cultures. Some investigators have argued that in cultures in which there are fewer color names, there is less ability to distinguish among colors. The prevailing view is that color naming is separate from color perception and that all individuals are able to distinguish an equally large number of colors.

5. There is a great variation in the manner in which different cultures divide and mark periods of the life span. Some cultures have clearly demarcated age grading; others have no such system.
6. The attribution of pregnancy differs among cultures, with many assuming that supernatural phenomena accompany sexual intercourse in leading to pregnancy. The role of the father in the pregnancy is also given different significance in different cultures. Pregnancy taboos and the diet of a pregnant woman vary widely.
7. While the mother is primarily responsible for infant care in most cultures, the proximity and contact of mother and child as well as the mother-infant interaction vary widely. Infants develop normally under a wide variety of divergent circumstances.
8. Whether it is presented formally or informally, a large part of early childhood education occurs through emulation of adult behavior.
9. Societies vary in terms of the age at which an individual is considered an adult and the length of the transition period from childhood or adolescence to adulthood. They also vary in terms of the clarity with which adult status is marked.
10. All cultures have some form of incest taboo, although attitudes and permissiveness toward sexuality vary extensively.
11. The nuclear family (consisting of father, mother, and offspring) is characteristic of Western culture, but it is only one form of family unit. In many cultures, the extended family (including three generations and more distantly related kin) form the typical family unit.
12. Age has different importance in various societies. In some, rigid age grading occurs; in others, age does not play a major part in determining an individual's role.
13. In contrast to many Western societies, the elderly of most primitive and peasant societies enjoy great status. In these societies old people are regarded as repositories of wisdom and knowledge rather than being considered obsolete.

Selected Readings

Bronfenbrenner, U. *Two Worlds of Childhood: US and USSR.* New York: Pocket Books, 1973. Dramatically contrasts child rearing in the United States and Russia with emphasis on the outcome of differing child-rearing practices.
Dennis, W. "Environmental Influences upon Motor Development." In *Readings in Child Psychology.* 2nd ed. Englewwood Cliffs, N.J.: Prentice-Hall, 1963. Description of classic research on the effect of different child-rearing practices on timing of motor development.
Kalish, R. S., and S. Yuen. "Americans of East Asian Ancestry: Aging and the Aged." *The Gerontologist,* 11 (1971), 42-53. Perspective of Eastern attitudes toward old age.
Whiting, J. W. M., and I. Child. *Child Training and Personality.* New Haven, Conn.: Yale University Press, 1953. Classic attempt to analyze effects of various child-rearing practices on personality from a psychoanalytic viewpoint.

IV BEHAVIORAL PROCESSES OVER THE LIFE SPAN

Psychology is said to be the science of behavior, and Part IV
deals with the major processes of human behavior. Here we find
a succession of chapters that progressively deal with more complex
types of behavior. Chapter 10 describes the processes of sensation
and perception, those processes that provide us with important
information about the environment and the state of our bodies.
We then proceed to learn about the processes of memory,
attention, and learning itself as these processes change with
maturation and adult development. Next in order come Chapters
12 and 13 that deal with language and intelligence, two of the
aspects of behavior that show the greatest development in humans
as compared with lower animals. The development of motivation
and emotions is presented in Chapter 14. The complexity of
these two aspects of development cannot be overemphasized.
Chapter 15 deals with our knowledge about the origins of sex
differences in behavior from both a biological and a
social-environmental point of view. Finally Chapter 16 puts
behavior in the context of the whole individual by discussing
personality.

Chapter 10

Sensation and Perception

How sensation and perception differ, and how they change over the life span

The development and structure of human sensory systems

How perceptual information is processed over the life span

Sensation or Perception?

Development and Aging in Sensory Systems

>   Cutaneous Processes (Touch, Pressure, Temperature, Pain)
>   Kinesthesis (Coordination and Postural Maintenance)
>   Vestibular Function (Balance and Upright Posture)
>   Olfaction (Smell)
>   Gustation (Taste)
>   Audition (Hearing)
>   Vision

Perceptual Information Processing

>   Perception and Cognition
>   Practical Applications of Perceptual Research

Introduction

What do newborn infants see and hear? What features of the environment draw their attention? Are their perceptions quantitatively and qualitatively different from those of siblings, parents, and grandparents? And what, if anything, does a fetus experience, floating during those months in the void of the mother's womb?

Such questions must have been in the mind of every parent since the beginning of human existence. Yet though these questions have been pondered and debated by philosophers for centuries, the answers remain elusive. Two adults can never totally communicate their personal sensations and perceptions (so that they know, for example, whether the blue of the sky and the green of the grass look exactly the same to them both). With infants, this problem of evaluating sensations and perceptions becomes even more complex. How do we ask babies what they see? Indeed, how do we go about measuring and comparing perceptions and sensations over the life span?

Developmental psychologists are becoming increasingly sophisticated at devising techniques to determine human perceptual responses—even those of newborn infants. Psychophysicists have also worked for a number of years to create methods for comparing sensations and perceptions among individuals of all ages. From these sources, an ever growing picture of human sensation and perception is emerging. While the picture is far from complete, this chapter attempts to answer some of the questions raised and to identify promising new sources and avenues of research into sensation and perception across the life span.

Sensation or Perception?

Generally, *sensation* is conceived in terms of the activity of sensory receptors and their coding and transmission of stimulus energy; *perception* is thought of as a higher-order process involving meaning and the extraction and interpretation of information from sensations. For generations psychologists have debated where to draw the line between sensation and perception. Indeed, many have argued that any distinction between the two processes must be arbitrary. The distinction is blurred from the moment stimulus energy impinges on an organism, because stimuli are never perceived directly. Rather, the nervous system *responds to* physical energy—such as wavelengths of light, frequencies of sound, and intensities of pressure, which are experienced as color, pitch, and pressure or pain, respectively.

Although these types of physical energies are different and are mediated through different sensory systems, all information about physical stimuli is coded in the nervous system in terms of the firing of nerve cells (neurons). Thus information is transduced in the nervous system; that is, it is transformed from its physical state in the environment and coded in a form that can be interpreted by the brain. This is why we say that human organisms never perceive the world directly. Objects exist in the world, which may or may not excite our sensory receptors. An object becomes a stimulus only when it excites a sensory receptor. We know that there are many kinds of physical energy in the environment to which we do not respond, such as the very high frequency waves that bats can emit and sense to guide them in flight. Thus organisms know the world only through their senses. And we, as human beings, are aware that our perceptual world is probably very different from that of organisms like the bat or even that of human infants.

Interpretation first enters the perceptual process at the level of the sensory receptor itself, in terms of the waxing and waning of the receptor to stimulation. This feature of sensory receptors is called the *threshold*. A threshold is the least amount of energy or smallest change in energy that can be detected by an observer. Moreover, in a given period of time, thresholds vary. We have to decide, for example, whether we actually saw a falling star or imagined it, whether we heard the telephone ring or not. With very weak stimuli, we have to guess. Thus from the moment stimulus energy impinges on and excites us, interpretation is involved.

In spite of this difficulty in distinguishing between sensation and perception, it is useful to discuss these processes in terms of simple and more complex integration of stimulus information. To identify the locus and cause of change over the human life span, it is essential for developmentalists to make these distinctions—to identify the level at which a change occurs. Therefore, for our discussion, *sensation* will be considered in terms of receptor functions, and *perception* will be discussed as higher-order processing of simple sensory information.

Development and Aging in Sensory Systems

That sensation and perception change over the life span is evident. It has been the task of developmental psychologists to describe, explain, and in some cases attempt to modify those changes that take place. One of the most obvious causes of change in a human organism's sensory and perceptual capacities is physiological change in the sensory receptors and in the nervous system. Indeed, some changes in sensation and perception over the life span can be attributed directly to changes in the nervous system. For this reason, it is essential in treating sensation and perception over the life span to consider the neural development and aging of sensory systems as well as study the changes on a behavioral level.

About three weeks after conception, when the embryo is barely 6/100 inch long, the nervous system begins to form a tube (review Figure 4.6). From this tiny tube grow the two great information processing and integrating structures that form the central nervous system: the brain and spinal cord. Peripheral nerves are formed by clusters of cells that gather along both sides of the tube, toward the back. These nerves lead both into the tube and out of the sense organs of the body. By the twenty-fifth day of life—when the mother may not even know she is pregnant—the tube is closed completely. It starts to close first around the neck region, then toward the head, and then toward the tail. The thicker, head part will grow into the brain, and the tail part—which is more cylindrical—will form the spinal cord. This order of growth is the first important clue to the sequence of behavioral development in human beings. The nervous system, which governs behavior, develops first from the neck up and then from the neck down. This trend is called *cephalocaudal development*. Another developmental regularity is the directional sequence of growth that occurs from the midline of the body outward. This trend is called *proximodistal development*.

By the time of birth, an infant's sensory systems are capable of functioning at least to some extent. In some cases, development in these sensory systems has begun twenty-five days after conception. Even so, at birth an infant's brain is only one-fourth the maximum size it will attain in adulthood, which means it weighs about ½ pound. (An adult's brain weighs, on average, 2 pounds.) Though the infant's brain has all the neurons it ever will have—about 100 billion—many of its cells and fibers are still growing. As described in Chapter 4, most postnatal growth involves the enlargement of neurons and the formation of interconnections among nerve cells. The growth of cells and fibers and their interconnections continues well into childhood, and myelinization (the growth of a protective sheath around large neurons, which may function to speed neural transmission) continues into young adulthood. Nonetheless, aging may begin in the human nervous system as early as age twenty-five, when neurons may start to die. Because the central nervous system contains billions of cells, losses are probably relatively insignificant, at least until very late in the life span. But other changes may be crucial to nervous system functioning in relation to perception in later life. For example, decreases in cerebral blood flow lower the supply of oxygen and vital nutrients to the brain, and increases in intracellular and intercellular materials within the nerve cells themselves may clog the system.

At birth, many parts of the brain have not yet been connected, either with each other or with various sense organs of the body, resulting in a baby's apparent inability to function in some respects. However, many functioning capacities are evident long before birth. The earliest sensation demonstrated by an embryo is touch. Anatomist and embryologist Davenport Hooker (1952) has established that at the early age of 7½ weeks the neck bends to one side if the mouth or the sides of the nose are stroked with a single human hair. Hooker arrived at this conclusion after examining 150 embryos and fetuses that had been delivered prematurely, because of spontaneous abortion or surgical intervention to save the mother's life. In another week's time, there is evidence of touch sensation in the upper trunk and shoulders, and a little later this sensation reaches the lower trunk, legs, and feet. This order of development mirrors the initial neck-up, neck-down closure of the neural tube; the earliest responses are elicited from stimulation of the lower part of the face. A little later in development, responses result from stimulation around the eyes and also the trunk of the body. Finally, by the fourth or fifth month of pregnancy, responses can be elicited by touching the limbs and feet of the fetus.

In early development, the *local senses* (those stimulated by immediate contact such as touch, temperature, pressure, pain) take precedence over the senses stimulated by less direct stimuli (hearing and vision). The local senses develop first presumably because they are involved with life-sustaining activities and must combat threats to survival. Taste is a local sense. Smell—though activated by *distal stimuli* (which do not come in direct contact with the receptor)—functionally figures in the early-developing senses because of its relation to food. Evidence indicates that in a number of species, including human beings, the order of development of four sensory systems is (1) *cutaneous* (touch), (2) *vestibular* (balance), (3) *auditory* (hearing), and (4) *visual* (sight). Thus a principle of development that has implications for survival—and that is generalized over many bird and mammal species—is that the senses develop in a fixed sequence, with the local senses becoming functional before the distal ones.

A related developmental principle noted by Hooker is that the last-acquired capacity is the first to be lost. That is, when the nervous system is threatened by exhaustion of its oxygen supply, the most recently acquired reflex is lost first (although severe oxygen deprivation affects the brain stem; see Chapter 4). In later life, also, only the more primitive reflexes may remain after trauma or shock to the nervous system. Thus when aged individuals suffer a stroke, more complex capacities may be lost whereas more primitive responses are retained.

This developmental hierarchy of the senses determines the order in which we discuss sensation and perception. We will begin with the earliest, most general senses—touch, the coordination of movement, and balance—follow with smell and taste, and then move to the later-developing senses of hearing and vision. This progression reflects the order and complexity that exists in the developing human brain.

Cutaneous Processes (Touch, Pressure, Temperature, Pain)

Cutaneous processes involve sensitivity to touch, pressure, temperature, and pain. As shown in Figure 10.1, various cutaneous receptors are involved, including the end bulbs of Krause, Pacinian corpuscles, Meissner's corpuscles, Ruffini's endings, and free nerve endings. The order and timing of appearance of these receptors in the fetus have not been determined precisely, but life span data after birth have been collected. Ronge (1943) counted the total number and concentration of Meissner's corpuscles in segments of skin taken from the index fingers of nine autopsied subjects ranging in age from one to eighty years. A steady decrease in the density of these receptors was found over the life span. During the first two decades of life, finger surfaces grow rapidly, causing the greatest drop in concentration of Meissner's corpuscles during this period. The drop is much more gradual after the second decade, and there appears to be a parallel decrease in the number of nerve fibers, Pacinian corpuscles, and end bulbs of Krause. Ronge (1943) also investigated touch sensation over the life span, finding a diminution in sensitivity up to the sixth decade. Thus there seems to be a parallel between declining touch sensitivity and the decreasing number of Meissner's corpuscles over the life span. However, it has not been established whether the change in sensitivity results entirely from the decreased number of receptors or whether the remaining receptors also function less effectively.

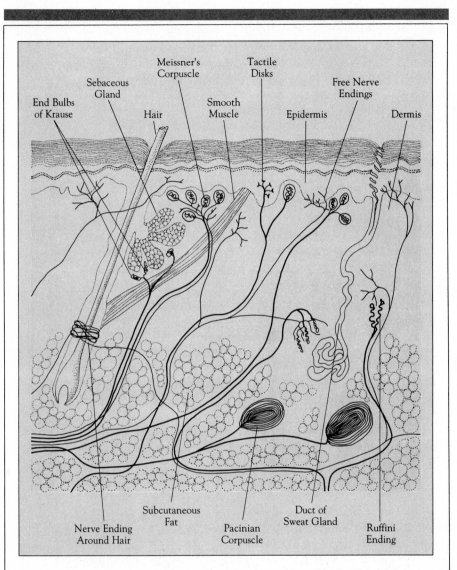

FIGURE 10.1
Cutaneous receptors. A schematic section of the nerve supply of the human skin, showing the receptors for mechanical energy (for example, touch, pressure, temperature, and pain).

After Woolard, from E. Gardner, *Fundamentals of neurology*, 4th ed., Philadelphia: W. B. Saunders Company, 1963.

Behavioral studies of the sense of touch have typically involved the use of hairs of different rigidity or weights of different amounts to deform a limited area of skin. For example, light contact with a hair elicits a response from a two-month-old embryo. The head region is most sensitive to such stimulation at this time. With increasing age the sensitivity of the fetus improves, and the response becomes more specific to the area stimulated. Pressure also elicits a response from the fetus, but Hooker (1952) has speculated that this may result not from touch and pressure receptors but from receptors in muscles, tendons, and joints that respond to muscle flexion and extension and deep pressure.

Sex differences in touch sensitivity have been identified in neonates and children, with females being more sensitive than males (Bell & Costello, 1964). Interestingly, females also appear to have a lower pain threshold, but a higher tolerance for pain than males have. Touch sensitivities over the life span have been determined for several areas of the body (Jalavisto, Orma, & Tawast, 1951). Generally, touch sensitivity declines slightly from childhood through age fifty or fifty-five, with a sharp decrease in sensitivity thereafter.

The prenatal environment maintains a relatively constant temperature, making it difficult before delivery to test fetal sensitivity in this regard. There is evidence, however, that temperature receptors are developed long before birth, and differential sensitivity to temperature changes is apparent at birth. Little is known about temperature sensitivity over the life span, but the scant existing evidence indicates that temperature sensation remains stable, with clinically testable deficits appearing in only 10 percent of an aged population (Howell, 1949).

The study of pain perception in fetuses and infants usually involves the stimulus of a needle prick. Crying, withdrawal, and general activity following such stimulation have been seen as evidence of pain sensitivity. The study of pain perception in children and adults has relied on verbal reports of a pricking sensation felt when a high-intensity light source is beamed on a spot of India ink painted on the skin (thermal stimulation). Results of these studies have shown pain sensitivity to be initially weak or absent in fetuses and newborns but developing within a week to ten days after birth. Pain sensitivity increases in older infants and remains relatively stable from childhood to the fifties; some studies, but not all, show a decline after sixty years. In newborn babies, McGraw (1941b) found no response to a light pinprick, though heavy pressure caused postural responses. McGraw concluded that it was impossible to know whether pain sensitivity was present at birth because the absence of a response to needle pricks could result from a lack of connections between sensory and somatic centers or between receptor centers and mechanisms controlling crying; it could also result from an undeveloped sensory mechanism. However, even a light pin prick elicited reactions after a week or ten days, and fewer pinpricks were required to elicit responses in older infants than in younger ones. A more localized response to noxious stimuli also develops with age, and the facial region always appears to be most sensitive.

In large samples of male and female subjects ranging in age from ten to eighty years, Hardy, Wolff, and Goodell (1943) and Birren, Shapiro, and Miller (1950) found no age changes in pain sensitivity to thermal stimulation. Yet Chapman (1944), using the same technique, found decreased sensitivity in older subjects. Procedural differences between the studies, as well as motivational and socio-cultural differences between subject populations, may account for discrepant results. When subjects were selected on the basis of educational and occupational similarity, pain sensitivity to thermal stimulation remained relatively constant until the fifties, with a sharp decline occurring after age sixty. Changes in the skin and in peripheral circulation could influence sensation to thermal stimulation so that, from these studies alone, it cannot be determined whether pain-receptor sensitivity itself changes with age. These authors also suggest that changes in other sensory modalities may influence pain perception, since the interpretation of a stimulus as being painful appears to be influenced by the level of sensory input. Moreover, pain sensitivity can be decreased by several processes unrelated to the threshold energy required to stimulate pain receptors. Thus if there is indeed a decrease in pain sensitivity with aging, it is not possible from available data to determine the nature of the change.

Kinesthesis (Coordination and Postural Maintenance)

Located in the muscles, tendons, and joints are *proprioceptors*—receptors that are stimulated by muscle flexion and extension and by deep pressure. Proprioceptors are probably functional in human beings eight weeks after fertilization (Hooker, 1952). Early kinesthetic responses are generalized, becoming more specific with development. Proprioception appears to remain stable throughout childhood and into middle age, but after age fifty may not function optimally. Laidlaw and Hamilton (1937) found age differences in thresholds of perception of passive movement (having the limb moved rather than moving it oneself) between subjects aged seventeen to thirty-five and those aged fifty to eighty-five. Older subjects made more errors and required more movement before reporting movement in the hip and knee, though there were no age differences in reports for upper extremities. Comparisons of vibration sensitivity in subjects ranging from five to seventy-nine years of age indicated threshold changes around the age of fifty (Cosh, 1958; Rosenberg & Adams, 1958). Hence kinesthetic sensitivity develops early and is stable throughout the life span until after the age of fifty, when it declines moderately.

Vestibular Function (Balance and Upright Posture)

The receptors involved in our sense of balance and ability to maintain upright posture, the *vestibular apparatus*, are located in the bony labyrinth of the inner ear and consist of three semicircular canals, the saccule, and the utricle (see Figure 10.2). These structures are well differentiated by the end of the second month of fetal development, and the neurons involved are among the earliest to become myelinated. However, the time of the onset of vestibular function is unknown (Langworthy, 1933). Righting reactions and nystagmic eye movements[1] have been observed early in the development of infrahuman species and in young fetuses. It is possible, however, that the responses attributed to vestibular receptors in these early stages of development are actually proprioceptive responses. At birth, normal reactions to rotation are clearly evident (Lawrence & Feind, 1953; McGraw, 1941a).

During the course of life, individuals are subjected to rotations, and postrotational vestibular responses are probably habituated over the life span. Thus newborn infants exhibit an unusually low threshold for and an especially long duration of nystagmus after they have been rotated (Groen, 1963; Galebski,

---

1. *Nystagmus* is the oscillation of the eyeballs from side to side following body rotation. It is the typical response used by neurologists to test vestibular function.

FIGURE 10.2
The vestibular appara-
tus. The human
membranous laby-
rinth, showing the
structural relations of
the cochlear to the
vestibular apparatus
(the semicircular
canals and the utricle
and saccule).

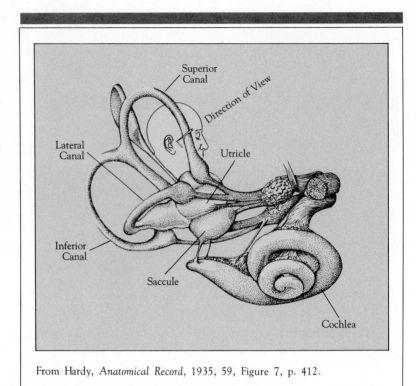

From Hardy, *Anatomical Record*, 1935, 59, Figure 7, p. 412.

1928) but the duration of nystagmus following rotation decreases with age (Arslan, 1957). Falls and dizziness are a common complaint of older persons, and these problems may be related to changes involving the vestibular appara-tus. Orma and Koskenoja (1957) studied postural dizziness in the aged and found it to exist in 81 percent of males and 91 percent of females over age sixty-five. Data from physical examination of these individuals led the inves-tigators to conclude that the dizziness probably resulted from transient circu-latory disturbances occurring during changes in body position rather than from age changes in the vestibular apparatus. Noting that Sheldon (1963) ob-served an increase in body sway after the age of fifty—and also noting that older people are more susceptible to falls—Szafran and Birren (1969) suggested that in addition to the circulatory disturbances that appear to affect it, the vestibular apparatus itself may change with age.

Olfaction (Smell)

Early in the life of the embryo the olfactory structures emerge as small pits in the ectoderm. These cavities enlarge and differentiate and receive innervation from olfactory nerves, which grow out from the brain. Because the fetus is submerged in amniotic fluid—and since liquid substances probably cannot stim-ulate the olfactory receptors—the fetus has no sensation of smell. The olfactory

The falls and dizziness that many older people experience may be related to changes in the vestibular apparatus.

Rhoda Galyn, Photo Researchers, Inc.

apparatus appears to function before birth, however, as premature fetuses respond to olfactory stimulation. Research on olfaction is especially difficult in the early stages of life, as it is hard to establish that an infant is responding to olfactory stimuli rather than to tactile irritation. Life-span data about olfaction are sparse and contradictory, also due to the difficulties in collecting accurate data. Olfactory receptors are incredibly sensitive, responding to as little as 1/460,000,000 milligrams of methyl mercaptan, the substance that gives garlic its odor (Best & Taylor, 1955). In addition to this extreme sensitivity of olfactory receptors, many variables affect the olfactory threshold, including temperature, humidity, altitude, genetic background, sex, and emotional and cognitive factors. Another impediment to life-span comparisons of olfactory sensitivity is that—relative to adults—infants and children work with a much reduced volume of air intake, thus reducing stimulation to filaments in the olfactory bulb. In spite of these difficulties, a tentative picture of olfaction over the life span has emerged.

Lipsitt, Engen, and Kaye (1963) demonstrated increasing sensitivity to an olfactory stimulus during the first four days of life, as well as differential reactions in human newborns to different odorants. The sense of smell is present in premature and term infants, and appears to be one of the most highly developed sensitivities in human newborns (Engen, Cain, & Rovee, 1968). In a life-span study of olfactory sensitivity in subjects ranging in age from six to ninety-four years, Rovee, Cohen, and Shlapack (1975) found no age differences. They concluded that the senses that develop earliest in the life span may also be the last senses to show decline. Preferences for odors appear to remain stable from childhood through at least early adulthood. Comparing the likes and dislikes for fourteen odors in two hundred subjects between the ages of seven and twenty-four years, Kniep, Morgan, and Young (1931) found no age differences in preferences. Odor preference in middle and old age has not been studied.

The senses of taste and smell develop very early in life and help an infant to explore the environment.

James Holland, Stock, Boston, Inc.

Gustation (Taste)

Taste buds are present by the third month of a fetus's life, and they are more numerous in fetuses than in newborn infants (Moncrieff, 1951). Newborns are amply supplied with taste buds, however, and Reese and Lipsitt (1970) suggest that an individual is perhaps more sensitive to taste stimuli at birth than at any other time in life. With age, the distribution of taste buds decreases; taste buds, located at birth throughout the mouth and tongue, eventually disappear from all but a few localized areas. In some of these localized areas, such as in the trench wall, the number of taste buds increases from birth to the second or third decade, and then declines. Adults retain about ten thousand taste buds, and the greatest loss of taste buds does not occur until old age.

Taste sensitivity appears to parallel changes in the gustatory apparatus. Sensitivity is present at birth, and appears to be acute by the age of two or three months, with infants noticing changes in the amount of carbohydrate in their formula or a change in milk mixtures. Infants at this age also demonstrate displeasure toward certain substances disagreeable to their taste. Typically, they explore their environment with the sense of taste until late in the first year, as every mother knows only too well. Toys, blankets, and anything within reach go into the mouth. Here, then, is a classic example of how the development of the nervous system affects behavior at specific points in the life span. The senses of taste and touch are better developed than vision and visual-motor coordination, and so infants explore objects with their mouths. Later in infancy and childhood, as the visual system becomes better developed, exploration will primarily be visual.

The few life-span studies that have been carried out concur that taste sensitivity is maximal in childhood, declines slightly in young adulthood, and declines greatly in old age (Bourliere, Cendron, & Rapaport, 1958; Harris & Kalmus, 1950; Richter & Campbell, 1940). Physiological differences in the gustatory apparatus probably account for the familiar age differences in taste preferences. Heightened sensitivity in children may cause them to dislike such flavors as spinach and liver and to prefer foods tasting less agreeable to adults. What tastes bland to parents and grandparents may be ambrosia to a child, and vice versa. For example, an increased preference for tart tastes and a decreased preference for sweetness have been found in older subjects. To 120 individuals ranging in age from twelve to sixty-eight, Laird and Breen (1939) presented five samples of pineapple juice ranging from tart to sweet. Although sweet preferences were predominant below age fifty, the older subjects preferred the tart taste. Preference changes were attributed to atrophy of taste buds in the front part of the tongue, where they are most sensitive to sweetness.

Learning and experience have profound effects on the development of taste preferences. Blood, spittle, sheep eyes, and insects, considered delicacies in various cultures, cause revulsion in most Americans (who, in turn, consume corn on the cob, peanut butter, and watermelon—to the distaste of many Europeans). Indeed, Wilentz (1968) suggests that the vast majority of the world's peoples might consider a cheeseburger an astonishing concoction. Distributing surplus foods and designing programs to feed the poor and hungry in different cultures become vastly complicated because, for the most part, children grow up adopting their parents' food preferences. Hence malnutrition can become accepted as a part of life, and attempts to substitute more nutritious foods often meet with failure. Another example of how learning affects taste preferences can be seen in gourmets and wine tasters, who develop the ability to detect minute differences in taste. Therefore, although physiological data over the life span suggest that adults should be less able than children to distinguish subtle taste differences, adults can compensate through learning.

Audition (Hearing)

Although the auditory apparatus is fully differentiated by the sixth month after conception, the ability of fetuses and newborns to respond to sound has been a controversial question for more than a century. As illustrated in Figure 10.3, auditory stimuli are vibrations that move the eardrum (*tympanic membrane*), which is attached to three small bones in the middle ear (collectively called *ossicles* and individually named *malleus, incus,* and *stapes*). Sound vibrations are transmitted from the eardrum to the ossicles, which are attached to the *cochlea,* a snail-shaped organ filled with fluid and a membrane covered with sensitive hair cells. Thus vibration causes fluid to move in the cochlea, which bends the hair cells and causes nerve cells to fire. The patterns of firing of these nerve cells are interpreted by the brain as sounds. Before birth the middle ear is filled with a gelatinous substance that makes mechanical movement of the eardrum and ossicles impossible. For this reason it has been assumed that fetuses and newborns are deaf until the fluid is drained, which occurs fairly rapidly after birth. Recent studies indicate that most infants are responsive to sound within the first few hours after birth.

FIGURE 10.3
The auditory apparatus. A semischematic drawing of the human ear.

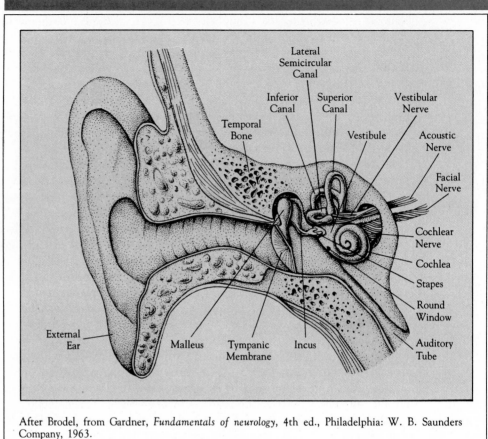

Lateral
Semicircular
Canal

Inferior   Superior   Vestibular
Canal   Canal   Nerve

Temporal   Vestibule   Acoustic
Bone   Nerve

Facial
Nerve

Cochlear
Nerve

Cochlea

Stapes

Round
Window

External   Auditory
Ear   Malleus   Tympanic   Incus   Tube
                          Membrane

After Brodel, from Gardner, *Fundamentals of neurology*, 4th ed., Philadelphia: W. B. Saunders
Company, 1963.

Anecdotal evidence, however, suggests that fetuses do respond to auditory stimulation late in development. Mothers report that fetuses move in response to loud noises, and Peiper concluded that such fetal movements can, indeed, be observed. In one case, the mother reported that she was sitting in a bathtub thirty-one days before her baby was born, when a loud banging noise caused the fetus to "jump." The feeling was much different from the typical kick or movement of the fetus. Five days later, under similar conditions, the experimenter made a similar noise and observed the woman's abdomen for movements. A fraction of a second after the noise there was a clearly observable "single quick rise of the anterior abdominal wall." The mother reported feeling the fetus jump as before, yet she had not been startled by the sound, and her muscles were relaxed at the time. When the experimenter attempted to elicit fetal response to tactile vibrations associated with the sound (in an attempt to determine whether the fetus was responding to tactile rather than auditory stimuli), there was no fetal movement. Hence the fetus apparently was responding to sound.

In subsequent observations of fetal response to loud sounds, similar conclusions have been drawn (Ray, 1932). In fact, several investigators have been able to condition fetal responses of movement and changes in heart rate to auditory stimulation (Spelt, 1948; Bernard & Sontag, 1947). Thus it appears that newborns and fetuses in late stages of development *can* hear, at least in the case of loud sounds. The question of whether they can distinguish tones, however, has not been answered clearly. Pratt, Nelson, and Sun (1930) observed fifty-nine infants from birth to twenty-one days of age and found that only 7 percent of the responses were made to a tuning fork, while the most responses (47 percent) followed the sound of banging a tin can.

Sounds have several qualities to which we respond, and though psychological perception does not always match the physical quality of the stimulus, the two are closely related. Loudness, or intensity, is one feature of sound; another quality is pitch, or frequency; and a third quality is phase, which is involved in sound localization. At its most acute, the human ear can respond to tones ranging in frequency from 15 to 20,000 cycles per second. This stage of greatest acuity is typically reached by age five, and it begins to decline around age twenty or twenty-five, especially at high frequencies. Women appear to lose less auditory acuity than men. The amount of hearing loss that results from such factors as interference with the blood supply (as in vascular disease) and the amount caused by environmental factors (such as noise and diet) have yet to be determined.

It is alarming to note that hearing loss is becoming a critical issue with the contemporary generation of adolescents who have exposed themselves to extraordinarily loud levels of rock and disco music. Contemporary adolescents receive far greater exposure to loud music than have previous cohorts of this age group, and research attention has been given to the issue of whether or not such exposure can be damaging. The noise level of rock and roll bands can be measured, so it is possible to predict the hazards of listening to such music. The noise levels of some live performances of rock bands have been found to exceed the level at which damage can occur to the ear. Rock music played at the level of 100 decibels of amplification appears to create little effect, but when the level reaches 110 decibels, some individuals sustain temporary hearing deficits that could lead to permanent hearing loss. Listening to the quieter rock band may be safe enough, but if the amplification/reverberation condition reaches 110 decibels, a sizable percentage of the people exposed to this music would be affected adversely—and probably permanently. Some music groups have registered 120 decibels, which not only creates havoc with most audiograms but probably causes severe hearing loss.

Although exposure to rock music is, in most cases, the option of the individual, exposure to environmental noise such as that caused by airplanes is frequently unavoidable. Research has demonstrated that living in the flight pathway of an airport not only is damaging to hearing but also can affect mental health. Sleeplessness and irritation caused by the abrupt onset of intense noise every five to seven minutes becomes telling on the individual's personality.

Employing traditional audiometric techniques, several large-scale studies have been undertaken to evaluate age differences in auditory acuity (for example,

Noise Pollution: Environmental Battle of the 1980s

SUSAN WALTON

The world is a noisy place these days, and as the cacophony grows, researchers and federal agencies are becoming more and more concerned about the possible ill effects of noise on humans. The Environmental Protection Agency (EPA) estimates that the amount of noise in America will double by the year 2000. Noise, it is becoming evident, can no longer be considered merely a nuisance....

Noise wreaks its most obvious damage on human hearing. The auditory effects of noise, which are irreversible, have been the subject of intensive investigation and government regulation by numerous federal agencies. But noise regulations, most of which were generated by the Noise Control Act of 1972, do not cover one increasingly apparent problem: The damage that noise causes does not stop at the ear.... Noise, by its very nature, attacks its victims on many levels at the same time—psychologically, socially, and physically. And there is a great deal of individual variation in noise susceptibility, even with regard to hearing loss. The difficulties in isolating noise as a variable, then, have rendered less useful many studies of its nonauditory, particularly cardiovascular, effects....

To remedy the shortcomings of existing studies, as well as to make a more realistic appraisal of the nonauditory effects of noise, EPA is sponsoring a four-to-five-year study of the cardiovascular effects of long-term noise exposure on rhesus monkeys.... So far the results are ominous: Not only does noise affect the monkey's cardiovascular system, but the effects linger after the noise stops....

Meanwhile, the fight to control noise is proceeding on a practical if somewhat limited level. EPA is attacking the problem by seeking to limit the noise from specific products and by encouraging consumers to buy, and manufacturers to produce, quieter products.... Such products will carry a "noise rating": a number indicating how many decibels of noise they emit. The same label will feature an outline of the decibel range for other manufacturers' versions of the same product....

EPA is also attacking some of the prime producers of urban noise: garbage trucks, buses, pavement breakers, bull-dozers, and front-end loaders. All garbage trucks manufactured after 1 October 1980 may not emit noise in excess of 79 dB measured at 7 meters: after 1 July 1982, the level will be 76 dB. The bus regulations should, according to EPA estimates, reduce the bus noise by nearly half. And the new regulations require motorcyclists to "roar into the sunset" at an average reduction of 5 dB.

For industrial workers, OSHA [Occupational Safety and Health Administration] now has an exposure standard of 90 dB for an eight-hour exposure, with a "time-intensity" trade-off for shorter exposures to louder noise....

"We need a dose-response criterion, and we have none yet for the nonauditory effects of noise," says one EPA official. "If the research proceeds and the effects are quantified, then the regulations would proceed from there."

Source: Reprinted, with permission, from the March 1980 BioScience, © American Institute of Biological Sciences.

National Health Survey, 1965). Concurrent results of such studies suggest that with increasing age (after about age thirty-two for men and age thirty-seven for women) there is always some hearing loss. Szafran and Birren (1969) summarize the following major features of age changes in auditory acuity:

1. Impairment occurs mainly at the upper end of the frequency spectrum—that is, individuals lose most acuity for the very high frequencies, and thresholds for frequencies below 2,000 Hz show no significant deterioration.
2. Surprisingly, the left ear shows a more pronounced loss in the largest proportion of cases, and the differences in threshold between the left and right ears are greatest at high frequencies.
3. The loss in the 4,000–6,000 range is greater than in any other frequency range and this holds true for both ears.
4. In some studies (but not all) there is a shortening of the loudness scale in older subjects, which is called *recruitment.*

Because of recruitment, older subjects perceive an increase in the intensity of an auditory signal as being much more rapid than it actually is. Although we know that perception does not always correlate perfectly with the physical qualities of a stimulus, in the case of recruitment, the discrepancy between the perceived and physical qualities of the stimulus is greater than normal.

Studying hearing loss in individuals aged seventy to eighty-eight, Schaie, Baltes, and Strother (1964) confirmed previous findings that loss was selectively greater at higher frequencies and that there were significant sex differences, with females retaining more acuity than males. This study also suggests that hearing loss in higher frequencies may be an important factor in the apparent intellectual changes that occur in advanced age. Age changes in auditory acuity impair an individual's ability to hear conversation and to communicate. Consonants, particularly, are difficult to perceive when acuity is diminished. Hearing aids amplify higher frequencies and enable older people to communicate and understand conversation. It appears essential—even for their mental alertness—that older individuals be kept in touch with their environment through auditory stimulation and the communication and social interaction it provides.

Vision

The eye is easily our most complex sensory receptor (see Figure 10.4). As was pointed out earlier, it is the last receptor to develop fully. Located in the back of the eye is the *retina,* which might be considered part of the brain itself, for processing of information takes place at the retinal level. Indeed, early in fetal development the retina originates as a small sac from the side of the brain and grows outward, leaving a stalk that connects it to the point of origin, the brain. This stalk becomes the *optic nerve,* and the sac at the end of the stalk becomes differentiated to form the layers of the retina, the *rods* and *cones,* which begin to develop at about three months. The skin around the optic sac thickens and forms a hollow, with the edges finally joining and forming a rounded mass of cells that develop transparency and become the *lens.* Other tissues in and

FIGURE 10.4
The visual apparatus.
A schematic view of
the horizontal section
of the right eyeball.

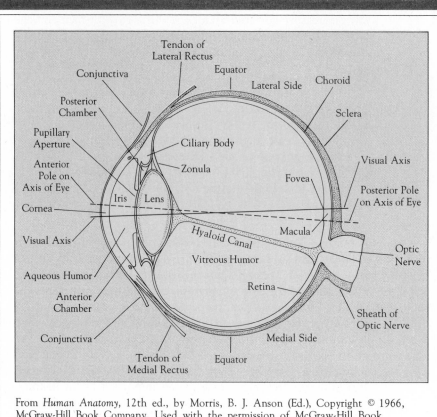

From *Human Anatomy*, 12th ed., by Morris, B. J. Anson (Ed.), Copyright © 1966, McGraw-Hill Book Company. Used with the permission of McGraw-Hill Book Company.

around the eye develop into the *cornea, eyelids, lachrymal glands,* and *eye muscles.*

Since there is no light in the intrauterine environment to stimulate receptors, fetal eye movements—which do occur—are probably made in response to the mother's movements when the vestibular apparatus is stimulated rather than in response to visual input. Prematurely delivered fetuses of seven months can differentiate between light and dark, and late fetuses also appear to respond to color. Because vision is such a critical feature of human perception, an extensive body of research has been devoted to the question of whether vision is innate and programmed into the organism or develops as a function of environmental input and learning. Proponents of the former position—called *nativists*—hold that vision is innately determined and depends on neural "wiring." They cite such evidence as the fact that newborn infants respond to light and that individuals who are blind from birth but then have their sight restored need little learning to see. Proponents of the position that all perception is based on prior experience—called *empiricists*—insist that proper interpretation and utilization of visual stimuli occur only after exposure to these stimuli. We will explore evidence gathered by both nativists and empiricists. Since each group has presented its case so persuasively, we undoubtedly will arrive at the currently popular position that both innate mechanisms and maturation of structures—as well as environmental input and learning—are essential for human visual perception.

A critical tenet of the empiricist position is that perception should improve with age, since it is based on prior experience. This position commits empiricists to a developmental perspective and illustrates the utility of the developmental approach in resolving issues basic to the area of perception. Nativists also recognize that development is a critical feature for perception, but they argue that maturation mediated by biological mechanisms (rather than learning mediated by environmental variables) is responsible for differences in how infants, children, and adults perceive the world. Two aspects of visual perception that have been studied most intensively with regard to the nativist-empiricist debate are depth perception and shape perception. We will consider the developmental aspects of these abilities in light of the nature-nurture controversy. Then we will continue our discussion of visual perception in relation to the cues of color and brightness, concluding with considerations of optical illusions and visual sensitivity and perception over the life span.

Depth Perception   An issue that has intrigued philosophers for centuries is how an individual can perceive the world in three dimensions given that the retinal surface is two-dimensional. In other words, how can we perceive space relationships, especially of distances between objects, in three dimensions? In adults, a number of cues are used. Seeing the world with two eyes provides us with two slightly different retinal images, and the magnitude of the differences between the images varies according to the distance of the object. This visual cue is called *binocular parallax*. With one eye, the rate in change in size of the retinal image as the object moves serves as a cue for moving objects, and head movement also causes the retinal images of nearer objects to move faster. Other monocular cues include texture and shadows. Empiricists have argued that individuals must learn to use these cues. Reese and Lipsitt (1970) relate an amusing anecdote indicating that, indeed, we must learn to understand the principles of size constancy (the experience that objects remain nearly invariant in their perceived size regardless of their distance from the observer). In their report a five-year-old boy, embarking on his first plane flight, was heard to ask his father as they gained altitude: "How come we aren't getting any littler yet?" Apparently the boy had observed that planes in the sky appeared very small, and he imagined that passengers in the plane would participate in this shrinking process.

One issue that might make untenable the nativist position that depth perception is present at birth is the maturity of the visual system of newborn infants. Haynes, White, and Held (1965) questioned the ability of an infant under one month of age to accommodate the lens enough for the image to be reproduced sharply on the retina, though by the time the infant is six months old this ability to focus on an object is as efficient as an adult's. *Conjugate eye movement* (movement of the two eyes together) is another ability essential to depth per-

FIGURE 10.5
The visual cliff used
by Gibson and Walk
to test depth percep-
tion.

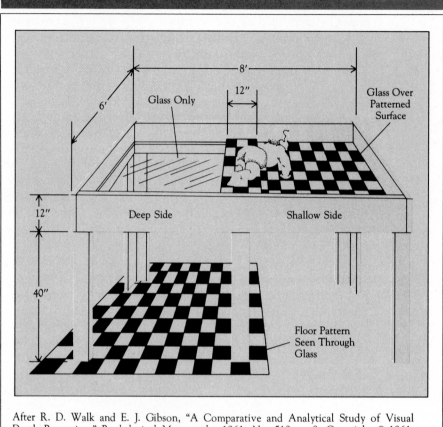

FIGURE 10.5
The visual cliff used
by Gibson and Walk
to test depth percep-
tion.

After R. D. Walk and E. J. Gibson, "A Comparative and Analytical Study of Visual Depth Perception," *Psychological Monographs*, 1961, No. 519, p. 8. Copyright © 1961 by the American Psychological Association. Reprinted by permission.

ception, for independent scanning by the two eyes yields conflicting information about distance. Apparently this ability is present most of the time in newborns. Nevertheless, it is not clear that all operations required to discriminate depth are functional in newborns.

Several direct attempts have been made to examine depth perception in infants. Gibson and Walk (1960) devised an apparatus that simulates a visual "cliff" (see Figure 10.5) and tested depth perception in human infants as well as in a number of subhuman species. The method in these studies is to place the infant on the edge of the cliff and have the mother on the other side coaxing the baby to cross over. Infants will not traverse the cliff, though they cry and exhibit other behavior indicating that they want to go to their mothers. Unfortunately, this type of experiment can be carried out only after infants are able to crawl, and so only human infants of six months to a year have been tested. Thus it is impossible to determine whether depth perception is learned or innate, since infants of this age have had a great amount of experience from which they might have learned depth cues.

The visual cliff has been used to measure depth perception in infants long before they were of crawling age by measuring their heart rates when they were placed on their stomachs over the "deep" and "shallow" ends of the cliff (Campos, Langer, & Korowitz, 1970). Two- and three-month-old infants had significantly slower heart rates when they looked over the "deep" side of the cliff. Because slower heart rates are associated with scanning the environment in search of meaning, it was concluded that the infants perceived the cliff and, hence, depth. These infants had not yet developed the fear response to looking down from heights.

A clever means of determining depth perception in younger infants was devised by Bower (1965), who conditioned infants seventy to eighty-five days old. Bower presented the infants with an interesting multidimensional visual and auditory display every time they moved their heads to one side in the presence of a 1-foot cube placed at a distance of 3 feet. (The infants presumably liked this show, since they were willing to perform to experience it.) Once the response was established, Bower tested the infants' ability to perceive depth by showing them (A) a 1-foot cube at a 3-foot distance; (B) a 1-foot cube at a 9-foot distance; (C) a 3-foot cube at a 3-foot distance; and (D) a 3-foot cube at a 9-foot distance. None of the responses were reinforced in this condition, and the number of head-turning responses to each stimulus was observed. If size of the retinal image is critical, infants should respond to stimuli A and D, but this is not what happened. The most responses were elicited by stimulus A, while stimuli B and C evoked about the same number of responses, and stimulus D evoked the fewest responses. Thus these infants discriminated depth, and they did not appear to use the size of the retinal image as a cue. In follow-up experiments to identify the significant cue(s) for the infants, Bower found that they could make the correct judgment as well with one eye as with both, and that the important cue was probably *motion parallax* (the rate of change in location of retinal image with eye movement). Thus from this research and the visual-cliff research with lower animals (Walk & Gibson, 1961) and older infants (Walk, 1966), Reese and Lipsitt (1970) concluded that sensitivity to depth cues—if not present at birth—quickly becomes part of an infant's repertoire.

Although infants may perceive depth cues, depth perception does appear to improve with age. Children at age three have a fairly well developed sense of size constancy, and this ability to equate two stimuli of the same size at different distances improves to the age of five or six, when it is essentially equal to adult levels of judgment. Smith and Smith (1966) compared children aged five to twelve with adults. Using a distance-estimation task, they found that in a free-viewing condition all groups were equal but that in reduced-viewing conditions older groups performed better. They concluded that in normal situations there is such a redundancy of information that even the youngest subjects have no trouble making size discriminations.

In a review of the size-constancy research, Wohlwill (1963) noted that in adults there appears to be a tendency to overconstancy. That is, older adults tend to judge a distant stimulus as being larger than it actually is relative to the near stimulus, whereas children judge the far stimulus as being slightly smaller or equal to the near one. Thus the main developmental change between early

Experimental condi-
tioning indicates that
physiological bases for
perceptual processes
interact with matura-
tion and experience
to influence how we
perceive the world.

Sol Mednick

childhood and maturity is not the gradual establishment of size constancy (which occurs much earlier) but the development of a stronger overconstancy bias. This change is not so much a deficiency in perception as it is a conscious correction imposed on perception—clearly a learned strategy.

In summary, it appears that depth sensitivity exists in young infants and that sensitivity to size and distance relationships in three-dimensional space exists in substantially complete form before children reach school. Additionally, a change toward overconstancy occurs during adolescence. From existing data, however, it is not possible to resolve the nativist-empiricist debate. Although there is some evidence for learning of depth cues, other evidence suggests the existence of depth perception in young infants. These data, along with research into other aspects of perception, indicate that neither a strict empiricist nor a rigid nativist position is tenable. There are clearly physiological substrates that make perceptual processes functional in newborn infants, but—as we will see in the next section—maturation and experience interact with brain structure to influence how we perceive the world.

Shape Perception Even as neonates, infants can discriminate some aspects of shape, though it is not clear which factors of a stimulus are the functional cues. Again, Bower (1966) provides significant data about this aspect of visual perception in infants. Using the conditioning technique to produce head-turning to a stimulus of selected shape, Bower tested infants' ability to generalize to (1) a physically identical shape at a different slant, which produces a different retinal image; (2) a physically different shape at the same slant, which again produces a different retinal image; and (3) a physically different shape at a different slant, which produces the same retinal image as the conditioned shape. Infants responded most consistently to the same shape at a different slant (stimulus 1), indicating their perception of shape constancy. These data provide evidence against the empiricist position, which would predict that infants could respond only to shape or slant alone, not the combination of both.

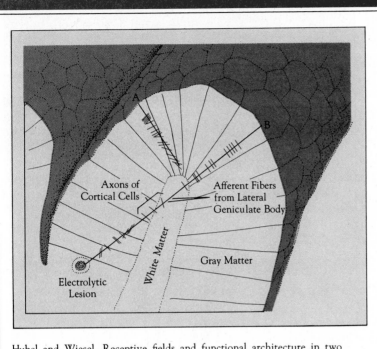

FIGURE 10.6
Organization of brain for form perception. The functional arrangement of cells in the visual cortex resembled columns, although columnar structure is not apparent under a microscope. Lines **A** and **B** show paths of two microelectrode penetrations; colored lines show receptive-field orientations encountered. Cells in a single column had the same orientation; change of orientation showed a new column.

Hubel and Wiesel, Receptive fields and functional architecture in two nonstriate visual areas. *Journal of Neurophysiology,* 1965, *28,* pp. 229-288.

Additional support for the nativist position was provided in the pioneering work of Hubel and Wiesel (1965), who identified neural substrates for line detection in cats, indicating that the brain is organized or "wired" for form perception. These researchers found single cells in the visual cortex that fired only to certain lines in certain orientations; other cells, firing to a particular line at a slant, appeared to be arranged in columns so that passing a line of a certain orientation across the visual field would fire a column of cells (see Figure 10.6). Such evidence provides compelling support for the nativist position. Recently, however, the developmental work of Spinelli, Hirsch, Phelps, and Metzler (1972) has indicated that environmental influences can have a profound effect even on something as basic as the receptive fields of visual cortical cells. By rearing kittens in an environment where they saw only one orientation of line, Spinelli and his associates demonstrated that only cortical neurons that fired to this orientation of line were developed. In other words, without normal environmental input, normal line detectors will not develop. Therefore, although the potential for normal wiring in the brain may be laid down in the genes and may be present at birth, the environment has a profound effect on the expression of this potential—even to the extent that it can affect the sensitivity and organization of neurons in the brain. The use of these structures apparently releases or establishes their function during development.

Throughout this book we have dealt with the critical effects of early experience on development in general, and many studies relevant to perception of form and depth have also demonstrated the importance of environmental stimulation. An early deprivation study was undertaken by Riesen and Aarons (1959), who raised four groups of kittens during the first six weeks of their lives in the following ways: (1) one hour of diffuse light per day in the absence of head movement; (2) one hour of patterned visual input per day without movement; (3) one hour of patterned visual input with head movement; and (4) when they were four to eighteen weeks old, normal rearing. All kittens were trained on a brightness discrimination task and on static versus moving form discrimination. While kittens in all groups could perform the brightness discrimination task, the kittens in groups 3 and 4 performed better at discriminating static from moving forms. The critical environmental feature for this type of form perception appeared to be patterned vision in the presence of self-initiated movement.

FIGURE 10.7
T-frame used by Held and Hein to investigate effects of movement on depth perception.

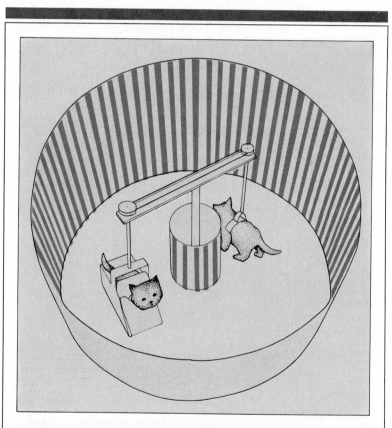

From Held and Hein, Movement-produced stimulation in the development of visually guided behavior. *Journal of Comparative & Physiological Psychology*, 1963, 56, 872–876. Copyright © 1963 by the American Psychological Association.

Held and Hein (1963) demonstrated the importance of self-induced movement for depth perception. Kittens were raised in the dark for eight to twelve weeks and were then exposed to visual stimulation for three hours per day in one of two manners. As shown in Figure 10.7, the kittens were yolked together in a movable T-frame; one kitten was allowed to walk, and the other was held just above the ground. Thus the nonwalking kitten was moved passively the same distance as the walking kitten. Testing visually guided paw placement, the investigators found that the passively moved kittens were retarded in development compared with the walking kittens. The passively moved group also took longer to develop a blink reflex in reaction to an approaching hand.

Although ethical considerations limit deprivation experiments on human subjects, some naturalistic studies have been carried out on individuals who regained their sight after being blind from birth. One man fifty-three years old was observed by Gregory and Wallace (1963). Soon after his sight-restoring operation, this man was able to identify shapes—but these were usually shapes he already knew through tactile experience. Complex shapes such as facial expressions were difficult for him to discriminate, and though he could perceive depth, he did not understand depth cues in two-dimensional drawings.

Facial perception in infants has been tested in a series of interesting studies carried out by Fantz and his coworkers (1965). Infants were placed on their backs in a criblike apparatus so that they could look up at the test stimuli.

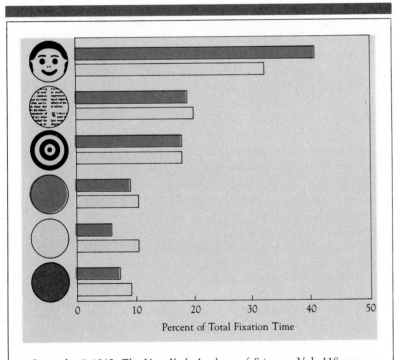

FIGURE 10.8
Results of tests of preferences for visual stimuli. The importance of pattern rather than color or brightness was illustrated by the response of infants to a face, a piece of printed matter, a bull's eye, and plain red, white, and yellow disks. Even the youngest infants preferred patterns. Colored bars show the results for infants from two to three months old; gray bars, for infants more than three months old.

Percent of Total Fixation Time

Stimuli were presented two at a time, and the corneas of the infants' eyes were observed to see which of the two stimuli was observed most, or preferred. Neonates under five days old as well as older infants were tested, and all infants displayed preferences for the more complex stimuli. The results are shown in Figure 10.8. In another study, infants appeared to prefer normally depicted faces to scrambled ones.

While nativists draw their most convincing evidence for innate mechanisms from studies of form perception, it is clear that environmental factors also play some role. Very young infants do appear to perceive form, but the normal maturation of receptor cells for form and pattern appears to depend on environmental input. Nevertheless, the studies on form and pattern perception by Fantz (1965), on depth perception by Gibson and Walk (1960), and on space and depth perception by Bower (1966) provide convincing evidence that the visual world of infants is better organized than empiricists would predict. After reviewing the research on perceptual development in infancy, Jeffrey and Cohen (1971) concluded that to make adequate statements about perceptual functioning researchers must be certain that their measurements of perception do not reflect the inability of infants to manifest a response or to attend to the experiment.

Visual Sensitivity over the Life Span   The general course of visual sensitivity over the life span is one of maturation and development in infants and young children and gradual decline in adulthood and old age. Many visual impairments, such as farsightedness and nearsightedness, can be compensated for with corrective lenses and increased intensity of the stimulus. However, some impairments are non-neural in nature, such as reduction in the size of the pupil and decreasing transparency or yellowing of the lens. In such cases, visual acuity may not be subject to compensation with our current level of science and technology.

Brightness is a quality of visual experience that is roughly correlated with the intensity of the light stimulus. Pupillary constriction occurs in newborn infants as a response to changes in light intensity, and sudden changes in the level of illumination also elicit blink reflexes and eye-neck reflexes (quick retractions of the head). These responses suggest that brightness is perceived by newborn infants. Brightness discrimination over the life span has not been studied extensively, but existing data suggest that it decreases with age, especially in subjects in their sixties and seventies. To attain the same degree of visibility, older subjects need an increase in lighting, and this is true throughout successive age decades (Guth, Eastman, & McNelis, 1956).

Other changes with regard to light sensitivity occur over the life span, particularly in relation to glare and dark adaptation. Evidence that infants can adapt to darkness has been gathered in a number of studies by measuring their activity level at various illuminations of light; the activity level changes as a function of the level of illumination. More precise threshold data have been collected over the life span, typically by testing subjects ranging in age from adolescence to old age, and remarkable changes have been observed. For example, the ability to detect small targets of light after sitting in darkness for thirty to forty minutes decreases dramatically with age. McFarland and Fisher (1955) observed a correlation of .89 between age and the final point of dark adaptation, and the intensity of illumination at threshold levels almost had to be doubled for each thirteen years of age between ages twenty and sixty. This correlation was among the highest reported in psychophysiological literature regarding age changes, and, using such data, McFarland and Fisher were able to predict a person's age with an accuracy of ±3 years. A striking feature of the data collected by McFarland and his colleagues was the magnitude of the difference in sensitivity between the very old and the young. For example, at the second minute of dark adaptation, young subjects were almost 5 times more sensitive than the very old; and at the fortieth minute they were 240 times more sensitive. The rate of dark adaptation is also slower in old age, and McFarland suggested that the decrease in sensitivity to light might provide an index to the aging process.

The implications of these studies are considerable. Besides the theoretical significance of the relationship between age and dark adaptation, the decline in light sensitivity with age has important significance for certain occupations (aviation) and certain activities (driving). McFarland (1968) describes a serious aviation accident in Tokyo harbor in 1966, in which the pilot descended rapidly from a brightly lit overcast sky into a low illumination level near the airport. Because the time for this descent was only six minutes—much less time than is required for dark adaptation—it is probable that the abrupt change in illumination led to a fatal error in judgment.

The decline in light sensitivity with age has important ramifications for older drivers.

Charles Harbutt, Magnum Photos, Inc.

Although most tasks do not require maximal sensitivity to light, tasks requiring partial adaptation to darkness (such as driving at night under conditions of intermittent and unpredictable changes in luminance) may tax our capacity—especially if we are older. The range of luminance in night driving is great, and so the rate of adaptation becomes exceedingly important. Older individuals are handicapped under these conditions, since they adapt to darkness at a much slower rate than the young do, and they are hampered further because they are particularly sensitive to glare. Wolf (1960) examined the ability of 112 observers aged five to eighty-five to detect targets at angular distances of 4, 7, and 10 degrees around a glare intensity that varied. From Figure 10.9 we can see that the intensity of target illumination needed for detection increases with age, with an abrupt increase around age forty. Comparing younger individuals (ages five to fifteen) with older ones (ages seventy-five to eighty-five), it was found

FIGURE 10.9
Target illumination and age. The light needed to detect an object increases with age, especially after age forty.

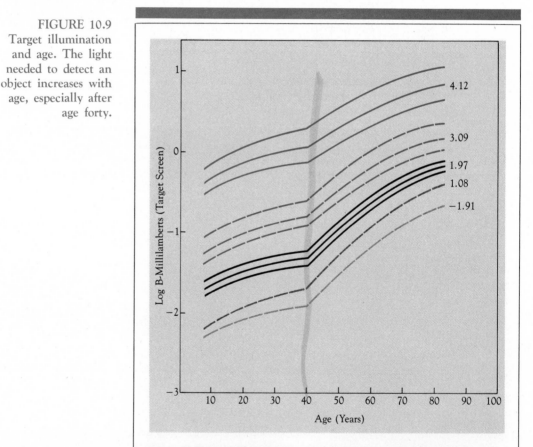

R. A. McFarland. The sensory and perceptual process in aging. In K. W. Schaie (ed.), *Theory and Methods of Research on Aging.* Morgantown, West Virginia, West Virginia University Press, © 1968, p. 955.

that the luminance of the target screen had to be increased 50 to 70 times for the older group to perform as well as the younger subjects. Thus the older individuals' handicap in the face of glare—coupled with their decreased ability to adapt to darkness—severely hampers them in situations such as driving at night.

It is difficult to separate responses to color from responses to brightness, since equal intensities of two different colors are perceived as different brightnesses. The human eye is selectively more sensitive to some colors (in bright light, it is most sensitive to middle green). In addition, the level of illumination affects color perception because the rods in the retina (which have lower thresholds in the dark and operate for peripheral vision) have a different luminosity curve than do the cones (which are responsible for detailed vision and color perception). Moreover, the center of the retina, where cone cells are congregated, does not mature fully until the age of five or six months, making the study of color vision in infants even more difficult. Thus the color spectrum may appear different to newborn infants than to adults, whose mature retina is pigmented. For all these difficulties, however, we do have evidence that infants perceive color, and this visual function has been identified even in premature infants.

Different languages use different numbers of words for color, indicating that different societies make more or fewer distinctions among different colors. Some languages discriminate among more colors by giving more names and identifying more colors, and it is interesting to speculate whether these language distinctions result in differences in perception of color. One way to test this notion is to study color perception in preverbal children. Follow-up tests could then yield data about the effects of language on color perception.

After infancy, when the retina becomes pigmented, there appear to be only small changes in color perception over the life span. Navrat (1965) tested children three to ten years old on a color-matching task and found improvement with age, while Pollack (1965) found no changes between ages seven and ten. Color appears to be a more salient stimulus feature for younger children than older ones. In a task that varies both the form and the color of two stimuli, children around age four match stimuli on the basis of color, whereas older children (age eight) match on the basis of form. Color preferences also seem to change with age. Infants indicate a preference for yellow, while most older children and adults prefer red to blue. These changes may be related to shifting spectral sensitivities in the retina between infancy and childhood, but they are probably also influenced by association with features of the environment. In old age, the lens of the eye yellows and the pupil constricts, which affects the perception of color. The amount and spectral distribution of light reaching an older retina decrease. Weale (1965) estimates that the retina of a sixty-year-old man receives approximately 30 percent of the amount of light reaching the retina of a twenty-year-old. In contrast, Guth, Eastman, and McNelis (1956) doubled the amount of light presented to the older eye and found that perception could be equalized across this age range. The changes in spectral distribution reaching the older eye appear to affect perception of short wavelengths of light, and older subjects may have difficulty discriminating blues and greens.

Visual acuity is a feature of sensitivity that shows great change over the life span. *Acuity* is defined as the minimum aspect of the test object dimension that can be identified correctly. The acuity of newborns has been tested by measuring eye movements in response to moving stripes. Examining the smallest width of stripe to elicit eye movements, Gorman, Cogan, and Gellis (1957) estimated the acuity of newborns to be equivalent to a Snellen Chart rating of 20/600. (The Snellen Chart is the familiar test used by eye doctors, and a 20/600 rating means that infants see at 20 feet what normal adults see at 600 feet.) Subsequent work indicated that some infants responded at the acuity of 20/350. Using more sensitive techniques to detect eye movements, Dayton and his associates (1964) concluded that infants under twenty-four hours old could respond to line widths of .032 inch, indicating a visual acuity of 20/150. Thus with more precise techniques, it may be found that infants' visual acuity is not as poor as originally estimated. According to Slataper (1950), average visual acuity for one-year-olds is 5/35 (seeing at 5 feet what a normal adult sees at 35 feet); at two years, acuity is 5/12; and at twelve years it is 5/5. Acuity reaches a maximum of 5/4.4 at the age of eighteen, and it remains stationary until the sixties. By the seventies, acuity may drop significantly because of senile changes in the eye.

An obvious functional change in vision over the life span is *presbyopia*—the impairment of our ability to focus on near objects. A normal eye at rest can focus objects at virtually an infinite distance, and it accommodates to focus near objects by shortening the focal distance of the lens. Maximal focusing accommodation is attained by around the age of five, with a gradual decline in accommodation up to age sixty, after which there is no further decline. The progressive decline in the focusing function results mainly from a loss of elasticity of the lens (McFarland, 1968). Thus most people become farsighted as they grow older, a decline that often begins in childhood. Because most of this inability to focus near objects can be corrected with convex lenses, it presents no major problem for visual perception in middle-aged and aged individuals.

Perceptual Information Processing

Up to this point we have considered age changes in sensation and perception as resulting mainly from structural changes in the eye. However, perceptual studies indicate that physical factors cannot be held solely responsible for the decrement in visual function with age. Equating older and younger subjects for visual acuity and increasing the light intensity for aged people do not adequately compensate for visual declines in old age. Such approaches have led investigators to conclude that processes of integration and decision making, which take place in the brain, also become relatively impaired with age. Thus declines in visual perception with age are seen as resulting from changes in the central nervous system as well.

One way to examine the higher-order organization and processing of visual information is to consider the susceptibility of individuals to illusions throughout the life span. In this manner psychologists attempt to understand perceptual processes by means of the "mistakes" made by the brain in interpreting information. We have all experienced optical illusions, and apparently this happens to a lesser or greater degree at different points in our lives. Figure 10.10 illustrates the Müller-Lyer illusion, which has been used in collecting most life-span data. In the presence of surrounding contours, the two physically equal lines in this figure appear to be different lengths. In general, susceptibility to this illusion decreases between ages six and twelve, rises slightly from fifteen to nineteen, reaches a plateau between twenty and thirty-nine, and increases thereafter (Comalli, 1970). Eisner (1968) obtained these results with longitudinal as well as cross-sectional data—he followed up subjects and observed changes in the effect of the illusion as well as comparing effects for subjects of different ages.

Pollack (1969) presents evidence that physiological mechanisms (such as increases in foveal pigmentation) can account for the decreased effectiveness of illusions among children. But Pollack has not tested this hypothesis in relation to the increased susceptibility among older subjects. Clearly, explanations that postulate that experiential factors lead to false interpretations of illusions cannot account for what happens with the Müller-Lyer figure because developmental functions indicate that susceptibility declines with experience and increases during old age. Pollack interprets such functions as relating to physiological mechanisms, which mature and then decline. He explains cases in which the optical illusion increases with age as being affected by intellectual mechanisms. In children, Pollack found high correlations between intelligence and the perception of those illusions to which susceptibility increases with age, but there were no relationships between intelligence and the perception of illusions that decrease with age. Again, these data were collected only for children, but their implications for old age—in which some measures of intelligence decline—are clear.

Comparing life-span data for four illusions, Comalli (1970) identifies two general ways in which the effects of illusions changed with age. First, a declining susceptibility with age in childhood remained stable until old age, when there was an increase in susceptibility. Second, increasing susceptibility with age

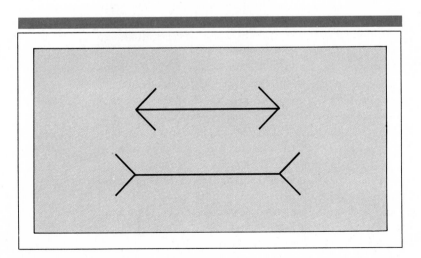

FIGURE 10.10
The Müller-Lyer illusion

attained some maximal level, after which there was a plateau and then a decline in old age. Comalli suggests that these illusion patterns are consistent with the developmental notion of early-life progression followed by late-life regression. In all cases for which data about susceptibility to illusions have been collected, the very young and the very old perceive illusions similarly—and in a fashion that is different from the perception of older children, adolescents, and adults.

Over the life span there do appear to be qualitative as well as quantitative changes in how perceptions are formed. Not only are there quantitative changes in sensory thresholds, but the way in which sensory information is processed may change. We have seen one example of this change in the degree to which certain visual information is perceived as an illusion. Kagan (1972) suggests that a qualitative change in visual perception occurs in infants around the age of two to three months, when they begin to notice how stimuli are discrepant from past experience. That is, they develop on the basis of past experience certain schematic representations for stimuli (Kagan calls these schema), and they test and compare new stimulus objects to these schema. When there is a discrepancy between an infant's schema and the stimulus object, the infant is capable of noticing this discrepancy. Qualitative changes in information processing may also occur at the end of life, as evidenced by the greater amount of time required to process information in old age as well as by changes on complex perceptual tasks. Now we will consider some evidence of perceptual changes among infants and children and evidence of qualitative perceptual changes in old age.

One perceptual ability that appears to change with age is the capacity to shift perceptual sets—that is, the ability to reorganize a given initial perception. Figure 10.11 is an example of an ambiguous drawing that has been used to test this capacity. The figure can be perceived as either an unattractive old woman ("mother-in-law") or an attractive young woman ("wife"). Older subjects appear to fixate on one of the two possible organizations of this figure, and they have difficulty in recognizing the alternative perception. Test yourself: how many times does this figure change for you in a one-minute period? Because this and other ambiguous figures shift less frequently for older subjects, it has been suggested that perception becomes more rigid with age.

Slowness on perceptual tasks—and indeed in all behavior—is a well-known characteristic of aged people. While some of the slowing can be attributed to changes in motor abilities, most of it appears to occur in the decision-making process itself. Increasing the complexity of a task widens the discrepancy between young and old subjects in terms of response speed, which suggests that there is some qualitative change in the central processing capacity with age. Thus just as Bower (1966) suggests that the amount of information processed by infants in a given period of time is less than the amount processed by adults, so too we may be witnessing in the aged a decreased capacity to process information. However, the degree of similarity between information processing in infantile and aged brains is unknown. While we may note parallels in the behavior of infants and elderly individuals on some perceptual tasks, the notion that their brains process information in the same manner is simplistic and most probably fallacious.

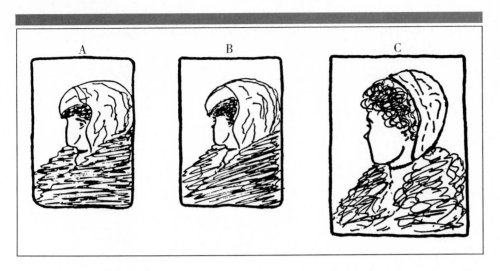

FIGURE 10.11
Ambiguous figure
used to test shifts in
perceptual sets

Perception and Cognition

A number of theories have been developed to explain how perceptual abilities develop and how they relate to our conceptions of and interactions with the environment. Although most theories deal exclusively with infancy and childhood, some have implications for adulthood and old age that should be clarified and refined.

Donald Hebb (1949) takes an empirical position in his cell-assembly theory, stating that perception is a mediating process between sensation and response that develops as a result of experience. According to Hebb, integrated neural networks are formed in the brain as a result of experience with certain regularities in the environment. Support for this theory comes from experiments measuring early environmental effects on perception. (See Chapter 6 and previous discussions in this chapter.) Research by Hubel and Weisel and by Spinelli regarding the organization of the visual cortex supports Hebb's theory. But work by Fantz (1965) and Bower (1966), identifying complex perceptual capacities in very young infants, along with evidence collected by Gregory and Wallace (1963) on the sophistication of perception in a congenitally blind man whose sight was restored, indicated that the brain may have more innate organization than was postulated by Hebb. The environment undoubtedly interacts with the maturing structure of the brain, but probably not all neural integration occurs as a function of environmental input.

While Kagan (1972) postulates that cognitive aspects such as hypothesis testing are involved in perception very early in development, Jean Piaget theorizes that perception and cognition are separate processes developing relatively independently. Piaget conceives of perception as the most direct or immediate possible knowledge of an object in one's sensorial field, and he feels that an individual can have knowledge by other means (such as through cognition) as well as perception. For example, in the case of the Müller-Lyer illusion shown in Figure 10.10, the lines in the illusion appear to be different lengths when we just look at or perceive them. However, if we were to measure the two lines, we would see that they are both exactly 2 inches long. In other words, it is possible to base a judgment on something other than simple perception; yet even knowing that the lines are equal, we perceive them to be unequal. This is the manner in which Piaget distinguishes between perceptual and cognitive processes. In such cases, conceptual knowledge is usually based on a broader body of information than the perception is, although it is not possible to integrate that broader knowledge into the perception.

For Piaget, one important development in a child's acquisition of conceptual thought is the gradual appearance of the effects of previous knowledge upon the child's thinking. A procedure used by Piaget illustrates this point. Figure 10.12 presents two arrangements of lines, all of which are equal in length. If sticks are held up to five-year-olds in the alignments depicted in the figure, they look of equal size; but to eight-year-olds, the top stick looks longer. With increasing age, the illusion diminishes. However, if one first holds up the sticks directly above each other, as in Figure 10.12b, and then in the child's presence moves the alignment to the position shown in Figure 10.12a, five-year-olds will usually say that the top stick is longer, whereas eight-year-olds are certain that the two lines are equal. This experiment demonstrates that the two ways of knowing these lines do not develop in parallel fashion. At age eight, when they experience the perceptual illusion to its fullest, children are capable of conceptually integrating two experiences separated in time and making a correct judgment, even though their perception is contradictory. Five-year olds, on the other hand—who do not experience the illusion even when the sticks are stationary— have not yet achieved a conceptual level of thinking and cannot integrate two experiences separated in time. Thus when the sticks are moved to the staggered position, they perceive the sticks as being unequal in length and believe them to be unequal. They operate at a preconceptual level, using perceptual information alone. As we grow older, we come to know that our senses sometimes play tricks on us.

FIGURE 10.12
Piaget's stick test. In this test devised by Piaget, two sticks of equal length are presented with one positioned ahead of the other (a) and juxtaposed (b). Children are asked if the lengths of the sticks are equal.

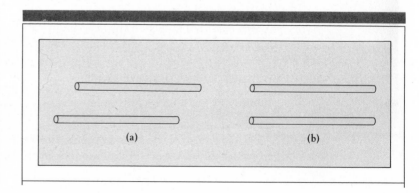

Rod-and-frame experiment. This field-dependence task is performed in the dark with only the luminous frame and rod visible. The chair is shown first upright and then tilted.

David Linton, © Scientific American, February 1959.

Another theory relating perception and cognitive styles has been developed by Witkin, who has studied the ability of individuals to make judgments that are free from environmental cues. Over the life span, individuals appear to change in the degree to which their judgments depend on environmental cues. Witkin used several tasks to test "field dependence" (reliance on environmental cues). From age eight to age seventeen, there appears to be a decrease in the amount of dependence individuals place on environmental cues, so that older subjects more quickly locate figures embedded in scrambled backgrounds. For example, older subjects were faster to adjust a rod and a chair to the true upright position. Males appear to be less field dependent than females, although some of this ability to respond independently of environmental cues appears to decline later in life.

One theory of perceptual development that has received widespread acceptance is that of Eleanor Gibson, who postulates that development brings greater differentiation and accuracy. As children grow older, they develop greater precision in recognizing similarities and differences among physical stimuli and in attaching labels to them. This process of perceptual differentiation undoubtedly continues throughout the life span. Indeed, the definition of development itself includes the notion of a continuing process of differentiation. One-year-olds have not yet learned labels to apply to discrete objects such as the array of tables and chairs and toys they might encounter in a playroom, and so these objects may not be differentiated or separated out in their minds. Thus one-year-olds might perceive the room as consisting of a mass of colors and shapes. Five-year-olds, however, are able to identify and label discrete objects and so can respond to them with a more adult perspective. To demonstrate this point, Gibson and Gibson (1955) carried out studies using scribbles as stimuli (see Figure 10.13) and asking children of different ages to sort cards by comparing the scribbles to standards they had seen previously. As shown in Figure 10.13, the scribbles differ only in subtle ways, and younger children were able to detect fewer differences between them than older children were. The children were required to repeat the card-sorting task after looking again at the cue stimuli, and they repeated sorting until they could perform the task correctly. As expected, younger children needed more sorts to eliminate all errors than did older children. Repetition of the task provided the children with experience and practice in differentiation. Such an experimental procedure may mimic normal development, in which children experience the world and find increasing differentiation in it.

Practical Applications of Perceptual Research

Although the study of perceptual development typically has drawn on traditional studies of perception (such as size, distance, shape, and illusions), the field may well have begun to draw on problems from the real world as well. Social problems of cultural and environmental deprivation are discussed elsewhere in this book, and this chapter has considered several practical aspects, such as driving at night and environmental noise. But many other aspects of perceptual

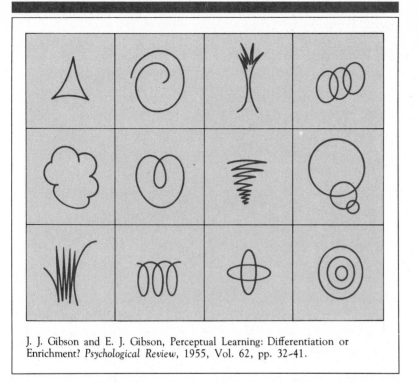

FIGURE 10.13
Scribble stimuli used by Gibson and Gibson. These are nonsense items differing on many dimensions.

J. J. Gibson and E. J. Gibson, Perceptual Learning: Differentiation or Enrichment? *Psychological Review*, 1955, Vol. 62, pp. 32–41.

development also have applications in the real world. Perceptual deficits are becoming recognized not only in blind and deaf children but in those with physical handicaps and learning disabilities. For example, children who have difficulties in learning to read because of letter reversals are now thought to have a perceptual problem in the functioning and interaction of the two hemispheres of the brain. Sensory deprivation among elderly individuals who receive less stimulus input is being considered in the design of nursing, boarding, and retirement facilities, and prosthetic devices such as artificial eyes and hearing aids have been designed on the basis of principles identified in studies of perception. Thus there is theoretical as well as practical significance in adopting problems from the real world for academic study. In the future, we might expect to see greater interaction between research into perceptual development and its application in our lives.

Summary

1. Systematic study of sensory and perceptual experience causes psychologists to make a distinction between sensation (registration of activity at the sensory receptor level) and perception (interpretation of sensory information). The

detection and interpretation of sensory information take place in the nervous system, which develops and begins to record information early in the fetal stage.

2. Those senses developing first are the proximal senses (such as touch), and distal senses (such as audition and vision) develop last. Early-developing senses also appear to be less vulnerable to processes of aging than are senses that develop later.

3. Development and aging take different courses in the various sensory systems. The first-developing sense, touch, is keen in early life, and its sensory thresholds remain stable over the life span until the sixties, when they show some decline. Temperature sensitivity appears relatively stable over the life span. Sensitivity to pain seems to develop later in infants, as it is difficult to elicit until shortly after birth; little decline in pain sensitivity is observed until after sixty years, and then not all studies show a decline. Kinesthetic responses are present early in fetal development; around the age of fifty, thresholds for kinesthetic sensation appear to increase. Balance is another early-developing sense; falls and dizziness in old age have been attributed to problems in the vestibular apparatus.

4. Taste sensitivity is maximal in neonates and shows some decrement throughout the life span. Smell sensitivity appears stable through late life. Although fetuses can respond to sound in the uterus, maximal auditory acuity is not attained until the age of five. In the mid-thirties, acuity for high tones diminishes, and most old people have reduced auditory capacity.

5. Some visual capacity is apparent in fetuses, but a controversy rages as to whether this capacity is innate or learned. Nativists have demonstrated that depth and shape perception exist in infants; empiricists point out that these abilities improve with age and are therefore affected by learning. Acuity in neonates is poor, and it is not until around puberty that adult acuity is attained. This level is maintained until very late in life.

6. The relationship between perception and cognition was examined through various theoretical perspectives such as the cell-assembly theory of Hebb, the notion of schema by Kagan, Piaget's cognitive approach, Witkin's field independence, and Gibson's concept of differentiation.

Selected Readings

Bower, T. G. R. "The Visual World of Infants." *Scientific American* (December 1966). A description of the fascinating research into what infants actually perceive.

Comalli, P. E., Jr. "Life Span Changes in Visual Perception." In *Life Span Developmental Psychology: Research and Theory.* Eds. L. Goulet and P. B. Baltes. New York: Academic Press, 1970. Pp. 211–227. A discussion of the research on visual illusions and how perception of illusions changes over the life span.

Cowan, W. M. "The Development of the Brain." *Scientific American* (September 1979). This article describes research on how the neurons in the embryonic brain find their place and make the right connections.

Eimas, P. D. Speech Perception in Early Infancy. In *Infant Perception: From Sensation to Cognition*. Eds. L. B. Cohen and P. Salapatek. New York: Academic Press, 1975. Pp. 193-231. Research strategies and results of probing the infant's ability to respond to speech.

Hubel, D. H., and T. N. Wiesel. "Brain Mechanisms of Vision." *Scientific American* (September 1979). An overview of the pioneering research of these investigators who have provided important insights into how we see.

Rovee, C. K., R. Y. Cohen, and W. Shlapack. "Life Span Stability in Olfactory Sensitivity." *Developmental Psychology*, 11 (1975), 311-318. A study that establishes estimates of the sensitivity of smell in subjects from infancy to old age.

Chapter 11

Learning, Attention, and Memory

The nature and development of learning processes, with particular emphasis on classical conditioning, operant conditioning, and modeling

How human beings select which information to attend to, and how attention affects learning

The attentional and arousal processes that regulate sleep and waking

The components and types of memory processes in human beings, and how they change over the life span

Learning

Classical Conditioning
Operant (Instrumental) Conditioning
Ethical Issues in the Use of Behavior Modification
Conditioning in Infants
Social Reinforcement over the Life Span
Imitation Learning (Modeling)

Attention

The Role of Attention in Learning
Measuring Attention: The Orienting Response
Developmental Determinants of Attention
Attention, Arousal, and Sleep

Memory

Components of Memory
Memory and Age Differences

Lifelong Learning and Education

Introduction

This chapter focuses on the processes that enable individuals to handle information. First we will discuss the nature and development of the learning processes that allow us to acquire new knowledge or information. Then we will examine the attentional and arousal processes that regulate sleep and waking and help us to select from available information that which is most relevant. Finally, we will consider the memory processes that make it possible to store and retrieve information that has been learned.

Although space limitations keep us from discussing all of the many different kinds of learning, attentional, and memory processes that human beings have, we will consider the nature and development of some of the more important ones. We will also examine the implications of research in this area, including such applications as the treatment of behavior disorders in children and the promotion of vigor and longevity in elderly individuals.

Learning

The question, What is learning? is more difficult to answer than it might seem. Indeed, there is considerable disagreement among learning theorists regarding what factors must be present for learning to take place. For example, does learning require that an organism make some kind of response (either an external motor one or an internal mental one)? And must that response be met with some kind of reward or reinforcement for learning to occur (for example, see Houston, 1976; Kimble, 1961)?

Controversy over such questions may in part reflect simply a semantic debate over how the term *learning* should be defined. However, it also reflects our ignorance of the biological bases of learning. The resolution of such debates is likely to require a more detailed understanding than we presently have about the biochemical and neural changes in the brain that underlie learning processes.

For all the debates about the nature of learning, there is also widespread agreement on certain points. For example, most psychologists would probably agree with the following defining characteristics of learning. First, learning involves a change in the *potential* for behavior, for an organism's competence or potential capacity to perform some action may not always be evident from a given performance. Second, learning involves a relatively long-lasting change in behavior potential that does not depend on temporary shifts in behavior arising from fatigue, distraction, memory lapses, or changes in motivation. (For example, in studying for an exam, you may have learned the meaning of a new word, but whether you in fact translate that learning into performance at a particular time depends on many factors. A cramp in your writing hand, test anxiety, or even tiredness may keep you from recalling the word during the exam.) Third, it is generally understood that learning is to be distinguished from changes in behavior resulting from such factors as maturation, disease, drugs, accidents, physiological aspects of aging, or sensory adjustments (such as the constriction of the pupil of the eye when exposed to bright light).

Learning involves a change in competence or capacity for certain behaviors. Whether this competence is shown in performance depends on other factors such as memory and motivation.

Paul Fusco, Magnum Photos, Inc.

Space limitations do not permit us to review exhaustively all of the various learning processes that have been described and researched by psychologists. Rather, we will focus on three of the most basic and intensively studied learning processes: classical conditioning, operant conditioning, and modeling.

Classical Conditioning

Classical, or *Pavlovian, conditioning* refers to learning that is established in the "classic" or traditional manner first set forth by the Russian physiologist Ivan Pavlov when conducting his Nobel Prize-winning research on digestion (Houston, 1976; Pavlov, 1927; Yerkes and Morgulis, 1909). In the course of these studies, which included the measurement of saliva secreted by a dog in the presence of food, Pavlov noticed that the dog came to salivate not only when eating the food but also when seeing it or the dish in which it was served, and even when hearing the sounds made by experimenters in preparing the food. Clearly, the dog had learned that various stimuli were associated with, and signaled the appearance of, food. Pavlov set out to investigate the properties of the learning involved.

By attaching a collecting tube to the dog's cheek and connecting it to a recording device, Pavlov measured the amount of saliva secreted at any one time. Then he showed that a particular stimulus, such as a tone, would not elicit saliva before it was paired with food. Next the tone was sounded, followed by presentation of meat powder. After several such conditioning trials pairing the tone with meat powder, Pavlov ran test trials in which the tone was sounded *without* presentation of meat powder. He found that the tone itself was enough to produce salivation. Thus "conditioning" had occurred.

Pioneering work by the Russian physiologist Ivan Pavlov on conditioning of salivation in dogs helped to establish the basic principles of classical conditioning.

The Bettmann Archive, Inc.

Because salivation in response to the tone was dependent on, or "conditional" to, being paired with food, Pavlov termed it the *conditional* response. In English translation and usage this has come to be known as the *conditioned response (CR)*. Similarly, the tone—which before pairing with food is a *neutral* stimulus—after pairing becomes a *conditioned stimulus (CS)*. By contrast, the meat powder in this situation acts as an *unconditioned stimulus (UCS)*, because it already can elicit salivation consistently. Finally, the *unconditioned response (UCR)* is the consistent response elicited by the UCS—in this case, salivation in response to meat powder.

Note that these terms (CS, CR, UCS, and UCR) are defined by the relations among stimuli and responses in a particular learning situation that involves classical conditioning. In other words, the same stimulus, such as a tone, might be the CS in one situation but the UCS in another. Moreover, the ability of the UCS to produce the UCR may be innate and reflexive (indeed, Pavlov initially used the term UCR to refer to an unconditional "reflex"), but it also may be learned. The important thing is that the UCS-UCR connection be strong and consistent enough so that it can be used to condition a previously neutral stimulus. Although the CR that results from classical conditioning tends to resemble the UCR, it still is distinct from it. Therefore, classical conditioning is not simply a matter of the CS coming to produce an exact replica of what was formerly the UCR.

If Pavlov had continued to present the tone to the dog *without* pairing it with food, the tone would gradually have lost its capacity to elicit the CR, until eventually the CR no longer would occur. This is called *extinction* of a response. And just as a CR can be extinguished, so too it can be *generalized*. In other words, after conditioning, organisms tend to display the CR not only to the CS but also to other stimuli that are similar to the CS. In fact, the more similar a stimulus is to the CS, the more likely it will also evoke the CR. These concepts of extinction and stimulus generalization in conditioning are the basis for one of the best-known experiments in the history of psychology.

John Watson, Little Albert, and Conditioned Fear   A classic study by John B. Watson and his student Rosalie Rayner investigated the conditioning of a fear response in a young infant named Albert. Watson and Rayner (1920) set out to see whether they could classically condition fear of a previously neutral stimulus—a furry white rat—and whether the fear would generalize to other, similar objects. They first made sure that their intended neutral stimuli would not evoke fear responses before conditioning: when Albert was nine months old, he was presented successively with a white rat and several other objects varying in similarity to the rat—for example, a rabbit, a dog, cotton wool, and burning newspapers.

A few days later a test was performed to make certain that the intended USC—a loud noise—would produce a fear reaction as expected. A steel bar was struck repeatedly with a hammer, causing Albert to startle and then cry. Clearly, the loud noise was an effective UCS for a strong fear response.

When Albert was eleven months old, conditioning began. Without Albert's expecting it, a white rat was presented to Albert. Just as he reached out and touched the rat, the bar was struck behind his head. After seven such conditioning trials in which the loud noises and white rat were paired, Albert began to cry the instant he saw the rat. On further testing Albert showed signs of fear not only of the rat but also of a rabbit, dog, fur coat, and even a hairy Santa Claus mask. The conditioned fear thus appeared to have generalized to other furry objects (though not to dissimilar objects such as toy blocks). Follow-up tests indicated that the conditioned fear persisted for at least a month.

Extinguishing a Conditioned Fear   A later study by another of Watson's students, Mary Cover Jones, would likely have a better chance of meeting today's standards of research ethics. Jones (1924, 1974) attempted to extinguish a fear of animals that already existed in a young boy, Peter, aged two years and ten months. One of Watson's and Rayner's motives in experimentally producing a conditioned fear was to provide scientific understanding that could be used to treat or desensitize irrational fears, or *phobias*. Watson suggested several methods by which such fear responses might be reduced or eliminated. These included (1) extinguishing the conditioned fear response by repeatedly presenting the CS in the absence of the UCS; (2) associating the CS with a pleasant UCS, such as erotic stimulation or food; and (3) teaching alternative constructive responses to compete with the fear response. Jones used these approaches in eliminating Peter's fear of animals.

A difficulty in eliminating phobias is that they often involve *avoidance learning,* in which one not only learns to associate a CS with a fearful UCS but also learns an avoidance response through which escape from the CS is rewarded by fear reduction. If the conditioned fear of the CS is to be extinguished, then the individual must learn that the CS is no longer associated with the UCS. But to do this, the subject must be kept from avoiding exposure to the CS. This can be done most easily through gradual *desensitization procedures,* in which a relatively mild form of the CS is introduced to the subject. When fear of this stimulus has been overcome—and this extinction, in turn, is generalized to other, similar stimuli—the subject is ready for exposure to another stimulus that would have been too threatening at first. Thus what initially was a terrifying stimulus (for example, letting the CS come within a few feet) now becomes only mildly threatening, and can be presented for extinction trials. This procedure is applied progressively until the initially fearful stimulus can be presented without inducing fear.

Jones used these techniques to eliminate Peter's fears of animals. Initially, when a white rat was placed in his crib, Peter responded with a paroxysm of fear. This fear was reduced progressively by introducing Peter to children his age who had no fear of the rabbit. The rabbit was always present during sessions in which Peter played with these children, who would hold and pet the rabbit. At first the rabbit was kept at a distance, but gradually it was brought into increasingly direct contact with Peter. Eventually Peter was able to touch the rabbit while it was being held by the experimenter and later to hold it on his own lap. Jones also fed Peter while the rabbit was nearby. In addition to eliminating fear of the rabbit, the extinction procedures also generalized so that Peter's fears of other animals were reduced as well.

Behavior Modification   The work of Mary Cover Jones represented a pioneering effort in the deliberate application of scientific learning principles to the problem of modifying problem behavior, an approach often called *behavior modication.* (When used to treat psychological disorders, the approach is called *behavior therapy* or *reinforcement therapy.*)

A fairly common example of the use of classical conditioning principles in modifying problem behavior is seen in the treatment of enuresis (bed wetting). Essentially, this involves a conditioning device (available in many stores) that consists of a bell and a special pad, which is wired so that even a small amount of urine will complete a circuit and set off the bell. Thus when an enuretic wets the bed during sleep, he or she is awakened immediately by the bell. In time, the individual learns to wake up *before* actually wetting the bed. Apparently, a form of conditioning occurs as a result of pairing the UCS (bell) with the CS (bladder tension or other bodily stimuli that precede urination and signal its need). In this case, the act of waking could be regarded as the CR.

Of course, enuresis can result from various causes, and medical specialists should be consulted. However, even when medical problems can be ruled out, some psychologists question whether behavior therapy is appropriate for treating enuresis. In particular, some psychoanalytically oriented therapists express concern that such problems as bed wetting are simply surface manifestations of underlying emotional conflicts. These therapists fear that if the superficial symptom is removed by behavior modification—without treating its underlying cause—then a new and possibly more dangerous symptom may arise as a substitute for the removed symptom.

The theory that failure to deal with supposed underlying causes of behavior problems will lead to *symptom substitution* has been raised frequently in criticism of behavior therapy. Behavior therapists respond that many problem behaviors represent the result of faulty conditioning, for which new learning experiences are the most direct and effective treatment (and certainly less expensive than lengthy psychoanalysis). Moreover, they point out, in some cases associated emotional problems may result from the learning problem, rather than cause it. For example, a child who is criticized or ridiculed by family members or peers because of bed wetting may develop poor self-esteem, anxiety, and other problems.

To investigate this issue, psychologist Bruce Baker (1969) studied a group of enuretic schoolchildren who had been screened to eliminate those who had obvious medical problems. He then randomly assigned the children into experimental and control groups. The experimental group received conditioning, using the mattress and bell device mentioned previously. Other children were assigned to a group designed to control for a possible *Hawthorne effect*, which refers to the fact that simply providing attention and introducing some novel treatment may by itself produce significant changes in behavior.[1] To determine whether any decrease in bed wetting or change in personality resulted from conditioning or from some more general Hawthorne effect, Baker placed in the bedrooms of control children a contraption that looked impressive but did not actually provide effective conditioning. (After the experiment, Baker did make an effort to provide effective conditioning treatment for the control children.) In fact, most children using this conditioning device did show a significant decrease in bed wetting. In addition, Baker attempted to measure how the children's personalities at home and in school might be affected by the treatment. Children who had learned to control bed wetting as a result of the conditioning showed, if anything, fewer behavior and emotional problems than did the control group. In this case, then, there was no support for the symptom substitution hypothesis (though it is possible that the hypothesis may apply to other psychological problems).

Operant (Instrumental) Conditioning

In learning research, classical conditioning is usually distinguished from *operant*, or *instrumental*, conditioning. Harvard psychologist B. F. Skinner (1938, 1953, 1976) was perhaps the first to outline scientific reasons for this distinction. He suggested that classical conditioning procedures be termed *respondent* conditioning, because the behavior being conditioned is made in response to stimuli that precede it. In contrast, Skinner focused his research on the conditioning of what he termed *operant* behaviors—responses that operate on the environment. In *operant*, or *instrumental*, *conditioning*, behavior is conditioned by the consequences that the behavior is instrumental in producing. In terms of the experimental procedures, at least, Skinner's distinction is rather clear. Classical conditioning modifies behavior by manipulating stimuli that precede it, whereas

---

1. The Hawthorne effect is named after a famous series of studies conducted by social psychologists at the Hawthorne plant, near Chicago, to see what kinds of changes in working conditions would most improve the morale and productivity of employees. They found that nearly *any* kind of change improved morale and performance. These and other results suggested that the nature of a specific change in working conditions was less important than the act of showing concern and providing attention.

operant conditioning modifies behavior by manipulating relevant stimuli that follow it.

Positive and Negative Reinforcement Only certain stimuli that follow the emission of an operant behavior are effective in modifying that behavior. Such stimuli Skinner termed *reinforcers*, and he distinguished between two basic types: positive and negative. *Positive reinforcers* are stimuli that increase the probability of a given behavior if they are presented as a consequence of that behavior. *Negative reinforcers* increase the probability of a given behavior if they are *taken away* as a consequence of that behavior. *Punishment*, by contrast, is designed to *decrease* rather than increase the probability of a behavior. Punishment involves the removal of desired stimuli or presentation of aversive stimuli as a consequence of behavior to be decreased.

Because of the ease, economy, and simplicity of using animals as experimental subjects, much of Skinner's research has involved the conditioning of simple behaviors in animals, particularly bar-pressing by rats and pecking by pigeons. Skinner often used a device known as a *Skinner box,* a small enclosure in which to house an animal in order to record its operant behaviors and quickly provide

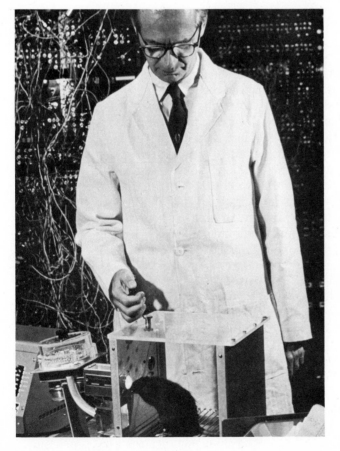

B. F. Skinner devised an apparatus to manipulate and control environmental variables so that he could study the effects of reinforcement on behavior.

Nina Leen, Life Magazine, © 1964, Time Inc.

reinforcers. In the case of rats, it was convenient for much of Skinner's research to use the pressing of a small bar in the box as the operant behavior and to provide a pellet of rat chow as the reinforcer. Behaviors and reinforcers can then be measured in discrete units; can be recorded and controlled automatically; and can be replicated by other investigators using standardized procedures. Skinner hoped by these means to discover principles of operant conditioning and reinforcement that could be generalized to a wide variety of situations and species, including human beings. He has, in fact, achieved remarkable success toward this goal.

Reinforcement Schedules   One major focus of Skinner's research has been to investigate the effects on behavior of different *schedules* for the timing of reinforcement. For example, very different effects result depending on whether a behavior is reinforced (1) according to a schedule of *continuous reinforcement,* in which every single response is followed by reinforcement; or (2) according to a schedule of *partial,* or *intermittent, reinforcement,* in which reinforcers are presented only after a certain interval of time has passed or for only a fraction of the responses made. More specifically, reinforcement schedules are distinguished according to whether they involve a fixed interval, a variable interval, a fixed ratio, or a variable ratio. These four types of reinforcement schedules typically produce different patterns of response over time (see Figure 11.1).

In a *fixed interval schedule,* for example, the subject is not reinforced for a response until a certain interval of time has passed—no matter how many responses are made during that interval. Once the time interval has passed, the first response in question is reinforced. Given such a schedule, most animals develop the appropriate strategy of emitting few if any responses during most of the interval. However, as the time period comes to an end, they respond with increasing frequency. As shown in Figure 11.1, this appears as a scalloped curve in which the flat regions correspond to periods of little or no responding and the more upward-sloping parts indicate periods of more rapid responding.

In a *variable interval schedule,* the period during which the subject must wait before being reinforced for a response varies over time, so that the interval might be a few seconds at one point but many minutes or hours at a later point. Because the subject cannot predict the length of the interval, such schedules tend to produce a rather steady rate of responding. As Figure 11.1 shows, the subject is less likely to devise a strategy that produces scalloping.

In a *fixed ratio schedule,* the subject is reinforced after a fixed number of responses, as when factory workers are paid on a "piecework" basis. And in a *variable ratio schedule,* the number of responses required before a reinforcement is delivered varies over time. Both fixed and variable ratio schedules produce high rates of responding.

In practice, if one is interested in modifying behavior, it is often efficient to begin with a continuous reinforcement schedule in order to establish the behavior and then gradually wean the subject onto a schedule that requires a higher ratio of responses per reinforcer. Indeed, by progressively increasing the ratio of responses required for reinforcement, it is sometimes possible to get animals to produce tens of thousands of responses before reinforcement. A related phenomenon is the fact that behavior learned under conditions of par-

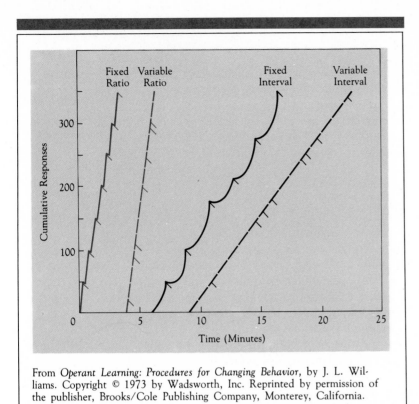

FIGURE 11.1
Stylized records of responses over time obtained under four common reinforcement schedules. Slash marks indicate presentations of reinforcements.

From *Operant Learning: Procedures for Changing Behavior*, by J. L. Williams. Copyright © 1973 by Wadsworth, Inc. Reprinted by permission of the publisher, Brooks/Cole Publishing Company, Monterey, California.

tial reinforcement—especially when a high ratio of responses is required—is very resistant to extinction once the response is no longer reinforced.

Shaping Behavior Skinner (1951) also demonstrated the power of operant conditioning for modifying behavior by a technique known as *shaping*. To increase the probability that a desired response will occur again in the future under similar circumstances, one can wait until the subject spontaneously emits the response and then quickly reinforce it. However, this strategy is obviously inappropriate if the behavior to be reinforced is one the subject rarely emits or does not know how to perform. In this case, Skinner tried to "shape," or mold, the animal's behavior in successive steps toward the desired response. By using this technique, he was able to teach animals remarkable new behaviors quickly and efficiently. He once even taught two pigeons to play a game of ping-pong. The animals held small paddles in their beaks and pushed a ball back and forth across a small table.

To shape this behavior, Skinner successively reinforced behaviors that were increasingly closer approximations to what he hoped to produce eventually. He began by requiring only, say, that the pigeon walk toward the paddle in order to be reinforced. Once the pigeon regularly approached the paddle, it would have to peck at the paddle before being reinforced. In such successive steps, the bird would be required to peck the paddle, put its beak around the handle, swing the paddle, and so on.

Using Operant Conditioning in Teaching Such methods of operant conditioning have been applied with considerable success in shaping human behavior. They have proved particularly useful in working with very young children and older individuals who because of psychological handicaps have difficulty understanding verbal instructions. For example, psychologists have used operant conditioning techniques to teach basic language skills to children afflicted with infantile autism (a form of childhood psychosis in which attentional processes as well as social, emotional, and language development appear to be severely disturbed). Such children often show a preoccupation with mechanical objects and a disinterest in or rejection of interaction with other people. Though certain abilities—such as memory for details—may be normal, the development of language skills tends to be markedly disturbed.

To help such children, Lovaas and his colleagues (1966) used techniques that have been successful in teaching communication skills to children who otherwise might not have developed them. For example, because praise and physical affection are often not positive reinforcers for autistic children, as they are for most children, such social reinforcers first may be paired with the presentation of food so that they become positive reinforcers through conditioning. These reinforcers can then be used to shape language behavior. If the children at first are virtually mute and completely ignore speech, the first step might be to reinforce them for attending to speech. Next an attempt might be made to develop their ability to articulate particular vowel and consonant sounds. Once these were mastered, the children might be reinforced for imitating syllables, then for imitating the pronunciation of words, then for labeling objects with appropriate words, then for combining words into simple sentences, and so on. (Note, however, that such learning differs in important respects from language development in normal children. The procedures used with autistic children may not be the most appropriate to use in encouraging normal children's language development, which is discussed in Chapter 12.)

These basic principles—of identifying existing reinforcers, conditioning new or acquired reinforcers if needed, applying immediate reinforcement to behaviors that successively approximate the desired goal, and breaking down complex behaviors into simple components—have been widely applied in the teaching of skills to retarded children and adults. By writing detailed teaching programs that break basic self-care behaviors into simple steps and by teaching parents or paraprofessional aides to apply principles of operant conditioning in teaching the skills, it is often possible to teach retarded individuals to care for their own basic needs, such as feeding, dressing, and personal hygiene. Teaching programs for the retarded have important benefits, not only in reducing their need for help but also in increasing their self-esteem and confidence. Success in learning basic skills is often important to individuals whose history of repeated frustration and failure in learning experiences prevents them from realizing their learning potential.

In general, learning theorists including Skinner have tended to emphasize the use of positive reinforcement instead of punishment. As Skinner noted in an interview (*Harvard Magazine*, 1977), "the power of positive reinforcement—that's what I've been pushing for 40 years." Skinner and others have noted that positive reinforcement is usually preferable because punishing contingencies often have undesirable side effects, such as producing fear in subjects or making them hostile toward the person who administers the punishment.

In some cases, however, strongly aversive or punishing procedures—even painful stimuli—have been considered appropriate. To take an extreme example, some children with infantile autism and other rare psychiatric disorders may engage in bizarre and injurious self-stimulatory behaviors. For example, they may repeatedly and severely bang their heads against the floor, or may bite their own flesh repeatedly until the bone is exposed. Such cases present a difficult choice: the child may be permitted to continue the behavior, with risk of serious injury; the child may be restrained in a straightjacket for an indefinite period; or punishing contingencies may be used to eliminate the behavior. Lovaas and some of his colleagues have argued that in this case punishment is the least of these evils. In some cases they have even used brief shocks from an electric cattle prod—momentarily a quite painful stimulus, but unlikely to cause lasting tissue damage. They were usually able to eliminate destructive behavior quickly, so that positive reinforcement procedures could be used to develop constructive behaviors. Even in extreme cases like this, however, the use of punishment is controversial. Lovaas and others would agree that positive reinforcement is generally more effective than, and preferable to, punishment as a means of influencing behavioral development.

Ethical Issues in the Use of Behavior Modification

Recent surveys of college students indicate that B. F. Skinner has perhaps the most widely recognized name of any living scientist. Skinner's fame (some say notoriety) probably results less from his important scientific work than from his more popular works, in which he has urged that learning principles be applied to child rearing and other social topics. For example, in his novel *Walden Two*, Skinner (1948) describes a utopian community based on principles of operant conditioning.

Skinner's political philosophy and attempts to apply principles of operant conditioning to social policy have drawn considerable criticism. A common concern—as expressed in the novel and movie *Clockwork Orange*—is that such applications represent a manipulation of human beings that threatens their freedom and dignity. Skinner replies that he simply wishes to help design programs of education and therapy so that society can shape citizens' behavior in constructive directions. Skinner sees himself as proposing control methods that are at once more effective and humane than methods involving punishment and coercion (such as jails, threats of imprisonment, execution, or war), which are used so widely as a means of behavior control.

Nonetheless, a number of psychologists have objected that Skinner's programs overlook important principles of human development. For example, humanistic psychologists such as Carl Rogers (1959) argue that an important goal of psychotherapy, education, and other efforts to foster mature development is to increase an individual's capacity for self-determination, for making his or her own responsible decisions. Rogers argues that the goal of such helping relationships should be not to bring the behavior of individuals under increasing control of the helper's reinforcement regime but rather to give people increasing freedom to make their own decisions. As Rogers points out, there is something of a paradox here, insofar as the goals of science have often been considered to include not only the understanding of natural phenomena but their prediction and control as well. However, Rogers argues that an important goal of successful helping relationships is to make a person's behavior less, not more, predictable and controllable.

An interesting practical research question involving these issues is the problem of how best to help children who are diagnosed as *hyperactive*. Excessive activity among some schoolchildren is a rather common complaint of teachers and parents. Actually, careful observation of such children (for example, by using activity meters attached to their wrists or ankles) indicates that they usually are no more active than other children in a general sense. Rather, they impress teachers and parents as being overly active because they are active at times judged inappropriate by the adults. For example, a hyperactive child may fidget or run around the room when he or she is supposed to be reading quietly. In laboratory tasks that demand sustained attention, hyperactive children have been found consistently to show greater motor restlessness and poorer performance compared with control children. This is especially so if the tasks are highly structured and are paced by the teacher or researcher rather than by the child. Thus the term *hyperactivity* is somewhat misleading, for what actually causes adults to label children as hyperactive is not a generally high activity rate per se, but inappropriate activity. This, in turn, is related to other psychological problems, such as attentional difficulties, distractibility, and impulsivity (Whalen & Henker, 1976). Indeed, the new diagnostic manual of the American Psychiatric Association (1980) has adopted the term *attention deficit disorder* in place of *hyperactivity*.

At present, psychostimulant drugs are used rather widely to help reduce hyperactive symptoms in schoolchildren—a matter of considerable controversy. Critics of such drug therapy argue that many children are diagnosed incorrectly, that making these drugs available to schoolchildren encourages hoarding of pills for sale on the black market, and that these drugs can have unfortunate side effects, such as some stunting of physical growth. Moreover, although the drugs often do seem to reduce temporarily the children's impulsivity, distractibility, and inappropriate activity, drug treatment does *not* seem effective in improving long-term social and academic adjustment. Existing studies have found that drug treatment did not seem to reduce the tendency for hyperactive children—as adolescents and adults—to have, on the average, lower self-esteem, fewer friends, and more trouble with the law (Whalen & Henker, 1976).

Treating hyperactive children with medication may also have harmful psychological side effects, for the fact that the children are receiving medication may tend to brand them as different and deviant in the eyes of parents, teachers, and peers. Moreover, the fact that the drug treatment often reduces some of the children's behavioral problems may lead others to conclude that the difficulties are something the children cannot change through their own efforts and that can be dealt with only by medical intervention. Although this conclusion is illogical, it is commonly drawn by people, including physicians and even the children themselves. Whalen and Henker (1976) cite the example of a ten-year-old who, when asked what would happen if she stopped taking Ritalin, replied, "I'd go nuts."

Depending on how they are designed, behavior modification approaches to the treatment of behavioral problems such as hyperactivity may also have potentially harmful side effects on a child's sense of self-control and personal effectiveness. University of California psychologists Bugental, Whalen, and Henker (1976) conducted a study in which hyperactive boys were tutored by college students over a period of two months in a classroom setting. Half of the boys were assigned to a behavior-change group that emphasized external monitoring and reinforcement by the tutors. For example, the tutors praised the children and gave them attention when they stayed with the assigned task, but they ignored the children if they showed inattentive or inappropriate behavior. In the second group, by contrast, the tutors encouraged the children to improve their own internal monitoring and regulation, and they taught the children techniques for doing so, such as self-controlling speech. For example, the tutors would model self-controlling speech and reinforcement for the children on a task that demanded sustained attention, and then encourage the children to imitate these behaviors. The children also were shown videotapes of behaviors in which they were able to apply such self-control strategies successfully. Before and after tutoring, the children were tested by means of a maze task on which hyperactive children tend to do poorly.

Which tutorial strategy was more effective in improving maze performance was found to depend on two factors: (1) whether the children were on medication, and (2) whether, when tutoring began, they tended to attribute their own success to personal effort or to external factors such as luck or how much the teacher liked them. Children who attributed their success more to their own efforts, and who were not taking medication, tended to show the most improvement if tutored according to the strategy that emphasized internal control rather than social reinforcement. On the other hand, tutoring that emphasized social reinforcement was most effective for children who attributed success to external factors and/or were taking medication.

These results illustrate the efficacy, over the short run, of tailoring a behavior-change program to fit a child's beliefs about his or her own personal causality. The results also suggest, however, that over the long run it is important to design behavior modification programs so that they not only teach children more desirable behaviors, such as reducing inappropriate activity, but also show the children how they themselves can be more effective at modifying their own behavior and development.

Principles of behavior modification have also been widely applied in experimental rehabilitation programs in prisons and correctional institutions for juvenile offenders. Besides punishing and housing convicted juveniles, a systematic attempt is made to shape their behavior in constructive directions through positive reinforcement. Such programs often use "token economy" systems to reinforce desirable behaviors. For example, such behaviors as studying, working diligently, engaging in vocational training, or helping to maintain order are reinforced quickly by some token reward such as poker chips or points that can be accumulated and cashed in later for rewards ranging from better food to earlier parole. This use of immediate positive reinforcement following clearly spelled-out guidelines seems fairer and more effective than a correctional system in which behavior is controlled primarily by fear of punishment (which often is applied in a delayed and even arbitrary manner).

Still, developmental psychologists such as Lawrence Kohlberg (1975), whose research has focused on cognitive and moral development, believe that behavior modification programs are far from ideal as means of rehabilitating criminal offenders. Kohlberg believes that correctional programs should do much more than simply bringing prisoners' behavior under the control of positive and negative reinforcers manipulated by the correctional staff. Rather, a truly rehabilitative program must promote moral education that involves the development of a new understanding of ethical principles.

Conditioning in Infants

Classical and operant conditioning can be demonstrated even in infants only a few days old, although their efficiency and the range of stimuli to which they can be applied increase with age. Lipsitt (1977) has reviewed a number of studies that use different stimuli and responses and have shown classical conditioning effects in young infants. For example, Marquis (1941) found that a previously neutral stimulus (the sound of a buzzer) came to elicit sucking movements in newborn infants after only a few days of presenting it before a bottle nipple was offered. Other studies have shown that, through classical conditioning, sounds and visual stimuli could come to act as conditioned stimuli not only for sucking movements but also for other reflex responses. As Lipsitt has noted, "Perhaps the first manifestations of socialization are seen in classical conditioning processes, wherein the young infant may quite quickly respond differently to the way in which the mother holds him, or how she addresses him with her voice just prior to offering the nipple" (p. 172).

Operant conditioning processes also operate in young infants. These processes can be used not only to shape behavior but also as a scientific tool to investigate which kinds of stimuli are reinforcing to infants. The basic idea is that, if a stimulus is reinforcing, then presenting it immediately after each desired response should increase the rate at which an infant makes that response. Conversely, the removal of reinforcement should extinguish conditioning so that the response rate declines toward its original baseline rate, before reinforcement. Of course, the response repertoire of young infants is limited. However, most infants are able to make simple responses such as sucking a nipple or turning their head for a large number of trials. Trehub and Chang (1977) provide experimental evidence that simply hearing human speech is positively reinforcing to infants aged five to fifteen weeks. Thirty-two infants were assigned randomly to one of four experimental groups. Presentation to one group of a speech sound was contingent on an infant's making a "high amplitude" suck. This group showed a significant increase in the rate of nonnutritive

Socialization may begin with conditioning processes in which infants respond differently to how they are held, talked to, and fed.

Ron Alexander, Stock, Boston, Inc.

sucking. (The nipple was attached to a pressure-sensitive recording device rather than to a bottle.) The three other groups (1) heard no speech sounds, (2) had speech sounds withdrawn when they sucked, or (3) heard speech sounds that were not contingent on sucking. None of these groups showed a change in sucking rate during the test period. Other researchers have reported similar findings, showing that infants increase their rate of nonnutritive sucking if new visual stimuli or vocal-instrumental music are presented as reinforcement for sucking (Butterfield & Siperstein, 1972).

Social Reinforcement over the Life Span

Particularly for human beings, the reinforcement supplied by other people—or *social reinforcement*—is an especially important shaper of development. Social reinforcers are important from the cradle to the grave. A number of well-controlled studies have shown that the rate of a particular response, such as vocalization or smiling, produced by young infants will usually increase dramatically if the infants are given immediate and consistent reinforcement in the form of an adult smiling, talking, or cuddling. Conversely, when such social reinforcement is removed, the response rate falls off rather quickly. The reinforcing power of adult attention is particularly powerful for institutionalized infants, who often have received little adult attention other than what is needed to satisfy basic physical needs.

Awareness of reinforcing factors and the effects of different reinforcement schedules can be of practical value to parents, teachers, and others responsible for child care. Not infrequently, the lack of such awareness leads us unintentionally to reinforce undesirable behavior. For example, schoolteachers sometimes unintentionally encourage disruptive or otherwise obnoxious behavior. For a child who is receiving less attention or other social reinforcement than he or she would like, a public scolding by the teacher may be reinforcing—even if not preferable to praise. Indeed, if a child has hostile or angry feelings toward a teacher, an outburst of temper or other signs of irritation might be reinforcing to the child. In such a case, an analysis of the reinforcement factors involved could help the teacher to devise a more effective sanction for unacceptable behavior (such as "time out"—placing the child alone in a hallway or room where he or she gets virtually no recognition or attention). By understanding reinforcement, a teacher can also help a child to learn more constructive ways of obtaining attention and social approval.

The inadvertent reinforcement of undesirable behaviors is often compounded by the fact that intermittent reinforcement tends to make it more difficult to extinguish reinforced behavior once reinforcement is withdrawn. In practical terms, this means that if attention-seeking misbehavior is reinforced only occasionally with adult attention, it may persist for some time even after the adult team has begun to withhold reinforcement. In such a situation, an understanding of the properties of reinforcement schedules may help one persevere.

Social reinforcement is also important for adults, of course, including the elderly, for whom a lack of social stimulation and reinforcement may contribute to a premature and unnecessary decline in mental functioning. Harvard gerontologist Alexander Leaf (1973) conducted a study of factors contributing to longevity and mental and physical vigor among the elderly in three regions around the world where people were blessed with unusually long lives. These regions were Vilcabamba, a village high in the Andes of Ecuador in South America; Hunza, a small principality nestled among the mountain peaks of the Karakoram Range in West Pakistan; and the highlands of Georgia in the Caucasus region of the Soviet Union. In each of these regions, an unusual percentage of the population is reputed to live past one hundred years of age. Although claims of longevity in some cases have been exaggerated, it does appear that the regions studied by Leaf are, indeed, characterized by unusual longevity. And many elderly people in these areas clearly show remarkable physical and mental vigor. Men and women in their eighties and nineties were observed by Leaf to be engaged daily in such activities as riding horseback, harvesting crops by hand, and bathing in icy mountain streams.

Leaf's study led him to conclude that several factors were likely contributors to the long life and vigor among the elderly in these three societies. The factors included heredity; diets low in calories and animal fats (obesity was virtually

Gerontologist Alexander Leaf studied factors affecting longevity and vigor among the elderly in three different regions; heredity, diet, exercise, and social reinforcement contributed to longevity. (Left: a party in Soviet Georgia; right: Leaf examines a Hunza man over 100.)

John Launois, Black Star

nonexistent among these elderly, and average caloric intake was actually less than the minimum recommended by the U.S. National Academy of Sciences); and regular, vigorous exercise—a virtual necessity in getting around these mountainous terrains on foot.]

In addition, Leaf felt that social conditions were an important factor in longevity. In each of these societies, the elderly tended to maintain an integral social role, continuing to work and make meaningful economic contributions by tending animals, harvesting crops, or baking bread. Many of the elderly sat on village councils of elders, contributing to the political decisions of their communities. This situation contrasts markedly with that in many industrialized societies, characterized by mandatory retirement and segregation of the elderly into nursing homes or retirement communities where they are relatively isolated from other people, often receiving little intellectual challenge or reinforcement. Leaf also found that married individuals in these societies seemed to live longer than those who lived alone.

Leaf's work thus raises the possibility that much of the decline in mental functioning often seen among the elderly is a function of social deprivation rather than unavoidable physiological deterioration. This view receives support from experiments by American psychologists William Hoyer, Gisela Labouvie, and Paul Baltes (1973). They studied the effects of practice and social reinforcement on the kinds of speeded clerical tasks that previous research had shown to decline especially with age. Results were striking: in a single practice session that involved immediate reinforcement for each correct answer, an experimental group of elderly American subjects showed significant improvement in performance. The reinforcement procedures contributed significantly to the improvement, for the experimental group showed much greater gains than control groups, which were chosen randomly from the same original population but did not receive reinforcement between the pretest and posttests. Indeed, several other studies have also found that various behavior modification procedures have successfully improved the initially poor performance of elderly subjects on intellectual tasks (for example, Labouvie & Gonda, 1976; Levendusky, 1978).

The results of these cross-cultural and behavior modification studies are supported by evidence from longitudinal studies, in which little decrease in the level of functioning is found among adults at most ages, over periods as long as fourteen years—*provided* those individuals have a complex environment and are involved in many relationships with other people. By contrast, major decreases in functioning were observed in individuals leading socially isolated lives (Schaie & Gribbin, 1975).

Finally, as Schaie and Willis (1978) have noted, many elderly persons perform well above the average of young adults (Schaie & Parham, 1977). That researchers have documented cases in which elderly persons did *not* show a decline on important psychological functions over time suggests that the average decline in functioning usually found in studies of people beyond age seventy may be related to pathological changes or may be susceptible to modification through social and educational programs.

Imitative Learning (Modeling)

We have noted that newborn infants seem capable of classical and operant conditioning. It is even more remarkable that some newborns have been reported to imitate the actions of other people. For example, developmental psychologist Thomas Bower (1977) notes that some researchers have reported what Bower believes is a form of social imitation in infants less than a week old. If the infant's mother or other adult makes a distinctive facial movement such as sticking out the tongue or fluttering the eyelashes, some infants were claimed to have been more likely to respond the same way in return than one would expect by chance. If these reports are correct, it suggests that the infant must have some knowledge that portions of the adult's face are somehow like the child's own face. Bower believes that such reciprocal social imitation between infant and caretaker is an enjoyable social game for the child.

As Bower notes, imitative games do not appear to require any extrinsic reinforcement such as food or relief from pain. Rather, the very act of imitation seems to be intrinsically reinforcing—rewarding in and of itself. Yet American psychologists, and particularly learning theorists, historically have tended to underestimate the importance of intrinsic reinforcement in certain kinds of learning. This kind of readiness to engage in social imitation is probably a very adaptive capacity for infants, not only serving to promote bonds of affection between parent and child but also acting as the basis for reciprocal imitation, social interchange, and verbal play. In short, social imitation seems to help teach children some of the fundamental skills of communication, out of which language skills can develop.

The powerful effects of imitative learning on behavioral development have been documented by a number of researchers, perhaps most notably Albert Bandura and his colleagues at Stanford University. First of all, Bandura, Ross, and Ross (1963) demonstrated the ability of even preschool children to learn new violent behaviors simply from watching adults—or even cartoon charac-

How Children Really Feel about Aging

BRENDA CROWE

"I'm never going to be old and ugly. Before that happens, I'll kill myself," confessed an intelligent, attractive teenage girl.

Among today's youth, such a reaction to aging is not unusual. Twenty-five percent say they'd rather die than grow old.

What about the other seventy-five percent? Some have a passive acceptance of aging: "Well, that's just the way it is." "There's nothing you can do about it." Others reject it: "Oh, not me!" "I don't want to get old. It's awful!" Only a few see old age as a stage of development which offers new pleasures and opportunities.

In a study of children ages three to eleven, the following descriptions of the elderly were prevalent: "They're all wrinkled and short." "They have gray hair." "They don't go out much." "They sit all day in a rocking chair and watch TV." "They chew funny." "They have heart attacks and die."

There were a few exceptional answers: "They could help me with my homework." "They could teach me things." "I can help him sail his boat." "We can ride his horse."

The differences in answers resulted from the various ages of the children and from the locations of the children's homes. Those from rural areas, who have more contact with the elderly, indicated that they considered older people to be somewhat more alive: "We could do chores together." "I could help him carry firewood." The younger children had more negative feelings about aging and the aged.

Even though these children had very little contact with the elderly—less than twenty-two percent were able to identify an older person they knew outside of the family—they still had strong attitudes and concepts of aging and the aged.

Where did these children get their views? As with most prejudices, children reflect the values of society—especially those of their parents and teachers. According to surveys, the public's perception of the aged is clearly negative and different ... from that of the older people's perceptions of themselves.

It is first the responsibility of parents, and teachers second, to initiate a change in children's attitudes toward aging and the aged.... What can parents and teachers do to give children a truer picture of aging and the aged?

By rejecting the myths of aging, they can introduce children to the values of age and the contributions the elderly make to society.

They can be careful not to make statements such as "I'm too old." "I can't do that anymore." "I'm not as young as I used to be."

They can be truthful about their ages. Being evasive indicates they are ashamed of their years.

They can avoid euphemisms such as "fading fast," "over the hill," "out to pasture," "down the drain," "finished," and "out of date."

By encouraging children to question society's value of physical beauty, they can introduce children to the many forms of beauty. They can discuss with children the role that television plays by emphasizing young and physical beauty.

They can supervise children's reading materials to insure that the children have more contact with literature that presents the elderly as active and creative.

And best of all, they can plan activities that involve both children and older people.

Source: *Marriage and Family Living,* April 1979. Reprinted with the permission of *Marriage and Family Living* magazine. © St. Meinrad Archabbey, St. Meinrad, IN 47577.

ters. In addition, it was found that the "vicarious" reinforcement resulting from children's observing an adult model being punished or rewarded for a violent act would also influence their subsequent tendency to *perform* the behavior. However, children still *learned* the behavior and were capable of performing it simply as a result of observing the model. In other words, no extrinsic reinforcement—not even a vicarious one—seems to be needed in order for observational learning to occur. This research thus is consistent with Bower's point: observational or imitational learning of *new* behaviors—like simple imitation using old behaviors—can occur without external reinforcement.

Attention

Organisms are continually bombarded with a vast array of potential information—much more than they possibly can "process" (that is, receive, transform, act on, and store for future use). But even though the range of physical information transmitted by our various sense organs is limited, it greatly exceeds the processing capacity of our central nervous system. Consider, for example, the enormous variety of sensory signals sent to our brains every second, only a tiny fraction of which we are aware of at any given time. Reflect on the multitude of sensations we are not aware of until attention is directed toward them: the pounding of our hearts, the sound of our own breathing, the feel of different parts of our bodies against different surfaces, the background sounds of voices or music, and so on. Clearly, it is impossible to be aware of, let alone respond to, all these stimuli at once. Some central filtering and switching mechanisms must determine which of many stimuli will enter awareness, be recorded in memory, and provide the immediate basis for response.

In much research and theorizing about learning, the definition of a stimulus has been taken for granted. In a given learning situation, the relevant stimulus is defined rather arbitrarily by the investigator. It is assumed that what is a stimulus for the investigator will also be a relevant stimulus for the subject. In the real world, however, identifying the relevant stimulus in a particular situation may be just as difficult for the subject—if not more so—than associating that stimulus with a particular response.

The Role of Attention in Learning

A dramatic illustration of the importance of attention in learning is provided by the research of Zeaman and House (1963) involving mentally retarded children. The study dealt with *discrimination learning,* in which subjects must learn which of two objects or patterns presented on a particular trial is the "correct" one that would be reinforced. For example, in a particular set of trials, subjects always would be presented with two figures that were distinguishable by color (red or green) and shape (triangle or circle). Regardless of whether the red figure was a circle or a triangle, or whether it was presented on the right or the left, the red figure would always be the correct choice and would be reinforced. (For a child, the reward might be praise or a piece of candy.) On successive trials, the color, shape, and position of figures were assigned randomly. Thus if subjects

How Can We Best Motivate Learning?

A provocative answer to this question is provided by psychologist Omar Khayyam Moore's computerized "talking typewriter," which teaches children by age 5 not only to read, write, and touch-type but also to use these skills in creative ways such as the composing, editing, and publication of a school newspaper. Moore's program is especially interesting because of the systematic philosophy of education that it evidences—and puts into practice with dramatic effects. The program teaches academic skills to preschool children in a way that relies on and fosters the children's own intrinsic motivation to learn. It also encourages children to use basic skills for higher-order, creative purposes.

The ideal educational environment, suggest Moore and his colleagues, (1) encourages the learner to adopt different *perspectives* toward the material to be learned, (2) is intrinsically rewarding, (3) is *productive* in the sense of being so structured that the learner can draw inferences about the material, and (4) is *personalized* and responsive to the needs and activities of each learner. For example, many adults feel that young children have a short "attention span." Moore's research suggests that this is an incorrect interpretation; rather, young children have a relatively short and unstable "perspective span," making it difficult for them to listen attentively to a lengthy presentation. Although preschool children may not be suited to "formal" education in this sense, Moore has shown clearly that they are capable of learning complex academic and symbolic skills if allowed to do so in an environment that permits flexibility in changing perspectives toward the material. One of the most important contributions of their research is to demonstrate that children can learn symbolic skills without the use of extrinsic reinforcers. Indeed, Moore suggests that such reinforcers are inherently distracting.

Children need to learn that the learning process itself—particularly the learning of symbolic skills—can be enjoyable. This goal has become particularly critical because of the technological explosion, which has brought with it the threat of annihilation through nuclear accident or war or ecological disaster. Increasingly, we will have to alter the traditional educational patterns in our society. We are shifting to a new pattern in which lifelong learning will be the mode, and people may expect to have several careers within the course of their lives. Such changes demand that our educational system emphasize the acquisition of a flexible set of highly abstract conceptual tools. Only symbolic skills of the greatest generality can help people cope with radical change.

That intrinsically motivating environments can teach young children academic skills has been demonstrated by Moore's learning laboratory, in which preschoolers were given complete freedom about whether or not to take their half-hour turn to play with the "talking" typewriter each day. One of the most remarkable things about this environment is that the children typically choose to come to it, day in and day out. In some cases several months would pass without even one of the sixty children refusing his or her turn.

tried to choose the correct figure simply on the basis of shape or right-left position, they would score at a chance level. Only by attending to the color dimension could subjects score significantly above chance, much less achieve a perfect or nearly perfect score.

On this kind of relatively simple discrimination problem, adults and older children of normal intelligence would learn within a few trials to choose the red figure consistently. Certain retarded children, however, might require over a hundred trials before they could choose the correct figure consistently. At first it might seem that the slowness of retarded children in learning the correct response was the result of poor instrumental learning, that is, of difficulty in associating the response with the reinforcer. However, on closer inspection it became apparent that the slowness of many retarded children in solving the discrimination problem lay largely in the fact that it took them longer to attend to the correct dimension—color. Once different groups of children had begun to show an above-chance level of performance on the discrimination problem (presumably, when they first began attending to the relevant cue), then all children progressed rather rapidly and at about the same rate toward near-perfect responding. Therefore, the major differences among these children lay not in the rate of instrumental learning but in how quickly they attended to the significant cue. Some do so almost immediately, whereas others do not attend until after days of practice, if at all.

Measuring Attention: The Orienting Response

How do we go about measuring something as elusive as attention? Verbal reports are often considered too subjective and, in any case, are not available when studying attentional processes in animals or young children. One approach is to make inferences on the basis of less direct evidence, as Zeaman and House did in studying discrimination learning. In addition, however, it would be helpful if we could find some means for directly and objectively measuring attentional processes.

In fact, there are certain observable behavioral changes that often accompany shifts in attention. Some of these are obvious. For example, Pavlov observed that besides the response of increased salivation in dogs, an *alerting*, or *orienting*, *response* could be conditioned to previously neutral stimuli. Thus after repeated pairings with food, the tone came to elicit other signs of attention in dogs, such as raising of the head, perking up of ears, and turning toward and visually searching for the source of the sound. Besides these rather obvious signs of attention, it has been found that a number of more subtle physiological changes also tend to accompany increased attentiveness to external stimuli. The following physiological responses are often components of the orienting response (Reese & Lipsitt, 1970; Lynn, 1966): (1) dilation of the pupils; (2) temporary quieting of ongoing activity and an increase in muscle tonus; (3) changes in the electrical activity of the brain, especially a decrease in alpha waves; (4) perspiration, which affects the electrical conductivity of the skin (the so-called galvanic skin response, or GSR); (5) constriction of blood vessels in the limbs and dilation of blood vessels in the head, resulting in increased blood flow to the brain; and (6) a change in heart rate, usually involving a deceleration if attention is directed to an interesting external stimulus. These physiological changes appear to increase an organism's capacity to perceive and respond to stimuli. For example, dilated pupils admit more light to the eye, providing for greater visual sensitivity. Of interest to developmental psychologists is the fact that such physiological indices of the orienting response can be recorded accurately on a second-to-second basis, especially with the aid of electronic recording devices like the electrocardiogram. This has made it possible to study attention even in very young infants.

Developmental Determinants of Attention

What is there to ensure that a young animal with no prior experience will select, from the large array of stimuli available, those that contain information important for the animal's survival? Experimental research suggests that many species possess certain innate guides or shapers of attentional processes. For example, ethological studies of seagull chicks reveal that they preferentially attend to, and peck at, moving objects of a certain color. This innate attentional preference helps a chick survive, because pecking at the bill of a parent gull stimulates the parent to feed the chick. And because the bills of certain species of adult gulls have a marking of a certain color, this innate tendency leads the chick to attend to and peck at the parent's beak, increasing its chances of being fed (Tinbergen, 1969; Hailman, 1969).

There is some evidence that similar innate attentional preferences exist in human infants. In experiments that presented different visual stimuli to newborn infants while cameras or observers recorded eye movements, infants were found to look longer at lights that move or flash than those that glow continuously. They also looked more at designs with a high degree of black-white contrast than at designs of a single color (Haith, 1966; Kagan, 1972). Indeed, Haith (1968) suggests that the visual attention of newborn infants can be described in terms of certain rules of searching. First, if the ambient light is not too bright, an alert infant will open his or her eyes. Next, an infant who sees no light will search for it. Third, an infant who sees light but finds no area of dark-light contrast will continue to search for one. Finally, once an area of contrast has been found, an infant will focus on that edge and repeatedly cross it. Such attentional strategies are likely to be adaptive for human infants, both because moving objects and areas of contrast generally provide more information and because crucial features of the human face—such as the eyes—possess a high degree of movement and dark-white contrast. Such stimuli attract the attention of infants, helping to ensure that they begin to develop an early recognition of parents' faces.

Identifying the factors that determine which stimuli will be attended to is of critical importance, for attention is a prerequisite for learning. One interesting question is the extent to which inborn attentional preferences encourage a developing child to attend to stimuli that are optimal for psychological development. Experiments with rats have shown that over time they will tend to choose a balanced diet if given the opportunity to select from a variety of foods. Swiss developmental psychologist Jean Piaget (1966) has pointed out that there are a number of similarities between intellectual and physical growth. Just as food substances are broken down during digestion and are reassembled in new structures to provide physical growth, so in cognitive development are stimuli that provide information about the environment broken down to be assimilated into existing cognitive structures and used to create change and new growth, or "accommodation." The question arises as to whether the attentional mechanisms in human beings are analogous to appetite-regulating processes observed in feeding rats. Do we also possess a kind of natural wisdom to select the optimal input, given the freedom to choose from a variety of stimuli? The question has important educational implications. For example, should efforts to foster intellectual development emphasize, on the one hand, attempts to measure a child's level of development and then match it with appropriate stimuli? Or should the emphasis be on providing a child with the opportunity to explore a wide variety of environments freely, relying on the child's natural wisdom to select those stimuli optimal for development at a given time?

Stimuli conducive to cognitive growth are likely to be those that represent an intermediate level of discrepancy from, and challenge to, a person's existing knowledge and abilities. Stimuli that are very familiar are likely to present little or no new information and little if any intellectual growth. Stimuli that are too discrepant from past experiences, on the other hand, may be difficult for the person to understand and assimilate with present mental structures. In short, very familiar or very discrepant stimuli are likely to be less than optimal for promoting cognitive development.

Harvard psychologist Jerome Kagan (1970, 1972) has reviewed a number of lines of evidence indicating that, between two and three months of age, a new attentional preference begins to appear to complement the preference for change in simple stimulus properties. This new attentional preference, Kagan suggests, is for stimuli that represent a moderate degree of discrepancy from cognitive representations (schemata) for past experience. For example, in an experiment by Hopkins et al. (1976), infants were presented with the opportunity to view a simple geometric figure moving slowly on a lighted turntable for a few seconds. The infants could determine how often they viewed the stimulus by pressing on a handle in front of them. After several presentations of the same stimulus, groups of infants were given the opportunity to view different test stimuli representing varying degrees of novelty or discrepancy. As indicated by a higher rate of handle pressing, infants showed greater interest in viewing moderately novel stimuli than they did in viewing familiar or extremely discrepant stimuli. Similar results were obtained by Kinney and Kagan (1976) in a study presenting auditory stimuli to infants 7½ months old. After eight presentations of a brief melody or verbal phrase, infants heard repetitions of a test melody or phrase. They showed greater attention (as indicated by looking toward the sound source and decreased heart rate) to auditory stimuli that were moderately discrepant from the initial stimulus.

As Kagan (1970, 1972) notes, stimulus discrepancy appears to become a factor in attention at about the same time that other notable changes are occurring in the development of the brain and behavior. For example, babbling begins to increase between two and three months of age. And *habituation,* or decreased attention to a repeated visual stimulus, can be established rather reliably. At this age, too, characteristics of electrical potentials in the cortex of the brain—as evoked by visual stimuli—become more like those seen in adults. Also, electroencephalographic characteristics such as the alpha rhythm become apparent for the first time (Ellingson, 1967). It appears that maturation of important areas of the visual cortex makes it possible for an infant of about three months to begin to discriminate complex visual patterns and store them in memory. With the storage of complex representations or schemas for experiences, discrepancies between new stimuli and schemas for past experiences can be detected and thus begin to influence attention.

Finally, Kagan suggests that toward the end of the first year an additional factor is added to those of movement, contrast, and stimulus-schema discrepancy in determining the degree to which a stimulus is likely to maintain attention. With the development of new mental abilities, particularly language capacity, children begin to try to interpret the meaning of a new stimulus, to ask simple questions, and, in a sense, to formulate hypotheses about its nature. As an example, Kagan (1970) cites the changing reactions of children observed at different ages between four months and three years of age as they were presented with clay masks portraying a regular and three distorted faces. Whereas the amount of time children spent attending to these faces declined from four to twelve months, it began to rise steadily from twelve to thirty-six months. Kagan suggests that the decline in fixation from four to twelve months occurred because the masks became less discrepant stimuli as the infants grew older. After a year, however, the length of time children spent looking at the masks increased. Kagan proposes that this was because the children had an increasing array of questions or hypotheses that they could pose in trying to interpret the novel stimulus. For example, in one mask stimulus, the major features are rearranged in a scrambled pattern. Upon seeing this stimulus, two-year-olds made spontaneous remarks that revealed their attempts to make sense of the strange stimulus: " 'What happened to his nose? Who hit him in the nose?' 'Who that, Mommy? A monster, Mommy?' " (Kagan, 1970, p. 304).

Attention, Arousal, and Sleep

Attention involves at least two basic aspects. One is stimulus selection, which we have discussed. In addition, there is clearly a dimension of arousal, ranging from intense alertness through drowsiness to deep sleep. The selection and arousal dimensions of attention are closely related, for repeated presentation of the same stimulus tends to produce habituation and cortical inhibition and is also conducive to drowsiness and sleep.

There is a rather consistent developmental trend over the life span in the average amount of time people sleep. As shown in Figure 11.2, the apparent decrease in the need for sleep is most rapid during infancy and early childhood, but it continues even into old age (Roffwarg et al., 1966). Note that a typical newborn spends two-thirds of the day asleep! During childhood, there is an especially marked decrease in the REM (rapid-eye-movement) components of sleep, as well as in the proportion of total sleep spent in the REM state. In adults, there is a rather regular alternation throughout the night between non-REM (NREM) and REM stages of sleep. REM sleep more closely resembles the waking state in terms of brain-wave or electroencephalographic activity. Sub-

FIGURE 11.2
Changes with
age in amounts
of total sleep
and types of
sleep

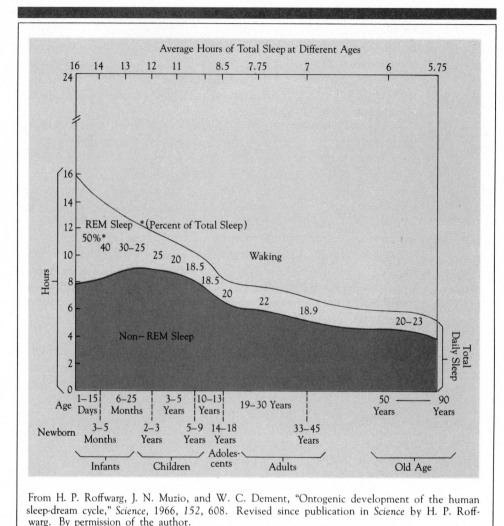

From H. P. Roffwarg, J. N. Muzio, and W. C. Dement, "Ontogenic development of the human sleep-dream cycle," *Science*, 1966, *152*, 608. Revised since publication in *Science* by H. P. Roffwarg. By permission of the author.

jects' voluntary motor movements are inhibited during REM sleep, and vivid dreams are associated more frequently with REM sleep, though they are not limited to it.

The physiological functions of different stages of sleep are not completely understood, but evidence suggests that sleep has a restorative role in both physical and psychological growth. Slow-wave, NREM sleep may be especially important for physical growth and repair, because the secretion of growth hormones peaks soon after a person falls asleep (the early period of sleep, when NREM sleep tends to be concentrated). Moreover, an increase in NREM sleep has been reported for some subjects following vigorous exercise (Johnson, 1977). Changes in REM sleep during development are even more dramatic, suggesting that REM sleep has a special purpose relating to psychological development during infancy and early childhood. There is some evidence to support the view that REM sleep is important for the consolidation of memory. Perhaps it is involved in the rapid brain development and the great amount of new perceptual organization and learning that occurs during early childhood.

If adult volunteers are selectively deprived of REM or NREM sleep, there occurs on subsequent nights a specific compensatory increase, or "rebound," in the type of sleep that was withheld. However, in studies of the effects of sleep deprivation on attention and memory, the total amount of sleep lost—rather than the type of sleep lost—seemed more important. As everyday experience suggests, subjects deprived of sleep perform more poorly on a variety of tests, including vigilance, long- and short-term memory, and reading speed and comprehension (Johnson, 1977). After two days of sleep deprivation, subjects are also more likely to report feeling depressed and hostile as well as less energetic, happy, or friendly.

Memory

The act of orienting oneself to a novel stimulus implies some kind of memory capacity involving a comparison between the new stimulus and the memory of previous stimuli. And habituation (declining interest in or responsiveness to repeated presentations of the same stimulus) suggests that an individual has formed a short-term memory for the stimulus and recognizes that new presentations are familiar. With the maturation of the cortex of the brain, infants about two months old show signs of habituation as well as *dis*habituation (recovery of interest, upon presentation of a novel stimulus). Individual differences in habituation and dishabituation seem among the most sensitive measures for studying early mental development. For example, Sigman et al. (1977) found that when normal four-month-old infants are shown a checkerboard pattern in four successive presentations, and then are given the choice of looking at the checkerboard or at a novel stimulus, they will show a marked preference for the novel stimulus. By contrast, infants who have an increased risk of brain injury because of prematurity or other obstetrical problems are less likely to show this preference for novelty.

Components of Memory

That there are different components or stages of memory formation is perhaps most dramatically illustrated by certain natural experiments involving brain injury. Patients in whom the hippocampal area of the brain has been damaged bilaterally (that is, in both hemispheres) show a remarkable pattern: they can recall events that occurred before the hippocampal damage, but they seem unable to retain memories of events that occur after the damage for more than a few minutes. It is as though the hippocampus is somehow needed to "consolidate" memory traces into a form that can last over long periods of time. Dr. Brenda Milner (1965) describes the memory loss of one such patient as follows:

As far as we can tell, this man has retained little if anything of events subsequent to the operation, although his I.Q. rating is actually slightly higher than before. Ten months before I examined him, his family had moved from their old house to a new one a few blocks away on the same street. He still had not learned the new address (though remembering the old one perfectly), nor could he be trusted to find his way home alone. He did not know where objects in constant use were kept, and his mother stated that he would read the same magazines over and over again without finding the contents familiar. On formal testing, it was clear that forgetting occurred the instant the patient's focus of attention shifted, although in the absence of distraction his capacity for sustained attention was remarkable. (pp. 104-105)

Milner notes that this memory loss for events occurring after the operation was tested by a variety of materials, including words, stories, objects, and drawings. For example, one patient who was asked to draw a dog sketched an outline with rather long legs, snout, and ears. When asked several minutes later to identify his own drawing, the patient could not recall having drawn it, and he called it a deer. Such patients also manifest loss of memory for events that occurred immediately before the damage—a so-called retrograde amnesia that covers a period from a few months to several years before the damage. Events that happened many years earlier were recalled with no difficulty. Milner notes that these patients show no deficit in concentration or attention; one patient was able to carry out complex arithmetic operations mentally with great skill.

Long-term memory for certain kinds of learning did *not* seem to be impaired, however. For example, one patient showed consistent improvement over time in the acquisition of a new motor skill—learning to trace the outline of a geometric figure while viewing it in a mirror. Milner suggests that the acquisition and memory of visual-motor skills thus may be independent of the hippocampal system.

Natural experiments such as this indicate that different memory processes or subsystems can be distinguished. In these patients, the registration, of *encoding*, of new information and its *retrieval* from a short-term memory system seem unimpaired; yet *storage* in a long-term, relatively permanent memory system seems destroyed. Moreover, memories that have been in permanent storage for many years seem to be retrieved in an relatively normal manner.

The existence of distinct encoding, storage, and retrieval processes in memory is also suggested by the differences usually found between *recognition memory* and *recall memory*. To take a commonplace example, you may have difficulty remembering the names of all your second-grade classmates (recall); yet, if given a list of their names and a group photograph of your second-grade class, you could probably name virtually all of them correctly (recognition). Clearly, our memories often contain much more information than we can retrieve voluntarily at any one time.

A more dramatic illustration of this point was observed by Canadian brain surgeon Wilder Penfield (1959) in the course of exploring the cortex of the brain with an electrical stimulating probe before performing surgery on certain diseased regions. (A mild electrical potential applied to the brain can stimulate neuronal firing in the surrounding region.) Penfield found that stimulation of those regions of the motor cortex that are concerned with controlling movements of the arms may cause involuntary arm movements; stimulation of areas mediating articulation of speech may cause involuntary speech. Stimulation of other cortex areas occasionally resulted in what the patient described as the feeling of reliving past experiences—some of which had occurred many years earlier and that the patient had not thought about since. Penfield has speculated that the probe might be activating old memories and that somewhere in the brain may be stored a "permanent record of the stream of consciousness." Many psychologists are skeptical of this hypothesis. They point out that it is difficult to confirm the accuracy of such anecdotal reports experimentally and that, in any case, the patients involved present unusual cases and are undergoing surgery because of brain diseases such as epilepsy.

Early childhood memories can often be recalled through strategems that provide a subject with special retrieval tricks or aids. As an example, take a moment right now to *print* your name with *very slow* strokes. For many people, this act brings back a flood of memories from early school years when they first learned to print words—memories they had not thought about in many years. Some psychologists have speculated that analogous devices might be used to help people recall memories from earliest childhood, which are inaccessible to most adults. Adults' so-called infantile amnesia regarding the events of early childhood might conceivably result not from the loss or decay of those experiences but from the fact that experiences of later childhood and adulthood are structured in a radically different form, making it difficult to retrieve the earliest memories. However, special circumstances—for example, being placed in a huge crib with giant faces hovering over one—might evoke long-forgotten memories of early infancy.

Memory and Age Differences

The general superiority of recognition over recall memory has been demonstrated in a number of experimental laboratory studies. Shepard (1967), for example, presented hundreds of magazine pictures to adult subjects, allowing them only a few seconds to look at each picture. The subjects could recall only a fraction of the pictures. However, on seeing them the next day intermixed with new pictures that they had not seen before, the subjects were able to *recognize* the old pictures with almost perfect accuracy. Several studies have shown that preschool children also have impressive recognition memory for pictures (for example, Brown & Scott, 1971; Scott, 1973). Brown and Campione (1972) found that preschool children in one study could identify which pictures they had seen a week before with better than 90 percent accuracy.

Several studies reviewed by Newcombe, Rogoff, and Kagan (1977) have indicated that recognition memory improves significantly with age. In their own study, Newcombe and her colleagues compared the recognition memory for single objects and multi-object scenes in six-year-olds, nine-year-olds, and adults. They found that recognition memory improved with age, with a particularly significant difference between the six- and nine-year-olds. Newcombe and associates suggest that two processes may explain the improvement in recognition memory. First, the older children and adults may scan a test picture before them more extensively and efficiently. Second, the older subjects may be more effective in comparing the features of the test picture they are inspecting with their memories for pictures seen previously.

Studies of the development of memory processes over time suggest that age affects recall even more strongly than recognition memory. Recall improves more than recognition does from childhood to adulthood and, in turn, shows a greater decline during old age.

A number of studies indicate that one reason recall memory improves with development is the increasing spontaneous use of various strategies or tricks to help recall information. For example, older children can label the recall stimuli verbally and can rehearse the items, keeping them in mind until asked to repeat them. Or, if shown an array of common objects, they can spontaneously group them into conceptual categories to aid recall.

One reason recall memory may improve with age is that older children and adults can label stimuli verbally, group them into categories, and rehearse the items.

Mimi Forsyth, Monkmeyer Press Photo Service

Belmont and Butterfield (1971) compared the short-term recall of lists of letters presented serially to normal children aged nine to thirteen years, to normal adults, and to mildly retarded subjects between ten and twenty years old. The normal adults were superior to the other groups, and their superior recall seemed to result from several factors. First, the normal adults were more likely to rehearse spontaneously the letters they had heard. In addition, older and more intelligent subjects were more likely to tailor their rehearsal strategies to the demands of a particular task, and to show increasing speed and accuracy in the retrieval of rehearsed material. It was found that when the retarded subjects were instructed to rehearse, their performance improved greatly. Similarly, other studies have found that young children of normal intelligence often do not spontaneously use rehearsal strategies. Thus Hagen (1971) found that five-year-olds were able to recall more pictorial information if they were induced to use rehearsal strategies. He concluded that young children who do not usually rehearse often can be taught to do so, with a resultant improvement in recall.

This improvement in recall memory with age may help to explain a baffling phenomenon of "memory improvement" that has been reported by Piaget and Inhelder (1973). A large body of experimental research confirms our everyday experience that memories fade with the passage of time. In fact, performance on memory tasks almost always declines with the passage of time. It is surprising, therefore, that Piaget and Inhelder reported finding, under certain conditions, that children's memories improve rather than decline with time. Children between four and six years old were shown pictures that, to be understood, require certain mental structures that Piaget believes undergo rather rapid development at these ages. For example, to grasp the significance of a picture showing an array of sticks arranged in order of increasing length, children must understand the concept of seriation. Similarly, to grasp the relevant details about a bottle half-filled with water and tilted at a 45-degree angle, they must understand the properties of fluids well enough to know that the surface of water in a stationary bottle will remain parallel to the floor, not to the sides of the bottle. Piaget and Inhelder report that children's memories for such pictures in many cases were better several weeks after seeing them than they were soon after viewing. Piaget suggests that memory improves if the initial presentation of a stimulus occurs when a child is rapidly mastering the mental structures required to understand the concepts implied in the pictures. In addition, acquisition of these new structures transforms the memory of the pictures.

An alternative explanation is suggested by recent research by Marsh (1977). In repeating Piaget's experiment, Marsh administered separate tests for recognition and recall. It was found that recall, but not recognition, increased over time for children of the right age. Apparently, the memory trace for events does fade with time, but in some cases older children's improved strategies for searching for and retrieving stored information more than compensates for this fading.

With increasing age, recall also seems to decline more rapidly than recognition. Several studies reviewed by Arenberg (1973) point in this direction. For example, Schonfield and Robertson (1966) presented a list of twenty-four target words to adults ranging in age from their twenties to their sixties and asked them to recall as many as possible. Across five age groups, the average number of words recalled decreased steadily with increasing age. Much smaller age differences were found in a recognition test, when subjects had only to identify the target words in a list that included a number of "distractor" words not presented previously. Because the recognition test procedure actually took longer than the recall procedure, there was more time for the memory traces of the words to decay in the recognition task. Nonetheless, age differences were minimal in this case, suggesting that faster decay was not the cause of poorer performance by the older subjects. The difference between recall and recognition is largely a matter of retrieval—which is much simpler in the case of recognition. These and other results suggest that a deficit in retrieval processes may be a major factor in the declining memory performance seen with increasing age.

Lifelong Learning and Education

Schaie and Willis (1978) have reviewed research evidence for a number of changes in information processing that occur over the life span, including implications of these changes for meeting the growing educational needs of older adults. Schaie and Willis point out that several factors are increasing interest in a lifelong approach to learning. The increasing numbers of older adults in the population results in an increasing demand for educational programs for the middle-aged and elderly. So, too, does the accelerating pace of scientific progress and technological change, which doubles the amount of information in many of the exact sciences every decade. Demographic factors such as increasing life expectancy and declining birth rates indicate that these trends will continue in coming decades in industrialized countries, leading to increasing proportions of older college students—the so-called "graying" of the university.

Successfully satisfying the burgeoning educational demands of older adults will require an understanding of how information processing develops over the life span. Schaie and Willis note that a number of age differences in learning, attention, and memory are likely to be important for designing educational programs for older learners. Several age-related differences involve the acquisition of new information. Older persons have been found especially likely to show deficits on paced tasks involving rapid presentation of material or requiring rapid responses from the learner. Older individuals' performance benefits from increased response time and self-pacing of learning tasks. The meaningfulness of the material to be learned also has been found to be more important for older than for younger adults in several studies; older adults did relatively much better on tasks involving meaningful versus nonsense content and concrete versus abstract content.

Age-related decrements on cognitive tasks are especially marked when attention must be divided—between two incoming stimuli, between incoming stimuli and the memory of older ones, or between memory and the response demands. In situations requiring subjects to attend to two different tasks, older persons tend to focus on one task while permitting performance on the other to deteriorate markedly. Age differences in short-term memory seem to be relatively slight; age-related difficulties in the acquisition of new information seem to be related more to processes involved in long-term memory.

Noncognitive factors play an increasingly important role in performance on cognitive tasks with increasing age during adulthood. Noncognitive factors include decreasing sensory acuity and speed of response, motivational changes such as an increasing tendency to avoid high-risk situations, and an increasing susceptibility to social pressure.

Many differences in performance on learning tasks are related to the increasing time needed by older adults to acquire information and retrieve it from memory. A slower pace of presentation of material, with longer periods for acquisition and response, is especially helpful for older adults. So, too, instructional programs that allow students to set their own pace should be especially beneficial for elderly learners.

Schaie and Willis note that individual variability in nearly every kind of intellectual ability increases over the life span. Just as extremes of individual ability in children (as in gifted or handicapped youngsters) usually require individualized instruction for the best results, so too the increasing variability in older adults is likely to mean that personalized and mastery-oriented instruction will be of special benefit for them.

Available research indicates that in the case of abilities for which speed of response is not inherently important, age changes in healthy populations are reliably seen only in the early sixties and are not really of great practical importance for educational purposes until even later in life. Schaie and Willis conclude that "reasonably healthy community-dwelling adults, if they were ever educable by reason of intellectual abilities, would retain such educability throughout life."

Summary

1. *Classical conditioning* refers to learning established in the classic manner described by Pavlov. As the result of being presented in association with an unconditioned stimulus (UCS), a previously neutral stimulus becomes a conditioned stimulus (CS) that can elicit a conditioned response (CR) similar to the unconditioned response (UCR) produced by the UCS. The CR tends to generalize to stimuli similar to the CS, and it can be extinguished by repeatedly presenting the CS in the absence of the UCS.

2. Pioneering studies by John Watson and Mary Cover Jones used classical conditioning procedures to condition and extinguish fears of animals in infants, foreshadowing desensitization procedures currently used for treating phobias.

3. The application of scientific learning principles in order to modify behavior is often termed *behavior modification* or—when used to treat behavior disorders—*behavior therapy*. When such therapy uses classical conditioning principles, it has proved effective for treating children with behavior prob-

lems such as enuresis. It also seems to reduce associated emotional problems rather than producing substitute symptoms, as some therapists had feared.

4. B. F. Skinner distinguishes classical, or *respondent*, conditioning from *operant*, or *instrumental, conditioning,* in which behavior is conditioned by its consequences. Skinner's research has clarified principles of operant conditioning, including the concepts of positive and negative reinforcement and the effects of different schedules of reinforcement.

5. Operant conditioning procedures have proved to be valuable teaching tools in varied settings, including the teaching of communication skills to children with infantile autism as well as the teaching of self-care skills to retardates. However, many of Skinner's far-reaching ideas for applying learning theory to child-rearing, therapy, and other helping relationships have been challenged by humanistic psychologists such as Carl Rogers. Rogers contends that the goal of helping relationships should be to give people increasing freedom and competence to make their own decisions, rather than to bring the behavior of individuals under increasing control.

6. The basic problem with most children whom parents or teachers label *hyperactive* actually seems to be an "attentional deficit disorder" involving impulsivity, distractibility, and socially inappropriate activity, rather than generally excessive activity. Behavior modification programs have helped many such children to control inappropriate activity without the use of psychostimulant drugs. Programs that teach strategies for self-control seem better for many children than programs that rely on external social reinforcement.

7. Research on moral development suggests that the usual behavior modification programs are ineffective at rehabilitating criminal offenders because true rehabilitation involves promoting a higher level of moral reasoning rather than simply bringing inmates' behavior under the control of reinforcement schedules manipulated by correctional authorities.

8. Classical and operant conditioning processes operate over almost the entire life span and can be demonstrated in infants only a few days old. Social reinforcement to help elderly persons remain socially and physically active seems to be a significant contributor to longevity and vigor in old age. Cultures characterized by unusual longevity seem to supply a great deal of such social reinforcement for their elderly members, and laboratory studies have shown that in elderly Americans reinforcement can produce striking improvements—even on the kinds of speeded clerical tasks that decline most markedly with age.

9. The capacity for social imitation is claimed by some researchers to be present in infants less than a week old; imitative games with parents seem to intrinsically reinforcing for infants and may help them learn early communication skills. Studies of preschool children have shown that they can learn how to perform aggressive acts simply by passively watching adults model the behavior. How the adult model is reinforced for the modeled behavior does not seem to influence the child's learning of the behavior, although it does influence the child's tendency to perform the behavior.

10. The importance of attentional strategies in learning is illustrated by studies of retardates, whose slowness in learning discrimination problems often lies in failure to attend to the right stimulus cue, rather than in an inability to associate stimuli and responses.

11. A newborn's attention is drawn to changes in simple stimulus properties. By two to three months, a second attentional preference develops, for stimuli moderately discrepant from cognitive representations of past experience. A third important influence on attention, developing toward the end of the first year, may involve the extent to which stimuli lead the child to pose hypotheses in an attempt to interpret them.

12. The average amount of time spent in sleep declines over the life span. During childhood, there is an especially marked decrease in the amount of time spent in the rapid-eye-movement stage of sleep.

13. Data for normal subjects as well as patients with certain brain injuries indicate the need to distinguish short- and long-term processes of memory storage. Although both recognition and recall memory seem to improve with age in children—and to decline in old age—the early increase and later decline seem more pronounced for recognition memory.

Selected Readings

Arenberg, D. "Cognition and Aging: Verbal Learning, Memory, Problem Solving, and Aging." In *The Psychology of Adult Development and Aging*. Eds. C. Eisdorfer and M. P. Lawton. Washington, D.C.: American Psychological Association, 1973. A succinct but scholarly review of research on learning, memory and aging.

Bower, T. G. R. *A Primer of Infant Development*. San Francisco: W. H. Freeman, 1977. A scholarly but readable introduction to recent research on the development of infant learning and perception. Includes extensive coverage of the ingenious experiments devised by Bower in his own work on infant development.

Fishbein, H. D. *Evolution, Development, and Children's Learning*. Pacific Palisades, Calif.: Goodyear, 1976. Provides good introductory reviews of research on the development of memory, attention, and language as well as moral and motor skill development in children; tries to relate this behavioral development to knowledge of human evolution and brain development.

Houston, J. P. *Fundamentals of Learning*. New York: Academic Press, 1976. A good introductory text on learning. Accurate yet written in an interesting manner, particularly for a subject that is often rather dry.

Leaf, A. "Getting Old." *Scientific American* (September 1973), 44-53. A fascinating description of Leaf's cross-cultural research on the sources for unusual vigor and longevity thought to characterize the peoples of three different cultures. Discusses possible factors relating to social reinforcement as well as diet, exercise, and heredity.

Skinner, B. F. *Walden Two*. New York: Macmillan, 1972 (paperback). This novel depicts a utopian community based on Skinner's research on scientific principles of learning. A long-term favorite of psychology students, it is not only lively reading and a thought-provoking introduction to Skinner's ideas but also has inspired a real-life utopian community.

Chapter 12

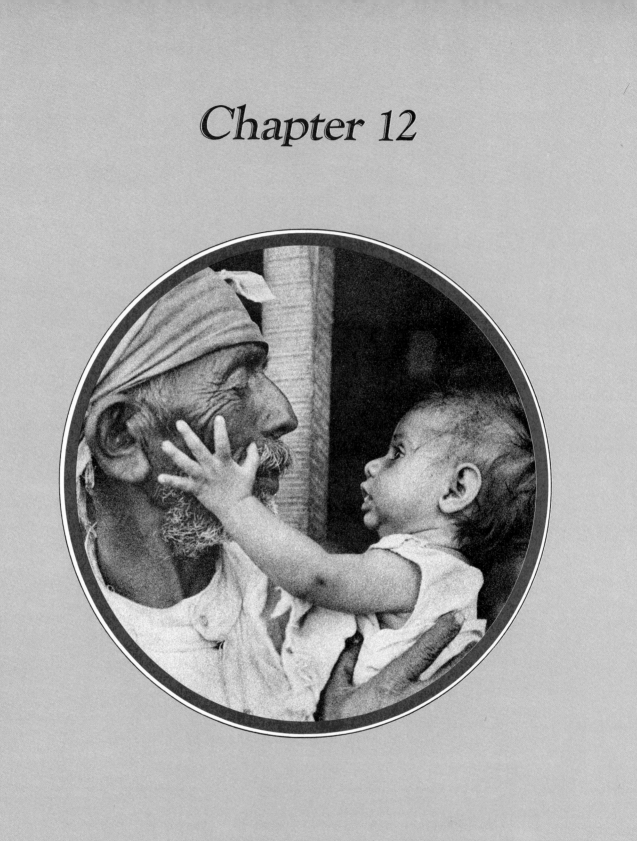

Language

Relationships between brain and language development

Various theoretical perspectives on language development

Theories about the syntax, or grammatical structure, of language, including an examination of children's syntax

Phonological development: how children acquire the sound pattern of a language

Semantic development: how children come to understand the meaning and functions of language

Sociolinguistics: the social and geographical factors involved in the use of language

Brain Lateralization and Language Development

Theoretical Perspectives on the Nature of Language
> Behaviorist Perspective
> Cultural Relativist–Determinist Perspective
> Interactionist Perspective
> Preformationist-Predeterminist Perspective

The Development of Syntax
> Behaviorist Model of Syntax
> Predeterminist-Preformationist Model of Syntax
> Children's Syntax

Phonological Development

Sematic Development and the Functions of Language
> Behaviorist Approach to Semantics
> Predeterminist-Preformationist Approach to Semantics
> Cognitive Development and Semantics
> Semantic Development over the Life Span

Dialects and Development

Introduction

Perhaps more than any other human behavior that we examine, language emerges quite early in life and remains relatively fixed over the life span. Language development is a unique and remarkable phenomenon, and it has been studied intensively by developmental psychologists, who have been concerned mainly with the acquisition of language in children. Therefore, although we will consider some aspects of language development over the life span, for the most part this chapter will be concerned with language development in early life.

Language acquisition is a robust phenomenon that occurs with remarkable regularity in children. Environmental factors such as social class or culture—which dramatically influence many of the behavioral processes discussed in this book—have little or no effect on the age at which children attain certain milestones in language acquisition. A child's first meaningful utterances usually occur between the ages of nine and eighteen months, and language development then proceeds in very predictable stages regardless of the language that is acquired. Oral language skills in a given culture are mastered rapidly by children with little deliberate instruction on the part of parents. Compared with other behaviors mastered between the ages of one and five, language is an incredibly complex synthesis of processes.

Attesting to the robust nature of the capacity to acquire language is the fact that acquisition occurs despite sensory impairment (for example, hearing deficits) or motor impairment (such as articulatory defects). Another unique feature of language is that it develops only in human beings; such a behavior is not exhibited in other species. These qualities make language development one of the most interesting areas of psychology. As a result, language study has received a flurry of recent activity and debate. Our investigation will begin with a discussion of the biological basis of language. After that, we will examine four theoretical perspectives on language development. Then we will explore the development of syntax, phonology, and semantics. The chapter concludes with a brief discussion of sociolinguistics—how various social factors affect language use.

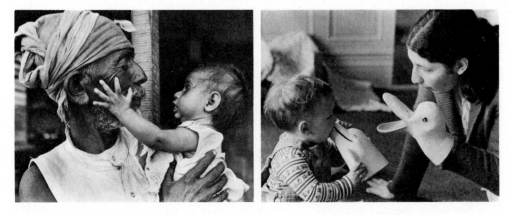

Although environmental factors like social class and culture dramatically influence many aspects of development, they have little effect on the age of acquiring language milestones.

Bhupendra Karia, Magnum Photos, Inc.   Christopher Morrow, Stock, Boston, Inc.

Brain Lateralization and Language Development[1]

There is mounting evidence that one hemisphere of the brain, typically the left, is specialized for processing language. Recent studies of the development of brain lateralization are changing our view about the onset of language processing. In the late 1960s specialists in cerebral lateralization (Bogen, 1969) and language (Lenneberg, 1967a) reported that the left hemisphere becomes specialized for language at around age two. These reports were based on clinical data collected on patients such as infants who had lost their left hemisphere. Lenneberg believed that lateralization of language occurred as a function of language acquisition. In this view, before the acquisition of language, neither hemisphere should be more involved in processing verbal stimuli. The brain became lateralized as a function of experience. Bogen (1969) agreed that the hemispheres had an equal potential for language during an infant's first years.

These conclusions were questioned when studies of the perception of language in infants indicated that receptive capacity for linguistic stimuli is present early in infancy (for example, Eimas, 1975). Infants much younger than two years of age responded to differences in verbal cues. Such data provided evidence of language acquisition and, hence, possible brain lateralization long before speech is produced in infants. Human beings appear to have the capacity to respond to language very early in life, even though they cannot yet produce it.

Early ideas about lateralization were challenged further when Witelson and Pallie (1973) reported marked anatomical asymmetry in the brains of human neonates, specifically in brain areas associated with language. The upper surface of the left temporal lobe was greater than that of the right. Hemispheric asymmetries in infants were comparable to those found in adults (Geschwind & Levitsky, 1968). Wada, Clarke, and Hamm (1975) replicated this work in one hundred infant and one hundred adult brains; the left temporal area was found to be greater in 90 percent of the brains. In addition, the asymmetry was greater in adults than in infants, suggesting it developed further after birth. The fact that anatomical asymmetry was found in neonates—in a brain area of known significance for language in adults—supported the idea that human newborns have a programmed biological capacity to process the sounds of speech.

Although recent studies indicate that some lateralization of the brain is present at birth, lateralization and cerebral dominance are not complete until at least the third to sixth year (Buffery, 1971; Kimura, 1963, 1967). An immature brain seems to be able to reorganize lateral specialization after injury up to age twelve (Hecaen & de Ajuriaguerra, 1964). There is also some evidence that cognitive difficulties arise when lateralization is slow to develop or incomplete. This can limit proficiency in school. Almost fifty years ago Orton (1934) suggested that problems like stuttering and dyslexia might result from poorly established cerebral specialization. Since then, many investigators have tried to relate poor lateralization to cognitive difficulties, with mixed results. In surveying this literature, Hecaen and de Ajuriaguerra (1964) concluded that no direct relation-

---

1. Portions of this section are based on "Brain Electrical Activity and Behavior Relationships over the Life Span" by Diana S. Woodruff in *Life-Span Development and Behavior*. Vol. 1. Ed. P. B. Baltes. New York: Academic Press, 1978, pp. 111-179.

ship has been shown between poor brain lateralization and cognitive impairment. However, they also argued that disorders of lateralization could have played a role in a certain number of cases.

One difficulty researchers faced in early lateralization studies was the lack of a valid measure of cerebral organization. Until recently, the only available index of lateralization was handedness, which is not always accurate. Nearly all right-handed people (98 to 99 percent) have left-dominant brains, with language being localized in the left hemisphere. Lateralization among left-handed people is more complex. Some 30 percent show right-brain localization of language, whereas the others have left-brain lateralization or less lateralization. Hecaen and his associates provided an extensive review of the neurological literature and a summary of their own clinical studies. They concluded that left-handers have more bilateral brain organization with less lateralization of language or spatial and tactile functions. These researchers distinguished between left-handedness that seems to be inherited, running in families, and left-handedness that may result from injury to the left hemisphere before birth. The inherited type may or may not have reversed language lateralization; the brain-injured type will have reversed or more bilateral cerebral representation of language. In the clinical studies, left-handers, people with little hand preference, left-handers who were "switched," or those with mixed hand and eye preference were considered likely to have less lateralized cerebral organization. Compared with the normal population, these people have higher incidences of problems such as dyslexia, stuttering, and specific learning disabilities.

Working with "split-brain" patients (those who for medical reasons have had the neural connections between their hemispheres surgically severed), Levy (1969) developed the *interference hypothesis*. This contends that left- and right-brain modes of processing are antagonistic; they interfere with each other when occurring in the same hemisphere. This hypothesis was supported by a study of left-handed subjects who were presumed to have less lateralized language representation (Levy, 1969). Also supporting Levy's concept of verbal-spatial antagonism is Sperry's (1973) contention that in cases of forced sharing of the same hemisphere for verbal and spatial modes of processing (for example, brain damage, early hemispherectomy, or congenital absence of the pathways connecting the two hemispheres), neither mode achieves top performance. The hemispheres committed to language are handicapped in the spatial, perceptual, nonverbal functions such as geometry, drawing, and sculptural and mechanical ingenuity. This is evident in left-handers. Although some left-handers have brains organized to favor nonverbal abilities (for example, Leonardo da Vinci, Raphael, and Michelangelo), more often the nonverbal functions are handicapped in favor of the verbal.

Such evidence of interference between right and left cognitive modes provides new support for Orton's (1934) hypothesis, that lack of cerebral lateral specialization plays a major role in dyslexia and stuttering. This hypothesis continues to hold interest, despite the lack of convincing direct evidence. Recently developed EEG techniques along with dichotic listening tests can provide more direct and sensitive means for investigating disorders of laterality than can measures based on hand, eye or foot dominance alone. Indeed, such studies are under way (Woodruff, 1978).

Besides their implications for the study of cognitive disorders, brain lateralization and hemispheric dominance have been linked to social and cultural differences. Several studies have suggested that different subcultures within the United States have different predominant cognitive modes (Bogen, DeZure, TenHouten, & Marsh, 1972; TenHouten, Thompson, & Walter, 1976; Thompson, Bogen, & Marsh, 1979). Middle-class individuals may be more likely to use the verbal-analytic mode, whereas the urban poor may rely more on the spatial-holistic mode. If such differences can be confirmed, it might partly explain the difficulties experienced by urban poor children in a school system that is oriented toward the middle class. Recognizing the importance of both cognitive modes, some educators emphasize the development of both verbal-analytical and spatial-holistic skills (Bruner, 1962). Galin and Ornstein (1973) have proposed that training procedures might be devised to help children use both cognitive modes appropriately.

Whether or not the implications of brain lateralization research lead to changes in educational curricula remains an open question. However, it now is clear that a measurable biological substrate for language influences behavioral development early in life. It also is evident that these brain substrates for language are shaped profoundly by experience.

Theoretical Perspectives on the Nature of Language

Historically, four principal theoretical perspectives have emerged concerning the nature of language and its acquisition. One major difference among these perspectives is the degree to which they attribute language acquisition to biological and maturational factors or to environmental and learning influences. Thus the nature-nurture controversy—which has emerged so often in this text—once again is seen as a salient issue.

Theories of language development range from the empirical or nurture-oriented perspective of the behaviorists to the nativist orientation of the preformationist-predeterminists. The former conceptualize language development in terms of simple mechanisms of association that govern learning in all species. The latter view language as being bounded by the set of potential rules emerging from the biological endowment of the human species.

The general characteristics of these four positions on language development are presented in Table 12.1. A concise summary of each theory is included, but not the arguments leveled by the various camps against one another. Nor is there an elaboration of the weaknesses of the models or detailed comments about the models' specific descriptions of language development. Instead, after examining the four models, we will look closely at *syntax* (the underlying grammatical structure of language), *phonology* (the sound system of a particular language), and *semantics* (the meaning of language). In this way we can compare the arguments, discrepancies, and weaknesses of the four theories of language development.

TABLE 12.1a
Overview of
Theoretical
Positions on
Language
Development—
General
Characteristics

Behaviorist	Cultural Relativist-Determinist	Interactionist	Preformationist-Predeterminist
1. Environmental orientation	1. Environmental orientation Less emphatic than behaviorists	1. Developmental orientation	1. Hereditary orientation
2. All learning is based on a few basic principles	2. Theory and methods borrowed from anthropology	2. Rooted in European psychological and developmental thought	2. Concern with generative linguistics Distinction between deep and surface structure Determination of way sentences are formed and related to one another Analysis of linguistic transformation
3. Language development is part of a universal learning system Anything that learns, learns the same way Anything that anyone learns, is learned the same way	3. Influence of culture on language and influence of language on thought	3. Concern with development of perceptions and relation between language and cognition Growth and development take place through organism's adaptation to environment and organization of conceptual schemes Language part of general scheme of human development	3. Emphasis on similarities among languages
4. Language mechanisms are simple Stimulus-response Operant behavior	4. Different cultures, languages and societies are unique Kinds of verbal responses that compose language differ for each linguistic system Perceptions of real world are shaped by language	4. Continuous interaction between hereditary structure of organism and input from environment	4. Goal of language study is development of language theory
5. Language is an acquired function Only innate aspect is ability to deal with stimulus-response Shared with all other creatures	5. Individual contributes little to his own linguistic and perceptual development	5. Concern with linguistic ontogeny Language develops as child passes through endogenously motivated stages Language develops along with capacity for logical thought	5. Linguistic structuring and acquisition is innate
6. Interest in language as an observable behavior	6. No biological predisposition for language acquisition	6. Belief that language and thought influence and reflect each other	6. Concern with question of internalized competence Syntactic structures Biological foundations

TABLE 12.1b
Overview of
Theoretical
Positions on
Language
Development—
Representative
Theorists

Behaviorist	Cultural Relativist-Determinist	Interactionist	Preformationist-Predeterminist
L. Bloomfield	*Benjamin Whorf*	*Jean Piaget*	*Noam Chomsky*
1. Structural linguist	1. Set forth hypothesis of linguistic relativity	1. Developmental orientation	1. Deals with generative linguistics
2. Dealt with language as a science	2. Language most important influence on development of thought patterns and perceptions	2. Growth and development take place through organism's adaptation to environment and organization of conceptual schemes	Ways sentences are formed and are related to one another
Stressed importance of eliminating introspective, mentalistic concepts from linguistics	Different linguistic systems lead to different ways of thinking	Involves assimilation and accommodation	Deep and surface structure
3. Viewed mechanics of language as fairly simple	Language patterns responsible for Western scientific and logical concepts	New elements from environment absorbed into organism's total structure	Linguistic transformation
Language a form of behavior that had to be taught by specific reinforcement	3. Without language, world would be perceived as undifferentiated continuum of sensory impression	Integrated into functioning	Concern for how language is organized within the mind of the speaker
Parent is conditioning agent	4. Words not just results of symbol-referent association	Represents continuous interaction between hereditary structure of organism and environment	2. Interested in psycholinguistics
Reinforce accidentally occurring sounds that resemble adult language		3. Language part of general scheme of human	3. Goal of language study should be development of language theory
Language becomes a habit			4. Emphasis on similarities among languages
Used for communication			Innate acquisition
			Linguistic universals

and for controlling environment
4. Item-arrangement grammar
Enumerate items comprising language
Arrange into grammatical utterance
Present data in taxonomic fashion
Assign linguistic elements to specific level of phonology, morphology, or syntax and to specific units within each level
No level-mixing
No ambiguity of classification
5. Concern for interlanguage diversity
Search for universals unscientific
Concentrate on description of observable linguistic behavior
Each language should be analyzed only in terms of its own features
Items composing each language and their arrangement into grammar patterns are unique to the language

Speakers confuse symbols and referents
Treat symbols as though connected with actual objects
5. Language arbitrary
Lacks biological basis
Seen in diversity of languages around world
Lack of conceptual framework
6. Important to understand world view peculiar to each language
Place linguistic descriptions in sociocultural framework
Use psychological criteria to set up linguistic categories
7. Goal of linguistic description to determine thought patterns and perceptions which correspond to structures of language in question

development
Concerned with linguistic ontogeny
Child passes through number of endogenously motivated developmental stages
Invariant throughout species
Uniform in ordering and age of onset
Each characterized by certain kind of cognitive organization and behavior
Language develops along with child's capacity for logical thought, judgment, reasoning
Reflects these capacities at each stage
4. Language and thought influence and reflect each other

5. Two categories of linguistic universals relevant to structuring of language
Substantive
Items of particular kind are drawn from fixed pool of such items
Theory of distinctive features of phonology
All language must have certain grammatical categories
Noun phrase, predicate phrase
Formal
All grammars of all languages meet formal conditions
Transformational component
Phonological rules
6. Formal and substantive universals built into biological language-learning mechanism
Noun/verb; Present/past
Child scans linguistic environment for examples of universal categories
Integrates into system
7. Every speaker has mastered and internalized generative grammar that expresses language knowledge

TABLE 12.1c
Overview of
Theoretical
Positions on
Language
Development—
Positions on
Six Questions
Concerning
Language
Theory

Question	Behaviorist	Cultural Relativist-Determinist	Interactionist	Preformationist-Predeterminist
1. How and why is language acquired?	1. Language acquired through selected reinforcement of natural babbling and shaping of such vocal behavior through operant conditioning Child learns what he is taught	1. Language acquired as social necessity Acquisition parallels development of thinking Does not have to be taught	1. Language acquired because of biological predisposition to language Acquisition not dependent on training Information received from others adapted by built-in genetic language-learning mechanism and integrated into system	1. Language acquired because of biological propensity of man to do so Has neurological structures specifically intended for language learning Does not have to be taught language or reinforced for acquiring
2. How is the concept *language* best defined?	2. Language a series of responses to stimuli Is equivalent to speech	2. Language a conceptual system Closely related to thought Words associated with objects Not just results of symbol-referent associations	2. Language defined in terms of conceptual and perceptual framework Form of behavior Internalized system	2. Language a system that associates sounds and meanings in a particular way Not equivalent to verbal behavior Characterized by variety
3. What is the best device or technique for describing language?	3. Language described by taxonomy or classification List parts of language	3. Language described by taxonomy with addition of psychological criteria Psychological criteria used to set up linguistic categories	3. Language described in terms of linguistic ontogeny Note utterances characteristic of each developmental stage and	3. Language described in terms of generative grammar Hierarchical and
4. To what extent is language peculiar to man?	4. Language a species-specific behavior Other species lack neurological apparatus for language			
5. Are there significant universals of language?	5. No universal grammar			
6. What form does the				

speaker's internalized competence take?

Search for universals unscientific	Important to understand world view peculiar to each language	type of cognition implied	multileveled
Interlanguage diversity more prevalent than interlanguage similarity	4. Language a species-specific behavior	Language the means by which concepts of space, time, causality are expressed	Three main components
Language best considered in terms of its own structure	Major factor dividing humans from animals	4. Language a species-specific behavior	Syntactic
	5. No universal grammar	Come from intellectual character of humans	Semantic
6. One talks by making stimulus-response associations among grammatical classes or response types	Individuals speaking one language live in different universe from those speaking another	5. Are universals in language development	Phonological
Classes unique	6. Speaker has mastered entire symbolic and conceptual system	All children use language about same way	Concern for organization of language in speaker's mind
Classes acquired through learning	Innate structure for language acquisition	Children learn language at about same ages	4. Language a species-specific behavior
	Internalized language substratum for thought	6. Several views:	Other species have biological mechanisms necessary language
		Piaget: Speaker has total conceptual system	5. All significant features of language universals
		Developed with, inseparable from rest of behavior	Substantive universals
		Linguistic competence integrated with cognitive process	All languages have grammatical categories
		Bruner: Separate linguistic competence in complex hierarchical system	Built into biological language-learning mechanism
			Child scans linguistic environment integrates
			Formal universals
			All grammars in formal conditions
			Transformational components
			Phonological rules
			Child has general ability to acquire these categories
			6. Every speaker of language has mastered and internalized generative grammar that expresses language knowledge

Source: S. Houston. "The Study of Language: Trends and Positions. In *Human Development and Cognition*. Ed. J. Eliot. New York: Holt, Rinehart and Winston, 1971, pp. 256–282.

Behaviorist Perspective

In the early 1930s Bloomfield fathered the behaviorist approach to the study of language. Taking the perspective that inductive generalizations would emerge when enough descriptive data were gathered, this approach produced vast records of descriptive data with little attempt to impose a theoretical structure on them. This position thus involved the active rejection of mentalistic concepts about language, such as concepts about underlying cognitive schema and physiological substrates of observable language behavior. The behaviorist approach was in direct conflict with the prevailing trend in European linguistics (represented in the work of Humbolt and de Saussure), which drew a marked distinction between observable linguistic *performance* and a theoretically posited inner linguistic *competence* that was thought to underlie the observed performance. Thus Bloomfield's thinking can be compared with Skinner's perspective, which rejected the idea that there is a *covert*, or nonobservable, competence underlying language.

The behaviorist position contends that language is acquired by the same simple mechanisms of association that govern learning in all species. Thus all linguistic phenomena can be understood fully in terms of the differential reinforcement of *observable* responses. In this model the random babbles of infants are differentially reinforced; sounds that approximate meaningful words (such as *dada* in English) elicit smiles and encouragement, whereas meaningless sounds are ignored. Rewarded responses are increased in frequency, whereas nonrewarded responses are dropped from the repertoire of sounds produced. The behaviorists do not believe that language differs very much from any other type of behavior—except, perhaps, that it is reinforced totally by other persons. The only unique native competence that the behaviorists associate with the human capacity for language is the complex of articulatory mechanisms underlying speech. Seen from this perspective, the feature that distinguishes human beings from other species in terms of language resides not so much in an underlying cognitive capacity as in the motor ability to articulate many sounds.

In the behaviorist model, complex language skills develop in the following manner. First, the babble of infants is reinforced differentially so that appropriate sounds increase in frequency. Following this acquisition of the sound system (phonology) and the development of a basic vocabulary, grammatical utterances then are shaped by those with whom the child interacts. Early in development the performance of verbal responses becomes controlled by environmental stimuli. That is, responses are reinforced by external or internal cues, thus establishing a strong verbal habit and increasing the level of verbal behavior. The regularities a child hears in language strengthen associations so that *classes* of words are formed (such as nouns, verbs, adjectives, and so on). Regularities in language also lead to either a strengthening or a weakening of associations between the different classes. For example, prepositions tend to precede articles, which precede nouns; that is, certain classes of words have a tendency to precede other classes. In this way, different grammatical classes are formed that have differing "privileges of occurrence" within the utterance, depending on what has come before. It is clear that sentences in this system are

The major theoretical perspectives on language development differ in the degree to which they credit biological or environmental influences.

Jim Harrison, Stock, Boston, Inc.

generated from left to right, for the beginning of the sentence determines what follows.

A behaviorist's definition of *language* might be "a network of interclass associations in which the classes are defined by the possible context of their occurrence" (Houston, 1971). Behaviorists argue that language is a behavior that develops entirely as a result of learning and that it requires no special endowment beyond the capacity for associative learning and the ability to generate a large number of sounds.

Cultural Relativist-Determinist Perspective

While still taking an environmentalist perspective, the cultural relativist-determinist approach focuses primarily on the role of language in determining thought. As such, it is concerned with internal, covert processes. This approach grew out of the work of Boas and Sapir and culminated in the writings of Whorf (1956). It represents the dominant position of anthropologists concerning language, for it asserts that each culture has a unique world view that is transmitted from generation to generation through the medium of language. Such perspectives are not transmitted by deliberate instruction but result from the structure of the language itself, which directly influences the course of perceptual and cognitive development. For example, the Eskimos have a number of words describing various states of snow and ice that denote distinctions in quality that English-speaking individuals might not make. Another example of how thought can be shaped by words is seen in the concept of God. The Chinese character (神) for this word consists of two components: 示 , which means "to indicate"; and 申 which means "to utter." So although Western theologians have debated about whether God is a self-revealing being, that debate is precluded in Chinese, for the very meaning of the word implies that God *is* a self-revealing being.

The cultural relativist-determinist position holds that the structure of language specifies which distinctions are to be made and which categories are to be formed in delimiting the individual's otherwise continuous sensory experience. For example, all languages include words to describe various hues on the color spectrum (a continuous range of light energy from shorter to longer wavelengths). However, the *number* of colors that are identified in different languages varies. The cultural relativist-determinist position would suggest that individuals perceive a greater or lesser number of distinct colors, depending on the number of words their language has for colors. Besides delimiting categories and specifying distinctions in perception, language in this view directly influences the manner in which categories can be related to each other. In short, language actually sets the bounds for thought.

Unfortunately, the cultural relativist-determinist perspective has not resulted in a model of language acquisition. Although proponents concede that there must be some innate basis for language acquisition, they feel that such a basis in no way specifies the course of language development or its final outcome. Thus experience is of primary importance in acquiring language, and each language embodies a unique spectrum of experiences characteristic of the world view of the culture in which the language is found.

In this model, language is defined as a conceptual system that is intimately involved with the development of thought processes. This position is determinist in that the direction of causality is from language to thought (that is, the thoughts and world views of individuals are shaped by the language they speak). The model is relativist in that it views an individual's concept of reality not as being absolute but as relative to the linguistic community in which the individual is raised. Further, this position holds that each language is unique and not merely the expression of the universal laws of associative learning—as behaviorists would hold. Cultural relativists and determinists also differ from behaviorists in their emphasis on mental processes. They view the human mind as being a unique biological endowment whose character is culturally (linguistically) determined during development.

Interactionist Perspective

As its name suggests, the interactionist approach proposes that there is a reciprocal relationship between the innate predisposition for language and the linguistic environment in which a child develops. This position is like the cultural relativist-determinist position, for it holds that language is bound up intimately in the process of intellectual development. It differs from both the behaviorist and the cultural relativist-determinist models in terms of when language development is initiated and what shapes its development. The former two models emphasize the importance of the environment in shaping language, whereas the interactionist model asserts that causality is not one-directional; rather, it views learning and maturation as being interdependent.

Piaget is the primary speaker for this position, and it is his model of intellectual development that provides the basis for the interactionist analysis of language acquisition. In Piaget's (1967) view, language is primarily a system of representation that facilitates cognitive functioning. Language is incorporated into the broader scheme of intellectual development through the processes of assimilation and accommodation (described in Chapter 13), which underlie all cognitive growth. Language is a part of the total conceptual system and is developed with and inseparable from the rest of behavior. Because there is a strong biological-maturational component to the process of intellectual development (according to Piaget), there also are universal characteristics of language development that are shared by all members of the human species, regardless of the culture or language spoken. These universals emerge from the interaction between a shared genetic predisposition for language and a common external environment.

Preformationist-Predeterminist Perspective

This approach finds its most complete exposition in the writings of Noam Chomsky (1957, 1965), and it represents the dominant theoretical position in modern linguistics. The most nativist of the four positions presented here, this is basically an attempt to explain the tremendous generative capacity of human linguistic competence in terms of an underlying system of innate linguistic universals. This model attempts to formulate a theory of linguistic competence in the form of a collection of rules whose application will allow the generation of every possible grammatical sentence—none of which will be ungrammatical. Such a group of rules is referred to as a *generative grammar*.

There are two major points in Chomsky's theory. First, he has asserted that there is an innate *language acquisition device (LAD)*, which provides the basis for human linguistic competence. Second, he posits that each sentence has both a *surface structure* (the actual form taken by the sentence) and a *deep structure* (the idea underlying the sentence). An example of the second concept can be seen in comparing the two sentences "The boy threw the ball" and "The ball was thrown by the boy." Both sentences clearly express the same idea, but their surface structures are quite different. According to Chomsky's theory, one sentence is recognized as a paraphrase of the other because both sentences have the same deep structure (the same idea or thought). In using the original idea to generate the passive form ("The ball was thrown by the boy"), the speaker applies the passive transformation to the deep structure, which results in this distinct surface structure. There can also be ambiguous sentences. For example, "They are eating apples" has one surface structure but two meanings or two deep structures. (The passive form tells us that a group of apples are for eating, and the active form tells us that a group of people are eating apples.) In order to recognize the identity of the active and passive forms and to be able to "disambiguate" such sentences as "They are eating apples," a developing child must be able to go beyond the information given in the surface structure. Thus it is necessary to postulate that a child has an innate knowledge of the possible transformations and grammatical relations found in the deep structure of the language.

Chomsky's position holds that all languages share the same rules at the level of deep structure, which is to say simply that grammatical relations in the deep structure are linguistic universals. Since no single language employs all possible rules, it is a child's task during development to determine which rules apply to the native language. Regardless of which language the child comes to speak, this language will be bounded by the set of potential rules in one's biological endowment. Thus the final outcome of linguistic development is, to a degree, *predetermined*, or in a sense *preformed*. A given language includes some subset of these biologically endowed rules, and it is this subset to which developing children conform, generating sentences that members of their linguistic community judge to be grammatical.

The Development of Syntax

Before analyzing the development of syntax, we need a clear statement concerning the nature of the syntactic (grammatical) structure of human language. Of the four theoretical positions presented, only two thus far have formulated explicit descriptions of the underlying grammatical structure of language. Skinner has presented the behaviorist model, and Chomsky has outlined the predeterminist-preformationist model.

Behaviorist Model of Syntax

The behaviorist position holds that all forms of sequential behavior are mediated by chains of associations; that is, what comes before serves as a stimulus for what follows. In this context, a sentence can be conceived of as a chain of word associations generated from left to right in much the same fashion that one reads or writes. Syntactic structure enters into this model when we recognize that words can be grouped into classes on the basis of where they tend to fall in sentences relative to other classes of words. At any point in a sentence chain, one class of words is said to have a "higher privilege of occurrence" than all other classes (Staats & Staats, 1963). Individual words thus are selected on the basis of semantic considerations (to be described later in the chapter). Therefore, the various associative strengths that exist between classes of words determine the permissible syntactic constructions that are to be found in a particular language.

In the behaviorist model, the process of language acquisition follows the rules of associative learning. The simplest example is that concerning prepositional phrases. In the course of listening to and imitating speech, children perceive and repeat numerous utterances following this form: preposition-article-(adjective)-noun. They hear the same prepositions along with the same article and noun. Eventually children develop a generalized class of prepositions. Throughout this process it is assumed that proper associations are strengthened by the differential reinforcement of correct imitations and spontaneous utterances. Thus language development should follow a steady course of progressive differentiations: the diffusely organized vocabulary of children develops into well-formed grammatical classes, which, when uttered in strings, come to approximate the grammatical structure of adult speech. The failure of developing children to demonstrate such trends would cause considerable difficulties in accepting this position.

The behaviorist model places great emphasis on the role of imitation, or *echoic behavior*. As a mother feeds her child, her vocalizations come to have secondary reinforcing value; and when the child later mimics these vocalizations, they are strengthened by this secondary reinforcing value. On the basis of this model, if imitation is responsible for the progressive development of syntax, then the grammatical level of a child's imitative vocalizations would be more advanced syntactically than when the child spontaneously vocalizes alone. In analyzing imitative and spontaneous vocalizations to test this prediction, Ervin (1964) presented results that did *not* support the behaviorist position: in both types of vocalization the grammatical level was the same. Ervin concluded, "There is not a shred of evidence supporting a view that the progress toward adult norms of grammar arises merely from practice in overt imitation of adult sentences" (p. 194).

An even more damaging critique of the role of reinforcement in the acquisition of syntax was provided by Brown, Cazden, and Bellugi-Klima (1969). Their analysis of records of parent-child verbal interactions found that reinforcement was not given on the basis of grammatical correctness but on truth value—that is, whether an utterance corresponded with reality.

As noted previously, behaviorists hold that the development of grammar involves a simple system of associated word classes in which context and associative strength determine a class's "privilege of occurrence." Therefore, the behaviorist model predicts that a child's acquisition of syntax will follow a smooth course of progressive development. Development should be gradual and continuous rather than in stages or discontinuous steps, for the system of associated word classes develops through the gradual strengthening of associations.

Careful observation, however, indicates that the development of syntax is not gradual and smooth. Ervin (1964) has shown that before developing the past-tense inflection of regular verbs (-*ed*), children use the correct past-tense form of irregular verbs (for example, *came, did, broke*). Remarkably, she found that when this past-tense inflection *does* enter a child's vocabulary, it makes its first appearance inappropriately, with the present tense of irregular verbs (*doed* or *breaked*), and before any observations of its use with regular verbs. Obviously, this could not have resulted from imitation. More to our point here, however, is the indication that a child's language behavior is guided by rules. It is difficult to imagine how the foreign combination *doed* could suddenly appear with greater habit strength than the previously employed correct form *did,* especially since the inflection -*ed* had never been used previously. Apparently, the child covertly formulated a "new" rule concerning the past tense on the basis of linguistic data obtained from listening to adult speech. Thus *doed* represented one of the child's first hypotheses. This same mentalistic, or rule-forming, behavior has also been demonstrated in the development of negation and interrogatives (Bellugi, 1965) and during the acquisition of Russian (Slobin, 1966).

Another criticism of the behaviorist position concerning the development of syntax arises from the consideration of such sentences as "John is eager to please" and "John is easy to please." The surface structure of these sentences is indistinguishable, but an attempt to paraphrase them reveals that they are grammatically very different in their deep structures (Palermo, 1970). In the first sentence John is the subject; in the second he is the object. "It is easy to please John" is an appropriate paraphrase of the second sentence, but "It is eager to please John" does not preserve the meaning of the first sentence. It is difficult to imagine how the grammatical structures of these two sentences—which resemble each other so closely on the surface (noun-verb-adjective-infinitive) but which, in fact, are syntactically so different—could result from a simple associative chaining procedure. It is precisely this sort of difficulty that the predeterminist-preformationist position attempts to clarify. Therefore, let us turn to the description of syntax as outlined in Chomsky's theory of grammar.

Predeterminist-Preformationist Model of Syntax

What impressed Chomsky most about language was its tremendous productive potential, despite the fact that it employs a limited vocabulary (basic units). He suggested that if you pick a sentence on the first page of a book and begin reading without interruption until you come across that sentence again, chances are that you will go through many books before you succeed—if, indeed, you can find that sentence again at all. This is what Chomsky meant by the *generative capacity* of language. There must be a set of covert rules that allow one to combine the units of a finite vocabulary and produce an unbounded number of grammatically correct sentences.

The behaviorists had pointed out the importance of *linear* word order in sentences, but, ultimately, this did not provide a complete description of syntax. The first attempts to overcome the deficiencies of this approach took the form of *phrase-structure grammars,* in which sentences are broken down into subunits (phrases) that also can be subdivided into smaller phrases, finally resulting in a string of units. Although linear order still provides some clues to the grammatical structure of a sentence, additional information must be sought in the rules that specify the *hierarchical arrangement* of the phrase structure. Because these rules tend to maintain certain linear order in the sentence structure, some behaviorists have attempted to modify their stance to accommodate such syntactic rules (Braine, 1963, 1965). However, many grammatical relationships can be handled by a phrase-structure grammar only with great difficulty. Problematic to phrase-structure grammar is the identity of active and passive sentences in their deep structures and the manner in which such sentences as "John is easy to please" and "John is eager to please" come to have such similar surface structures (when their deep structures are so dissimilar). Phrase-structure grammars cannot handle such difficulties, because the rules involved in generating these sentences involve substantial shifts in word order.

The same rules are applied to derive the passive form (the sentence meaning "apples are for eating") as for the active form (the sentence meaning "some people are eating apples"). At some point, however, the passive *transformation* rule is applied, which results in a substantial alteration of the meaning.

Somewhat more complicated are the derivations of "John is easy to please" and "John is eager to please." As Dale (1976) points out, each of these sentences contains two simpler sentences in its deep structure: (It is easy) (Someone pleases John); and (John is eager) (John pleases someone). Thus transformations must be applied in order to combine these two sentences and effect substantial changes in word order.

A system that includes deep and surface structures, phrase-structure rules, and transformations appears unnecessarily complicated at first. In fact, however, this system is far more parsimonious than other analyses that incorporate numerous rules to account for the irregularities that occur in language (at least it is more economical when the transformational rules are not employed).

More significant than the relatively parsimonious analysis of language is the fact that Chomsky's system of deep-structure relations and transformational rules are the same in all languages. Considering the vast differences in the surface structures among the various languages of the world, this universality not only is remarkable but also provides very persuasive support for Chomsky's position. Additionally, a variety of psycholinguistic data has been gathered that tends to support the psychological reality of transformational grammar. A typical example of such support is a study by Savin and Perchonock (1965) in which subjects were presented with a sentence followed by a list of words. After the two presentations, they were asked to repeat from memory both the sentence and the words. On all trials, sentences of equal length were used, but they differed in the number of transformations involved in their derivations. Since it had been demonstrated that subjects remember a sentence by independently encoding its underlying form and transformational rules, it was predicted that the sentences involving more transformations would take up more space in memory, thus decreasing the number of words remembered from the list that followed. This prediction was borne out in the subjects' performance.

While providing a psychologically plausible description of syntax, the predeterminist-preformationist viewpoint has not resulted in an explicit theory of how language is learned. Rather, it is postulated that an innate language acquisition device (LAD) enables children to sort out the rules of grammar for their particular language from the adult speech they hear. A number of observations support this concept, some of which have been mentioned. Primarily, proponents of this view find it necessary to postulate an innate knowledge of grammatical rules to account for the acquisition of deep-structure relationships and transformational rules that are not encoded in the surface structure of the speech children hear. Since children's only potential source of information concerning syntax is found in the surface structure (the speech they hear), and since the acquisition of syntax appears to follow a pattern not predictable solely on the basis of surface-structure exposure, the predeterminist-preformationist viewpoint postulates an innate mechanism for language acquisition.

Are Those Apes Really Talking?

Pupil (rolling on ground): You tickle me.
Laura: Where?
Pupil (pointing to leg): Here.
Laura (after tickling him): Now you tickle me.
Pupil (tickling her): Me tickle Laura.

This dialogue between Laura and her charge might not seem unusual, except for one thing: the pupil was not a human child but a young chimpanzee named Nim. Like several others of his primate kin, Nim had been taught to communicate with humans in American Sign Language, a system of hand gestures developed for the deaf. He eventually learned to make and recognize 125 signs. But the frisky little chimp and other apes who have received such "language" instruction are now the center of a raging academic storm. The issue: can apes really master the essence of human language—the creation of sentences? . . .

No one has done more to stir doubts than Columbia University Psychologist Herbert Terrace in his work with little Nim (full name: Nim Chimpsky, a play on the name of Linguist Noam Chomsky of the Massachusetts Institute of Technology, a staunch proponent of the idea that language ability is biologically unique to humans). The object of Terrace's experiment was to prove Chomsky wrong—to show that creatures other than man could, indeed, conquer syntax and link words into sentences, however simple.

Toward that goal, Terrace, with Laura Petitto, a student assistant, and other trainers, put Nim through 44 months of intensive sign-language drill, while treating him much as they would a child. In some ways the chimp was an apt student, learning, for example, to "sign" *dirty* when he wanted to use the potty or *drink* when he spotted someone sipping from a Thermos. Nonetheless, Nim never mastered even the rudiments of grammar or sentence construction. His speech, unlike that of children, did not grow in complexity. Nor did it show much spontaneity; 88% of the time he "talked" only in response to specific questions from the teacher.

Armed with his new insights, Terrace began reviewing the reports and video tapes of other experimenters. Careful study of the record showed the same patterns with other apes that Terrace had noted in the work with Nim. There were rarely any "spontaneous" utterances, and what had seemed at first glance to be original sentences now emerged as responses to questions, imitations of signs made by the teacher, or as rote-like repetitions of memorized combinations. For instance, when Lana, a chimp at Yerkes, said *Please machine give apple,* the first three words seemed to mean nothing more to her than a mechanical prelude to obtaining something she wanted. Says Terrace . . . "The closer I looked, the more I regarded the many reported instances of language as elaborate tricks [by the apes] for obtaining rewards." . . .

As for the man in whose honor Nim was named, he has no doubts. Says Noam Chomsky: "It's about as likely that an ape will prove to have a language ability as that there is an island somewhere with a species of flightless birds waiting for human beings to teach them to fly."

Source: *Time,* Mar. 10, 1980, pp. 50, 57. Copyright 1980 Time, Inc. All rights reserved.

The concept of an innate (species-wide) linguistic competence is given support by the very universality of deep-structure relationships and transformational rules. Further, it is argued that many characteristics of language acquisition resemble genetically controlled physiological maturation (Lenneberg, 1967). For example, the onset of language acquisition occurs at roughly nine to eighteen months of age and is complete by age six in children throughout the world—despite the facts that rearing practices are quite different and that at no point during this time is deliberate instruction needed for the development of linguistic behavior. Similarly, the sequence of developmental stages and the actual structure of early grammars are much the same in all cultures, despite differences among languages. Notably, genetic or hormonal defects such as Down's syndrome or hypothyroidism, which retard the course of physiological maturation, also expand the time scale for language acquisition. What is more, language can be acquired in the face of minor sensory (hearing) or motor (articulatory) deficits. Thus language seems to take care of its own development—much as though it were "wired in."

The concept of the innate endowment of language was emphasized by McNeill (1966), who pointed out that child languages form similar grammatical classes during their early stages in all cultures and that these classes are distinct from the adult grammars into which they eventually will evolve. Not only does this suggest an innate competence, but the unique character of early child grammars provides a strong argument against the behaviorist approach. Since the grammar of children's early utterances does not resemble that of the adult language, it is doubtful that children could learn such grammars by imitating the speech they hear. Therefore, the evidence concerning the development of syntax is weighted heavily against the behaviorist position and supports in a general fashion the predeterminist-preformationist position. Remember, however, that no explicit hypotheses about the acquisition of syntax have been presented by the predeterminist-preformationists. Therefore, we must analyze the actual course of syntactic development as seen in the recorded speech of children in order to examine how such development is accomplished.

Children's Syntax

The first step in syntactic development occurs early in the second year and has been called the *holophrasic stage,* when a child's verbal behavior is characterized by one-word utterances. The words are generally nouns, adjectives, or "self-invented words"; and they usually take the form of directions concerning actions to be taken by the child or by another (Dale, 1976). Such utterances are interpreted as communicating the meaning of an entire sentence, such as the child's statement "Milk!" which is translated as "Bring me some milk."

By the age of eighteen to twenty months, a child's vocabulary begins to split into two distinct classes. Braine (1963) has designated these the *pivot class* and the *open class.* The pivot class is the smaller group of the two; however, its words occur more frequently in a child's speech than do words from the open class. The open class, as its name suggests, is a more diffuse collection of vocabulary items that is continually expanding. Examples of pivot- and open-class vocabularies compiled for individual children are presented in Table 12.2.

The following rules summarize a child's grammar at this point in develop-ment. (P = pivot-class words; O = open-class words; and parentheses indicate that use is optional.)

1. S (single-word sentence)
2. $S \rightarrow [(P) + O]$ or $[O + (P)]$
3. $P \rightarrow$ [pivot-class words]
4. $O \rightarrow$ [open-class words]

The position for the pivot word is fixed for any particular child, but it can be found in either a preceding or a following position among different children. Soon after the distinction between pivot and open classes is established, a second group of pivot-class words is formed, which assumes the alternate posi-tion, and utterances involving two open-class words appear. Thus rule 2 is expanded to:

2. a. S ($P1$) + O
   b. O + ($P2$)
   c. O + O

TABLE 12.2
Pivot and Open
Classes from
Three Studies of
Child Language

Braine (1963)		Brown (1970)		Ervin (1964)	
Pivot Class	Open Class	Pivot Class	Open Class	Pivot Class	Open Class
allgone	boy	my	Adam	this	arm
byebye	sock	that	Becky	that	baby
big	boat	two	boot		dolly's
more	fan	a	coat		pretty
pretty	milk	the	coffee		yellow
my	plane	big	knee		come
see	shoe	green	man		doed
night-night	vitamins	poor	Mommy	the	other
hi	hot	wet	nut	a	baby
	Mommy	dirty	sock		dolly's
	Daddy	fresh	stool		pretty
		pretty	tinkertoy		yellow
					arm
				here	baby
				there	dolly's
					pretty
					yellow

Source: D. McNeil. "Developmental Psycholinguistics." Reprinted from *The Genesis of Language* by F. Smith and G. A. Miller by permission of The MIT Press, Cambridge, Massachusetts. Copyright © 1966 by The MIT Press.

In addition to studying word classes, Bloom (1970) has identified a number of functional relationships that exist between words within each sentence during this first stage of syntactic development. An interesting example of this concerns the sentence "Mommy sock," which was uttered by a young girl in two different situations. In the first instance, the child was referring to her mother's sock; this sentence is an example of a possessor-object relationship. Later, the child uttered the same sentence when her mother attempted to put the girl's own sock back on the child's foot. In this case the relationship is one of agent-object. The mother (agent) does something with the sock (object). In a cross-cultural study of children's speech, Brown (1970) was able to specify roughly twelve such relationships in the speech of every child, regardless of the language being acquired (see Table 12.3). These relationships can be thought of as *structural meanings,* and Dale (1976) speculates that the difference between such structural relationships and syntactic form (pivot-open class distinctions) might be a precursor of the later division of syntax into deep and surface structures.

Dale (1976) notes that the complexity of a child's language increases rapidly after this first stage of syntactic development. Three-word sentences appear that are usually combinations of the previous two-word structural meanings (a commonly occurring example of which would be agent-action-object). Most important, the child begins to expand the object category into a rudimentary noun phrase that occurs in the same relative position as individual nouns did previously. This occurs with the gradual *differentiation* of a larger class of general modifiers into smaller classes, such as articles and adjectives. Besides such dif-

TABLE 12.3
The First
Sentences in
Child Speech

Structural Meaning	Form	Example
1. Nomination	that + N, it + N	that book
2. Notice	hi + N	hi belt
3. Recurrence	more + N, 'nother + N	more milk
4. Nonexistence	allgone + N, no more + N	allgone rattle
5. Attributive	Adj + N	big train
6. Possessive	N + N	mommy lunch
7. Locative	N + N	sweater chair
8. Locative	V + N	walk street
9. Agent-action	N + V	Eve read
10. Agent-object	N + N	mommy sock
11. Action-object	V + N	put book
12. Conjunction	N + N	umbrella boot

Source: Reprinted with permission of Macmillan Publishing Co., Inc. from *Psycholinguistics* by R. Brown. Copyright © 1970 by The Free Press, a division of Macmillan Publishing Co., Inc.

ferentiation, new classes are formed by the reclassification of words within the child's vocabulary—a process that is not yet well understood.

In addition to an innate knowledge of potential syntactic organization, clues to the syntactic structure of a sentence are signaled by two principal sources in its surface structure: *word order* and *inflections*. During the early stages of syntactic development, word order is of primary importance and is characteristic of the early acquisition of language in all cultures, regardless of whether the adult language relies more on order (English) or inflections (Russian) (Dale, 1976). Inflections, which primarily indicate number and tense (-*s*, -*es*, -*ed*, -*ing*, and so on), usually make their first appearance after the onset of three-word sentences (Slobin, 1970). This illustrates a major characteristic of language acquisition—the tendency of a child toward "overregularization" (Dale, 1976). An example given earlier in the chapter was the child's overgeneralization of the past-tense inflection -*ed*, resulting in such inappropriate utterances as *doed* or *breaked*.

Up to this point in development there has been no sign of the use of transformational rules. Between the ages of three and five, rapid progress occurs in this regard. Transformational rules that allow the generation of negative sentences and interrogatives (such as yes/no questions and *wh-* questions) have been studied most fully during this period, but the analysis of such development is beyond the scope of this chapter. By the age of five or six a child's spontaneous utterances are almost indistinguishable syntactically from adult speech. Though subject-verb agreement and endings on personal pronouns (for example, "Him and her went") need improvement, and occasional double negatives must be eliminated, the acquisition of syntax as seen in speech is virtually complete. Yet in studies of comprehension of syntactically complex sentences, it is apparent that some further syntactic development is needed, which is not obvious from a child's speech (Chomsky, 1969).

Although language acquisition appears to proceed normally without formal direction, a question remains concerning the nature of the interaction between a child's native competence and the environment needed to facilitate mastery of the particular language involved. Earlier in this chapter, evidence was cited to rule out the role of imitation and reinforcement as major factors in such a development. Another possibility involves a more active linguistic interchange between the child and the environment. This interchange takes three basic forms: prompting, echoing, and expansion. *Prompting* and *echoing* basically involve asking questions in a form that is syntactically more accessible to the child. In the absence of a response to "What do you want?" the mother might ask, "You want what?"—which does not involve the interrogative transformations but rather makes the child's task one of sentence completion. Similarly, in response to an unintelligible "I going ow nah," the father might respond with, "You're going where?" (examples from Dale, 1976). More interesting, however, is *expansion*, which involves responding to a child's grammatically inferior utterance with a grammatically improved form of that utterance. For example, the child might say, "Baby highchair," to which the mother might respond, "Baby is in the highchair" (Dale, 1976).

Cazden (1965) conducted a most revealing study on the importance of this sort of interaction. A large group of day-care children was divided into three

It is important for children to be presented with a rich linguistic environment that provides meaningful responses to their own verbal behavior.

Elizabeth Hamlin, Stock, Boston, Inc.

experimental conditions. The first group received expansions for every utterance during a forty-minute period each day. The second group also received forty minutes of well-formed sentences in response to their speech each day, but the responses were relevant answers to the children's utterances. The third, control group received no special attention except forty minutes of the experimenter's presence each day. It was found that although the control group showed somewhat less improvement than the expansion groups, the second group showed considerable improvement over both other groups.

Such results are not completely unequivocal (since the experimenter could have been providing inappropriate expansions), but they do suggest that it is most important during development for children to be presented with a rich linguistic environment in terms of meaningful responses to their own verbal behavior. As has been evident in other chapters in this text, innate and environmental factors interact to produce the observed behavior. Neither nature alone (in terms of the innate LAD) nor environment alone (in terms of the speech of parents, siblings, and others) determines the development of syntax. Results like those of Cazden's study and the appearance of much verbal play on the part of children have led many psycholinguists to conclude that the acquisition of syntax is an active and interactive process. A child's behavior is not unlike that of a linguist—generating hypotheses about what makes up grammatical speech and testing those hypotheses on reality.

In light of the fact that syntax acquisition is an active and interactive process, concern has arisen about the effect of television and its imposition of a passive role on the child at a time when verbal skills should be developing. The role of television in amplifying aggressive and paranoid behaviors has been established empirically, but it has been suggested more recently that television viewing may have other negative influences (Winn, 1977). When young children could be playing actively with parents or peers or developing verbal skills through reading, many of them are watching television. Television viewing is a major activity of many preschool and school-aged children, with some of them spending as much as fifty-four hours a week at this pastime. Since watching television involves activation of visual-spatial processes, Winn has suggested that television may stimulate the development of the right hemisphere of the brain, which has been shown to be involved with these processes. She argues that excessive stimulation of the right hemisphere may result in delayed or inhibited development of the left hemisphere, which is involved in verbal-analytic information processing. As a result of passively watching television instead of actively engaging in verbal interaction, children may be limiting their capacity for language and logical thought.

The notion that visual-spatial processing is antagonistic to verbal-analytic processing has received empirical support (Levy, 1969), and it also has been documented that these two modes of processing are carried out in different hemispheres of the brain (Sperry, 1973). Evidence has yet to be accumulated that television viewing actually affects brain organization and consequent verbal and spatial processing. However, the mere possibility of such an effect should stimulate more research on this problem and should serve as an additional reason for parents to limit their children's access to television—both because of the content of programming and because of the time spent in this passive manner.

Phonological Development

The two major theoretical perspectives on the acquisition of sound are the same two perspectives we have been examining with regard to the acquisition of syntax. The behaviorists maintain that the sound system of a particular language grows in a continuous fashion by the process of selective reinforcement of appropriate sounds and breath patterns that occur in a child's early cries and babblings. Opposed to this is the predeterminist-preformationist position, which argues that there is a definite discontinuity between the babbling stage and the appearance of the phonemic regularities of language. Again, from this perspective, innate predispositions play a major role in the acquisition of the sound pattern of language; and, once more, a distinction is drawn between surface and deep structure—this time in the phonemic organization.

Before examining the points at which the two positions diverge, we will consider their points of agreement. There is little disagreement over the basic phonemic composition of language. All languages comprise two basic types of sound: vowels and consonants. The distinction between the two is based on the degree of obstruction involved in the passage of air across the vocal chords and through the vocal cavities. With *vowels* there is no obstruction of air; with *consonants* there is. Within the category of consonants there are many subdivisions, depending on whether the obstruction is *complete* (*stops*, such as /t/, /p/, /b/, /d/) or *partial* (*fricatives*, or *continuants*, such as /s/, /f/, /z/, /v/); *voiced* (such as /d/, /b/, /v/) or *voiceless* (such as /s/, /t/, /p/, /f/); produced by placing the tongue at the ridge behind the teeth (*alveolar*, such as /t/, /d/, /z/, /s/) or by touching the lips together (*labial*, such as /p/, /b/, /v/, /f/); and so forth. It is clear from these English examples that the subsets are overlapping. Besides vowels and consonants, two other groups of sound fall between those categories (in that they involve some obstruction of air flow but do not create the characteristic turbulence of consonants); these are called *liquids* (/r/ and /l/) and *glides* (/w/ and /y/).

The English language contains twelve vowel sounds, twenty consonants, two glides, and two liquids—for a total of thirty-six phonemes. A *phoneme* is defined as a class of sounds that are considered equivalent in a given language (and thus are relevant to the particular language under consideration).

While the phonemes make up the segmental components of the sound system, also important are the overall sound patterns that result from intonational contour and stress. Intonational contour follows the breath group (the course of exhalation) that occurs over the duration of a sentence, affecting its tonal quality and in a sense defining its boundaries. The most common pattern, found in almost all languages, is a drop in the fundamental frequency at the end of the sentence (except in the case of interrogatives, which usually end with a rise in the fundamental frequency).

In support of the behaviorist position, there is some evidence that these overall sound components show continuous development from birth to the completion of the acquisition process. However, there are also a number of observations that suggest that the predeterminist-preformationist position provides a superior analysis of the development of segmental sound features. We will consider these two perspectives and their strengths and weaknesses by examining them in relation to the course of phonological development as presented by Kaplan and Kaplan (1971).

The Kaplans divide phonological competence into two abilities: sound production and sound reception. These two abilities develop essentially simultaneously, and the stages of each are presented in Table 12.4.

The main point of dispute between behaviorists and predeterminists-preformationists centers on the transition from stage 3 to stage 4 in the development of a child's productive abilities. The behaviorists note that practically every sound found in human language is emitted at some point by the child in stage 3, and they argue that the transition from stage 3 to stage 4 is the result of a process in which sounds not utilized by the language are extinguished whereas sounds belonging to the language are strengthened by reinforcement. The predeterminist-preformationist viewpoint instead maintains that there is an important distinction between randomly emitted sounds and intentionally voiced phonemes.

The empirical evidence appears to be on the side of the latter position. In phonemic development, not all sounds appear simultaneously (Irwin, 1957), as the behaviorist position would predict. There is, in fact, a definite order of appearance during stage 3. This seems to be universal and quite different from

TABLE 12.4
The Course of
Phonological
Development:
Production and
Reception

Production:

Stage 1: Crying
        first 6 months
        develops characteristic breath patterns
        angry cry
        pain
        etc.
Stage 2: Pseudo-cry and noncry vocalizations
        from 3 weeks to 4–5 months
        first use of articulatory organs to produce temporal and frequency
        patterns
Stage 3: Babbling and intonated vocalizations
        till end of first year
        development of adult intonation patterns
        appearance of vowel and consonant-like sounds
Stage 4: Patterned speech
        onset 9–12 months
        systematic differentiation of "phonemes"
        appearance of first words

Reception: (Stages less clearly defined)

Stage 1: Neonate responsiveness to auditory stimuli
        locate source
        discriminate frequency, intensity, and pattern
Stage 2: At 2 weeks begins to discriminate human from nonhuman sounds
Stage 3: At the end of second month can discriminate affective qualities
Stage 4: At 5–6 months begins to attend to and discriminate supra-segmental
        features of adult speech
Stage 5: At the end of the first year begins to attend to and discriminate
        segmental features of adult speech

Source: Based on E. Kaplan and G. Kaplan. "The Prelinguistic Child." In *Human Development and Cognition.* Ed. J. Eliot. New York: Holt, Rinehart and Winston, 1971.

(very nearly the reverse of) the order in which these sounds are incorporated into wordlike utterances in stage 4 (Jakobson, 1968). An example is the sound /r/, which is heard frequently in a child's early babbling. Later, as the child enters stage 4, this sound virtually disappears from spontaneous utterances until much later in phonemic development. Predeterminists-preformationists also argue that the universality of the stages of both productive and receptive phonological development—despite differences in languages and cultural practices—supports the position that such development is influenced strongly by an innate competence.

Therefore, as was the case with the acquisition of syntax, the principles of learning as set forth by the behaviorists have failed to provide an adequate model of phonological development. We are left to take recourse in the predeterminist-preformationist model, which is not totally satisfying in that it postulates an innate (and unexplained) competence. This competence is manifested in what appears to be rule-governed behavior on the part of the child.

Jakobson (1968) argues that three overriding principles are present in the universally ordered appearance of sounds in children's phonemic vocabulary. These principles are concerned with the differentiation of what has been described as "distinctive features"—a system of binary contrasts that underlies the production of all phonemes. These distinctive features were alluded to earlier, in our discussion of the various subgroups within the larger category of consonants (continuant versus stop, voiced versus voiceless, alveolar versus labial, and so forth). Within a matrix of roughly fifteen such contrasts, all the known phonemic categories can be described. A portion of that matrix is shown below (from Dale, 1976):

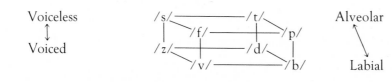

As these articulatory contrasts develop, more and more consonants appear. Certain of these are universal in that they appear in every language.

Jakobson's first principle, the *universality of contrasts*, stipulates that contrasts occur in every language and that those contrasts that seem to be universal in all languages are the first to appear in individual development. The laws of *irreversible solidarity*, Jakobson's second principle, then govern the order in which the rest of the phonemes appear. For example, some languages have front consonants without having back consonants, but no language has the reverse. (Front and back consonants are distinguished on the basis of where they are articulated in the mouth.) Thus front consonants can be considered to be a prerequisite for back consonants, and they will emerge first in languages that have both types (Dale, 1976). Jakobson's third principle, involving frequency of phonemes in the languages of the world, implies that it is *frequency of occurrence in all languages* (not just in the particular language under consideration) that determines which phonemes will appear earliest in children's speech. This principle suggests that the more universal a phoneme is, the earlier it will occur in development. Clearly, Jakobson aligns with the predeterminist-preformationist camp by suggesting an innate biological competence with which all human infants are endowed to account for generalities in language acquisition that occur regardless of the specific language being acquired.

As development progresses, children begin to combine phonemes into units called *morphemes*, which represent the smallest meaningful units within a language. English examples include *car, book, un-, -ful, and,* and *-ed*. That there are laws of phonemic combination is apparent from the fact that certain combinations are never formed. Dale (1976) gives the example of the words *brick,* *blik,* and *bnik.* The first is an English word; the second could become an English word; but the third will never become an English word because the combination *bn* is forbidden in English (whereas *bl* is allowed). Rules specifying permissible combinations of phonemes are called *morpheme structure rules* (Chomsky & Halle, 1968). As was the case with syntax, these rules operate on an underlying representation (deep structure) of the morpheme to produce the surface, phonetic representation.

It is interesting to note that there is a greater correspondence between the structure of written words and their underlying representations than there is between the written words and their phonetic equivalents—the surface structure heard in speech. As a result, there are often severe departures from an idealized one-to-one correspondence between the phonemic representation one hears and the *graphemic* representation (written letters of the alphabet) that one reads. This has a number of implications for the teaching of reading. First, since the goal of reading is to obtain the meaning that the author wished to convey, less emphasis should be placed on relating the written to the spoken word in a perfect one-to-one fashion (which ultimately will fail). Rather, an effort should be made to convey to children the more direct relationship that the written word has to the underlying meaning. Table 12.5 presents an example of this principle.

For the reasons presented above, practice at reading aloud in a sense runs at cross-purposes with the ultimate goal of reading. However, a child of five or six who is just starting to read may not yet have mastered this dual phonological system of relating deep and surface structures, which is, in fact, the last step in phonological development. Thus the only way the child can gain access to the meaning is through the sound. One method of dealing with this problem is first to present words for which the grapheme-to-phoneme correspondence is high

TABLE 12.5
The Relationship
of Written
Versus Spoken
Words to
Meaning

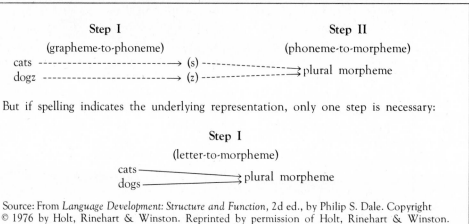

	Step I	Step II
	(grapheme-to-phoneme)	(phoneme-to-morpheme)
cats	----------------------→ (s)	--------------→ plural morpheme
dogz	----------------------→ (z)	--------------→ plural morpheme

But if spelling indicates the underlying representation, only one step is necessary:

Step I

(letter-to-morpheme)

cats ———→ plural morpheme
dogs ———→ plural morpheme

Source: From *Language Development: Structure and Function,* 2d ed., by Philip S. Dale. Copyright © 1976 by Holt, Rinehart & Winston. Reprinted by permission of Holt, Rinehart & Winston.

and then later to introduce word groups that will enable the child to construct the underlying representations of words with less grapheme-to-phoneme correspondence (Dale, 1976). Such a process not only will facilitate reading development but also will contribute to the completion of phonological development as a whole.

Semantic Development and the Functions of Language

The study of *semantics*, or the meaning of language, is one of the most difficult problems confronting psycholinguistics and is presently one of the least understood areas of human psychology. Not the least of our difficulties here is the fact that meaning is among the knottiest of philosophical problems, and the source of little agreement. In the absence of a clear statement regarding the nature of semantics, it becomes all the more difficult to formulate an outline of its development. Although a number of theoretical positions have been presented, each deals with only a small range of phenomena taken in isolation. When confronted with the vast number of things that may be discussed and the variety of ways in which we can discuss them, all theories ultimately prove inadequate.

Behaviorist Approach to Semantics

According to the behaviorist position, the meaning of a word in a sentence is a function of the situation in which it is emitted and the response that it elicits. In the Skinnerian model, a child's verbal behavior comes under stimulus control when he or she is reinforced for emitting the appropriate word or words in response to either internal stimuli (for example, saying "Milk" when hungry) or external stimuli (saying "Doggie" when a dog is nearby). Skinner refers to the first situation as *manding* (presumably, from "demanding"), and he calls the second *tacting* (for coming verbally in "contact" with an external object). In the behaviorist approach, then, meaning is derived from reference. As Dale (1976) points out, however, this explanation has three notable deficiencies. First, sentences can contain several phrases that have the same referent but different meanings. The two phrases "Sir Walter Scott" and "the author of *Waverly*" provide an example. In the sentence "Sir Walter Scott is the author of *Waverly*," both phrases have the same referent; but if they also had the same meaning, the sentence would be pointless. Thus in this example there is not a one-to-one correspondence between the meaning and the referent. A second problem is that one word can have two referents. Obvious examples are such words as *I, you, here, there, yesterday,* and *tomorrow.* The meaning of each will vary with who is speaking, where, and when. Third, there are words such as *and, but, to, if, is,* and so forth that have no referents but can greatly influence the meaning of a sentence. Similarly, on the response side of the behaviorists' definition of meaning, a single sentence can elicit different and often quite unexpected or irrelevant responses, yet that does not alter the meaning of the original sentence. Furthermore, many sentences are meant simply to be informative. In such cases the response is most often covert, mentalistic, and idiosyncratic.

Predeterminist-Preformationist Approach to Semantics

The predeterminists-preformationists do not fare much better in explaining the development of semantic knowledge. The most substantial attempt at providing a description of the semantic structure of language from this perspective can be found in a paper by Katz and Fodor (1963), and the book by Katz and Postal (1964) that followed. Their main contribution to semantic theory was the notion that each word carries with it a number of semantic *markers,* or words that give clues about the meaning of key words. Often a single word can give rise to two strings of semantic markers; that is, one word can have two meanings. An example is the word *bat*:

$$bat = (noun) \nearrow \text{(inanimate), (wooden stick), (baseball)} \dots$$
$$\searrow \text{(animate), (flying mammal), (nocturnal)} \dots$$

Within a sentence, the appropriate branch of the semantic tree is chosen on the basis of certain *selection restrictions* that operate between the semantic markers of different words (indicated above in parentheses). Thus if the word *wing* also appeared in a sentence with *bat*, it is likely that the branch leading to "flying mammal" represents the appropriate meaning.

The selection restrictions also operate between syntactic markers in the tree, which accounts for the role of syntax in word selection and semantics as seen in a study conducted by Miller and Isard (1963). These investigators asked subjects to "shadow" (repeat what they were hearing while they were hearing it) sentences of three different types. The sentences were presented amid noise (meaningless sound). Some sentences were grammatical and meaningful ("Grammatical"); some were grammatical but meaningless ("Anomalous"); and some were neither grammatical nor meaningful ("Ungrammatical"). Subjects were scored on the number of correctly perceived words or strings of words, examples of which follow:

Grammatical   Colorless cellophane packages crackle loudly.

Anomalous   Colorless yellow ideas sleep furiously.

Ungrammatical   Sleep roses dangerously young colorless.

Because subjects do better on the anomalous strings than on those that are ungrammatical, it can be argued that syntactic factors restrict the possibilities for each word and thus make the task somewhat easier. When the semantic component is added, of course, performance again improves.

McNeill (1970a) conducted a modified version of this study using children of different ages. While obtaining comparable results, he also showed that performance on anomalous and ungrammatical sentences improved little with age between five and eight years. Performance on grammatical sentences, on the other hand, improved gradually up to age seven, and then rose quite rapidly, far outstripping the other two types of word strings. Thus it was concluded that semantic development is far from complete by the age of seven, at which time it improves quite significantly.

Cognitive Development and Semantics

Relevant to the above findings is the fact that, when discussing semantic development, we must take general cognitive growth into consideration. At issue in this regard is the principal direction of causality between linguistic and cognitive development. We have discussed this earlier and noted that cultural relativists-determinists believe that the direction of causality is strictly from language to thought. There are two levels at which this can occur in the model. First, the various vocabulary items available to a speaker tend to divide the world into different categories in different cultures. For example, the Eskimos recognize three types of snow and have a word for each, whereas the English language has only one word for all three types. At a deeper level, the grammatical relationships embodied in a language are held to greatly influence the course and content of thought. Whorf (1956) points to the language of the Hopi Indians, which has grammatical forms for indicating the validity of statements but none for indicating tense. This, Whorf believed, gives the Hopi's philosophical outlook a timelessness in which there is an absence of any sense of historical progression. Unfortunately, it is quite difficult to determine which came first—the philosophical outlook or the grammatical structure of the language. Therefore, Whorf has been criticized for being circular in his interpretation.

Brown and Lenneberg (1954) conducted a study to investigate the effects of word categories on cognitive functions in the perception of colors. In this study, a color chip was presented briefly, and later the subjects were asked to select the chip from a group of similar chips in which it was placed. The investigators rated the subjects' performance (percentage correct) against the color's "codability," which was determined by the length of the phrase needed to categorize the color and the amount of agreement among the subjects in their categorizations. The shorter the phrase and the greater the subject agreement, the higher the codability score. A small positive correlation was found between codability and accuracy of recognition; when the task was made more difficult by lengthening the memory interval, the correlation rose. Colors that were delimited more precisely by language were remembered better, suggesting that language may affect what is perceived. The same experiment was conducted with Zuni Indians, and the same results were obtained. The only exception was that different colors had different codabilities between the two linguistic communities. For example, Zunis do not distinguish in a highly codable fashion between blue and green, for which they have only one word to describe the entire color range.

This experiment and several others have led psycholinguists to conclude that languages differ not so much in what can be said in them but in what is relatively more or less difficult to say in them (Hockett, 1954). It is not clear from the above experiments if it is actually more difficult for Zunis to *perceive* various shades of blue than it is for English-speaking people. However, the cultural relativist–determinist position, which postulates that language shapes thought, would suggest that this would be the case—that language would shape the way the world is perceived.

Interactionists have taken a somewhat more conservative stance on the issue of how language affects thought, and they argue among themselves over the exact function of language in aiding cognitive growth. In Bruner's opinion (Bruner et al., 1966), language can facilitate the transition from nonconserving thought to the attainment of conservation (see Chapter 13 for a discussion of conservation ability). Piaget, on the other hand, maintains that language simply facilitates the expression and manipulation of these notions once they have been obtained. For Piaget, maturation and interaction with the environment foster cognitive development. Use of language itself does not cause cognitive growth. Until the knowledge communicated in the linguistic symbolization of that knowledge is acquired through maturation and experience, according to Piaget and his colleagues, the linguistic symbols cannot bring about real understanding. This is a profound and philosophically well-taken position, as it becomes difficult for Bruner to explain how his linguistic "goads" to understanding gain their ability to overcome the compelling perceptual evidence that misleads the child in the conservation task. Piaget takes the position that rather than containing the knowledge itself, the language is an extremely fluid symbolic medium in which to manipulate one's thoughts. Further, he believes that the laws of grammar are an expression of the very processes that underlie all perceptual and cognitive growth, and are thus the innate source of linguistic competence. However, we then must ask what is going on in children of nine to eighteen months that—from the perspective of intellectual growth—can rival the maturation of a unique LAD. In this period a child's conception of reality is being broadened gradually from its original perceptually immediate stage to one that is more symbolic and less constrained by immediate considerations of space and time. Sinclair-DeZwart (1969) provides an interesting example of this development:

First, one sees action-schemes appear out of their proper context as representations (for instance, pretending to be asleep); then, these representations become detached from the subject (for instance, putting a doll to sleep). Slowly these deferred imitations become interiorized, and constitute sketchy images, which the child can use to anticipate further acts. (p. 319)

Thus the processes of symbolic play, deferred imitation, and mental images reflect a state of cognitive development that is ripe for the advent of language. With maturation, language is explored and manipulated until it attains its central function in hypothetico-deductive thought. In introducing one of Piaget's books, Elkind observes:

Thought derives from the abstraction of one's own actions upon things. Ordering objects, putting them into groups, transforming them in multiple ways in motor manipulations provide the basis for those abstractions which become mental operations. (Piaget, 1967, p. xvi)

These, then, provide the form and substance of grammatical transformations such as negation and passive construction. In this sense it is not language that shapes cognition. Language is rather an outgrowth of sensorimotor manipulations that also form the rudimentary beginnings of complex cognition.

Russian psycholinguists such as Vygotsky (1962) take a somewhat different view of language and cognition. They believe that cognition develops as an internalization of a previously oversocialized external speech that is basically emotive or imitative in nature and meant solely for social interaction. As language develops, a child's verbal behavior splits along two functional paths: one maintains the primarily communicative function; the other becomes more highly egocentric and idiosyncratic. In the latter case, unnecessary words are streamlined away, leaving a "language" that consists primarily of predicates. Gradually children cease to utter this egocentric speech, internalizing it as the basis for their cognitive processes. Luria (1961) argues that in its earliest stages language is used simply as might be any guiding physical stimulus, as a signal in the regulation of behavioral sequences. Words act simply as impulses that tell a child to "act now." It is only later that language assumes its symbolic or semantic regulating properties. Unfortunately, the manner in which this is accomplished is not particularly clear.

Semantic Development over the Life Span

From this discussion of various theoretical perspectives on the development of semantics, it is clear that the manner in which the meaning of language is acquired is poorly understood. Compared with syntax and phonology, semantic development appears to be the last of the three linguistic competencies to develop fully, and it is also the competence that continues to grow over the life span.

We have discussed language development almost entirely from the perspective of infancy and childhood, and this seems justified in the case of syntactic and phonological development, which appear to be completed early in life. Our scant knowledge about semantic development in childhood is matched by the paucity of study of semantic development beyond childhood. Indeed, it appears that simple semantic development in terms of understanding the meanings of words is one of the competencies that shows a continuous increment. Vocabulary is greater in old age than it is in middle or young adulthood (Birren, 1964).

Although increasing verbal proficiency appears to accompany age, the ability of individuals to process information in a meaningful way may decrease with age. Recent approaches to the study of memory have emphasized the *depth of processing* concept. The idea is that the more deeply the material is processed, the better it will be remembered. It has been demonstrated that when people process information in a meaningful way—when they use semantic processing— they remember more than if they do not process the information meaningfully. A typical example of semantic processing would be to think of words as pleasant or unpleasant. Counting the number of *e*'s and *g*'s in words, on the other hand, is a nonsemantic task. Young subjects remember more words in the semantic than in the nonsemantic condition. The same is true for old people, although

Language development and aging must receive greater research attention.

Paul S. Conklin

the differences between young and old in the semantic condition are great (Eysenck, 1974; Smith, 1979). The ability of old people to process and remember words in a meaningful way appears to have declined. While additional research is needed, it has been suggested that the old have difficulty with the semantic task because they no longer are capable of the depth of processing possible in young adulthood.

Given the vast individual differences in interpretations of meaning within a given language—not to mention the variety encountered when all languages are considered—it is questionable if many generalizations about semantic development in adulthood will emerge. At this point in developmental psychology, it is clear that development and aging in terms of adult language and thought must be given greater consideration and research attention if we are to understand and discover lawful patterns of behavior in later stages of life.

Dialects and Development

So bimeby she tell me, "Florsheim, you gotta go night school learn speak haole no kanaka," and I tellem, "Go to hell. I ketchem airplane Hawaii," and she speak me, "Wha' you gonna use money da kine?" and I tellem, "Seven hunnerd dollars I scoop f'um you," and she speak, "You dirty boa', you filthy mountain pig!" and what I tellem den, I ain't gonna repeat.

James A. Michener, *Hawaii* (1959)

I seen all the towns. I seen all of them. When the bus got to going good, I found out I was jest about wore out for sleep. But there was too much I hadn't never saw before. We run out of Jefferson and run past fields and woods, then we would run into another town and out of that un and past fields and woods again, and then into another town with stores and gins and water tanks, and we run along by the railroad for a spell and I seen the signal arm move, and then I seen the train and then some more towns, and I was jest about plumb wore out for sleep, but I couldn't resk it.

William Faulkner, *Two Soldiers* (1933)

And for ther is so gret diversite
In Englissh, and in writyng of oure tonge,
So prey I god that non myswrite the,
Ne the mys-metre for defaute of tonge.

Geoffrey Chaucer, *Troilus and Criseyde* (1385)

Although most English-speaking people can recognize what is being said in the three quotations above, there is a vast difference in how the language is articulated. All three quotations are examples of dialects of contemporary English; however, the third quotation reflects standard English as it was years ago. *Dialects* are variants of the standard form of a language. It is characteristic of a dialect that some of the phonological or syntactic rules have been modified. The dialect remains recognizable to the native speaker because the dialect retains a substantial proportion of the basic grammatical structure of the original language.

The first two quotations above reflect social and geographical differences in the English language, with pidgin English representing a dialect used primarily by lower-class Hawaiians and rural Southern English representing the speech of less educated people living in rural sections of the American South. Variations in dialect as a function of social and geographical conditions are the primary focus of study for sociolinguists. In the past, linguists were concerned primarily with dialect differences resulting from geographical variation. Sociologists were interested in the effect of social class on language. However, Dale (1976) points out that the study of one aspect without the other leads to significant oversights, and so the field of sociolinguistics was developed to combine the insights of both perspectives.

Another factor that leads to changes in language and to different dialects is time. As indicated in the third example above, the language spoken by our English ancestors and even by our American forebears was vastly different from contemporary speech. Indeed, language changes so rapidly that within a person's lifetime his or her colloquialisms often become obsolete. Many parents have difficulty communicating with their adolescent children, and not only because of emotional barriers. Often the young develop their own slang to provide themselves with a unique way of communicating. Slang changes with each generation so that the youth of the 1980s would not have been able to understand youthful expressions of 1910. For this reason, Monge (1971) was able to construct a vocabulary test on which old people scored extremely well whereas middle-aged and young adults failed. Monge simply chose words that were obsolete in contemporary usage but had been popular at the beginning of the century. Sometimes it is even possible to determine an individual's age by his or her speech, for people tend to continue to use the language of their youth throughout their adult lives.

Even though people often use the language form prevalent during their youth, one would not expect a contemporary forty-year-old to use terms like "daddy-o" or "cool." These slang terms were undoubtedly standard during that person's adolescence, but individuals modify their own dialect as a function of their age, situation, profession, social class, and even the geographical region in which they speak. Besides the differences in dialects between groups, individuals adopt different speech patterns at different times. Labov (1970) demonstrated differences between groups as well as within individuals in different settings in the use of the endings -in' and ing. The less formal -in' changed in its frequency of usage by a given individual depending on whether the speech was casual, careful, or read. Different social classes also used the two endings with different frequency. The use of the dialect form -in' decreased with increasing social class within any given context. However, as an individual in any one social class moved from a less formal to a more formal context, the use of the dialect form decreased.

Dialects identify differences among individuals, and for centuries prejudice has flourished against those who speak differently from the majority. Snobbishness and mistrust arise when people of different social classes detect their differences through language. The mere sound of a Yankee twang once was enough to evoke hatred in the American South. Indeed, one's life might depend on the appropriate dialect, as in the following Biblical anecdote:

The Gileadites seized the fords of the Jordan and held them against Ephraim. When any Ephraimite who had escaped begged leave to cross, the men of Gilead asked him, "Are you an Ephraimite?", and if he said "No," they would retort, "Say Shibboleth." He would say "Sibboleth," and because he could not pronounce the word properly, they seized him and killed him at the fords of the Jordan. At that time forty-two thousand men of Ephraim lost their lives.

Judges 12: 5-6: New English Bible

Today the forfeit of life is no longer the cost of speaking a dialect, but dialects do exist that are not popular with most English speakers. Perhaps the best-known English dialect is that spoken by many black Americans, which is now formally called Black English. This is probably the most widespread nonstandard dialect and the one on which there has been the greatest amount of research. Not all blacks speak this dialect, of course, nor is it unique to blacks. Many southern regional dialects carry the same features. However, it is the dialect most often spoken by blacks, and it is spoken or understood by a large number of this minority group. Studies have identified syntactic and phonological differences between Black English and standard English, and the vocabulary is also somewhat distinct.

Stewart (1964) has shown that in the Washington, D.C. area there are two forms of this dialect. The first, *acrolect*, is closer to standard English and is spoken primarily by adults and older children; the second, *basilect*, is spoken chiefly by young children. At the age of seven the dialect of the child usually switches to acrolect, but this does not seem to result from formal education. What does seem to be important is that the child's peer-group status at this time changes from that of being, say, a "little boy" to being a "big boy." Accordingly, some argue that the peer group is more important for language learning than the parents. However, Dale (1976) points out that this belief arises out of a confusion of linguistic performance with linguistic competence. In the Labov (1970) study described previously, performance improved with the context; however, no one would argue that the competence improved also. Similarly, the young children in Stewart's study had no trouble understanding their parents and thus must have had competence in both forms of Black English. Apparently, when the child changes peer groups, motivational factors influence the choice of the competence on which the child comes to rely.

Many have argued that black children have less competence because of their use of Black English. It has been suggested that the language is impoverished or retarded and that this results in poor school performance and deficient intelligence. It is possible that some black children do have difficulties in language development. However, Dale (1976) argues persuasively that the verbal-deficit hypothesis is based on questionable assumptions and evidence. For example, the position that Black English leads to poor school performance assumes that language plays a predominant role in thinking. This is an extremely controversial position, and many cognitive specialists maintain that the capacities for thought and language have parallel development. Language development does not necessarily cause cognitive development. Another problem with the verbal-deficit hypothesis is that it does not separate structure from function. Are the children unable to master the linguistic system, or are they unable to use language in various cognitive tasks? Third, race and social class usually are confounded in studies supporting the verbal-deficit hypothesis, because middle-class whites are compared with lower-class blacks. The effects of poverty on cognition are well documented and should not be confused with the effects of language. Finally, samples of black speech taken by white examiners fail to reflect the capacity of the children, who are undoubtedly uncomfortable and unnatural in the testing situation. There is great emphasis on verbal fluency in the black culture, but this is missed by many white examiners. Furthermore, on most tests of comprehension of standard English, there is evidence of considerable knowledge of the mainstream language by black children. Black English has been poorly understood by psychologists, educators, and others, who perhaps have overrated it as a source of difficulty in cognitive development.

Summary

1. Language emerges early in life and remains relatively fixed over the life span. Language development is a robust phenomenon occurring with remarkable regularity in spite of environmental or physical variation.
2. Language capacity in most people is localized primarily in the left side of the brain. Anatomical asymmetries in the left and right halves of the brains of neonates suggest that the brain may be specialized for language at birth.

Slow or deficient brain lateralization may be associated with problems of language and proficiency in school.

3. There are four major theoretical perspectives on the nature of language and its acquisition. Of these, the *behaviorist position* emphasizes learning and experience most. This position stipulates that language is acquired by the same simple mechanisms of association that govern learning in all species. Reinforcement of sounds and appropriate utterances accounts for the acquisition of language.

4. The *cultural relativist-determinist position* emphasizes the environment and focuses on the role of language in determining thought. The structure of language affects the individual's world view. This position does not have a model for language acquisition.

5. The *interactionist model* stresses the interactive nature of the environment and innate capacities in the development of language. Learning and maturation are interdependent in this model. Language emerges as a system of representation that facilitates general cognitive functioning.

6. The *preformationist-predeterminist position* represents the dominant theoretical model in modern linguistics. It emphasizes the significance of innate language capacity, postulating a language acquisition device (LAD) that is unique in the human brain. All sentences are seen as having a surface structure (or form of the sentence) and a deep structure (or idea underlying the sentence). At the level of the deep structure, all languages share the same rules.

7. The development of syntax or grammar does not appear to occur as predicted by behaviorists. Development of syntax is not gradual and smooth but appears to be guided by a child's rule-forming behavior.

8. Preformationists-predeterminists attempt to account for the ability to generate an unlimited number of sentences with a limited vocabulary. They postulate the existence of an underlying set of rules that allow an individual to combine the units of a finite vocabulary to produce an unlimited number of grammatically correct sentences. The LAD enables children to sort out the rules of grammar for their particular language.

9. The first stage of syntactic development occurs when a child utters one-word sentences (holophrases) early in the second year. By eighteen to twenty months of age, a second stage is reached when two-word sentences are uttered.

10. Phonological development, or the development of a sound system, appears to be explained best as primarily an innately developing phenomenon.

11. The manner in which the meaning of language, or semantics, is acquired is poorly understood. Full semantic development appears to occur later than syntactic or phonological development, and it is a competence that continues to grow over the life span. However, meaningful processing of material may decline in late life.

12. Dialects vary as a function of social class, geographical location, age, and social situation. Black English is the most widespread American dialect. While some have attributed poor school performance in black children to the use of Black English, the evidence for this position is not strong.

Selected Readings

Dale, P. S. *Language Development: Structure and Function.* 2nd ed. New York: Holt, Rinehart and Winston, 1976. A comprehensive overview of the recent research on language development.

Lenneberg, E. H. *Biological Foundations of Language.* New York: Wiley, 1967. Presents the predeterminist-preformationist approach to language development.

Skinner, B. F. *Verbal Behavior.* New York: Appleton-Century-Crofts, 1957. Presents the behaviorist approach to language development.

Whorf, B. *Language, Thought and Reality.* Cambridge, Mass.: MIT Press, 1956. Language development from the perspective of the cultural relativist-determinist position.

Chapter 13

Intelligence

Two basic approaches to defining intelligence: the quantitative approach and the qualitative approach

The major theories about intellectual development and intelligence

How intelligence is measured throughout the life span

The uses and problems of intelligence tests and how to improve them

Introduction

Almost everyone holds some sort of concept about what constitutes intelligent behavior. Yet surprisingly enough, neither psychologists nor laypeople have been able to define intelligence in a way that receives universal acceptance. The problem of definition becomes even more difficult when we consider intelligence from a developmental perspective. Intelligent behavior in an infant does not constitute intelligent behavior in a four-year-old or an adult. Furthermore, it is difficult to predict intelligence on the basis of performance as an infant. This problem arises because we use sensorimotor behavior to assess intelligence in infancy, whereas verbal and symbolic behavior are used to measure intelligence in children and adults.

The discrepancy in measurement illustrates a basic issue in the study of intelligence: we have to rely on observable behavior in order to evaluate what we believe to be an innate capacity of an organism. So although the concept of intelligence has been used to encompass the totality of the human mind and

The study of intelligence runs into problems both with definitions and with predictions.

499

imagination, performance on one or another of the numerous intelligence tests has become the critical measure of intellectual capacity.

If we could "look" into the brain and examine that entity that is intelligence, it would be possible to predict an infant's cognitive capacity for life, just as it is possible to examine an infant's bone structure and predict fairly accurately the adult size that will be attained. Although it is assumed that there are probably some physiological substrates of intelligence, we cannot yet examine those substrates, for the biological mechanisms of intelligence are not understood. Hence, in the absence of brain damage, physiological correlates of intelligence are difficult to identify. However, attempts *are* under way to relate physiological measures (such as a brain-wave measure called the *averaged evoked potential*) to behavioral measures of intelligence. This work is in very early stages, however, and presently the clearest criterion we can use to evaluate the validity of intelligence tests is that of usefulness. In short, does the test provide reliable predictions about other behavior?

Some Definitions of Intelligence

Intelligence has been defined in at least four ways:

1. The ability to carry on abstract thinking (Terman, 1921)
2. The aggregate or global capacity of an individual to act purposefully, to think rationally, and to deal effectively with the environment (Wechsler, 1944)
3. Adaptive thinking or action (Piaget, 1950)
4. Innate, general, cognitive ability

These definitions refer to intellectual capacity in an individual. However, we must observe behavior in order to evaluate intelligence. Thus inferences about intellectual capacity must be drawn from observable performance on some task, and intelligence tests consist of samples of behavior on a variety of tasks designed to tap whatever the investigators' definition of intelligence may include. Reese and Lipsitt (1970) suggest that the particular tasks that go into each intelligence test vary as widely as do the psychologists' definitions, so that what constitutes intelligent behavior in one test battery may not even be considered on another test battery.

Is intelligence consistent over the life span? The data we will explore in this chapter suggest that there does appear to be some consistency over the life span in terms of scores achieved on intelligence tests. On the other hand, we learned in Chapter 3 that such scores can be influenced by a variety of environmental factors. We will explore different approaches to intelligence and thinking, noting that these topics can be approached from a qualitative as well as a quantitative perspective. In other words, the structure of cognitive behavior as well as the number, variety, and speed of responses can be evaluated, and these qualitative and quantitative aspects are not always highly related. The qualitative approach has been taken by the eminent Swiss psychologist Jean Piaget, whereas the quantitative approach was used originally by the French psychologist Alfred

Binet, who devised the notion of the intelligence quotient (IQ). The quantitative approach later was taken by such well-known psychologists as Terman, Spearman, Guilford, and Cattell.

Quantitative Approaches to Intelligence

Intelligence testing began in France early in the twentieth century with Alfred Binet, who worked with Théodore Simon, a psychiatrist, to identify backward children in the schools of Paris. School authorities sought to separate students who lacked motivation and interest from those who clearly did not have the capacity to perform well in the regular school curriculum. Binet began by carefully observing his own children and the development of their ability to master certain tasks. He believed he would be able to measure the general level of any particular child's intelligence much as one would measure with a ruler; in this manner Binet wanted to devise a metric scale of intelligence. His end product consisted of a series of ingenious and carefully graded tests of comprehension, memory, judgment, ability to detect absurdities, capacity to resist foolish suggestion, cleverness, and penetration. Grading was achieved by ordering the tests by level of difficulty, administering them to large numbers of schoolchildren, and noting the average age at which each task could be completed. The *intelligence quotient* was a score assigned to a child on the basis of performance relative to other children in the age group. Thus if a seven-year-old passed all the questions typically passed by ten-year-olds, that child was assigned a mental age of ten. The IQ would then be computed by dividing the mental age by the chronological age and multiplying by 100. Thus

$$IQ = \frac{\text{Mental age}}{\text{Chronological age}} \times 100$$

Much remains of the legacy of intelligence testing first generated by Binet—for example, the intelligence quotient, the variety of tasks used in the test, and the selection of items based on the ability of children of a given age to pass them. Binet's test was brought to the United States by Lewis Terman, and a modified and updated version of this test is still used widely and is considered to be one of the best measures of IQ for children. This American version is known as the *Stanford-Binet Intelligence Scale*. In a landmark study, Terman used the Stanford-Binet to identify and follow up individuals of extremely high intelligence, and his longitudinal studies of genius have provided some of the most interesting and provocative life-span data on IQ available. These fascinating data are an important source for our knowledge of intelligence over the life span, since Terman's subjects have been observed from childhood to adulthood (hopefully, data also will be collected when the subjects reach old age).

Virtually every individual who has gone through the United States public school system in the past several decades has received some type of IQ evaluation. Intelligence test items are thus familiar aspects of the educational experience. For example, the examiner might say to a seven-year-old, "Do you see this book? Put it on the chair by the door. Then open the door. Then come

The Stanford-Binet
Intelligence Scale—
brought to the United
States by Terman—is
still used widely and
is considered one of
the best measures of
IQ for children.

back here." To pass the item, the child must carry out all three commands
without error. In another type of item, the examiner reads five numbers (for
example, 3, 2, 5, 9, 6), and the child's task is to repeat the numbers either
forward or backward. Or a child might be asked to arrange five cubes that look
much the same but that vary in weight in order from lightest to heaviest, or to
look for a few seconds at several designs and then to draw them from memory.
The child might also be asked to identify what is wrong with a statement like
"Yesterday the police found the body of a girl cut into eighteen pieces. They
believe that she killed herself." Cattell (1971) reports that this ghoulish item
was used in the European versions of Binet's tests but was omitted from the
American translation.

The variety of questions asked is intended to tap a number of different
abilities that are thought to be components of intelligence. Whether all these
abilities are related to one general intelligence factor or whether intellectual
abilities are independent and non-overlapping is one of the continuing debates
concerning intelligence. This debate began early in the history of intelligence
testing, with Charles Spearman, the other prominent psychologist (along with
Binet) who was concerned with intelligence around 1900.

Spearman was more interested in the theoretical issues surrounding the concept of intelligence, whereas Binet sought to solve the practical problem of
identifying retardates. Binet's assemblage of a variety of seemingly unrelated
tests appeared to imply that intelligence consisted of a group of unrelated abilities. But Spearman considered that intelligence might involve a large single,
general capacity as well as some specific abilities. He sought answers to questions like, "Could a person be quite a genius at mathematical problems, a perfect

fool at expressing himself in writing, and an average man in handling sensitive social situations?" Such divergence in abilities in one individual seemed improbable to Spearman, who very early and very clearly asked some of the most critical questions about the nature of human intelligence.

Spearman also developed a highly original and effective method for answering questions about the generalizable aspects of intelligence (Cattell, 1971). His technique, known as *factor analysis,* involves a statistical methodology for observing the relationships among a large number of items (such as the ones found on intelligence tests). With this technique it is possible to observe whether certain types of items tend to be answered in the same way—that is, whether they tend to be related, or correlated. Groups of items that are highly intercorrelated are identified as *factors,* and a typical intelligence test is composed of a large number of items that fall into at least several different factors. Unfortunately, factor analytic techniques have not resolved whether there are one or many components of intelligence, for different factor analytic techniques yield different results. Views range from Spearman's position that there is one general (g) factor of intelligence, to Thorndike's view that there are a "few big abilities," to the view that appeared in Binet's work and was stated more strongly by Watson (1913) and other learning theorists that intelligence is a vast collection of specific acquired competencies.

For developmental psychologists, the concept of factors of intelligence raises a whole new group of questions. For example, are intellectual factors the same over the life span, or are there different components of intelligence that are different at different ages? Do some factors remain stable while others change? Does the interrelation among factors and the number of factors remain constant? Thus the emergence of intelligence as a multivariate trait makes the issue of the development and aging of intellectual behavior all the more complicated.

Although intelligence testing techniques represent an important advance in the search for objective answers about human ability, IQ scores have become such a critical means of categorizing and labeling individuals that their usefulness may have been overgeneralized. Tests developed and standardized on urban middle-class white students may be unfair when used for rural or minority students, who have had different life experiences. Even "culture-free" tests must be administered in a circumscribed manner by specific types of testers for their results to be optimal. Furthermore, situational factors can influence tests so much that scores can fluctuate ten to twenty points within a short time period. Thus to take a test score obtained at one sitting by one examiner and then to classify a child as belonging within a certain environment for several years is a practice that reflects a great overestimation of the reliability and validity of intelligence tests.

Qualitative Approaches to Intelligence

Besides the pragmatic approach to intelligence that was initiated by the test construction methods of Binet, observational techniques have been used to build theories of intellectual development by such psychologists as Piaget, Kagan, and Bruner, among others. Rather than emphasizing the *number* of tasks children can do at a given age, these psychologists have chosen to describe the *nature* of children's thinking at various ages. This qualitative approach has led to the identification of stages of thinking through which normal children proceed. It has been determined that children at different stages conceptualize problems in qualitatively different ways, at first most influenced by immediate perceptual cues and at later stages more tempered by cognitive experiences. Recent research suggests that some of these qualitative changes in thinking may be reversed in old age. Therefore, although most applications of qualitative analysis to human thinking have been made at the early stages of development, some researchers have also pointed out the applicability of these methods to the study of cognition in middle and old age (for example, see Birren, 1969; Papalia, 1972).

Theories of Cognitive and Intellectual Development

Just as intelligence has been measured and studied from qualitative and quantitative approaches, so have theories of intellectual development been constructed from both approaches. The following discussion explores theories about cognition that most directly deal with developmental issues and that have the most relevance for a life-span perspective. Although many theories involve intellectual development in children, few have been concerned with mental growth and change after maturity. This state of affairs is typical of the life-span material on cognition. Although theories of intellectual development have been worked out to some degree for the early stages of the life span, the development of adult intellectual abilities has been approached mainly through

Although studies of intellectual development in the early stages of life are based to some degree on theory, adult intellectual abilities have been studied mainly through empirical approaches.

Constantine Manos, Magnum Photos, Inc.

empirical and descriptive strategies that pay relatively little attention to theory. Because our interest as developmentalists centers on cognitive theories that are relevant for life-span conceptualizations of intelligence, we will examine three theoretical approaches to intelligence: those of Piaget, Guilford, and Cattell and Horn.

Piaget: Periods of Cognitive Development

A general theory of cognitive growth is the product of the careful observations, clever insights, and systematic studies of Swiss psychologist Jean Piaget and his colleagues, who have investigated the development of cognition for over sixty years. It would be hard to overemphasize the impact of Piaget's viewpoint on developmental psychology. Besides its conceptual value, Piaget's theory has stimulated a tremendous literature on the development of thinking that has implications for students of language, perception, and education as well as for those studying intelligence and cognition. In essence, Piaget demonstrated just how different a child's thinking is from an adult's.

Piaget generated his theory by employing a case study method. He observed and recorded the play behavior or motor movement of his own three children during infancy, manipulating the children's environment to test his speculations about their thought processes triggered by their behavior. Although this method may not be particularly strong in terms of scientific evidence, the force of Piaget's genius and imagination—along with innumerable systematic studies involving children of all ages—have led to the creation of one of the most highly regarded theories in developmental psychology.

According to Piaget, adult intelligence is qualitatively different from that of a child, but all levels of intelligence are defined in terms of "adaptive thinking and action." Children arrive at the adult stage by passing through the four major stages of conceptualization presented in Table 13.1. Piaget believes that the ages at which individuals attain the various stages are somewhat variable and depend on environmental influences, but that the sequence of development is always the same. Thus the formal operational stage can be attained only if a child has progressed first through the sensorimotor, the preoperational, and the concrete operational stages (in that order). This process begins in infancy with the processing of sensorimotor information and progresses to the formal operational stage, typically attained by age fifteen.

Stage	Age
Sensorimotor	0–2
Preoperational	2–7
Concrete operations	7–12
Formal operations	12–adult

TABLE 13.1
Piaget's Periods of Cognitive Development

Piaget and the Scientific Basis for Open Education

Piaget's cognitive-developmental theory has several important implications for educational practice, including the ideas that (1) a child's individual development proceeds through an orderly sequence of stages and that instruction should suit the level or stage of the learner; (2) human beings are intrinsically motivated to learn, to move toward higher and more sophisticated levels of thinking, and to be most interested in intellectual materials that best promote further development; and (3) human beings learn best if they become actively involved in the material. The concern of those advocating the "open classroom" approach has been to give individual students more freedom and more active roles in their own learning—ranging from greater freedom to move about the classroom (or even beyond it) to more responsibility and greater choice concerning when and in which particular activities to engage.

The basic pedagogical principles derived from the work of developmental psychologists such as Piaget have brought about a profound restructuring of the educational system in British primary schools—a restructuring that is generally in the direction of open education. The results have been encouraging for the most part, and the model has become the standard toward which all British primary schools should aim, as endorsed by the massive Plowden Report evaluating British primary education.

The results of open education programs in the United States are mixed—with disappointments in some schools and encouraging progress in others. One reason for the failure of many well-intentioned but poorly planned open schools may have been a prevalent misconception that confuses the open approach with a laissez-faire one. Many people misperceive the open school as one in which students are active while the teacher is passive and nondirective. In fact, *both* teacher and students are likely to play a highly active role in a well-run open classroom. However, the teacher's task in effectively playing an active role is demanding. The teacher is asked to stimulate the intellectual development of each child, to diagnose each child's learning strengths and weaknesses, and to provide a variety of interesting materials that promote balanced and vigorous intellectual growth and mastery of academic skills. Moreover, this must be accomplished in a way that encourages children to become active problem-solvers and to take increasing responsibility for, and enjoyment in, their own learning. Another important teaching role is to promote personal growth by showing respect for the feelings and cognitive and personal styles of each student. The teacher must strive for warmth and honesty in all encounters with the students.

Far from assigning the teacher a passive role, then, the effective open school is likely to require greater effort, energy, and planning than in the more traditional schools. The effort is worthwhile, however, in terms of greater potential rewards for teachers and students alike.

A large and growing body of research tends to support the Piagetian view that the sequence of cognitive development is universal. Although not every person may attain the highest stage, individuals of every culture and background pass through the same stages. Following is a description of the various stages of cognitive development as outlined in Piaget's theory.

The behavior of young children indicates that their world is perceived as a kaleidoscope of continuously changing objects and events.

Frank Siteman, Stock, Boston, Inc.

Sensorimotor Stage   In the early stages of infancy, behavior occurs as though the world was perceived as a kaleidoscope of continuously moving and changing objects and events. Young infants appear not to perceive permanence in objects; they behave as though they believe that objects that disappear from their sight no longer exist. The maxim "Out of sight, out of mind" appears to be literally true for infants. They can be engrossed in playing with a toy or a person, but if that object disappears from sight, they behave as though it no longer exists. This behavior begins to change during the closing months of the first year, when infants learn to seek out objects that have disappeared, thus attaching permanence to objects that are not present in sensory experience. At this point infants cry when left by their mother. Hence one of the major cognitive achievements of the sensorimotor period is the establishment of *object permanence*—the ability to be aware of the existence of objects even when they are not within sight or within a range where they can be touched, smelled, tasted, or heard.

Another major cognitive achievement in the sensorimotor stage is the acquisition of the notion of *causality*. During this period infants begin to note the results of their actions and to anticipate certain results before they occur. For example, infants learn to play and get attention by throwing their toys out of their crib. When they knock a toy out of the crib, they may look to the floor in anticipation that it will fall, and they also may anticipate an adult's reaction of picking up the toy and returning it. *Spatial concepts* are also established during this period, as infants learn (only too well) how to gain access to every part of their home.

During the first two years of life, infants make remarkable progress in their thinking about the world. Their concepts develop from perceiving the world only in terms of immediate sensorimotor experience to gaining a notion of object permanence, causality, and space. These changes are so extensive that Piaget breaks the first two years of life into a series of six substages. Before describing the specific events of infancy, however, we need to examine some Piagetian concepts that relate to cognitive development as a whole.

Although infants in their first years of life do not acquire the ability to represent the world internally, Piaget feels that the sensorimotor stage is significant because infants construct all the cognitive substructures that will serve as a point of departure for the development of perception and thinking. During this stage there is a continuous progression from spontaneous movements and natural reflexes, to acquired habits, to behavior clearly reflecting intelligence. Thus adaptive thinking, which is the basis for adult intelligence, has its foundation in the earliest years.

Piaget finds evidence for two forms of cognitive adaptation during the early stages of infancy: accommodation and assimilation. By *accommodation* Piaget means the ability of an organism to adapt to external stimuli (rather than to respond mechanically to stimuli); by *assimilation* he means the integration of stimuli into the organism's existing cognitive structures. An analogy often used to express the concepts of accommodation and assimilation is digestion (Ginsburg & Opper, 1969). For example, accommodation to food in the digestive system occurs when the muscles of the stomach contract, when organs secrete acids, and so forth. In short, the body changes itself in response to the food stimulus. Assimilation occurs when the food is acted upon by the body and is transformed into something the body can use.

The following psychological examples of accommodation and assimilation were provided by Piaget (1970):

> For example, the infant who assimilates his thumb to the sucking schema will, when sucking his thumb make different movements from those he uses in suckling his mother's breast. Similarly, an 8-year-old who is assimilating the dissolution of sugar in water to the notion that substance is conserved must make accommodations to invisible particles different from those he would make if they were still visible. (p. 708)

In the case of an infant, accommodation is a motor activity involving a reshaping of the sucking behavior; in the case of an eight-year-old, the accommodation is conceptual. That is, children must accommodate their former concepts of sugar to include the concept of sugar in a dissolved state in order to understand, or assimilate, what actually occurs when sugar is dissolved in water. A younger child, who is not able to accommodate the concept of sugar in this manner, believes that the sugar disappears.

Additional psychological examples of accommodation and assimilation are quoted from Piaget's observations of his children's development in the following paragraphs, which describe the six substages of the sensorimotor period.

Stage 1. In the first month of life, an infant increasingly perfects certain reflexes such as sucking. For example, in the first few days after birth, the baby finds the nipple more quickly and more easily (*functional assimilation*). Then the sucking reflex occurs in response to other objects as well as developing merely as an ongoing behavior of the infant (*generalizing assimilation*). Finally, toward the end of this stage, the infant appears to recognize the nipple as being different from other objects and to respond to it (*recognitive assimilation*).

Both accommodation and assimilation occur early in life. The following example of accommodation comes from Piaget's observations of his son, Laurent:

At 0; 0 (26) [26 days] Laurent ... feels the nipple in the middle of his right cheek. But as he tries to grasp it, it is withdrawn 10 cm. He then turns his head in the right direction and searches. This time he goes on to touch the nipple, first with his nose and then with the region between his nostrils and lip. He raises his head in order to grasp the nipple. (1952, p. 29)

In this example Laurent moves his body to reach the stimulus. He has accommodated in a very obvious and overt physical manner. Piaget views this rudimentary sensorimotor form of accommodation as the precursor of complex mental accommodation, in which, for example, an adult can accommodate his or her perspective to empathize with the viewpoint of a friend. An intermediary stage of accommodation might occur in a child who initiates a behavior that was not performed before. The child accommodates his or her manner of thinking and action to model another behavior. However, with these more complex examples of accommodation, we are getting far ahead of cognitive development as it occurs during the sensorimotor stage.

Stage 2. Primary circular reactions, such as systematic thumb-sucking, appear in stage 2 of the sensorimotor stage. Now an infant can bring the thumb to the mouth in order to suck, whereas in stage 1 the thumb would be sucked only if it randomly happened to end up in the mouth. Such reactions are termed *circular* inasmuch as they appear to be self-reinforcing, and they are *primary* because the content of the behavior seems to have biological origins. Thus primary circular reactions involve actions centered on the infant's own body that are at first random but that lead to an event that is of value to the child. The infant then learns to repeat the behavior in order to reinstate the event, and these circumstances result in an organized behavioral scheme such as thumb-sucking.

At 0; 1 (3) [1 month, 3 days] ... after a meal ... his arms, instead of gesticulating aimlessly, constantly move toward his mouth ... it has occurred to me several times that the chance contact of hand and mouth set in motion the directing of the latter toward the former and that then (but only then), the hand tries to return to the mouth.... [Later] it is no longer the mouth that seeks the hand, but the hand which reaches for the mouth. Thirteen times in succession I have been able to observe the hand go back into the mouth. There is no longer any doubt that coordination exists. (1952, p. 51)

Clearly, accommodation is occurring as the infant modifies the previously aimless hand movements to ensure that they will reach the mouth. The strategy of

moving the mouth to the hand failed, and so Laurent accommodated his behavior until he was successful in bringing the hand to the mouth.

Stage 3. Whereas reactions in stage 2 center on the infant's body, stage 3
involves events or objects in the external environment. The infant learns to
repeat movements that by chance have caused, for example, the mobile over
the crib to move or rattle. At first the baby observes the result and, in pleasure,
may squirm and move and thus accidentally cause the event to occur again.
When the baby initiates the movement and shows anticipation of the result
(perhaps by blinking the eyes or flinching), the behavior is called a *secondary
circular reaction.* It is *secondary* inasmuch as it involves events or objects apart
from the infant's body, and it is *circular* because it will be repeated and is
reinforcing in and of itself.

During stage 3, then, the infant is interested in the external environment and
is able to have some crude appreciation of a causal sequence of events. Behavior during this stage is not viewed as constituting intelligent response, however,
for two major reasons. First, the infant discovers the cause and effect quite by
accident. The child is not set on a goal at the outset of this behavior, for the
goal must be discovered before the baby repeats the behavior. Second, the
behavior that has occurred in the past is duplicated, and there is no attempt to
invent new behavior. Only in stage 4 does an infant finally demonstrate intention and, therefore (according to Piaget), intelligence.

Stage 4. When infants are around eight to twelve months old, they develop
an ability to solve simple problems. They can find an object under a pillow or
can knock down an obstacle to reach a desired object. Such behavior is the first
reflection of true intelligence, for it involves the origination of a goal in the
infant and the devising of a unique means to attain that goal. Piaget gives the
following example:

At 0; 6 (0) [6 months] I present Laurent with a matchbox, extending my hand
laterally to make an obstacle to his prehension. Laurent tries to pass over my
hand, or to the side, but he does not attempt to displace it. As each time I
prevent his passage, he ends by storming at the box while waving his hand. . . .
Finally, at 0; 7 (13) [7 months, 13 days] Laurent reacts quite differently almost
from the beginning of the experiment. I present a box of matches above my
hand, but behind it, so that he cannot reach it without setting the obstacle
aside. But Laurent after trying to take no notice of it, suddenly tries to hit my
hand as though to remove or lower it; I let him do it to me and he grasps the
box. I recommence to bar his passage, but using as a screen a sufficiently supple
cushion to keep the impress of the child's gestures. Laurent tries to reach the
box, and bothered by the obstacle, he at once strikes it, definitely lowering it
until the way is clear. (1952, pp. 217-218)

Piaget goes on to note that striking has been a characteristic behavior of
Laurent up to this point and has served as an end in itself (a secondary circular
reaction). Now, however, the act of striking is not self-reinforcing but is a
means to attain a goal.

At this stage infants will also begin to search for an object that has been
hidden, whereas in earlier stages they act as though the object no longer exists
once it is hidden from view. The qualities of *substance* and *permanence* are

attributed to objects during this stage. However, when the movement of an object becomes too complicated for the infant to follow, the child falls back on past actions that proved successful, rather than correctly solving the problem. Following is an example of the surprising manner in which children respond during stage 4:

At 0; 10 (18) [ten months, 18 days] Jacqueline is seated on a mattress without anything to disturb or distract her (no coverlets, etc.). I take her parrot away from her hands and hide it twice in succession under the mattress, on her left, in A. Both times Jacqueline looks for the object immediately and grabs it. Then I take it from her hands and move it very slowly before her eyes to the corresponding place on her right, under the mattress, in B. Jacqueline watches this movement but at the moment when the parrot disappears in B she turns to her left and looks where it was before, in A. (Piaget, 1954, p. 51)

Apparently, children at this stage of development are not able to recognize the continuous processes in the environment, and so they instead repeat acts that have been successful in the past. Infants do not yet understand that an object will be at the end point of the path along which they have seen it moving; and if they cannot follow movements visually but must imagine them, they appear to lose the concept of object permanence and to revert to associating the object with the spot where it once was found.

Stage 5. During this stage infants begin to show trial-and-error experimentation in behavior, which Piaget calls *tertiary circular reactions*. Children are interested in novelty, and they begin to manipulate objects and observe the results. For example, they will drop an object and watch it fall; then they will hold the object in a different way and drop it again, perhaps noting the different spot where it lands. Another feature of this stage is that children learn to accomplish the same goal through several different means. They might observe that kicking the mobile over the crib makes it swing and jangle, and so they will kick it again—or hit it, or pull at it. The difference between these responses and the behavior shown during stage 3 (secondary circular reactions) is that children modify and vary their movements and accommodate in a very intentional manner. They are involved with the novelty of their actions, and they seek to achieve the same ends in a variety of ways.

Stage 6. A major step is taken by children during stage 6: they begin to use mental symbols and words to represent absent objects. This is the beginning of internalized thought. In previous stages children are limited to immediate experience, and although they can invent solutions to problems through experimentation during stage 5, they are still more or less tied to the present. Until stage 6 they cannot solve a problem in their heads or represent objects symbolically. Consider the dramatic strides in terms of internal representation in the following example, in which Piaget hides a chain in a matchbox.

I put the chain back into the box and reduce the opening to 3 mm. It is understood that Lucienne is not aware of the functioning of the opening and closing of the match box and has not seen me prepare the experiment. She only possesses two preceding schemes: turning the box over in order to empty it of its contents, and sliding her fingers into the slit to make the chain come out. It is of course this last procedure that she tries first: she puts her finger inside and gropes to reach the chain, but fails completely. A pause follows during which Lucienne manifests a very curious reaction. . . .

She looks at the slit with great attention; then, several times in succession, she opens and shuts her mouth, at first slightly, then wider and wider!

At this point . . . Lucienne unhesitatingly puts her finger in the slit, and instead of trying as before to reach the chain, she pulls so as to enlarge the opening. She succeeds and grasps the chain. [Age 1 year, 4 months] (1952, pp. 337-338)

During stage 5 a child randomly experiments until the problem is solved, but Lucienne solved this problem mentally—with no manipulations. Her only observable behavior was to open and close her mouth, which Piaget interpreted as showing that she was thinking about solving the problem. Not yet proficient at full representation in mental terms, Lucienne used mouth movement to help her think through the problem.

Other behaviors that emerge during stage 6 are *deferred imitation* and *complete object permanence*. Children can now imitate a behavior hours or days after they have observed it, and they have also formed a mental image of an object so that they can follow it through a series of complex displacements even if they cannot see it. Thus infants who in stages 4 and 5 would revert to searching for an object in the location where they previously found it (even though they observed it being hidden in a different spot) can no longer be fooled in this way. Now they follow the object to the point at the end of its movement and immediately look for it there.

Throughout this remarkable sensorimotor stage of development children progress from basic reflex activities and a constantly changing world view to the state where they can devise simple solutions in their heads and can begin to form symbolic representations of objects. They have laid down the basis for all future cognitive growth, and with their ability to represent objects and events mentally, they open the way to conceptual thought and a new stage of cognitive development.

Preoperational Stage Between the ages of about two and six, children develop the ability to use symbols, which is the major accomplishment of the preoperational stage. Language development is a significant component of this stage, and there is also the emergence of symbolic play, dreaming, and deferred imitation. Mastery of *symbolic function* means that children are able, by themselves, to produce symbolic representations. This is a major aspect of language, but symbolic function is also evident when children are able to imagine, say, that the kitchen table is a tent in the woods; when they have dreams and nightmares; and when they are able to imitate Superman several hours after they have seen their hero on television.

Two aspects of the sensorimotor stage are signals and signs. *Signals* are stimuli that, through conditioning, have come to elicit certain behavior (for example, mother's putting on her coat is associated with her leaving, which thus elicits crying). *Signs* are part of the object represented (for example, daddy's voice is a sign of daddy). However, not until the preoperational period are children able to manipulate true *symbols,* which are produced by an individual

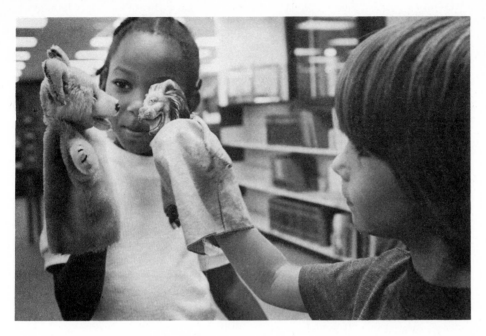

The major accomplishment of the preoperational stage is that children learn to use symbols; a new world emerges.

Bruce Roberts, Photo Researchers, Inc.

to represent something. When children can maintain and express internal representations of objects and events, they are prepared for further cognitive growth into what Piaget calls concrete operations.

Concrete Operations Stage It is during this stage that children begin to form notions of class, relations, and number. While preoperational children can use the language symbol *doggie* to stand for a specific dog, Rover, they also use the word *doggie* interchangeably with the dog's name as well as to identify all other dogs and perhaps bears, foxes, and wolves too. In other words, they cannot distinguish between using *doggie* for a single member of the class and for the class as a whole.

Between the ages of six or seven and eleven or twelve, children emerge into the "age of reason" inasmuch as they develop the ability to internalize actions and to reason in an elementary fashion. They can deal with classes and can manipulate them in a manner analogous to elementary arithmetical operations. In this way they understand that apples and oranges are part of the overriding class of "fruit," or that boys and girls fit within the logical class "children." Furthermore, they can reason that when boys are removed from the category of children, what is left is girls. During this period children become able to deal with the concept of time and can learn to read the clock and to understand historical time. Reasoning is internalized so that children can work out problems in their heads rather than attempting to solve them in the trial-and-error fashion that characterizes the preoperational stage. During the period of concrete operations children become aware of constancies in their environment and recognize them as such, even in the face of seemingly contradictory perceptual

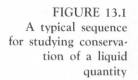

FIGURE 13.1
A typical sequence
for studying conserva-
tion of a liquid
quantity

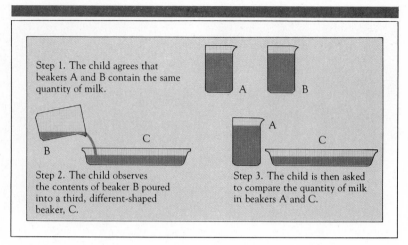

Step 1. The child agrees that beakers A and B contain the same quantity of milk.

Step 2. The child observes the contents of beaker B poured into a third, different-shaped beaker, C.

Step 3. The child is then asked to compare the quantity of milk in beakers A and C.

evidence. One of the best-known examples of this phenomenon is the conservation of quantity, an example of which is illustrated in Figure 13.1.

Piaget believes that most children under seven years old do not fully understand that when liquid from beaker B is poured into a narrower beaker or a wider one C, the amount of liquid remains the same. However, by the time children are seven or eight and have attained concrete operations, they know the amount of liquid is conserved. They will explain that even though the column of liquid is higher in beaker A than beaker C, this is made up for by the fact that it is also narrower. Moreover, the child will note that the amount remains the same, because the transformation of shape can be reversed by pouring the liquid back into the original beaker B. Piaget thinks that the ability of the child to conserve reflects the development of a new system of coordinated mental operations. With increasing age and experience, these operations are generalized to a wide variety of situations. For example, Piaget and his co-workers asked children what happened when lumps of sugar dissolved in water. Preoperational children thought the sugar simply disappeared. By seven or eight, however, children thought the substance of the sugar was conserved, but not its weight or volume. Still later children recognized that weight and volume were also conserved. Piaget believes that the development of concrete operations also affects children's social relations and moral judgments. In studying children's understanding of games with rules, Piaget found that before the age of about seven, children tended to regard such rules as " 'sacred, untouchable, and of transcendent origin' (parents, the government, God, etc.). Older children, on the contrary, regard rules as the result of agreement among contemporaries, and accept the idea that rules can be changed by means of a democratically arrived at consensus" (Piaget and Inhelder, 1969, p. 127).

Formal Operations Stage Progression from concrete to formal operations occurs during early adolescence (between ages eleven or twelve and fifteen).

Adolescents in the formal operations stage can think about thinking; they can conceptualize thoughts and understand why they have arrived at conclusions.

Charles Harbutt, Magnum Photos, Inc.

In this adult stage of cognitive development an individual is able to reason with logical propositions as well as with concrete objects. For example, if children during the concrete operations stage are *shown* two blocks of which the first is smaller than the second, and then they are shown a pairing of blocks in which the third is greater than the second, they can reason that the third block is greater than the first without comparing the two directly. If, however, we were to say that room 1 is larger than room 2 and that room 2 is larger than room 3, concrete operational children would have difficulty in reasoning that room 1 is larger than room 3. During the formal operations stage, this problem can be solved, and an individual is also able to deal with a number of classes of relations at once. (During the concrete operations stage, only two classes at most can be dealt with.)

Other types of thinking also occur only during the formal operations stage. For example, now individuals can think about thinking. They can conceptualize their thoughts, and they understand why they have arrived at certain conclusions. Reese and Lipsitt (1970) present the following example. If children are asked, "Can a dog be a Protestant?" they might answer, "No, because they won't let him into church." Adolescents would have a better perspective of the issue and would answer, "No, because dogs wouldn't understand things like that." Other attainments during the formal operations stage include the ability to think about ideal or counterfactual situations and metaphors and to be able to reason from them, and the ability to understand mathematical concepts involving proportions and the laws of probability.

Formal operations enable one to use "hypothetico-deductive" or "formal" reasoning. Faced with a problem, one can now think through all of the logical combinations of factors that might account for a situation, deduce the consequences of each of these possible hypotheses, and then test to see which is correct. Piaget and his colleague Inhelder posed children with a problem involving five jars of colorless liquid, labeled A through E. Each child was asked to discover which combination would produce a yellow color. (In fact, the answer was A, C, and E). Children in the concrete operations stage tried different combinations of liquids, but in a haphazard way, and almost never solved the problem. By contrast, formal operational children methodically tested all possible hypotheses involving combinations of two, three, four, or five jars, until the solution was found. Acquiring formal operations also enables one to think at a new and higher level about such topics as social justice, beauty, or philosophy. Piaget believes these new powers of reasoning often lead adolescents to engage in flights of speculation about hypothetical political or social systems, or to develop strong emotional commitments to abstract ideals.

Cognitive Development in Adulthood   Piaget has been concerned with the development of cognition in children, and he posits the formal operations stage as being the equivalent of adult thinking and seems to make the assumption that this is the final and most mature stage of reasoning. He also assumes that once the period of formal operations has been attained, it can never be lost—that is, he assumes that cognitive development is progressive and cumulative and that there can be no regression. Both these assumptions about cognition in adulthood and old age have been challenged. Riegel (1973) suggests a fifth stage of reasoning, the *dialectical stage*, in which adults are able to deal with contradictions and multiple levels of meaning. In addition, a body of evidence is accumulating that suggests that there is regression in old age to the earlier Piagetian stages of cognition.

Riegel (1973) acknowledges the insight and accuracy of Piaget's theory of cognitive development for thinking in children, but he feels compelled to extend the theory beyond the stage of formal operational thinking. He believes that adults spend most of their time reasoning in a manner that is different from formal operations. According to Riegel, the early periods in Piaget's theory involve *dialectic thinking*, that is, the acceptance of contradictions. Piaget, however, views cognitive development as gradually moving away from the acceptance of contradictions in thinking—to the formal operations stage, in which there are no contradictions. Conflicts and contradictions in thinking drive developing children to higher levels of reasoning in which they develop stable structures that allow them to consolidate contradictory evidence into consistent interpretations. According to Riegel, however, conflicts and contradictions are fundamental properties of thought, which individuals accept. Thus in addition to Piaget's four stages of cognitive development—and apart from them—is the fifth stage of dialectic reasoning.

Whether or not Riegel's ideas can be documented remains to be seen. Clearly, however, he has made a contribution to life-span developmental psychology by drawing attention to a possible alternative to Piaget's model for adult thinking. Piaget (1972) has also commented on thinking during late adolescence and adulthood and has suggested that the passage from adolescence to adulthood raises a number of unresolved questions. The period of young adulthood involves the beginning of professional specialization and, consequently, a number of widely divergent courses of cognitive growth. Piaget questions whether this level of development involves any common cognitive structures that are expressed differently in individuals with different aptitudes or whether special structures are developed depending on the aptitude and interest of the individual. He acknowledges that he does not yet have enough evidence to draw any conclusions.

One of Piaget's foremost advocates in the English language, John Flavell, has also commented on cognitive changes in adulthood (Flavell, 1970). He reasons that cognitive changes during childhood have a specific set of formal properties, probably because they stem from biological-maturational growth processes in the nervous system. Since no such clearly documented physical changes take place in the nervous systems of adults, there may not be such universal changes in adulthood as in childhood. Thus the cognitive changes occurring after maturity result from environmental and experiential influences. Since these are different for different individuals, adults do not exhibit the commonality of cognitive change that is clearly observable in childhood. Flavell (1970) suggests that there might be some experience-based adult changes that do occur uniformly across individuals, but feels that the identification of such changes has just begun.

Piaget has assumed that cognitive development is progressive, cumulative, and without regression. For this reason he has not considered it necessary to collect life-span data relative to cognition. Other investigators (for example, Denney, 1974; Hooper, Fitzgerald, and Papalia, 1971; Papalia, 1972) have speculated about life-span changes on Piagetian measures of intellectual ability and have collected data about these tasks for young and old adults as well as for children. These investigators found that old subjects perform more poorly on some intelligence measures and that while abilities based on stored information (*crystallized intelligence*) hold up well with age, active problem-solving behaviors requiring immediate solutions of novel problems (*fluid intelligence*) appear to be impaired during the normal aging process. Since the abilities tapped by Piagetian measures may be the same or similar to abilities tested in fluid measures of intelligence, it was hypothesized that old subjects would perform less well than young on some of the more complex Piagetian measures. This hypothesis has been documented. For example, Papalia (1972) found that subjects over age sixty-five performed more poorly than did adolescents and adults in tasks involving the conservation of quantity. Denney (1974) demonstrated that the classification skills of older adults were more similar to the behavior of young children than to the responses of adolescents. Denney was able to train her subjects to improve their performance, thus demonstrating that they were capable of a higher level of performance. Nevertheless, the decline in the ability of the aged to demonstrate higher levels of reasoning as exemplified in tasks of classification and conservation has led some investigators to hypothesize that the decrements reflect neurological impairment inherent in the aging process (Hooper, Fitzgerald, & Papalia, 1971; Papalia, 1972).

Guilford: The Structure of Intellect

J. P. Guilford has devised a model of the structure of intellect that can best be described as a taxonomy, or system, of classifying intellectual abilities. Guilford (1967) set out to identify all the types of intelligence that exist, and he has done this by developing a three-dimensional model that posits 120 different subcategories of ability. Three types of organizing principles provide the three dimensions of the model: content, operations, and products. The dimension of *content* involves the mode in which the intelligence is expressed, and Guilford identified four such modes: figural, symbolic, semantic, and behavioral. *Operations* categories reflect ways in which information can be manipulated or worked upon, and there are five categories of operations: evaluation, convergent production, divergent production, memory, and cognition. The third dimension of this model, *products*, involves six levels of complexity or organization involved in thinking: units, classes, relations, systems, transformations, and implications. All possible combinations of the four content categories, the five operations principles, and the six products result in a rectangular solid consisting of 120 cells (4 × 5 × 6). Guilford hypothesized that intelligence can be expressed as any of these 120 intellectual abilities.

When Guilford began devising his model of the structure of intellect, only about 40 intellectual factors had been identified. One of Guilford's contributions has been to stimulate research designed to identify additional abilities predicted by the model. To date, over 90 factors fitting into the model have been identified. Guilford and his associates produced many of these factors by devising tests to measure abilities predicted by the model and by confirming the predictions with factor analytic techniques. That is, they would devise certain questions to tap a predicted but previously unidentified ability in the model, and embed these questions in a large number of general intelligence test items. Through factor analysis, it was possible to determine whether the new items would be related and would emerge as independent factors among the other factors in the general intelligence test. Using this method, Guilford and his coworkers confirmed the existence of 90 of the predicted 120 abilities, and work is continuing to demonstrate the existence of the additional 30 factors. One example of this kind of work was undertaken by O'Sullivan, Guilford, and DeMille (1965), who demonstrated 6 factors in the behavioral content category that were predicted by the model. According to Cunningham (1974) this work represented the first methodologically satisfactory explication of the construct of social intelligence. So, although most people have some notion that there are individual differences in the ability to engage in social interaction—and although this ability had been predicted in the model—the empirical demonstration of social intelligence occurred only in the last decade, as a result of Guilford's predictions.

One unique feature of this model is the postulation of a great number and variety of abilities. Guilford criticized Spearman's conception of intelligence because it consisted of only eight cells in the model and therefore represented an incomplete picture of human intelligence. Models postulating hierarchies of intellectual ability (Burt, 1955; Vernon, 1951) are also criticized because they employ constructs that are not sufficiently basic or elemental. In defense of the models concerned with the more general nature of intelligence, it can be said that Guilford's factors may be too specific and therefore of no great consequence in the larger picture of intelligence. Thus between these theories there is a philosophical conflict regarding the nature of human intelligence: Spearman, Cattell, Burt, and Vernon emphasize a global perspective, whereas Guilford stresses a molecular structure of intellectual constructs.

From a developmental perspective, Guilford's theory provides an empirical definition of adult intelligence but does not explain how individuals arrive at the point where they possess all the abilities proposed by Guilford. The model merely makes assertions about the kinds of abilities that exist, and it attempts to explain to some extent why those abilities exist. Although a large amount of experimental and observational data have been fitted systematically into the model, explicit predictions about developmental changes are few. If intelligence is conceived of as continuously differentiating with maturation and aging, then at some point this developmental perspective will conflict with the model, which postulates a clear end point upon the development of 120 abilities. Furthermore, whereas Piaget suggests that not all individuals will necessarily attain the highest stage of mental growth, Guilford appears to suggest that human intelligence includes all these capacities naturally, with individual differences residing in the quantitative amount of each of these abilities rather than in the number of abilities. Piaget's notion of cognitive abilities is hierarchical, with complex thinking developing from simpler perceptual-motor forms of cognition. Guilford's view, however, appears to attribute equal significance to all intellectual abilities.

The only dimension in Guilford's model that involves increasing complexity is the products dimension, since units are viewed as being less complex than classes, classes are considered less complex than relations, and so on. Although it might be possible to examine the sequence within which the capacity to deal with these various products emerges, little attempt has been made to do so. Therefore, though Guilford's model represents the most extensively developed theory in the area of human intelligence, it has not been devised from a developmental perspective. Moreover, its implications for the development and maturation of intellectual abilities have hardly been tested.

One developmental application of Guilford's model that has received limited attention is the examination of age changes in the various abilities. Guilford considers human intelligence to consist of a large number of relatively independent abilities, so it is possible that these abilities develop at different rates. Cunningham (1974) has attempted to fit some empirical data regarding age changes in adult intelligence into the model. Longitudinal data collected from a college sample in which subjects were tested in the second and fifth decades of their lives were consistent with the extensive literature showing that verbal abilities—and especially vocabulary (cognition of semantic units, in the model)—are highly resistant to decline over the life span. Symbolic and figural materials appeared less resistant to decline with aging. Cunningham suggested that the model should be used by developmentalists to determine precisely which of the test properties are most and least resistant to changes with age.

Such a research perspective would represent an important analytical and theoretical advance.

Cattell-Horn: Fluid and Crystallized Intelligence

In contrast to Guilford's model of the structure of intellect (which posits that a large number of relatively independent abilities represent the nature of human intelligence) is the *two-factor theory* of fluid and crystallized intelligence formulated by Raymond Cattell and supported and extended over the life span by Cattell's former student, John Horn. The Cattell-Horn theory is the conceptual descendent of Spearman's notion that intelligence consists of one or two basic and general factors (Cattell, 1971). The only major similarity between the positions of Cattell-Horn and Guilford is that both theories have been developed on the basis of factor analysis. Because the theorists hold opposing notions of intelligence, they used different factor-analytic methods. Cattell and Horn maintain that the higher-order factors they obtain with their method are more important than the many individual factors of Guilford, and that the larger concepts can account for more of the variance in intelligence tests.

The theory of fluid and crystallized intelligence suggests that intellectual abilities can be organized into two general types of intelligence, which are fairly independent of one another. *Fluid intelligence* (G_f)[1] reflects the integrity and efficiency of the nervous system, the physiological structure upon which intellectual processes must be constructed. These influences operate through the agencies of heredity and injury. Thus fluid intelligence reflects the innate capacity of an organism, the ability with which we are born. Fluid intelligence is measured by tests that call for a capacity to perceive relations, to maintain the span of immediate awareness, to form concepts, and to reason and abstract. Subtests on intelligence batteries that measure fluid intelligence include word analogies (for example, "Dog is to cat as bear is to (1) rug, (2) cub, (3) lion); memorizing pairs of words; solving nonsense equations; and perceiving relationships among complex figures.

Crystallized intelligence (G_c), on the other hand, reflects influences such as acculturation, learning, and education. It is the product of experience and environmental influences. Hence tests of word comprehension (for example, "What is the meaning of the word *finite*?"); information ("What is the capitol of the state of California?"); mechanical information and skills; and numerical ability (once it is learned) reflect crystallized intelligence. Fluid intelligence operates whenever the sheer perception of complex relations is involved and is present in tests in which borrowing from stored, crystallized, judgmental skills brings no advantage. Fluid ability is an expression of the level of complexity of relationships that an individual can perceive and act upon without recourse to complex answers already stored in memory. Behavior in crystallized ability tasks appears to be determined largely by the repertory of an individual's stored information. Thus the acquisition of basic knowledge is highly dependent on G_f, but the

---

1. This notation is taken from Spearman's concept of the *g*, or general, factor of intelligence, of which fluid intelligence is one part.

Crystallized intelligence reflects learning experiences and is considered to increase throughout life.

Hugh Rogers, Monkmeyer Press Photo Service

retention and subsequent deployment of information can be carried out with G_c even if the powers of G_f have declined.

Cattell and Horn have included in their theory of fluid and crystallized intelligence a developmental perspective of these abilities over the life span. Crystallized intelligence is held to increase throughout life, since it reflects cumulative learning experiences. Fluid ability, on the other hand, is seen to increase throughout childhood and young adulthood; to level off during early adulthood; and to decline steadily during middle and old age. This is predicted because fluid intelligence is related to physiological efficiency, which is thought to decline after young adulthood. Since learning continues throughout life, crystallized intelligence (which reflects acquired knowledge and a generalized ability to solve problems) continues to increase over the life span.

To test the hypothesis that crystallized abilities improve but that fluid abilities improve, level off, and then decline with age, Horn and Cattell (1967) tested 279 teen-agers and adults drawn from a wide range of socioeconomic levels, with a particularly large representation from less educated groups. The results of this study were consistent with their predictions, although they must be viewed with qualifications. First, only five individuals in the sample were over age fifty-one; second, this was a cross-sectional study and thus involved cohort differences as well as age changes (see Chapter 2 for a discussion of this methodological issue). Finally, the available longitudinal data do not provide evidence of a large drop in fluid intelligence with age, as predicted by Cattell and

Horn. Data collected by Schaie and Labouvie-Vief (1974) in a combined cross-sectional and longitudinal (sequential) study; by Granick and Patterson (1971) in a longitudinal follow-up study of healthy older men; and by Cunningham (1974) in a follow-up study of men and women tested twenty-seven years previously all failed to corroborate large decrements in fluid ability after young adulthood. Although slight decrements in fluid intelligence appeared in these samples, they were in no way near the magnitude of the changes predicted by the theory of fluid and crystallized intelligence. On the other hand, the finding that individuals improve with age on tests measuring vocabulary and stored information (crystallized abilities) has been well documented by both longitudinal and cross-sectional studies.

Although currently available data fail to support fully the developmental hypothesis of Cattell and Horn, this theory has important implications for life-span studies of intelligence. First, the theory is one of the few that posits an explicit hypothesis regarding changes in adult intelligence, and so it serves as a model for future theories of intelligence. Second, the Cattell-Horn notion has stimulated interest and research in the area of adult intelligence, contributing to a clearer understanding of the issues involved. Additionally, there is clear empirical support for the ideas that crystallized intelligence improves with age and that all changes in fluid intelligence are in the direction predicted by Horn and Cattell. However, the changes do not approach the magnitude predicted by these investigators.

Measurement of Intelligence over the Life Span

Large groups of individuals of varying ages have been tested on a number of intelligence batteries, and from these data a generalized picture of intellectual functioning over the life span has emerged. Very simply stated, the average trend is a gradual improvement of overall intellectual performance up to about ages fifteen to twenty-six, when a plateau is reached that extends over adult life and into old age. Finally, performance drops rather sharply a few years before death.

Figure 13.2 presents a schematic representation of the generalized growth curve of intelligence over the life span. It serves as a summary statement for a large number of studies of intellectual development over the life span, some of which we will describe. It must be emphasized that the general curve represents an average, with individual fluctuations being smoothed out by group data. Individual growth curves of intelligence reflect varying degrees of increments and decrements in scores that can arise from situational testing factors, environmental events, and fluctuations in individual biological growth rates of intelligence. Figure 13.3 presents longitudinal data from the Berkeley Growth Study of intellectual changes for 61 individuals during the first thirty-six years of their lives. Clearly, not all individuals conform to the generalized pattern of intellectual growth in childhood and adolescence; the picture that emerges in Figure 13.3 represents an average of Bayley's data for all subjects. It is from Bayley's (1970) data that we have drawn the first part of our generalized growth curve of intelligence, and indeed, these represent the only available longitudinal

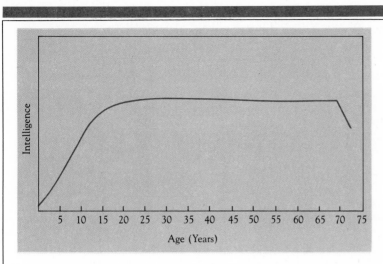

FIGURE 13.2
Intelligence over the life span. Early development is gradual; this is followed by a plateau in adulthood and a terminal drop several years before death.

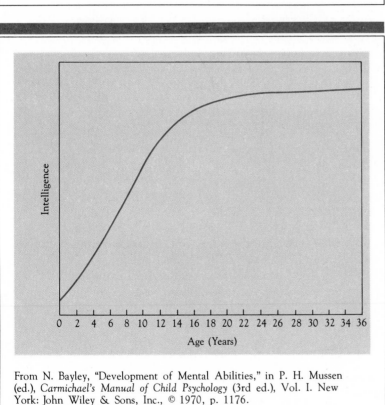

FIGURE 13.3
Theoretical curve of the growth of intelligence, based on Berkeley Growth Study.

From N. Bayley, "Development of Mental Abilities," in P. H. Mussen (ed.), *Carmichael's Manual of Child Psychology* (3rd ed.), Vol. I. New York: John Wiley & Sons, Inc., © 1970, p. 1176.

data on intelligence from infancy to adulthood. No life-span longitudinal studies of intelligence include individual behavior from infancy to death, and so we must rely on composite pictures drawn from longitudinal and cross-sectional studies at various points in the life span.

That the level of performance on mental tests normally increases with chronological age has been fairly well established, although fluctuations in growth rates occur in individuals. Furthermore, children who give evidence of mental precocity tend, for the most part, to maintain their high position relative to a group of age peers. Terman and Oden (1947) demonstrated this with a group of intellectually gifted children who maintained their superior position in college and in everyday life. Forty years after the gifted children first were tested, most of them still were fulfilling the promise they had shown as children (Oden, 1968). Other studies have demonstrated that low IQ scores are also fairly accurate predictors of low achievement in school and in life, although changes in individuals' patterns of IQ scores and achievement have been observed (Bayley, 1968; Skeels, 1966).

The upper limit of intellectual growth has been set variously by different investigators using different inventories. By "upper limit," we are referring to competence in such processes as verbalizing, remembering, and reasoning that is not exceeded at a later point. This does not imply that new learning ever ends, but suggests that the processes used to acquire information and skills reach some optimal level that is not surpassed. This level as scored on the Stanford-Binet Test is reached by age fifteen, when scores no longer improve significantly. Thorndike (1926) collected data suggesting an upper limit between ages eighteen and twenty, and Wechsler (1944) supported Thorndike with data showing age twenty as the end point for the growth curve. In contrast, Bayley (1968, 1970), using longitudinal data, found a leveling-off point around age twenty-six. Thus for our generalized growth curve of intelligence we see a leveling off somewhere between the ages of fifteen and twenty-six, with performance maintained at this high point until late in life, when there is a rapid drop in intelligence scores immediately preceding death.

Intelligence in Infancy

Before the age of one year, an infant's intellectual capacity is evaluated by intelligence measures that rely almost exclusively on sensorimotor development. (Development at a sensory and motor level has been described in Chapters 4, 6, and 10.) After the age of one it is possible to include tests involving increasing numbers of items to measure symbolic material and verbal ability. Because of an infant's level of functioning, the infant scales must be administered individually, and at this level the problems of reliable testing and scoring are especially acute.

Given the difficulty of measuring intelligence in infancy, why do psychologists persist in attempting to do so? It would be helpful to be able to identify intellectual potential in infancy for a number of reasons. In the first place, most parents are anxious to know whether or not their baby is "normal." Allaying parents' fears, satisfying their curiosity, or helping them prepare for dealing with a retarded child who may need extra care and attention are all obvious motives for developing infant IQ tests. Such tests could also be of use to adoption agencies in placing babies in homes best suited for their intellectual development, and to pediatricians and child psychologists in diagnosing problems and progress in an infant's early development. Early diagnosis of retardation, which would lead to early treatment, is clearly important; indeed, it can be critical, as in the case of PKU (see Chapter 3), where irreversible brain damage occurs if the disease is not detected and treated early in life.

Another pressing reason for developing good tests of infant intelligence is the need for objective measures to evaluate the effectiveness of day-care and intervention programs designed to stimulate the cognitive development of infants—particularly infants from disadvantaged backgrounds. As Lewis (1976) points out, most of these programs have as part of their avowed purpose the stimulation of intellectual development. Yet in evaluating the success of such programs psychologists have used infant intelligence tests that are very poor in their prediction of intelligence scores and academic achievement in later childhood and adulthood. Similarly, in assessing the effect on mental ability of attempts to improve the quality of prenatal and delivery care, it would be extremely valuable to have a reliable test of infant intelligence, so that one would not have to wait until children are four or five years old to evaluate how successful such efforts have been.

Regrettably, developmental psychologists have not yet been able to design tests of infant ability that correlate very highly with later IQ scores. Not until children reach the age of two or three years do correlations between existing infant tests and later IQ scores edge above .3 (see Table 13.2). The one exception to this seems to be in the case of infants who are severely retarded as a result of brain damage; in these cases the present infant tests may predict future IQ rather well. For example, mental deficiency was predicted in the first year of life with 75 percent accuracy by Illingworth (1961), on the basis of modified Gesell tests, the history of the infant, and clinical judgment. If these extreme cases of mental deficiency are excluded, however, predictive efficiency of the tests drops to near zero.

This low predictive validity of infant tests holds true despite great efforts by psychologists to devise valid measures. Many different infant scales have been

Ages	Number of Children	Correlation Coefficients
3 mos.–5 yrs.	91	.008
6 mos.–5 yrs.	91	−.065
9 mos.–5 yrs.	91	−.001
12 mos.–5 yrs.	91	.055
18 mos.–5 yrs.	91	.231
24 mos.–5 yrs.	91	.450

Source: Adapted from J. E. Anderson. "The Limitations of Infant and Preschool Tests in the Measurement of Intelligence." *Journal of Psychology*, 8 (1939), 351–379.

TABLE 13.2
Correlation Coefficients Between Infant Intelligence Tests Given at Various Ages and Stanford-Binet IQ at Five Years

developed, carefully standardized, and tested on large numbers of babies (see Bayley, 1970). Gesell (1928) was the first to report infant tests, and he established a well-known scale giving norms for "key ages" at weeks 4, 16, 28, and 40 and at months 12, 18, 24, and 36. Behaviors were categorized into four scales: motor, adaptive, language, and personal-social. Developmental age is assigned to infants on the basis of their behavior on these scales in relation to a large number of other infants of the same age.

The Cattell Infant Intelligence Scale involves many of the items used on the Gesell adaptive and language scales, and it begins testing infants at two months. Perhaps the best standardized and most widely used infant intelligence test is the Bayley Scale of Mental and Motor Development, which consists of 163 items. The Bayley Scale is similar to the Gesell and Cattell scales and was derived from scores earned in a series of repeated testings on the Berkeley longitudinal sample. Bayley's mental scale includes materials selected to elicit adaptive responses (such behaviors as attending to visual and auditory stimuli, grasping, manipulating, and combining objects, shaking a rattle, ringing a bell, smiling, cooing, babbling, and later, vocabulary). The motor scale includes such abilities as holding up the head, turning over, sitting, creeping, standing, walking, going up and down stairs, and manual skills such as grasping small objects and throwing a ball. An Infant Behavior Record is also used to rate various social, emotional, and other reactions observed incidentally during the test.

Bayley has argued that, although infant tests have relatively little predictive validity (in contrast to tests of school-age and older subjects), they do appear to have high validity as measures of an infant's cognitive abilities at the time of testing. Given that in the first year these tests mainly measure motor and nonverbal behaviors, it is not surprising that they do not predict that well how children will score on tests designed for older age groups. A number of studies have reported low- and zero-order correlations between scores on infancy tests and scores achieved at school age or older. Anderson (1939), who examined the correlations between infant tests (given at three, six, nine, twelve, eighteen, and twenty-four months) and the Stanford-Binet scores of the same children at age five, found correlations ranging from −.065 to .450, the latter being the correlation between test performance at twenty-four months and at five years. Anderson's study illustrates two principles about the predictability of infant tests that have been generalized over a number of studies. First, infant scores have very low correlation with scores achieved in later childhood; second, the relationship between test scores increases the closer the two tests are administered, with tests given at older ages showing the greatest predictability.

Although infant intelligence tests do not appear to provide sufficient information to predict later intelligence accurately, some evidence of success in predicting childhood intelligence emerges from clinical assessment of a more global nature. MacRae (1955) asked examiners who had administered an infant intelligence battery to a child to also rate the child as being superior, above average, average, below average, borderline, or mentally defective. These subjective impressions of global capacity correlated quite highly with test scores achieved by the children when they were nine. Tests given before eleven months, at twelve to twenty-three months, and at twenty-four to thirty-five months correlated .56, .55, and .82, respectively, with the nine-year-olds' retest results.

Why have the infant intelligence tests been relatively unsuccessful in predicting intellectual performance later in life? The following factors are commonly held to account for the low correlations:

1. The nature of intellectual functioning may change so radically in infancy that it is impossible to measure.
2. The infant tests are primarily sensorimotor in content and overlap very little with the primarily verbal content of the later tests.
3. Sensorimotor development may not be related to, and hence cannot be correlated with, verbal and symbolic development.
4. Infant tests are difficult to administer, since the examiner must make judgments about when the infant is attending, or shows surprise at novelty, and so forth. (Such behaviors are variable and are difficult to identify precisely.)
5. Infants may fluctuate more in their performance than do children—that is, they may be more variable within a given level of intelligence.
6. The range of behavior that can be observed in infancy is limited, and so there is little room for the display of individual differences.
7. Early temperament variations such as activity level may affect early achievement differently than the manner in which they affect later performance.

Let us now examine some of these explanations for the failure of infant intelligence tests to predict IQ in childhood and adulthood.

It may be inherently impossible to devise an infant intelligence test because the nature of intellectual functioning changes so radically during the first two or three years of life. It well may be, for example, that neurological computers in the cerebral cortex (which are critically important for language capacity and the ability to manipulate symbols and engage in complex forms of problem solving and abstract thinking) simply are not yet functioning fully in infants. Individual differences in these abilities might not appear until the cortical centers mediating such differences have, in fact, matured to the point where they are functional.

A sophisticated variant of this theory has been advanced by behavior geneticist Gerald McClearn (1971). Developmental genetics now recognizes that only a fraction of the genes in an organism's genetic constitution are actually turned on and actively synthesizing proteins at any given time. Most genes are being inhibited, held in a dormant state until they are to be activated at an appropriate time later in the life cycle. McClearn suggests, therefore, that differences in adult IQ might reflect differences in genetic constitutions, and that the impact of these genetic differences might not manifest itself completely during early infancy. Only a small proportion of the genes influencing differences in intellectual development might be activated during the first two years. With increasing age, however, as more and more of these genes are "turned on," the person's IQ would come increasingly to reflect his or her genetic potential for intelligence, and the person's IQ scores would become increasingly stable over time. (See Chapter 3 for a fuller discussion of this idea and related concepts.)

Psychologists simply have not yet found the appropriate measures of intelligence in young infants. A baby, particularly during the first few months of life, is a rather helpless animal that cannot make many responses. How, after all, does one test the intellectual capacity of a babe who can neither understand questions nor manipulate very skillfully, if at all, possible test objects? Perhaps the most obvious and dramatic developments during the first year are in the area of sensorimotor development, and it is the major motor milestones such as sitting up, crawling, standing, and walking that are most likely to concern parents. The neighbor's baby, Wilbur, has been walking for three weeks now, but baby Orville (who is actually a week older) hasn't taken his first step yet. Does this mean that Orville is retarded and will have a low IQ? Probably not, since precocity in the development of sensorimotor items—particularly in the acquisition of gross motor skills like sitting and walking—does not appear to have much relation to later IQ, unless the baby shows extreme retardation.

Consequently, though sensorimotor acts may represent the earliest form of intelligent behavior (and, indeed, this point has been emphasized by Piaget), early development of sensorimotor skills does not serve as a good predictor of intelligence in later life. Bayley (1955) suggests that it might be unreasonable to expect that the precocious development of such sensorimotor skills as auditory acuity or pupillary reflexes should predict capacity for more complex acts that also require neuromuscular development. Bayley's point is that complex cognitive processes require a number of capacities that may have relatively independent growth curves. Thus an infant who is precocious in one simple skill may not be precocious in all skills and thus may lose some of the early advantage. Only when verbal and symbolic processes, including language, begin to emerge do intelligence test scores begin to predict ability in later life.

Indeed, as Kagan (1969) notes, even Piaget seems to have overemphasized the importance of infant sensorimotor skills as precursors and predictors of intellectual skills in later childhood and adulthood. More recent studies suggest that early childhood and infant tests would be better predictors of later intelligence if they paid less attention to sensorimotor items and focused on how infants use and respond to verbal stimuli, on how they process and store sensory information about events around them, and on how well they can solve simple problems.

For example, correlations between infants' Stanford-Binet IQ scores at age ten and eighteen months have been found to be on the order of .35 (Honzik, MacFarland, & Allen, 1948). Bloom (1964), however, concluded from extensive analyses of longitudinal studies that the correlations between early and later IQ would be much higher if sensorimotor items were disregarded. If this is done, then the correlation between IQ at age three years and age seventeen years rises to about .65, and the correlation between IQ at age five years and age seventeen years rises to about .80.

Cameron, Livson, and Bayley (1967) report somewhat similar results from analyses of longitudinal data with IQ scores going all the way back to the first months of infancy. In examining their data again, they found that, whereas their original measures of infant intelligence (including a variety of sensorimotor items) did not predict later IQ very well, a cluster of items tapping precocious verbal development *did* correlate remarkably well with IQ, even at twenty-five years—although the correlation seemed to hold only for female babies. Although the items are primarily concerned with how infants use or respond to verbal utterances, babies who were precocious in these areas also seemed to be precocious in a simple type of problem solving that involved recognizing that a toy could be obtained by pulling on a string that was attached to it.

Moreover, Lewis (1971) reports that rapid habituation to repeated presentation of the same stimulus in infants a year old is significantly correlated with IQ later in childhood. Lewis suggests that this rapid habituation may in some cases reflect how rapidly an infant can process and remember information in the environment—how rapidly, if you will, the nervous system can construct, store, and retrieve accurate models of stimuli and relationships in the environment.

Thus it may well be that as psychologists devise more subtle and sophisticated items to test infants' capacities for processing information, for understanding their experience, and for solving simple problems, they will be able to develop reasonably good tests of infant IQ.

Intelligence in Childhood and Adolescence

The impetus for measuring intellectual capacity arose from the desire of French educators to identify schoolchildren who did not have the capacity to succeed in the school system. Thus intelligence testing began with children, and intelligence tests realize their greatest success in predicting school achievement. Indeed, that is what they were designed to do. In this sense, intelligence tests are valid measures of ability in childhood.

It has been pointed out earlier that childhood is the time of the most rapid growth of mental ability and that mental growth peaks late in adolescence or early in adulthood. During this period, IQ stabilizes and becomes much more predictable on the basis of previous test scores. The correlations for several studies of scores obtained at various childhood ages and at maturity are presented in Figure 13.4. Tests obtained in early childhood are predictive of mature scores, and test-retest correlations are higher the later in childhood the tests are given.

Although test performance appears to stabilize during childhood, there can be wide individual fluctuations of scores. Honzik, MacFarland, and Allen (1948) report that almost 60 percent of the 252 children in the Child Guidance Study had scores that changed fifteen points or more in the period between the ages six and eighteen. This means that it is a dangerous practice to test an individual once and then assign that score for life. Environmental factors clearly influence the expression of the genetic potential for intelligence, and prevailing influences at a given time may cause individuals to score in an uncharacteristic manner. Some of these environmental influences on IQ—such as socioeconomic status and educational level of parents, ethnicity, and school environment—have been discussed in Chapter 8.

Intelligence in Adulthood

The early cross-sectional studies of adult intelligence that compared the scores of younger and older individuals on various test batteries are probably most

FIGURE 13.4
Correlation of test
scores obtained at
various ages and at
maturity

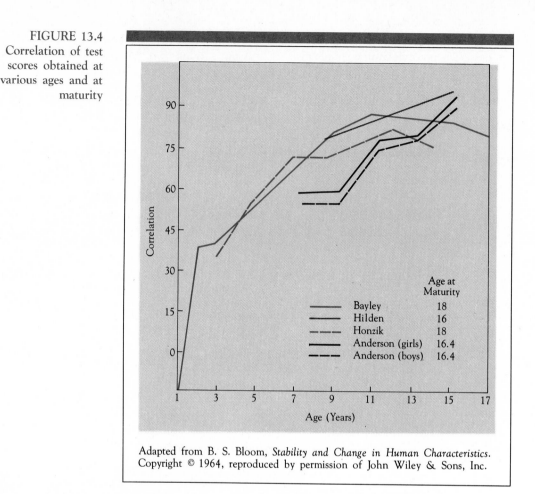

Adapted from B. S. Bloom, *Stability and Change in Human Characteristics.*
Copyright © 1964, reproduced by permission of John Wiley & Sons, Inc.

responsible for the current picture of intellectual decline in old age. Among the
best known of the early studies are the work undertaken by Miles (1934) involving the brief form (fifteen minutes) of the Otis Self-Administering Test of
Intelligence and the research of Jones and Conrad (1933) involving the Army
Alpha Examination. Both studies reported sizable drops in intelligence scores
over the life span, and they represented a large number of cross-sectional studies
of intelligence. Indeed, Wechsler, who constructed the most widely used intelligence scores for adults, built in scoring norms for his tests based on what he
believed to be the empirically supported notion that intelligence declined with
age. Wechsler designed his scoring so that normal IQ was 100 at all age levels,
so an assigned score of 100 is achieved with a different actual score depending
on the individual's age. In other words, because Wechsler believed that the
normal age function of intelligence was a declining one and because he wanted
to assign scores on the basis of an individual's position relative to his or her
own age group, he kept the norm at 100 regardless of the absolute score. Thus
to receive a Wechsler score of 100, a younger individual would have to achieve
a higher absolute score than would an older individual.

TABLE 13.3
The Wechsler
Intelligence Scale
for Children
(WISC-R)

Verbal Scale	Performance Scale
1. Information—A series of questions to assess the general knowledge of the child beginning with easy items such as, "How many ears do you have?" to more difficult items such as "What are hieroglyphics?"	**1. Picture completion**—Incomplete pictures are shown, and the child must state what is missing (e.g., teeth from a comb).
2. Similarities—The child must identify the quality that two words have in common (e.g., *shirt* and *hat* are both pieces of clothing).	**2. Picture arrangement**—The child must order a series of pictures so that they tell a story.
3. Arithmetic—A series of problems is presented orally, and the child must solve them in his or her head in a fixed amount of time.	**3. Block design**—Blocks with colored parts must be arranged to match a presented design in a limited time period.
4. Vocabulary—A list of words of increasing difficulty must be defined (e.g., "What does *knife* mean?")	**4. Object assembly**—The child is given the name of an object for which the parts are presented, and he or she must assemble the parts in a fixed time period.
5. Comprehension—The child is asked to explain certain phenomena or solve situational problems (e.g., "What is the thing to do when you cut your finger?")	**5. Coding**—Objects such as a star and a ball are presented with lines through them, and the child must replicate the lines in additional blank stars, balls, and so on in a fixed time period.
6. Digit span (optional)—From three to nine digits are read, and the child must repeat them. A second part of this test has the child repeat the digits backwards.	**6. Mazes (optional)**—Drawings of mazes are presented, and the child must trace through them in a fixed time.

Another input from Wechsler was the separation of intellectual abilities into subcategories or dimensions. He thus included ten subtests grouped in the categories of Verbal (the subscales are Information, Comprehension, Arithmetic, Similarities, Vocabulary) and Performance (Digit Symbol, Picture Completion, Block Design, Picture Arrangement, and Object Assembly). Table 13.3 gives some examples of Wechsler's items. The subtests made it possible to examine age differences on various dimensions of intelligence. It was observed that old people scored more poorly on the performance subscales than on the tests of verbal ability, thus suggesting that different facets of intelligence declined at differential rates. This has become established as a classic pattern in aging—that verbal abilities and stored information show relatively little deficit, whereas psychomotor skills, especially those involving speed and perceptual-integrative abilities, decline to a greater extent.

Although early cross-sectional studies indicated that intelligence declined with age, when data became available reflecting IQ scores of the same individuals over time, a different picture began to emerge. Owens (1953) was among the first to report intelligence scores of college freshmen who originally had been tested in 1919 on the Army Alpha Examination and whom he found and retested in 1949–1950, when they were approximately forty-nine years old. The scores of these subjects actually increased in the thirty-year interval since they were first tested. Similar results were reported by Bayley and Oden (1955), who retested over one thousand adults within a twelve-year period, and by Schaie and Strother (1968), who tested and retested a large cross-sectional sample of adults over a seven-year period. Schaie and Labouvie-Vief (1974) subsequently followed up the same sample after fourteen years and again found some improvement. Thus, whereas cross-sectional studies produced age functions pointing to an early intellectual decrement, longitudinal studies suggested stability or even improvement well into adulthood. Several additional considerations will help to clarify the confusion arising from these apparently contradictory results.

One major difference between studies reporting intellectual decline over the life span and those reporting increments is found in the way subjects were sampled. Cross-sectional studies (which sample individuals from different generations or cohorts at one point in time) involve comparisons of test scores among individuals who have had different life experiences. Warner Schaie (1965) was among the first to point out that different cohorts may differ in terms of genetic potential, and certainly they differ in experiential backgrounds such as education. Schaie argued that we should not expect cross-cohort (cross-sectional) and within-cohort (longitudinal) comparisons to result necessarily in the same age functions. More recently, Baltes and Schaie (1974) have argued that the decline in IQ scores described in cross-sectional studies is artificial and can be accounted for mainly in terms of differing educational opportunities for younger and older cohorts. These authors suggest the use of educational intervention strategies to bring older cohorts to a functioning level that is equivalent to the level of younger cohorts.

Whereas cross-sectional studies may overestimate intellectual decline in the aged, longitudinal studies may present an unrepresentative picture in terms of increment. Numerous studies have demonstrated that people who volunteer for longitudinal studies may be a select sample in the direction of above-average intelligence when compared with the norm for the population. Even in longitudinal studies in which great effort is taken to select representative samples, those individuals who are available for retesting over the years tend to have higher IQs and, indeed, are better off in terms of a number of health, economic, and behavioral categories than are the subjects who drop out. Continued retesting of the sample may also elevate test scores, and since longevity appears to be related to higher intelligence, the aged individuals remaining in the sample will be ones who score higher on the IQ tests.

As a result, when we conceptually combine the results of cross-sectional and longitudinal studies in an attempt to determine what occurs to intelligence on the average in the population, we arrive at the general curve described earlier—

of increment up to ages fifteen to twenty-five followed by a leveling off until the late years of life. Remember, however, that this is an average curve, and does not negate the phenomenon of intellectual increment over the life span as reported in longitudinal studies. Those individuals did show an increase in their scores, and the increase was typically in verbal ability such as vocabulary. Nevertheless, they appear to be a somewhat select group. When the general population is considered, with its increasing susceptibility to poor health with age, it is safe to assume that decrements in the IQ scores of some individuals also occur.

Age-related decline in intellectual function may reflect health factors rather than the normal aging process. Birren (1963) found that even in a group of old men who were selected as being in the best of health, the IQ scores of some individuals suffering from subclinical diseases were somewhat lower than the scores of the healthiest men. This led Birren to suggest that intellectual decline in old age, when it is observed to occur in verbal measures such as vocabulary and information, reflects changes in health status. On the other hand, Birren observed psychomotor slowing in all the aged subjects, suggesting to him that slowing in the central nervous system is a natural phenomenon occurring in all aging individuals.

Since psychomotor slowing appears to be a correlate of normal aging—and since many of the performance tests are speeded—we may expect that old people, whether tested cross-sectionally or longitudinally, will show deficits on speeded tests. Therefore, scores on some performance measures will decline with age. Why, then, have we presented the general age function of intelligence to be stable over the life span, knowing that psychomotor slowing occurs? Although older people perform more poorly on tasks such as Wechsler's digit symbol, they improve on verbal tests such as vocabulary and information. Thus the increments and decrements cancel out, and the average picture shows no change. Remember, however, that this is an oversimplified picture that represents an average of all the more subtle changes taking place in intellectual capacity. Baltes and Schaie (1974) can state that educational intervention strategies for the aged will change the picture presented by cross-sectional studies because educational experience will improve the learned abilities that are tested on verbal intelligence measures. Thus increments on the verbal measures for older adults who have had less educational experience would compensate for the decrements on performance measures and present a general picture of no change. This picture then would be more compatible with the picture presented by longitudinal studies representing individuals who, for the most part, have benefited from educational opportunities to a greater extent than most of the population.

With increasing age there is increasing mortality, and death is preceded and/or indicated by an accelerated change in certain functions. In the case of intelligence, a large drop in performance is manifested several years before death. Indeed, it has been suggested that the accelerating rate of IQ drop in very old age might be used as a predictor of impending death. Baltes and Labouvie (1973) present a simulation of this effect, depicted in Figure 13.5. The example demonstrates that, with increasing age, a greater proportion of subjects pass

FIGURE 13.5
Effect of age-related
increase in frequency
of terminal change
patterns on mean age
functions: Hypotheti-
cal example. (Note: *
= time of death; . =
raw score; ● = mean
performance.)

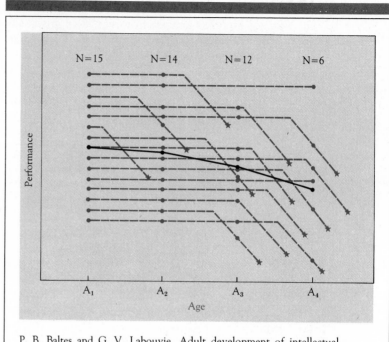

FIGURE 13.5
Effect of age-related
increase in frequency
of terminal change
patterns on mean age
functions: Hypotheti-
cal example. (Note: *
= time of death; . =
raw score; ● = mean
performance.)

P. B. Baltes and G. V. Labouvie, Adult development of intellectual
performance: Description, explanation and modification. In C. Eisdorfer
and M. P. Lawton (Eds.), *The Psychology of Adult Development and Aging.*
Washington, D.C.: American Psychological Association, 1973, pp.
157-219.

through a period of terminal change, resulting in an age function that exhibits a
continuous but increasing rate of decrement. Clearly, this average function
does not well represent the actual individual change patterns, which is one
reason that cross-sectional studies overestimate intellectual decline. Nevertheless, despite the fact that this terminal drop represents a bias in cross-sectional
studies (where group means are used to predict an average age curve), it does
appear to occur in all individuals. For this reason it is reflected in the last part
of the "normal age curve" of intelligence for an average individual.

Current Issues in Developmental Psychology:
IQ Tests

Few areas in the history of psychology have created so much confusion and
controversy as the question of intelligence testing. There exists a truly vast
body of research and theory about tests of intellectual abilities, and it would
require volumes to discuss this entire body of scientific literature fully. In this
section, therefore, we will attempt only to (1) make some basic conceptual

distinctions concerning the nature of intelligence and its development, (2) point out some important potential uses and abuses of intelligence tests, and (3) briefly discuss some interesting recent approaches to devising better intelligence tests.

Finding a Definition of Intelligence

In most fields of human endeavor, it is helpful to be as clear as possible about what one is discussing. The creation of special vocabularies or nomenclatures with greater clarity and precision than that permitted by lay language has proved an important aid to scientific advance. Much controversy and disagreement over intelligence testing appears to have resulted from the fact that there is no clear consensus among psychologists about what the term *intelligence* should mean. Scientists have differed greatly not only in how they conceptualize the nature and development of intellectual capacity but also in how they use the term *intelligence*.

Unless we are more careful to distinguish among different types of intellectual abilities, we will not be able to expand our scientific understanding of intellectual development and how it can best be measured. For example, Gagné (1970) has distinguished at least eight different types of learning, and earlier in this chapter we discussed the theories of Piaget, Guilford, and Cattell and Horn, who distinguish many qualitatively different forms of intelligence. Furthermore, if we are to create useful tests of intelligence, we must also keep in mind the nature of development and the various influences that shape it. Ideally, then, a good battery of intelligence tests should distinguish at least six different developmental types of intellectual potential, competence, or performance:

1. Genetic potential
2. Congenital potential
3. Neurological potential
4. General intellectual competence
5. Specific intellectual competence
6. Intellectual performance

Genetic Potential At the moment of conception, the fertilized egg may be viewed as having a rather broad set of potential intellectual outcomes. Its particular chromosome set not only would lay out the upper and lower levels to which it might develop various types of abilities but also would specify what types of environments would be optimal for developing this genetically determined potential to the fullest. As development proceeds, the potential range of intellectual outcomes is likely to become progressively narrower, since the particular environmental history of an individual increasingly specifies which of these potential outcomes will, in fact, be realized.

Congenital Potential A person is born with a range of intellectual potential that is already narrower than his or her potential at the time of conception, for that potential now reflects the interaction between the person's genotype and events occurring during pregnancy and delivery.

Neurological Potential The neurological potential of the child or adult at some time after birth would reflect the person's congenital potential as well as the quality of the postnatal environment, including not only abnormal "physical" events (such as lead poisoning, brain infection, malnutrition, and head injury) that produce grosser forms of brain damage, but also more "normal" changes in brain function as a result of maturation or aging. Finally, it would include the effects of more subtle "psychological" factors that can produce microscopic but no less real or irreversible changes in brain structure.

General Intellectual Competence This represents a person's general repertoire of attitudes, learning sets, and problem-solving strategies, which largely determines the capacity to solve new problems or to learn new material. This is perhaps closest to the way the term *intelligence* is used in everyday discourse, as when a teacher or employer says that a person is "bright" or "dull."

Specific Intellectual Competence How much does the specific person know, and how well could he or she do if performing at an optimal level? Both linguists and learning theorists, as we have seen, consider it critically important to distinguish between the competence a person possesses and the performance that is displayed. They cite dramatic examples of cases in which the competence-performance distinction is unusually clear, for example, rare cases of children who speak hardly a word until they are three or four years old, when they suddenly begin to speak in complete sentences. (Clearly, such children were acquiring competence in the complex rules of language for many months; but, for whatever reasons, they chose not to use their knowledge to produce actual utterances.) Note that competence in this sense would include various skills and abilities as well as vocabulary and factual information. The person's level of competence would reflect his or her general competence as well as previous opportunities to have learned the material.

Intellectual Performance As demonstrated in a particular setting (for example, a standardized intelligence test), intellectual performance would reflect not only the level of competence that an individual potentially was able to display under ideal conditions but also such factors as whether the person was sleepy or well rested, ill or in good health, distracted or able to concentrate, bored or eager to do well, and so on.

Ideally, a good intelligence test should enable us to distinguish and measure each of these six different types of intelligence, if we are to achieve some of the more important goals of intelligence testing.

Uses and Abuses of Intelligence Tests

Questions concerning the goals of intelligence testing are crucial. Why, indeed, should we have intelligence tests at all? What useful purpose, if any, can they ideally serve? Well-designed and well-implemented tests of ability can be ex-

Although intelligence testing can be abused, it also can help identify the causes of a child's learning problem.

Sybil Shelton, Monkmeyer Press Photo Service

tremely valuable tools in achieving a variety of important goals. Let us briefly consider just a few of these.

First, such tests would be of great help to both individuals and society as a whole in understanding, predicting, and influencing psychological development. Take, for example, the case of a child who is having difficulty learning some school subject, such as reading. Clearly, it would be helpful to know the cause or causes of the child's learning problem. (Is it lack of motivation? Poor preparation? Brain damage? An inherited form of visual memory deficit or some other factor? Or is it a combination of factors?) Knowing how a child compares in performance and competence with other children the same age and identifying the likely reasons for such performance are clearly important. If a child is not achieving up to his or her potential, it is important to realize this and to find out why. Particularly if the child comes from an educationally deprived background, poor performance in school may lead the child as well as parents and teachers to fail to recognize the child's true potential. This would be a loss both to the child and to society. Conversely, a child may actually be trying very hard but still may fail to satisfy the achievement demands of parents or teachers because they have overestimated the child's true potential. In this case, because adults have misdiagnosed the child's poor performance as resulting from low motivation, they may make the child miserable. They may punish or goad the child, leading to feelings of guilt or shame because of failure to live up to the standards of siblings or to other unrealistic expectations the parents may have set.

Intelligence tests ideally should prove useful for placement and prognosis as well as for diagnosis. Thus an accurate sampling of a schoolchild's present level of knowledge and his or her capacity for further learning and development can be extremely helpful in designing an educational program that will be optimally challenging for stimulating that child's educational development.

Similarly, for an adolescent or adult beginning or changing a career, knowledge of one's particular strengths and weaknesses is also likely to be particularly helpful. A person may discover, for example, some strength or talent not previously noted; conversely, one might find that one lacks the ability to compete realistically in some other profession. Of course, ability or potential is by no means the sole determinant of achievement and satisfaction in a given area of endeavor. Such factors as interests, drive, and persistence are clearly also very important. Still, it is generally true that we tend to enjoy the things we do well.

From the standpoint of society, well-designed tests of ability can serve an extremely valuable diagnostic function—by providing a profile of the variety and distribution of talents in the national pool. Standardized testing on a wide scale provides a kind of census of the country's most important national resource: human talent. Moreover, if properly constructed, such tests will help social institutions to use human talent in the fairest and most productive manner so that positions of great power and responsibility are filled by those with the greatest talent for the job. In addition to these diagnostic and allocation functions, tests may also help society to identify the most effective and humane ways of developing needed talents in the population—approaches that may range from genetic counseling to better health care and educational methods and opportunities.

One important potential service that good tests ideally could perform is that of identifying talent among the disadvantaged, so that positions requiring certain types of special talent would be assigned on the basis of true merit (rather than irrelevant factors such as sex, appearance, ethnicity, or social status) and on potential for long-term development (rather than the level of present achievement). One tragic failure of many existing intelligence tests is that for the most part they have not achieved this goal and often do not provide a good measure of learning potential in educationally and economically deprived persons. This is particularly true in the case of individuals from our society's minority subcultures.

We assume that differences in performance on an intelligence test (our "type 6" intelligence) will accurately reflect differences in general intellectual potential only if those being tested are fairly equal both in their motivation to take the test and in their opportunities for learning the material to be tested. These assumptions most likely are violated in the case of minority children in the United States today.

Sociologist Jane Mercer and her colleagues at the University of California at Riverside (Mercer et al., 1973a, 1973b) have documented the fact that schools are more likely than other social agencies to label persons as mentally retarded and also share their results more widely with others in the community. Mercer's data also indicate that, compared with Anglo children, a much higher percentage of black and Chicano children are labeled as retarded. Additionally, Mercer and her colleagues suggested that the retarded label is more likely to be inappropriate and damaging for minority than for white children, for at least two reasons. First, data suggest that, in the case of minority children, a low score on an IQ test is much more likely to represent lack of opportunity to learn the material being tested. For example, data show that many black and Chicano children who score in the borderline retardate range on IQ tests are able to function rather well outside the school setting and can do such things as go to school or the store by themselves or hold a responsible job. In contrast, white children who score in the retarded range are, for the most part, retarded in their social adjustment and behavior outside the school. Mercer also showed that the more closely the home environment of minority children approaches that of the typical white home, the higher the minority children score on the average. If one matches white and minority children on enough demographic variables (such as family size, parental income, and parental education), their average IQ scores are the same. This suggests, though it does not prove (since the data are correlational rather than experimental), that the major factor accounting for the higher percentage of minority children scoring in the retarded range is inequality of opportunity.

Of course, the practical use of IQ tests began when Binet was commissioned by the Parisian school system to devise a simple test that would distinguish children who could handle the regular school curriculum from those who would need to be placed in special classes. This continues to be one of the major uses of IQ tests today. Why should anyone object if a child who scores poorly on an IQ test is placed in a smaller class that can provide extra help and attention? Perhaps the major reason people object to this is the fear that labeling a child as "retarded" is itself likely to be damaging, since it tends to stigmatize the person as being someone who is different and inferior—in the minds of teachers, parents, fellow students, and perhaps even the child. Much of this concern grows out of the famous studies on teacher expectancy conducted by psychologist Robert Rosenthal (1976; Rosenthal & Rosnow, 1969). Rosenthal and colleagues carried out an ingenious experiment in which they administered an IQ test to a group of elementary schoolchildren and then informed the children's teachers that, on the basis of test scores, certain children were likely to be "bloomers" who would show increases in IQ. In fact, Rosenthal had no such information but had chosen children randomly to be labeled as having great potential. His interest was in experimentally manipulating the *expectancy* that teachers had about a child. Rosenthal found that children labeled as "bloomers" did, in fact, tend to show larger increases—though the effect seemed to be confined primarily to the early grades and seemed stronger in the case of minority children.

A number of researchers have attempted to replicate Rosenthal's findings, with mixed results. Some have found the self-fulfilling prophecy to hold true; others have not. Tentatively, we suggest that present data indicate that a low IQ score is most likely to act as a negative and self-fulfilling prophecy for a child if the child's teacher has not yet formed a confident impression about the child's potential. This is perhaps most likely if the child is of a different ethnic status or from a disadvantaged background, and if the child is just beginning school, so that the teacher has no prior information about the child's ability (such as report cards or informal comments from teachers in earlier grades at the same school). For reasons like these, a number of states—including the two most populous, California and New York—have now passed laws restricting the use of IQ tests as a basis for placing children in classes for the retarded.

Designing Better Intelligence Tests

How can we avoid the potential dangers and realize the potential gains of IQ testing? Several approaches to this have been attempted. One is to devise so-called culture-free intelligence tests that attempt to measure reasoning abilities with a minimum of reliance on words or content that might be specific to a particular culture. One of the more widely used examples of this approach is Raven's Progressive Matrices, which uses nonverbal test materials. Each test problem involves a matrix or array consisting of a series of geometrical designs that vary in an orderly way according to a logical set of principles. One design is missing from each array, and the subject's task is to select the missing design from a multiple-choice set of similar designs. This approach is clever, because solution of the matrix problems requires one to infer the logical rule explaining the sequence of changes in the pattern of designs, and then to deduce what new pattern that rule would predict for the place in the array occupied by the missing design. The test thus measures certain reasoning and problem-solving abilities, yet it can be presented to subjects with any language background—even those who are deaf and mute.

However, while this approach is clever, it is probably a misconception to consider such tests "culture-free" (Vernon, 1979). Indeed, psychologists Patricia Greenfield and Jerome Bruner argue that it makes little sense to talk about a culture-free intelligence test, since one of the most important functions of a culture is to provide its members with various intellectual tools and strategies for thinking and problem solving. Intellectual performance and competence (intelligence types 4, 5, and 6)—by their very nature—embody what the individ-

Some psychologists argue that it makes little sense to devise "culture-free" intelligence tests, since it is culture that provides the tools and strategies needed for intellectual competence.

Carol J. Minar, Stock, Boston, Inc.

ual has learned within the culture. On the other hand, there are likely to be important differences in individual capacities to acquire the intellectual tools offered by the culture (intelligence types 1, 2, and 3). The trick is to devise an intelligence test battery that can assay each of these different levels.

Mercer (1973a, 1973b) suggests that one approach may be to develop separate IQ norms for each ethnic group, so that black children or Chicano children are assigned IQ scores on the basis of comparisons with other children of the same ethnic group rather than on how they compare with all American children, who are predominantly white. Other psychologists have noted that some of the more widely used IQ tests deliberately have discarded items that did not yield average IQ scores that were similar for boys and girls. Why then, do we not treat ethnicity in the same way, simply eliminating items that yield higher total

IQ scores for whites than for nonwhites? Although this procedure may avoid some potential dangers of culturally biased IQ tests, it also seems likely to reduce the chances of gaining some potential benefits of IQ tests. If certain abilities *are* more prevalent among one sex or ethnic group, then we would, in effect, be ignoring this fact. In addition, we would be excluding items that measure those abilities, thus missing the opportunity to discover the reasons for group and individual differences regarding them. For example, a team of researchers including neurologist Joseph Bogen and cultural anthropologist Warren TenHouten (Bogen et al., 1972) have presented data suggesting that more analytical activities mediated by the left cerebral hemisphere tend to be more developed, on the average, in urban whites. By contrast, the same test data suggested that other mental abilities that rely more heavily on the right hemisphere of the brain may be more highly developed in such groups as blacks and Hopi Indians. The subjects in the latter groups had higher mean scores than urban whites on visual pattern recognition tests—which other evidence indicates rely more heavily on the right hemisphere of the brain.

Rather than eliminating items that may identify differences in ability, it may be possible to devise new and more sophisticated tests that systematically will distinguish and measure abilities in each of the six different intelligence types we have identified. To distinguish performance from specific competence, for example, will require more determined and sophisticated efforts toward identifying situational factors that elicit the best performance from a given child.

More sophisticated attempts to ensure that one has elicited a child's best possible performance would be, however, only the first step to a good IQ test. Even children who are completely comfortable and optimally motivated may have very little intellectual competence to demonstrate if they have had little opportunity to acquire that competence. One solution to this problem is to administer tests that include material that the child—especially a child from a minority ethnic or cultural background—is likely to have been exposed to. Black sociologist Adrian Dove has designed a "Counterbalance General Intelligence Test," or "Chitling" test, with thirty multiple-choice questions as a halfserious attempt to show that many black children are exposed to a very different world and speak a very different dialect than the typical white middleclass child. Some examples from Dove's test not only serve as an interesting illustration of why standard IQ tests are likely to be a poor measure of many inner-city children's intellectual competence and neurological potential, but also suggest better approaches to measuring that potential (cited in Haskins & Butts, 1973):

1. A "handkerchief head" is: (a) a cool cat, (b) a porter, (c) an Uncle Tom, (d) a hoddi, (e) a preacher.
2. Which word is most out of place here? (a) splib, (b) blood, (c) gray, (d) spook, (e) black.
3. Cheap chitlings (not the kind you purchase at a frozen-food counter) will taste rubbery unless they are cooked long enough. How soon can you quit cooking them to eat and enjoy them? (a) 45 minutes, (b) two hours, (c) 24 hours, (d) one week (on a low flame), (e) one hour.

4. T-Bone Walker got famous for playing what? (a) trombone, (b) piano, (c) "T-flute," (d) guitar, (e) "Hambone."[2]

A third approach to measuring a person's general competence and neurological potential is to evaluate achievement in light of learning history and opportunity, as judged by the home, neighborhood, and school environment. Mercer, as we noted, has made a beginning at this approach by identifying sociological variables such as family income and parental education that correlate with average student performance. An index of such socioeconomic factors could then serve as a crude indicator of the quality of a child's opportunity for acquiring school-related skills. On reflection, however, such an approach is likely to be too crude a measure of opportunity. For example, Tulkin (1968) has shown on the basis of careful home observations that mothers with the same socioeconomic standing may treat their children in extremely different ways. Indeed, some parents may provide very different opportunities and encouragement for some of their children than for others.

A more promising general approach, therefore, seems to be one suggested long ago by the Russian psychologist Vygotsky (1962). It was he who noted that, in evaluating a person's ability to learn, one should be guided not so much by what the person has already learned but by how much new material he or she can learn, given the opportunity under controlled conditions. A group of researchers at the Cambridge Research Institute in Massachusetts (Babad & Budoff, 1974) did, in fact, develop a form of this approach known as the *test-coach-retest procedure*. Among other things, this method has proved fairly successful in distinguishing between children who score at the retarded range because of inadequate opportunity and those who, in fact, have low neurological potential. An example of the approach would be to test a child's capacity to solve simple reasoning problems like those in Raven's Progressive Matrices. The child then would be coached or tutored by an adult, and finally would be tested again. The degree to which the score improved would then give a better indication of the child's capacity to benefit from instruction.

A fifth approach is to attempt to measure the functioning of the brain directly. After all, if one wants to examine an individual's neurological potential, why not do so as directly and simply as possible? One interesting example of this approach is provided by the work of Hungarian-born Canadian electroencephalographer John Ertl, whose interest in designing better IQ tests was initiated when, as a graduate student, he made a score of 77 on an IQ test. Ertl has tried to find different patterns of "brain waves," or electrical potentials generated by the brain, that might fairly consistently distinguish people with high and low IQs. Ertl has looked, for example, at the timing, amplitude, and slopes of the potentials evoked in the cerebral cortex of the brain by various stimuli such as repetitive flashes of light. Ertl suggests that an evoked potential (which can be used to measure the time it takes for neural impulses registering such flashes to travel from the retina to the cortex) may be a fairly good index

2. Those who are not "culturally deprived" will recognize these correct answers: 1 (c), 2 (c), 3 (c), 4 (d).

of speed of information transmission in the brain, thereby providing important information as an adjunct to more traditional intelligence tests.

Other EEG experts, however, are somewhat more cautious and suggest that any correlations among populations in which severely brain-damaged individuals have been excluded are likely to be artifactual—reflecting, for example, the fact that smart people simply may become bored and less attentive to the strobe light (Ertl, 1966). Although Ertl's approach and the interpretation of his results must be viewed with caution, they do illustrate an interesting approach to measuring intellectual potential.

However, even if Ertl and his fellow electroencephalographers are eventually able to develop direct measures of intellectual capacity in the brain, this would not provide us with the complete answer. A person's neurological potential at age twenty or even age two years may only poorly reflect genetic potential. To assay intelligence types 1 and 2, we need better measures of infant development and a more sophisticated understanding of how genetic factors influence mental development. (For a more extensive discussion of these matters, see Chapter 3 and the section in this chapter concerning infant intelligence tests.)

In conclusion, it appears that the answer to past misuses of intelligence tests is not to abandon them altogether but rather to devise better tests that will assess different types of intellectual ability more fairly and accurately. We also must be more intelligent and imaginative in our use of such tests, so that, for example, they are used not simply to assign a child to a normal or a retarded class but rather to tailor-make educational programs to meet each person's needs. Such tests would be more complex and expensive than present tests, but they would pay for themselves many times over if they helped us to manage more successfully the enormous investments of time and energy that now are devoted to learning in school and on the job.

Race, IQ, and Equality of Opportunity

Our discussion of intelligence testing and different types of intelligence provides a useful perspective on one of the most controversial issues in developmental psychology—that of the sources of racial differences in IQ. Within each ethnic or racial group, there are individuals who score at every level of performance on standard IQ tests. At the same time, however, significant mean IQ differences have been consistently found between certain ethnic or racial groups. Particular concern has focused on why the mean IQ of certain minority groups in the United States is about 15 points below the general population's average on standard IQ tests. Because those groups tend to be most disadvantaged economically and educationally, the predominant view among behavioral scientists is that the mean IQ differences largely reflect differences in equality of opportunity.

This view, however, has been challenged by a vocal minority of scientists, most notably the educational psychologist Arthur Jensen. In a controversial 1969 article, Jensen concluded that these mean ethnic differences in IQ largely reflect differences in genetic potential for intellectual attainment. For over a decade, a heated debate has raged among Jensen and a small number of scientific supporters (for example, 1969, 1973) and a variety of critics representing the majority of geneticists and behavioral scientists (for example, *Harvard Education Review*, 1969; Bodmer & Cavalli-Sforza, 1973). In some ways this debate has been destructive. For example, some of Jensen's arguments were distorted and misused to rationalize racial discrimination, which Jensen himself has denounced. On the other hand, irresponsible critics have threatened Jensen's right to speak, and even his life has been threatened.

The debate also has had constructive effects, for it has stimulated new research and theory on factors influencing intellectual development. Of special interest are several studies that indicate that certain kinds of test bias and environmental handicaps can, indeed, significantly depress IQ test performance of disadvantaged minority children. The results of experimental research deserve special attention, since the experimental method is such a powerful tool for studying causal relationships among different variables.

Tests, Testers, and Motivational Factors   The average American minority child seems to face a number of handicaps in competing with white counterparts on the more widely used intelligence tests. First of all, there is the nature of the test and the situation in which it is given. Jensen (1969) himself notes that in his experience disadvantaged and minority children were handicapped in the standard testing situation with a strange examiner—who frequently is of a different race. He also notes that when the examiner first took time to play games and otherwise establish rapport with the child, one routinely could produce a gain of five to ten points.

Experiments (for example, Zigler, Abelson, & Seitz, 1973; Seitz et al., 1975) have shown that motivational factors may depress test performance of disadvantaged children by several points. Such children often may simply see less reason to try to do well on a strange, abstract task that has no obvious relevance. A number of attitudinal factors may prevent a person's test performance from accurately reflecting true capability or competence. High anxiety, low self-confidence, or a feeling of fatalism are all likely to depress test performance.

Indeed, Dickstein (1974) showed that motivational factors may even account for much of the differences between male and female college students on tests of language and mathematical ability. Dickstein found that whereas bright females did less well than male students under a control condition on a test of mathematical reasoning, under a condition of special motivation the females' scores improved by the equivalent of about ten IQ points.

Pregnancy and Obstetrical Care   We have noted that poor obstetrical care was more prevalent among disadvantaged groups and carried with it greater risk of impaired brain and cognitive development. Poor nutrition during pregnancy is a factor of special concern, and nutritional surveys in the United States have found poor nutrition to be more prevalent among disadvantaged minorities. A dramatic demonstration of the impact of improved prenatal nutrition on the IQ of offspring was provided by a team of Columbia University researchers (Harrell et al., 1955) who randomly assigned numbers of disadvantaged expectant American mothers to either an experimental condition (in which they received vitamin and mineral supplements) or to a control condition (in which they received placebos). When children of these mothers were tested five years later, those whose mothers had received dietary supplements tested some five points higher on the average.

Home Environment and Preschool Learning Opportunities Impressive documentation of the effects of home environment on IQ and the educational handicap that can be associated with growing up in a slum environment was provided by Heber and his colleagues at the University of Wisconsin (Garber & Heber, 1976). They assigned children of very poor low IQ mothers in the economically deprived Milwaukee ghetto areas to (1) an experimental group, who received for their first five years intensive preschool tutoring designed to foster intellectual growth, or (2) a similar control group who did not receive special encouragement. For most of this preschool period and during the early school years, the experimental group maintained an average IQ of over 100, roughly 25 points higher than the control group. This occurred even though both groups received an equal amount of practice in taking the same IQ tests. Although the program did not prevent retardation in all children in the experimental group, it clearly had an impact on many.

The Milwaukee study involved the use of extremely intensive tutoring of children (forty hours per week for five years). Other studies have also shown sizable gains as a result of more modest tutoring. Blank (1969), for example, was able to produce average IQ gains of fifteen points through a four-month program of daily and individualized but short (fifteen-minute) sessions in which the preschool teacher focused on improving the disadvantaged child's "ability to organize thoughts, to reflect upon situations, to comprehend the meaning of events, and to structure behavior so as to be able to choose among alternatives." Also interesting are the more careful analyses of the cognitive effects of Head Start programs, which suggest that although most children may not have made significant gains in intellectual development as a result of participating, some groups—particularly black children from large-city ghettos—did show consistent benefits.

Convergent evidence for the impact of home environment on IQ comes from adoption studies conducted by researchers at the University of Minnesota (Scarr & Weinberg, 1976). These researchers studied children from different racial and social backgrounds who were placed in adoptive homes at varying ages. Black children who had been adopted into middle-class homes by the time they were two or three years old had an average IQ of 106. White children placed in these homes by age two or three had similar IQs. Moreover, the earlier the children were placed in these adoptive homes—and the higher the educational background of the adoptive mother—the higher the average IQ of the adopted child.

Implications for Equality of Opportunity These empirical demonstrations of environmental handicaps are particularly impressive if one considers that these different handicaps are likely to have a cumulative effect. Thus no one factor—such as test bias, poor care during pregnancy and delivery, growing up in a slum environment, or going to poor and segregated schools—may by itself account for a disadvantaged minority group's scoring an average of fifteen points below the general population. Still more impressive is some evidence that such handicaps may be not only cumulative, but synergistic—that is, their combined effects may be even greater than one would expect from the sum of the individual effects. There is evidence, for example, that infants who are at risk for minimal brain damage from poor prenatal care may be especially vulnerable to the effects of growing up in a deprived environment (Willerman, Broman, & Fiedler, 1970). In sum, then, it seems not unreasonable to suppose that if the average disadvantaged child were given truly equal opportunity, he or she would be likely to have an IQ that was average or even above average.

In conclusion, three other points regarding IQ differences and equality of opportunity should be emphasized. First, as geneticists have noted (Bodmer & Cavalli-Sforza, 1973), it will not be until we have eliminated widespread racial prejudice and discrimination from our society that we will really be able to provide complete equality of opportunity for ethnic minorities and draw accurate conclusions about the causes of average racial differences in IQ.

Second, one critical point on which even Jensen and his critics agree is that, since the full range of talents is present in all races and classes, discrimination on the basis of race, creed, or color is not only unjust but nonsensical from the standpoint of scientific genetics. Moreover, to be most meaningful and effective, equality of opportunity must entail a range of different opportunities so that individuals may, as much as possible, choose the environment that allows them to fulfill personal individual needs and potential.

Third, high heritability for important talents such as intelligence is itself one of the strongest arguments for equality of opportunity. That is, the greater the individual differences in inherited potential for talent, the more important it is to place that talent where it can do the greatest good in society, and the more society will suffer from denying that talent the opportunity to develop itself. Indeed, one could argue that the most important way in which the majority suffers from discrimination against minorities is through the loss of minority talents and intelligence that would otherwise benefit the entire society. This same argument applies, of course, not only to other disadvantaged ethnic minorities but also to groups such as women who comprise an actual majority of the population. In conclusion, we should note that the importance of equal opportunity applies more generally: we *all* stand to gain by extending equality of opportunity to everyone, regardless of race, creed, color, or sex.

Summary

1. There is no universal definition of intelligence on which all psychologists and laypeople agree. Thus intelligence is measured in numerous ways.
2. Taking a quantitative approach to intelligence, Binet constructed the first intelligence test, which was designed to identify schoolchildren who were not capable of learning in the regular school system.
3. Intelligence tests typically tap a wide variety of abilities. Some investigators

argue that the different abilities assessed in an intelligence test all have some underlying general component in common. Others feel that there are independent and nonoverlapping intellectual abilities.

4. Qualitative approaches to intelligence stress the nature of the development of thinking. The most prominent theory of intellectual development is that of Jean Piaget, which traces the rudiments of intelligence to the early responses of newborn infants and follows the development of thought to adulthood.

5. According to Piaget, adult thinking is qualitatively different from thinking at earlier ages. There are four major developmental stages: sensorimotor, preoperational, concrete operational, and formal operational. An individual passes through these stages by assimilating and accommodating to the environment. Although it has been suggested that adult thinking may develop beyond the stage of formal operations, no clear additional stages have been identified.

6. One quantitative model of intelligence, designed by J. P. Guilford, posits 120 types of abilities. While this taxonomy of human intellectual abilities is useful, the means for the development of various abilities have not been described.

7. The quantitative model of crystallized and fluid intelligence presented by Horn and Cattell posits two major dimensions of intelligence. *Fluid intelligence* is related to biological capacity and is thought to deteriorate after early adulthood; *crystallized ability* is associated with learning and is thought to increase throughout life. Not all data support this formulation, although it is based in part on empirical evidence.

8. Although there are many individual fluctuations in patterns of development and aging, on average, intellectual ability increases over the childhood years and remains stable in adulthood with decline in very old age.

9. Infant intelligence tests provide useful information for assessment in infancy, but scores on these tests are poor predictors of intelligence in childhood and later life.

10. Although intelligence tests have been abused, they are still extremely useful in the diagnosis and prognosis of intellectual development.

11. Measures to avoid the dangers and to realize the potential of intelligence testing include designing culture-free tests, establishing norms within various ethnic and racial groups, ensuring that the best possible performance is elicited from the individual, assessing opportunity and environment as well as behavior, assessing ability to learn new material, and assessing the nervous system.

12. Among the most controversial questions in psychology is why the *average* IQ for certain disadvantaged ethnic groups is below the national average. Most scientists today believe such differences largely reflect inequalities of opportunity, rather than differences in genetic potential. Evidence supporting this view comes from many studies, including those in which children born to disadvantaged parents developed above average IQ when reared in advantaged adoptive homes, or after receiving special preschool tutoring. Whatever the sources of average group differences in IQ, responsible scien-

tists agree that racial discrimination is irrational, and that a high heritability for a trait such as intelligence only strengthens the argument for equal opportunity.

Selected Readings

Baltes, P. B., and K. W. Schaie. "Aging and IQ: The Myth of the Twilight Years." *Psychology Today*, 7 (1974), 35-40. An overview of research on intelligence and aging, with the perspective of the mistakes that can be made in the interpretation of data.

Bayley, N. "Behavioral Correlates of Mental Growth: Birth to Thirty-six Years." *American Psychologist*, 23 (1968), 1-17. A description of a large body of research relating aspects of behavior that correlate with intellectual development in early life.

Birren, J. E. "Age and Decision Strategies." In *Decision Making and Age*. Eds. A. T. Welford & J. E. Birren. New York: S. Karger, 1969. Pp. 23-36. An attempt to evaluate adult intelligence in a manner more relevant to the lives of older adults.

Elkind, D. "Infant Intelligence." *American Journal of Diseases of Children* (1973). A discussion of the instability and inconsistency of intelligence test behavior in infants and the relation to evaluation of current infant stimulation programs.

Zajonc, R. B. "Dumber by the Dozen." *Psychology Today* (January 1975). Examines the relationship between birth order and intelligence and presents a hypothesis to explain why children born earliest in the family score highest.

Chapter 14

Motivation and Emotions

The basic motivations of living organisms and how they impel us toward goals

The physical bases of motivations and emotions: to what extent human responses are programmed by genetic and physiological factors

How motivations, goals, and activities develop and change over the life span

How our tendencies to action can be seen as basic components of personality

Motivation

Spontaneous Activity
Play
Motivation as a Pull Factor
The Smile and the Frown
Motivation as a Push Factor

Neurobiological Bases of Motivation

The Hypothalamus and Motivation
Emotions and Motivation
Learning and Emotional Responses
Mixed Motivational States
Pheromones
Bonding of Newborn and Mother

Motivation and Maturity

Secular Trends in Adolescent Interests
Changes in Interests with Age
Motivation and the Audience Effect
Crime and Age
Exercise and Age
Goals
Motivation Toward Goal Realization
Personality and Motivation

Introduction

A wind-up toy truck and the child who plays with it have something in common: they both have an energy source and a control system inside them that impels them to action. The spring of the wind-up toy can be replaced by a battery and an electric motor, but an energy source is still there. And in the case of the child there is an energy source in muscle cells, which, when released, gives rise to contraction.

Physiologists now know that the human energy source is a product of metabolism and can be identified with phosphorus-rich chemical compounds in the cell. Psychologists, however, are less interested in the energy source itself than in the pattern of behavior shown in its release. Terms like *motivation, drive, needs,* and *emotions* imply that human organisms are organized and ready for action—indeed, that they initiate action.

To say that we are motivated implies that we are impelled to action toward some goal. We may be reminded that we are hungry by the sight of food; but if we are sufficiently hungry, we seek food even if it is not in view. Similarly, if we are thirsty, we seek some water and drink it. And if we are cold, we may seek a warm place in the sun or build a fire. If we did not do these purposive or motivated activities, we would not survive. Hence motivation seems almost synonymous with life.

It is impossible to think of a living but unmotivated person, though we might consider individual differences or day-to-day variations in the strength of the motivation (sometimes we are hungrier than at other times). How do the purposive or goal-directed behaviors become organized, and what is their course over the life span? This chapter deals with behaviors ranging all the way from drinking, feeding, and sexual activity, which have a biological base, to highly abstract behaviors like achievement motivation and interest in games, which have a wide variety of expression. Some psychologists speak about the need for achievement or accomplishment as a source of motivation and also as a way of defining the goals of certain patterns of behavior. Clearly, *something* drives us on to achievement even through pain and deprivation. How does such strong motivation become developed and channeled in its expression?

Motivation

Motivation may be defined as the impulsion of an organism to expend energy and to organize behavior in order to reach some goal. The term usually implies a relatively sustained state of behavior in contrast to momentary or eruptive acts. Thus a human being is said to be highly motivated if he or she shows persistence in seeking a goal and is willing to endure frustration and perhaps even anxiety and pain.

As a first step toward understanding motivation, we will examine some behaviors associated with it. Then we will investigate the physiological bases of this great energy source (like the mechanics of our wind-up toy). Finally, we will explore the ways in which motivation is expressed throughout the life span.

553

People are highly mo-
tivated if they are
willing to endure
frustration and even
anxiety and pain in
the pursuit of some
goal.

Guy LeQuerrec, Magnum Photos, Inc.

Spontaneous Activity

One of the clearest examples of a force impelling animals to action is seen in the spontaneous wheel-turning activity of small rodents such as squirrels, rats, and mice. When placed in an activity wheel, such animals often turn the wheel several thousand times in a twenty-four-hour period. Many years ago psychologists first observed the wheel-turning activity of rats in relation to age. Spontaneous wheel-turning activity was found to increase during the first third of life and then gradually to decline toward old age and death (Richter, 1922–1923). The amount of nest-building activity roughly paralleled the amount of activity in the revolving wheel, suggesting a common internal source of the drive toward activity.

That such spontaneous activity reflects an *internal* state of the animal is shown by the fact that female rats increase their spontaneous activity every fourth to fifth day. Female rats do not mate except during a period of "heat," or estrus, which occurs every fifth day. In the wild state, a female rat in heat increases her probability of mating by increasing her field exploration and running. From this behavior, we can easily imagine a course of evolution of the species in which animals whose activities bring them into contact with mates during the phase of estrus tend to reproduce. Selection favors those animals whose behavior increases the probability of successful mating.

Play

Children often impress adults with their energy. Parents may wearily describe their children as being "always on the go" and "always playing." In fact, children who have time on their hands often make up games and become very noisy and active in pursuing them. One senses from the behavior of children that they are prone to action and that games become a vehicle for expressing their impulse to activity. With age, play activities become more formal or structured, and some forms of play behavior may drop out. Yet throughout the life span, human beings like other animals are active, not passive. Unlike an automobile or a light switch, living organisms are not shut off at night. They continue their active metabolism. Indeed, sleeping human beings dream, and electrical recordings from the brain indicate that there is ongoing activity of the brain during sleep.

Healthy children and adults are energetic and active. Although play often involves the expenditure of high amounts of energy, the activity itself seems to be pleasurable. Parents often detect illness in children because their playing has stopped. A healthy kitten or puppy is also playful; when it stops playing, we wonder whether the animal is ill. In short, a reduction of activity is an adaptive way to conserve energy and help the process of self-repair in illness.

Some years ago two psychologists followed children around during their usual daily activities (Barker & Wright, 1955). They found that on a normal day an eight-year-old child engaged in several thousand transactions occurring in about six hundred situations. Some of these many activities are seen to reflect *primary* motivation, whereas others are regarded as *secondary* motivation, which derives from the primary sources. Play in the spontaneous sense is regarded as a primary source of motivation. In fact, some forms of play in animals are highly patterned, suggesting that they are a rehearsal for behavior that will become important for survival. Thus play improves skills and increases fitness for survival during the adult phase of life.

Seemingly, the more complex an animal is, the more complex the play demonstrated by its young. Kittens and puppies, for example, engage in rough-and-tumble play with their littermates. They pounce, growl, bare their teeth, jump up, and chase each other—all activities that would be useful in the presence of a real adversary. The similarity between these activities and behaviors used for survival as adult animals has led many psychologists and ethologists to conclude that play activities are in large part genetically programmed. The reasoning is that lines of animals that have survived are those in which the young practiced adult behaviors. Indeed, we should point out that play brings with it some risks. In wild animals, the noise of play behavior of the young may attract the attention of predators. In human beings, children's play may lead to the irritation of adults and result in punishment. However, adult fitness seems to be improved by the practice and experience of play, even though it is nonproductive for the young in terms of energy expenditure and risks of injury. It is in the short run that play involves risks of injury. There is an element of risk taking in a present play situation, such as in the mock aggression and chasing of children that often results in sprains and broken limbs. So, although play seems to be pleasurable for the participants, its basis in the species would seem to be the later selective survival advantage it imparts.

In discussing sociobiology, Edmund Wilson (1975) points out that in play the numerous elements of adult behavior can be varied, and that an advantage is conferred by the fragmenting and recombining of behavior in play:

Among the higher mammals, where it is more free-ranging, play loosens the behavior repertory in each generation and provides the individual with

The motivation to
play seems to come
from within; play
serves no apparent
purpose, is sought
after, and is pleasur-
able.

J. Berndt, Stock, Boston, Inc.

opportunities to depart from the traditions of its family and society. Like sexual reproduction and learning, generally, it is evidently one of the very broad adaptive devices sustained by second-order natural selection. At its most potent, in human beings and in a select group of other primates that includes the Japanese macaques and chimpanzees, playful behavior led to invention and cultural transmission of novel methods of exploiting the environment. (p. 167)

In wild chimpanzees the frequency of play increases with age during the infant years and then declines in adolescence and adulthood. For an adult female with a child, however, the frequency of play again increases to the level of adolescence (Van Lawick-Goodall, 1968; cited in Wilson, 1975). This is not unlike the human mother, whose play increases because of her interactions with a baby or small child. Similarly, when men become fathers, they too often increase their time in play, spending considerable time in playing games with their children. Some of the games come back readily from the parents' past experiences of childhood and are expressed in the particular idiom of their culture.

With the foregoing evidence of play in mind, it is perhaps time to ask the question, What is play? One chief characteristic of play seems to be that it appears to serve no apparent purpose. Other attributes are that play is sought after, is pleasurable, and is "fun." The motivation to play seems to come from within an organism, and healthy young animals seem to convert available objects in their environment into play objects. For kittens, a piece of paper in the wind becomes something wild to stalk and pounce upon. Similarly, the toys of children are converted into other toys for fantasy games. Wagons become spaceships, and boxes become boats. In these examples, the original purposes of an object are subverted for the purposes of playing. The goal of play seems to be less in the reward of the outcomes of the behavior than in the exercise of the behavior itself.

How, then, do we recognize play? Partly we recognize it by its apparent purposelessness, in that a child or an adult seems to be doing something that is pleasurable but pointless when considered from the viewpoint of energy expenditure and risk. To be told to "stop playing" means to become serious and to behave for "real." Nonetheless, intelligent mammals do make up games to "play," and human adults may continue to play many games throughout their lives. Men and women eighty or ninety years old play cards and other games with great frequency and apparent enjoyment. It seems as though we create games so that we can act and react. Birren (1964) points out that games share the following characteristics: "a moderate element of suspense governing gains or losses; a semi-ritualized setting with familiar aspects; activities carried out in a setting of social approval at least by the in-group; and some element of mastery, which makes a difference in overcoming the level of suspense" (p. 225). Resolution of game suspense appears to be pleasurable, and people of all ages seem to enjoy the development and resolution of created suspense, such as is experienced in reading a mystery novel.

Motivation as a Pull Factor

Motivation should be viewed not only as a push from within but as a pull from outside an organism. Words like *needs, drives, wishes, desires,* and *wants* refer to an inner impulsion toward a goal. But the external environment pulls the attention; that is, stimuli can be made attractive. Indeed, the term *attractive nuisance* refers to the fact that adults may be legally responsible if a child is injured on their property because an irresistible but dangerous object was left unattended. Thus an unattended swimming pool or a piece of machinery are viewed as being unusually inviting to a child, who may be in danger of injury as a result of the attraction. The law holds the owner accountable because through common sense a responsible adult ought to recognize the impulsive curiosity of the child. The tendency to explore the unfamiliar is widely accepted. To show curiosity seems to be a fundamental characteristic of lower animals as well as of people.

Repetitive situations may be pleasurable up to a point, but they then become "boring," and animals will try to vary the situation. Along with a "curiosity drive," some psychologists also believe there is a "manipulation drive" (Harlow, Harlow, & Meyer, 1950). Puzzles are intriguing and invite hours of activity, which may result in learning that is useful to the individual and to the species. But there is no obvious extrinsic gain or reward to be realized.

As mentioned earlier, a distinction is sometimes drawn between primary and secondary drives. Given that animals and people seek stimulation and seem to be basically curious, it is probably not possible to insist on a rigid distinction between primary and secondary drives. That is, any goal-seeking behavior is a mixture of inborn and acquired motivation. The level of arousal of an organism is also a mixture, an interaction among centers in the brain that monitor

"Job Burnout": Growing Worry for Workers, Bosses

AN INTERVIEW WITH PROFESSOR CARY CHERNISS

Q Professor Cherniss, some people say they dread getting up in the morning and going to work because they're unhappy and frustrated in their jobs. Is that a widespread complaint?

A Everyone has that feeling occasionally. When people experience it regularly, day in and day out, we call it "job burnout."

Q What does that mean?

A It refers to a situation where a person has been experiencing high levels of stress and hasn't been able to cope with it.

Such a person gets more and more discouraged, and finally just gives up and withdraws from things. So burnout is really a reaction to a stressful job.

Q Can you describe the symptoms and give us an example of burnout?

A Probably the most common one is exhaustion—emotional as well as physical. It's the feeling that one just can't go any further.

There are more-subtle symptoms, too, such as cutting corners at work or losing one's idealism. The latter reaction shows up particularly among young professionals who are new to their jobs. I recall a young woman lawyer in her first year of practice, dealing with people at the poverty level.

She had been a student activist, was very idealistic and felt that poverty law would be her life's work—an opportunity to do something

constructive for the needy.

Within a few months, she had become extremely frustrated. She found that her clients would lie to her and were ungrateful for her efforts on their behalf. They considered her a part of the "system."

She was robbed at gunpoint a couple of times by clients. Her car was stolen. She got little support from her colleagues, all of whom were young and overworked.

She started using drugs heavily and put on a lot of weight. Her attitude changed dramatically. She considered going to work for the prosecutor's office, she said, so she could "put these people behind bars." Hers was a classic case of burnout. . . .

Q What kind of impact can burnout have on one's personal life—on family relationships and on health?

A People who experience burnout tend to have a lot of health problems. The physical symptoms include headaches, problems with sleeping, gastrointestinal disturbances. Those are all reactions to stressful and frustrating work situations. People who are bored or frustrated at work show differences in blood chemistry. They tend to have more ulcers also.

We're just becoming aware, though, of the kind of spillover effect that burnout and dissatisfaction in work can have within the family. People who are burned out are more likely to have marital problems. And there is much more tension within the family from the stresses that they bring home from the job. . . .

Q Do you believe there are specific on-the-job conditions that can lead to this type of problem?

A One of the biggest factors is simply lack of control over one's work environment. Often we think of the assembly-line worker as epitomizing that situation. But it applies to people at higher levels, too.

(continued)

Administrators in public agencies, for instance, frequently feel that they must deal with so many constituencies, so many pressure groups, so many regulations that they have little control over their own organizations.

And it's that lack of control—the sort of thing a teacher might feel in an inner-city classroom with 30 active kids—that is a major factor that can contribute to burnout. . . .

Q How do you advise people who are experiencing job burnout? What is the solution?

A While there are clearly things that individuals can do, I would emphasize the importance of personal control and effectiveness within the workplace. When a job is structured in a way that really limits the worker's self-control and his chances for experiencing a sense of success and competence, then that person is going to experience frustration and burnout.

The emphasis really has to be on what employers can do to structure jobs and work settings to make them more meaningful to workers.

Q Aren't there some lines of work where it would be almost impossible for an employer to make those kinds of changes?

A Obviously there are limits on what can be done within the workplace. Needs for productivity and efficiency will limit what can be done. But in most work situations, some changes can be made to increase the extent to which workers can exercise control over their own jobs.

Something as minor as having workers periodically fill out a survey in which they rate their supervisor's performance is an example.

Not only does that sort of thing give workers a feeling that they are being consulted, but it also has been found that many supervisors respond positively to the feedback and do, in fact, change in ways that the workers find desirable. And when that happens, then the workers feel they have been given some control over their own work lives.

physiological needs, stimulation from the environment, and past learning. Some behavior even appears to have the goal of keeping an individual at a desired level of arousal. For example, although play is an activity, it can also be thought of as an arousal mechanism, because it leads to stimulation. This has been illustrated dramatically by brain stimulation experiments with rats. Rats with electrodes embedded in their brains will actively press a lever to receive small electric shocks of about 120 microamperes (Olds, 1958, p. 316). Moreover, the areas of the brain in which electrodes can result in the seeking of increased electrical stimulation are quite broad (Olds, 1962, p. 595). Thus the view that mammalian motivation and behavior result only from attempts to reduce drives and correct internal physiological deficits is untenable. Not only do animals seek to avoid internal deficit states and noxious conditions, but they also seek stimulation and anticipate needs and pleasures.

Besides seeking stimulation, animals also anticipate deficit states. For example, when we eat lunch or drink, we may not be responding to an existing internal deficit state so much as anticipating one. In the same way, we may plan next year's vacation and arrange the stimulation to which we want to be exposed. In anticipating the vacation, we may plan to learn new skills, such as surfing or a foreign language. Thus selective anticipation directs and organizes our activities, resulting in more effective learning. Motivation pushes and pulls us toward the part of the environment that is attractive.

Two kinds of motivated behavior patterns may be distinguished: those resulting in *approach behavior* (such as eating, sex, and exploration) and those leading to *withdrawal behavior* (the avoidance of danger). It has been suggested that approach and avoidance are expressions of positive and negative reinforcing systems, both of which are adaptive and use fixed behavior patterns characteristic of the species (Wong, 1976, p. 281). We will now discuss one of the more interesting examples of human social behavior to illustrate some of the issues of motivation: the smile and the frown.

The Smile and the Frown

Because both the smile and the frown appear early in newborn infants, they are excellent specific behaviors by which to study the relative contributions of genetic organization and learning. The smile appears more frequently as infants mature; therefore, we might assume that it is acquired by learning or by mimicry of parents who smile. Research has shown that the amount of smiling decreases in premature babies as a function of the elapsed time from estimated conception. This suggests that the basic mechanism for the organization of smiling behavior has already matured in the fetus while it is still in the mother's uterus and not exposed to external stimulation. In addition, shortly after birth, a newborn's smile appears to be associated with light sleep that is accompanied by eye movements (REM sleep). Logically this seems to reduce considerably the possibility that smiling is a learned behavior. Rather, it is a pattern of motor

Although smiling may not be a learned behavior, over a lifetime it comes to be used as a stimulus to elicit a desired response.

Jean-Claude Lejeune, Stock, Boston, Inc.

behavior organized below the level of the cortex—specifically, in the brain stem. It is doubtful whether smiling among newborns can be regarded as a social signal even as a reflex. However, over a lifetime of learning, the smile and the frown are used both as a stimulus to elicit a desired response in another person and as a response to signal displeasure.

For a while after a baby's birth, smiling decreases in frequency; then it increases and becomes elicited more and more often by the appearance of friendly faces and pleasant vocalizations of doting relatives. Later the smile appears not only as a response but as a means to anticipate friendly actions. The child will smile first, using the behavior as a social signal or to stimulate others.

The frown also appears early in newborn infants and, like the smile, seems to be organized in the subcortical structures of the brain. Thus the initial organization of both the smile and the frown as patterns of behavior is not learned. However, the social *uses* of the smile and the frown are learned in association with environmental events. Frowning, smiling, and laughing are used in human cultures throughout the world, and there are clear analogies if not homologies in the facial expressions of monkeys and apes (Wilson, 1975, p. 556). Social primates use the smile as a signal for friendly contacts and to invite approach behavior, and they use the frown to communicate aversion or disapproval.

Motivation as a Push Factor

An important discovery in the neurosciences is the existence and influence of a structure in the brain stem called the *reticular formation,* a mesh or network of cells whose level of excitation may rise and fall (see Figure 14.1). Excitation of the reticular formation is transmitted through pathways to higher centers of the brain, including the cortex itself. The apparent role of ascending excitation from the reticular formation is to activate the cortex or modulate its activity. Stimulation of the reticular formation in a sleeping animal arouses it to wakefulness; if a surgical lesion is made in the reticular formation, the animal shows a lack of arousal and sleeps. The reticular formation is also a source of enhancement of motor responses. For example, if one strikes the knee of a monkey to get a reflexive jerk and simultaneously stimulates the reticular formation electrically, the motor response of the knee jerk is increased (Luria, 1973, p. 49). Finally, activity of the reticular formation influences the arousal of the cortex and the sensitivity to sensory stimulation.

Also of major significance is that the cortex and other brain structures can send their influences downward into the reticular formation so that, in turn, its state of excitation is modified by sensory input, anticipation, and emotions. Thus the descending reticular formation provides "a system by means of which the higher levels of the cortex, participating directly in the formation of intentions and plans, recruit the lower systems of the reticular formation in the thalamus and brain stem, thereby modulating their work and making possible the most complex forms of conscious activity" (Luria, 1973, p. 60). Here lies the pull factor in motivation, the recognition of stimuli in the environment, which lead the organism to expect events and to plan action. Learning and environmental stimuli modify the level of activity in the reticular formation, which, in turn, prepares the organism for voluntary action.

FIGURE 14.1
Human nervous
system

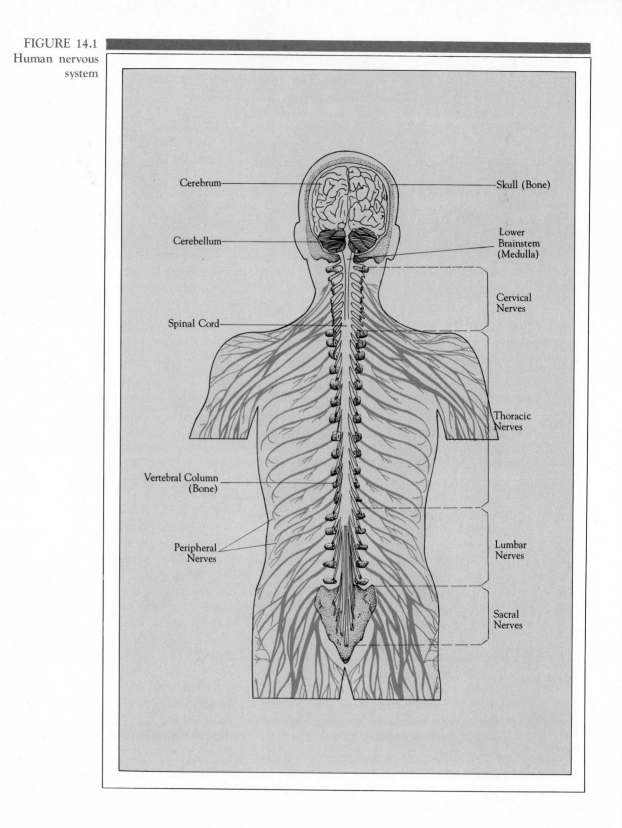

Cerebrum

Cerebellum

Spinal Cord

Vertebral Column
(Bone)

Peripheral
Nerves

Skull (Bone)

Lower
Brainstem
(Medulla)

Cervical
Nerves

Thoracic
Nerves

Lumbar
Nerves

Sacral
Nerves

FIGURE 14.1
(continued)

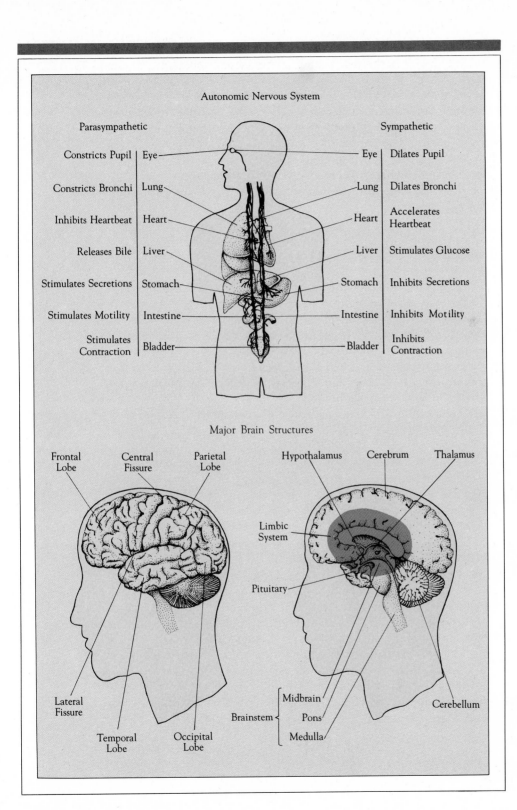

In the reticular formation we have an activation system whose activity rises and falls in accord with bodily needs and environmental input. It provides a tonic background state of excitation and acts as a push factor in motivation. Discoveries about the neurophysiology of the reticular system revealed how the motivational state of an organism responds both to the push factors of internal bodily needs and to the learned interpretations of the environment as well as to current sensory input. Most important is the alerting and anticipatory organization of behavior in accord with expected actions. This also is part of motivation, a part that is highly influenced by learning but that requires the participation of neural systems organized on a genetic basis. We will examine these neural systems next.

Neurobiological Bases of Motivation

Increasingly, the organization of behavior is being related to the biochemistry of the nervous system, or *neurochemistry* (Ordy & Kaach, 1976). As shown in Figure 14.1, that part of the peripheral nervous system that organizes an animal for fight or flight is the sympathetic nervous system. The substance released at the ends of the nerve fibers of this system is closely related to the hormone secreted by the adrenal glands (located above each kidney) when an organism is aroused to fight or flight. It has what is known as an *adrenergic action* (that is, "like the adrenal"). Actually, it is the fibers of the sympathetic nervous system originating in the *hypothalamus* that stimulate the adrenal glands to release their hormone (called adrenalin or epinephrine).

What is important in considering motivation is the fact that there are fibers in the central nervous system that release the hormone norepinephrine (or noradrenalin). These fibers project diffusely to large numbers of cells in the cortex of the brain. This would seem to establish them as being involved with a broad or general arousal of the nervous system that results from threat or some disturbance of the internal milieu, such as a shortage of water or glucose (Stricker & Zigmond, 1976). Actually, a second chemical substance, dopamine, is closely related to norepinephrine chemically and is also involved in the diffuse arousal or activation of the nervous system. Other evidence for this comes from clinical studies of depression, in which individuals who show general apathy and loss of interest in food, sex, appearance, and recreation will improve if given energizing drugs to increase the availability of norepinephrine and dopamine in the central nervous system. Depressed individuals also may improve if given a monoamine oxidase inhibitor to retard the action of monoamine oxidase in destroying the two adrenergic neurotransmitters (norepinephrine and dopamine). To raise the levels of these two transmitters in a depressed person, one either increases the substrate for synthesizing the transmitters themselves or decreases the concentration of the chemical that destroys the transmitters.

We refer here to the chemical treatment of depression to indicate the close relationship between the chemistry of the brain and our moods and motivations. The essential points are that there is a diffuse arousal system in the brain and that this system has chemical specialization. For example, research on animals shows that destruction of dopamine-containing fibers in the central nervous system leads to loss of activity and to failure to eat and drink. Interestingly, animals so treated show relatively little response to weak sensory stimulation and an intolerance of intense stimuli. This is not unlike the behavior of individuals under high stress, in that they overreact to stimuli—that is, they are "irritable." It seems likely that in a few years we will know much more about the chemistry of motivation and moods and that we will reduce the gap in understanding between the physiology of our bodies and how we feel and think.

The Hypothalamus and Motivation

The fact that human beings and other animals play and make up games when "there is time to kill" suggests that conservation of effort is not necessarily the prime goal of healthy organisms. Indeed, it is sick organisms that make energy conservation a prime factor. A sick dog crawling out of its corner to eat and drink—the minimal activity to sustain life—and then curling up to sleep again illustrates this. Our main point is a complex organism acts only minimally out of considerations of energy conservation. Rather, the arousal and directions of the organism arise from the selection of directions or goals by the central nervous system. More specifically, the starting, maintaining, stopping, and directing of behavior involve the limbic system, which includes the hypothalamus. As shown in Figure 14.1, the hypothalamus is a relatively small area of the brain above the pituitary and below (hypo) the thalamus. It is the center from which arise basic influences on the organized directions of behavior. The energizing of an organism's patterns of activity to satisfy some need is the essence of what we call motivation.

The biological needs of an organism for food, water, and a warm body temperature are expressed in *drives*. This term is meant to suggest that less learning is involved in detecting such needs and the patterns of behavior to satisfy them than is the case for such needs as affection or achievement. However, in complex organisms like human beings there is always interaction between the environment and internal bodily needs, making it practically impossible to separate completely learned or "psychological" needs from "biological" ones.

The hypothalamus is sensitive to the levels of substances in the blood, and its cells may initiate responses to increase or decrease them. The hypothalamus is a detector center that monitors a wide range of physiological activities and initiates appropriate corrective internal adjustments such as blood pressure or overt behaviors such as eating. To some extent the hypothalamus resembles the thermostat on the wall of a room, which detects the temperature of the environment and regulates the large energy source of a furnace. The temperature level at which the thermostat is set determines the energy expenditure of the furnace. Experiments on the brains of small animals show that specific points or nuclei in the hypothalamus regulate basic biological motivations such as adjustments to temperature. Destruction (lesions) produced in very small areas of the hypothalamus dramatically changes an animal's expressions of hunger. Stimulation of one area will lead to eating, and stimulation of another area will stop eating. Thus such centers can be regarded as *excitatory* or *inhibitory*. Sleep, sexual behavior, drinking, eating, and activity are among the behaviors that seem to be localized specifically.

As pointed out, the hypothalamus not only monitors bodily needs and initiates appropriate overt behavior but also detects hormone levels and initiates internal adjustments. For example, the hypothalamus monitors the level in the blood of testosterone, a male sex hormone secreted by the testes. If the level is too high, the hypothalamus will initiate a corrective action by causing the pituitary gland to reduce stimulation of the testes and lower the level of testosterone in the blood. Thus by serving as a monitoring and feedback center, the hypothalamus regulates vital processes and maintains an optimal internal state.

The name *homeostasis* has been given to the tendency of an organism to maintain physiological and chemical stability in its internal environment while it pursues other goals that may be necessary for survival. The capacity to maintain homeostasis develops in young organisms, and children fluctuate more in physiological functions than do mature adults. In late life the capacity of an organism to maintain homeostasis may again decline, perhaps because of a lowered sensitivity (higher threshold) of the hypothalamus. For example, old people placed in high or low temperatures will show less ability to adapt and maintain a nearly constant internal temperature. Evidence that diminished hypothalamus sensitivity does occur with advancing age has been collected by Everitt and Burgess (1976). Such a change as that certainly would influence the biological basis of motivation. One such change in later life for women is menopause, the cessation of fertility and monthly menstrual cycles, which probably results from imprecise timing in the release of pituitary-stimulating hormones by the hypothalamus.

Generally, the strength of motivation is a function of the amount of activity in excitatory centers in the hypothalamus. Given that the centers for hunger and other drives such as sex are located near the center that controls physical activity, it is easy to see why a hungry animal becomes diffusely active. Similarly, under high sexual arousal—as in an estrus female—diffuse activity is increased. On the surface, this increase in activity with hunger goes against logic, for a hungry animal should conserve energy and reduce activity. However, it also appears to be a survival mechanism, because a more active animal is likely to explore the environment more thoroughly, increasing the probability of finding food or a mate. Such increased activity is noted only up to a point; in a starved or emaciated animal, activity is reduced as in any ill animal. A small tumor in the hypothalamus area of an eighteen-year-old girl resulted in her having a voracious appetite. When hungry, she became angry, and her rage could be managed only by allowing her to eat to satiation (Stellar, 1974). This patient's behavior clearly demonstrates the importance of the hypothalamus in regulating the intensity of motivation—in this case, for food—and of hedonic experiences such as hunger, anger, or discomfort.

We should not expect neurochemical research to establish that the hypothalamus is *the* exclusive center regulating motivation. Daily experience shows that we have many simultaneous needs and goals. Behavior aimed at reaching these goals is modified by learning and by the sensory input our brains receive from both inside and outside the body. An analogy can be drawn to a busy airport where many planes are circling to land and other planes are waiting to take off. The total level of activity in the airport's control tower is like the arousal of an organism: there is pressure to take many actions, but only one can be processed at a time. The control tower receives various pieces of information—about, say, the fuel level of a landing plane, or a mechanical disability that might give the plane priority to land before its arrival time, or the number and types of planes in the area. The tower is like the central nervous system: it makes choices on the basis of many inputs and many goals while maintaining the efficiency of the system and preventing its destruction.

If we are intensely interested in our work, we may work through lunch time without noticing it. On another day, boredom may lead us to an early lunch. Even when we are uninterested in food, an attractive lunch may entice us and we might say, "I didn't know how hungry I was." Clearly, many factors modulate the selection and strength of goal-directed patterns of behavior over the life span. One of the strongest of these is anticipation acquired through past experience. For example, someone with a strong religious dietary prohibition might avoid food entirely for a long time if only the prohibited food is available. And if such a person eats the prohibited food unknowingly, and then is told about it, the individual might vomit.

The hypothalamus is the most important center for collecting information about the internal milieu of the body and for raising the predisposition to behaviors that will reduce physiological deficits. Raising an organism's disposition to activities that will meet specific needs is the nub of what we call motivation. The hypothalamus is not the only part of the nervous system that helps determine the relative strength of behavior predispositions. It is part of a dynamic information system whose ultimate output is a choice of behavior. Seen in this way, an organism's learning, culture, sensory information, habits, and previous activity all influence its central nervous system, helping the "control tower" to choose which behavior deserves attention first.

Emotions and Motivation

It is almost impossible to speak of motivation without discussing emotions. The term *emotion* refers to our feeling tone and the state of affective arousal. We may speak of how events stimulate our emotions and, in turn, of how our emotions influence our actions and thinking. Again, as when considering motivation itself, we are involved in circular processes. This is not merely because we are trapped by the use of language but because of how the nervous system is organized.

In regard to language, the Greeks believed words had three attributes: *cognitive*, which refers to recognizing or knowing; *connotative*, which has to do with action; and *affective*, which relates to feeling. All our verbal expressions appear to be an interplay of these three components. However, some writing—like poetry—may be oriented primarily toward one quality and may evoke affective responses, whereas other writing is oriented toward information, or cognition, and still other writing focuses on action. Similar relationships can be seen in the development of human hypothalamic centers. They are well developed at birth and are necessary for a baby to survive outside the womb. Later, more complex emotional responses appear. And still later in development—extending over the life span—we experience continuing cognitive development. This continuing development is a process of differentiating among the *kinds* of events and stimulation that result in emotional states and complex overt responses.

In 1937 a distinguished neuroanatomist, Papez, presented a picture of the anatomical organization of emotions that is still valid. He said that incoming stimuli are carried over sensory pathways that split into three routes in the thalamus. One pathway conducts impulses to the lateral cerebral cortex, where they are analyzed in terms of thought processes. Another pathway of impulses goes to the inner wall of the cerebral hemispheres and evokes feelings. This area of the brain, which is concerned with feelings, is now called the *limbic system*. Papez pointed out that sensory excitation within this threefold pathway receives emotional coloring from the limbic system en route to the cerebral cortex—where, presumably, cognitive processes and thinking occur. The human brain thus has specialized divisions for thinking, action, and feeling. In animals, stimulation or destruction of a portion of the limbic system will tame a ferocious animal or turn a tame animal into a wildly attacking one.

The development of the large cortex of the brain is most characteristic among human beings. Indeed, the cortex is the largest part of the human brain and the most different from the brains of lower animals. Presumably, the cerebral cortex provides us with a broad basis for learning new combinations of stimuli and responses.

The development in human beings of the large new brain, the *neocortex*, results in a greater range of behavioral complexity not merely because of increased effector circuits but because of an increased inhibitory control over built-in response patterns. A considerable part of the human nervous system is already organized at birth and reflects our genetic programming for differentiation of nervous tissue into sensory components, interneurons, and effector neurons. After birth, the developing nervous system shows a growth of cells that modulate the built-in response patterns and enlarge the number of alternative behavioral responses to environmental circumstances. Plasticity, or the ability to shift among built-in responses, is made possible by an increase in the number of a specialized type of nerve cell. Their function is primarily inhibitory, so that "instinctive" responses can be withheld, and adaptive responses to environmental challenges can be released. Now identified with this inhibitory role are the GABA neurons, which secrete a substance (gamma aminobutyric acid) that prevents effector neurons from firing. This is done by increasing the electrical polarization of the effector nerve cells so that it becomes difficult for the cells to receive enough electrical stimulation to depolarize, or "fire" (Roberts & Matthysse, 1970). Modulation or controlled release of our built-in response predispositions or those based on learning is expressed in the relative amounts of excitatory and inhibitory neurotransmitters present.

Although the cortex enables us to recombine behaviors in new ways, it is the more primitive limbic system that emotionally tones or colors events that are "interpreted." In this manner the limbic system helps to determine our goals and whether in a real-life situation we will be pleased, sexually aroused, or enraged. The interaction of the cortex and the limbic system determines the choices of goals in our behavior. The interaction is an interplay among our current states—our physiological needs, our feelings, and our stable traits. Thus we may not go to the movie if we are tired, or we may not play tennis if we are having a bad day. It is probably the limbic system that helps to give our behavior the particular individual qualities known as personality—that is, our predisposition to view the world and respond with feeling tones and emotional qualities that are characteristic of us.

Learning and Emotional Responses

Convincing evidence that emotional responses are not learned but are inherent in the genetic organization of the nervous system has been obtained from stimulation of the brains of small animals. By electrically stimulating the hypothalamus of a cat that has had its cerebral cortex removed surgically, one can observe physiological responses like those of rage—such as the raising of fur, dilatation of the pupils of the eye, and so on. However, further research has shown that though the hypothalamus is involved in organizing or programming the pattern of emotional expression, it is not involved in the experiencing of emotion. In a sense, a "feelingless" response of emotions can be evoked by stimulating areas of the hypothalamus. Thus all physiological responses seen in emotional states can be evoked, such as increased blood pressure, change in facial expression, baring of teeth, increased heart rate, sweating, decrease in movement of the gastrointestinal tract (peristalsis), and increase in blood sugar. Such an emotional response without feeling can be called a *pseudoemotional response*, since the organism shows no memory of an affective experience and will immediately resume previous activity without apparent disturbance by the "emotional display" (Delgado, 1960). Electrodes implanted in human beings whose brains were exposed for purposes of surgery indicated that elicitation of responses of fear, friendliness, and pleasure could be evoked by stimulating specific cerebral structures.

Emotional responses apparently are organized in one area of the brain (the hypothalamus) and are facilitated or inhibited in other areas by association with particular sensory stimulation and responses. The balance and integration of emotional predispositions and their expression make up a large part of what we call personality. Perhaps the most important point to be repeated about development in this regard is that we don't have to learn emotions. Rather, we learn with which stimuli the various emotions are associated through a continuous process of learning. Learning results in the regulation of emotional states through inhibition and facilitation. Unfortunately, strong stimulation—as is experienced by victims of violent crimes—can establish incapacitating fear responses that are demonstrated long after the events with which they were appropriate. Similar responses may result from such disasters as fires, floods, and wars.

Mixed Motivational States

Wild fish are shy and tend to avoid the sight of human beings and other animals. This presumably is a survival mechanism; shy animals live longer and are more likely to reproduce. Fish avoid moving objects, so in order to spear them a person should be very still. But fish may be hungry as well as shy; so if a nearby human being throws food on the water, the more hungry fish will— within limits—approach and eat. On subsequent days one may move closer to the fish as they eat, thus taking advantage of a clear gradient of the strength of avoidance and approach. Over time, the avoidance (or shy) response becomes inhibited in favor of the approach to food, despite the presence of other animals or human beings. Hungry fish are thus more trainable than sated ones, because they will approach and—in overcoming their native fear response—may risk more danger (though animals that have been fed recently may approach simply out of curiosity). It is a common practice to train small animals or birds in the wild state by having a trainer remain still and over subsequent days dropping food closer and closer to the trainer so that the animals or birds eventually eat out of the trainer's hand, a feat impossible at first because of the strength of their aversion to foreign animals. In this example we can recognize the interaction of several push and pull factors operating simultaneously.

Acquired inhibition can also be seen in control of the tendency to micturate (urinate) when the bladder is full. Rather than voiding continuously, babies accumulate urine and then void in a steady stream when the urinary sphincter is relaxed and the bladder contracts. When a baby's diaper is removed, the infant may urinate because of the stimulating effect of exposure to cool air. However, as the nervous system matures, the baby acquires voluntary inhibitory control over the urinary sphincter and will urinate only when it is socially acceptable. Also, the child acquires control and learns not to urinate spontaneously during the night. Adult human beings with brain damage may revert and void reflexively, since the reflex system remains organized at a subcortical level.

Similarly, many older men experience a frequent desire to urinate because of enlarged prostate glands. The prostate gland encircles the urinary tract, and its normal function is to provide viscous lubrication of the tract for the passage of sperm during ejaculation. Enlargement of this gland may be benign, or noncancerous, and its causes are unknown. One result, however, is that older men may awaken several times throughout the night with the desire to urinate. The point is that sensory input from the bladder changes the level of arousal in the reticular activating system and induces wakefulness so that individuals can execute appropriate complex behaviors, such as turning on the light and getting out of bed to use the toilet instead of voiding reflexively and wetting the bed.

Earlier in this century much attention was given to the matter of toilet training. Some psychologists and psychoanalysts have maintained that early rigid efforts at toilet training have persistent effects throughout an individual's life. A study with this issue in mind was carried out on kindergarten children

(Hetherington & Brackbill, 1963). According to this study, the age at which toilet training was started, the time to complete the task, and the emphasis on training by parents had little subsequent influence on behavior. While undoubtedly sound, these results do not exclude individual instances in which unfortunate emotional circumstances of the early toilet training may have resulted in lasting attitudes toward urination or defecation that generalized into other areas of behavior. Other studies of toilet training do suggest that severe and early training can carry over into a later predisposition of the child to be overly aggressive, negative, or timid (Mussen, Conger, & Kagan, 1974). One variable difficult to assess is the actual emotional state of a child during toilet training (such as arousal, anxiety, or fear) that *focuses* undue attention and opportunities for incidental learning surrounding the circumstances of toilet training. In bowel and bladder training, control is transferred from the reflexive emptying of the bladder or rectum to voiding under socially approved circumstances, which requires a delay made possible by an active inhibition of the lower neural centers.

Motivation, then, may be divided into two types: that arising from internal deficit states resulting from tissue needs and that arising from nondeficit states of learned incentive, such as working for money. The amount of the physiological deficit is usually related to the strength of motivation that results from it, whereas, in acquired nondeficit motivation, increased deprivation leads to reduced motivation. In other words, in the case of an acquired need, the strength of the motivation increases with the probability of satisfying the need. This is not the case with tissue needs, which is evidenced by a child whose need to urinate leads to increasingly agitated or diffuse motor behavior. Because of such obvious examples, it might be thought that all biogenic needs are initiated from within an organism. However, the next section discloses that scents have been discovered to evoke typical response patterns in animals.

Pheromones

Because of the importance of vision and hearing to human beings, there has been a tendency to overlook chemical communication. However, chemical substances called *pheromones* are now known to be secreted by members of many species in order to communicate vital information. These chemical messages are biogenic. They motivate the recipients of a message to some form of action. (Evidence of chemical communication has been found even among bacteria and algae, but in this discussion the emphasis is on chemical communication among complex organisms such as insects and mammals.)

Pheromones have a bearing on motivation because the exposure of an organism to a pheromone of its species will arouse the animal and evoke a characteristic response. In response to pheromones, motivation and the impulsion to action and the behavior response are *unlearned*. Remarkably, a chemical alarm signal in a bee colony may, in fact, arouse other nearby insects, not only bees.

Animals lay down chemical scents in order to attract mates, label territory, mark trails, and signal an alarm, for nest construction and defense, and so on. In fact, so many pheromones exist that one may speak of the *chemical vocabu-*

lary of a species. In studies of one species of deer, pheromones have been found to be released from seven different sites of the body: in the urine and feces, on the leg, foot, and forehead, and around each eye (Wilson, 1975, p. 234). The trail marking of ants can be disturbed merely by rubbing a finger across the trail, which results in much confusion and scurrying of ants until the pheromone marking of the trail is reestablished.

Since other primates use pheromones in communication, it seems unlikely that evolution would have stopped at Homo sapiens. Probably we still release pheromones. However, the relatively small olfactory lobe of the human brain and the little use we put it to in detecting odors make it unlikely that chemical communication is important to us. Still, pheromones *are* used as sexual attractants by both male and female primates, and Comfort (1971) holds open the possibility of their existence and use in human beings. A pheromone has been identified chemically in the vaginal secretions of female dogs in heat (Goodwin, Gooding, & Regnier, 1979). If a synthetic preparation of this substance is applied to the vaginal area of a female not in heat, or a spayed female, males exhibit intense overt sexual behavior toward her and attempt to mount. Application of the synthetic pheromone to a female *not* in heat does not induce receptivity in her, however, and she resorts to barking and other avoidance behavior to discourage unwanted sexual advances from males aroused by the synthetic pheromone.

The communication of territoriality and dominance in rats by means of pheromones has a strong motivating effect on exploring rats. Unlike the simple deficit and nondeficit incentive sources of acquired motivation, pheromones exert a *pull* factor that elicits behavior that is organized genetically. But what elicits activity and complex behavior in humanity over the life span? We seem to mature from a bundle of tissue needs and specific behaviors related to satisfying those needs into beings whose complex behaviors are elicited by symbols and abstractions.

Bonding of Newborn and Mother

Much attention is being given at present to those conditions of birth that may have lasting effects on the response patterns of both mother and child. Instead of being hurried away immediately after birth to be washed and safely stowed away in a nursery, newborn infants are placed quickly on the mother's breast. Apparently, in the early few moments after birth, a child and mother become attached or *bonded*, in such a way as to result in a more secure child and a more confident, responsive mother (Lozoff et al., 1977). Possibly, at the time of birth a mother and child may release pheromones that give them a basis for special recognition and emotional bonding, with subsequent emotional toning of their relationship.

Although the sense of smell in human beings is not as well developed as in other species, the nose *is* able to detect extremely small concentrations of molecules in the air. Of significance is the fact that the sensory nerve fibers from the nose—the olfactory tracts—connect directly with the areas of the brain related to emotional behavior. In fact, humans appear to show an evolutionary heritage from the lower animals in which the sense of smell contains the most important

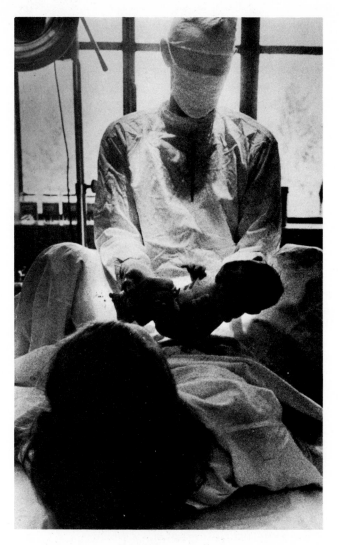

Some researchers suggest that in the early moments following birth, a child and mother become bonded emotionally.

Eve Arnold, Magnum Photos, Inc.

cues, for example, about approach-avoidance behavior and fight, or flight. The area of the brain identified with feelings is the limbic system, into which the olfactory tract feeds excitation. It is difficult from our vantage point to realize that lower animals depend less on sight and hearing and more on smell to identify friend and foe. In animals, the senses of sight and hearing may be used more to alert and orient them to attend to other signals, of which olfaction may be the most important in directing them to appropriate action, whether friendly responses or aggression. Newborns within most species are so similar in appearance that smell is usually the dominant sense used by a mother to identify individuals. Because of the close relationship between feelings and smells, strong associations become established even in human beings between feelings and the odors of perfumes, flowers, liquors, and foods. For example, adults may respond with anticipation and pleasant feelings when they smell a particular kind of familiar food. Thus the sense of smell has been overlooked as an evocative source of motivation and as a determinant of directions of behavior. Yet the consequences may begin with the birth experience itself; hearing and sight in a newborn infant have not developed as well as smell, and are not as useful in discriminations.

The expression of emotion and the strength of motivation concern the organism as a whole. Such states of arousal determine the goals of our behavior, and they color our perception of reality. Babies appear to be reasonably trusting after birth; but as they mature and their awareness increases, they may become shy and may want to be held only by their mother or father. Later they usually again become responsive to outsiders and, in fact, may have to be restrained in their openness to strangers, particularly if the family lives in an area where strangers may be less than kind.

Motivation and Maturity

As we mature, we develop more control over our primary emotions. That is, we cry less often and are aroused to anger more slowly. Maturity seems to bring mastery over emotions and to establish a balance that serves our long-range goals. In mature and wise adults, emotions appear to be in balance, and individuals do not dart off to pursue each new attractive object in the environment or react dramatically to each frustration. This suggests that maturity is accompanied by more stability in the energizing aspects of motivation, by more voluntary control, and by more stability of directions and goals. Even given this tendency with development or age to establish a consistent pattern of traits we call personality, individual differences remain. The question arises, How stable *are* our interests and personality?

One longitudinal study was conducted at the Institute of Human Development (Berkeley, California) on males and females between the ages of about fourteen and thirty-three. The most stable characteristic found in boys was the expression of aggression. That is, boys (and later, men) tend to retain their relative positions regarding drive aggression (corrected correlation .91; Tuddenham, 1971, pp. 395–403). The grouping of characteristics suggests that a cluster of factors remains typical of the boys when seen later as men. The stable traits can be described as being related to expressiveness and spontaneity and—at the opposite pole—to constriction of action. Another cluster includes drive aggression and drive control. In the females, a cluster of characteristics relating to masculinity versus femininity appeared stable. Whereas drive aggression was the most stable trait in males, the most stable trait in females was social prestige (correlation .81). Unstable for both males and females were the traits of pleasing expression and attractiveness.

There is evidence of considerable behavior change over adolescence, and group standards also change. Apparently, the skills and personal attributes valued highly by the group change from age to age, so that many adolescents undergo radical shifts in self-confidence and popularity. Some become more self-confident and popular as they grow older; others become less so. Given the responsiveness of young people to peer-group pressures, we can wonder how the relative stability of male and female aggression, expressiveness, and spontaneity will be affected if studied again during a historical period that emphasizes equal opportunities for females in sports, work, and education.

In boys, being expressive and outgoing is found to be related to being gregarious as a man. Such a boy or man seems better off than his withdrawn and reserved peers in terms of intrapersonal and interpersonal adjustment. An expressive, outgoing girl, on the other hand, seems to demonstrate a level of activity or aggressiveness not in accord with how we expect girls to behave. As a result, she has had less favorable adjustment (Bronson, 1971, pp. 386-395). Mussen and Jones (1971) add a note of caution to the idea that high masculinity and good adjustment in adolescent boys will maintain a favorable relationship later in adulthood. The point is that in adulthood men may have to work in a more socially interactive context. If they cannot modify their masculine tendencies, they may lose self-confidence and self-acceptance and may feel inadequate for leadership roles.

Tuddenham's (1971) research did not find evidence to support Frenkel-Brunswick's (1942) hypothesis that personality characteristics at a "deep level" should prove more stable and predictable than characteristics that seem more dependent on a given situation. Although the results do not refute the idea completely, they make us pause a bit in accepting the belief that some core of personality can be characterized for an individual and will remain stable in that individual over a lifetime.

Secular Trends in Adolescent Interests

As noted in Chapter 4, a *secular trend* has been observed in the physical development of boys and girls; that is, physically they mature earlier than in past generations. It seems appropriate in examining motivation to ask whether there has also been a change in adolescent interests. Fortunately, we have some information about this question. M. C. Jones (1971) periodically measured the interests and attitudes of adolescents in a California community over a twenty-year period during which, luckily, the population remained relatively stable. We thus have longitudinal data about individuals first measured in 1935 as well as samples of different subjects at the same age level over two decades.

Adolescent boys and girls studied in 1959 tended to have interests that were more mature than those of boys and girls seen several decades earlier. Thus ninth-graders in 1959 were more like eleventh- and twelfth-graders twenty years earlier. For example, both boys and girls showed increased interest in reading about science and in talking about politics. A surprising finding was that more adolescents in 1959 spent time earning money than did adolescents in 1935. They also spent more time talking about what they wanted to do when they grew up. In sum, the information indicates that adolescents today are more mature socially than were adolescents during the Depression years.

As might be expected from their earlier physical maturing, girls show an earlier sociosexual development as measured by interest in the opposite sex. Another notable secular trend in girls is a shift from passive to active interest in

Research indicates that today's adolescents are more mature socially than were their counterparts during the Depression years.

Charles Gatewood, Stock, Boston, Inc.

athletic activities and sports. The author raised a question about the impact of this shift on boys: "We might conjecture that, for this sample at least, boys may be staking out a new claim in the borderland of social respectability involving betting and gambling. On the other hand, the increased heterosexual orientation of ninth-grade boys suggests that they may not be averse to sharing interests in some areas with girls" (Jones, 1971, p. 264).

Changes in Interests with Age

As mentioned earlier, young children appear to be more active physically than either young or old adults. With development, physical activity seems to become more focused. Also, as children move into adulthood, the simple expenditure of energy no longer seems to be so pleasurable. Older males tend to watch sports events on television rather than to engage in them. Adult men and women both tend to read more, and for many there is "a trend away from participation to spectatorship, a trend towards less energetic and less hazardous activities, and a trend toward self-paced and passive interests, such as gardening, reading, television viewing and simple amusements" (Bromley, 1974, p. 236).

From the studies of Lehman (1953) regarding age and achievement it is apparent that age brings changes not only in what we are good at but also in how we invest our time. Younger poets write lyric poetry, whereas older poets write epic poetry. Younger composers write chamber music and other forms of music, whereas older composers write operas. Young adults read more fiction, whereas older adults read more biographies. Such differences very likely reflect changes in motivation. The goals of life evolve or do not remain constant. One senses with age the movement from a focus on highly personal feeling states to an identification with the culture of which one is a part. Moral judgments are also

An organization called Senior Olympics encourages adults of all ages to compete in athletics.

Payton Jordan—competing in 10th annual Senior Olympics. Joe Landis Production.

thought to change with development, with the highest form of moral development coming later in life as a result of identification with the broadest type of morality and altruism (Kohlberg, 1973). It is reasonable that we are reinforced for our competence and are encouraged by rewards so that, as we grow older, we identify more broadly with the family group, society, and culture.

The above might suggest that there are dramatic changes over the life span in leisure-time interests. Actually, some individual interests remain quite stable throughout the adult years (Palmore, 1968; Stone & Norris, 1967), although middle-aged and older adults often comment that they have less energy to pursue their interests than they once did (Birren, 1969). It is difficult to decide what roles health and opportunity play in modifying adult leisure-time interests. Some older adults may be interested in strenuous physical activity, but health concerns may restrict their choices to less active ones. An organization called Senior Olympics now encourages adults of any age to compete in a wide range of athletic events. Individuals with previous heart disabilities participate, and some are as old as ninety. The existence of the Senior Olympics provides evidence that our ideas are changing dramatically about what is appropriate activity for older adults.

Being strongly influenced by peers, adolescents are pressured to conform— even if the conforming behavior lies outside parental or societal rules.

Erika Stone, Peter Arnold, Inc.

Motivation and the Audience Effect

Children tend to be socially shy when brought into groups of strangers. Although this shyness is overcome later, even into adulthood there remains an *audience effect*. By this we mean that our arousal and performance are affected by the presence or absence of a group of people. The presence of a group can influence us to increase our drinking or eating or even to display aggressive behavior. In the past, sociologists used the term *contagion* to refer to the spread of a group influence, as in a riot situation. The point is that the presence of a group tends to be arousing to an individual and potentiates simple dominant responses such as eating or drinking. Thus if we are running, we will tend to run faster when others are watching.

Because adolescents appear to be under peer influence more than parental influence, it seems reasonable that adolescents are generally more responsive to audience and group effects than are adults. Gang behavior—in which there is social pressure to become more aggressive—can also involve a conformity influence, a desire to show that one is tough and willing to engage in breaking society's laws and rules and parental restrictions. Given that many adolescents are alienated from society (in the sense that they have not entered the adult social roles and stand on the sidelines looking in on society and social power), they turn to a peer group that will provide them with status. When adolescents fail to achieve some personal status and are unable to participate in a social system that allows the development of a positive self-evaluation, they move into alternative activities that offer the possibility of higher self-esteem. One such activity is participation in a gang; another is fantasy escape and television viewing. A summary of television viewing (Berelson & Steiner, 1964) indicated that emotionally insecure, duller children watch a great deal of television. Evidence suggests that adolescents who achieve more in school or athletics tend to view television less. It appears that extensive television viewing may in part compensate for the lack of recognition of personal qualities.

As young people mature, they become less susceptible to social conformity. Studies by Klein (1972) indicate that retired adults also conform more than younger adults in the sense of agreeing with group opinions—even when those opinions were contrived to be wrong. When the experimenters arranged conditions so that the retired adults had better opinions of their competence, they became less socially conforming. Apparently, large numbers of adolescents and retired adults have feelings of low self-esteem and insecurity because of their alienation from major social roles. Presumably, it is for this reason that they are more swayed by group opinion in determining the goals of their behavior.

Crime and Age

Data about the frequency of types of crimes committed by different age groups have bearing on motivation. As shown in Table 14.1, adolescents—particularly males—commit crimes of short duration or crimes of impulse. Youths steal cars in great numbers, whereas older men commit crimes that are more premeditated, such as embezzlement or planned burglary. Girls and women commit fewer crimes than do boys and men.

Exercise and Age

An interesting relationship to consider is that between exercise and age. Young children tend to be spontaneously active, whereas older men and women appear to keep up their physical activities with the thought that "it is good" for them. There is much physiological and psychological evidence that exercise is, indeed, good for health. However, the rewards for exercise are diffuse and do not appear immediately. In fact, during the process of exercise there can be an impulse to stop in order to avoid discomfort and strenuous effort. Countering this is the strong social effect of the peer group and the audience effect, amplifying the incentive, the thought, or the abstraction that exercise will result in good health and that a person is likely to live longer and better through regular exercise. The sensory input to the "executive brain" (regarding physical discomfort) in contrast to the strength of the conviction that exercise is good

TABLE 14.1a
Crime in the
United States by
Type and the
Age of the
Offender

Offense charged	Grand total all ages	Ages under 15	Ages under 18	Ages 18 and over	Age							
					10 and under	11–12	13–14	15	16	17	18	19
TOTAL	9,029,335	725,866	2,170,193	6,859,142	77,716	156,013	492,137	422,162	507,380	514,785	521,721	491,690
Percent distribution	100.0	8.0	24.0	76.0	.9	1.7	5.5	4.7	5.6	5.7	5.8	5.4
Criminal homicide: (a) Murder and nonnegligent manslaughter	17,163	215	1,670	15,493	14	21	180	258	523	674	826	850
(b) Manslaughter by negligence	2,933	42	327	2,606	7	8	27	38	112	135	164	233
Forcible rape	25,800	1,081	4,257	21,543	53	176	852	748	1,146	1,282	1,550	1,558
Robbery	122,514	10,309	39,259	83,255	503	1,997	7,809	7,597	10,258	11,095	10,622	9,371
Aggravated assault	221,329	10,392	36,182	185,147	1,062	2,266	7,064	6,430	9,133	10,227	10,830	10,922
Burglary	454,193	87,624	233,904	220,289	9,369	19,393	58,862	47,099	52,491	46,690	38,282	29,150
Larceny-theft	1,006,915	188,110	431,747	575,168	22,655	49,002	116,453	78,248	86,058	79,331	67,753	55,285
Motor vehicle theft	135,196	18,727	71,648	63,548	455	2,152	16,120	18,030	19,351	15,540	10,737	8,064
Violent crime	386,806	21,997	81,368	305,438	1,632	4,460	15,905	15,033	21,060	23,278	23,828	22,701
Percent distribution	100.0	5.7	21.0	79.0	.4	1.2	4.1	3.9	5.4	6.0	6.2	5.9
Property crime	1,596,304	294,461	737,299	859,005	32,479	70,547	191,435	143,377	157,900	141,561	116,772	92,499
Percent distribution	100.0	18.4	46.2	53.8	2.0	4.4	12.0	9.0	9.9	8.9	7.3	5.8
Subtotal for above offenses	1,986,043	316,500	818,994	1,167,049	34,118	75,015	207,367	158,448	179,072	164,974	140,764	115,433
Percent distribution	100.0	15.9	41.2	58.8	1.7	3.8	10.4	8.0	9.0	8.3	7.1	5.8
Other assaults	399,584	27,387	76,386	323,468	3,240	6,519	17,628	13,560	17,001	18,438	19,824	19,688

TABLE 14.1a
(continued)

	Age														
	20	21	22	23	24	25-29	30-34	35-39	40-44	45-49	50-54	55-59	60-64	65 and over	Not known
	453,665	419,610	378,052	342,904	312,534	1,149,665	737,356	536,470	433,864	364,649	300,153	198,077	113,788	97,454	7,490
	5.0	4.7	4.2	3.8	3.5	12.7	8.2	5.9	4.8	4.0	3.3	2.2	1.3	1.1	.1
	833	890	814	769	810	3,161	2,064	1,382	957	739	564	351	194	280	9
	157	179	148	158	140	485	285	172	152	109	81	65	31	45	2
	1,578	1,565	1,418	1,382	1,227	4,633	2,791	1,624	902	579	352	180	91	101	12
	7,980	7,191	6,450	5,542	4,734	16,726	7,334	3,401	1,736	1,038	576	244	76	193	41
	10,911	10,779	10,266	9,752	8,908	36,364	24,316	16,602	11,982	8,696	6,329	3,872	2,245	2,278	95
	22,560	18,438	15,310	12,901	11,074	36,131	16,072	8,346	4,868	3,107	1,848	947	392	438	425
	46,187	39,841	34,822	30,679	27,056	98,201	53,925	33,510	24,020	19,284	15,853	11,279	7,310	9,562	601
	6,192	5,088	4,262	3,623	3,171	10,292	5,184	2,807	1,698	1,088	686	325	91	141	99
	21,302	20,425	18,948	17,445	15,679	60,884	36,505	23,009	15,577	11,052	7,821	4,647	2,606	2,852	157
	5.5	5.3	4.9	4.5	4.1	15.7	9.4	5.9	4.0	2.9	2.0	1.2	.7	.7	(+)
	74,939	63,367	54,394	47,203	41,301	144,624	75,181	44,663	30,586	23,479	18,387	12,551	7,793	10,141	1,125
	4.7	4.0	3.4	3.0	2.6	9.1	4.7	2.8	1.9	1.5	1.2	.8	.5	.6	.1
	96,398	83,971	73,490	64,806	57,120	205,993	111,971	67,844	46,315	34,640	26,289	17,263	10,430	13,038	1,284
	4.9	4.2	3.7	3.3	2.9	10.4	5.6	3.4	2.3	1.7	1.3	.9	.5	.7	.1
	20,227	19,553	18,803	17,462	16,434	64,618	42,109	28,292	20,353	14,228	10,359	5,669	2,849	2,687	313

Source: Crime in the United States, 1977. FBI Uniform Crime Reports. U.S. Department of Justice. Washington, D.C.: U.S. Government Printing Office, October 18, 1978.

TABLE 14.1b
Crime in the
United States by
Sex of the
Arrested
Offender

Offense charged	Number of persons arrested			Percent male	Percent female
	Total	Male	Female		
TOTAL	9,029,335	7,581,262	1,448,073	84.0	16.0
Criminal homicide:					
(a) Murder and nonnegligent manslaughter	17,163	14,670	2,493	85.5	14.5
(b) Manslaughter by negligence	2,933	2,605	328	88.8	11.2
Forcible rape	25,800	25,518	282	98.9	1.1
Robbery	122,514	113,399	9,115	92.6	7.4
Aggravated assault	221,329	192,923	28,406	87.2	12.8
Burglary	454,193	426,881	27,312	94.0	6.0
Larceny-theft	1,006,915	687,211	319,704	68.2	31.8
Motor vehicle theft	135,196	124,211	10,985	91.9	8.1
Violent crime	386,806	346,510	40,296	89.6	10.4
Property crime	1,596,304	1,238,303	358,001	77.6	22.4
Subtotal for above offenses	1,986,043	1,587,418	398,625	79.9	20.1
Other assaults	399,854	344,570	55,284	86.2	13.8

Source: Crime in the United States, 1977. FBI Uniform Crime Reports, U.S. Department of Justice. Washington, D.C.: U.S. Government Printing Office, October 18, 1978.

creates a dynamic balance between the desire to stop and the desire to continue. Marathon runners speak of going through the "wall" of pain about halfway through the twenty-six miles. In this situation the tissues are "screaming" for the runners to stop, yet strong cognitive control may override that impulse because of an intense desire to complete the run, if not win. One wonders if long-distance runners do not create a state of autohypnosis that enables them to gate, or "turn off," the pain input from bleeding legs and feet and exhausted muscles.

Goals

We can also view motivation from the vantage point of our goals. Being highly cerebral or cognitive animals, human beings develop goals that persist for many years. Buhler and Massarik (1968) see our major goals as being established during the first twenty years of life, followed by a period of goal attainment and realization. Later, persons who are better adjusted and more successful achievers reexamine the goals of their early adult life and reorient their efforts. This and similar views of life are based on a concept of three phases of motivation over the life span: growth, realization, and constriction. In the growth phase, we acquire direction to our arousal and define specific goals for achievement, such as financial security, a good professional or personal reputation, having children, or enjoying social success. Such desires may be realized or gratified in middle age. Then, during the constriction phase in late middle age, retirement and changes in health may bring the goal of a strategic retreat from life. Older people may maximize their potentials for loss rather than anticipate and plan for further gains and expansion.

In a view similar to Buhler's, Erikson sees our lives as consisting of eight stages, of which the early ones generally are marked by expansion (Erikson, 1964, 1968). However, for Erikson the later stages of life are marked not so much by the inevitability of constriction but by struggles between opposite tendencies. For example, his last stage of life is called *integrity versus despair*. At this point an individual's life either makes sense because of some human principles or is marked by a sense of despair, because it seems meaningless. Erikson's view is not unlike that of Jung (1971), who believed that, although the direction of attention in the late years may be inward, such introspection carries with it the possibility of integrating experience so that life ends with a sense of meaningfulness and intactness rather than an existential void. These views of personality over the life span recognize the impulsion of an individual toward goals and the normality of individuals undergoing a development or progression of goals.

Data on personality traits of identical (one-egg) twins and fraternal (two-egg) twins suggest that their similarity from childhood to young adulthood was never able to explain over half the variance. That is, the similarity between twins never accounted for more than half the total of individual differences on such traits as dominance and sociability (Carter, 1935). Generally, the data suggest that our personality traits are not rigidly stable over long periods of years, with the need for achievement being among the more stable traits.

Motivation Toward Goal Realization

Psychologists have viewed much of the motivation behind human behavior as being directed toward extending mastery over the environment. This view has been developed by a number of distinguished psychologists, including Maslow (1950), White (1959), and Rogers (1959). Of these, perhaps Maslow is best known for his characterization of human striving for self-actualization. He proposed a hierarchy of needs in the following order of decreasing urgency: (1) physiological requirements, (2) safety, (3) love and belongingness, (4) esteem, and (5) self-actualization. Presumably, we have to satisfy the earlier, biological needs before progressing toward higher needs. Thus some people are free to pursue self-actualization because they have satisfied the four prior levels of needs. Self-actualizing persons are thought to have better-than-average psychological health; to show better perception of external reality and better acceptance of one's self, other persons, and nature; to show greater spontaneity and an increased focus on problems outside themselves; and to show a greater need for privacy and detachment as well as more autonomy and independence from their environment and culture (Maslow, 1954, 1962, 1967).

Maslow's hierarchy of needs generally follows a developmental course. That is, only a relatively mature adult with experience could be self-actualizing. Buhler holds a parallel view of a pattern in the development of motivation from childhood through old age (Buhler et al., 1973, pp. 816–917). She describes the sequence this way: "the tendency to need satisfaction, predominating in infancy and early childhood; the tendency to self-limiting adaptation, predominating in later childhood; the tendency to creative expansion, predominating in adolescence and adulthood; and the tendency to upholding and resorting the internal order, predominating in late adulthood and old age" (1973, p. 872).

The statements by Buhler and Maslow are made in "program language," the language we use in communicating experience. Not specified are the biological and social interactions in terms of an organism's "machine language"—that is, the brain centers and neurochemistry involved. One senses, however, that these psychologists view motivational development as proceeding upward from the dominance of mechanisms in the brain stem, to the hypothalamus, to other components of the limbic system, and finally to domination by the neocortex of the two hemispheres when an individual has mastered the self and the environment and lives by evolved principles rather than tissue needs.

Personality and Motivation

Personality can be defined as the characteristic way we behave and respond to our environment. The consistency in the way we behave is what enables others to predict how we will react to particular situations. Among the components of personality are our tendencies to action. Howarth and Cattell (1973) call these motivational components of the personality *ergs*. They define an *erg* as "an innate psychophysical disposition which permits its possessor to acquire reactivity to certain classes of objects more readily than others, to experience a specific emotion in regard to them, and to start on a course of action which ceases more completely at a certain specific goal activity" (p. 808). For Howarth and Cattell, ergs include curiosity, gregariousness, self-assertion, and many other predispositions to action.

Besides the tradition of quantitative measurement used by Howarth and Cattell, another trend emerged on the intellectual scene in the 1960s—*humanistic psychology*, which emphasizes the purpose of human beings, our intentionality or will to action. The humanists also stress our intentions, aspirations, and capacity to transcend daily existence (Sargent, 1973, pp. 817–825). Maslow (1968) reacted to what he felt was a lack in the psychopathological views of humanity held by earlier psychologists. He identified self-actualizing people as those who show the particular quality of being motivated for reasons of personal or self-growth. Like most personality theorists and humanistic psychologists, he regarded human beings as striving for some kind of internal consistency in values or in the way the self is viewed.

Erikson's late stage of adult development, called *ego integrity*, refers to a consolidation or integration of life's experiences. There are many pathways or attempts to achieve integration, and one of them is to seek selectively the explanations of events that justify one's behavior. People in this mode are like lawyers who collect evidence to defend the meaning of their lives in some ultimate trial or judgment. Studies on communication do, in fact, indicate that people attend to and respond most to communications that are in accord with their predispositions. That is, we tend to listen to, read, and seek communication that is likely to reinforce positions already held, rather than to seek challenging or contradicting evidence (Berelson & Steiner, 1964, pp. 539-543). Seen from this point of view, the human mind is too often a rationalizer of life as it is lived rather than a force in seeking an objective understanding of it. Nevertheless, there are some people who seek honest answers to penetrating questions.

Some evidence on the changing patterns of behavior with age comes from a longitudinal study of Harvard undergraduates (Vaillant, 1977). A total of ninety-five men were followed for over thirty years from the time they were sophomores. As middle-aged men they used fewer immature mental devices (so called ego-defenses) than they did when first interviewed. In their middle years they tended to use more of such devices as humor and altruism and less of fantasy and projection in handling frustrations and mastering their motivations in relation to reality. Apparently there is a process of maturing in adults that, despite some declines in the efficiency of bodily processes, results in an improved integration of experience, a lessening of tensions, and an earned feeling of mastery. Whatever an individual's style, it appears that achieving an integration of experience, as in acquiring a high level of internal self-consistency, is positively related to good mental health. Such integration also appears to equip an individual to surmount stress more readily, including the most difficult of life's crises: facing death with poise. Two major philosophical issues of life are the integration of our own thinking about the meaning of life and the parallel matter of our feelings and thoughts about the end of life, death itself.

Summary

1. Living organisms are motivated; that is, they have an impulsion to expend energy and to organize behavior in order to reach a goal. An individual is said to be highly motivated if he or she shows persistence in seeking a goal and a willingness to endure frustration, fear, or pain.

2. Small animals will engage in spontaneous wheel-turning in captivity, indicating that there exists a background arousal or motivation toward activity. Healthy young mammals, including children, show a great deal of spontaneous activity in play, which is thought to express a need to rehearse behaviors to be used as adults. Young animals may pounce, growl, bare their teeth, and chase each other in a kind of mock adversary relationship.

3. The widespread occurrence of playlike activities in young mammals suggests that these activities have an evolutionary basis and may have played a role in selective survival. The curiosity expressed by young organisms may also be a preprogrammed tendency to explore the environment and provide the basis for an expanding repertory of experiences and behaviors that make an individual more likely to survive.

4. Physiological deprivations such as lack of food or water lead to increased activity to relieve the deprivation. Such biologically based motives are often referred to as drives. In human offspring drives are well developed at birth, enabling an infant to survive outside the mother. Later the expression of drives such as the need for water, food, temperature regulation,

elimination, and sex become socially conditioned and are expressed in organized, socially approved ways that are typical of the culture in which a child is raised.

5. A small region of the brain, the hypothalamus, is concerned with monitoring biological needs and with activating response patterns leading to satiation of those needs. Maturation of the central nervous system brings about an increase in the capacity for inhibiting built-in response patterns and adjusting them to fit the circumstances for expression. Thus infants void urine as a reflexive action, whereas adults postpone urination until it can be done under socially approved conditions. Socially derived motives and interests continue to change over the life span.

6. Homeostasis is the tendency of organisms to maintain physiological and chemical stability, a capacity that increases during development (although very elderly persons may be less able to maintain or reestablish such internal states as body temperature).

7. Besides the built-in response mechanisms to satisfy biological needs, there also are emotional patterns that are organized in advance of such experiences as fear and anger. The capacity for these responses is programmed or organized largely by genetics. What is learned during development are the associations of the response predispositions with particular stimuli.

8. The portion of the brain that contains the organized emotional patterns is referred to as the limbic system. Through progressive approaches that use food as a reward, shy animals can learn to eat out of one's hands and "overcome" their fear. Over time, the fear, or avoidance response, becomes inhibited in favor of the approach response (the desire to secure food).

9. Longitudinal studies show that adolescents today appear more mature in the sense that their interests are more like those of older adolescents several decades ago. Changing social attitudes toward careers and sports for women may produce a new generation, a cohort of girls and women who will be more achievement minded in work and athletics.

10. Older adults tend to move away from participatory activities and toward spectator (less physically active) roles, but it is not clear whether this is a result of a change in internal biologically based motivation or social conformity. With the removal of narrow age and sex restrictions on what is regarded as appropriate behavior, more choices will be available to individuals as they grow up and grow old.

11. The increasing options available to individuals in contemporary society require people to spend effort and time to integrate their capacities, goals, and opportunities. Motivation toward realizing one's potentials also requires effective mental strategies by which, in fact, a wise older adult may bring about more contentment and a lessening of tensions while being more effective in the face of some physical declines.

Selected Readings

Elias, M. F., and P. K. Elias. "Motivation and Activity." In *Handbook of the Psychology of Aging*. Eds. J. E. Birren and K. W. Schaie. New York: Van Nostrand Reinhold,

1977, pp. 357–383. An attempt to integrate information about motivation in nonverbal animals with information about human beings. The advantages of using animals as models for research are described. Both young and old animals will work to increase the amount of stimulation to which they are exposed.

Scientific American (September 1979), Vol. 241. This entire issue is devoted to the structure of the brain, its chemical and functional organization, its disorders, and the ways of studying and thinking about it.

Wigdor, B. T. "Drives and Motivations with Aging." In *Handbook of Mental Health and Aging.* Eds. J. E. Birren and R. B. Sloane. Englewood Cliffs, N.J.: Prentice-Hall, 1980, pp. 245–261. Information has been drawn from studies of young persons as well as older adults together with clinical studies in an attempt to understand the role of motivation and incentives over the life span. The individual is regarded as adapting to changes in the internal and external environment while attempting to maintain goal-directed behavior.

Chapter 15

Sex Differences and Sexual Behavior

The myths and realities about sex differences: what traits really *do* differentiate between males and females?

Biological and environmental influences on sex differences

Major theories relating to sex-role development

Changing patterns of sex roles and sexual behavior

Sexual behavior over the life span

Sex Differences: Myths and Realities

Sex Differences That Appear to Be Real
Traits That *May* Differentiate the Sexes
Myths About Sex Differences

Mediators of Sex Differences

Biological Bases for Sex Differences
Social and Cultural Bases for Sex Differences
Variations in Home Environments

Theories of Sex-Role Development

Psychoanalytic Approach
Social-Learning Approach
Cognitive-Developmental Approach

Changing Patterns of Sex Roles and Sexual Behavior

Erosion of Traditional Sex-Role Differentiations
Changes in Sexual Behavior and Attitudes

Sexual Behavior over the Life Span

Puberty and Adolescence
Sexuality and Aging
Sexuality in Old Age

Introduction

Despite the impact of the feminist movement on contemporary life in the United States, and regardless of the changing status of women and men, people still rely on stereotypes to characterize masculine and feminine roles. It has been more than two decades since Talcott Parsons devised the terms *instrumental* and *expressive* to characterize males and females, respectively. Yet these stereotypes—which characterize men as being active and dominant and women as being gentle, nurturant, and dependent—still prevail today.

Current evidence for the existence of sex-role stereotypes comes from studies of college students, which have been replicated in several parts of the country (McCandless, 1975). For example, Rosenkrantz and associates (1968) asked students to write essays about the roles of men and women and then culled adjectives from these essays to be evaluated for "maleness" and "femaleness." Of the 122 categories evaluated, 41 exemplified stereotypes about which 75 percent or more of both sexes agreed in terms of the direction of the masculine-feminine difference. Another 48 items could be differentiated reliably between the sexes, although not to as great a degree as the first group. Some of the items agreed upon as being most characteristic of males and females are presented in Table 15.1. Examination of these items suggests that males are characterized by more desirable traits than females are, and college students have agreed that more masculine traits are socially desirable (for example, Broverman et al., 1970, 1972; Rosenkrantz et al., 1968).

Thus in a period when a great deal of attention and effort is focused on equalizing roles and opportunities for males and females, it is clear that stereotypes still reflect inequities. One question this chapter will examine is the extent to which such stereotypes reflect reality. *Are* there differences in ability between the sexes? What are the myths about sex differences and what is reality? After examining the nature of the differences between the sexes, we will consider the explanations for sex differences in behavior and in sex-role development. Finally, we will consider changing patterns of socialization in the United States and examine the consequences for sex-role development and sexual behavior at various points of the life span.

Sex Differences: Myths and Realities

From the time parents begin to think about having a child, they conjure up widely divergent images according to whether they imagine having a male or a female child. Such divergence was characterized in the musical *Carousel* in a scene occurring just after the hero learns he is to become a father. Immediately he assumes the child will be a son, and he sings about how tall and tough the boy will be. This prospective father sees his son as being able to wrestle, herd cattle, run a riverboat, drive spikes—all the "masculine" jobs characteristic of the period and locale. It will be acceptable for the child's mother to teach the boy manners, but she must beware of making him a sissy. The future father sings on, and then he suddenly has an insight: the child may be a daughter! The music becomes softer, and the song takes on a wholly different tone. His

TABLE 15.1
Stereotypic
Sex-Role Items
(Responses from
74 College Men
and 80 College
Women)

Competency Cluster: Masculine Pole Is More Desirable

Feminine	Masculine
Not at all aggressive	Very aggressive
Not at all independent	Very independent
Very emotional	Not at all emotional
Does not hide emotions at all	Almost always hides emotions
Very subjective	Very objective
Very easily influenced	Not at all easily influenced
Very submissive	Very dominant
Dislikes math and science very much	Likes math and science very much
Very excitable in a minor crisis	Not at all excitable in a minor crisis
Very passive	Very active
Not at all competitive	Very competitive
Very illogical	Very logical
Very home oriented	Very worldly
Not at all skilled in business	Very skilled in business
Very sneaky	Very direct
Does not know the way of the world	Knows the way of the world
Feelings easily hurt	Feelings not easily hurt
Not at all adventurous	Very adventurous
Has difficulty making decisions	Can make decisions easily
Cries very easily	Never cries
Almost never acts as a leader	Almost always acts as a leader
Not at all self-confident	Very self-confident
Very uncomfortable about being aggressive	Not at all uncomfortable about being aggressive
Not at all ambitious	Very ambitious
Unable to separate feelings from ideas	Easily able to separate feelings from ideas
Very dependent	Not at all dependent
Very conceited about appearance	Never conceited about appearance
Thinks women are always superior to men	Thinks men are always superior to women
Does not talk freely about sex with men	Talks freely about sex with men

Warmth-Expressiveness Cluster: Feminine Pole Is More Desirable

Feminine	Masculine
Doesn't use harsh language at all	Uses very harsh language
Very talkative	Not at all talkative
Very tactful	Very blunt
Very gentle	Very rough
Very aware of feelings of others	Not at all aware of feelings of others
Very religious	Not at all religious

Table 15.1
(continued)

Warmth-Expressiveness Cluster: Feminine Pole Is More Desirable

Feminine	Masculine
Very interested in own appearance	Not at all interested in own appearance
Very neat in habits	Very sloppy in habits
Very quiet	Very loud
Very strong need for security	Very little need for security
Enjoys art and literature	Does not enjoy art and literature at all
Easily expresses tender feelings	Does not express tender feelings at all easily

Source: P. S. Rosenkrantz, S. R. Vogel, H. Bee, I. K. Broverman, and D. M. Broverman. "Sex Role Stereotypes and Self-Concepts in College Students." *Journal of Consulting and Clinical Psychology, 32,* (1968), 287–295. Copyright 1968 by The American Psychological Association. Reprinted by permission.

daughter will have ribbons in her hair and be pretty like her mother, and she will attract many men. The expectant father realizes that a daughter must be protected and that he better have enough money to raise her properly and in a setting where she will be able to meet the right man to marry.

The differentiation of parental roles as a function of the sex of the child may be dramatized in this example; however, it reflects distinctions made by most parents. Pink and blue blankets are only the initial signs of the many ways parents and relatives differentiate boy and girl babies, and we will examine the extent to which such differentiation is reliably manifested in the developing individual.

Sex Differences That Appear to Be Real

The most exhaustive examination of the current literature concerning sex differences was published by Eleanor Maccoby and Carol Jacklin (1974). Evaluating all the published data about sex differences in behavior, these scholars found four major traits on which males and females could be differentiated clearly: verbal ability, visual-spatial ability, mathematical ability, and aggression. It must be emphasized that sex differences in the distributions of scores show great overlap. Only when the group averages are computed do the differences emerge.

Verbal Ability Female superiority on verbal tasks is one of the more solidly established generalizations in the field of sex differences. Although Maccoby and Jacklin (1974) suggest that the early studies indicating sex differences in verbal ability (even at the babbling phase in infancy) have not been replicated more recently, the sexes begin to diverge at about age eleven. Female superiority increases through high school, and many studies indicate that women maintain or increase this superiority during adult life. Though the two sexes perform in a similar manner on a number of verbal tasks, whenever a sex

Even before a child is born, parents hold widely divergent images of how their boy or girl will grow up.

David Strickler, Monkmeyer Press Photo Service

difference is found in verbal abilities, it favors females. Verbal fluency, vocabulary, spelling, reading, creative writing, and analogies—all are tasks on which females typically excel.

Visual-Spatial Ability In adolescence and adulthood males are consistently superior on visual-spatial tasks. An example of such a task is presented in Figure 15.1. In general such tasks involve the ability to visualize rotations of objects or different perspectives of objects in space. The male advantage shows up in some studies as early as the ages of eight or ten, but it is not consistent until early adolescence.

Mathematical Ability Although the two sexes perform equally well on tasks requiring quantitative ability and show equal mastery of arithmetic in grade school, boys show more rapid advancement beginning around the age of twelve or thirteen. The magnitude of this difference in ability appears to be smaller than the difference in visual-spatial ability, and it varies depending on the populations studied. Maccoby and Jacklin (1974) note that some math problems can be solved with both verbal and visual-spatial strategies, whereas other problems are resolved with visual-spatial skills alone. Therefore, they suggest the variation in the magnitude of sex difference in mathematical ability may occur because different studies use different types of problems. Sex differences in mathematical ability do *not* seem to be entirely the result of the fact that, in the adolescent years, when the differences begin to show, boys tend to take

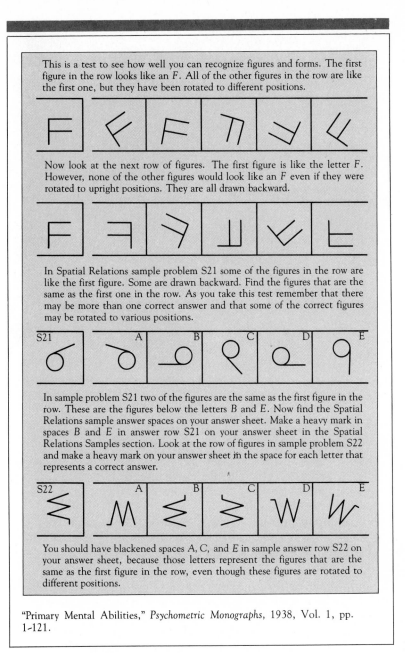

FIGURE 15.1
Visual-spatial task. This is an example of a task testing visual-spatial ability. It is taken from the Spatial Relations subtest of the Primary Mental Abilities Test.

"Primary Mental Abilities," *Psychometric Monographs*, 1938, Vol. 1, pp. 1-121.

more math classes than girls do. Maccoby and Jacklin point out, however, that the question of the effect of classes of mathematics on the differential performance of adolescent boys and girls has not been studied extensively.

Aggression   More than any other trait or ability, aggression differentiates males and females. In all cultures in which relevant observations have been made,

From early childhood into young adulthood, there is a significant difference between the sexes in terms of aggression.

Paul S. Conklin

and across many subhuman species, the results are similar—males are more aggressive than females. They are more aggressive both physically and verbally, and they manifest this trait to a greater degree in any form in which it has been measured (such as mock fighting or aggressive fantasies). As soon as social play begins (around age two), boys express aggression more than girls do. This sex difference appears throughout childhood and into young adulthood, and at every point in the life span at which it has been measured. Thus aggression is a trait on which there is a large magnitude of difference between the sexes, and this difference appears early in life. With age, the difference between the sexes on aggression declines, but it is still apparent in young adulthood. Data for later adulthood are not available.

Traits That *May* Differentiate the Sexes

For a number of abilities or traits there are suggestive data about sex differences. In no instance, however, are the data completely consistent in terms of indicating a superiority for one sex. Hence we will consider the following behaviors only as likely candidates for differentiating the sexes. The final decision must be reserved for some later time, when more studies of these behaviors have been completed. In no cases are the differences between the sexes on the following traits as clear as on the four traits discussed previously.

Tactile Sensitivity Most studies in which sex differences have been analyzed in terms of sensitivity to touch have been done with infants. A number of studies indicate no sex differences; when a sex difference *is* found, however, it is in favor of females. Female infants may be more sensitive to touch than males, and a few studies also have found greater sensitivity in females after infancy. Pain sensitivity may also be greater in females.

Fear, Timidity, and Anxiety Studies in which individuals are observed in various situations find no differences between the sexes in fearful behavior, but ratings by teachers and self-reports usually find females to be more timid or more anxious than males. Perhaps girls are more willing to admit they feel anxious, and thus the self-report data may merely reflect a response bias. Maccoby and Jacklin (1974) point out that willingness to assert that one is fearful may lead to fearful behavior. Thus the distinction between reporting and experiencing anxiety may be meaningless. At this point, however, the meaning of girls' greater self-attribution of fears is not clear.

Activity Level Although male and female infants are not different in activity level, boys appear to be more active by the time they engage in social play, around two years of age. When sex differences *are* found during the preschool years, boys are more active. The fact that many studies show no sex differences in activity level led Maccoby and Jacklin (1974) to compare various studies in this area, and they concluded that much of the variance can be accounted for by the measurement situation. If children are measured in a social situation, boys are more active—especially in the presence of other boys. The precise nature of situational control over activity level has not been established, however.

Competitiveness Studies of competitive behavior often show no sex differences, but males are more competitive when differences *are* found. One reason that studies of competition may show an absence of sex differences is the way in which the studies are designed. In the games typical of such studies, competition is seen as maladaptive, and so the children win if they cooperate. In such studies cultural differences in competition are much more apparent than are sex differences. Speculation on the basis of male competitiveness in sports would suggest that, when rewarded for competitiveness, males might compete more than females, but such data are not available. Clearly, the age of the subject and the identity of the opponent make a difference. For example, when heterosexual interests develop, adolescent girls are reluctant to compete with boys, and young women hesitate to compete against their boyfriends.

Dominance Just as little boys show spurts of activity in the presence of other boys, so do boys appear to exhibit more dominance behavior in groups of boys. Boys are also more likely to attempt to dominate adults. In girls' groups, dominance appears to be much less of an issue. There is little attempt at heterosexual dominance during childhood because children tend to play in sex-segregated groups; and in the studies where boys and girls are grouped together, it is not clear which sex influences the behavior of others. Formal leadership tends to go to males in adult mixed pairs of groups, especially in the beginning of the interaction. The longer the relationship lasts, however, the more sex-equal it becomes, with decisions and labor being divided by competency. Indeed, there is some evidence that in aged couples the female becomes dominant, and older men and women perceive older women as being more powerful than do middle-aged men and women.

Compliance This is a behavior in which sex differences are extremely specific to the situation and age of the individuals. In childhood, girls tend to be more compliant to adults, whereas boys are more likely to comply with peer pressure. Neither sex appears willing to comply consistently with the wishes of the other.

Nurturance and "Maternal" Behavior The only clear evidence that females are more nurturant comes from cross-cultural studies that suggest that girls from ages six to ten are more often found to behave in a nurturant manner. Comparisons of boys and girls in the United States do not lead to this conclusion, but in most cases observations of children have been made in settings where much younger children are not present. Hence the elicitors of such behavior have not been available. Although maternal behavior in human females may be under the control of hormones, as it is in lower animals, there is no direct evidence that this is the case. Additionally, if there *is* a sex difference in nurturant behavior, it does not generalize to altruistic behavior in all situations, for males are as likely as females to be altruistic, depending on circumstances.

Myths About Sex Differences

We all hold stereotypes about what is feminine and masculine, and the material presented up to this point suggests that some aspects of these stereotypes have a factual basis. Some clear differences in behavior exist between the sexes, and some differences that may be more subtle appear to be somewhat reliable. One of our tendencies as human observers, however, is to overgeneralize and to develop expectancies that we remember when they are confirmed and ignore when they are disconfirmed. This tendency of the human mind to categorize and label can lead to fallacious conclusions. Following are some of the myths we have created about sex differences in behavior.

Sociability We tend to consider females to be more "social" than males, but this assumption is fallacious on several grounds. First, both sexes are equally interested in social stimuli, and they learn equally well through imitation of models. Second, in childhood girls are no more dependent on their caretakers than are boys, and neither sex is more willing to remain alone. Both sexes are responsive to social reinforcers, with males being as responsive as females. Girls do not spend more time playing with other children than boys do, and at some ages boys are more responsive to peers than girls are. In most of the studies that have been done concerning empathy, or understanding the emotional reactions of others, the two sexes have performed equally well.

Females are no more "social" than males; both sexes seek social stimuli, and both learn equally well through modeling.

Cary Wolinsky, Stock, Boston, Inc.

If there are any differences between the sexes in terms of sociability, the differences are qualitative rather than quantitative. Boys tend to play in larger groups and are oriented more toward the peer group, whereas girls interact in pairs or small groups and may be oriented more toward adults.

Suggestibility Females have been considered to be more subject to external influence than males. The data indicate that spontaneous imitation is equal in both sexes and that persuasive communications and face-to-face social-influence situations are equally effective on males and females.

Self-Esteem The data indicate that, contrary to the myth, the two sexes are similar on measures of self-satisfaction and self-confidence throughout childhood and adolescence. Although there are not many data concerning adulthood, those available also suggest no sex difference in terms of self-esteem. Where differences in self-esteem do exist, they involve areas of self-attributed competence. Females feel more confident about their social abilities, whereas males more often see themselves as strong, powerful, and dominant. During the college years men are more likely than women to express feelings of control over their own fate and to predict higher levels of performance for themselves on school-related tasks. However, such differences are not observed in children or in adults beyond college age.

Cognitive Abilities In part because females achieve better grades in school and males realize greater career success, it has been postulated that females are better at rote learning and simple repetitive tasks and that males excel in tasks requiring higher-level cognitive processing and the inhibition of previously learned responses. This myth is exploded by data showing that neither sex is more susceptible to simple conditioning or excels in simple paired-associates or other forms of "rote" learning. On tasks involving discrimination learning, reversal shifts, and probability learning—all of which have been interpreted as involving some inhibition of response—the sexes perform equally well. Early in development, when the male's nervous system is immature compared with the female's level of development, boys are somewhat more impulsive (or lacking in inhibition) than girls. After the preschool years, however, the sexes do not differ in their ability to wait for a delayed reward or to inhibit early (wrong) responses.

Males have also been considered more "analytic" than females, and this assumption is also a myth. The only tasks involving analysis on which males perform better are tasks involving spatial visualization. In all modalities except the visual mode, females and males both ignore surrounding contexts and find features embedded in the surround. This suggests that the analytic skills are equal in the sexes, although—as mentioned previously—males excel in spatial visualization. In cases where specific aspects of a task must be analyzed while other aspects are ignored, the two sexes are distracted equally by irrelevant stimuli.

Achievement Motivation   Since girls' achievement imagery was not found to be as responsive to competitive arousal as was the achievement imagery of boys, it has been thought that females lacked achievement motivation. Actually, in neutral conditions, girls scored higher than boys on tests of achievement motivation. To bring their achievement imagery up to the level of girls', boys need to be challenged. Observational studies of achievement strivings have either found no sex differences or have found females to be superior.

Visual Versus Auditory Sensory Modality   Since females excel in verbal skills and males show visual-spatial superiority, attempts were made to find differences in responding to visual and auditory stimuli. Females were considered to attend more to auditory information, whereas males were more interested in visual stimuli. These notions were contradicted by studies of infants' response to sounds, the majority of which report no differences in responding between the two sexes. There also appear to be no sex differences in memory for sound. Studies of visual fixation in the first year of life find no consistent sex differences. Moreover, from infancy to adulthood, the sexes are highly similar in terms of their interest in visual stimuli, ability to discriminate among visual stimuli, identification of shapes, distance perception, and a variety of other measures of visual perception.

Mediators of Sex Differences

We have seen that stereotypes about sex differences in behavior persist in our society, even among those whom we might expect to be least likely to retain them—contemporary groups of college students. We have also seen that parts of the stereotypes are based on measurable differences between males and females. For example, females are considered to be more talkative, and, indeed, they do appear to excel on tasks requiring verbal skills. Males are viewed as being very aggressive, and they clearly are more aggressive than females. The evidence is less clear, however, regarding one notion held by most college students—that males are more dominant and females are more nurturant—although the data are not inconsistent with such images. The evidence contradicts some of the stereotypes, such as that females are more influenced by persuasive others or that males are more ambitious. In part, then, the stereotypes appear to be based on accurate perceptions of differences between the sexes, but they also reflect the human tendency to overgeneralize.

Given that children are raised by individuals who hold notions about the capacities of males and females, do these children merely conform to societal expectations when they manifest sex-typed behavior? If this is the case, how are sex-typed behaviors transmitted? We will examine these questions later in our discussion of theories of sex-role development. It is also important to ascertain whether sex differences in behavior are more than a reflection of societal expectations. Do parents respond to sex differences in their children that are evident at birth? Is there a biological basis for any of the sex differences in behavior? It is this last question that requires consideration first.

Biological Bases for Sex Differences

Throughout the life span, from conception to death, on average males are more vulnerable to insult and are less likely to survive than females. Males are conceived in greater numbers than females, the ratio at conception being estimated at 120 males to 100 females. By birth, this ratio has dropped to 106:100. More spontaneous abortions are of male than of female fetuses, and following birth male infants continue to die in greater numbers than female infants. Around the age of fifteen the ratio of males to females has dropped to 104:100, and by the age of twenty-nine males outnumber females only by 101:100. In the years between ages thirty and forty-four the ratio reverses, with 91 males surviving for every 100 females; and by the age of sixty-five, men are outnumbered by women by a ratio of 72:100. Another way of showing the greater male vulnerability is to note that male life expectancy is sixty-nine, whereas female life expectancy is seventy-seven years—an eight-year difference. Although not all sex difference in longevity can be attributed to biological sex differences, biological differences clearly play a role.

Another biological sex difference involves maturation. Some data suggest that newborn girls may be more mature than boys on average in aspects of anatomical growth such as skeletal development. The adolescent growth spurt for height also occurs earlier on average in girls. However, different systems mature at different rates, and it is not clear that brain maturation is more rapid in girls. Thus, boy and girl infants seem to attain sensorimotor milestones at similar ages.

Differentiation of the developing organism begins shortly after conception and is mediated through hormones. In the presence of the Y chromosome (the

Norm Hurst, Stock, Boston, Inc.

Although not all differences in longevity result from biological sex differences, females have the definite advantage.

genetic determinant of maleness; see Chapter 3), gonads develop and produce *androgens,* or male hormones. These hormones in turn affect the developing brain. (Specifically, they affect a structure in the brain—the *hypothalamus*—which controls the endocrine system; see Chapter 14.) The hypothalamus then regulates and affects all further development. In the absence of a Y chromosome, or in the absence of early androgenic influence, the organism will develop into a female.

In an attempt to assess the influence of hormones on fetal and neonatal development, Phoenix, Goy, and Resko (1969) injected pregnant monkeys with the male hormone testosterone. When the monkeys were pregnant with genetic females, the hormone had a striking effect. Daily injections of testosterone (administered beginning in the second quarter of pregnancy and continued at least throughout the second quarter) produced *pseudohermaphrodites.* These are genetically female monkeys that possess the external genitalia of males—well-developed scrota and well-formed but small penises. The animals also possess ovaries. In addition to the male physical characteristics, the pseudohermaphrodites exhibited male patterns of behavior. In general, the androgenized females were more aggressive. They manifested more threatening gestures, less withdrawal to approach or threat by other animals, more mounting behavior, and more rough-and-tumble play. Hence male hormones influenced not only the physical characteristics of the genetically female infants but also their behavior.

Aggression appears to be one human behavior for which there is a biological basis for a sex difference. We noted earlier that very young boys show more aggressive behavior patterns than girls do and it appears that these sex differences may be mediated by hormones. Although most of the evidence is indirect and is based on work with animals, the picture of hormonal influences on aggressive behavior is becoming a compelling one.

Injecting male hormones into female monkeys after birth but before puberty masculinizes the behavior of the animals, making them more assertive. Female monkeys given this treatment have even become the dominant member of their monkey troop—a position always reserved for males in the absence of hormonal intervention.

Testosterone mediates aggressive behavior in a number of mammals that have been studied. Phoenix and associates (1959) found physical and behavioral changes in guinea pigs. This finding was replicated in rats by Grady, Phoenix, & Young (1965) when they administered testosterone during pregnancy and immediately after birth. Adult female rats also can be turned into aggressive animals by spaying them and injecting them with testosterone (Levine, 1966). Additionally, testosterone levels in dominant animals are high, and they drop quickly and remain low in male animals that have lost a fight and been dominated.

The subhuman data are quite clear: hormonal injections and high levels of circulating testosterone affect behavior, particularly in the area of aggressive play. It is difficult to determine whether these results generalize to human beings because in the rare instances when hormones have been manipulated in human subjects there was also evidence of social and biological mediation of masculinized behavior patterns.

A small number of cases have been studied that involved human pregnancies and androgen injections. In some instances androgens such as progestin have been administered to prevent threatened miscarriages. Money and his colleagues studied genetically female children whose mothers were treated with progestin during the crucial part of the prenatal period (Ehrhardt & Money, 1967), as well as children experiencing various prenatal hormonal anomalies (Money, Hampson, & Hampson, 1957; Money, 1961; Money & Ehrhardt, 1972). The effect of high prenatal levels of androgen on human development appears to be feminization of the male and masculinization of the female, which results in sexually ambiguous infants. For example, female infants with normal internal female reproductive organs are born with an enlarged clitoris that resembles a penis and labial folds that often are fused and resemble a scrotum. Even when they are raised as girls, these children exhibit masculine behaviors and are considered "tomboys." They are active in vigorous sports; prefer simple, functional clothing; show little interest in jewelry and cosmetics; and assert themselves and are high achievers. They also have above average IQs, although data are not yet available to determine whether they show the "male" IQ pattern (higher scores on mathematical than on verbal abilities).

Comparing these girls with the pseudohermaphrodite monkeys produced by Phoenix and associates leads to a consistent picture of the masculinizing effect of prenatal androgen levels. It is tempting to conclude from these studies that the behavior patterns of human hermaphrodites result from hormonal influences. However, the impact of social forces on these girls cannot be overlooked. Knowing that their children are sexually ambiguous may influence the way parents raise them. Parents may be more tolerant of tomboyish behavior in girls who are born with some of the physical characteristics of boys.

It appears that with hermaphrodites the critical determinant of sex-role identity is not their hormones but the sex their parents "assign" to them. Money

(1971) studied a number of children who were sexually ambiguous at birth and were raised either as boys or girls. Thus some children's parents decided to rear them as boys while other parents reared them as girls. Matching the children for physical appearance, Money found that the children reared as boys considered themselves male and adopted masculine behavior patterns, whereas those reared as girls behaved in a more feminine manner. If gender was reassigned after the first few years of life, maladjustment resulted. This has led to the conclusion that there is a critical period for the establishment of gender-role identity between the ages of eighteen months and three years. Therefore, though it is plausible that some behavioral differences between human males and females may be affected by prenatal hormone levels, it is also clear that the environment has a tremendous impact on sex-role identification and behavior. These results led Money (1971) to state:

> Despite whatever sexual dimorphism may already have differentiated in the central nervous system, the human organism at birth is still largely bipotential for dimorphism of gender-identity differentiation. More simply said, the individual's gender-identity and role . . . will differentiate in response to and in interaction with stimuli encountered after birth. (p. 209)

In spite of this powerful effect of rearing, we still are left with the fact that female hermaphrodites show masculine behaviors even though they consider themselves females. Such data led Bee (1974) to conclude that, although children consider themselves to be whichever sex they are assigned and attempt to fill the role assigned to that sex, we still know little about the determinants of behavior of children whose assigned sex differs from their biological sex. Do such children still show some of the cognitive and behavioral patterns of their biological sex because hormones are influencing their behavior? Such issues are being studied in research currently under way.

Hormonal effects on cognitive development have been studied at several points of the life span. Data from Money's laboratory indicate that both males and females who have been exposed to high prenatal androgen levels show elevated scores on intelligence tests. Speculation is that androgens may play a role in the development of the cerebral cortex. Broverman and associates (1968) believe that increases in hormone levels during adolescence affect cognitive development and are involved in the cognitive sex differences that become more apparent at that time. Most of this work has been done with adolescent males, who experience a sharp increase in androgen level at puberty. For example, college-aged males with higher androgen levels performed better on simple repetitive tasks and more poorly on restructuring tasks (Klaiber, Broverman, & Kobayashi, 1967), and testosterone injections in two boys who were slow in pubertal development resulted in an improvement in repetitive task performance (Klaiber et al., 1971). Comparable data about the effects of increased estrogen levels in adolescent girls may clarify the significance of the data for males. At this point the data merely provide evidence that adolescent changes in hormone levels affect cognitive performance. The data do not support the hypothesis that the observed divergence in cognitive ability between the sexes in adolescence—especially in mathematical skills—results from hormonal changes.

So far we have seen that biological effects mediated through hormonal differences between the sexes probably account for some of the observed sex differences in aggressive behavior. Hormonal effects on cognition are less clear, but we have noted an association between androgens and cognitive performance.

Another behavioral difference between the sexes—visual-spatial ability—may also result from a biological sex difference. The mechanism for the mediation of visual-spatial ability has not been determined; however, studies of the heritability of this trait suggest that it is linked genetically to sex. To attribute a sex difference in behavior to a genetic difference, it must be demonstrated that the behavior is controlled by a gene or genes carried on the X or Y chromosome. This is because it is only the sex chromosomes (X and Y chromosomes) that are *always* different between males and females. (As Chapter 3 noted, males have one X and one Y chromosome, whereas females have two X chromosomes.) Several researchers (Stafford, 1961; Bock & Kolakowski, 1973; Harlage, 1970) note high correlations between the spatial ability of children and their opposite-sexed parent. Boys' scores on spatial abilities are predicted by their mothers' scores, and girls' scores are best predicted by their fathers'. Because it is not very plausible to hypothesize that fathers teach their daughters visual-spatial skills whereas mothers teach the same skills only to their sons, a hypothesis involving sex-linked heritability has been postulated.

Stafford (1961) explains the cross-sex heritability by speculating that at least one important genetic component coding for high spatial ability is carried on the X chromosome and that it is recessive. If this is correct, then individuals with two X chromosomes (females) would have to inherit the recessive gene from both parents in order to show the trait; males would have to inherit the trait from only one parent, their mothers. This means that there is an increased probability for males to be high in spatial ability, since they have only one X chromosome, which they inherit from their mothers. Thus a boy's visual-spatial ability would be more likely to be like his mother's ability, because her X chromosome determined the boy's ability. The fathers of girls with high spatial ability would have high spatial ability themselves, since they have only one X chromosome, whereas the mothers of high-ability girls may or may not have the trait (since the gene is recessive). Thus females of high or low visual-spatial ability would have a higher probability of being like their fathers. The evidence we have to support this hypothesis is that father-daughter and mother-son scores on visual-spatial tasks are correlated. Additionally, more direct evidence for this hypothesis has been provided by Goodenough et al. (1977) in a study described in Chapter 3.

Genetic and hormonal sex differences may directly mediate such behavioral phenomena as aggression and visual-spatial ability, but they also may mediate variations in the kinds of social and sensory input received by males and females. We mentioned previously that males appear to be more active than females, and it has been suggested that early in life male and female neonates come to be treated differently as a function of their behavioral differences. Moss (1967) reports that on average, three-week-old female infants sleep more, fuss less, and show less irritability than males. In addition, mothers hold and respond more to their male babies during this period. This may be because a male infant is awake and fussing more, for when a female child does fuss, she is more likely to get attention than is a male. According to Moss, mothers may receive more reinforcement for soothing female infants because the infants fuss less and are soothed more easily. Because males fuss more and are harder to comfort, their mothers may learn to attend to them less. Support for this notion comes from observations of three-month-old boys. The fussiest of these infants got the least attention. Thus innate sex differences in activity level shape caretakers' behavior, which in turn affects the responding of the infants. In this example, caretakers are responding differently to babies not because of cultural notions about boys and girls but as a function of innate differences in the infants. We also know that caretakers "read in" sex differences between male and female infants that are not apparent at birth. For example, although male infants are more vulnerable and maturationally younger than female infants, they are handled more roughly.

Having established that biological and innate behavioral differences do exist between the sexes, we will now examine the environment to identify additional influences that can account for observed sex differences in behavior.

Social and Cultural Bases for Sex Differences

The profound effect of assigning a sex to an infant has been noted in our discussion of Money's work with hermaphrodites. Regardless of the genetic sex of these individuals, they identified themselves with and attempted to assume the sex role of the gender they had been assigned. Somehow children acquire information from the environment that leads them to pattern their behavior in masculine or feminine ways. Parental teaching and shaping of behavior, imitation of adults who typify behavioral sex differences, and other less direct environmental influences all operate to shape sex-typed behavior in developing children.

Given the prevalent notions about male and female behavior in our society and the degree to which colors, clothes, and toys for infants are classified almost exclusively by sex, we assume that boys and girls are treated differently from birth. A number of studies do show different socialization practices for males and for females. Nevertheless, overviews of the research concerning early socialization conclude that, on the whole, the sexes are treated very similarly during preschool years. Bee (1974) states that though many studies showed differences, the direction of the differences was not consistent. Furthermore, such variables as the child's ordinal position within the family, the educational level of the mother, and the behavior of the father versus the mother were more relevant than the sex of the child in terms of how the caretaker responded to the child.

Examination of all the variations and similarities of socialization of boys and girls in the literature led Maccoby (1972) to conclude that there were two general areas of agreement. First, boys are handled somewhat more roughly than girls, and parents indicate more concern about their daughters' physical well-being. Second, boys are physically punished more and are given more direction than girls.

Little girls can cross "sexual boundaries" with less social disapproval than boys can.

Sam Sweezy, Stock, Boston, Inc.

One study leading to such conclusions was carried out by Minton, Kagan, and Levine (1971), who observed the interactions of nearly one hundred mothers with their two-year-olds in the homes of these individuals. Both lower-middle and middle-class mothers were rather intrusive, interrupting their children every six to eight minutes to reprimand or command them. Sons were reprimanded and physically punished more frequently than daughters; and the lower the educational level attained by the mother, the more inclined she was to be intrusive.

Besides being punished more in general, boys also seem to be punished more than girls for behaviors that are inappropriate for their sex. The masculine role in our society is regarded with greater respect and status; it is more clearly defined than the female role; and there appears to be greater pressure for boys than girls to conform to sex-appropriate standards. When asked to respond about sex-appropriate behaviors for boys and girls, parents of young children responded more negatively to opposite-sex choices for boys than for girls (Lansky, 1967). Little girls who climb trees and play with toy soldiers are tolerated to a much greater degree than are little boys who cry, play with dolls, or like to play at dress up (especially if it involves dressing up in mommy's clothes).

Because they are punished for exhibiting sex-inappropriate behaviors, it is not surprising that boys are more consistent in their adoption of sex-typed behaviors and adopt them earlier than girls do. When asked whether they would like to be boys or girls, young boys are far more likely than young girls to select

FIGURE 15.2
Degree of masculine
preference by boys
and girls, kindergar-
ten through grade 5.

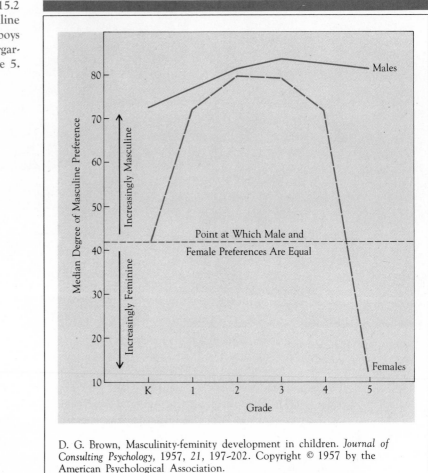

D. G. Brown, Masculinity-feminity development in children. *Journal of Consulting Psychology*, 1957, *21*, 197-202. Copyright © 1957 by the American Psychological Association.

their own sex. It is not until the age of ten that a majority of girls state that they prefer to be female (see Figure 15.2). These results may occur because girls have observed the greater advantages accorded to males and state a preference for their own sex only as a result of preadolescent social pressures. An alternative explanation is that girls are not punished as frequently as boys for sex-inappropriate choices and hence are less fearful of expressing their honest preference.

Apart from their greater permissiveness with females and rougher handling of males, parents treat young children in a remarkably similar fashion. For example, there are no consistent findings regarding differential treatment of aggressive behavior, in spite of the fact that sex differences along this dimension are clear. Extensive studies in England (Newson & Newson, 1963) and in the United States (Sears, Rau, & Alpert, 1965) found no differences in how parents treated aggressive behavior of boys and girls. In the absence of different training during preschool years, how can we explain the sex differences that are known to exist? Besides the biological explanations already presented, we can take an environmentalist perspective and suggest that most of the observed sex differences in behavior are not manifested clearly until school-age years or later. The only real sex difference showing itself early in development is that of aggressive behavior. Other behavioral and cognitive differences are most apparent after the age of ten, while most of the data concerning rearing practices deal with preschool children. It may be that parents exert more pressure to conform with sex roles as children grow older and that such pressure, along with the expectations of teachers and peers, leads to greater differentiation.

The Newsons (1963) found that parents were equally permissive with young boys and girls in regard to independence and physical movement, but began to restrict their girls more around the age of seven. Teachers expect different responses from boys and girls in the classroom. Levitin and Chananie (1972) examined the manner in which teachers responded to aggression and dependency in boys and girls. Forty teachers were assigned to four groups; after reading descriptions of individual children, they were asked to rate the children. All teachers received the descriptions of two children. One description always involved an achieving child, but the name of the child was varied to indicate a male or a female. The second description was of either a dependent or an aggressive child, and again the sex of the child was varied by changing the name. Teachers approved of and rated as normal girls who were dependent and boys who were aggressive, and they liked the high-achieving student more if the child was a girl rather than a boy. The least-liked student was an aggressive child who was also female. Thus teachers appeared to reinforce sex-role stereotypes in boys and girls by reporting that they preferred children who reflected the stereotype. Studies like this one and others that have yielded similar results indicate that even if little pressure is exerted on preschoolers to conform to sex-role norms, by the time they enter school they elicit more approval when they behave according to expected patterns.

The evidence that aggressive females receive the most disapproval from teachers concurs with the work of Horner (1970), which indicated that young women have a tendency to fear success and predict bad outcomes for women who have been assertive and have achieved. Horner presented unfinished stories about achieving men and women to college students and asked the students to complete the stories. Negative outcomes were used to complete the stories about achieving women by 65 percent of the women but only 10 percent of the men. Female subjects were especially likely to predict unhappiness for women who were successful in their careers, but both males and females told stories with happy endings for men who were achievers. Teachers (who are usually female) disapprove of aggressive females in elementary school, and this message apparently carries over to adulthood, when women express negative feelings about female achievement.

Elementary school appears to be the time when patterns of masculinity and femininity become apparent and well established. Although gender identity may be formed by the age of three, it is not until children enter school that they have a clear conception of sex differences that generalizes. Until then, children make mistakes in identifying gender and will, for example, be as likely to call a cow "he" as "she." Longitudinal data also indicate that adult heterosexual behavior can be predicted from sex-typed interests in elementary school. Kagan and Moss (1962) report results from the Fels Institute Study showing that boys who were interested in competitive games, gross motor skills, and topics such as mechanics were more likely to be involved in sex-typed behaviors in adulthood than were girls who liked cooking, sewing, reading, and noncompetitive games in elementary school. Boys were more stable than girls in their sex-typed preferences: a finding that is congruent with the data presented earlier suggesting that sex-role preference is established earlier in boys than it is in girls.

From the data presented thus far we see that a few sex differences in behavior are apparent early in life but that most sex-typed behavior appears later in childhood and early adolescence. This may be a consequence of what appears to be relatively undifferentiated treatment of preschool boys and girls by parents, followed by greater emphasis on sex-role conformity by parents, teachers, and peers in later childhood. Such a picture may minimize the role parents play in shaping behavior on the basis of sex, for when we examine other sources of data—such as comparisons of parents' child-rearing practices as a function of socioeconomic status, comparisons of father-absent and father-present homes, and comparisons of homes in which the mother works or remains unemployed—we see that even in preschoolers there are differences in terms of sex-role behavior.

Variations in Home Environments

In Minton, Kagan, and Levine's (1971) study of mothers' interactions with their two-year-olds, reported earlier, differences in sex-role training were observed as a function of social class. Lower-middle-class mothers are more restrictive and punish their sons more than middle-class mothers do. Sex-typing appears to be even more rigid in families with lower socioeconomic status, and children learn appropriate behaviors accordingly. Rabbin (1950) found that lower-class boys prefer sex-appropriate toys by age four or five; middle-class boys and lower-class girls do so by about seven; and middle-class girls prefer such toys by age nine. Sex-role standards are also more differentiated by class during adolescence, at which time bullies are leaders in lower-class but not middle-class groups of boys, and "sissies" are outcasts from both groups (Pope, 1953).

The differences in behavior between the two classes have been attributed to differences in parental reinforcement of sex-typed behavior. Lower-class members delineate sex roles more clearly; they make more rigid demands for conformity to sex standards; and parents provide more sex-stereotyped models. Thus early in childhood the differential effects of social-class environment become apparent in the different ages at which sex-role preferences are manifested.

Children's attitudes about sex-role behavior appear to be influenced greatly by the roles their parents play. For example, children of families with low socioeconomic status are more likely to observe their mother in traditional feminine roles both at home and in terms of they type of employment she can obtain (typically involving cooking, housework, or child care). Men of such families often work in occupations regarded as uniquely masculine. Thus parents in lower socioeconomic categories have particularly traditional roles, which probably explains in part why their children have more traditional attitudes about sex roles.

Since it is less traditional for women to work, it might be expected that children of working mothers would have less traditional attitudes about female sex roles—*if* parental roles affect children's attitudes about sex roles. Vogel and associates (1970) found this to be the case in a group of college students. Regardless of social class, students whose mothers had worked held less sex-stereotyped notions about the roles open to females. That is, children of working mothers identified fewer roles as being open only to one sex or the other. Daughters of working mothers appeared to be especially influenced in this way, seeing more opportunities for themselves and more available roles for females than did daughters of nonworking mothers. Thus we have seen examples of how parental sex-role training affects children early in life in the comparisons of lower-class and middle-class families, and of how sex-role models set by parents carry over to attitudes expressed in adolescence.

Father absence also plays a role in the gender identity of children. If we use as standards the traditional sex-role stereotypes of "instrumental" for males and "expressive" for females, we find that boys raised in homes where the father is absent are more "feminine" (Carlsmith, 1964; Hetherington, 1966). Father absence has more impact on the sex-role identity of male children. The main aspect affected in female children is their ability to develop heterosexual relationships during adolescence. Adolescent girls who have not had a father have been observed to be either more shy or more promiscuous with males (Hetherington, 1972). It seems that their ability to interact with males is affected when they do not have a father, whereas boys tend to act less masculine themselves when they have no male model. Sutton-Smith, Rosenberg, and Landy (1968) report that the effects of father absence are mitigated when other males are a part of the family. For example, in a father-absent home where there are at least two boys in the family, those boys will exhibit more masculine characteristics than will a boy who is raised in a father-absent home alone or with only female siblings.

In attempting to assess the role of parents in sex-role development, it appears that parents seem to have more or less impact—depending on the approach researchers have taken. We find few sex differences in behavior during the preschool years, the period when children spend the most time with parents and are most under their influence. The only behavior that consistently distinguishes males and females at this stage is aggression. Additionally, parents do not appear to treat their preschool children in a remarkably different fashion on the basis of sex. Preschool boys and girls are socialized in a fairly similar fashion, especially in the treatment of aggressive behavior. When we examine parental influences by comparing variations in parental behavior, however, it seems that parents have a great impact on sex-role development. In families that hold more traditional and more rigid concepts of sex roles—such as families of lower socioeconomic status and families in which the mothers are not employed outside the home—children have more stereotyped notions about sex roles. Also, the sex-role identities of both males and females appear to be affected when the father is not present. Father absence has its greatest impact during the first five years of life—the very period in which few sex differences have been found and in which differential treatment of boys and girls has for the most part been too subtle to register or measure. Now we will turn to the theories that have been devised to explain the subtle and not so subtle influences that lead to sex-typed behavior.

Theories of Sex-Role Development

In discussing biological mediation of sex differences, Money (1971) concluded that in spite of the role of hormones in differentiating the sexes, sex-role identity was dependent on socialization. That is, regardless of their genetic sex, children who are physically ambiguous will take on the identity of the gender they are assigned by their parents. A number of theories have been devised to explain this identification process. We will examine the three most prominent theories of sex-role development: the psychoanalytic approach, the social-learning approach, and the cognitive-developmental approach.

Psychoanalytic Approach

Freudian theory has been presented in Chapter 2; therefore, we will limit this discussion to the relevance of the theory to sex-role development. According to Freud, physical differences between the sexes predestine them to have radically different personality configurations. "Anatomy is destiny" when it comes to sex roles—with girls being born to have their empty spaces filled with babies and penises, and boys being built to insert themselves into and fill those spaces. This destiny is learned and accepted during the *phallic stage*, which involves the resolution of the *Oedipal complex* (for boys) or the *Electra complex* (for girls). In this view a boy, having a penis, desires his mother and becomes a rival of his father. Aware of the father's greater strength and power and fearing castration, the boy renounces his desire for his mother, identifies with his father, and thus completes his gender identity when he passes through this third stage of psychosexual development, around the age of five or six. In this manner a boy—who probably spends most of his time with his mother, the primary caretaker—still manages to identify and pattern his behavior after his father.

Girls do not need to switch their identification from their first love object—their mother. According to Freud, however, they do go through the phallic stage, during which they develop penis envy and desire their fathers. Like boys, they resolve the competition with their same-sexed parent by identifying with that parent and behaving in a sex-appropriate manner. The sex-role identity attained at this period will be maintained throughout life, and fixation at this stage may cause lifelong patterns of abnormal sex-role identification.

Psychoanalytic theory stresses the importance of early development in shaping lifelong patterns of behavior, and it does not view sex roles as flexible. Biological and psychological aspects of individuals are the organizing properties for sex-role identity, which—once crystallized—will be maintained for life.

Sex differences are learned, after which a child's identification is formed.

Ed Buryn

Although Freud was the first to report the increased interest in sexual phenomena in children around the ages of four to six, which coincides with the completion of gender identity by the age of six or seven, his postulation of Oedipal and Electra complexes has proved difficult to test empirically. Furthermore, behaviors observed during this period can be explained by alternative hypotheses. Especially damaging to the psychoanalytic interpretation is the known flexibility of sex-role behavior over the life span, as well as the recent secular trends indicating that traditional sex-role differentiations are breaking down.

Social-Learning Approach

Social-learning theorists such as Bandura (1969) and Mischel (1970) have emphasized the significance of social contingencies and external environmental influences as the main shapers of gender identity. Patterns of reinforcement, verbal instruction, the behaviors of models, and the publicly observable consequences of the models' behaviors (vicarious learning) are the means through which children acquire sex-role identification. Through observation of anatomy, children learn that there are two types of individuals, or two sexes, and that all of the forces in the environment indicate that people are differentiated on the basis of these physical characteristics. Children come to have a broad concept of maleness and femaleness on the basis of their experiences. Sex differences are learned, and once this learning takes place, a child's identification is formed.

The social-learning approach emphasizes the flexibility of sex-role behavior and the potential for changing sex-role stereotypes. If the environment is constantly shaping behavior, then alterations in the environment can lead to alterations in attitudes and behaviors of males and females. From this perspective, secular changes that may lead to mismatches between early sex-role socialization and later role requirements will not be terribly traumatic, because sex-role identity is not seen as being laid down indelibly in the first five years of life (as in Freud's view), nor is it seen as being so intimately linked to anatomy.

Cognitive-Developmental Approach

On the basis of Piaget's cognitive theory, Kohlberg (1966, 1969) has explained sex-role development as a cognitive phenomenon. Whereas social-learning theorists view the environment as being the organizing force in sex-role identity, cognitive-developmental theorists see the organizing force as being the interactions between an individual and the environment. A child's general cognitive level shapes his or her social responses, and sex-role development progresses through a series of stages, beginning with the formation of a sex-typed identity—rather than culminating in it, as postulated by psychoanalytic and social-learning theories.

The developmental trends presented for males' sex-role development during childhood are (1) formation of gender identity; (2) increasingly sex-typed interests, attitudes, and values; (3) greater imitation of male figures, including the father; and (4) greater attachment to male figures, including the father. By carefully documenting the sequence and age at which these behaviors emerged, Kohlberg (1966) attempted to demonstrate that cognitive-developmental theory could account for the observations better than could the social-learning or psychoanalytic approaches. Kohlberg insisted that perceptions of gender-role differences and perceptions of the self as being more similar to same-sexed individuals occur even before a child identifies with the same-sexed parent and before modeling and attachment to the same-sexed parent. Both psychoanalytic and social-learning theorists instead predicted that a child's identification was formed *after* modeling. The importance of the environment is not denied in cognitive-developmental theory, but an individual is seen as playing a more active role in organizing environmental input and initiating behavior as a function of this organization, rather than merely being passively organized by the environment.

Changing Patterns of Sex Roles and Sexual Behavior

Any theory of sex-role development must be able to account for changes in sex-role behavior at various points in the life span as well as for secular changes in sex-role definitions. Emmerich (1973) notes that secular changes can lead to mismatches between early sex-role socialization and later role requirements, and he also points out that developmental discontinuities in sex-role requirements are not recent phenomena. For example, we have already described differences in sex-role norms that exist between different social classes. Socially mobile individuals thus have experienced discontinuities between the sex role in which they were socialized and the role they experience in later life.

Erosion of Traditional Sex-Role Differentiations

Recent secular trends indicating that traditional sex-role differentiations are breaking down will lead to greater numbers of individuals experiencing discontinuities between early socialization and later life experiences. Females who have been socialized consistently and strongly to favor traditional feminine activities and interpersonal behaviors are likely in later life to experience circumstances or opportunities calling for more traditional masculine role behaviors. Social movements such as women's liberation can be expected to accelerate societal redefinitions of traditional sex roles. Additionally, recent analyses of socialization during adulthood indicate that adult statuses and roles change rather continually throughout adult life (Brim, 1966; Neugarten, 1968; Riley et al., 1969). All these factors led Emmerich (1973) to suggest that sex-role distinctions should be subordinated to the development of a broad range of competencies in both sexes.

The changing status of women has had profound effects on American society—including attitudes and traditional relationships between the sexes.

James Holland, Stock, Boston, Inc.

Sex Differences in Sports

P. S. WOOD

There has been, it seems fair to say, an explosion in women's competitive sports. If women have not yet achieved equal rights or equal time on the playing fields of America, or equal space in the halls of fame, they have, as they say, come a long way, and they are moving up fast. . . .

New research on the physical and athletic differences between men and women, as well as interviews and observations, prompts one, under the circumstances, to report at the start that in some respects women may be a good deal tougher than men. As more and more women enter long-distance events, such as the marathons and multievent supermarathons, evidence is growing that their endurance may be equal or perhaps even superior to men's in some ways, and their systems may be more efficient at turning stored fats into energy. Women's bodies are, indeed, constructed so that certain crucial organs are better guarded from injury; ovaries, for instance, are located internally and float in a large sac of fluid, far better placed for protection than the testicles.

Source: *New York Times Magazine*, May 18, 1980, pp. 30–34, 95–100. © 1980 by The New York Times Company. Reprinted by permission.

Nor does the folk wisdom seem correct that other elements of the female anatomy make women athletes more vulnerable. The suspicion that severe bruises cause breast cancer is evidently not borne out; breasts are less susceptible to injury than knees or elbows, whether male or female. And the old idea that, at certain times of the month, women do not operate at peak performance is generally not true for athletes. World and Olympic records have been set by women in all stages of their menstrual cycles. Moreover, at certain intense levels of training, menstruation conveniently turns off for many women, a phenomenon that has been linked to a reduction in body fat.

The point here is that, if concern for safety is a determining factor, women should have the same rights or opportunities to participate in competitive athletics as men. And, by and large, they have the same reasons for wanting to do so. . . .

No one suggests now that equal experience is going to lead to equal performance in all things athletic, or even that the average woman can match the performance of the average man. The physical plant is not the same. Men are bigger and stronger, can run faster, throw and jump farther. But the fact that women are genetically ordained through most of life to compete with less powerful bodies, far from tarnishing their performance, makes it more worthy.

Public opinion appears to favor breaking down the barriers based on sex. A Harris poll taken at the end of 1975 found that 63 percent of Americans favored "most of the efforts to strengthen and change women's status in society," while 25 percent disagreed. As recently as 1970 only 42 percent had favored such a statement, as opposed to 41 percent against. *Time* magazine called 1975 the "Year of Women" and found an immense variety of women altering their lives, entering new fields, and functioning with a new sense of identity, integrity, and confidence. The claim was made that in 1975 the women's drive penetrated every layer of society and matured beyond ideology to a new status of general and sometimes unconscious acceptance. Across the broad range of American society, women's lives are changing profoundly—along with men's attitudes and the traditional relationship between the sexes.

The changing status of women is having an impact on individuals at all points of the life span. New attitudes about sex roles in young parents are affecting the manner in which they socialize their children. We already have seen that adolescent children (and especially girls) raised in families of working mothers have less stereotyped notions about sex roles (Vogel et al., 1970). With more and more women entering the work force (almost 50 percent of mothers of children eighteen or younger), it appears certain that growing numbers of children will develop less rigid attitudes about appropriate sex-role behavior. Midlife is another period in which rapid changes are taking place. Longer life expectancies, earlier completion of child-rearing responsibilities, and increasing economic pressures are leading more and more older women to establish careers. In late life, retirement forces men into greater role equality with their wives, and Neugarten (1968) notes that sex-role distinctions are blurred in later life. Hence in the cohorts most socialized into traditional sex roles—those individuals of retirement age and beyond—secular change has led to great discontinuities between early socialization and later-life experience.

Changes in Sexual Behavior and Attitudes

Besides personally experiencing some of the most drastic shifts in sex-role behavior, older people today probably represent the cohort that initiated the sexual revolution. This statement may seem surprising, given the relatively recent advent of improved birth control methods and associated sexual liberation for younger cohorts of women. However, although we tend to associate increased sexual activity with younger generations (a fact to which we will return later), some of the greatest changes in attitudes and acceptance of premarital sex were promoted by the grandparents of contemporary adolescents.

The Kinsey data suggested that the greatest changes in sexual activity occurred among females, who began to increase their premarital sexual activity during the 1920s. Of women born before 1900, only 2 percent had premarital intercourse before age sixteen, 8 percent before age twenty, and 14 percent before age twenty-five. The daughters of this generation of women were more active sexually before they were married. Twice as many (4 percent) had sexual relations before age sixteen, 21 percent before age twenty, and well over a third (37 percent) had premarital intercourse before age twenty-five. More recent studies (Sorensen, 1973) indicate that premarital intercourse among young women is continuing to rise, and dramatically. Almost a third (30 percent) of female adolescents below age sixteen in 1973 said that they had experienced premarital intercourse, and 59 percent had the experience before age nineteen. These data and the data for males are presented in Table 15.2. It is clear that men have not changed their patterns of sexual activity to the degree that women have, but the availability of sexually active women probably has been associated with a drastically reduced involvement with prostitutes by males. In 1948 Kinsey reported that at least 20 percent of a sample of college men re-

TABLE 15.2
Percentage of
Contemporary
Adolescents
Reporting
Experience with
Sexual
Intercourse
Compared to
Reports from
Members of Their
Parents'
Generation

	Intercourse Before Age 16	Intercourse After Age 20
Contemporary adolescents (1973)		
Males	44%	72%
Females	30%	57%
Parental generation (1948, 1953)		
Males	39%	72%
Females	3%	20%

Source: R. C. Sorenson. *The Sorenson Report: Adolescent Sexuality in Contemporary America*. Cleveland, Ohio: World Publishing, 1973; A. C. Kinsey, W. B. Pomeroy, and C. E. Martin. *Sexual Behavior in the Human Male*. Philadelphia: Saunders, 1948; A. C. Kinsey, W. B. Pomeroy, C. E. Martin, and P. H. Gebhard. *Sexual Behavior in the Human Female*. Philadelphia: Saunders, 1953. Copyright 1948, 1953 by The Institute for Sex Research.

ported having experience with prostitutes, whereas less than 4 percent of adolescents questioned two decades later reported that experience (Kinsey, Pomeroy, & Martin, 1948; Packard, 1968).

Apparently, the increased sexual activity among contemporary adolescents does not represent an increase in promiscuity. Respondents typically report serious emotional involvement with their sexual partners, and one of the biggest cohort differences in sexual behavior appears to be in attitudes about sex. In the last decade adolescents have taken a more honest approach to sexual activity and have openly sanctioned behaviors that previously were engaged in but not discussed. In 1966 *Look* magazine reported a survey in which 75 percent of respondents thirteen to twenty years old reported that attitudes among their contemporaries were changing. These adolescents felt that they had not lowered their moral standards from the standards of their parents, but they believed themselves to be more honest. They felt that adults were phony and dishonest about sex—demanding that their children conform to a set of standards to which they themselves paid only lip service. The adolescents favored openness. Of this middle-class sample, 98 percent wanted sex education in school, and they wanted more than just biological information. Sexual techniques, the meaning of sex in and out of marriage, and consideration of the relationship between sex and love were all topics considered to be of critical importance in terms of sex education.

There appeared to be a qualitative difference between their attitudes and the attitudes of individuals in the parental generation. The middle-aged cohort appeared to be more rule oriented, whereas the adolescent cohort was oriented more toward individual situations. Adolescents considered sex a matter of personal choice rather than an issue for public concern. They favored open dorms and access to contraceptive information and devices so that individuals would have the freedom to choose whether to engage in sexual relations without negative consequences. This did not mean that the adolescents favored promiscuity. They emphasized the quality of a relationship. Premarital intercourse for a couple who were in love or engaged was viewed as more permissible than petting for a couple who had no affection for one another. Middle-aged adults felt the opposite. They supported petting without affection rather than premarital intercourse for couples in love. Whereas adolescents favored the meaningfulness of the relationship, middle-aged individuals favored conventional social standards of right and wrong.

Although many in society were shocked by what appeared to be the sexual excesses of adolescents in the late 1960s and early 1970s, surveys indicated that promiscuity was not sanctioned by the majority of this cohort (Luckey & Nass, 1969; Packard, 1968). Only 37 percent of the males and 11 percent of the females interviewed favored casual sex. The majority felt that couples who engaged in intercourse should at least be dating one another exclusively, and the majority of females felt that the couple should be engaged. Adolescent women were clearly more conservative than men, and 40 percent of the women felt that a couple should be married before having intercourse.

As with all controversial topics, premarital sexual activity was viewed with a wide range of opinions in the adolescent samples. Young adolescents tended to be more conservative, as did females, although career-oriented women had fewer conflicts about premarital intercourse than did women with no career plans. Blacks were less conservative than whites, and students from the East and West coasts favored more liberal stances to premarital sex than did students on other campuses.

In spite of these differences among various segments of the adolescent cohort, their attitudes were more similar to the attitudes of their peer group than to the attitudes of adults. The biggest difference involved intercourse for engaged couples, with the majority of adolescents finding it morally acceptable; only a minority of adults held that view. Evidence supporting adolescents' attitudes that adults are hypocrites when it comes to sexual behavior came from data suggesting that the number of adults who expressed approval for premarital intercourse was much smaller than the number who reported that they had had premarital intercourse. Adolescents, far more than adults, matched their behavior with their ideals.

Sexual Behavior over the Life Span

Sexuality is an aspect of an individual's behavior throughout the life span. Although Freud was maligned in the late nineteenth century for suggesting that young children's play had a sexual dimension, contemporary empirical observations support Freud's contention that there is increased interest and attention to genital areas and sexual matters in four- and five-year-olds. Old age is another point in the life span where consideration of sexuality has been taboo. Only in the last decade have experts on human sexuality presented data concerning sexual activity after age sixty, and many younger people still titter in discomfort at the thought of their grandparents in bed. Nevertheless, data suggest that the

The upper age limit on sexual capacity results more from psychological and cultural inhibitions than from physical limitations.

Ginger Chih, Peter Arnold, Inc.

capacity for heterosexual relations—once developed—is typically maintained from puberty until death. It is psychological and cultural inhibitions, more than physical limitations, that put an upper age limit on human sexual capacity.

Puberty and Adolescence

While various components of sexual behavior (such as masturbation and petting) are engaged in by children, it is not until puberty that individuals have the capacity to engage in full-blown sexual relations. Puberty is attained by females fully two and one-half years earlier than males, and until recently there has been a secular trend to earlier onset of puberty in Western countries. The average developmental sequences of sexual maturation in boys and girls are presented in Figure 15.3 and 15.4. Wide variations around the norms exist, and these variations cause many adolescents to be shy and embarrassed.

During this period of the life span, when the peer group is so important, late or early puberty appears to have social and personal significance. Faust (1969) points out that early puberty in girls can be distressing if it occurs in elementary school, when a girl may feel awkward because she is larger than her classmates and because she has experienced menstrual flow when many of her friends have not yet learned about it. Prepubertal girls are more popular than pubertal girls according to evaluations by sixth-grade classmates. The picture changes in slightly older groups, however, and the budding young adolescent female in junior high school is favored over her prepubescent friends. Eichorn's (1963) data clearly show that maturing early is always an advantage for boys. Peers favor the larger and stronger male who can best succeed in sports and who is most likely to be chosen as a leader. Jones (1957) demonstrated that the consequences of maturing early continued to affect men as adults. Being selected to take more responsibility as a result of older physical appearance in adolescence apparently provides men with social skills and confidence that leads them to be better adjusted to their occupations, even in their thirties.

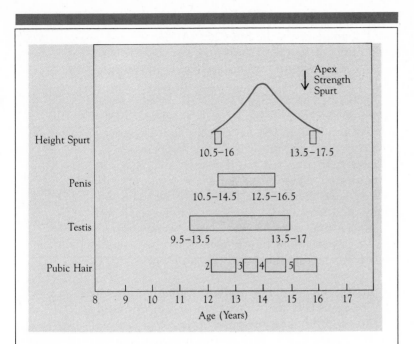

From W. A. Marshall and J. M. Tanner. Variations in the pattern of pubertal changes in boys. *Archives of the Diseases of Childhood*, 1970, **45**, 13. By permission.

FIGURE 15.3
Average developmental sequence of sexual maturation in boys. An average boy is represented. The range of ages within which some events may begin and end is given below them.

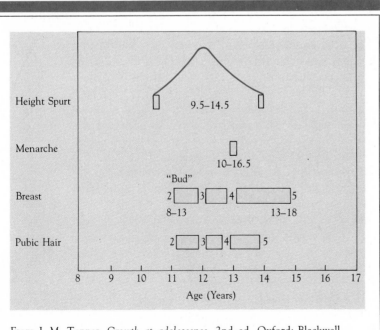

From J. M. Tanner, *Growth at adolescence*, 2nd ed. Oxford: Blackwell Scientific Publications Limited; Philadelphia: Davis, 1962. By permission.

FIGURE 15.4
Average developmental sequence of sexual maturation in girls. An average girl is represented. The range of ages within which some events may begin and end is given below them.

The interplay among biological, social, and psychological aspects of sexuality is apparent in adolescence and at all points in the life span. At puberty, when there is a dramatic increase in hormone levels, there is also a great increase in sexual drive. This appears to be especially true for males. Earlier in this chapter we associated increased testosterone levels in animals with an increase in masculine behaviors such as mounting and aggression. Clearly, in adolescence the increased levels of testosterone in males serve to greatly heighten sexual arousal, and this drive is focused and specific. Sexual capacity in males reaches its peak between puberty and the age of fifteen. It is during this period in the life span when males have the shortest latency in terms of erection and ejaculation, and when they have the greatest capacity for multiple orgasm. It is also during this time that males may have the most difficulty with their sexuality, having to find sexual discharge in a manner that does not burden them with guilt and having to control their drive without developing excessive inhibitions. The mean frequency of total sexual outlets for males peaks between the ages of twenty-one and thirty, reflecting the degree of opportunity to engage in sex.

Sexual drive in pubescent females is more diffuse and ambiguous and rises to a peak much later in the life span—usually during the mid to late thirties or beyond. Mark Twain noted the lack of synchronization between males' and females' peak sexual drives and considered it one of the ironies of human existence. Although both males and females show a dramatic increase in sexual activity and interest during adolescence, the increase in sexual activity and masturbation is greater in adolescent males. Females during this part of the life span are more conservative in their attitudes and behavior (Zubin & Money, 1973).

The causes of sex differences in attitudes and sexual activity are not clear and may reflect a combination of social and physiological factors. In addition to a double standard concerning activity for men and women (which, if disappearing in today's scene, has affected all but the most contemporary cohorts of Americans), hormonal and anatomical differences may result in different drive levels. Female sex organs are less prominent and less likely to be manipulated spontaneously. Thus young females are less likely than males to discover spontaneously the pleasure of masturbation. They also have much lower levels of testosterone, which appears to be related to high levels of sexual drive.

When sexual capacity is considered—as opposed to sexual drive—females appear to have more. Masters and Johnson (1966, 1970), in their pioneering studies of human sexual response, have documented the fact that the basic female capacity surpasses that of males. This research team also demonstrated that sexual behaviors such as frequency of orgasm and masturbation vary over much greater ranges for women than for men, and the variation in a given woman is also greater than in an individual man. Although men appear to be aroused more easily, women can respond to a greater degree.

In contrast to the Victorian era, when the question of women's sexuality was a topic not even to be discussed, many contemporary young women dispute the contention that men are aroused more easily. Social influences have a profound effect on the manner in which sexual activity is considered and expressed.

Women during the Victorian era were considered abnormal if they found sex pleasurable; today, some groups of young, liberal women express more sexual arousal than some groups of men. The wide cultural divergence in sexual behavior indicates that learning plays a critical role in determining sexual response patterns.

Formal sanctions for sexual behavior in the United States are extended only by marriage, and though this pattern is not subscribed to by a majority of adolescents, we still discourage sexual activity in childhood and adolescence. In many parts of the country parents spend years teaching children to inhibit sexual responses—presumably to prepare them for a time when they will be expected to make these responses. Children are taught to respond to sex with anxiety in early life, yet they are expected to perform without anxiety as adults. It appears that anticipatory socialization for sexual responses in our society often leads to sexual conflict rather than adaptation. Cross-cultural studies have indicated that individuals in societies where training involves inhibition of sexual responses late in childhood—without excessively severe prohibitions—are much less likely to experience guilt and conflict about sexual matters than individuals in societies where training is early and involves severe restrictions. Sexual training has a tremendous impact on the appeal of sex, and whether it is viewed as pleasurable and matter of fact or as sinful and dangerous is determined in part by training in childhood. The openness and honesty expressed by contemporary adolescents toward sexual matters suggests that the sexual revolution has been occurring in the United States for several generations. These youths have grown up in an atmosphere of less sexual repressiveness than did their parents, who in turn were raised by a generation rebelling against the repression of the Victorian era. Given the emphasis of contemporary youth on affection and mutuality in sex, future American cohorts may be less likely to experience guilt and anxiety over sexual matters, which still express themselves in the behavior and attitudes of middle-aged and older cohorts.

Sexuality and Aging

Sexual activity appears to peak early in life—usually during the first few years of marriage when an interesting and available partner is present. The frequency of intercourse appears to decline fairly steadily with age (Kinsey et al., 1948). These data are presented in Figure 15.5. Changes in male patterns of activity most likely pace the age changes for both males and females. With age, both single and married men have fewer orgasms. On the other hand, the age change for single women is minimal. A married woman's decline in frequency of orgasms apparently results from age changes in her husband's sexual patterns, since her own sexual capacity continues to increase until midlife.

Although many individuals enjoy an active sex life throughout middle and old age, it is in midlife that individuals often experience problems with sexuality (McCary, 1973). Women during this period of their life span are still close to the peak point of their activity, and many report an increase in sexual interest—either because they incorrectly assume that they soon may lose sexual

FIGURE 15.5
Sexual activity and aging in males

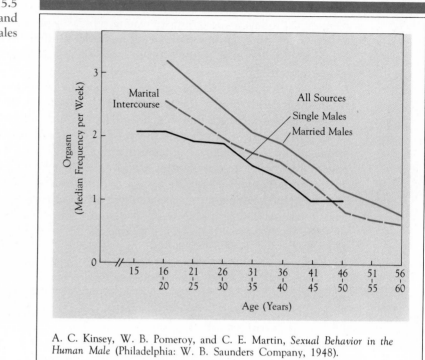

A. C. Kinsey, W. B. Pomeroy, and C. E. Martin, *Sexual Behavior in the Human Male* (Philadelphia: W. B. Saunders Company, 1948).

satisfaction with the onset of menopause or because they are relieved not to have to worry about unwanted pregnancy. At the peak of their careers in middle age, men may be less interested in sexual activity and may experience impotence for the first time. The inability to have an erection during intercourse increases in incidence during middle age, and Masters and Johnson (1970) report that after age fifty the incidence of sexual inadequacy increases dramatically in men. This is not normally a result of physiological age changes in males, who experience a gradual reduction in testosterone level as they age (as opposed to a rapid drop of estrogen production for females during menopause). Impotence in middle-aged men appears to be caused largely by social and psychological factors. Masters and Johnson listed six major factors in male impotence: (1) monotony of a repetitious sexual relationship, (2) preoccupation with career or economic pursuits, (3) mental or physical fatigue, (4) overindulgence in food or drink, (5) physical and mental incapacities of the individual or his spouse, and (6) fear of performance resulting from any one or a combination of the other categories. Although physical changes in both males and females make sexual responses slower and of less magnitude, these slight and gradual declines can in no way account for the inability to maintain an erection or achieve orgasm.

Menopause occurs in middle-aged females as a dramatic sign that their reproductive years have ended. It is probably the symbolic significance of menopause that has the most impact on women, rather than the slight physical discomfort they may experience. Research suggests, however, that even the stressful psychological aspects of menopause are overrated.

For most women the menstrual cycle ends between the ages of forty-five and fifty, and estrogen and progesterone are no longer produced by the ovaries. Since satisfying sexual activity is not affected by estrogen and progesterone levels, sexual pleasure need not decline after menopause. Also, as mentioned previously, some women experience an increase in sexual interest and activity at this point, since they no longer are anxious about pregnancy. The physical symptoms of menopause include hot flashes, breast pains, dizzy spells, headaches, and heart palpitations, and the incidence of these symptoms varies among individual women. The depression and anxiety reported by some women do not appear to be an inevitable result of menopause, for many women are free of such symptoms (Neugarten, 1967). Physical changes such as loss of elasticity of the skin, hot flashes, appearance of facial hair, and changes in the breasts and genitals can be retarded by treatment with estrogen. Although many specialists advocate the use of estrogen therapy to retard physical aging in appearance and function, others warn of the danger of increased incidence of cancer. Women and their physicians should be aware of the benefits of estrogen replacement, but they must also be alerted to the potential dangers of this treatment. Additional research is under way to evaluate more clearly the relative benefits and risks of such treatment.

A cross-sectional study of women's attitudes toward menopause indicated that half of the middle-class women in the sample had extremely negative attitudes toward this change, whereas the other half had more favorable attitudes (Neugarten et al., 1963). Women beyond age forty-five (who presumably had experienced menopause) saw more favorable aspects of this period than did younger women. Older women and women who were better educated also saw the change as less stressful, suggesting that education reduces the problems associated with menopause. Women reported that one of the worst things about menopause was not knowing what to expect. Also rated as negative aspects were the pain and discomfort and the indication that one was getting older. Most felt that menopause had no effect on sexual relations or on physical and mental health.

Although most men do not experience an analog to menopause in women, some men may experience a *climacterium*, or lessening of reproductive ability, late in life, when fertile sperm are no longer produced. The rapid decrease in hormone level experienced by women during the menopause is responsible for some of the physical symptoms of that period, and recently there have been reports of analogous symptoms in about 10 to 15 percent of men in their mid to late fifties or early sixties (Ruebsaat & Hull, 1975). It appears that in this small proportion of men there is a rapid rather than a gradual drop in hormone level, and men who experience this rapid hormone drop are subject to physical and sometimes psychological discomfort. Hot flashes, dizziness, and depression have been reported by men experiencing this syndrome. So although there is no male menopause involving both the loss of reproductive capacity and the rapid decline of hormones, some men do experience a rapid drop in hormone level (unrelated to the later-occurring climacterium), leading them to experience symptoms similar to the symptoms of menopausal women.

Survey of Aged Reveals Liberal Views on Sex

JANE E. BRODY

A questionnaire survey of 800 older Americans living in communities throughout the country challenges many long-standing beliefs about the sexual interests and activities of the elderly. . . .

An overwhelming majority of the survey participants, includings widows, widowers and divorced or unmarried people, said that they were sexually active; 93 percent said they liked sex.

The respondents, 35 percent of whom were men, ranged in age from 60 to 91, with 36 percent between 70 and 79 and 9 percent over 80. All were living independently in their own homes or apartments or in residences for senior citizens throughout the country.

The study was conducted by two psychologists, Bernard Starr, a professor at Brooklyn College and research associate at the CASE Center for Gerontological Studies, and Marcella Bakur Weiner, adjunct professor of psychology at Brooklyn College. . . .

The findings "can give us tools to help the elderly who do not now express themselves sexually, but would like to," Dr. Starr said. They also "raise serious questions about the sexual fate of older women, whose sexual lives have always been tied to men," he said.

Source: *New York Times*, April 22, 1980, pp. C1–C2. © 1980 by The New York Times Company. Reprinted by permission.

The researchers concluded that sexual feelings and needs are "as vital a part of the lives of old people as when they were younger.". . .

Gerontologists have long suspected that the elderly are far more interested in sex than is commonly assumed, but most previous sex studies gathered only limited information on older persons. . . .

To conduct the new study, the Brooklyn psychologists addressed gatherings of older people primarily in senior citizens' centers and then distributed the 50-question survey to be filled out anonymously at home. On average, 14 percent returned completed questionnaires.

Contary to the researchers' expectations, there was wide acceptance of nudity, little self-consciousness about aging bodies and little anxiety about the decline of sexuality as the individuals got even older. Nearly two-thirds of the entire group and three-fourths of those who were still sexually active reported that their lovemaking had actually improved with the years.

Factors that contributed to the improvement included relief from the pressures of childrearing and the fear of pregnancy, greater privacy at home, fewer inhibitions and, with retirement, more time and opportunity.

"The frequency of sex may be less at age 75 than 25, but that doesn't mean it is better or more meaningful at 25," the researchers said. Many of those who completed the questionnaire said they were now more relaxed about their sexuality and more willing to explore new avenues of sexual expression than in their younger years.

Sexuality in Old Age

A great number of misconceptions about sex in old age are held by most people and, more tragically, by many physicians as well. Recent emphasis on sex education and on the research of Masters and Johnson, which has received widespread coverage by the media, may be affecting public awareness of sexual potential in old age. A study of Brandeis students undertaken in the 1950s (Golde & Kogan, 1959), in which the students were asked to complete the sentence "Sex for old people is . . . ," yielded pessimistic answers such as "unimportant," "past," and "negligible." A more recent survey involving students in a gerontology class at the University of Southern California led to a more positive picture. Students polled in the 1970s were unanimous in their acknowledgment that sex continues to play an important role in the lives of old people. Students completed the sentence with descriptions such as "O.K., but strange"; "Fine"; "Important and gratifying"; "Good"; "Fun"; "A matter of personal ability, attitude, and opportunity"; "As important as it is for people of all ages for psychological well-being"; "It depends upon individual needs and appetite"; "Whatever they want to make it"; "Great, if they are both capable of doing it"; "Out of sight"; "Not necessarily different than for younger people"; "Based on puritanical fallacy"; "Beneficial"; "Groovy but infrequent"; "Great, as long as they can and do still dig it"; "Necessary in some way"; "Probably more desired than had." Lastly, this insightful reflection was offered: "Still a part of life, and since they are still alive, it's cool."

Such data are encouraging, not only because they reflect positive attitudes about aging but because they indicate that future cohorts of elderly people may have more active sex lives. It appears that the best correlate of sexual activity in old age is patterns of sexual activity in earlier years. Thus healthy attitudes about sex in old age decrease the probability of a self-fulfilling prophecy. Those individuals who have a positive attitude about sex and who derive sexual satisfaction in early life will have the best change to enjoy a rich sex life when they are old (Butler, 1975).

Masters and Johnson point out that psychological factors play at least as great a role as hormones in determining the sex drive of older individuals; yet misinformation about sex in the later years often exaggerates fears and misconceptions that sexually incapacitate the aging. There is an amazing amount of misinformation—even among physicians. For example, if intercourse is painful for an older woman as a result of slight atrophy in her vulva and vagina, many physicians are apt to say "What do you expect at your age?" Hormone therapy might alleviate these problems, but the physician does not consider the issue important enough to consider therapy.

One of the most important features of an active sex life in old age is an interesting and interested partner. Pfeiffer, Verwoerdt, and Wang (1970), in a longitudinal study of 254 men and women aged sixty to ninety-four, found that 50 percent of the subjects in their sixties were still engaged in sexual activity, and that 10 to 20 percent of those in their eighties maintained sexual relations. The drop in activity in the seventies resulted in part from physical illness, but the availability of partners becomes an issue at this age as well. Women are particularly at a disadvantage, because they usually outlive their husbands and have little chance of finding available partners. Thus in addition to the social and economic constraints facing them, widows also lose the opportunity for sexual interaction. Nevertheless, for those fortunate individuals to whom an active sexual partner is still available, there is no time limit drawn by the advancing years to their sexuality.

Summary

1. Sex-role stereotypes are prevalent, with males being categorized by more traits that are desirable than are females.

2. Among the wide variety of behaviors that have been sampled, four behaviors show measurable differences between the sexes: verbal ability, visual-spatial ability, mathematical ability, and aggression. Additional behaviors for which there is suggestive evidence of a sex difference are tactile sensitivity, fear, timidity and anxiety, activity level, competitiveness, dominance, compliance, and nurturance.

3. There appear to be no sex differences in behaviors such as sociability, suggestibility, self-esteem, cognitive abilities, achievement motivation, or visual versus auditory sensory modality.

4. Biological factors account for some of the sex differences in behavior. Males are more vulnerable than females from birth. They also develop more slowly than females. The hormone testosterone appears to be associated with higher levels of aggression. High visual-spatial ability may be an inherited trait that is related to the X chromosome.

5. Socialization has a profound effect on sex-role development. Regardless of the genetic sex of an individual, socialization causes one to attempt to assume the sex role of the gender that has been assigned by parents.

6. Parents handle boys more roughly than girls, and they indicate more concern about the girl's physical well-being. Boys are more frequently punished physically, and they are given more direction than girls are.

7. Few sex differences in behavior are apparent early in life; most sex-typed behavior appears later in childhood and early adolescence.

8. On average, families of lower socioeconomic status appear to practice sex-typing more rigidly than do families in the middle socioeconomic range.

9. Psychoanalytic theory postulates that sex differences lead to widely different personality configurations in males and females. These personality differences are attributed to sex differences in anatomy and in interactions with parents. Psychoanalytic theory emphasizes the importance of early development and sees sex roles as being inflexible.

10. Social-learning theorists emphasize the significance of social contingencies and external environmental influences as the main shapers of gender identity. Sex differences are a function of learning, and sex-role behavior is flexible and has the potential to change.

11. Cognitive-developmental theorists view sex-role development as a cognitive phenomenon in which sex-typed identity forms before sex-typed interests, imitation, and attachment to the same-sexed parent can occur.

12. Sex roles appear to be changing in the United States, and the changing status of women is having an impact on individuals during all periods of the life span.

13. Sexual behavior has changed dramatically in the twentieth century, with the greatest changes occurring in women's behavior. Premarital sexual activity is dramatically more frequent in contemporary society than it was at the turn of the century.

14. Although contemporary adolescents are more sexually permissive, the majority of them do not condone promiscuity but favor caring relationships.

15. Though early maturation is always an asset to young males, it can cause difficulty in social adjustment for young females.

16. Sexual activity appears to peak early in life, usually during the first few years of marriage when an interesting and available partner is present. The frequency of intercourse declines with age, but sexual activity is still enjoyed and experienced throughout most of the adult life span, well into old age.

Selected Readings

Bee, H. L. "Part I. Sex Differences in Development." In *Social Issues in Developmental Psychology.* 2nd ed. New York: Harper & Row, 1978. Pp. 3-97. An overview and collection of important articles on sex differences at various stages of development.

Bernstein, A. C. "How Children Learn About Sex and Birth." *Psychology Today,* 10 (1976), 31-35. An interesting overview of contemporary American parents' approaches to providing sexual information to children.

Butler, R. "Sex After Sixty." In *The Later Years.* Eds. L. Brown and E. Ellis. Acton, Mass.: Publishing Sciences, 1975. An overview of the sexual potential of older people.

Neugarten, B. L. "A New Look at Menopause." *Psychology Today,* 1 (1967), 42-45. A realistic perspective of women's attitudes and experiences in menopause.

Sorenson, R. C. *The Sorenson Report: Adolescent Sexuality in Contemporary America.* Cleveland, Ohio: World Publishing, 1973. A national survey of American teenagers' sexual attitudes and behavior.

Chapter 16

Personality

The main theories of personality and their implications for development over the life span

The constitutional and environmental influences on personality development

The main developmental tasks an individual faces during different stages of the life span

In what ways personality remains stable or changes over the life span

How developmental psychologists describe the progress of an individual's personality as it unfolds and differentiates

Theories of Personality and Their Implications

Static (Descriptive) Personality Theories
Dynamic (Functional) Personality Theories

Constitutional and Environmental Factors

Genetic Influences
Prenatal Influences
Hormonal Influences
Body Types
Developmental Tasks

Consistency and Change in Personality over the Life Span

Traits and States
Disengagement and Defense

Some Personality-Related Constructs

The Self-Concept
Attitudes
Goals and Values
Subjective Feelings and Perceptions
Life Satisfaction and Morale

Life-Span Personality Profiles

Personality Questionnaires
Clinical Approaches

Introduction

The total psychological makeup of an individual is often referred to as *personality*. But this term is not a specific characteristic. Instead, it describes the combination of different terms used by personality theorists to indicate the "quality of the individual's total behavior" (Woodworth & Marquis, 1947). We will encounter several rather different definitions of personality, each of which may emphasize different developmental events. A minimum number of definitions, however, is required for any useful personality theory. Thus all theories considered here are concerned with the stimulus situation, with an organism that has specific characteristics, and with the organism's responses. However, because theories differ in what aspects they emphasize they also differ in the variables they measure to describe personality development and change.

The dynamics of individuals as they interact with others and confront environmental events include several dimensions. First, there are certain givens. These include the constitutional factors limiting the range of behaviors available to any individual within genetically transmitted potentials as well as the limiting constraints of favorable or unfavorable environments, both before and

A person's total psychological makeup, or "personality," arises from a combination of inherited and environmental factors that interact with developmental processes.

Charles Gatewood

after birth. These influences may lead to the development of distinct personality types or styles. Second, there are the socializing influences of early childhood, as well as other environmental influences occurring over extended periods of time. These result in what are generally called *personality traits*. Finally, there are the specific effects of situational events in eliciting behavior patterns. These have been described as *personality states*.

This chapter briefly examines the developmental implications of some major personality theories, which either have been explicitly stated by the theorist or can be deduced logically from the theory.[1] Next we examine constitutional factors that appear to be important in determining personality types and consider environmental demands (developmental tasks) facing most individuals over the life span. Although many theorists propose that personality patterns, once formed, remain stable throughout life, there are grounds to argue for a more flexible position. Therefore, we will examine some evidence concerning consistency and change in personality over the life span. Any discussion of personality must also consider certain related constructs, and so we investigate the development of self-concept, attitudes, goals and values, aptitudes and interests, subjective feelings and perceptions, and life satisfaction and morale. Finally, we discuss how developmental psychologists describe life-span personality profiles by using personality questionnaires and clinical assessment studies.

Theories of Personality and Their Implications

Two systems of personality theory make rather different contributions to our understanding of human development. The first system includes what might be called *static*, or *descriptive, personality theories*. These theories deal with facets of behavior that characterize an organism in the present, without necessarily inferring the antecedents that have led to the present situation. Trait theories and type theories fall into this category. Their implications for development relate primarily to changes in how personality may be organized at different life stages.

The second system includes *dynamic*, or *functional, personality theories*. Most theories emphasizing the relationship of events occurring early in life to later behavior fall into this category. Criteria for a dynamic theory include the assumptions that (1) behavior of all living organisms is functional, (2) behavior always involves conflict or ambivalence, (3) behavior can be understood only in relation to the field or context within which it occurs, and (4) all living organisms tend to preserve a state of maximal integration or internal consistency (Mowrer & Kluckhohn, 1944). In contrast to static theories, dynamic theories chart the manner in which personality changes from one developmental stage to the next.

The distinction between static and dynamic theories of personality is not, however, hard and fast. For example, psychoanalysis uses some rather struc-

1. For more detailed discussions of personality theory and its developmental implications, readers are referred to Cartwright (1974) and Rappaport (1972).

tural and thus static aspects in its emphasis on concepts such as the id, ego, and superego. Similarly, many trait theorists introduce dynamic concepts, such as the *ergs,* or energizing forces, mentioned by Cattell (1965) and the differentiation between stable traits and transient states. With these thoughts in mind, we are ready to examine the major theories of personality.

Static (Descriptive) Personality Theories

Trait and Factor Theories   Personality theories of this kind are derived in an inductive manner by sorting empirical data obtained from behavior observations that are ordered into a logical system by means of statistical operations. Falling into this category are the *typologies,* or broad categories of behavior descriptions, provided by Cattell (1957), Eysenck (1952), Guilford (1959), and Leary (1957). A brief description of Cattell's model will illustrate the basic concept of a representative trait theory.

The basic data units for trait theorists consist of the descriptive entities that can be obtained from observing the behavior of others, from self-description, or from performance on an objective test. Trait theory thus begins by cataloguing everyday descriptions of behavior. But the English language contains as many as 17,953 terms to describe human behavior (Allport & Odbert, 1936). Cattell refined this large list to a smaller group of 171 terms, which were reduced further to a set of 42 clusters. Subjects were then rated by observers who knew them in terms of each of the traits.

In trait description a person is observed to react in a certain way in a specified situation, but no attention is given to the reasons for the observed behavior. A distinction is made between *phenotypical (surface)* traits and *genotypical (source)* traits.[2] Cattell called the observable surface traits the "mask" aspects of personality description, and he used statistical methods to define more stable and pervasive source traits. In this way Cattell discovered fifteen basic source traits, including such dimensions as dominance versus submissiveness, naiveté versus shrewdness, confidence versus timidity, and so on. Further analysis of the fifteen source traits led to the discovery of several higher-order factors, the most important of which are introversion-extroversion and anxiety.

Factor analysts consider source traits to be the building blocks of personality. They seek to discover which behaviors distinguish individuals who score low on a given factor from those who score high. The major developmental questions involved are whether personality structure (in terms of both the number and the types of factors) changes, and whether the level of factor scores changes with age. Current evidence (see Schaie & Marquette, 1972; Schaie & Parham, 1976) suggests that only a few known factors change with age but that there are marked cohort (generational) differences for many factors. Because such studies are difficult, there is not yet evidence that personality factor structure changes across age, even though differences in factor structure have been shown for different cohorts (Costa, 1973).

2. Note that the terms *genotype* and *genotypical* are used here somewhat differently than in genetics, where *genotype* refers to the genetic constitution and *phenotype* to the observable trait (see Chapter 3).

Type Theory Compared with a trait, a type is a broader classification of behavior that may include many trait descriptions. Therefore, the data unit in type theory often consists of a set of observations or scores on a self-description questionnaire. By this means, observed individuals are assigned to types. Although typologies can result empirically from the operations used by trait theorists, more often they are derived from an armchair formulation of psychological categories for which empirical validation is sought later. Examples include Jung's (1923) introvert-extrovert typology, Sheldon's (1942) description of body types, discussed later, and the description of mental disease provided by the *Diagnostic and Statistical Manual* (DSM III, 1980), which forms the basis of modern psychiatric nomenclature. The value of a typology depends on how well it describes individual behavior patterns, on how consistent it is as a descriptive system, and on how well it permits the prediction of future behavior. For developmentalists it is important to know whether people can shift from one personality type to another and whether different types of personalities show differential patterns of behavior over time.

Dynamic (Functional) Personality Theories

Stimulus-Response (S-R) Theory S-R theory stresses associative learning of those responses that reduce the tensions experienced by an organism. However, the S-R relations may be simple or complex, and the reinforcement required to establish a response may involve elaborate behavior chains that can be difficult to trace. For example, an individual may learn a response without being aware of the S-R connections. This model is best defined by Guthrie (1952), who describes personality as "those habits and habit systems that are stable and resistant to change." S-R theorists argue that S-R connections relating to drive states and motives are the most adequate units to describe personality and that their formation can best be understood and studied through general laws of learning.

A particularly important variant of S-R theory is Skinner's (1953) model, which prefers to ignore intervening or mediating variables. Though this model is prominent in currently fashionable behavior intervention programs, it nevertheless requires the assessment of overt personality traits in order to identify the operants to be manipulated and to chart the frequency of response. Radical operant psychologists (see Baer, 1973) propose that developmental processes are not time dependent and that, consequently, personality traits can be modified at will—once the necessary technology is known.

Social Learning Theory An extension of learning concepts as applied to personality is provided by Rotter (1953). He argues for a social learning model of personality because most basic modes of behaving are learned in social situations and so are fused with needs that must be satisfied through the involvement of other persons. The unit of analysis for studying personality is therefore the interaction between an individual and the meaningful environment. Rotter suggests that a person's experiences influence each other and that new experiences are in part a function of old experiences. However, the meanings of such old experiences are changed by new experiences.

Bandura and Walters (1963) extend social learning theory by calling attention to the necessity of role models and the importance of imitation in the development of personality traits. In particular, they note that children often do *not* do what adults tell them but rather model their behavior on what adults *actually* do. Social learning theory might provide a model for two subjects discussed later in the chapter: the differential personality styles observed in old age (Reichard, Livson, & Petersen, 1962) and the phenomena described by disengagement theory (Cumming & Henry, 1961).

Phenomenological Theories In contrast to strict behaviorists, who make observable behavior the primary data base, phenomenologists propose that individual behavior can be understood only from the viewpoint of the behaving organism (Allport, 1961). In this system personality develops as the result of changes in an individual's phenomenal (perceived) field that are caused by changing needs and consequent alterations of perceptual relationships. The most important construct in this theoretical model is the *self-concept,* defined as those parts of an individual's perceptual field that have been differentiated by that person as being stable characteristics. Units of analysis for phenomenologists consist primarily of self-report data and of discrepancies in behavior as judged by self and others. Also important is congruence between the perceived actual self and the idealized self (Wylie, 1961). Currently the most prominent phenomenological model is probably that of Carl Rogers (1947). In this model, continuous experience implies continuous growth and self-actualization, and so personality differentiation is seen to continue throughout life.

Personology The work of Henry Murray (1938) focuses on the forces and motives that make an individual respond rather than on the response itself. Personality studies following this model may be quite general or may emphasize specific motives, such as achievement (McClelland et al., 1953). Needs or motives and environmental *presses* are the basic units of analysis, along with their interaction (called *thema*). This model infers personality from both manifest content and fantasy material obtained from the observed individual. Although the model is neutral on the issue of changes in need hierarchy over the life span, there is some evidence of shifts from young adulthood to old age (see Schaie & Strother, 1968).

Psychoanalytic Theory Of broad historical impact on the thinking of many developmentalists—as well as of major interest in its own right—are classical Freudian theory and its modern derivatives. Freud's major concern was with the development of sexual energy (the *libido*) and the destructive drive, or death wish (sometimes called *Eros* and *Thanatos*). Personality structure is conceptualized as being partitioned into the id, ego, and superego. The *id* represents the source of the person's drives and motivations, governed by what Freud called the "pleasure principle." The *ego* refers to the rational, reality-oriented part of the person. And the *superego* relates to the moral and ethical parts of the person (often referred to as "conscience"). Thought processes that are involved with id-based impulses for immediate gratification—whether in the everyday activities of a young child or in the dreams and fantasies of an adult—are called *primary processes.* Reality-oriented thinking that deals with practical life circumstances as well as moral and ethical considerations is called *secondary process* (Freud, 1923).

As noted in Chapter 2, psychoanalytic theory emphasizes early experience as being of major importance in forming personality patterns that may persist throughout life. This development goes through a series of so-called psychosexual stages, beginning with the *oral-passive period* in infancy (before the eruption of teeth) and shifting to the *oral-sadistic period* thereafter. According to Freud, an infant uses the mouth to gratify libidinal needs both by incorporating and by "destroying" food as a source of satisfaction. During toddlerhood the major source of erotic gratification shifts from the mouth to the digestive tract, as the child enters the *anal phase.* During this period conflict arises between the child and the parents, who wish to control the child's bowel movements. Tendencies to develop compulsive personality patterns are thought to arise out of inadequate resolution of such conflict.

If weaning (during the oral period) and toilet training (during the anal period) have been accomplished successfully, the *phallic stage* is reached during the preschool years. This period is differentiated from an adult's mature *genital period* in that gratification of needs is sought without concern for the feelings of others. The phallic stage culminates in what are called the *Oedipus* and *Electra complexes.* These simply describe the struggle between the child and the same-sex parent for the affection of the opposite-sex parent. Mechanisms involved in the resolution of these complexes involve so-called castration anxiety in boys and masculine protest in girls. As a consequence, mechanisms such as repression, substitution, and sublimation come into play, permitting the child to develop socially acceptable solutions to unrealistic needs (see Freud, 1933).

An individual's personality pattern is established by successful movement through these psychosexual states, including a latency stage, to the adult genital level. Also important is *fixation,* or partial arrest, resulting from insufficient gratification or overgratification during one of the earlier stages. Adult changes in personality are accounted for primarily by the principle of *regression,* which implies that as a result of traumatic experiences—say the stress of losing a spouse—an individual reverts to a behavior pattern that was appropriate at an earlier life stage. Thus personality changes in old age are seen as a reversion to childlike patterns, a model that is unsatisfactory.

Neo-Freudian Theories   Several variations on the basic psychoanalytic theme relate to the need to incorporate social forces in addition to the libidinal principles advocated by Freud or to introduce other sources for that libidinal energy. On the latter issue, we can list Jung (1933), already encountered as a type theorist, who advocated concern with the racial unconscious and archetypes; Otto Rank (1929), who emphasized the importance of birth trauma and the will; and Adler (1927), who was concerned with organ inferiority as expressed through sibling rivalry and compensatory behavior.

Concerns oriented more toward society were expressed by neopsychoanalysts such as Harry Stack Sullivan (1953), Karen Horney (1945), and Erich Fromm (1947). For these writers, it is not the intrinsic id chaos but the evil of modern civilization that creates anxiety and neurosis. Of greatest interest is the work of

Erik Erikson (1959, 1963), the only psychoanalytic theorist who has made specific contributions to our understanding of personality development across the life span. Erikson proposed a modified eight-stage model of psychosocial development, with specific personality patterns depending on the assumption that at each stage a person is confronted with a psychosocial crisis requiring the integration of personal needs with the demands of the culture. Erikson's stages and their associated psychosocial crises are as follows:

1. Infancy is the stage of trust versus mistrust.
2. Toddlerhood (ages two to four) is the stage of autonomy versus shame and doubt.
3. In early school years (ages five to seven) the emphasis is on initiative versus guilt.
4. The middle school years (from eight to twelve) focus on industry versus inferiority.
5. In adolescence (thirteen to eighteen) the issue is identity versus role confusion.
6. Young adulthood (nineteen to thirty) is concerned with intimacy versus isolation.
7. Middle adulthood (thirty-one to fifty) confronts generativity versus stagnation.
8. Late adulthood (after fifty) deals with ego integrity versus despair.

Maturational Theories   In contrast to the strong environmental positions expressed by the models discussed thus far, another group of theorists sees maturation as a critical explanatory principle for personality development. Maturational theorists see learning as the activation of new structures. It is not surprising that cognitive and emotional development are linked closely in such a model, represented best by the work of Gesell and Amatruda (1941), Werner (1957), Piaget (1972), Flavell (1963), and Kohlberg (1973).

Werner's *orthogenetic principle* is a good example of the maturational position. This principle specifies that all living organisms grow from an initially simple and undifferentiated state toward a state of complex differentiation and organization. Thus in an infant or otherwise primitive organism, emotional and cognitive functions are intertwined. The immature personality is characterized by diffuseness, rigidity, concreteness, and syncretic (undifferentiated) function. In the mature adult, however, cognitive and emotional functions are differentiated. In this view personality is characterized by its articulation, abstractness, flexibility, and discrete organization of function. Such a view would propose a regressive return in later life to the original primitive state (see Comalli, 1970).

In a similar vein Piaget has described a child's maturing as the unfolding of cognitive structures ranging from behavior dominated by sensorimotor functions to what he calls the level of formal operations of logicomathematical modes of thought. No clear distinctions are made between intellectual processes and personality. However, Piagetian models underline the stages of moral development provided by Lawrence Kohlberg (1973). These stages are of particular interest to life-span developmentalists, since Kohlberg has described stages of development ranging from the egocentric behavior of young children

The Cognitive-Developmental Approach to Moral Education

LAWRENCE KOHLBERG

Aims of Moral and Civic Education

Moral psychology describes what moral development is, as studied empirically. Moral education must also consider moral philosophy, which strives to tell us what moral development ideally *ought to be*. Psychology finds an invariant sequence of moral stages; moral philosophy must be invoked to answer whether a later stage is a better stage. The "stage" of senescence and death follows the "stage" of adulthood, but that does not mean that senescence and death are better. Our claim that the latest or principled stages of moral reasoning are morally better stages, then, must rest on considerations of moral philosophy. . . .

The conception that a moral choice is a choice made in terms of moral principles is related to the claim of liberal moral philosophy that moral principles are ultimately principles of justice. In essence, moral conflicts are conflicts between the claims of persons, and principles for resolving these claims are principles of justice, "for giving each his due." Central to justice are the demands of *liberty, equality,* and *reciprocity.* At every moral stage, there is a concern for justice. The most damning statement a school child can make about a teacher is that "he's not fair." At each higher stage, however, the conception of justice is reorgan-

Source: from *Phi Delta Kappan*, 1975, 46 (10), 670–677. © 1975, Phi Delta Kappa, Inc.

ized. At Stage 1, justice is punishing the bad in terms of "an eye for an eye and a tooth for a tooth." At Stage 2, it is exchanging favors and goods in an equal manner. At Stages 3 and 4, it is treating people as they desire in terms of the conventional rules. At Stage 5, it is recognized that all rules and laws flow from justice, from a social contract between the governors and the governed designed to protect the equal rights of all. At Stage 6, personally chosen moral principles are also principles of justice, the principles any member of a society would choose for that society if he did not know what his position was to be in the society and in which he might be the least advantaged. Principles chosen from this point of view are, first, the maximum liberty compatible with the like liberty of others and, second, no inequalities of goods and respect which are not to the benefit of all, including the least advantaged. . . .

Why are decisions based on universal principles of justice better decisions? Because they are decisions on which all moral men could agree. When decisions are based on conventional moral rules, men will disagree, since they adhere to conflicting systems of rules dependent on culture and social position. Throughout history men have killed one another in the name of conflicting moral rules and values. . . .

Planned Moral Education

. . . In the cognitive-developmental view, morality is a natural product of a universal human tendency toward empathy or role taking, toward putting oneself in the shoes of other conscious beings. It is also a product of a universal human concern for justice, for reciprocity or equality in the relation of one person to another. . . .

(continued)

In terms of moral discussion, the important conditions appear to be:

1. Exposure to the next higher stage of reasoning
2. Exposure to situations posing problems and contradictions for this child's current moral structure, leading to dissatisfaction with his current level
3. An atmosphere of interchange and dialogue combining the first two conditions, in which conflicting moral views are compared in an open manner

Studies of families in India and America suggest that morally advanced children have parents at higher stages. Parents expose children to the next higher stage, raising moral issues and engaging in open dialogues or interchange about such issues.

to the transcendent thought processes of mature adults who make societal contributions.

Kohlberg described seven stages organized into three levels. The premoral level occurs between ages four and ten. *Stage 1* is characterized by an obedience orientation; that is, the child is obedient in order to avoid punishment. This phase soon changes into a naive instrumental hedonism *(stage 2)*, where the child functions at a morally opportunistic level designed to maximize personal needs and objectives. Between ages ten and thirteen the main theme or morality consists of conventional role conformity. Two stages can be distinguished: *stage 3*, in which actions are evaluated in terms of whether they lead to the approval of others, particularly adults; and *stage 4*, in which authorities impose morality by emphasizing a person's role and duty in maintaining the established social order. The third level of morality obtains from about age thirteen to adulthood, although for many it may never be reached. *Stage 5* represents the maintenance of self-respect. It involves adherence to interpersonal and social contracts, the acceptance of democratically imposed laws, and respect for the rights of others. *Stage 6* maximizes the importance of the individual's conscience. It involves respect not just for rights but also for the integrity of other persons, and it tempers the principled enforcement of social rules with concern for judgment and the individual's and society's welfare (Kohlberg & Kramer, 1969).

Kohlberg also specifies a seventh stage, demonstrated in his opinion by such great universal thinkers as Spinoza, Gandhi, and Martin Luther King, Jr. Such individuals transcend principled moral integrity by moving away from despair with human fallibility into a cosmic or infinite perspective. Kohlberg has recently found in analyzing empirical data that few, if any, individuals meet his criteria for the sixth and seventh stages (Kohlberg, 1980).

Field Theory Not unrelated to maturational theory is the Gestalt-influenced field theory of Kurt Lewin (1935). Although Gestalt theory is in principle a nondevelopmental approach, Lewin became interested through studies of children in applying the concept of the *life space* to developmental issues. The life space defines aspects of the environment that an individual identifies as being immediately meaningful. It contains goal objects that have positive or negative valences, and an individual moves or is immobilized by these valences and thus takes available courses of action. Lewin indicated that the life space becomes increasingly differentiated in the course of development, and he viewed regression as the *dedifferentiation* of the life space. Although it uses quite different methods of analysis, this approach is similar to that of Werner. Schaie (1962) describes implications of field theory for adult development, in particular relating the development of flexibility-rigidity to field theory.

Constitutional and Environmental Factors

Although different theorists argue about the importance of biological and environmental factors in personality development, it is certain that all behaviors must be mediated by such matters. Therefore, we must examine to what extent personality factors are subject to genetic, prenatal, and hormonal influences, and whether or not certain body types account for personality variables. In addition, we must examine the effects of society's demands and expectations on the maturing individual.

Genetic Influences

Chapter 3 described the genetic transmission of traits and the methods by which behavior and genetics are studied. Most research into the inheritance of personality has involved the *co-twin method,* that is, comparing identical with fraternal twins. It is argued that when the correlation of a trait is greater among identical than among fraternal twins, that trait is likely to be subject to hereditary influences. Much of the strongest evidence regarding the inheritance of what might be called personality traits has been obtained from animal studies (McClearn & DeFries, 1973), particularly with respect to such matters as activity level, emotionality, aggression, and mating behavior. However, there also are a number of studies that implicate hereditary influences in human populations.

Much of the literature concerning the inheritance of personality traits has been summarized by Vandenberg (1969), who concludes that genetic sources have been shown to influence at least three traits: activity level, emotional expressiveness, and the tendency toward long-range planning. Emotional expressiveness includes such traits as sociability and extroversion. In this regard, the heritability of introversion-extroversion appears to be greater for females than for males (a correlation of .71 versus .33) in studies of twins using the Minnesota Multiphasic Personality Inventory and Sixteen Personality Factor Questionnaire (Gottesman, 1963). Similar findings were obtained in several studies using the California Personality Inventory for the traits of sociability, social presence, self-acceptance, and dominance (see Loehlin, 1975, for a review). And Eysenck (1967) reports that a number of studies involving performance tests of extroversion have shown heritability for that trait.

Among other traits, genetic factors influence emotional expressiveness.

Cary Wolinsky, Stock, Boston, Inc.

It appears likely, then, that it is primarily those traits involving a person's temperament, energy level, and emotional control that are particularly subject to genetic influences. In addition, there is evidence that some major personality disturbances (particularly schizophrenia) may be affected by hereditary factors, although the evidence is less clear in the cases of neuroses or alcoholism (see Chapters 3 and 4).

Prenatal Influences

An infant's first environment, of course, is the mother's womb. And because of the two-way relationship, the fetus is affected by the mother's stressful experiences. Though it is well known that infectious diseases and birth trauma can severely affect a child's intelligence, it is not always recognized that such factors may influence personality. For example, it has been shown that changes in the mother's hormonal balance and emotional state can influence the fetus (Sontag, 1944). And it has been shown experimentally in rats that shocking a pregnant animal results in more fearful offspring (Thompson, Watson, & Charlesworth, 1962). There is also evidence that infants of disturbed mothers may be hyperactive in responding to stimuli and may fluctuate more in heart action and gastrointestinal function—all of which indicates emotionally unstable behavior (Spelt, 1948).

The event of birth itself not only is an experiential trauma (Rank, 1929) but also is accompanied frequently by minor birth injuries resulting in particular from lack of oxygen, pressure, and other accidents of delivery. Intensive follow-up studies of children who suffered what has been called "minimal brain damage" show that they are often hyperactive, distractable, demanding, and highly impulsive (Wender, 1971).

Hormonal Influences

Another important constitutional factor is the influence of the endocrine system on personality, a field that has received systematic attention only recently. Hormonal effects on personality may be triggered by gene factors. These factors may be activated early or late in life, they may be activated only under certain environmental conditions (see Schaie et al., 1975), or they may be elicited by abnormal glandular conditions.

Endocrine glands that are known to have some effect on personality include the thyroid, adrenals, gonads, and the pineal gland. Thus persons suffering from excessive hormone production (hyperthyroidism) tend to show increased tension, excitement, and anxiety. On the other hand, individuals with thyroid deficiency (hypothyroidism) are often described as lethargic, depressed, and distrustful (Stagner, 1974). Pineal gland malfunction may interfere with the ability to learn from punishment (Schoenfield, 1971), and high production of male sex hormones has been shown to correlate with high scores for need dominance, the desire to make a good impression, responsibility, and socialization (Jones, 1957).

Adrenocortical hormones are released in response to stress, and individuals showing relatively low response appear to have greater "ego strength" and less emotional disturbance (Gerard & Phillips, 1953). At rest, the adrenal medulla produces a substance called *norepinephrine,* whereas in a stress situation it secretes *epinephrine.* Funkenstein, King, and Drolette (1957) conducted an intensive study of personality patterns associated with physiological stress as measured by such adrenal secretions. A number of complex relations were found, but the major conclusion was that both immediate response and delayed reactions to stress are related differentially to a variety of personality patterns. Further support for these studies was provided by Frankenhaeuser (et al., 1968), who found that individuals who successfully handled a stressful task had greater increments of norepinephrine than did subjects who failed the task. Differences in arousal level mediated by hormonal secretions also have been described in stress reactions among the aged (Wilkie & Eisdorfer, 1973).

Beyond such fairly well described hormonal effects on personality, there is a plethora of more detailed biochemical events that may affect an individual's expression of personality. The tremendous variety of such biochemical influences and expressions is well described by the eminent biochemist Roger Williams (1963). It suffices here to note that subtle biological differences among individuals may account at least in part for why human beings show such different responses to the same environmental stimulation.

Body Types

People obviously can be distinguished by a number of physical features, such as appearance, shape, and muscular development. These features are often described as a person's *physique,* or *body type.* One of the earliest scientific advocates of the concept of body type was Kretschmer (1925), who studied the physical appearances of individuals who had been diagnosed as schizophrenic or manic-depressive. He proposed that schizophrenic individuals are the abnormal version of a *schizoid type*—long, lean people who are characterized as unsociable, quiet, and prone to disassociation. By contrast, manic-depressive individuals are the abnormal version of the *cycloid type*—short, blocky people who are described as sociable, good-natured, humorous, and impulsive. Kretschmer called individuals with the schizoid body type *leptosomes* and those with the cycloid body type *pyknics.*

Kretschmer's typology loosely fits the body types of psychotics, but does not work so well with normal individuals. Sheldon (1942) consequently proposed some refinements, developing a theory that incorporates both physical appearance and temperament. Sheldon examined the front, side, and rear views of several thousand individuals and found that these could be scaled with respect to three "primary structural components" of physique. He called these components *endomorphy, mesomorphy,* and *ectomorphy* and rated them on a scale of from 1 to 7. A high rating on endomorphy is given to individuals who are barrel-chested, soft, fat, and big-bellied; an extreme endomorph is virtually circular in shape. A high rating on mesomorphy is obtained by muscular individuals who are broad-shouldered and narrow-hipped; an extreme mesomorph is like a triangle with the base on top. By contrast, ectomorph individuals can best be described as shaped like verticals lines; their external body surface is large in relation to their weight, and they are slender and flat-chested. Figure 16.1 illustrates Sheldon's body types among boys 11½ and 15 years of age.

Sheldon postulated three personality patterns to go with his body types. Endomorphy is associated with *viscerotonia,* which is characterized by love of comfort, sociability, and affection. The mesomorph's personality pattern is named *somatotonia,* which involves assertiveness, interest in muscular activities, and risk-taking tendencies. Ectomorphy is associated with *cerebrotonia,* which involves inhibition, low sociability, and excessive restraint. Sheldon (1942) reported high correlations between body type and associated personality pattern (.83 for ectomorphy, .82 for mesomorphy, and .79 for endomorphy). But Child (1950) attempted to replicate this work and obtained much lower correlations (.27, .38, and .13). On the other hand, Davidson, McInness, and Parnell (1957) studied seven-year-old children and were able to support Sheldon's theory by showing a .65 correlation between emotional disturbance and ectomorphy.

Of perhaps greater interest than the correlations between body type and personality characteristics may be the social reactions elicited because people *think* body types represent personality variables. Brodsky (1954) found that

FIGURE 16.1
Front and rear views
of Sheldon's body
types

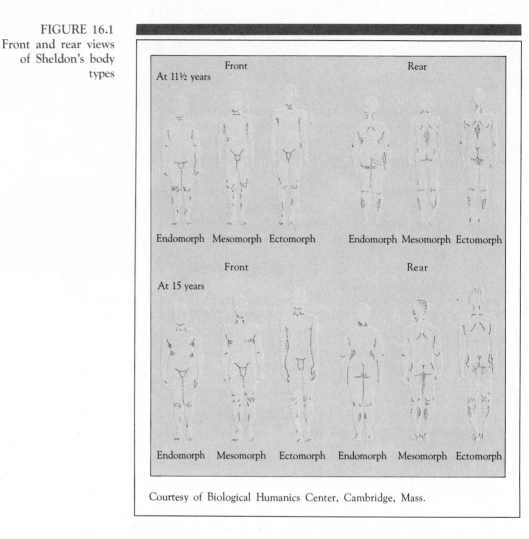

Courtesy of Biological Humanics Center, Cambridge, Mass.

raters ascribed negative traits to silhouettes of endomorphs, highly favorable traits to mesomorphs, and relatively favorable traits to ectomorphs. However, these traits may well be in the minds of the raters, since Wiggins and Wiggins (1969) showed that preferred female body types correlated highly with the personality characteristics of male raters.

Developmental Tasks

Besides the constitutional environmental factors that mediate personality development, attention must be called to a further organizing principle, the *developmental tasks* introduced by Havighurst in 1948. That is, maturing individuals find themselves facing consecutively new demands and expectations from the society in which they live.

Some tasks arise from physical maturation, others from cultural pressures of society, and yet others from an individual's personal values and aspirations

Maturing individuals constantly face new developmental tasks—demands and expectations from the society in which they live.

Cary Wolinsky, Stock, Boston, Inc.

(Havighurst, 1972). All of these tasks have biological, psychological, and cultural bases, and all must be mastered at an appropriate stage of the life span if an individual is to become a successful human being. Some developmental tasks appear to be the same across different cultures; others are more culture-specific. The former are typically tasks that depend on biological maturation, whereas the latter involve social demands that vary from one culture to another.

The following six developmental stages have been described for middle-class Americans, with some variation occurring for both lower- and middle-class individuals:

1. Early childhood (birth to age six)
2. Middle childhood (ages six to twelve or thirteen)
3. Adolescence (ages thirteen to eighteen)
4. Early adulthood (ages eighteen to thirty-five)
5. Middle adulthood (ages thirty-five to sixty)
6. Later maturity (beyond age sixty).

Tasks of Infancy and Early Childhood Although the common tasks of infancy and early childhood relate most directly to biological survival, they nevertheless include behavioral objectives that clearly are mandated by socialization. The tasks at this level include such things as learning to walk and take solid foods, initiating verbal communication, controlling the elimination of bodily wastes, and learning the social implications of sex differences and demands for sexual modesty. Toward the end of this period, more specific tasks begin to appear. Children are expected to form concepts and to learn language that describes both social and physical reality. Next they must learn to distinguish right from wrong and must begin to develop what is commonly referred to as a conscience. And, in preparation for further socialization, children must get ready to read—to learn that signs can stand for words.

Tasks of Middle Childhood During middle childhood, individuals are thrust from the home into the peer group, their neuromuscular skills are developed by means of games and simple work, and they begin to encounter adult levels of logic and communication. The specific tasks listed by Havighurst for this period include learning the physical skills needed for ordinary games; building wholesome attitudes toward oneself as a growing organism; learning to get along with age-mates; learning an appropriate masculine or feminine social role; developing fundamental skills in reading, writing, and calculating; developing concepts needed for everyday living; developing conscience, morality, and a scale of values; becoming an autonomous person; and developing social attitudes that are basically democratic.

Tasks of Adolescence Adolescence is the period of physical and emotional maturing. Although such changes are mainly internal, adolescent experience is clearly affected by society. Within recent decades, values in affluent societies have changed from *instrumental activities* (which may involve current sacrifices for future gains) to *expressive activities* (which involve enjoying the present moment without regard for the future). Nevertheless, the basic psychosocial tasks of this period remain concerned with what Erikson (1950) calls *achievement of identity*. The relevant tasks include achieving more mature relations with age-mates of both sexes; learning a socially approved adult masculine or feminine social role; accepting one's physique and using the body effectively; achieving emotional independence from parents and other adults; preparing for marriage and family life; preparing for an economic career; acquiring a set of values and an ethical system as a guide to behavior; and desiring and achieving socially responsible behavior.

Tasks of Early Adulthood Early adulthood has been described as the most lonely and individualistic period. During this period individuals must tackle some of the most important tasks in life, those involving the establishment of a new family unit and an independent life role. Havighurst lists the following specific tasks for this stage: selecting a mate, learning to live with a marriage partner, starting a family, rearing children, managing a home, getting started in an occupation, taking on civic responsibilities, and finding a congenial social group.

Tasks of Middle Age During this period individuals reach their peak of influence in society. At the same time, however, they begin to feel the biological changes of aging. Developmental tasks in middle age are programmed both by changes within the organisms and by environmental pressures, including influences deriving from an individual's own needs and aspirations. The following tasks are described for this life stage: assisting teen-age children to become responsible and happy adults, achieving adult social and civic responsibilities, attaining and maintaining satisfactory performance in one's career, developing adult leisure-time activities, relating to one's spouse as a person, accepting and adjusting to the physiological changes of middle age, and adjusting to aging parents.

Tasks of Later Maturity The final stage of life may involve disengagement from more active participation in society or re-engagement in new life roles, whether as grandparent, as involved citizen, or even in a new career. Certain constrictions seem inevitable in our present social environment, but much task-oriented behavior during this stage is related to adapting to and compensating for biological and societally mandated losses. Havighurst describes the following common tasks: adjusting to decreasing physical strength and health, adjusting to retirement and reduced income, adjusting to the death of one's spouse, establishing explicit affiliations with one's age group, adapting social roles in a flexible way, and establishing satisfactory physical living conditions. Thomae (1975) provides detailed examinations of the developmental tasks of aging, confirming the usefulness of this approach in relation to the last part of life.

Consistency and Change in Personality over the Life Span

We are now ready to turn to what should be the most interesting question developmentalists might ask about personality: does personality remain stable over the life span, or does it change? Two very different positions have been taken. The first—typical of psychoanalytically oriented theorists but also implicitly advocated by some learning and type theorists—argues that personality structure is determined by early-childhood socialization experiences within the constraints of applicable genetic and constitutional factors. In this view, all further development is seen simply as an expression of the established personality pattern under unique interactions between the person and the environment, but no further systematic development occurs. The opposing position—taken by organismic theorists and some who are phenomenologically oriented—is that there are transformations both in physiological structure and in common experience, and that these transformations occur at different life stages. This view sees personality as developing and changing throughout life.

It is important to distinguish between developmental changes and changes that occur in response to an individual's unique experiences. Support for continuing developmental change requires evidence that adult personality changes are as universal and systematic as those observed in early childhood. The latter position simply affirms that human beings are flexible and can respond to both favorable and unfavorable environmental circumstances within the limits of previous experiences and capabilities.

Two different types of evidence will help to illuminate whether personality remains stable or changes past early childhood. The first kind of evidence involves the longitudinal study of particular traits and personality constructs over long periods of time within the same individuals. The second kind of evidence concerns studies of personality organization at different life stages to

Personality
and Disease

MATT CLARK

Nearly three decades ago, Dr. Caroline Bedell Thomas of Johns Hopkins University set out on an intriguing search to identify personal characteristics—both physical and emotional—that might be linked to the development of various diseases later in life. Between 1946 and 1964, she and her colleagues gave meticulous physiological and psychological examinations to more than 1,000 students as they passed through the Baltimore medical school and followed them up with detailed annual questionnaires as they went on to their careers. Now, as the participants enter middle age and illnesses start to take their toll, the investigators have begun to assemble a comprehensive picture of the interplay of mind and body in the susceptibility to heart disease, high blood pressure, cancer, mental illness and suicide.

Most studies that seek to identify factors leading to disease are retrospective; the researchers look into the past histories of persons already ill. Other studies that try to identify risk factors before a disease strikes are usually conducted on persons who have already reached middle age and thus may no longer be typical normal subjects. In choosing medical students, Thomas could study subjects who were young and, if anything, healthier than average.

Among the participants, most of whom are men now ranging from 35 to 60 years of age, 131 have developed one of the disorders under study and 47 have died. Forty-three developed cancer, fourteen have had heart attacks, twenty have high blood pressure, 38 have experienced mental illness, and sixteen have committed suicide.

As might be expected, both the suicides and the victims of mental illness showed high test scores for depression, anxiety and nervous tension. The suicides were among the heaviest smokers in the study. They also tended to be underweight and to have skinny "ectomorphic" physiques. The victims of mental disorders were heavy coffee drinkers and tended to suffer from insomnia. . . .

Most surprising, in Thomas's view, was the discovery of a link between personality patterns and cancer. The cancer victims were among the lowest scorers with respect to anxiety and depression. On the whole, they showed placid, gentle and nonaggressive dispositions. But they shared with the suicides and victims of mental illness a remarkable lack of closeness to their parents. On perusing the medical literature, Thomas has since found several retrospective studies that have disclosed a similar cancer-prone personality, characterized by alienation beginning in early childhood. . . . Most cancer experts now think that the body's immune system plays an important part in protecting against malignancies. A person with an unresolved emotional conflict from childhood, Thomas speculates, may be peculiarly susceptible to stresses involving the loss of strong relationships—spouses or jobs—and such stresses might produce hormonal changes and failure of the immune system.

determine whether the interrelations remain similar across age and successive generations. Review of evidence for specific personality traits has been provided by Mischel (1969), and multivariate studies of personality have been reviewed by Schaie and Marquette (1972).

In this section we will show that most personality traits are quite stable across life, even though situationally determined personality states are not. By contrast, there are a few traits—most of which involve temperament and energy level—that, because of their probable genetic and constitutional determinants, show fairly well-determined developmental patterns. We will also examine the extent to which the supposed disengagement of the aged is determined by development or constructed as a defense against an increasingly less supportive social and interpersonal environment.

Traits and States

The distinction between personality traits and states can be illustrated by focusing on anxiety. *Trait anxiety* refers to the relatively stable differences among people in their tendency to respond to situations perceived as threatening by the kind of psychological and physiological responses described as anxiety. *State anxiety,* on the other hand, is a transitory emotional state that is characterized by consciously perceived feelings of tension and apprehension, including heightened activity of the autonomic nervous system. In other words, trait anxiety indicates the predisposition of an individual to manifest an anxious reaction, given a certain situation, whereas state anxiety is an empirical reaction taking place at a particular time and at a specified level of intensity. Whether or not people who differ in their level of trait anxiety show corresponding differences in state anxiety depends on the extent to which a specific situation is perceived as dangerous or threatening, a perception greatly influenced by that individual's past experience (Spielberger, Lushene, & McAdoo, 1976).

It follows, then, that the expression of a trait in a given situation may differ markedly, which might make it seem as though there is considerable personality change across age, even though the trait is substantially stable. In other words, because stimulus situations may differ markedly across life stages, it is not unreasonable that situations that elicit a state such as anxiety may occur more frequently during one stage than another, without implying that personality actually has been reorganized.

The study of a wide array of personality traits yields a relative scarcity of traits showing significant change across the life span but a prevalence of traits exhibiting substantial differences that are likely to arise from shifts in patterns of child rearing and socialization across generations. Schaie and Parham (1976) describe three kinds of variables among personality traits and attitudes that would seem to have different life courses. The first of these is referred to as *biostable traits*—behaviors that either are determined genetically or are shaped by influences that occur early in life, perhaps during a critical imprinting period. All such traits show significant sex differences but few if any age variations. Nevertheless, such traits may be affected by transient sociocultural changes or by generational differences. Examples include such traits as reactivity to threat, expressed honesty, and attitudes toward science and community involvement.

In contrast, the second set of traits, called *acculturated traits*, is overdetermined by environmental events occurring at different life stages and is subject to rapid modification through sociocultural change. Such traits ordinarily show no sex differences, and apparent age trends turn out, on analysis, to result from interactions of generational differences and transient sociocultural trends. Examples of such traits include extroversion, low self-sentiment, superego strength, dominance, and positive attitudes toward supporting society.

The type of trait that is observed least frequently is called a *biocultural trait*. Such traits have clear ontogenetic patterns and sex differences that are modified in a similar manner by generational shifts or sociocultural events at all age levels (see Figure 16.2). Examples of such traits include excitability and surgency (expression of energy level).

Patterns for specific traits have been examined over much of the adult life span (Schaie & Parham, 1974, 1976), emphasizing the great degree of stability. But examination of a single twenty-five-year study that emphasized stability for a more global measure of personality—the California Personality Inventory—illustrates what is found in the more analytic studies of specific traits. Woodruff and Birren (1972) retested subjects—who first described themselves as adolescents in 1944—twenty-five years later, when they were middle-aged. Interest-

FIGURE 16.2
Life course of the biocultural trait of excitability

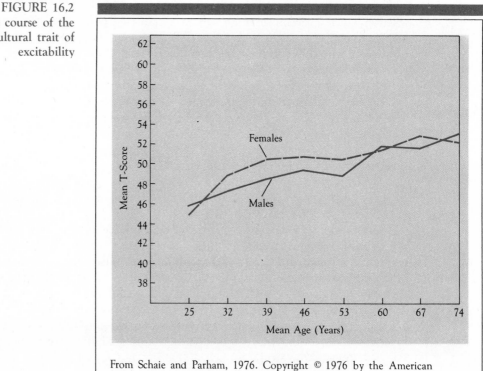

From Schaie and Parham, 1976. Copyright © 1976 by the American Psychological Association. Reprinted by permission.

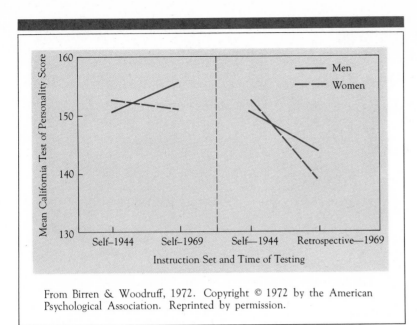

FIGURE 16.3
California test of personality scores for persons born in 1924 and tested in 1944 and 1969

From Birren & Woodruff, 1972. Copyright © 1972 by the American Psychological Association. Reprinted by permission.

ingly enough, their descriptions were similar to those given earlier, even though the subjects thought in retrospect that they had given a less favorable description of themselves than they actually had (see Figure 16.3). When the investigators obtained a new sample of adolescents in 1969, these later cohorts described themselves far less favorably than had the adolescents in 1944. In other words, although this study shows stability of personality at least from adolescence to midlife, there are substantial differences between successive generations.

While the apparent stability of personality traits may be reassuring, we must remember that we are talking about evidence from studies averaged *across* large numbers of different persons. Indeed, one important variable may be the stability of behavior within an individual. For example, in a study of ten- and eleven-year-old children, Labouvie and Schaie (1974) showed that children who differed in stability on the Child Personality Quiz (Porter & Cattell, 1960) over a one-year period also showed a variety of important differences on other traits. In addition, the number of behavior dimensions needed to describe the behavior of the unstable group was greater than was needed to describe the stable group. In particular, the boys in the stable group seemed better socialized and more advanced in their development than the girls.

Disengagement and Defense

So far, we have made the argument that traits either are programmed genetically or, more frequently, are acquired early in life; then, after some vacillation during childhood, they remain relatively stable throughout life except for the intervention of major changes in the environment or in an individual's specific

The elderly do not
have to disengage;
there is a positive re-
lationship between ac-
tivity and morale.

Sybil Shackman, Monkmeyer Press Photo Service

life circumstances. When life circumstances change quite uniformly because of
events such as retirement practices, it may appear as though the changes are
accompanied by personality reorganizations. Such thinking led Cumming and
Henry (1961) to formulate their *disengagement theory,* in which they conclude—
erroneously, we think—that the process of psychological and social withdrawal
frequently observed in old people arises from psychological events within a
person rather than as a response to societal exclusion and role limitations (compare Schaie, 1973).

Disengagement theory has three basic postulates. It claims that (1) social and
psychological withdrawal is optimal for aging adults, (2) the disengagement
process is both inevitable and intrinsic, and (3) disengagement is not simply a
correlate of successful aging but is in essence a necessary condition for successful
aging. Cumming (1963) further specifies that successful disengagement involves
a decrease in new contacts, interaction in fewer roles with present contacts, a
shift away from achievement orientation, and less affective involvement in
remaining social relationships.

Several prominent gerontologists have taken exception to the disengagement
position. For example, Maddox (1964) disputes that happy old people could or
would be disengaged and provides evidence for positive relationships between
activity and morale in aged persons (Maddox & Eisdorfer, 1962). Indeed, it
may be argued that disengagement is not an inevitable adaptive response or a
normative personality reorganization of old age but rather represents a defensive response to societal pressure emanating from its middle-aged members

(Schaie, 1973). Additionally, disengagement may represent but one of many lifestyles found among the elderly.

In fact, several lifestyles other than disengagement have been described among the elderly. For example, in a study of eighty-seven males, five personality types were identified (Reichard, Livson, & Petersen, 1962). Three of these were accepting of aging: mature, philosophic individuals who enjoyed whatever they were doing at the moment; "rocking-chair" men who enjoyed ease and relaxed into old age; and "armored" men who used activity as a defense against old age, arguing that they had to keep active or die. The two other groups consisted of individuals who aggressively blamed others for the disappointments and frustrations of old age, and self-haters who were depressed and gloomy. Similar types were described by Neugarten, Havighurst, and Tobin (1968) in a study of men and women in their seventies. Further evidence that seems incompatible with the adaptiveness of disengagement in old age is provided by Lieberman (1971), who suggests that grouchiness or combativeness may be essential for survival into very old age. And Gutmann (1971) points out that combativeness, not withdrawal, is characteristic of the longest-lived men in various preliterate societies.

With these exceptions, then, it appears that personality patterns are quite stable through life but that the expression of such patterns may be affected markedly by individual crises, some of which have greater probability of occurring during one life stage than another. Just as disengagement is only one way of coping with the crises of old age, so will coping styles differ in handling other crises (Brim, 1968; Lowenthal, Thurnher, & Chiriboga, 1975). Finally, it may be important whether the crisis occurs at a time of life when it is anticipated (Neugarten, 1970), and whether a particular event is perceived to be threatening or innocuous (Back & Morris, 1974).

Some Personality-Related Constructs

Not all behavioral dimensions associated with the concept of personality can be packaged neatly in a discussion of personality traits or other global personality dimensions. Therefore, we will now examine some additional dimensions that have received attention in developmental research.

The Self-Concept

Humanistic and existential psychologists view the self as the prime subject of inquiry for those seeking to understand human personality (Buhler & Allen, 1972). Indeed, they argue that the development of conscious awareness of self is one of the central events of early childhood (Rappoport, 1972). The emergence of the self-concept during childhood is described by Allport (1961). He suggests that before age three, a child first acquires a sense of *bodily self*. Next, a sense of continuing *self-identity* is acquired, which leads to the development of *self-esteem*. Somewhat later, at from four to six years of age, there is an *extension of self* as evidenced by possessiveness toward objects and people. At about five years, an *extended self-image* develops that may be an initial approximation of the conscious self-appraisal and value system characteristic of a mature person.

The self-concept emerging in childhood frequently must be altered radically in adolescence because the individual no longer can rely on the social support provided by parents and peers. In addition, adolescents must deal with the unfamiliar physical changes of puberty. Value conflicts with parents also require frequent reorganization of the self-concept to permit establishment of one's identity.

In maturity, the self-concept once again changes as successful individuals engage in what Rogers (1947) describes as *self-actualization*. Allport (1961) suggests six qualities possessed by adults who have developed a mature self-concept: extension of the sense of self, or ego-involvement with and commitment to others; warmth in relating to others; emotional security, or self-acceptance; realistic perception and good judgment; self-objectification, including insight and humor; and finally, some kind of unifying philosophy of life.

Changes in self-concept in old age largely reflect the stereotypes expressed by others toward the aged (see Ahammer & Baltes, 1972). An older person's self-concept must come to grips with the many "insults" of old age, such as the loss of physical attractiveness, the loss of supporting loved ones, the loss of status and of useful and respected roles, and the lessening of physical health and vigor (Havighurst, 1959). Note, though, that such changes are not determined developmentally but occur as a function of changes in individual circumstances. They are not tied inevitably to the advent of old age. Indeed, literature and life are replete with individuals who exhibit positive, well-integrated self-concepts even into advanced age.

Attitudes

Attitudes summarize a person's evaluation of specific objects, persons, or social issues. Such evaluation may be an important part of how an individual's personality is expressed. In contrast to personality traits—which we have defined as an individual's patterns of habit or response—attitudes may say much about a person's stereotype without necessarily revealing what his or her expressed behavior would be. Nevertheless, attitudes may have a utilitarian function, leading us to continue interacting with persons or using objects that we have found to be rewarding in the past. Whether benevolent or bigoted, attitudes may be simple codes that help us summarize our reaction to classes of objects or persons. Then again, they may serve to let others know what kind of person we are, helping us to deal with otherwise ambiguous feelings about objects or persons (McGuire, 1969). Attitudes that have received the most attention are those relating to conservatism-radicalism, tough-mindedness versus tender-mindedness, and feelings toward other races and authoritarianism (Cartwright, 1974).

From a developmental point of view, attitudes seem to become firm fairly early in life, and studies of adult development indicate that they are quite resistant to change over time within individuals (Haan & Day, 1974). One exception, however, is that humanitarian concern seems to increase with age (Schaie & Parham, 1976). Other attitudes, such as interest in science and community involvement, increase across successive generations but appear to be quite stable within each generational group across adult development.

Goals and Values

Although describing an individual's attitudes may help us understand that person's belief system, other constructs may be linked more closely to behaviors that predict an individual's response tendencies in certain situations. For example, social learning theory makes a good deal of the fact that different behavior potentials may influence each other because they have a common *goal* (Rotter, Chance, & Phares, 1972). In other words, if human behavior is purposive, then it must lead toward personal goals, and it would be useful for us to know how such goals develop. But the concept of goal-directed behavior is not very different in meaning from the term *value*, which often is preferred by humanistic and phenomenologically oriented writers (for example, Frankl, 1962; Madison, 1969).

Goals and values express themselves as judgmental sets that markedly influence behavior and the expression of personality traits. They probably are acquired during childhood as part of the early socialization process. As such, goals and values are affected markedly by social class and ethnic background (McCandless, 1967). The conflicts of adolescence—particularly the resocialization effects of college and exposure to peers and prospective mates who hold other value orientations—may lead to significant transformation stages (Madison, 1969). Nevertheless, values seem to be transmitted within families, as has been demonstrated by several studies of three-generation families (Hill et al., 1970; Kalish & Johnson, 1972). But consecutive generations are more likely to be more similar, and children's values are often more like those of their parents than those of their grandparents (Bengtson & Black, 1973). Again, within generations it appears that goals and values generally are maintained over the life course, even though significant experiences may alter the personal objectives of some individuals.

Subjective Feelings and Perceptions

The role of perceived age-related behavior may be crucial to an understanding of the developmental process because change in a person's behavior is often preceded by the person's perception that, indeed, environmental change has occurred (Thomae, 1970). Of particular importance in this process are both the salient characteristics of the perceived person or situation and the characteristics of the perceiver (Warr & Knapper, 1968). A substantial body of research has focused on stereotypes prevalent at different age levels toward the perceived group. Interestingly enough, it has been shown that subjectively perceived age differences across generations do not match actual age differences (Nardi, 1973). For example, Ahammer and Baltes (1972) compared actual and perceived age differences for adolescents, adults, and the elderly in terms of the desirability of certain personality traits. In this study adults perceived adolescents as placing a higher value on autonomy than they actually did. Similarly, both the young and the middle-aged subjects perceived older people as valuing autonomy less than they actually did. Another interesting finding was that the middle-aged group was never misperceived by the other two groups, whereas the oldest group was always misperceived by the younger groups.

The literature dealing with subjective feelings and perceptions of others across age suggests that what seems to be changing is the perception of individuals at life stages other than our own. Not surprisingly, it is easier to identify correctly where we have been than where we will go.

Life Satisfaction and Morale

Although happiness is a personality construct, psychologists readily concede that it may be important to know whether people consider themselves to be happy. Some studies have raised this question directly, but more information about developmental changes in feelings of contentment has become available through studies of the concepts of life satisfaction and morale. These concepts are mostly present-oriented in childhood, involving such issues as acceptance by parents and peers and congruence between the child's expectations of material surroundings and what actually can be provided by the family.

In adulthood, on the other hand, life satisfaction seems to be intimately related to satisfaction with one's marital partner and to attainment of expected social status by appropriate advancement in a career. Satisfaction and happiness in marriage tend to be greater for those who have traditional expectations, and are greater among working-class than among middle-class individuals (Cutler & Dyer, 1965). But marital satisfaction differs by life stages. Honeymooners, couples whose children have left home, and elderly couples report greater satisfaction than do parents of young children or teen-agers. And childless couples are much more satisfied with marriage than those married the same length of time who have children (Feldman, 1964).

Contrary to widespread belief, there is no evidence for a marked decline in job satisfaction. For the past decade, 90 percent of samples of the working population report satisfaction with their occupational roles. In fact, there appears to be an increment from young adulthood (when about 75 percent describe themselves as being satisfied) into middle age, and most dissatisfied workers are at the lower level of occupational status (Quinn, Staines & McCullough, 1974).

This writer and associates in several longitudinal studies have always questioned subjects about the state of their feelings concerning happiness and life satisfaction (Schaie, 1974). No generational differences or age changes have been noted. However, this is not to say that there are no life circumstances that affect life satisfaction. For example, Neugarten, Havighurst, and Tobin (1968) found substantially higher life satisfaction among old people who were described as well integrated than among those who were not so described. And Lowenthan and Haven (1968) reported substantially higher life satisfaction

People who have a confidant report greater happiness and life satisfaction.

George Bellerose, Stock, Boston, Inc.

among people over sixty who had no serious illness and were married or still working, compared with those who had serious physical illnesses or were widowed or retired. These authors also reported, however, that the presence of a confidant seemed to offer a buffer against feelings of low morale. That is, in all categories, those who had a confidant reported greater life satisfaction than those who did not have a confidant.

Life-Span Personality Profiles

How can we describe the progress of personality as it unfolds and an individual's pattern differentiates—whether it remains characteristic of socialization patterns affecting the population cohorts or whether it deviates because of significant individual experiences? First of all, we can attend to the major attempts to describe personality by means of questionnaires. Next we can look at the more clinical approaches, including the projective techniques used in some major longitudinal studies that followed groups of the same individuals over significant periods of time.

Personality Questionnaires

Pencil-and-paper tests of personality are simply self-administered standard interview procedures. Their virtues include simplicity, economy, and relative objectivity. However, this objectivity may be impaired by test items that lead test takers to describe themselves not as they are but as they may wish the examiner to view them. In fact, "faking" on personality tests is frequently an unconscious matter, since persons will often answer a test item affirmatively because that seems socially desirable, whether or not the test item applies to the person answering.

Another problem with personality questionnaires is that they depend on the assumption that the people taking the test have sufficient information about themselves that they are willing and able to reveal. Also, many popular self-report questionnaires have been developed and normed by using college populations. The meaning of items may well differ when applied to other groups whose members may misunderstand or fail to understand the language used.

Personality inventories differ in their method of construction and, consequently, in the problems and populations to which they might be applied. Three major types are described below, with examples. These are *criterion-group measures*, which attempt to show how well a given person fits into a particular personality type based on traits; *inventories derived from factor analysis*, which try to describe the standing of an individual in terms of a personality genotype or genotypes; and *construct-based inventories*, which assign an individual to a position on the basis of constructs derived from a particular personality theory.

Criterion-group Measures These are constructed by selecting statements that reflect personal behaviors and attitudes (traits) that sample the broad domain of personality as defined by the investigator. Such items are then administered to criterion groups to determine which test items distinguish among such groups. For example, on the California Psychological Inventory (CPI)—a questionnaire designed to survey the personality of adolescents and college students—items were selected for a scale of "responsibility" by having high school principals nominate their "most" and "least" responsible students and then picking items that differentiated best between the two groups (Gough, 1964). Once a pool of test items has been established, it is possible to construct as many scales as there are identifiable criterion groups.

When inventories such as the CPI or the MMPI (Minnesota Multiphasic Personality Inventory) are used to compare individuals of different ages or to monitor behavior change across time in the same person, we sometimes find that comparable criterion groups do not exist at all ages. Thus the validity of such questionnaires for answering developmental questions is in serious doubt, because observed changes or differences may simply imply different genotypic meaning of the scales at different ages or for different cohorts.

Construct-based Inventories These result from a theoretical model that specifies dimensions of personality or some subsphere of personality. Depending on the theory used, the questionnaire constructor deduces the variables to be included and then writes a set of items that, in the tester's opinion, best represents the construct to be measured. The questionnaire is then administered to a large group of normative subjects, and validity studies are conducted to determine whether the new scale does, in fact, relate to the construct it purports to describe. For example, Edwards (1959) constructed a questionnaire describing individual need hierarchies by identifying items that he judged to be relevant to fifteen of the needs described in Murray's (1938) study of normal adult personality. Edwards controlled for social desirability (attempts to guess the "normal" response) by pairing items for each need that had been judged equal in social desirability value. This particular scale does not provide absolute values for a given person's needs. Rather, it describes the rank order of the fifteen needs within the person's need hierarchy. Such a comparison may have considerable utility in developmental studies, because it may be more significant to know what happens to the organization of personal needs than it is to assess their absolute level. For example, it is interesting to know that achievement need still occupies a prominent position in aged college graduates' need hierarchy, even though overall achievement need may well be lowered (Schaie & Strother, 1968).

Factor-analysis Method This is a data-based approach to questionnaire construction that, by contrast, requires no preconceived notions about the dimensions of personality. As in the criterion-group approach, the questionnaire constructor collects a large pool of items to represent as closely as possible the behavior domain to be surveyed. The pool of items is administered to a large heterogeneous sample of normal subjects; intercorrelations between items are then computed and factor analyzed. The resulting personality dimensions are identified by determining which items load on these dimensions. Items that identify the factor dimensions most clearly are then combined into scales, and additional items are selected for scales that are not as long as desired.

An advantage of the factor-analytic approach is that once the scales are constructed, they can be used to study any number of criterion groups. It is not necessary to build new scales, as would be the case with the criterion-group approach. Also, once the structure of the domain to be assessed has been determined, it is relatively easy to build parallel forms to measure the same factors at different language levels—an important consideration for life-span studies.

Perhaps the most prominent example of a factored personality questionnaire is the Sixteen Personality Factor Test (16 PF), for which the pool of items was derived from the original studies of personality traits (Cattel, Eber, & Tatsuoka, 1970). Factor analysis of these items resulted in the sixteen personality dimensions listed in Table 16.1. Two forms of the test make it possible to retest the same subjects after a brief period of time, and there is an alternative form for subjects who have a low level of literacy. In addition, new factor analyses of item pools at lower levels of language difficulty led to the establishment of alternative scales measuring the same factors. Currently available are the High School Personality Quiz (HSPQ), for adolescents; the Children's Personality

TABLE 16.1
Factor Scales of
the Sixteen
Personality
Factor
Questionnaire

A: Reserved versus outgoing
B: Low intelligence versus high intelligence
C: Ego strength versus proneness to neuroticism
D: Excitability versus insecurity
E: Dominance versus submissiveness
F: Expedient versus conscientious
G: Timid versus uninhibited
H: Tough-minded versus tender-minded
I: Trusting versus suspicious
L: Practical versus imaginative
M: Unpretentious versus polished
O: Guilt proneness versus confidence
Q1: Radicalism versus conservatism
Q2: Self-sufficiency versus group dependency
Q3: High self-sentiment versus low self-sentiment
Q4: Relaxed versus tense

Source: R. B. Cattell, E. W. Eber, and M. M. Tatsuoka, *Handbook for the Sixteen Personality Factor Questionnaire.* Champaign, Ill.: Institute for Personality and Ability Testing, 1970. Copyright 1970 by The Institute for Personality and Ability Testing. All rights reserved. Reproduced by permission of the copyright owner.

Quiz (CPQ), for ages eight to twelve; the Early School Personality Quiz (ESPQ), for ages five to eight; and the Pre-school Personality Quiz (PSPQ), for nursery school children. Not all factors can be identified reliably for all ages, but there is enough continuity to permit long-range clinical studies of a single individual.

Clinical Approaches

Going beyond the description of personality structure at different life stages requires more detailed assessment procedures than those just described. A variety of projective techniques have been designed to identify personality dynamics and subconscious needs and defense structures as well as to identify physiological growth (particularly in childhood), which provides the context of changes in personality patterns. As yet, no single study has followed personality variables throughout life. However, several studies have employed extensive assessment batteries to follow children into middle adulthood, and adults into old age. Several of these studies are described below.

The Fels Study Beginning in 1929 at the Fels Research Institute of Yellow Springs, Ohio, eighty-nine children were studied from birth. This study was reported extensively during its first thirty years (Kagan & Moss, 1962), and further data are still being collected. In this study, researchers made half-day visits to the homes of mothers and children twice a year, until the children were six. They then made annual visits until the children were twelve. In addition, children were observed in nursery school from ages two-and-a-half to five, and in day camp from ages six to ten. School observations and mental testing were continued annually from ages six to fourteen. Between ages eight and seventeen, personality tests were given at three-year intervals, and at approximately age twenty-four interview data were obtained from five to six hours of taped interviews. These studies resulted in data about four major personality patterns: passivity and dependency, achievement and recognition strivings, sex-role identification, and social interaction anxiety.

The main findings from this study were that passivity and dependency remained reasonably stable in females (but not in males) during childhood and from childhood to young adulthood. From ages three to six, achievement and recognition striving in both sexes remained stable through the remainder of childhood and into adulthood. Sex-role identification was also stable; in boys the degree of masculinity at ages three to six correlated with vocational choices made in adulthood, with the more masculine boys choosing less intellectual vocations. Finally, social interaction anxiety was unstable between childhood and adolescence but stable from adolescence into young adulthood. It was also found that the origin of anxiety was rooted more deeply in childhood for males than for females.

The Berkeley Growth and Guidance Studies   In California, a group of children born in Berkeley in 1928–1929 and a group of adolescents in an Oakland high school in 1933 have been followed by means of an intensive set of psychological and anthropometric measures (Jones, 1967). These studies have been important in developing our understanding of physiological growth rates and personality. For example, data from these studies have led to the recognition of differences in personality patterns between early- and late-maturing boys (Jones & Bayley, 1950). Moreover, the large array of data collected for individuals between twenty-one months and eighteen years of age have been used by experts to arrive at a "basic" personality description for longitudinal subjects, and these data were used to predict psychological adjustment in adulthood. It is interesting to note that early-childhood behavior was not predictive of adult adjustment, but both preadolescent and adolescent behavior were predictive of adult adjustment (Livson & Peskin, 1967; Peskin 1972).

The Kansas City Study of Adult Life   This short-term longitudinal study of adult personality followed 159 adults ranging in age from forty-eight to eighty-eight years over a six-year period, from 1956 to 1962. This study placed particular emphasis on the variables of personal and social engagement (Havighurst, Neugarten, & Tobin, 1968). Psychological engagement was assessed by means of the Thematic Apperception Test (TAT) developed by Murray (1938) to yield measures on the dimensions of ego-energy and ego-style. The TAT is a projective technique that uses pictures for which respondents free associate and make up stories. The stories are analyzed to yield data about life themes and needs. The Kansas City study provided evidence of a drop in ego-energy over the six-year period. Also, cross-sectional data suggested that a passive ego-style was more prevalent among the oldest subjects. This study also provided information about the relation of activity to life satisfaction in old age; people with lower activity levels showed less satisfaction. With respect to disengagement and life satisfaction, this study made it clear that life satisfaction may interact significantly with an individual's personality type. Among a group of subjects in their seventies, life satisfaction was uniformly higher for integrated and armor-defended personalities than for the other type.

None of the studies mentioned here was designed in such a way that it could differentiate developmental age changes from the effects of sociocultural change and generation differences. Nevertheless, these methods illustrate important ventures in the systematic description of personality change over significant life periods. As a result, they have markedly affected our understanding of the normal development of personality.

Summary

1. There are two types of personality theory. Static theories describe current facets of personality; dynamic theories emphasize antecedent-consequent relationships.
2. Trait and factor theories describe how people behave in certain ways in a specific situation, whereas type theories classify people according to common patterns of trait organization.
3. Stimulus-response and social learning theories describe personality as the pattern of learned associations that characterizes an individual's typical behavior.
4. Phenomenological and personological theories consider an individual's perception of self and others in the context of that person's needs and motivations and how they interact with the environment.
5. Psychoanalytic and neo-Freudian theories emphasize early experience as having major formative effects on personality that may persist throughout life.
6. Maturational theories consider personality as an unfolding process that develops from a diffuse egocentric pattern into one that is increasingly differentiated and sensitive to environmental influences and moral imperatives.
7. Constitutional factors such as genetic, hormonal, and prenatal influences primarily affect personality traits related to temperament, energy level, and emotional control. But subtle biological differences among individuals may in many instances determine why different persons react in a different manner to the same enviromental stimuli.
8. Body type may affect personality not only because it characterizes biological differences but also because others respond to the stereotypes commonly associated with physical appearance.
9. In maturing, an individual faces a succession of developmental tasks that are unique at different life stages: early childhood, middle childhood, adolescence, early adulthood, middle adulthood, and later maturity (Havighurst, 1972).

10. Personality changes over the life span depend on the early experiences that are common to most people as well as on unique events that affect an individual. For many personality traits stability is the rule, but others do change.

11. Personality traits are the stable characteristics that differentiate among people throughout much of their lives and across many situations. Personality states are response patterns that are specific to a particular circumstance or situation and that change readily over an individual's life.

12. Biostable traits are behaviors that are determined genetically or are shaped by early influences; acculturated traits are determined by environmental events; and biocultural traits represent both genetic and environmental influences.

13. Disengagement is the withdrawal of an older individual from active participation with the environment, either because of difficulty in coping with the environment or more likely because meaningful roles are reduced and the societal stereotype expects older people to withdraw progressively.

14. The self-concept is one of the organizing principles that individuals use to understand their own behavior. The self-concept emerges gradually during childhood and changes progressively to permit the individual to achieve some congruence between perception of self and how others perceive that person.

15. Attitudes, goals, and values represent a person's evaluation of specific objects, people, and events. They help us understand the individual's belief system, which may influence observed behavior.

16. Stereotypes about the elderly often involve misperceptions by other age groups. Only the middle-aged are perceived correctly by other age groups.

17. Life satisfaction and morale seem to be related to absence of illness and to satisfactory work roles and interpersonal relationships. In old age morale is higher for people who have confidants.

18. Life-span personality profiles can be studied by means of personality questionnaires. These are of three types: criterion-group measures, inventories derived from factor analysis, and construct-based inventories.

19. Clinically oriented studies of the life span involve the description of personality at different life stages by means of longitudinal studies involving detailed assessment of individuals and their life situations. Examples of such studies described in this chapter are the Fels study, the Berkeley Growth and Guidance Studies, and the Kansas City Study of Adult Life.

Selected Readings

Baltes, P. B., and K. W. Schaie, eds. *Life-span Developmental Psychology: Personality and Socialization.* New York: Academic Press, 1973. This edited volume of substantive reviews of research covers many facets of life-span personality development described in this chapter.

Cartwright, D. S. *Introduction to Personality.* New York: Rand McNally, 1974. An excellent review of personality theory and empirical research from the vantage point of a writer committed to a trait view of personality.

Maas, H. S. and J. A. Kuypers. *From Thirty to Seventy*. San Francisco: Jossey-Bass, 1975. A series of case studies involving personalities and lifestyles of men and women from early midlife into old age.

Neugarten, B. L. "Personality and Aging." In *Handbook of the Psychology of Aging*. J. E. Birren and K. W. Schaie. New York: Van Nostrand Reinhold, 1977. An interesting theoretical and historical review of personality research in adulthood.

Rappoport, L. *Personality Development: The Chronology of Experience*. Glenview, Ill.: Scott Foresman, 1972. A comprehensive presentation of personality theory and an interpretation of empirical data from the psychoanalytic vantage point.

V EPILOGUE

This section points out some of the implications of the fact that people are living longer than ever before. The longer length of life and the opportunities of a changing society present individuals with more choices. Questions are raised in Chapter 17 about how we want to exercise our individual responsibility for our style of life. Prospects exist for a healthier and more productive life, and many of these prospects are to some extent under our control. Chapter 17 explores some of these potentials for human development.

Chapter 17

Potentials for Individual Development

How the human species developed within the physical environment

The prospects for further physical and psychological development

The potentials for further cognitive and emotional development

The role of religion in modern life

The Meaning of Death

Individual Responsibility and Lifestyles

The Evolution of Our Species
    Effects of Environment on Physical Characteristics
    Health Potentials

Prospects for Further Improvements in Society
    Human Suffering
    Psychological Choices and Controls
    The Development of Rational Beings

Potentials for Cognitive Development

Emotional Potentials

Religion and Modern Life

Introduction

Over the past century the length of the average human life span has increased more than it did from prehistory to the beginning of modern times. Even in the days of the Roman Empire, people could expect to live only about thirty years. An increase of such magnitude (over 50 percent in the last hundred years) might be expected to have many consequences for families and society.

Along with this much longer life expectancy has come a fall in the birth rate, which has resulted in an impressive shift in the age composition of Western societies. In the past, individuals over the age of seventy were rare; now they are commonplace. This has brought changes in family structures. Indeed, it is now possible for five generations of a single family to be alive at one time. We know a woman who visited her ninety-two-year-old grandmother in a residence for the elderly and later the same day babysat for her young grandson!

Earlier chapters have documented many of the psychological and social changes that have accompanied the dramatic changes in longevity and age structure. Particularly intriguing are the ramifications of these changes for individuals throughout the life span. Specifically, changes in longevity and the age structure have caused us to reexamine the meaning of death and to reappraise our personal responsibility for how we live.

The Meaning of Death

In past centuries the short life span brought with it a constant reminder of death. Parents were grateful if their children survived even the growing phase of life, and many individuals did not survive beyond early childhood. People lived with death as an experience, even personifying it as a "Grim Reaper" who daily claimed family members and friends. Against this backdrop attention was focused on the meaning of death. In early centuries religion emphasized the existence of an eternal life after death—as explanation and compensation for a short, seemingly meaningless life. Reassurance and a sense of meaning undoubtedly were thus developed through the elaboration of a belief structure that focused on life after death.

Today, however, the average person survives into what was formerly called "old age." From the vantage point of a seventy-year life, the implications of death are decidedly different. Because of increased longevity, society has shifted its orientation from the child to the adult. And people's preoccupation with the meaning of death has changed to concern about the meaning of life. Adolescents and young adults, who have lived but a portion of the full course of life, regard the concept of death differently from older adults, for whom most of the life span is past. Young people use the future as a repository of their hopes for achievement and well-being. In contrast, older adults are more concerned with the interpretation of life as it has been lived; they care less for what lies ahead in an abstract sense. Young persons are anxious about death itself, whereas older adults are concerned about the process of dying, about being alone, breaking a leg, having a heart attack out of reach of assistance, or having

Are Old Folks Really Poor?

ALVIN RUBUSHKA AND BRUCE JACOBS

A commonly held image of misfortune and need underpins the broad-based support that many programs for the elderly enjoy. This negative image is reinforced by widespread news-media coverage of a select few among the elderly who may suffer from poverty, forced retirement, job discrimination, crime, malnutrition, poor housing, social isolation and serious health impairments. This stereotyped view of aging holds that a great many of our senior citizens cannot lead independent lives, that they are in desperate need of money, nutritious meals, decent housing, comprehensive health care and other vital social services.

These preconceptions are largely inaccurate and are contradicted by the facts of aging. Based on our interviews with more than 1,500 elderly homeowners around the United States and other studies, we can sketch a much brighter picture.

To begin with, less than 5 percent of the elderly live in institutions. Fully 70 percent live in their own houses and nearly nine of every 10 elderly homeowners make no mortgage payments. Every state has some form of property-tax relief for this group, and all older Americans are eligible for other state and Federal tax benefits. Social Security recipients are among the very few who receive a tax-free yearly increase in cash income indexed to inflation. Moreover, the Supplementary Security Income program guarantees a minimum income to all older Americans. Food stamps, housing benefits, and Medicare and Medicaid provide in-kind income to millions of older persons.

Despite a national image of poverty among the aged, the number of officially counted "poor" elderly has fallen since 1959 from 33 percent of the elderly population to as low as 6 percent when noncash benefits are added to greatly increased retirement benefits.

Elderly Americans also have more than $300 billion of home equity, an enormous source of potential income. In California, for example, elderly homeowners can defer their property taxes by granting the state a lien on their homes for the amount due plus annual interest charges of 7 percent. Experimental programs offering "reverse annuity mortgages" will allow a homeowner to obtain a loan based on the equity he owns and use the loan to purchase a lifetime annuity. These measures allow the elderly to retain an independent life in their own homes.

The aged are generally well-housed. The Government's annual housing survey shows that homes owned by the elderly are in no worse shape than those of younger families. Moreover, the owners of homes that had problems did not consider the problems significant. Only 3 percent said there was a serious problem they would not fix because of lack of money.

Older people do suffer disproportionately from a variety of chronic health problems. But the great majority are able to lead independent lives. Serious systematic decline in physical capacity typically sets in only after age 75 and medical developments continuously extend healthy living. Most surveys disclose that fewer than one in five elderly Americans regard themselves as in poor health.

The notion of widespread social isolation also turns out to be false. Fully 80 percent have children living nearby, and a 1974 Louis Harris survey found that 80 percent had seen one or

(continued)

more of their children within the previous week! Many government and private-sponsored social activities give ample opportunity for those elderly who wish to participate.

Although the elderly are not disproportionately victims of violent crime, we did find that fear of crime is their chief concern.

A small number of older Americans are indeed among the unfortunate. They may be poor, victimized by inflation, and unable to maintain an independent life in their own homes. The care of these people has and should be viewed as a responsibility of society, so long as these elderly do not have the financial resources to take care of themselves. But we must not confuse the plight of the few with the condition of the many. The fact is that we must pay for increased benefits for the elderly just as we must for any other group. If we do not focus our programs on those truly in need, the bill will be very expensive.

to endure pain. Having lived a long and full life, an elderly person is concerned about the circumstances of the transition from life to death and the achievement of a perspective on life as it has been lived. To an older person death itself may be welcome as one comes to grasp that life as it has been known has run a full course. Elderly people may accept death as coming appropriately; it need not be accompanied by deep regrets and fears. In contrast, for young people death is difficult to explain or accept. Its ultimate unfairness and unreasonableness present a philosophical challenge that religions have addressed. Solace has been provided through a belief system.

It initially seems paradoxical that the recent shift from a child-centered society to an adult-centered one has substituted a focus on the meaning of life for preoccupation with the meaning of death. The attainment of a perspective on the meaning of a fully lived life is a task for older adults, just as the meaning of death is an issue to be resolved by young adults.

Individual Responsibility and Lifestyles

In earlier centuries piety and morality were emphasized as prerequisites for an eternal heavenly life. Today, because death has been delayed so dramatically for most persons, attention has focused on our responsibility for how we lead our lives on this earth. Although having long-lived grandparents ensures that an individual has a greater average life expectancy than others might have, it is what that individual does in life that determines to a greater extent than heredity how long life will be and what quality it will have. At present, how we lead our lives is more important in determining how long and how well we live than is genetic background or medical intervention. New considerations indicate that individuals must accept responsibility for their lives. Such responsibility, as well as their roles in the social system, can be manifest in the extent

What parents do with
and for children may
have significant ef-
fects when the
children "grow up."

Constantine Manos, Magnum Photos, Inc.

to which they seek information about physical and mental health. Individuals who regularly exercise, who limit the amount and types of food ingested, and who can manage the consequences of stress are much more likely to lead long, competent lives of higher morale than are those who ignore such responsibilities.

In summary, those circumstances of life that are under our control are at present more important in how well and how long we live than are the benefits we might expect to secure from medical science. To realize our potentials for individual development, then, we should seek information about advances in science with a view toward using them for personal gain, rather than expecting scientific gains to be transmitted passively to us.

One goal of developmental psychology is to provide knowledge that will increase the prospects for maximizing our individual potentials as adults. In this regard there may be important sleeper effects; that is, the things we do with and for children may have significant outcomes for their characteristics as adults. Of chief importance are the later-life outcomes of childhood development and early experience—what they contribute to the development of competent adults.

One of the common and powerful curiosities people have concerns their prospects for a satisfying way of life. People wonder what their potentials are in terms of intellectual capacities, skills, and health. Children think about what they are going to be like "when they grow up." Some adults are so intrigued or concerned about their future that they consult fortune tellers, hoping to forecast their lives through the use of a crystal ball, cards, palmistry, or tea leaves. In addition to such superstitious curiosity, there is value in speculating about future prospects for our development so that we will not be taken completely by surprise.

One factor that makes forecasts about our development difficult is the rapidly changing nature of our physical and social environment. Nonetheless, we repeat that the prospects for improving the limits or potentials of humanity in the immediate future appear to arise primarily from improvements in the environment rather than from improvements in our genetic background. First we will consider the evolution of our genetic characteristics; then we will examine some of our potentials in light of environmental interactions and our human creativity in developing new views of existence.

The Evolution of Our Species

The evolution of modern human beings from our earliest tool-making ancestors took about a million and a half years and involved perhaps four major changes in the species, particularly with regard to brain size. One conjectural tracing of the emergence of modern human beings suggests that our type *(Homo sapiens sapiens)* replaced Neanderthal beings about thirty-five thousand years ago. The development of culture has accelerated since the appearance of our abilities to make tools and to transmit information, thereby extending dominance over other species and our environment and extending our range of adaptations to environmental change. However, the likelihood that major genetic changes will occur in the human species within a matter of a few hundred years is slight. Much current biological research is concerned with experimental genetics, with synthesizing genes and perhaps ultimately changing cells or the cellular environment in order to suppress the appearance of undesirable traits. Genetic engineering may come to a reality in which we eliminate or reduce the consequences of diseases that have a genetic basis. However, our capacity to build machines that change the environment in which genetic capacities are expressed is even more important for the immediate future than are the prospects for genetic change. Therefore, for the immediate future it seems likely that improvements in our species will come from manipulating the cellular, physiological, and social environments rather than from major genetic changes or spontaneous mutations that would be favorable to our future potentials. We shall not anticipate the speedy development of a genetic super race, free from disease, highly intelligent, resistant to emotional stress, and able to lead productive social lives. Rather, we must look to environmental factors as offering the greatest immediate promise for advancing human potentials and development.

Effects of Environment on Physical Characteristics

Past evidence suggests that the environment in which we grow up influences how tall and how heavy we become. For example, the military draftees of World War II were, on average, about two-thirds of an inch taller than the draftees of World War I. Similarly, analyses of college records show that sons and daughters are taller and heavier than their parents were when they were in school. In addition, we have some indication of regional environmental influences. World War II draftees from the western states were taller than those from the northwestern states (5 feet, $8^2/5$ inches as compared with 5 feet $7^2/5$ inches); the shortest recruits came from the northeastern states.

Our genetic backgrounds may set the upper limits on the development of our bodies, but whether we reach these limits depends on the quality of our environment. This includes the amount and types of food eaten and the amount of exercise, sunshine, and activity. Such factors influence the height and weight we attain as well as our rate of development and how long we live. Infectious diseases also influence the rate of development, both psychologically and physically.

Chapter 4 noted and described the secular trend in development, the fact that present-day adolescents arrive at puberty much earlier than previous generations did. How long this trend toward an earlier pubescence will continue is not clear, although it will probably level off at between ages ten and eleven for most girls and somewhat later for boys. This trend may represent the consequences of a better physical environment, but it may also reflect increased psychosocial stimulation. That is, the stimulation children receive through movies, reading, and social learning in peer groups may result in stimulation of the hypothalamus, which facilitates the early onset of menarche and ovarian cycling in girls, assuming an otherwise healthy individual. The fact that present-day boys and girls have matured physically earlier than did their parents and their grandparents has been a source of conflict in family life, for today's children want to engage in more differentiated social and sex roles—and at a much earlier age—than was acceptable in the past.

Health Potentials

One way to estimate the potentials for human development in the near future is to compare regions of the United States with countries of the world that have the most advantageous position regarding some statistical characteristic. For example, infant mortality is relatively high in America, given the country's technological development. We might contrast this rate with that of a country like Holland, which has relatively few infant deaths. Within America itself we can also see large variations. A region that is high in infant mortality may have double the rate of a region that is low; but the low region of America probably still has about twice the rate of infant death as the best country in the world.

Similar comparisons may be made concerning the outlook for length of life. The United States does not show outstanding life expectancy among the countries of the world. Comparisons with a very long-lived country like Norway might be used to estimate what American life expectancy could be if we were to improve our physical and social environmental conditions and health services. From this we might judge that men might be expected to improve their life expectancy more than women. The middle years seem to be the phase of life in which the greatest gains could be made in life expectancy because of the very high rates of male mortality resulting from cardiovascular disease. It seems much more likely that the United States can add to the average life expectancy by reducing deaths during the middle years than by dramatically increasing the life span or the number of very long-lived people.

One consequence of the relatively short life expectancy for men in the United States is the large number of widows. Because men live somewhat shorter lives than women do and tend to marry women younger than themselves, men tend to remain married throughout their life span; in contrast, women are frequently widowed. In 1980 there were about 7.5 million widows over age sixty-five in the United States.

Prospects for Further Improvements in Society

Pessimists in the sciences feel that we cannot forecast trends in the development of our species because of the widespread changes in our physical and social environments. Still, this century has shown clear trends of improvement in terms of infant and maternal mortality and an increased average life expectancy. Although individuals have grown taller and heavier, they have also arrived at physical maturity at an earlier age than in past generations. There is also a higher level of educational attainment than in the past, and in some instances a rise in scores on standardized intelligence tests. Were such trends to continue, we could be optimistic about improvements in subsequent generations.

Along with such optimism, however, there is an ever-present basis for pessimism because of persistent problems of human suffering among many nations of the world. It seems desirable, therefore, to use a dual approach in strengthening

One source of optimism today is the higher level of educational attainment that many people achieve.

Richard Kalvar, Magnum Photos, Inc.

The Forever Factor

EDWARD EDELSON

The search for immortality is starting to show its age.

For decades, biologists have been looking at the aging process with every method at their command. They have discovered any number of changes associated with aging in the cells and tissues of the body. Every discovery has led to the hope that the secret of aging has been discovered at last, and that science can finally begin to slow or reverse the aging process. But each time, success has remained tantalizingly out of the reach of researchers.

And so the emphasis in research on aging has shifted in the last few years.

The new emphasis, in the words of Dr. Richard Greulich of the National Institute on Aging, is on "improving the quality of life, not the quantity"—that is, on helping people stay vigorous and healthy longer, rather than simply trying to lengthen the life span. . . .

But the age-old dream of banishing old age, of finding an elixir, a drug or a treatment that could extend life for decades more, still lives on among many researchers. Indeed, some scientists believe that the goal is nearly within reach, and that perhaps it is time to start testing—with human volunteers—some techniques designed to prolong life.

One of those scientists is Dr. Charles Barrows of the National Institute on Aging. He has been working with a technique that is both amazingly simple and amazingly effective in laboratory animals. The technique is to cut back on the amount of food that an animal eats.

The result, in species after species, has been an increase in life span of anywhere from 10% to more than 30%.

Diet restriction, as the method is called, was discovered more than 40 years ago by Dr. Clive M. McCay, a nutritionist at Cornell University. McCay worked with rats, giving them all the vitamins and minerals that they needed but keeping their calories well below the recommended level. The rats grew up stunted, but they lived much longer than rats eating a normal diet.

Barrows says that research in his and other laboratories seems to have pinpointed the specific dietary factor that is responsible for the increased life span.

"We feel it's the dietary protein that is the most important nutrient being restricted," he said. "When we cut protein from 24% of the diet to 12% of the diet, we increased the life span of rats by 35% of their life expectancy. . . .

At the University of Nebraska, another gerontologist, Dr. Denham Harman, thinks that the time is ripe for human trials of another simple technique for lenthening life span. . . .

Harman says that he takes 100 milligrams a day of vitamin E. The recommended dietary allowance is 12 milligrams a day. The larger amount of vitamin E, he says, "has no adverse effect and potentially can have some beneficial effects."

It sounds convincing, until you talk to a former vitamin E taker, gerontologist James R. Smith of the W. Alton Jones Cell Science Center in Lake Placid, N.Y. A few years ago when he was working at the Veterans' Administration Hospital in Martinez, Calif., Smith and a colleague, Lester Packer, dropped a bombshell by reporting that vitamin E doubled the life span of a cell culture. If vitamin E could help cells live longer in laboratory glass, Smith and Packer said, it probably could also help humans live longer. Both researchers said then that they were taking daily doses of Vitamin E.

(continued)

Smith isn't taking vitamin E any more because no one has been able to reproduce the results of that cell culture experiment. Smith and Packer tried again. So did scientists in a number of other laboratories. . . .

In broad outline, there are two basic theories. One holds that aging is built into all living beings and is an inevitable part of life. The second is that aging is the result of accidents and diseases that slowly rob a living being of the ability to meet the challenges of life.

Either theory leaves open the path toward the fountain of youth. If the inevitability theory is true, immortality might be possible—if scientists could break the genetic code of aging and insert an immortality gene. If aging is the result of an accumulation of accidents and physical insults, eternal life might be possible by finding a way to prevent the damage. . . .

It is much more realistic, Greulich maintains, to focus more of our research on an effort to make life better for the increasing number of Americans who are old right now.

"Those people in the main are not terribly interested in how they got old or in research on the aging process," he said. "They are interested in what research can do to make their lives more comfortable and rewarding, and to contribute to a situation in which they are not burdens to the family and society.". . .

the prospects for the continuing development of humanity. One approach has to do with the opportunities for potentiating the most positive characteristics of the species. For example, we could develop an elitist approach that is concerned with the upper limits of humanity's potentials and we might seek to ensure the environmental conditions that might encourage the development of the most favored individuals. The other approach has to do with reducing the major causes of human suffering, those resulting in premature death, poor mental health, twisted lives, and a failure to develop personal characteristics among individuals at the lowest socioeconomic level. Death rates from all causes are higher at the lowest socioeconomic level of society (Birren & Bernstein, 1978).

Some of the problems of human suffering and limited personal development arise from naturally occurring disasters such as earthquakes, hurricanes, fires, and floods. Loss of life, the destruction of family homesteads, and the breakup of families can leave lasting and limiting marks on the behavior of survivors. In addition to such events there are also shortages of food and even famines, as well as the occurrence of infectious diseases. All these factors may damage an individual's prospects for reaching the limits of physical and intellectual development.

Other occurrences, though outside an individual's control, seem to offer prospects for limiting and reducing human suffering. For example, accidents are the sixth highest cause of death for all ages together. In this century more deaths in our society have been caused by accidents than by war. Of all accidents, motor vehicles cause about 45 percent of deaths; falls and burns are the next most frequent cause. Many of these can be prevented through higher safety standards and a commitment from both companies and unions to insist on conformity to such standards. A good part of the economic loss resulting from accidents also may be saved with better safety standards. The economic loss from accidents was estimated by the National Safety Council to be about $47 billion in 1975. Reductions in accidents would free large amounts of money for constructive efforts in education, preventive medicine, and other socially desirable activities.

Human Suffering

Unfortunately, this century offers much evidence of the continuation of human aggressiveness as expressed in international wars and local insurrections. Tendencies in recent years toward guerrilla warfare and political philosophies that justify bombings, fires, and the taking of hostages have resulted in the loss of lives and maiming of innocent victims. Torture as a political tool seems to have been widely used in recent years in many countries of the world. Power cliques have justified torture as a means of obtaining political information and the killing of opponents as a means of maintaining political power. Although the United Nations has struggled to develop statements of individual rights, there clearly is no universally agreed upon set of principles to govern human behavior in these areas. Pessimistically viewed, it would seem that there has been an abdication of responsibility by the political leaderships of many of the major countries of the world—at least when it comes to reducing the problems of human suffering. Instead, leaders have devoted their efforts to maintaining power. In the United States we have seen the use of illegal burglaries to obtain political and criminal information about individuals. The Watergate scandal that forced former President Richard M. Nixon from office involved over thirty lawyers—all graduates of major universities—who seemingly did not respond to the issues of the legality of their own behavior but were concerned only in justifying adversary activity. Their mismanagement of political power was not inhibited by the values and ethics that, presumably, they should have acquired through their schooling or their profession.

Besides external sources of human suffering such as disease and malnutrition, some causes of human suffering are related to the personal habits of individuals. The abuse of alcohol and other drugs causes much suffering in our society. Yet other, less obvious, causes involve the lack of understanding about how our political and social systems work. Thus individuals may unrealistically believe that there is a lack of opportunity for employment; that is, they have not been socialized in such a way as to understand their options and opportunities in our technological society. Some of such suffering results from a lack of information and from the misperceptions of individuals. Much of it tends to affect people at the lower end of the socioeconomic scale.

Some human suffering results from insufficient information available to the leadership—those persons at the top of our society who have the responsibility for policies and the administration of programs. For example, research has yielded an explosion of knowledge that is beyond the grasp of any individual or small group. Because educated people—no matter how hard they try to—cannot grasp many of the main lines of this knowledge expansion, let alone its details, leadership is often confused. The knowledge explosion has provided more information and more potentials than society can pursue. We have not yet progressed to the point where we can evaluate large masses of new information with regard to social policy and the guidance of society. Given that it would be impossible for all individuals at all levels of society to evaluate the mass of information available, we must trust appointed persons to evaluate and interpret portions of it. As long as a society has a reasonable basis for trust in those who are responsible for evaluating information, we can live with a sense of security. At present, however, new problems of health and environmental pollution have arisen because of technological advances. The knowledge gap has caused many individuals to be suspicious of those responsible for the evaluation of information and the control of adverse influences in our society.

Psychological Choices and Controls

In his book *The Two Cultures and the Scientific Revolution,* writer C. P. Snow describes two worlds of thought, one derived from the humanistic tradition and the other from science. Some humanists today perceive a threat to freedom by scientific psychology. Humanists essentially regard freedom of choice as the ultimate principle of society. The humanistic tradition sometimes perceives that scientific developmental psychology would shape individuals and could produce masses of brainwashed individuals who adhere to mass-produced goals. American psychologist B. F. Skinner has received much critical comment because of his thoughts about producing an ideal society by developing controls over the kinds of reinforcements that individuals are given for behavior. The issue for society is not to cultivate an absence of restrictions on behavior but to promote *desirable* controls and inhibitions on behavior. Perhaps as research provides a greater understanding of our nature—of our wishes, needs, and the circumstances under which we feel content, are productive, and use freedom to our best advantage—there might be a better basis for agreement about the kinds of behavior we would like to reinforce within individuals and about the kinds of social controls we would impress upon transgressors.

Skinner's book *Beyond Freedom and Dignity* offers insights into how we are controlled, even if that control is for our so-called welfare. For a long time, lack of control, freedom, and inherent goodness have been associated as though they belong together. More recently, society has come to suspect that a permissive environment that establishes no differential rewards or controls can result both in individuals who are unable to make choices and in self-destructive behavior. Skinner holds that the environment always exercises control. He believes that the essential task is not to press for moral struggle and to display virtues, but to make life in a society less punishing. Further, the thought is to use the time and energy that normally goes into the avoidance of punishment to pursue more productive activities that will help to develop more effective people. The issue is not to design an "ideal" human being but to design an environment with the proper controls. Skinner is among the most influential scientists of our day, and he must be taken seriously. Yet with regard to the development of our species, he does perhaps view the individual as being excessively plastic and responsive to the reinforcements of society. Skinner considers growth itself as a metaphor rather than as a determinant process characteristic of most individuals. He minimizes the importance of the genetic background—both of the species and of individuals—which must influence how we grow up and grow old.

The followers of Skinner's point of view make up an important contemporary school of thought, which believes that behavior is shaped primarily by reinforcement. Although these followers accept the fact that the species has evolved by selective pressures regarding which persons will survive, they believe that development consists of shaping and maintaining the behaviors of individuals by selective reinforcements in the social environment. In contrast, a new point of view, called *sociobiology*, considers a behavior like altruism as having been selected for; it thus will make its appearance if only it is given the opportunity. In this view, the organization of altruism is inherent in an organism. At present it seems likely that many patterns of behavior are latent in the individual, requiring only release by the environment rather than organization or shaping by reinforcement. It remains to be seen whether the behavioristic approach of Skinner and his followers can be adapted to modifying the behavior of those individuals who are at the low end of the socioeconomic scale and who have little entrée into the social system and the advantages of progress. Their approach would seem to have little to offer to the educated or leadership level of society, for whom principles may be grasped as abstractions from reading or from insights gained by personal communication. Behavioral analysis of the reinforcement contingencies in the environment—though it appears to offer techniques for improving the quality of life in our society—does not fit in well with the concept of rational behavior that has been evolving in our culture.

The Development of Rational Beings

Parallel with the cultivation of behaviorism, some psychologists have emphasized the pursuit of personal development through thought and meditation. Of this, Skinner says:

It is in the nature of an experimental analysis of human behavior that it should strip away the functions previously assigned to autonomous man and transfer them one-by-one to the controlling environment. The analysis leaves less and less for autonomous man to do. But what about man himself? Is there not something about a person which is more than a living body? Unless something called a *self* survives, how can we speak of self-knowledge or self-control? To whom is the injunction "know thyself" addressed? (1971, p. 189)

If rationalism is only an illusion that we cultivate to make us feel more personally omniscient, then perhaps Skinner is right. On the other hand, the insights that come to wise individuals would seem to have a pervasive effect in families and on the community. One should not jump with enthusiasm to throw out the old, since many cultures have spent thousands of years cultivating meditation and contemplation as a form of control over their lives. Such principles do not seem to be derived directly from environmental contingencies but from reflection upon experience. In contrast to behaviorism, an attempt to explain phenomena of consciousness was made by Robert E. Ornstein in *The Psychology of Consciousness* (1972). Ornstein examined the concepts of humanity that have been developed through the contemplative and mystic religions. He also reviewed a considerable amount of physiological evidence about the physiological correlates of thought processes and the responsiveness of physiological patterns to the mental state of the individual. Ornstein produced a wedding of physiology with mysticism—paying little attention to the role of reinforcement. Perhaps to humanists and to behaviorists, as well as to mystics, science has not yet revealed all it will. Perhaps, too, without being aware of it, we may be on the verge of new scientific breakthroughs in understanding our own nature that will permit a synthesis of the different traditions of thought.

Potentials for Cognitive Development

One point we have noted already is that parents, teachers, psychologists, pediatricians, and others who are concerned with children should view their task as one of raising adults, not children. The point is that children are en route to becoming adults. Thus the criterion of successful child raising is whether the individual is intellectually and emotionally competent as an adult, and wise as an elder.

Many aspects of higher cognitive processes are involved in living an effective adult life. It is important that we have occupational skills and that we acquire skills in reading and in verbal communication. In addition, however, some individuals are able to use cognitive abilities and skills in such a way as to result in novel and unusually high-quality productions. Such persons are spoken of as being highly creative. It is important that the circumstances under which individuals become maximally creative be studied and recognized. Currently the trends toward short-term careers and multiple careers during the life span mean that individuals will have to develop a high level of creativity and flexibility in shifting to new opportunities and in reorienting—if not retraining—themselves.

Not only do we need educational systems that will encourage creativity in children and adolescents, but we also need an approach to education throughout the life span that will continue to stimulate creativity in older adults. Creativity may characterize not only productions such as those in the arts, science, and industry but also achievements in the personal lives of individuals. One part of creativity would seem to fall into what might be called the "nonaptitude aspects" of personality. By this we mean the cognitive capacity involved in creativity of a product that is not only original but is of such high quality that we give recognition or awards for unusual performance. Individuals become known as being creative; that is, they can be counted on to take unusual stances, to provide powerful insights, or to uncover rare elements in a situation that other people have missed. It seems very important in developmental psychology that we increase the creative potentials of the population so that more such persons are developed. Society obviously gains much from greater creative productivity.

American psychology has spoken about creativity in terms of abilities, and Guilford (1959–1967) believes that creativity can be broken down into component abilities. By contrast, British psychologist Vernon (1967) believes that one should not regard ability tests as tapping creativity per se. British researchers avoid the term *creativity* and tend to use the term *divergent thinking* (in contrast to *convergent thinking*). Convergent thinkers are people who do better at tests requiring a single correct answer, whereas divergent thinkers do much better at tests that are open-ended.

Independent of the approach that attempts to measure creativity with tests, the *product-centered approach* examines the level of productivity of individuals with age. Lehman (1953) and Dennis (1956) both looked at the products of outstanding people in relation to age. Lehman analyzed the productivity of outstanding people and determined the age at which the single most outstanding product was generated. He also looked at the total productivity with age and found that individuals tended to produce their most outstanding works early in their careers (although they may maintain a relatively high level of productivity throughout their lives). The various fields of science and art differed in the age at which outstanding contributions were made. As developmental psychologists, we should ask, What are the conditions under which we can maintain a high level of creativity throughout the life span? This leads us to consider other factors that influence creativity.

One such factor in the creative process is the *set,* or attitude, that an individual has in response to questions, problems, or situations. For example, in the production of novel thoughts, an attitude of fantasy obviously would encourage a great diversity of responses and could also influence performance on tests of divergent thinking. Such tests usually measure three qualities: fluency, flexibility, and originality. Thus a highly creative person would be one who can produce a large number of original responses while showing high flexibility in shifting among the different categories of thought processes and also showing a large quantity of different responses. Although intelligence is involved in such performance, Anderson (1960) thought that after some minimum level of intelligence is reached, creative functioning no longer depends on intelligence itself. Torrance (1962) suggests that above an IQ of about 120, intelligence no longer predicts creativity. Presumably, for a person with a high level of intelligence, attitude is more important for creativity than is the level of intelligence.

Obviously our schools should potentiate the development of intelligence. However, they also should attend to the style of thinking that uses intelligence. For example, Hudson (1967) showed that science students who are high achievers show a convergent style of thinking, whereas those in the arts are predominantly divergent in their pattern of thought. This, of course, would fit with the conventional notion of artists as being highly novel, divergent, and unconventional in behavior and attitudes. In contrast, science students are thought to be more focused on a specific point. Hudson maintained that the arts and the science curricula mold attitudes that bias the manner in which intelligence is deployed. Other studies have also reported that science majors are predominantly convergent in their style of thinking (Cropley & Field, 1968). However, Cropley (1969), who looked at the pattern of thinking in individuals who were in the top group of science honors program, found that honor graduates in science tended to be almost exclusively divergent in their

A creative person can produce many original responses while remaining flexible in shifting among the different types of thought processes.

Photographed by Marcia Weinstein, © 1976

pattern of thinking. One may conclude from the literature that convergent thinking is a style favored by middle-level individuals in science, whereas top-level individuals in science show divergent styles of thinking—not unlike individuals in the arts. Another suggestion, from the work of Field and Poole (1970), is that divergent thinkers in science take a while to catch up to but then surpass convergent thinkers. The convergers may do relatively well in the early stage of mastering their science. Perhaps top-level scientists can alternate between convergent and divergent modes of thinking suitable to the phase of the problem they are studying. That is, there is a phase when one must generate many alternative solutions or hypotheses, but there is also a phase of testing and developing one particular solution that can be accepted or discarded. There is little doubt that flexibility of thinking is an attribute of creativity, but the suggestion here is that flexibility may be involved even in a self-controlled alternation in which the individual comes to know when it is good to be divergent and when it is good to be convergent in one's thinking.

Besides convergent thinkers and divergent thinkers, there is a mixed group that Renner and Rowell (1975) call "all arounders." These individuals are not simply convergent or divergent. Such classification refers to their characteristic bias or attitude toward intellectual activity. Here we have suggested that highly creative individuals may be able to shift from divergence to convergence, depending on the requirements of the situation, unlike those who might be limited to one attitude. Given this possibility, education should encourage students to show both divergent and convergent thinking in approaches to problem solving. This, of course, would require that teachers themselves alternate their orientation to problem solving. Torrance (1964) notes that authoritarian teachers or highly defensive teachers have difficulty learning techniques that facilitate creativity in children. Tense students often model themselves after the teacher. If the teacher has one dominant mode, the students are likely to adopt that. For example, Torrance (1962) found that teachers often judged the responses of creative boys as naughty, silly, or wild and tended to encourage socially acceptable behavior rather than creativity. Convergent activity is easier to control in the classroom than divergent activity is. Clearly, more attention must be paid to the social system that can, at intervals, alternate between divergent and convergent activity. However, the teacher or parent must have a high level of tolerance for ambiguity, since the production of novel divergent responses often leads to contradictory and irrational responses that might be intellectually distasteful and socially disorganizing. Yet in the flow of many such responses, there are likely to emerge high-quality, highly original responses.

Divergent thinking can be encouraged in a gamelike atmosphere in which the performance of individuals are not evaluated in the usual sense of being graded by the teacher. The student in a relaxed manner under game conditions might generate many alternative responses and increase scores on divergent tests of thinking. It is perhaps easiest to think about the encouragement of creative activity of children in classroom situations and alternate between convergent and divergent tasks. It is less easy to see the context for improving the creative output of mature adults. For one thing, adults have been taught in past-school situations that were generally unsympathetic to divergent thinking. It is only in small classroom situations where divergent activities can be encouraged immediately. Older individuals—because of career influences as well as early education—will tend to be more focused on convergent thinking and to avoid risk-taking situations. With a convergent mode of thought, they will avoid making creative decisions about important life circumstances. Older adults often show caution and thereby restrict the alternatives to be used in meeting life crises. For example, older adults prefer to deal with less complex visual stimuli on the Barron-Welsh art preference scale (Alpaugh, 1975). This preference reflects a desire to avoid ambiguous situations and to be cautious. Avoidance of complexity, plus a tendency to be cautious and an acquired characteristic of load-shedding, results in an approach that reduces the intellectual effort of older individuals to be creative. There is thus less pressure within the individual to develop many novel ideas. With age, there may be a personal reluctance to tolerate the dissonance or ambiguity that arises with creative alternatives. Whereas young adults will sometimes regard speculation of wild alternatives as fun, older individuals may have come to abhor such brainstorming.

Our best opportunity for maximizing our potentials for creative thinking clearly lies in education, but the classroom context must expose children to tasks that encourage alternating between convergent and divergent approaches.

Classes for older adults particularly should encourage the exercise of divergent thinking, since it is likely to fall into disuse in adults. Apparently, a lack of confidence among mature adults may underlie caution and an unwillingness to show innovative thinking and deviate from group opinion. Klein (1973), for example, discovered that raising the level of self-perceived confidence in older adults makes their judgments more independent of the social group. By raising the level of perceived competence, by reassurance and encouraging novel and divergent responses, we may help older adults take a more creative stance in their personal lives. We also may encourage new approaches to undertaking second and third careers, along with a willingness to undertake risks and to put effort into the acquisition of new skills. There is little doubt that an important aspect of the encouragement of innovation lies in the atmosphere in which an adult's or child's education is conducted. The attitudes of the teacher, the physical organization of the classroom, the techniques, and the manner of instruction are important. An atmosphere that encourages attention to the one right answer through punishment and devaluation for the wrong answer must be balanced with an atmosphere in which individuals are rewarded for bringing up novel and unusual ideas without fear of depreciation. Instructors can become so concerned with getting the one right answer that they forget that students, particularly older adults, need encouragement to experiment with new thoughts. There are circumstances in life in which a convergent solution is the desired one. But there also are many circumstances in which people should be encouraged in a relaxed manner to explore novel alternatives and to exercise creativity that will lead to the creation of new systems of thinking, new material products, new insights, and new creative styles of life that will be more rewarding. Counseling is probably an essential ingredient—both for young students and for older adults—to reduce the insecurity many individuals feel when they engage in classroom activities. Classroom situations may make older adults feel extremely awkward and insecure particularly if they enter classes with younger college students.

Although we know very little as yet about the chemical events that take place in the brain when creative closure is attained on a problem, we do know something about the characteristics of individuals who are creative. In addition, we now know something about the conditions of the social environment that foster creativity. Society needs the creative potential of individuals for both economic and personal reasons. To realize our potentials as individuals, we should seek opportunities to participate in situations that encourage us to show fluency, flexibility, and originality in a pattern of divergent thinking. Such participation can maximize our potentials in using cognitive abilities across the life span.

Emotional Potentials

Cognitive abilities are but part of our capacities for leading effective lives. Emotions play a vital role as well. Many individuals lead truncated lives far short of their potentials because they have emotional problems. Still others have lives that are destroyed because of intense emotional problems that cannot

Emotions play a vital role in our capacity to lead effective lives, but mental health is not simply a matter of avoiding emotional stress.

Roger Malloch, Magnum Photos, Inc.

be resolved. Emotional difficulties often involve abuse of drugs and alcohol and often have such consequences as suicide or permanently damaged bodies. An adaptive person uses cognitive abilities in such a way that they work in harmony with emotions and are congruent with his or her behavior—not in conflict. A congruency or balance between the emotional and cognitive aspects of life can be viewed as optimal mental health (Birren & Renner, 1980).

One view of good mental health is that we can obtain it by protecting individuals from stresses in the environment. However, the notions that an ideal environment can be created that exposes individuals to little change or stress and that we gain good mental health from stability and avoidance of stress emphasize the wrong side of the personal equation. Life—no matter how much we might try to stabilize it—contains new events that challenge us and have the potential to precipitate crises. Naturally occurring events associated with fires, hurricanes, accidental deaths, and economic depressions are usually unpredictable. The changes in our society that Toffler documented so well in *Future Shock* (1970) imply that we can all expect to be challenged by unpredictable events throughout our lives. Although we should strive as much as we can to make life predictable and controllable, the large factor in our personal effectiveness and mental health is how we adapt to environmental changes and crises (Birren & Sloane, 1980).

One consequence of exposure to stress is an increase in the activity of the adrenal glands, those two small endocrine glands located just above each kidney. The adrenal gland has two portions—the outer layer, called the *cortex*, and the inner core, known as the *medulla*. When we are exposed to stressful stimuli, the brain initiates activity in the pituitary gland, which, in turn, releases a hormone (ACTH, adrenocorticotrophic hormone) that stimulates the adrenal cortex to release its hormones to help the body combat the impending or actual stress. The hormones released by the adrenal cortex (17-OHCS) reflect psychological influences. That is, there is increased activity of the pituitary gland and thereby of the adrenal cortex in response to the perception of stress or the anticipation of stress. It should be remembered that there are interactions between the brain and the endocrine glands. Hormones influence the brain, and the brain also influences the levels of hormones. There are large individual differences in such physiological responses to stress as increased blood pressure or heart rate. Some part of the individual differences in the physiological response to stress is genetic. That is, individuals vary in their inherent intensity and duration of response to stress. Other differences arise by virtue of how individuals deal with stress, that is, their coping devices or strategies for handling difficult situations.

From the foregoing it is clear that one cannot judge the magnitude of an individual's physiological response solely from an event that has occurred. There are large individual differences in the psychoendocrine responses to the same situation. Thus no matter how severe the life-threatening aspects of a situation may be, individuals will not experience the same magnitude of emotional or physiological arousal. Social factors play a role in individual differences in stress response, as do the characteristic ways in which an individual copes with stress.

We are not passive responders to the hormones our bodies synthesize, but our endocrine glands are regulated by the way we handle or cope with stressful stimuli. Environmental events or psychological stimuli are important influences on pituitary-adrenal activity and thereby have the potential for producing disorganizing breakdowns in behavior associated with high levels of 17-OHCS. As mentioned earlier, our personal ways of dealing with stress may either reduce or elevate the endocrine response. An important issue for maximizing our potentials as human beings is how to develop ways of handling stress so as to minimize excessive responses of our endocrine system. Increasing emphasis is being placed on the psychological factors in response to stress, since over a lifetime our stress responses are important in determining the diseases we develop and how long we will live (not to mention, for example, the depressive emotional climate that may exist over much of a lifetime because of the style and effectiveness of psychological defenses). In this context, *psychological defenses* refer to the way we cope with threatening situations; *coping styles* and *adaptive mechanisms* refer to the ways we meet changes or anticipated changes around us. How do we as individuals handle the prospect of going to the dentist, of having a surgical operation, of failing a course in school, of having someone close to us become terminally ill, of losing a friend or lover, or of having to move? Not all stressful events are negative. Even positive, sought-after changes such as taking a new and better job also can have stressful implications. The effects of such events on our emotional life or health in part depend on the meaning of the event to us, the stability of our emotions, and, as said earlier, how we deal with the events.

Some events or circumstances can be converted into lifelong tensions because of the way we handle them. For example, a non-college-educated person may rise to a job level at which almost all colleagues are college educated. This discrepancy has been called *social status incongruity*. It often occurs in marriage as well, if one or the other partner marries well above his or her previous family's socioeconomic status. If the individual is sensitive about the discrepancy but tries to put it out of mind or overcompensates for the feelings of inadequacy, the social status incongruity may become a source of stress throughout life.

Actual or threatened stress may provoke either withdrawal or anger on the part of the individual. Withdrawal is often associated with depression. Hamburg and Barchas (1975) point out that there is an evolutionary background for the emotions and for our responses of anger or depression. From an evolutionary point of view, an individual tends to do what the species has done in similar previous situations in order to survive. Emotions thus reflect a heightened state of arousal to use a pattern of behavior evoked many times earlier in the evolutionary history of the species. One of the maladaptive behavior patterns is that of the depression that occurs in response to loss or separation from parents. Chimpanzees show a severe depression if their mothers die before they are separated in the normal course of development. Indeed, an adolescent monkey may die if the mother dies. In the account of Hamburg et al., an 8½-year-old chimpanzee died twenty-five days after his mother's death; during the time of his "grief" he became increasingly tense and apathetic, huddled for long times, and lost interest in what was going on around him. He ate little and "his eyes had a wide, frightened look which never left them" (Hamburg et al,., 1975, p. 248).

Human beings also show reactions to the death of an important other person. Such grief reaction may last for several months. But for some individuals the relatively normal pattern of grief may move into a depression with a chronic loss of interest in the environment and other persons and a feeling of hopelessness. The individual's handling of psychological loss can maximize grief and lead to depression or, after a period, can lead to resumption of normal human relationships.

Coping styles include the use of a variety of devices such as denial, repression of emotional responses, a stoical outlook that accepts what is, or displacement of the stress. Thus a person threatened with a personal problem may become increasingly hypochondriacal, complaining of many physical ailments.

One adaptive response to loss or threat is to affiliate or associate with others. Apparently, affiliation reduces stress and the emotional states surrounding crises. By contrast, the unfortunate aspect of withdrawal and depression in response to loss is that it reduces the chances for gaining new information and the reduction of tension that comes with affiliation with others. Generally, to increase one's potential for handling stress, one should seek the company of others during loss or threat.

We have much to learn about coping styles so that we can better manage the stresses in our lives. In meeting such problems, there seems to be both a cognitive component, in which we think about events and our strategies for resolving them, and an emotional component, such as the neuroendocrine response to the events. Certainly the best strategy regarding the cognitive level is, as mentioned, to encourage affiliation. People who are isolated increase the consequences of stress, and their isolation increases the probability of long-term depression and alienation from the group. Although we cannot eliminate change from our lives, we can look more closely at the ways we manage stress and can thus attempt to cushion the unwanted physiological and emotional consequences.

It is apparent that there will be many new stresses in our society. For example, the changing role of women has implications for both sexes. One cannot change the role of one sex without influencing the other. Changes in family life as child-free women seek careers have implications for men, some of whom may see the changes as a loss of status. Education for women is changing, as is their role in marriage, childbearing, and career. There are now more female heads of households (Van Dusen & Sheldon, 1976). Generally, the trend has been toward a decreasing importance of family life for women and the lessening of the importance of the social difference between married and unmarried women. Given women's traditional family and nurturant roles—sometimes evidenced in volunteer community roles—questions remain concerning the long-term impact of such changes. If both men and women work, how will the responsibility be managed for the needs of aging parents, let alone for growing children? Shared roles are likely to become more common for pairs of men and women who remain together as a family unit.

One of the relatively rare but dramatic changes in individuals is that brought about by surgery to change one's sex. Many questions remain concerning the lifelong consequences for the identities of children who may have been born of such individuals before they had transsexual surgery. These dramatic issues are but a sample of the unforeseen stresses that may arise in the future. Although we cannot prevent social change, we can prepare ourselves to cope with it by understanding our emotional responses better and by adopting stress-reducing strategies. Research, counseling, and self-education are the keys to unlocking our potentials for a better life. Educated persons in the future will more likely seek professional help before serious problems arise and thereby may prevent some of the debilitating stresses that many persons now experience.

Religion and Modern Life

Religious belief and religious ritual have been a part of human development and have played a large role in the establishment of culture. Observance of religious customs varies from time to time, and in recent years there has been a decline in Western societies in collective or group observance of religious customs, such as attending church or suitably marking religious festivals. In Great Britain church attendance has dropped to such a low that many churches are kept more as museums than as places to gather to observe religious rituals. In the United States, following a resurgence of religious attendance after World War II, attendance has also dropped in recent years, particularly in what one would regard as the mainline churches. Paradoxically, one sees a decline in attendance in the more intellectual or rational religious groups and an increase in interest of some youth in some of the fundamentalist and communal relig-

Religious belief plays a
central role in the
establishment of
culture; significantly,
there is a trend today
toward emotionally
oriented religions.

James Holland, Stock, Boston, Inc.   Bill Aron, Jeroboam, Inc.

Alex Webb, Magnum Photos, Inc.

ions. Such increased interest in the fundamentalist and evangelical sects, particularly among adolescents, may indicate a groping for something to meet an unfilled need in their lives. This can be expressed in the identification with a fundamentalist religious group that offers a fixed canon of observance with which to achieve security.

The waxing and waning of various emphases of youth on religion and / or other commitments suggest that there is a search for a durable belief in a set of ideas. Perhaps they reflect an unmet underlying motivation or need. This leads to the question of what educated men and women believe today and what they are prepared as rational beings to pass on as the basis for their children's principles of life and goals. Revivalist religions urge us to be saved and encourage our possession by or submission to the spirit of God, Jesus, Allah, or some other god force, thereby improving not only our individual condition but society itself, which thus will be made benevolent and moral.

In the nineteenth century, Western society began to develop a strong confidence in the scientific method. Indeed, science became the belief system for those who rejected the superstitions and rituals of earlier organized religion. The scientific method and science appeared to offer a pathway out of ignorance toward understanding and control over the destiny of both the species and individuals. Members of university faculties began to be free to make statements about religion that, in previous centuries, might have led to their being killed, tortured, or banished. Tribal confidence would have been so shaken in earlier centuries by a skeptical individual who challenged beliefs in the tribal gods and the observance of rituals that people were afraid of retribution and would sacrifice the blasphemous person. By the nineteenth century some were observing that there appeared to be no major differences in ethical or moral behavior between individuals or nations that believed in the same God and those that did not, and that being blessed had little effect on natural outcomes. Scientists could challenge the deity by suggesting that a priest might pray over one farmer's field and not over another to see what the difference would be in crop production and thereby test the efficacy of prayer. Simply suggesting that the efficacy of prayer could be subjected to scientific testing would earlier have been judged sinful and would have warranted punishment. By 1914 William James, professor of philosophy and psychology at Harvard University, had the temerity to write a book called *The Varieties of Religious Experience* (Longman's Green, London, 1914). James suggested that religious experience could be studied from a rational or natural science perspective and that it could be reduced to principles that transcend the elements of any particular belief or ritual.

Early in the twentieth century, confidence in the scientific method was growing; indeed, science yielded advances in biology that led to the control of diseases. Labor-saving machines could be designed on the basis of physical principles, and the social sciences were beginning to study the organization of society and how it affected the behavior of individuals. However, new uncertainties about science were arising, since devastating wars were still being fought. Furthermore, as a product of World War II, the atomic bomb was developed through science, and it was used to destroy people with a force and an extent that produced an emotional revulsion. This led many to question their belief in the scientific method. But if they had detached themselves from a belief in tribal gods and rituals, to what did they turn to maintain hope and manage their fear if science failed them? Between the world wars the intellectual and scientific elite of the world were often identified with science per se and less with their national origins. Following World War II, however, science became nationalistic, and the products of science were weapons of the "tribe" to be used not only against the natural enemies of climatic disaster, parasites, and disease but also against other nations. The realization became more commonplace that science and the scientific method in and of itself was not benign and moral. This led many to search for new vantage points from which to observe humanity and to draw inferences about our inherent nature as rational and emotional beings.

One of the present authors offers the following personal experience to illustrate the dilemmas involved. Shortly after World War II a distinguished scientist from Japan asked this author whether he felt Japan should import Christianity as a form of social control. After World War II, family control in Japan was breaking down, customary religious beliefs such as Shintoism were declining, and emperor worship was replaced with the concept of the emperor as an ordinary mortal being. The consequences of the decline of these strong belief systems resulted in an increase in deviant behavior in youth such as taking of drugs, adolescent suicides, and lack of participation in family life. In brief, the view was that the decline of the older belief systems led to erosion of society and declining mental health of individuals, particularly young people. The important point, however, is that the person raising this question could conceive of adopting a religion empirically as a form of social control to achieve societal aims. Those who believe in religion as being divinely revealed could not countenance such a question, let alone answer it. Religious belief is customarily taught as a supreme belief that is inherently correct and is not subject to revision by natural law or empirical scrutiny. Usually, one does not believe in religion because it is good for one—in the sense that it is an anxiety reducer or a penicillin against evil spirits—but rather because it is inherently correct.

In our technologically developed society, what can we teach growing children to believe in order to provide a basis for their value systems now and as mature adults? America's separation of church and state takes the position that a religious belief may not be taught in the schools, but religions may be taught in the community and in the home—despite the fact that some religious and state principles are at times mutually contradictory. This gives rise to the question of the nature of belief itself, regardless of the substance of the belief.

People with strong belief systems do appear at times to have immunity against stresses and the ability to deal with catastrophes better. Uncertainty is disquieting, for it gives rise to anxieties and fears. Perhaps belief in and of itself, however arbitrarily based, may offer individuals a way of escaping anxiety and physiological and psychological tensions. Indeed, belief, while sometimes causing nightmares and panics, may offer protection against fears generated by the unexpected or the presently inexplicable. At this time our understanding of our own nature and the nature of the universe of which we are a part is limited. While there appears to be a design to biological and physical systems, we have widely varying scientific ideas about the origins of these designs. We do not know whether there are other intelligent beings in the universe who are watching us with amusement or with hostility, whether there are benevolent forces or hostile destructive forces awaiting us. High uncertainty would seem to carry with it pressure for strong belief systems.

In *The Mind Possessed* (1975), William Sargant, a distinguished English psychiatrist, has made a survey of the psychophysiology of faith healing, mysticism, and religious practices. One begins with the thought that the mind or the nervous system under stress has characteristic ways of reacting. Under stress, the mind may become highly suggestible, leading to imprinting or bonding of a set of stimuli and responses. Sargant's survey of many religious beliefs and mystical rituals throughout the world suggests that not all the formal aspects of these beliefs can be correct. Certainly, not all the worshipped gods can exist at the same time in the sense of verifiable reality, though they all may exist in the minds of some people. The possession of individuals by the god Dionysius (before the birth of Christ), by the Holy Ghost, by Pepos in Kenya, by the god Shango in Brazil, by Bablou in Cuba, or by Loa in voodoo cult in Haiti: it seems impossible for all these to be correct simultaneously. Given the perspective of a William James or a William Sargant, one begins to have the distinct feeling that there are common motivational bases of religious beliefs throughout the world and that an important element is the motivation toward the development and holding of these beliefs rather than the content of the beliefs themselves. Such an inference, however, represents the tradition of a rational person believing in the scientific method. One may admit that a hysterical blindness or paralysis may be cured by a priest in Ethiopia or by a medicine man in Zaire, or that a Maori may die because of a transgression of the sacred soils, without holding a belief in the causality these groups propose.

To some extent religious belief represents forms of dealing with collective uncertainties. Sargant poses the question, "What are we to think, then, about the truth or falsity of the numerous creeds and faiths that have been physiologically implanted in human beings in different societies and at different periods?" Theology and other branches of philosophy may be concerned with the analysis of the content of belief. Psychology, however, must be concerned with the mechanisms of belief—the consequences—and perhaps from this can suggest some alternative to viewing belief systems. Given that our species has evolved a nervous system that can be programmed through learning and experience, the human nervous system is to some extent plastic and thereby suggestible. There is typically insufficient opportunity for experience in the life span of one individual to provide a basis for deciding about the validity of a particular belief. However, in the collective system of scientific information, one can look at generations of individuals who develop new beliefs and ideas and examine them for implications about the physiological and psychological well-being of the believers and their societies. One of the great issues in our political systems is how we can respond appropriately to appeals of such demagogues as Hitler, who might encourage us to believe that we are being moral and constructive by killing off other people who are labeled undesirable.

Within the traditions of science, developmental psychology should have as its goal the expansion of the rational control of behavior through reasoning about information rather than through appeals to emotional bases of action or adherence to principles that cannot be either proved or disproved. At present, what we know is that there is a great deal in common among faith healing, religious belief, and the cures of behavioral disturbances by mental health specialists.

A question for each individual and for each parent is "Should you teach or advise another person to adopt an arbitrary belief solely because it seems useful?" Arbitrary beliefs may later restrict the psychological development of the individual if they also protect against insights that are more threatening. Many individuals do not undertake psychotherapy, for example, because they fear what might be revealed. They therefore use their belief systems and denial as a way of protecting themselves against the consequences of facing what they may fear are the ultimate unrevealed truths about their lives. Some fear that they may be discovered unlovable, unwanted, or evil or perhaps that they have transgressed inviolable laws.

Grouping together, whether among animals or people, seems to reduce fear; in collectivity there seems to be emotional security. This principle transcends the content around which the grouping occurs. Developmental psychology would seem to hold promise for the improvement of society by bringing us closer to an understanding of such behavior and our own emotional needs. It may open avenues through which we might obtain emotional support from others or from professionals when needed. It is hoped that more of us can become emotionally and intellectually strong so that we may not be brainwashed readily by demagogues or those who might manipulate us to their own personal gain. The future of humanity depends not only on what we know and what we believe but also on our emotional well-being. Developmental psychology has an expanding role to play in increasing our prospects for the development of emotionally strong and wise people.

In the present century there has been an embracing of psychology by many theologians. Thus, religion and science need not be on opposite sides in building a society that produces more wise, ethical, and emotionally strong people. Developmental psychology, along with religion, must continue to search for answers to basic questions about growing up and growing old in ways harmonious with our natures and our relationships with the universe we are exploring.

GLOSSARY

Accommodation: In Piaget's theory, the tendency to change psychological structures in response to environmental demands.

Acculturated traits: Behaviors that are overdetermined by environmental events and are subject to rapid modification through sociocultural change.

Acrolect: The more sophisticated form of black dialect.

Acuity: In vision, the minimum aspect of the test object dimension that can be correctly identified.

Adaptation: In Piaget's theory, the ability to change in accordance with internal and environmental demands. It consists of two complementary processes: assimilation and accommodation.

Adaptive mechanisms: The ways we meet changes or anticipated changes in our lives.

Adrenal cortex: The outer layer of the adrenal gland.

Adrenal medulla: The inner core of the adrenal gland.

Adrenergic action: An adrenalin-like action of the sympathetic nervous system involving fight-or-flight arousal.

Adrenocortical hormones: Hormones produced by the adrenal cortex in response to stress.

Affect: In intergenerational solidarity, the degree of sentiment among family members.

Affective: Relating to affect or emotion.

Age grade: A category or division within an institution based on age.

Age set: An institution into which one is admitted by an initiation ceremony.

Alerting (orienting) response: Various changes in behavior, such as turning the head, which indicate that an animal is attentive.

Alleles: Variant forms of a gene at a given locus.

Alveolars: Consonants produced by placing the tongue at the ridge behind the teeth.

Amino acids: The chemical building blocks of proteins.

Amino acid urias: Forms of mental retardation characterized by the lack of an enzyme needed to metabolize a particular amino acid. Examples include PKU and maple syrup urine disease.

Amniocentesis: The process of removing amniotic fluid from a pregnant woman. The fluid is analyzed to see if the fetus has any genetic defects.

Anal phase: In Freudian theory, the second phase of psychosexual development, during which libidinal energy is focused on the anal region.

Androgens: Hormones promoting male characteristics.

Animistic thinking: A characteristic of the preoperational period in which objects are regarded as being alive or aware.

Anoxia: A lack of oxygen which frequently results in brain injury.

Antisocial person: Someone who is aware of social expectations but has developed an antagonistic stance toward the reference group so that he or she does not conform.

Approach behavior: Motivated behavior patterns for interacting with the environment.

Archetypes: Recurring themes of the collective unconscious.

Assimilation: In Piaget's theory, dealing with environmental demands by incorporating them into existing cognitive structures.

Association: In intergenerational solidarity, the objective interaction between generations.

Attachment: An affectional bond between two people that endures over time and space and produces a desire for close contact as well as distress during separation.

Attitudes: A person's evaluation of specific objects, persons, or social issues.

Audience effect: The common finding that arousal and performance levels are affected by the presence or absence of a group of people.

Authoritarian parent: A rigid style of parenting in which rules and decisions are made irrespective of the child's ideas, needs, wishes, desires, and so on.

Authoritative parent: A flexible style of parenting in which parental authority is exercised but the child's point of view is considered.

Autism: A severe childhood disorder marked by withdrawal, poor social relatedness, language disturbances, and an insistence on preservation of sameness in the environment.

Autocratic classroom: Classroom setting in which the teacher announces what is to be done.

Autosomes: The forty-four chromosomes that are not associated with the determination of sex.

Avoidance learning: Learning not only to associate a conditioned stimulus with a fearful unconditioned stimulus but also learning an avoidance response to use to escape the conditioned stimulus (and fear).

Axons: Neuronal processes that transmit information to other cells.

Basilect: A form of black dialect spoken mainly by younger children.

Behaviorism: A school of psychology founded by John Watson which rejects introspective techniques in favor of studying overt, observable behavior.

Behavior modification: The deliberate application of scientific learning principles in order to alter existing problem behavior.

Behavior (reinforcement) therapy: The use of scientific learning principles in the treatment of psychological disorders.

Binocular parallax: The difference between the two retinal images of the eyes.

Biocultural traits: Behaviors with clear ontogenetic patterns and sex differences that are modified by generational shifts.

Biofeedback: Methods that provide an individual with information concerning his or her own biological states and responses.

Biological age: Index to an individual's position within the potential life span.

Biostable traits: Behaviors that are either determined genetically or shaped by early life influences.

Birth order: An individual's sequential position among siblings.

Blastula: The single-layer spherical formation of cells surrounding a fluid center that results from the rapid, repeated division of the zygote as it travels through the fallopian tube.

Body type: An individual's physical appearance, shape, and muscular development.

Bonding: The attachment of mother-to-infant (and vice-versa) during the moments immediately after birth.

Canalize: To channel development along genetically determined pathways.

Causality: A concept concerning cause-and-effect relationships.

Cell migration: The orderly movement of nerve cells to their proper location at the proper time in development.

Cephalocaudal development: The tendency for development to begin in the head and proceed downward.

Cerebrotonia: The pattern of inhibition, low sociability, and excessive restraint associated with ectomorphy.

Chromosomes: Long stretches of DNA which carry the genes. There are normally forty-six chromosomes in human cells (except in the egg and sperm).

Classical conditioning: A form of learning first described by Pavlov. A neutral stimulus is paired with a meaningful stimulus until eventually the neutral stimulus elicits the response originally made only to the meaningful stimulus.

Climacterium: A lessening of reproductive ability late in life when fertile sperm are no longer produced.

Clinical studies: Research that combines observation with interview techniques.

Cochlea: A snail-shaped organ filled with fluid and a membrane covered with sensitive hair cells which transmits sound vibrations from the eardrum to the ossicles.

Codon: A triplet sequence of the four nucleotide bases in the genetic code.

Coefficient of variation: A statistic used to describe the range of individual differences on a particular scale.

Cognitive: Referring to recognizing or knowing.

Cohort: A group of individuals born at a particular time and sharing certain historical events and trends.

Collective unconscious: Jung's concept that there is an unconscious element of personality which contains the beliefs and myths of the human race.

Concrete operations: The third stage of cognitive development in Piaget's theory, when thought becomes reversible. Conservation is evidenced during this stage.

Conditioned response: In classical conditioning, the response to the formerly neutral stimulus that was originally made only to the meaningful stimulus.

Conditioned stimulus: In classical conditioning, the neutral stimulus after it has been paired with the meaningful stimulus to elicit a conditioned response.

Cones: Receptor cells in the retina that are specialized for color vision.

Conjugate eye movement: The movement of the two eyes together.

Connotative: In Greek philosophy, the action component of language.

Consensus: In intergenerational solidarity, the agreement of values and opinions across generations.

Conservation: In Piaget's theory, the ability to recognize that certain properties of an object or set of objects (for example, weight, volume) remain invariant despite irrelevant changes in shape, length, or position.

Consonants: Language sounds produced when air is obstructed as it crosses over the vocal chords and through the vocal cavities.

Construct-based inventories: Personality inventories that assign an individual to a position on the basis of constructs derived from a particular theory.

Content: In Guilford's taxonomy, the mode in which intelligence is expressed.

Continuants: Consonants in which air obstruction is partial.

Continuous reinforcement: A schedule in which every single response is followed by reinforcement.

Contrasts: In phonology, fifteen binary contrasts underlying all phonemes produced, for example, voiced vs. voiceless and continuant vs. stop.

Control group: A group of subjects who do not receive any experimental treatment and are compared to the experimental group.

Convergent thinking: Thought patterns that result in the single correct response to a question or problem from the gathering of relevant data.

Coping styles: The ways we meet changes or anticipated changes in our lives.

Cotwin method: Comparing identical with fraternal twins to estimate genetic factors in behavior.

Creativity: Unique thought patterns that generate novel solutions to problems.

Criterion-group measures: Personality inventories that attempt to show how well a given person fits into a particular personality type based on traits.

Critical period: A period crucial for development of an organ or a behavior; often a time when development is most rapid and vulnerable to environmental influence.

Cross-cultural perspective: The comparison of behaviors, development, and so forth in different cultural groups.

Cross-sectional design: Research in which groups of subjects are seen at only one age or point in time; contrasted with longitudinal designs in which subjects are followed over time.

Crystallized intelligence: Abilities based upon stored information reflecting influences such as acculturation, learning, and education.

Culture: A given society's norms, values, and customs.

Culture-free intelligence tests: Intelligence tests that attempt to measure reasoning abilities with a minimum of reliance on words or content that might be culture-specific.

Cutaneous processes: Sensitivity to touch, pressure, temperature, and pain.

Cycloid type: Short, blocky body type.

Deep structure: The idea underlying a sentence.

Deferred imitation: The ability to imitate a behavior some time after observing it without the opportunity to practice it while observing or immediately following observing it.

Democratic classroom: An educational setting in which students and teachers decide jointly what specific ways learning activities are to be implemented.

Dendrites: The processes of nerve cells that receive information from other cells.

Deoxyribonucleic acid (DNA): The basic molecular substance in genetic material.

Dependency: The tendency of an individual to seek support and affection from others.

Dependent variable: In an experimental study, the behavior that is expected to change as a result of the experimenter's manipulations of the independent variable.

Deprivation dwarfism: A stunting of growth, apparently due to inadequate love and attention.

Deprivation experiments: Research in which an animal is reared under conditions in which it has no opportunity to learn a certain behavior or be exposed to certain stimuli.

Descriptive research: Research that describes an event or sequence of events.

Desensitization: A form of behavior therapy in which increasingly frightening forms of a feared object are gradually introduced until, eventually, the phobia is extinguished.

Developmental psychology: The scientific study of

how individuals and psychological processes develop over the life span, and the factors influencing their development.

Developmental task: A task that persons in a given culture are expected to master at an appropriate stage of the life cycle, such as learning to walk in infancy or to read in middle childhood.

Dialectical stage: Riegel's "fifth stage" addition to Piaget's theory in which adults are able to deal with contradictions and multiple levels of meaning.

Dialects: Variants of the standard form of a language.

Differentiation: The process of increasing specialization of functioning, complexity, and organization that is evident in both physical (for example, cellular) and psychological (for example, cognitive structures) development.

Discrimination learning: Learning to discriminate or distinguish which stimulus in a situation or trial is the one that will be reinforced.

Disengagement theory: The position that the process of psychological and social withdrawal commonly observed in old people arises from internal psychological events rather than in response to societal exclusion and role limitation.

Dishabituation: Following habituation, a recovery of interest upon presentation of a novel stimulus.

Distal senses: Senses stimulated by indirect stimuli such as vision and hearing.

Distant-figure role: Grandparents who make only formal and infrequent contacts with their grandchildren.

Divergent thinking: Thought patterns that result in a variety of novel answers to an open-ended problem.

Dominant gene: A gene whose effects on a trait dominate those of another (recessive) gene.

Down's syndrome: A form of mental retardation attributable to the presence of three number-21 chromosomes.

Drives: Motives based on biological needs.

Dynamic (functional) personality theories: Theories emphasizing antecedent-consequent relationships in an individual's current behavior patterns.

Echoic behavior: The imitation of language.

Echoing: The simplification of the interrogative form by a mother asking her small child a question following an unintelligible statement by the child.

Ectomorphy: A primary structural component of physique associated with linearity.

Edema: The swelling of body tissue due to water retention.

Educational psychology: The application of psychological research and theories to address school-related issues such as learning and motivation.

Ego: In Freud's theory, the rational element of personality.

Electra complex: In Freud's theory, the conflict between a girl's love for her father and jealousy of her mother which should be resolved by the girl's identification with her mother.

Embryo: Earliest stage of growth. In humans, the period from conception to the end of the second month.

Embryonic disc: A thickened mass of cells on one side of the blastula from which the embryo and supportive structures develop.

Emotion: Our feeling tone and state of affective arousal.

Empiricists: People who believe that behavior or development is determined mainly by environmental rather than biological factors.

Encoding: The registration of new information in memory.

Endocrine glands: Ductless glands (for example, the gonads and adrenals) that secrete hormones directly into the bloodstream.

Endomorphy: A primary structural component of physique associated with soft, round body features.

Epinephrine: Adrenalin, an adrenal medulla hormone.

Equilibrium: In Piaget's theory, balance between the psychological structures and environmental events.

Eros: In Freud's theory, the life-supporting or sexual drive.

Erythroblastosis fetalis: A disease resulting from an immunological incompatibility between a pregnant woman and her baby.

Ethology: A biological science of behavior: its evolutionary and individual development, survival value, and innate and learned components.

Excitatory: Causing the onset of an activity.

Expansion: Responding to a child's grammatically inferior utterance with a grammatically improved form of that utterance.

Experimental research: Research in which the researcher controls and manipulates certain variables in order to study their effects on particular behaviors.

Expressive activities: Activities that involve enjoying the present moment without regard for the future.

Extended family: Three generations living together in a single household.

Extinction: In classical conditioning, the loss of effectiveness of a conditioned stimulus to elicit the conditioned response due to the discontinuation of the pairing of the conditioned stimulus with the unconditioned stimulus.

Factor analysis: A statistical method for observing relationships among a large number of items. Clusters of items that are highly intercorrelated are identified and termed *factors.*

Fetotoxic: Toxic (poisonous) to the fetus.

Fetal period: The period in human development from the end of the second month to birth.

Field work: Obtaining data "first-hand" by living with the group being studied.

Fixation: In Freud's theory, partial arrest at a particular phase due to under- or overgratification during that period.

Fixed interval schedule: A reinforcement schedule in which the subject is reinforced for a response only after a certain time interval regardless of how many responses occur during the interval.

Fixed ratio schedule: A schedule of reinforcement in which the subject is reinforced after a fixed number of responses.

Fluid intelligence: Active problem-solving behaviors that enable immediate solution of novel problems reflecting the integrity and efficiency of the nervous system.

Formal operations: In Piaget's theory, the final stage of development, which begins in early adolescence.

Formal role: A style of grandparenting in which grandparents bestow gifts and treats but otherwise adopt a "hands-off" policy in child training.

Fricatives: Consonants in which air obstruction is partial.

Functional age: A person's relative ability to perform tasks (compared to peers).

Functional assimilation: In Piaget's theory, the tendency to exercise a structure, for example, nonnutritive sucking.

Fun-seeking role: A style of grandparenting marked by an informal relationship in which grandparents and grandchildren are companions in enjoyable activities.

Generalization: In classical conditioning, the ability of stimuli similar to the conditioned stimulus to elicit the conditioned response.

Generalizing assimilation: In Piaget's theory, the extension of a structure to a variety of objects.

Generative capacity: In Chomsky's theory, the possi-bility of producing an infinite number of sentences from the limited lexicon of a language.

Generative grammar: In Chomsky's theory, a group of rules of syntax that would allow the generation of every grammatically correct sentence in every language but no ungrammatical sentence.

Genes: The basic units of heredity.

Genetic counseling: Counseling persons or their families about the risks and consequences of inheriting or transmitting genetic disorders or factors.

Genital phase: In Freud's theory, the final stage of development (after age twelve) during which mature heterosexual activity is achieved.

Genotype: The genetic makeup of an individual.

g factor: Spearman's notation for general intelligence.

Glia: Cells that provide nutritive and structural support to the neurons. They also form the myelin sheaths.

Glides: Language sounds in which air is obstructed but the characteristic turbulence of consonant sounds is not created.

Graphemic: Concerning written letters of the alphabet.

Gregarious person: A person who has mastered the social aspects of group interaction and has also received much reinforcement from others.

Gustation: Sense of taste.

Gyri: The rounded elevations of the cerebral cortex.

Habituation: Decreased attention or response to a stimulus that is repeated or has become familiar.

Hawthorne effect: The fact that simply providing attention and introducing a novel treatment may produce improved morale or performance.

Heredity: The biological transmission of characteristics from parent to child.

Heritability: The proportion of the observed variation of a trait in a group that results from gene effects.

Heterozygous: Possessing different alleles for a given locus.

Holophrastic stage: The period when a child's speech is characterized by one-word utterances, which many believe represent entire sentences.

Homeorhesis: The innate control mechanisms that keep maturation on a genetically predetermined track.

Homeostasis: The process whereby various critical physiological factors (for example, body temperature) are maintained in a steady state that is compatible with life.

Homogeneous: Having uniform parts or composition.

Homologous chromosomes: Two matched chromosomes having the same genetic loci.

Homo sapiens: The human species.

Homozygous: Possessing identical alleles at a given locus.

Humanistic psychology: A branch of psychology that emphasizes the purpose of human beings, our intentionality or will to action.

Hypothalamus: A central brain structure involved in autonomic nervous system and limbic system functioning which is believed to be instrumental in motivation and emotional functioning.

Hypothesis: A tentative theory to explain existing data and make predictions for further research.

Id: In Freud, the most primitive system of personality, which is driven by instinctual needs.

Identification: The process by which children perceive similarities between themselves and another person leading them to adopt that person's behaviors.

Identity: A relatively stable sense of being the same person at various times in various settings.

Imprinting: A kind of rapid learning occurring during a critical period and determining a later behavior (as when a duckling "imprints" on its mother).

Inbreeding depression: A decline in behavioral performance over generations due to inbreeding.

Independent variable: The factor in an experimental study that is controlled and manipulated by the researcher.

Infantile marasmus: Severe emaciation in a child due to insufficient caloric and protein intake.

Infantile pyloric stenosis: A congenital defect of a valvelike muscle in the stomach that results in projectile vomiting early in infancy.

Inferiority complex: Adler's concept of a lifestyle of self-depreciation.

Inflections: Word endings such as *-ed, -s,* or *-ing* that modify the meaning of a word.

Inhibitory: Blocking (inhibiting) a behavior or event.

Initiation rites: Rituals used in some cultures to mark the transition from childhood to adulthood.

Instrumental activities: Activities that may involve current sacrifices for future gains.

Integration: The coordination of functioning.

Integrity vs. despair: The eighth and final stage of development in Erikson's theory. At this point, an individual's life either makes sense because of some human principles or is marked by despair because it seems meaningless.

Intelligence: A broad term referring to an individual's thought capacity and abilities. .

Intelligence quotient (IQ): A score assigned to a person on the basis of performance relative to other people in the same age group.

Intergenerational solidarity: A physical, emotional, and attitudinal closeness between generations that facilitates the transmission of cultural and behavioral norms.

Internal standard: An individual's personal gauge of accomplishment, which is relatively independent of societal expectations.

Intervention: Steps taken to alter the course of events rather than simply allowing them to follow their natural course.

Irreversible solidarity: Jakobson's principle governing the acquisition of nonuniversal phonemes.

Kachinas: In Hopi Indian culture, the spirits of the ancestors who will punish disobedient children.

Kinesthesis: Coordination and postural maintenance.

Klinefelter's syndrome: A disorder, often resulting in mental retardation, in which a male carries two X and one Y chromosomes (instead of one of each).

Kwashiorkor: A syndrome occurring when a child's protein intake is insufficient. It is characterized by edema, skin lesions, and reduced synthesis of proteins.

Labials: Consonants produced by touching the lips together.

Language Acquisition Device (LAD): A hypothetical innate structure that guides children's acquisition of syntax or other aspects of language.

Latency period: In Freudian theory, the period during childhood (age five to twelve) when sexual desires are repressed and the child concentrates on acquiring important social, educational, and work skills.

Lateralization: The specialization of the cerebral hemispheres. Typically, the left hemisphere is specialized to play a dominant role in language functions.

Law of Effort: An ethological principle stating that the strength of imprinting increases proportionately with the amount of effort exerted to imprint.

Learning: A relatively long-lasting change in the potential for behavior that is not attributable to maturation, biological status, or temporary states of the organism.

Libido: In Freud's theory, sexual or creative energy.

Life space: In field theory, the aspects of the environment that an individual identifies as being meaningful.

Limbic system: An area of the brain believed to be related to emotion.

Liquids: Language sounds in which air is obstructed but the characteristic turbulence of consonant sounds is not created.

Local senses: Senses stimulated by immediate contact, such as pain, pressure, temperature, and touch.

Longitudinal design: A group of people, all of whom are the same age, are studied over a period of time.

Low-birthweight babies: Babies weighing less than 2,500 grams at birth, regardless of gestational age.

Major gene disorders: Psychological defects resulting from genes at a single locus on a chromosome pair.

Markers: Words within a sentence that give clues to the meaning of key words.

Maturational age: A person's level of maturation relative to his or her peers.

Meiosis: The process by which chromosomes are sorted out during the formation of sex cells.

Membership identities: Associations with groups that forge a link between an individual and the formal and informal organizations of community life.

Menarche: A woman's first menstrual period.

Mental age: A person's relative ability to think compared to peers.

Mesomorphy: A primary structural component of physique associated with high muscular development.

Microcephaly: A congenital disorder in which the skull and brain are abnormally small resulting in severe mental retardation.

Mitosis: Reproduction of genetically identical cells.

Modeling: Learning by imitation.

Modified extended family: A nuclear family that maintains close ties with family members of other generations.

Morphemes: The smallest meaningful units within a language.

Morpheme structure rules: Rules specifying permissible combinations of phonemes in a language.

Motion parallax: Greater apparent movement of near than far objects as an observer changes position.

Motivation: The impulsion of an organism to expend energy and to organize behavior in order to reach some goal.

Motor development: The development of motor skills such as walking, grasping, and so on.

Myelinization: The development of myelin sheaths around the axons of nerve fibers.

Myelin sheath: An insulating, protective covering surrounding many nerve fibers that facilitates neuronal transmission.

Myelogenetic cycle: The period of myelinization for a particular fiber system of the brain.

Myopia: Nearsightedness.

Nativists: People who believe that behavior or development is innately determined.

Natural experiment: An experiment involving individuals who have been exposed to unusual developmental conditions.

Natural selection: The differentiation of species during evolution, based on the idea that characteristics which aid survival will persist.

Negative eugenics: Attempts to improve the human race by decreasing the frequency of harmful genes.

Negative reinforcers: Stimuli whose removal after an operant decreases the chances it will recur.

Neonate: Newborn. The human infant during the first month or two after birth.

Neural plate: In the first phase of nervous system development, a flat sheet of cells on the outer surface of the embryo.

Neuroblast: An early stage of nerve cells.

Neurochemistry: The biochemistry of the nervous system.

Neurons: Nerve cells.

Nonsocial person: A person who has not mastered the expectations and behaviors of his or her relevant reference group and has not developed the appropriate attitude toward that group.

Norepinephrine: The hormone produced by the adrenal medulla. Also a neurotransmitter in the brain.

Normative events: Events that most individuals growing up in a culture are expected to encounter.

Norms: Cultural expectations for behavior at certain ages.

Nuclear family: Mother, father, and children.

Nystagmus: The oscillation of the eyeballs from side to side following body rotation. Used by neurologists to test vestibular functioning.

Object permanence: The ability to be aware of the existence of objects even when they are not perceptually available.

Observational learning: Learning that occurs by observing the performance of a model.

Oedipal complex: In Freud's theory, the conflict between a boy's love for his mother and jealousy of his father, which should ultimately be resolved by the boy's identification with his father.

Olfaction: Sense of smell.

Ontogeny: The development of an individual.

Operant: An emitted response that "operates" on the environment and is controlled by reinforcement.

Operant (instrumental) conditioning: A form of learning, first described by Skinner, in which behavior is controlled by the consequences it produces.

Operations: In Guilford's taxonomy, the ways in which information can be manipulated or worked upon.

Operator genes: Genes that control the action of the structural genes.

Optic nerve: The major nerve running from the retina to the brain, transmitting visual information.

Oral period: In Freud's theory, the first stage of psychosexual development, during which gratification is obtained primarily through the mouth.

Organismic: In Werner's theory, emphasis on the total organism and development throughout the life span.

Orthogenetic principle: In Werner's theory, the concept that development proceeds from a state of globality and nondifferentiation toward states of increasing differentiation and hierarchic integration.

Ossicles: The three small bones of the middle ear.

Ovum: The egg cell.

Partial (intermittent) reinforcement: Reinforcement schedules in which reinforcers are presented only after a certain time interval or in a certain fraction of the instances of the response.

Participant observation: A cross-cultural research technique in which the researcher "immerses" himself or herself in the group being studied, becoming, as much as possible, a member of the group.

Patrilineal family: Family traditions and inheritance patterns based upon the male's line of descent.

Patrilocal family: A family based on home territory of the male's family or tribe.

Perception: The process of extracting, interpreting, and categorizing sensory stimulation.

Permissive classroom: An educational setting in which children initiate activities under the teacher's guidance.

Personality: The characteristic way we behave and respond to our environment.

Personality states: The specific effect of situational events in eliciting behavior patterns.

Personality traits: Relatively enduring characteristics of one's personality.

Phallic stage: In psychoanalytic theory, the third stage of psychosexual development (age thirty months to five years), during which sex role behavior develops through the process of identification.

Phenocopy: An environmentally induced mimic of a typically hereditary phenotype or condition.

Phenotype: The actual physical or behavioral traits manifested, as distinguished from an individual's genotype, or genetic make-up.

Phenylketonuria (PKU): A major gene disorder which can result in mental retardation if diet control is not instituted at birth.

Pheromones: Chemical substances secreted by various species to communicate certain information.

Phobias: Unrealistic and exaggerated fears of specific things.

Phocomelia: A birth defect in which the limbs are reduced and deformed so as to resemble flippers.

Phoneme: A class of sounds that are considered equivalent in a given language.

Phonology: The sound system of a particular language.

Phrase-structure grammars: Linguistic analyses that break sentences into increasingly smaller phrases finally resulting in a string of units.

Phylogeny: The evolutionary development of a species.

Pivot-open classes: A system devised by Braine to characterize children's two-word utterances.

Pleiotropy: Production by a single gene of multiple phenotypic effects.

Polygenic: Affected by many genes at different loci.

Polypeptides: Long chains of amino acids.

Positive eugenics: Attempts to improve the human race by increasing the frequency of beneficial genes.

Positive reinforcers: Stimuli that, if presented after an operant, increase the chances it will recur.

Pre-eclamptic toxemia: A pregnancy disorder involving high blood pressure, edema, and kidney malfunction.

Prenatal: Occurring during the period of pregnancy.

Preoperational thought: In Piaget's theory, the second stage of cognitive development lasting from approximately ages two to seven years. Symbolic thought appears during this stage but thought is highly egocentric.

Prepared childbirth: Birth based on techniques to prepare parents for the birth process thereby reducing the need for drugs during labor and delivery.

Presbyopia: The impairment of the ability to focus on near objects.

Primacy factor: The concept that early life experience has a disproportionately strong influence on later development.

Primary circular reaction: In Piaget's theory, a behavioral sequence initially produced by chance that is repeatedly reproduced and practiced by the infant.

Primary prevention: Intervention designed to reduce the frequency or avoid the occurrence of specified problems.

Primary processes: In Freud, thought processes involved with id-based impulses for immediate gratification.

Product-centered approach: A method of evaluating the development of creativity by examining the level of productivity of individuals as they age.

Products: In Guilford's taxonomy, the six levels of complexity or organization involved in thinking.

Projective tests: Tests that consist of unstructured, ambiguous stimuli. Subjects' descriptions of these stimuli are analyzed to ascertain motivational, emotional, and attitudinal states.

Prompting: A characteristic of speech to a young child in which questions are asked in a simplified format.

Proprioceptors: Receptors that are stimulated by muscle flexion and extension and by deep pressure.

Proximodistal development: The tendency for growth to start at the midline of the body and proceed outward.

Pseudoemotional response: A response in which all the physiological aspects of an emotional reaction are present but there is no affective component.

Pseudohermaphrodite: In animal research, a condition induced by the administration of testosterone during fetal development in which genetically female monkeys have male external genitalia but female ovaries.

Psychoanalytic theory: Theory formulated by Sigmund Freud to explain personality development and functioning.

Psychological age: An index of an individual's adaptive capacities such as perception, learning, and memory.

Psychological defenses: The way we cope with threatening situations.

Quantification: Arranging data into hierarchical categories that can be meaningfully numbered for the purpose of statistical analysis.

Quasi-experimental research: Research whose designs have some of the advantages of experimental methods; for use when true experiments are not possible.

Random sampling: The process of selecting a representative subset (sample) from a group (population) so that every member of the population has an equal chance of being chosen.

Recall memory: The ability to remember events or information without any cues.

Recessive gene: A gene whose effect on a trait is only seen in homozygous states (see Dominant gene).

Recognition memory: Ability to recognize that something was previously learned or experienced.

Recognitive assimilation: In Piaget's theory, a primitive form of recognition, appearing in early infancy, in which the infant shows discrimination in the application of schemes under certain circumstances.

Recruitment: A shortening of the loudness scale in older subjects.

Regression: In Freudian theory, reversion to a behavior pattern appropriate to an earlier life stage as a result of a traumatic experience.

Regulator genes: Genes that activate and deactivate the structural genes.

Reinforcers: Consequences following an operant that increase the likelihood the behavior will recur.

Reliability: The accuracy of reproduction or replication of data.

Religious communities: Communities in which interpersonal and family relationships are governed primarily by a set of religious principles.

REM sleep: The rapid eye movement phase of sleep.

Reservoir of family wisdom: A style of grandparenting in which the grandparent passes on special skills and knowledge rather than controlling the child's behavior.

Reticular formation: A network of cells located in the brain stem whose activity is linked to arousal states of the organism.

Retina: The inner layer of the eye containing the light-sensitive receptors (rods and cones).

Retrograde amnesia: A form of memory loss in which recent events are forgotten but events of the distant past are easily recalled.

Rods: Retinal receptor cells sensitive to dim light; important for night (but not color) vision.

Role-playing activities: Rehearsal devices that eventually will aid role enactment.

Rubella: "German measles," which if contracted during pregnancy may result in birth defects or fetal death.

Schedules: Sequences for giving reinforcement.

Schemas: In Piaget's theory, organized thought processes or motor activities.

Schizoid type: Lean-bodied, quiet, unsocial person.

Schizophrenia: A serious form of mental illness marked by disturbances in logical thought, attention, emotional well-being, and social relationships.

Secondary circular reaction: Similar to primary circular reaction except that external objects and events (rather than the infant's body) are involved.

Secondary prevention: Intervention designed to reduce the duration of problems.

Secondary process: In Freud, reality-oriented thinking dealing with practical life circumstances as well as moral and ethical considerations.

Secular trend: A long-term historical trend (for example, toward more rapid physical maturation).

Self-concept: In phenomenological theories, those parts of an individual's perceptual field which have been differentiated by that person as being stable characteristics.

Semantics: The meaning system of language.

Senile dementia: Progressive mental deterioration in the aged, marked by confusion, disorientation, and memory impairment.

Sensation: The stimulation of the sensory receptors (eye, ear, skin, and so on) and the coding and transmission of stimulus energy.

Sensorimotor intelligence: In Piaget's theory, the first stage of cognitive development occurring from about birth to age two years. Thought during this period is nonrepresentational and dominated by action schemas.

Set: A readiness to attend, perceive, or respond in a certain way to stimuli or situations (for example, different sets may help or hinder creativity).

Sexual identity: Identification of gender and behaviors associated with it.

Shaping: The process of reinforcing successive approximations of a behavior until, gradually, a complex behavior is emitted.

Short-gestation babies: Babies who are born prior to the completion of a normal-length pregnancy (forty weeks).

Short-term memory: The ability to recall material immediately or soon after it has been presented. Information is quickly lost from short-term memory.

Signals: Stimuli which, through conditioning, come to elicit certain behaviors (in Piaget's theory).

Signs: A part or characteristic of the object being represented (in Piaget's theory).

Skinner box: A small enclosure in which an animal is housed in order to record its operant behaviors and quickly provide reinforcers.

Social deprivation: The state in which opportunities for social influences are denied to a developing individual.

Socialization: The life-long process of learning to carry forward society's institutions and to adopt social roles and behaviors associated with the roles.

Social learning: The manner in which social behavior is formed from stimuli provided by other people and the physical environment.

Social person: A person who has learned and adopted the approved behaviors of his or her relevant reference group and is, therefore, able to interact with others in a positive manner.

Social reinforcement: The reinforcement supplied by other people.

Social roles: A pattern of behavior expected of a person of a certain age or position.

Social status incongruity: A discrepancy between an individual's background and his or her position within a group.

Sociobiology: A perspective which argues that certain behavioral traits are selected for in the evolutionary process.

Somatotonia: The assertiveness, interest in muscular activity, and risk taking associated with mesomorphy.

Spatial concepts: Concepts concerning relationships between objects and space.

Spines: Budlike formations along a dendrite that increase its receiving area.

Split-brain patients: Patients who, for medical reasons, have had the neural connections between the cerebral hemispheres surgically severed.

Stage: A distinct period of development within a sequence of developmental levels.

Standard deviation: A statistic used to measure the dispersion of scores around an average score.

Stanford-Binet: A common standardized intelligence (IQ) test used with both children and adults.

State anxiety: A transitory emotional state characterized by consciously perceived feelings of tension and apprehension.

Static (descriptive) personality theories: Theories dealing with facets of behavior that characterize an organism at present without necessarily inferring the antecedents.

Stops: Consonants in which air obstruction is complete.

Structural genes: Genes that carry the actual blueprint for synthesizing a particular protein and direct the synthesis of that protein when activated.

Structural meanings: The functional relationships or functions of early childhood utterances.

Sulci: The furrows of the cerebral cortex.

Superego: In Freud's theory, the system of personality imbued with societal norms and rules; the conscience.

Surface structure: The actual form of a sentence.

Surrogate mothers: In Harlow's studies, artificial "mothers" constructed of wire or terry cloth used to investigate determinants of attachment in rhesus monkeys.

Surrogate parent role: Grandparents who assume responsibility for the care and discipline of their grandchildren.

Symbolic function: The ability to produce by oneself mental symbols or representations.

Symbols: Personal (and perhaps idiosyncratic) representations of objects or events.

Synapse: The junction between the axon of one neuron and the receiving area of another neuron.

Syntax: The underlying grammatical structure of language.

Teratogenic: Capable of producing congenital deformities.

Tertiary circular reactions: Similar to secondary circular reactions except that, in an effort to produce moderate novelty, the child makes slight variations in the event when reproducing it.

Tertiary prevention: Intervention designed to reduce the amount of time needed by an individual to return to normal life.

Test-coach-retest procedure: A method of administering IQ tests that helps to differentiate children who score at retarded range due to cultural deprivation from those who are neurologically impaired.

Thanatos: In Freud's theory, the destructive drive or death wish.

Theory: A set of statements and principles designed to organize and explain existing data so that behavior may be predicted and controlled.

Threshold: The least amount of energy or smallest change in energy that can be detected by a receptor.

Toxoplasmosis: A disease caused by a parasite which may cause brain damage or death to a fetus if contracted during pregnancy.

Trait anxiety: Relatively stable differences among people in their tendency to respond to situations perceived as threatening with anxiety.

Transformation: In Chomsky's theory, rules of syntax that facilitate the translation of deep structure into surface structure.

Trimesters: The three three-month periods of pregnancy.

Trisomy-21: Down's syndrome.

Turner's syndrome: Disorder involving girls with only one X chromosome. Usually sexual development is abnormal.

Tympanic membrane: The eardrum.

Type A personality: A pattern of behavior marked by competitiveness, ambition, impatience, and achievement orientation that is thought to be conducive to heart attacks.

Typologies: Broad categories of behavior descriptions.

Unconditioned response: In classical conditioning, the meaningful stimulus that consistently elicits a particular response prior to conditioning.

Unconscious: In Freud, the portion of the mind containing feelings, experiences, ideas, and so forth that we are unaware of in our daily functioning.

Universality of contrasts: Jakobson's principle that contrasts exist in every language and those contrasts which are universal in all languages appear first in development.

Unsocial person: Someone who has not achieved mastery of social processes and therefore is forced to spend much time alone.

Utopian communities: Communities formed around shared philosophies about ideal lifestyles.

Validity: The extent to which measurements truly measure or predict the thing they are intended to predict.

Variable interval schedule: A reinforcement schedule in which the time interval between reinforcers varies.

Variable ratio schedule: A reinforcement schedule in which the number of responses between reinforcers varies.

Vesicles: Tiny packets of molecules of neurotransmitters.

Vestibular sense: Sense of balance.

Viscerotonia: The love of comfort, sociability, and affection associated with endomorphy.

Visual cliff: A research apparatus designed to produce the optical illusion of a dropoff used to test depth perception in infants.

Visual-spatial ability: The ability to visualize rotations or different perspectives of objects in space.

Voiced consonants: Consonants for which the vocal cords vibrate during production.

Voiceless consonants: Consonants for which the vocal cords do not vibrate during production.

Voluntarism: The philosophy that voluntary will is the major determinant of behavior.

Vowels: Language sounds produced without the obstruction of air passing over the vocal chords and through the vocal cavities.

WAIS (Wechsler Adult Intelligence Scale): A standardized intelligence scale for adults which measures verbal and performance IQ.

WISC (Wechsler Intelligence Scale for Children): A standardized intelligence scale for children that measures verbal and performance IQ.

Withdrawal behavior: Motivated behavior patterns for avoiding danger.

Word order: The sequencing of words in an utterance to reflect their syntactic and semantic relationships.

Young society: A society in which there is a high proportion of young people.

Zygote: Fertilized egg.

REFERENCES

Abelson, P. H. A damaging source of air pollution. *Science*, 1967, *158*, editorial page.

Adams, B. N. Birth order: A critical review. *Sociometry*, 1972, *35*, 411-439.

Adams, B. N., & Butler, J. E. Occupational status and husband-wife social participation. *Social Forces*, 1967, *45*, 501-507.

Adler, A. *Understanding human nature*. New York: Greenberg, 1972.

Ahammer, I. M., & Baltes, P. B. Objective versus perceived age differences in personality: How do adolescents, adults, and older people view themselves and each other? *Journal of Gerontology*, 1972, *27*, 46-51.

Ahern, F. M., & Johnson, R. C. Inherited uterine inadequacy: An alternate explanation for a portion of cases of defect. *Behavior Genetics*, 1973, *3*(1), 1-12.

Ailor, J. W. The church provides for the elderly. In R. R. Boyd & G. G. Oakes (Eds.), *Foundations of practical gerontology*. Columbia: University of South Carolina Press, 1969.

Ainsworth, M. D. *Infancy in Uganda: Infant care and the growth of love*. Baltimore: Johns Hopkins University Press, 1967.

Ainsworth, M. D. S. The development of infant-mother attachment. In B. Caldwell & H. Ricciuti (Eds.), *Review of child development research* (Vol. 3). Chicago: University of Chicago Press, 1973.

Alder, A. *Practice and theory of individual psychology*. New York: Harcourt, Brace & World, 1927.

Allen, G. *The colour-sense: Its origin and development*. London: Trubner, 1879.

Allport, G. W. *Pattern and growth in personality*. New York: Holt, 1961.

Allport, G. W., & Odbert, H. S. Trait names: A psycholexical study. *Psychological Monographs*, 1936, *47* (Whole No. 211).

Alpaugh, P. K., & Birren, J. E. Are there sex differences in creativity across the adult life span? *Human Development*, 1975, *18*, 461-465.

Altman, J. Postnatal growth and differentiation of the mammalian brain, with implications for a morphological theory of memory. In G. C. Quarton, T. Melnechuk, & F. O. Schmitt (Eds.), *The neurosciences: A study program*. New York: Rockefeller University Press, 1967.

American Psychiatric Association. *Diagnostic and statistical manual of mental disorders* (3rd ed.). Washington, D.C.: American Psychiatric Association, 1980.

Anderson, J. E. The methods of child psychology. In C. Murchison (Ed.), *A handbook of child psychology*. Worcester, Mass.: Clark University Press, 1931.

Anderson, J. E. The limitations of infant and preschool tests in the measurement of intelligence. *Journal of Psychology*, 1939, *8*, 351-379.

Anderson, J. E. The nature of abilities. In E. P. Torrance (Ed.), *Education and talent*. Minneapolis: University of Minnesota Press, 1960.

Anonymous. Harris poll, 1976.

Anonymous. The open generation. *Look*, September 20, 1966, *30*, 52.

Anonymous. Women of the year: Great changes, new chances, tough choices. *Time*, 1976, *107*, 6-16.

Antown, R. T. *Arab village—A social structural study of a Transjordanian peasant community*. Bloomington: Indiana University Press, 1972.

Arenberg, D. Cognition and aging: Verbal learning, memory, problem solving, and aging. In C. Eisdorfer & M. P. Lawton (Eds.), *The psychology of adult development and aging*. Washington, D.C.: American Psychological Association, 1973.

Arey, L. B. *Developmental anatomy* (8th ed.). Philadelphia: Saunders, 1974.

Arslan, M. The senescence of the vestibular apparatus. *Practica Oto-Rhino-Laryngologica*, 1957, *19*, 475-483.

Atchley, R. C. *The social forces in later life* (2nd ed.). Belmont, Calif.: Wadsworth, 1977.

Aubenque, M. Note documentaire sur la statistique des tailles des étudiants au cours de ces dernières années. *Biotypologie*, 1957, *18*, 202-214.

Babchuck, N., & Bates, A. P. The primary relations of middle-class couples: A study in male dominance. *American Sociological Review*, 1963, *28*, 377-384.

Back, K. W. The ambiguity of retirement. In E. W. Busse & E. A. Pfeiffer (Eds.), *Behavior and adaptation in later life* (2nd ed.). Boston: Little, Brown, 1976.

Back, K. W., & Morris, J. D. Perception of self and the study of whole lives. In E. Palmore (Ed.), *Normal aging II: Reports from the Duke longitudinal studies*. Durham, N.C.: Duke University Press, 1974.

Bacon, F. *The historie of life and death*. London: I Oakes, 1638.

Baer, D. M. The control of developmental process: Why wait? In J. R. Nesselroade & H. W. Reese (Eds.), *Life-span developmental psychology: Methodological issues*. New York: Academic, 1973.

Bajema, C. J. Relation of fertility to educational attainment in a Kalamazoo public school population: A follow-up study. *Eugenics Quarterly*, 1966, *13*, 306-315.

Baker, Bruce L. Symptom treatment and symptom substitution in enuresis. *Journal of Abnormal Psychology*, 1969, *74*, (1), 42-49.

Baltes, P. B., & Labouvie, G. V. Adult development of intellectual performance: Description, explanation, and modification. In C. Eisdorfer & M. P. Lawton (Eds.), *The psychology of adult development and aging*. Washington, D.C.: American Psychological Association, 1973.

Baltes, P. B., & Schaie, K. W. Aging and IQ: The myth of the twilight years. *Psychology Today*, 1974, *7*, 35-40.

Bandura, A. Social learning through imitation. In M. R. Jones (Ed.), *Nebraska symposium on motivation*. Lincoln: University of Nebraska Press, 1962.

Bandura, A. The role of modeling processes in personality development. In W. W. Hartup & N. L. Smothergill (Eds.), *The young child: Review of research*. Washington, D.C.: National Association for the Education of Young Children, 1967.

Bandura, A. Social-learning theory of identificatory processes. In D. A. Goslin (Ed.), *Handbook of socialization theory and research*. Chicago: Rand McNally, 1969.

Bandura, A., Ross, D., & Ross, S. A. Imitation of film-mediated aggressive models. *Journal of Abnormal and Social Psychology*, 1963, *66*, 3-11.

Bandura, A., & Walters, R. H. *Social learning and personality development*. New York: Holt, 1963.

Barker, R. G., & Wright, H. F. *Midwest and its children*. Evanston, Ill.: Row Peterson, 1955.

Barnes, A. B., Colton, R., Gunderson, J., Noller, K. L., Tilley, B. C., Strama, T., Townsend, D. E., Hatab, P., & O'Brien, P. C. Fertility and outcome of pregnancy in women exposed in utero to diethylstilbesterol. *New England Journal of Medicine*, 1980, *302*, 609-613.

Baumrind, D. Current patterns of parental authority. *Developmental Psychology Monographs*, 1971, *4*, 99-103.

Baumrind, D. Some thoughts about child rearing. In U. Bronfenbrenner (Ed.), *Influences on human development*. Hinsdale, Ill.: Dryden, 1972.

Bayley, N. On the growth of intelligence. *American Psychologist*, 1955, *10*, 805-818.

Bayley, N. Behavioral correlates of mental growth: Birth to thirty-six years. *American Psychologist*, 1968, *23*, 1-17.

Bayley, N. Development of mental abilities. In P. H. Mussen (Ed.), *Carmichael's manual of child psychology*. New York: Wiley, 1970.

Bayley, N., & Oden, M. H. The maintenance of intellectual ability in gifted adults. *Journal of Gerontology*, 1955, *10*, 91-107.

Beals, R. L., & Hoiger, H. *An introduction to anthropology*. New York: Macmillan, 1971.

Beattie, W. The design of supportive environments for the life-span. *Gerontologist*, 1970, *10*, 190-193.

Bee, H. *Social issues in developmental psychology*. New York: Harper & Row, 1974.

Bell, R. Q., & Costello, N. S. Three tests for sex differences in tactile sensitivity in the newborn. *Biologia Neonatale*, 1964, *7*, 335-347.

Belloc, N. B., & Breslow, L. Relationship of physical health status and health practice. *Preventative Medicine*, 1972, *1*, 409-421.

Bellugi, U. The development of interrogative structures in children's speech. In K. Riegel (Ed.), *The development of language functions* (University of Michigan Language Program, Report No. 8). 1965.

Belmont, J. M., & Butterfield, E. C. What the development of short-term memory is. *Human De-*

velopment, 1971, *14*, 236-248.

Bengtson, V. L. Inter-age differences in perception and the generation gap. *Gerontologist*, 1971, *11*, 85-90.

Bengtson, V. L. Generation and value effects in value socialization. *American Sociological Review*, 1975, *40*, 358-371.

Bengtson, V. L., & Black, K. D. Intergenerational relations and continuities in socialization. In P. B. Baltes & K. W. Schaie (Eds.), *Life-span developmental psychology: Personality and socialization.* New York: Academic, 1973.

Bengtson, V. L., & Cutler, N. E. Generations and intergenerational relations: Perspectives on age groups and social change. In R. H. Binstock & E. Shannas (Eds.), *Handbook of aging and the social sciences.* New York: Van Nostrand Reinhold, 1976.

Bengtson, V. L., Olander, E., & Haddad, A. "The generation gap" and aging family members: Toward a conceptual model. In J. F. Gubrium (Ed.), *Time, self, and roles in old age.* New York: Behavioral, 1976.

Bennett, J. W. Individual perspective in fieldwork. In R. N. Adams & J. J. Preiss (Eds.), *Human organization research.* Homewood, Ill.: Dorsey, 1960.

Benson, R. C. *Handbook of obstetrics and gynecology.* Los Altos, Calif: Lange Medical Publications, 1974.

Berelson, B., & Steiner, G. A. *Human behavior.* New York: Harcourt, Brace & World, 1964.

Berger, B., Hackett, B., Cavan, S., Zicklin, G., Millar, M., Noble, M., Thieman, S., Frarrell, R., & Rosenbluth, B. Child rearing practices of the communal family. In D. Flapan (Ed.), *American social institutions.* New York: Behavioral Publications, 1972.

Berle, B. B., & Javert, C. T. Stress and habitual abortion. *Obstetrics and Gynecology*, 1954, *3*, 298.

Bernard, J. *The future of marriage.* New York: World, 1973.

Bernard, J., & Sontag, L. W. Fetal reactivity to tonal stimulation: A preliminary report. *Journal of Genetic Psychology*, 1947, *70*, 205-210.

Bernstein, A. C. How children learn about sex and birth. *Psychology Today*, 1976, pp. 31-35.

Berreman, G. D. Behind many masks (Monograph No. 4, Society for Applied Anthropology). Ithaca, N.Y.: Cornell University Press, 1962.

Best, C. H., & Taylor, N. B. *The physiological basis of medical practice.* Baltimore: Williams & Wilkins, 1955.

Bijou, S. W. The mentally retarded child. *Psychology Today*, 1968, *2*, 46-51.

Biller, H. B. The mother-child relationship and the father-absent boy's personality development. *Merrill-Palmer Quarterly*, 1971, 17, 227-241.

Biller, H. B., & Weiss, S. D. The father-daughter relationship and the personality development of the female. *Journal of Genetic Psychology*, 1970, *114*, 79-93.

Birch, H. G. Health and the education of socially disadvantaged children. *Developmental Medicine and Child Neurology*, 1968, *10*, 580-599.

Birch, H., & Gussow, J. *Disadvantaged children: Health, nutrition, and school failure.* New York: Harcourt Brace Jovanovich, 1970.

Birren, J. E. Principles of research on aging. In J. E. Birren (Ed.), *Handbook of aging and the individual.* Chicago: University of Chicago Press, 1959.

Birren, J. E. *The psychology of aging.* Englewood Cliffs, N.J.: Prentice-Hall, 1964.

Birren, J. E. Age and decision strategies. In A. T. Welford & J. E. Birren (Eds.), *Decision making and age.* Basel: Karger, 1969.

Birren, J. E., & Bernstein, L. Health and aging in our society: Perspectives on mortality and the emergence of geriatrics. *Transactions of the Association of Life Insurance Medical Directors of America,* 1978, *62*, 135-152.

Birren, J. E., Butler, R. W., Greenhouse, S. W., Sokoloff, L., & Yarrow, M. R. (Eds.). *Human aging: A biological and behavioral study.* Washington, D.C.: U.S. Government Printing Office, 1963.

Birren, J. E., & Gribbin, K. The elderly. In D. Spiegel & P. Keith-Spiegel (Eds.), *Outsiders USA.* San Francisco: Rinehart, 1973.

Birren, J. E., & Renner, V. J. Concepts and issues of mental health and aging. In J. E. Birren and R. B. Sloane (Eds.), *Handbook of mental health and aging.* New York: Van Nostrand Reinhold, 1980.

Birren, J. E., Schapiro, H. B., & Miller, J. H. The effect of salicylate upon pain sensitivity. *Journal of Pharmacology and Experimental Therapy*, 1950, *100*, 67-71.

Birren, J. E., & Sloane, R. B. (Eds.). *Handbook of mental health and aging.* New York: Van Nostrand Reinhold, 1980.

Bischoff, L. J. *Adult psychology.* New York: Harper & Row, 1969.

Blank, M., & Solomon, F. A tutorial language program to develop abstract thinking in socially disadvantaged preschool children. *Child Development*,

1968, *39*, 379-389.

Blau, Z. S. *Old age in a changing society.* New York: Franklin Watts, 1973.

Bloom, B. S. *Stability and change in human characteristics.* New York: Wiley, 1964.

Bloom, L. *Language development: Form and function in emerging grammars.* Cambridge, Mass.: MIT Press, 1970.

Bloomfield, L. *Language.* New York: Holt, 1933.

Bock, D. R., & Kolakowski, D. Further evidence of sex-linked major-gene influence on human spatial visualizing ability. *American Journal of Human Genetics,* 1973, *25,* 1-14.

Bodmer, W. F., & Cavalli-Sforza, L. L. Intelligence and race. *Scientific American,* 1970, *223,* 19-29.

Bogen, J. E. The other side of the brain. I, II, III. *Bulletin of the Los Angeles Neurological Society,* 1969, *34,* 73-105; 135-162; 191-220.

Bogen, J. E., DeZure, R., Tenhouten, W. D., & March, J. F. The other side of the brain. IV. The A/P ratio. *Bulletin of the Los Angeles Neurological Society,* 1972, *37,* 49-61.

Bortner, R. W., & Hultsch, D. F. Personal time perspective in adulthood. *Developmental Psychology,* 1972, *7,* 98-104.

Bossard, J. H. S., & Boll, E. S. *The sociology of child development* (4th ed.). New York: Harper & Row, 1966.

Boston Children's Medical Center. *Pregnancy, birth, and the newborn baby: A complete guide for parents and parents-to-be.* Boston: Delacorte Press/Seymour Lawrence, 1971.

Bourliere, F., Cendron, H., & Rapaport, A. Modification avec l'age des seuils gustatifs de perception et de reconnaissance aux saveurs salée et sucrée, chez l'homme. *Gerontologia,* 1958, *2,* 104-112.

Bower, T. G. R. Stimulus variables determining space perception in infants. *Science,* 1965, *149,* 88-89.

Bower, T. G. R. Slant perception and shape constancy in infants. *Science,* 1966, *151,* 832-834.

Bower, T. G. R. *A primer of infant development.* San Francisco: Freeman, 1977.

Bowerman, C. E., & Elder, G. H. Variations in adolescent perception of family power structure. *American Sociological Review,* 1964, *29,* 551-567.

Bowers, P., & London, L. Developmental correlates of role-playing ability. *Child Development,* 1965, *36,* 449-508.

Bowes, W. A. Obstetrical medication and infant outcome: A review of the literature. *Monograph of the Society for Research in Child Development,* 1970, *35* (4, Serial No. 137).

Bowes, W., Brackbill, Y., Conway, E., & Steinschneider, A. The effects of obstetrical medication on fetus and infant. *Monograph of the Society for Research in Child Development,* 1970, *35* (4, Serial No. 137).

Bowlby, J. *Attachment and loss: Attachment* (Vol. 1). New York: Basic Books, 1969.

Bragg, B. W. E., Ostrowski, M. V., & Finley, G. E. The effects of birth order and age of target on use of persuasive techniques. *Child Development,* 1973, *44,* 351-354.

Braidwood, R. J. The agricultural revolution. *Scientific American,* September 1960.

Braine, M. D. S. The ontogeny of English phrase structure: The first phase. *Language,* 1963, *39,* 1-13.

Braine, M. D. S. On the basis of phrase structure: A reply to Bever, Fodor, and Weksel. *Psychological Review,* 1965, *72,* 483-492.

Brazelton, T. B. Psychophysiologic reactions in the neonate: II. Effect of maternal medication on the neonate and his behavior. *Journal of Pediatrics,* 1961, *58,* 513-518.

Bresler, D. E., Ellison, G., & Zamenhof, S. Learning deficits in rats with malnourished grandmothers. *Developmental Psychobiology,* 1975, *8,* 315-323.

Brim, O. G., Jr. Adolescent personality as self-other systems. *Journal of Marriage and the Family,* 1965, *27,* 156-162.

Brim, O. G., Jr. Socialization through the life cycle. In O. G. Brim, Jr., & S. Wheeler (Eds.), *Socialization after childhood: Two essays.* New York: Wiley, 1966.

Brim, O. G., Jr. Adult socialization. In J. A. Clausen (Ed.), *Socialization and society.* Boston: Little, Brown, 1968.

Brim, O. G., Jr., & Wheeler, S. *Socialization after childhood.* New York: Wiley, 1966.

Brodsky, C. M. *A study of norms for body form-behavior relationships.* Washington, D.C.: Catholic University Press, 1954.

Brody, E. M. The transition from extended families to nuclear families. In R. H. Williams, C. Tibbits, & W. Donahue (Eds.), *Processes of aging* (Vol. 2). New York: Atherton, 1963.

Bromley, D. B. *The psychology of human aging.* Middlesex, England: Penguin, 1974.

Bronfenbrenner, U. The changing American child—A speculative analysis. *Merrill-Palmer Quarterly,*

1961, 7, 73-84.

Bronfenbrenner, U. The psychological costs of quality and equality in education. *Child Development*, 1967, *38*, 909-925.

Bronfenbrenner, U. Reality and research in the ecology of human development. *Proceedings of the American Philosophical Society*, 1975, *119*, 439-469.

Bronson, G. W. Infants' reactions to an unfamiliar person. In L. J. Stone, H. T. Smith, & L. B. Murphy (Eds.), *The competent infant.* New York: Basic Books, 1973.

Bronson, W. C. Early antecedents of emotional expressiveness and reactivity control. In M. C. Jones, N. Bayley, J. W. McFarlane, & M. P. Honzik (Eds.), *The course of human development.* Waltham, Mass.: Xerox College, 1971.

Broverman, D. M., Klaiber, E. L., Kobayashi, Y., & Vogel, W. Roles of activation and inhibition in sex differences in cognitive abilities. *Psychological Review*, 1968, *75*, 23-50.

Broverman, I. K., Broverman, D. M., Clarkson, F. E., Rosenkrantz, P. S., & Vogel, S. R. Sex-role stereotypes and clinical judgments of mental health. *Journal of Consulting and Clinical Psychology*, 1970, *34*, 1-7.

Broverman, I. K., Vogel, S. R., Broverman, D. K., Clarkson, F. E., & Rosenkrantz, P. S. Sex-role stereotypes: A current appraisal. *Journal of Social Issues*, 1972, *28*, 59-78.

Brown, A., & Campione, J. Recognition memory for pictures in preschool children. *Journal of Experimental Psychology*, 1972, *95*, 55-62.

Brown, A., & Scott, M. Recognition memory for pictures in preschool children. *Journal of Experimental Child Psychology*, 1971, *11*, 401-412.

Brown, R. *Psycholinguistics: Selected papers of Roger Brown.* New York: Free Press, 1970.

Brown, R., Cazden, C. M., & Bellugi-Klima, V. The child's grammar from I to III. In J. P. Hill (Ed.), *Minnesota Symposium.* Minneapolis: University of Minnesota Press, 1969.

Brown, R., & Lenneberg, E. H. A study in language and cognition. *Journal of Abnormal and Social Psychology*, 1954, *49*, 454-462.

Brueckner, G. H. Untersuchungen zur Tierziologie, inbesondre der Aufloesung der Familie. *Zeitschrift für Psychologie*, 1933, *128*, 1-120.

Bruhn, J. G. an ecological perspective of aging. *Gerontologist*, 1971, *11*, 318-321.

Bruner, J. S. On knowing: Essays for the left hand. Cambridge: Harvard University Press, 1962.

Bruner, J. S., Oliver, R., Greenfield, P. M. (Eds.) *Studies in cognitive growth.* New York: Wiley, 1966.

Buffery, A. W. H. Sex differences in the development of hemispheric asymmetry of function of the human brain. *Brain Research*, 1971, *31*, 364-365.

Caldwell, B. M. The development of social behavior. *American Psychologist*, 1961, *16*, 377.

Callaway, E. *Brain electrical potentials and individual psychological differences.* New York: Grune & Stratton, 1975.

Cameron, J., Livson, N., & Bayley, N. Infant vocalizations and their relation to mature intelligence. *Science*, 1967, *157*, 331-333.

Campbell, D. T., & Stanley, J. C. Experimental and quasi-experimental designs for research on teaching. In N. L. Gage (Ed.), *Handbook for research on teaching.* Chicago: Rand McNally, 1963.

Campbell, R. F. Tomorrow's teacher. *Saturday Review*, January 14, 1967, 60-73.

Campos, J. J., Langer, A., & Krorowitz, A. Cardiac responses on the visual cliff in prelocomotor human infants. *Science*, 1970, *170*, 196-197.

Carey, S. Cognitive competence. In K. Connolly & J. Bruner (Eds.), *The growth of competence.* New York: Academic, 1974.

Carlsmith, L. Effect of early father absence on scholastic aptitude. *Harvard Educational Review*, 1964, *34*, 3-21.

Carp, F. M. Person-situation congruence in engagement. *Gerontologist*, 1968, *8*, 184-188.

Carter, H. D. Twin similarities in emotional traits. *Character and Personality*, 1935, *4*, 61-78.

Carter, L. J. Auto safety: Coleman to act on controversial air bag issue. *Science*, 1976, *103*, 1219-1222.

Cartwright, D. S. *Introduction to personality.* New York: Rand McNally, 1974.

Casler, L. Maternal deprivation: A critical review of the literature. *Monographs of the Society for Research in Child Development*, 1961, *26*, 1-64.

Cattell, R. B. *Handbook for the IPAT Anxiety Scale.* Champaign, Ill.: Institute for Personality and Ability Testing, 1957.

Cattell, R. B. *Personality and motivation: Structure and measurement.* Yonkers-on-Hudson, N.Y.: World, 1957.

Cattell, R. B. *The scientific analysis of personality.* Baltimore: Penguin, 1965.

Cattell, R. B. *Abilities: Their structure, growth and action.* Boston: Houghton Mifflin, 1971.

Cattell, R. B., Eber, E. W., & Tatsuoka, M. M. *Handbook for the Sixteen Personality Factor Questionnaire.* Champaign, Ill.: Institute for Personality and Ability Testing, 1970.

Caudill, W., & Plath, D. W. Who sleeps by whom? Parent-child involvement in urban Japanese families. *Psychiatry,* 1966, *29,* 344-366.

Caudill, W., & Weinstein, H. Maternal care and infant behavior in Japanese and American urban middle class families. In R. Konig & R. Hill (Eds.), *Yearbook of the International Sociological Association,* 1966.

Cavan, S. R. Speculations on innovations to conventional marriage in old age. *Gerontologist,* 1973, *13,* 409-411.

Cazden, C. *Environmental assistance to the child's acquisition of grammar.* Unpublished doctoral dissertation, Harvard University, 1965.

Chapman, W. P. Measurements of pain sensitivity in normal control subjects and in psychoneurotic patients. *Psychosomatic Medicine,* 1944, *6,* 252-255.

Chess, S., Korn, S. J., & Fernandez, P. B. *Psychiatric disorders of children with congenital rubella.* New York: Brunner/Mazel, 1971.

Chiarelli, A. B. Comparative cytogenetics in primates and its relevance for human cytogenetics. In A. B. Chiarelli (Ed.), *Comparative genetics in monkeys, apes, and man.* New York: Academic, 1971.

Child, I. L. Relation of somatotype and self-ratings on Sheldon's temperamental traits. *Journal of Personality,* 1950, *18,* 440-453.

Child, I. L. Socialization. In G. Lindzey (Ed.), *Handbook of social psychology.* Reading, Mass.: Addison-Wesley, 1954.

Chomsky, C. S. *The acquisition of syntax in children from 5 to 10.* Cambridge, Mass.: MIT Press, 1969.

Chomsky, N. *Syntactic structures.* The Hague: Mouton, 1957.

Chomsky, N. *Aspects of the theory of syntax.* Cambridge, Mass.: MIT Press, 1965.

Chomsky, N., & Halle, M. *The sound pattern of English.* New York: Harper & Row, 1968.

Chwast, J. Sociopathic behavior in children. In B. B. Wolman (Ed.), *Manual of child psychopathology.* New York: McGraw-Hill, 1972.

Clark, A. W., & Van Sommers, P. Contradictory demands in family relations and adjustments to school and home. *Human Relations,* 1961, *14,* 97-111.

Clark, M., & Anderson, B. *Culture and aging.* Springfield, Ill.: Charles C. Thomas, 1967.

Clark, M., Gosnell, M., & Coppola, V. A gonorrhea vaccine? *Newsweek,* August 6, 1979, p. 83.

Clark, M., Kager, M., & Shapiro, D. Epidemic of senility. *Newsweek,* November 5, 1979, p. 95.

Cohen, D. J., Dibble, E., Grawe, J. M., & Pollin, W. Separating identical from fraternal twins. *Archieves of General Psychiatry,* 1973, *29,* 465-470

Coleman, J. *The adolescent society.* New York: Free Press, 1961.

Collins, J. K., & Thomas, N. T. Age and susceptibility to same-sex peer pressure. *British Journal of Educational Psychology,* 1972, *42,* 83-85.

Comalli, P. E., Jr. Life span changes in visual perception. In L. R. Goulet & P. B. Baltes (Eds.), *Life span developmental psychology: Research and theory.* New York: Academic, 1970, pp. 211-227.

Comfort, A. Likelihood of human pheromones, *Nature,* 1971, *230,* 432-433.

Conel, J. L. *Postnatal development of the human cerebral cortex* (Vols. 1-6). Cambridge: Harvard University Press, 1939-1963.

Connolly, K. J., & Bruner, J. S. Competence: Its nature and nurture. In K. Connolly & J. Bruner (Eds.), *The growth of competence.* New York: Academic, 1974.

Cooper, R., & Zubek, J. Effects of enriched and restricted early environments on the learning ability of bright and dull rats. *Canadian Journal of Psychology,* 1958, *12,* 159-164.

Coppen, A. J. Psychosomatic aspects of pre-eclamptic toxaemia. *Journal of Psychosomatic Research,* 1958, *2,* 241-265.

Cornell, E., & Gottfried, A. W. Intervention with premature infants. *Child Development,* 1976, *47,* 32-39.

Cosh, J. A. Studies on the nature of vibration sense. *Clinical Science,* 1958, *12,* 131-151.

Costa, P. T. *Age differences in the structure of 16 PF surface traits.* Paper presented at the Eighty-First Annual Meeting of the American Psychological Association, Montreal, 1973.

Cowan, M. The development of the brain. *Scientific American,* 1979, *241,* 112-133.

Crain, A. J., & Stamm, C. S. Intermittent absence

of fathers and children's perceptions of parents. *Journal of Marriage and the Family*, 1965, *27*, 344-347.

Cravioto, J., DeLicardie, E. R., & Birch, H. G. Nutrition, growth and neuro-integrative development: An experimental and ecologic study. *Pediatrics*, 1966, *38*, 319.

Cravioto, J., & Robles, B. Evolution of adaptive and motor behavior during rehabilitation from kwashiorkor. *American Journal of Orthopsychiatry*, 1965, *35*, 449.

Cropley, A. J. Creativity, intelligence, and intellectual style. *Australian Journal of Education*, 1969, *13*, 3-7.

Cropley, A. J., & Field, T. W. Intellectual style and high school science. *Nature*, 1968, *217*, 1211-1212.

Culliton, B. J. Penicillin-resistant gonorrhea: New strain spreading worldwide. *Science*, 1976, *194*, 1395-1397.

Cumming, E. Further thoughts on the theory of disengagement. *UNESCO International Social Studies Journal*, 1963, 15, 382.

Cumming, E., & Henry, W. *Growing old: The process of disengagement.* New York: Basic Books, 1961.

Cunningham, W. R. *Age changes in the factor structure of intellectual abilities in adulthood and old age.* Unpublished doctoral dissertation, University of Southern California, 1974.

Curtiss, S., Fromkin, V., Rigler, D., Rigler, M., & Krashen, S. An update on the linguistic development of Genie. In D. P. Dado (Ed.), *Developmental psycholinguistics: Theory and applications.* Washington, D.C.: Georgetown University Press, 1975. (Georgetown University Roundtable on Languages and Linguistics)

Cutler, B. R., & Dyer, W. G. Initial adjustment process in young married couples. *Social Forces*, 1965, *44*, 195-201.

Cutler, N. E., & Harootyan, R. A. Demography of the aged. In D. S. Woodruff & J. E. Birren (Eds.), *Aging: Scientific Perspective and Social Issues.* New York: Van Nostrand Reinhold, 1975.

Dale, P. S. *Language development: Structure and function.* Hinsdale, Ill.: Dryden, 1972.

Darwin, C. *Origin of species.* New York: Philosophical Library, 1951. (Originally published, 1859.)

Davids, A., Holden, R. H., & Gray, G. B. Maternal anxiety during pregnancy and adequacy of mother and child adjustment eight months following childbirth. *Child Development*, 1963, *34*, 993-1002.

Davids, A., Spencer, E., & Talmadge, M. Anxiety, pregnancy, and childbirth abnormalities. *Journal of Consulting Psychology*, 1961, *25*, 74-77.

Davidson, M. A., McInness, R. G., & Parnell, R. W. Distribution of personality traits in seven-year-old children: A combined psychological, psychiatric, and somatotype study. *British Journal of Educational Psychology*, 1957, *27*, 48-61.

Davison, A. N., & Dobbing, J. Myelination as a vulnerable period in brain development. *British Medical Bulletin*, 1966, *22*, 40-44.

Davison, K., & Bagley, C. R. Schizophrenia-like psychoses associated with organic disorders of the central nervous system: A review of the literature. In R. N. Herrington (Ed.), *Current problems in psychiatry* (*British Journal of Psychiatry* Special Publication No. 4). Ashford, Kent: Headley, 1969.

Dayton, G. O., Jr., Jones, M. H., Aiu, P., Rawson, R. H., Steele, B., & Rose, M. Developmental study of coordinated eye movements in the human infant. I. Visual acuity in the newborn human: A study based on induced optokinetic nystagmus recorded by electro-oculography. *Archives of Opthalmology*, 1964, *71*, 865-870.

deFries, J. C. Paper for the C.O.B.R.E. Research Workshop on Genetic Endowment and Environment in the Determination of Behavior, October 1971, 3-8, Rye, N.Y.

Dejnozka, E. L. School board members: Their opinions, status, and financial willingness. *Journal of Educational Sociology*, 1963, *36*, 193-199.

Delgado, J. M. R. Emotional behavior in animals and humans. In L. J. West & M. Greenblatt. *Explorations in the physiology of emotions* (*Psychiatric Research Report*, No. 12, American Psychiatric Association), 1960.

Dennis, W. Age and achievement: A critique. *Journal of Gerontology*, 1956, *11*, 331-333.

Dennis, W. Environmental influences upon motor development. In *Readings in Child Psychology* (2nd ed.). Englewood Cliffs. N.J.: Prentice-Hall, 1963.

Denny, N. Classification abilities in the elderly. *Journal of Gerontology*, 1974, *29*, 309-314.

DeVos, G., & Hippler, A. Cultural psychology: Comparative studies of human behavior. In G.

Lindzey & E. Aronson (Eds.), *Handbook of social psychology* (Vol. 4). Reading, Mass.: Addison-Wesley, 1969.

DiCara, L. V., & Miller, N. E. Instrumental learning of vasomotor responses by rats: Learning to respond differentially in the two ears. *Science,* 1968, *159,* 1485-1486.

Dickstein, L. S., & Brown, N. Effect of role orientation and instructions regarding competition on cognitive performance of college females. *Psychological Reports,* 1974, *34,* 291-297.

Dodge, J. A. Psychosomatic aspects of infantile pyloric stenosis. *Journal of Psychosomatic Research,* 1972, *16,* 105.

Dohrenwend, B. S. Life events as stressors: a methodological inquiry. *Journal of Health and Social Behavior,* 1973, *14,* 167-175.

Douvan, E., & Adelson, J. *The adolescent experience.* New York: Wiley, 1966.

Drell, S. D., & von Hippel, F. Limited nuclear war. *Scientific American,* 1976, *235,* 28-37.

Drillien, C. *The growth and development of the prematurely born infant.* Baltimore: Williams & Wilkins, 1964.

Dubos, R. Biological individuality. *Columbia Forum,* 1969, *12,* 5-10.

Dubos, R. *A god within.* New York: Scribner, 1972.

Duvall, E. M. *Family development* (4th ed.). Philadelphia: Lippincott, 1971.

Eckensberger, L. H. Methodological issues of cross-cultural research in developmental psychology. In J. R. Nesselroade & H. W. Reese (Eds.), *Life-span developmental psychology: Methodological issues.* New York: Academic, 1973.

Edwards, A. L. *Manual for the Edwards Personal Preference Schedule.* New York: Psychological Corporation, 1959.

Ehrhardt, A. A., & Money, J. Progestin induced hermaphroditism: IQ and psychosexual identity in a study of ten girls. *The Journal of Sex Research,* 1967, *3,* 83-100.

Eibl-Eibesfeldt, I. *Ethology, the biology of behavior.* New York: Holt, 1970.

Eichorn, D. H. Biological correlates of behavior. In H. W. Stevenson (Ed.), *Child psychology.* Chicago: University of Chicago Press, 1963.

Eimas, P. D. Auditory and phonetic coding of the cues for speech: Discrimination of the (r-l) distinction by young infants. *Perception and Psychophysics,* 1975, *18,* 341-347.

Eimas, P. D. Speech and perception in early infancy. In L. B. Cohen & P. Salapatek (Eds.), *Infant perception: From sensation to cognition. Vol. 2. Perception of space, speech, and sound.* New York: Academic, 1975.

Eimas, P. D., Siqueland, E. R., Juscyk, P., & Vigorito, J. Speech perception in infants. *Science,* 1971, *171,* 303-306.

Eisner, D. *Age changes in perceptual functioning in the aged.* Unpublished master's thesis, West Virginia University, 1968.

Ekman, P., Friessen, W. V., & Ellsworth, P. *Emotion in the human face.* New York: Pergamon, 1972.

Ellingson, R. J. Study of brain electrical activity in infants. In L. P. Lipsitt & C. C. Spiker (Eds.), *Advances in child development and behavior.* New York: Academic, 1967.

Emmerich, W. Socialization and sex-role development. In P. B. Baltes & K. W. Schaie (Eds.), *Life-span developmental psychology: Personality and socialization.* New York: Academic, 1973.

Engen, T., Cain, W. S., & Rovee, C. K. Direct scaling of olfaction in the newborn infant and the adult human observer. In N. Tanyolac (Ed.), *Theories of odor and odor measurement.* Istanbul, Turkey: Robert College, 1968.

Engen, T., Lipsitt, L. P., & Kaye, H. Developmental changes in the olfactory threshold of the neonate. *Child Development,* 1963, *34,* 371-376.

Erikson, E. *Childhood and society.* New York: Norton, 1950, 1963, 1964.

Erikson, E. Identity and the life cycle. *Psychological Issues,* 1959, *1* (Whole No. 1).

Erikson, E. *Identity: Youth and crisis.* New York: Norton, 1968.

Erlenmeyer-Kimling, L., & Jarvik, L. F. Genetics and intelligence: A review. *Science,* 1963, *142,* 1477-1479.

Ertl, J. P. Evoked potentials and intelligence. *Revue de l'Université d'Ottawa,* 1966, *36,* 599-607.

Ervin, S. Imitation and structural change in children's language. In E. H. Lenneberg (Ed.), *New directions in the study of language.* Cambridge, Mass.: MIT Press, 1964.

Estvan, F. J. Relationship of nursery school children's social perceptions as to sex, race, social status and age. *Journal of Genetic Psychology*, 1965, *107*, 295-308.

Everitt, A. V., & Burgess, J. A. (Eds.) *Hypothalamus pituitary and aging.* Springfield, Ill.: Charles C. Thomas, 1976.

Eysenck, H. J. *The scientific study of personality.* London: Routledge & Kegan Paul, 1952.

Eysenck, H. J. *The biological basis of personality.* Springfield, Ill.: Charles C. Thomas, 1967.

Eysenck, M. W. Age differences in incidental learning. *Developmental Psychology*, *1974, 10*, 936-941.

Falade, S. *Le développement psycho-moteur de jeune Africain originaire du Sénégal au cours de la première année.* Paris: Foulon, 1955.

Falkner, F. General considerations in human development. In F. Falkner (Ed.), *Human development.* Philadelphia: Saunders, 1966.

Fantz, R. L. Visual perception from birth as shown by pattern selectivity. *Annals of the New York Academy of Sciences*, 1965, *118*, 793-814.

Faust, M. S. Developmental maturity as a determinant in prestige of adolescent girls. *Child Development*, 1969, *31*, 173-184.

Feldman, H. *Development of the husband-wife relationship.* New York: Cornell University Press, 1964.

Ferreira, A. J. Emotional factors in prenatal environment: A review. *Journal of Nervous and Mental Disorders*, 1965, *141*, 108-118.

Field, T. W., & Poole, M. G. Intellectual style and achievement of arts and science undergraduates. *British Journal of Educational Psychology*, 1970, *40*, 338-341.

Fish, B. Visual-motor disorders in infants at risk for schizophrenia. *Archives of General Psychiatry*, 1973, *28*, 900-904.

Fish, B. Biologic antecedents of psychosis in children. In D. X. Freedman (Ed.), *Biology of the major psychoses.* New York: Raven, 1975.

Flavell, J. H. *The developmental psychology of Jean Piaget.* New York: Van Nostrand, 1963.

Flavell, J. Cognitive changes in adulthood. In P. B. Baltes & L. R. Goulet (Eds.), *Life-span developmental psychology.* New York: Academic, 1970.

Frankenhaeuser, M., Mallis, I., Rissler, A., Bjorkvall, C., & Patkai, P. Catecholamine excretion as related to cognitive and emotional reaction patterns. *Psychosomatic Medicine*, 1968, *30*, 109-120.

Frankl, V. E. *Man's search for meaning.* New York: Simon & Schuster, 1962.

Freedman, D. An ethological approach to the genetical study of human behavior. In S. G. Vandenberg (Ed.), *Methods and goals in human behavior genetics.* New York: Academic, 1965.

Freedman, D. G. Smiling in blind infants and the issue of innate vs. acquired. *Journal of Child Psychology and Psychiatry*, 1964, *5*, 171–184.

Freedman, J. L., Klevansky, S., & Ehrlich, P. The effect of crowding on human task performance. *Journal of Applied Social Psychology*, 1971, *1*, 7-25.

Freedman, R., & Coombs, L. Child spacing and family economic position. *American Sociological Review*, 1966, *31*, 631-648.

Frenkel, J. K. Toxoplasma in and around us. *BioScience*, 1973, *23* (6).

Frenkel-Brunswick, E. Motivation and behavior. *Genetic Psychology Monographs*, *26*, 121-265.

Freud, S. *The ego and the id.* New York: Norton, 1962. (Originally published, 1923.)

Freud, S. New introductory lectures on psycho-analysis. In J. Strachey (Ed.), *The standard edition of the complete psychological works of Sigmund Freud* (Vol. 22). London: Hogarth, 1964. (Originally published, 1933.)

Freud, S. *A general introduction to psychoanalysis.* New York: Liveright, 1935.

Friedenberg, E. Z. *Coming of age in America: Growth and acquiescence.* New York: Random House, 1959.

Friedman, M., & Rosenman, R. H. *Type A behavior and your heart.* New York: Knopf, 1974.

Frisch, R. E. A method of prediction of age of menarche from height and weight at ages 9 through 13 years. *Pediatrics*, 1974, *53*, 384-390.

Fromkin, V., Krashen, S., Curtiss, S., Rigler, D., & Rigler, M. The development of language in Genie: a case of language acquisition beyond the "critical period." *Brain and Language*, 1974, *1*, 81-107.

Fromm, E. *Man for himself.* New York: Rinehart, 1947.

Fuller, J. L., & Clark, L. D. Genotype and behavioral vulnerability to isolation in dogs. *Journal of Comparative and Physiological Psychology*, 1968, *66*, 151-156.

Fuller, J. L., & Thompson, W. R. *Behavior Genetics.* New York: Wiley, 1960.

Funkenstein, D. H., King, S. H., & Drolette, M. E.

Mastery of stress. Cambridge: Harvard University Press, 1957.

Gagné, R. W. *The conditions of learning.* New York: Holt, 1970.

Galebski, A. Vestibular nystagmus in newborn infants. *Acta Oto-laryngologica,* Stockholm, 1928, *11,* 409-423.

Galin, D., & Ornstein, R. Hemispheric specialization and the duality of consciousness. In H. Widroe (Ed.), *Human behavior and brain function.* Springfield, Ill.: Charles C. Thomas, 1973.

Garber, H. L., & Heber, F. R. *The Milwaukee Project: Indications of the effectiveness of early intervention to prevent mental retardation.* Paper presented at the Fourth International Congress, of the International Association for the Scientific Study of Mental Deficiency, Washington, D.C., August 1976.

Garcia, J., Hankins, W. G., & Rusiniak, K. W. Behavioral regulation of the *milieu interne* in man and rat. *Science,* 1974, *185,* 824-831.

Garcia, J., & Koelling, R. Relation of cue to consequence in avoidance learning. *Psychonomic Science,* 1966, *4,* 123-124.

Gardner, L. I. Deprivation dwarfism. In *The nature and nurture of behavior: developmental psychobiology.* San Francisco: Freeman, 1973.

Geber, M., & Dean, R. F. A. The state of development of newborn African children. *Lancet,* 1957, *1,* 1216. (a)

Geber, M., & Dean, R. F. A. Gesell tests on African children. *Pediatrics,* 1957, *30,* 1055-1065. (b)

Gelfand, D. M. *Social learning in childhood.* Belmont, Calif.: Brooks Cole, 1975.

Gerard, D. L., & Phillips, L. Relation of social attainment to psychological and adrenocortical and reactions to stress. *AMA Archives of Neurology and Psychiatry,* 1953, *69,* 350-354.

Geschwind, N., & Levitsky, W. Human brain: Left-right asymmetries in temporal speech region. *Science,* 1968, *161,* 186-187.

Gesell, A. *Infancy and human growth.* New York: Macmillan, 1928.

Gesell, A., & Amatruda, C. S. *Developmental diagnosis.* New York: Hoeber, 1941.

Gesell, A., & Ilg, F. L. *Infant and child in the culture of today.* New York: Harper & Brothers, 1943.

Gewirtz, J. L. Mechanisms of social learning: Some roles of stimulation and behavior in early human development. In D. A. Goslin (Ed.), *Handbook of socialization theory and research.* Chicago: Rand McNally, 1969.

Gibson, E. J., & Walk, R. D. The "visual cliff." *Scientific American,* 1960, *202,* 64-71.

Gibson, J. J., & Gibson, E. J. Perceptual learning: Differentiation or enrichment. *Psychological Review,* 1955, *62,* 32-41.

Ginsburg, H., & Opper, A. *Piaget's theory of intellectual development: An introduction.* Englewood Cliffs, N. J.: Prentice-Hall, 1969.

Gladstone, W. E. *Studies on Homer and the homeric age* (Vol. 3). Oxford: Oxford University Press, 1858, pp. 457-499.

Goetzel, T. Generational conflict and social change. *Youth and Society,* 1972, *3,* 327-352.

Golde, P., & Kogan, N. A sentence completion procedure for assessing attitudes toward old people. *Journal of Gerontology,* 1959, *14,* 355-363.

Goodenough, D. R., Gandini, E., Olkin, I., Pizzamiglio, L., Thayer, D., & Witkin, H. A. A study of X-chromosome linkage with field dependence and spatial visualization. *Behavior Genetics,* 1977, *7,* 373-387.

Goodwin, M., Gooding, K. M., & Regnier, F. Sex pheromone in the dog. *Science,* 1979, *203,* 559-561.

Gordon, C. Development of evaluated role identities. *Annual Review of Sociology,* 1976, *2,* 405-433.

Gorman, J. J., Cogan, D. G., & Gillis, S. S. An apparatus for grading the visual acuity in infants on the basis of opticokinetic nystagmus. *Pediatrics,* 1957, *19,* 1088-1092.

Gottesman, I. L. Heritability of personality: A demonstration. *Psychological Monographs,* 1963, *77,* (Whole No. 9).

Gottlieb, G. The call of the duck. *Natural History,* October 1977, 40, 44, 46.

Gough, H. G. *Manual for the California Psychological Inventory.* Palo Alto, Calif.: Consulting Psychologists, 1964.

Gradey, K. L., Phoenix, C. H., & Young, W. C. Role of the developing rat testis in differentiation of the neural tissues mediating mating behavior. *Journal of Comparative and Physiological Psychology,* 1965, *59,* 176-182.

Granick, S., & Patterson, R. D. (Eds.), *Human aging II: An eleven-year followup biomedical and behavioral study* (Publication No. (HSM) 71-9037). Washington, D.C.: U.S. Government Printing Office, 1971.

Greenough, W. T. Experiential modifications of the developing brain. In I. L. Janis (Ed.), *Current trends in psychology: Readings from American Scientist.* Los Altos, Calif.: William Kaufman, 1977.

Gregory, R. L., & Wallace, J. G. Recovery from early blindness: A case study. *Experimental Psychology Society Monographs* (Cambridge), 1963 (No. 2).

Griffitt, W. B. Personality similarity and self-concept as determinants of interpersonal attraction. *Journal of Social Psychology,* 1969, *78,* 137-146.

Grimwade, J. C., et al. Human fetal heartrate change and movement in response to sound and vibration. *American Journal of Obstetrics and Gynecology,* 1971, *109,* 89-90.

Groen, J. J. Postnatal changes in vestibular reactions, *Acta Oto-Laryngologica, Stockholm,* 1963, *56,* 390-396.

Groff, P. J. The social status of teachers. *Journal of Educational Sociology,* 1962, *36,* 20-25.

Grosch, D. S., & Hopwood, L. E. *Biological effects of radiation* (2nd ed.). New York: Academic, 1979.

Gruman, G. J. *A history of ideas about the prolongation of life: The evolution of prolongevity hypotheses to 1800.* Philadelphia: American Philosophical Society, 1966.

Guilford, J. P. *Personality.* New York: McGraw-Hill, 1959. (a)

Guilford, J. P. Three faces of intellect. *American Psychologist,* 1959, *14,* 469-479. (b)

Guilford, J. P. *The nature of human intelligence.* New York: McGraw-Hill, 1967.

Gustavson, C. R., Garcia, J., Hankins, W. G., & Rusiniak, K. W. Coyote predation control by aversive conditioning. *Science,* 1974, *184,* 581-583.

Guth, S. K., Eastman, A. A., & McNelis, J. F. Lighting requirements for older workers. *Illumination Engineering,* 1956, *51,* 656-660.

Guthrie, E. R. *The psychology of learning* (rev. ed.). New York: Harper, 1952.

Gutmann, D. L. Dependency, illness and survival among Navajo men. In E. Palmore & F. C. Jeffers (Eds.), *Prediction of life span.* Lexington, Mass.: Heath, 1971.

Haan, N., & Day, D. A longitudinal study of change and sameness in personality development, adolescence to later adulthood. *Aging and Human Development,* 1974, *5,* 11-39.

Haber, A., and Runyon, R. P., *Fundamentals of psychology.* Reading, Mass.: Addison-Wesley, 1974.

Hagen, J. W. Some thoughts on how children learn to remember. *Human Development,* 1971, *14,* 262-271.

Hailman, J. How an instinct is learned. *Scientific American,* 1969, *221*(6), 98-106.

Haith, M. M. The response of the human newborn to visual movement. *Journal of Experimental Child Psychology,* 1966, *3,* 235-243.

Haith, M. M. Visual scanning in infants. Paper presented at the Regional Meeting of the Society for Research in Child Development, Clark University, Worcester, Mass., March 1968.

Hall, G. S. *Adolescence* (Vols. 1 & 2). New York: Appleton-Century-Crofts, 1905.

Hamburg, D., Adams, J. E., & Brodie, H. K. H. Coping behavior in stressful circumstances: Some implications for social psychiatry. In A. H. Leighton (Ed.), *Further explorations in social psychiatry.* New York: Basic Books, 1975.

Hamburg, D. A., Hamburg, B. A., & Barchas, J. D. Anger and depression in perspective of behavioral biology. In L. Levi (Ed.), *Emotions: Their parameters and measurement.* New York: Raven, 1975.

Hanaway, T. P., & Burghardt, G. M. Girls, boys, and books. *Psychology Today,* 1976, *67.*

Handsfield, H. H. Disseminated gonococcal infection. *Clinical Obstetrics and Gynecology,* 1975, *85*(1), 131-141.

Handsfield, H. H., Hodson, W. A., & Holmes, K. K. Neonatal gonococcal infection. *Journal of the American Medical Association,* 1973, *225*(7).

Hardy, J. D., Wolff, H. G., & Goodell, H. The pain threshold in man. *American Journal of Psychiatry,* 1943, *99,* 744-751.

Harlow, H. F. Love in infant monkeys. In *The nature and nurture of behavior: Development psychobiology.* San Francisco: Freeman, 1973. (a)

Harlow, H. F. *Learning to love.* New York: Ballantine, 1973. (b)

Harlow, H. F., & Harlow, M. K. Social deprivation in monkeys. *Scientific American,* 1962, *207*(5), 136-145.

Harlow, H. F., & Harlow, M. K. Social deprivation in monkeys. In *The nature and nurture of behavior: Developmental psychobiology.* San Francisco: Freeman, 1973.

Harlow, H. F., Harlow, M. K., & Meyer, D. R. Learning motivated by a manipulation drive. *Journal of Experimental Psychology,* 1950, *40,* 228-234.

Harlow, H. F., Harlow, M. K., & Soumi, S. J.

From thought to therapy: Lessons from a primate laboratory. In I. L. Janis (Ed.), *Current trends in psychology: Readings from American Scientist.* Los Altos, Calif.: William Kaufman, 1977.

Harrell, R. F., Woodward, E., & Gates, A. E. *The effects of mothers' diets on the intelligence of offspring: A study of the influence of vitamin supplementation of the diet of pregnant and lactating women on the intelligence of their children.* New York: Teachers College, Columbia University, 1955.

Harris, H., & Kalmus, H. The measurement of taste sensitivity of phenylthiouria. *Annals of Eugenics,* 1950-1951, *15,* 24-31.

Harshbarger, D. Some ecological implications for the organization of human intervention throughout the life span. In P. B. Baltes & K. W. Schaie (Eds.), *Life-span developmental psychology: Personality and socialization.* New York: Academic, 1973.

Hartlage, L. C. Sex-linked inheritance of spatial ability. *Perceptual and Motor Skills,* 1970, *31,* 610.

Hartup, W. W., Glazer, J. A., & Charlesworth, R. Peer reinforcement and socio-economic status. *Child Development,* 1967, *38,* 1017-1024.

Hartup, W. W., & Lempers, J. A problem in life-span development: The interactional analysis of family attachments. In P. B. Baltes & K. W. Schaie (Eds.), *Life-span developmental psychology: Personality and socialization.* New York: Academic, 1973.

Harvard Education Review (Eds.). *Environment, Heredity, and Intelligence* (Reprint Series No. 2). Cambridge, Mass.: Harvard Education Review, 1969.

Harvard Magazine. I am not a dangerous man. It is my ideas that are said to be dangerous (An interview with B. F. Skinner). July-August 1977, 53-58.

Haskins, J., & Butts, H. F. *The psychology of black language.* New York: Barnes and Noble, 1973.

Hasler, A. D., & Larsen, J. A. The homing salmon. In *Psychobiology: The biological bases of behavior.* San Francisco: Freeman, 1967.

Havighurst, R. J. Social and psychological needs of the aging. In L. Gorlow & W. Katkovsky (Eds.), *Readings in the psychology of adjustment.* New York: McGraw-Hill, 1959.

Havighurst, R. J. *Developmental tasks and education.* New York: McKay, 1948, 1972.

Havighurst, R. J., Neugarten, B. L., & Tobin, S. S. Disengagement and patterns of aging. In B. L.

Neugarten (Ed.), *Middle age and aging.* Chicago: University of Chicago Press, 1968.

Haynes, H., White, B. L., & Held, R. Visual accommodation in human infants. *Science,* 1965, *148,* 528-530.

Healthy people: The U.S. surgeon general's report on health promotion and disease prevention (Serial No. 017-001-00416-2). Washington, D.C.: U.S. Government Printing Office, 1979.

Hearn, H. L. Career and leisure patterns of middle-aged urban blacks. *Gerontologist,* 1971, *11,* 21-26.

Hebb, D. O. *The organization of behavior.* New York: Wiley, 1949.

Hecaen, H., & de Ajuriaguerra, J. *Left-handedness, manual superiority and cerebral dominance.* New York: Grune & Stratton, 1964.

Heilbrun, A. B., & Fromme, D. K. Parental identification of late adolescence and level of adjustment. *Journal of Genetic Psychology,* 1965, *107,* 49-59.

Held, R., & Hein, A. Movement-produced stimulation in the development of visually guided behavior. *Journal of Comparative and Physiological Psychology,* 1963, *56,* 872-876.

Henneborn, W. J., & Cogan, R. The effect of husband participation on reported pain and probability of medication during labor and birth. *Journal of Psychosomatic Research,* 1975, *19,* 215-222.

Hess, E. H. "Imprinting" in animals. In *Psychobiology: The biological bases of behavior.* San Francisco: Freeman, 1967.

Hess, E. H. The ethological approach to socialization. In R. A. Hoppe, G. A. Milton, & E. C. Simmel (Eds.), *Early experiences and the process of socialization.* New York: Academic, 1970.

Hess, E. H. "Imprinting" in a natural laboratory. In *The nature and nurture of behavior: Developmental psychobiology.* San Francisco: Freeman, 1973.

Hess, R. D., & Shipman, V. Early experience and the socialization of cognitive modes in children. *Child Development,* 1965, *36,* 869-886.

Hetherington, E. M. A developmental study of the effects of sex of the dominant parents on sex-role preference, identification, and imitation in children. *Journal of Personality and Social Psychology,* 1965, *2,* 188-194.

Hetherington, E. M. Effects of paternal absence on sex-typed behaviors in Negro and white preadolescent males. *Journal of Personality and Social Psychology,* 1966, *4,* 87-91.

Hetherington, E. M. Effects of father absence on

personality development in adolescent daughters. *Developmental Psychology*, 1972, *7*, 313-326.

Hetherington, E. M., & Brackbill, Y. Etiology and covariation of obstinacy, orderliness and parsimony in young children. *Child Development*, 1963, *34*, 919-934.

Hetzel, B. S., Bruer, B., & Poidevin, L. O. S. A survey of the relation between certain common antenatal complications in primiparae and stressful life situations during pregnancy. *Journal of Psychosomatic Research*, 1961, *5*, 197-282.

Hickey, T. L., Hickey, L. A., & Kalish, R. A. Children's perceptions of the elderly. *Journal of Genetic Psychology*, 1968, *112*, 227-235.

Higgins, J., Reed, S., & Reed, E. Intelligence and family size: A paradox resolved. *Eugenics Quarterly*, 1962, *9*, 84-90.

Hill, R. Decision making and the family life cycle. In E. Shanas & G. F. Streib (Eds.), *Social structure and the family: Generational considerations*. Englewood Cliffs, N.J.: Prentice-Hall, 1965.

Hill, R. *Family development in three generations*. Cambridge, Mass.: Schenkman, 1971.

Hill, R., & Aldous, J. Socialization for marriage and parenthood. In D. Goslin (Ed.), *Handbook of socialization theory and research*. Chicago: Rand McNally, 1969.

Hill, R., Foote, N., Aldous, J., Carlson, R., & MacDonald, R. *Family development in three generations*. Cambridge, Mass.: Schenkman, 1970.

Hobbes, Thomas. *Leviathan*, Part 1, Chapter 13, 1651. (Quotation cited in *Bartlett's Familiar Quotations*.)

Hockett, C. F. Chinese vs. English: An exploration of the Whorfian thesis. In H. Hoijer (Ed.), *Language in Culture*. Chicago: University of Chicago Press, 1954.

Holmes, T. H., Hawkins, N. G., Bowerman, C. E., Clarke, E. R., Jr., & Joffe, J. R. Psychosocial and psychophysiologic studies of tuberculosis. *Psychosomatic Medicine*, 1957, *19*, 134-143.

Holmes, T. H., Rahe, R. H. The social readjustment rating scale. *Journal of Psychosomatic Research*, 1967, *11*, 213-218.

Honzik, M. P. Developmental studies of parent-child resemblance in intelligence. *Child Development*, 1957, *28*, 215-228.

Honzik, M. P., MacFarland, J. W., & Allen, L. The stability of mental test performance between 2 and 18 years. *Journal of Experimental Education*, 1948, *17*, 309-324.

Hooker, D. *The prenatal origin of behavior*. Lawrence: University of Kansas Press, 1952.

Hooper, F., Fitzgerald, J., & Papalia, D. E. Piagetian theory and the aging process: Extensions and speculations. *Aging and Human Development*, 1971, *2*, 3-20.

Hopkins, J. R., Zelazo, P. R., Jacobson, S. W., & Kagan, J. Infant reactivity to stimulus-schema discrepancy. *Genetic Psychology Monographs*, 1976, *93*, 27-62.

Horn, J. L., & Cattell, R. B. Age differences in fluid and crystallized intelligence. *Acta Psychologica*, 1967, *26*, 107-129.

Horner, M. S. Femininity and successful achievement: Basic inconsistency. In J. M. Bardwick, E. Douvan, M. S. Horner, & D. Gutman (Eds.), *Feminine personality and conflict*. Belmont, Calif.: Brooks/Cole, 1970.

Horney, K. *Our inner conflicts*. New York: Norton, 1945.

Houston, J. P. *Fundamentals of Learning*. New York: Academic, 1976.

Houston, S. The study of language: Trends and positions. In J. Eliot (Ed.), *Human development and cognition*. New York: Holt, 1971.

Howard, J., & Howard, M. Youth and the counterculture. In D. Spiegel & P. Keith-Spiegel (Eds.), *Outsiders USA*. San Francisco: Rinehart, 1973.

Howarth, E., & Cattell, R. B. The multivariate experimental approach to personality research. In B. B. Wolman (Ed.), *Handbook of general psychology*. Englewood Cliffs, N.J.: Prentice-Hall, 1973.

Howell, T. H. Senile deterioration of the central nervous system. *British Medical Journal*, 1949, *1*, 56-58.

Howell, W. W. The distribution of man. *Scientific American*, September 1960.

Hoyer, W. J., Labouvie, V., & Baltes, P. B. Modification of response speed deficits and intellectual performance in the elderly. *Human Development*, 1973, *16*(3), 233-242.

Hubel, D. H., & Wiesel, T. N. Receptive fields and functional architecture in two nonstriate visual areas (18 and 19) of the cat. *Journal of Neurophysiology*, 1965, *28*, 229-288.

Hudson, L. *Contrary imaginations*. Middlesex, England: Penguin, 1967.

Hulse, F. S. Exogamie et hétérosis. *Arch. Suisses d'Anthr. Gen.*, 1958, *22*, 103-125.

Hunt, M. M. *The world of the formerly married*. New York: McGraw-Hill, 1966.

Hurlock, E. B. *Child development* (5th ed.). New York: McGraw-Hill, 1972.

Huttel, F. A., Mitchell, I., Fischer, W. M., & Meyer, A. E. A quantitative evaluation of psycho-prophylaxis in childbirth. *Journal of Psychosomatic Research*, 1972, *16*, 81–92.

Illingworth, R. S. Predictive value of developmental tests in the 1st year. *Journal of Child Psychology and Psychiatry*, 1961, *2*, 210–215.

Irwin, O. C. Phonetical description of speech development in childhood. In L. Kaiser (Ed.), *Manual of phonetics*. Amsterdam: North Holland, 1957.

Jackson, C. M. Some aspects of form and growth. In W. J. Robbins, S. Brody, A. F. Hogan, C. M. Jackson, & C. W. Green (Eds.). *Growth*. New Haven: Yale University Press, 1929.

Jacobs, J. *Fun City: An ethnographic study of a retirement community*. New York: Holt, 1974.

Jacobsen, B., & Kinney, D. Perinatal complications in adopted and nonadopted schizophrenics and controls. *Acta Psychiatrica Scandinavica*, Supplement 285, 1980, *62*, 337–346.

Jacobsen, M. Report of research showing caffeine in pregnant animals produces birth defects. Washington, D.C.: Center for Science in the Public Interest, 1976.

Jacobson, C. B., & Berlin, C. M. Possible reproductive detriment in LSD users. *Journal of the American Medical Association*, 1972, *222*.

Jahoda, G. Retinal pigmentation, illusion susceptibility and space perception. *International Journal of Psychology*, 1971, *6*, 199–208.

Jakobson, R. [*Child language, aphasia and phonological universals*] (A. R. Keiler, Trans.). The Hague: Mouton, 1968. (Originally published, 1941.)

Jalavisto, E., Orma, E., & Tawast, M. Aging and relation between stimulus intensity and duration in corneal sensibility. *Acta Physiologica Scandinavica*, 1951, *23*, 224–233.

James, W. From a letter to H. G. Wells, September 11, 1906. (Quotation cited in *Bartlett's Familiar Quotations*.)

Janes, W. *The varieties of religious experience*. London: Longmans Green, 1914.

Jarvik, L. F. & Blum, J. E. Cognitive declines as predictors of mortality in twin pairs: A twenty-year longitudinal study of aging. In E. Palamore

and F. Jeffers (Eds.), *Prediction of lifespan*. Lexington, Mass.: Heath, 1971.

Jarvik, L., & Cohen, D. A biobehavioral approach to intellectual changes with aging. In C. Eisdorfer & M. P. Lawton (Eds.), *The psychology of adult development and aging*. Washington, D.C.: American Psychological Association, 1973.

Jeffrey, W. E., & Cohen, L. B. Habituation in the human infant. In H. W. Reese (Ed.), *Advances in child development and behavior* (Vol. 6). New York: Academic, 1971.

Jencks, C. *Inequality: A reassessment of the effect of family and schooling in America*. New York: Basic Books, 1972.

Jensen, A. R. How much can we boost IQ and scholastic achievement? *Harvard Educational Review*, 1969, *39*(1), 1–123.

Jensen, A. R. *Educability and group differences*. New York: Harper & Row, 1973. (a)

Jensen, A. R. *Genetics and education*. New York: Harper & Row, 1973. (b)

Joffe, J. M. *Prenatal determinants of behavior*. New York: Pergamon, 1969.

Johnson, L. C. Are stages of sleep related to waking behavior? In I. Janis (Ed.), *Current trends in psychology*. Los Altos, Calif.: William Kaufman, 1977.

Jones, B. *Good things for babies*. Boston: Houghton Mifflin, 1976.

Jones, H. E., & Conrad, H. S. The growth and decline of intelligence: A study of a homogeneous group between the ages of ten and sixty. *Genetic Psychology Monographs*, 1933, *13*, 223–294.

Jones, K. D., Smith, D. W., Ulleland, C. N., & Streissguth, A. P. Patterns of malformation in offspring of chronic alcoholic mothers. *Lancet*, 1973, *11*, 999.

Jones, M. C. A laboratory study of fear, the case of Peter. *Pedagogical Seminary*, 1924, *31*, 308–315.

Jones, M. C. The later career of boys who were early or late-maturing. *Child Development*, 1957, *28*, 113–128.

Jones, M. C. A report on three growth studies at the University of California. *Gerontologist*, 1967, *7*, 49–54.

Jones, M. C. Changes in the attitudes and interests of adolescents over two decades. In M. C. Jones, N. Bayley, J. W. McFarlane, & M. P. Honzik (Eds.), *The course of human development*. Waltham, Mass.: Xerox College Publishing, 1971.

Jones, M. C., Albert, Peter, and Watson, John B.

American Psychologist, August 1974, 581–583.

Jones, M. C., & Bayley, N. Physical maturing among boys as related to behavior. *Journal of Educational Psychology*, 1950, *41*, 129–148.

Jones, M. C., & Mussen, P. H. Self-conceptions, motivations, and interpersonal attitudes of early- and late-maturing girls. In M. C. Jones, N. Bayley, J. W. McFarlane, & M. P. Honzik (Eds.), *The course of human development*. Waltham, Mass.: Xerox College Publishing, 1971.

Jung, C. G. *Psychological types*. New York: Harcourt, Brace, 1923.

Jung, C. G. *Modern man in search of a soul*. New York: Harcourt, Brace, 1933.

Jung, C. G. The stages of life. In J. Campbell (Ed.), *The Portable Jung*. New York: Viking, 1971.

Kagan, J. Inadequate evidence and illogical conclusions. *Harvard Educational Review*, 1969, *39*, 274–277.

Kagan, J. The determinants of attention in the infant. *American Scientist*, 1970, *58*, 298–306.

Kagan, J. Do infants think? *Scientific American*, 1972, *226*, 74–82.

Kagan, J., & Klein, R. E. Cross-cultural perspective on early development. *American Psychologist*, 1973, *28*, 947–961.

Kagan, J., & Moss, H. A. *Birth to maturity: A study in psychological development*. New York: Wiley, 1962.

Kahana, B., & Kahana, E. Grandparenthood from the perspective of the developing grandchild. *Developmental Psychology*, 1970, *3*, 92–105.

Kalish, R. A. (Ed.). *The dependencies of old people* (Occasional Paper No. 6). Ann Arbor: University of Michigan Institute of Gerontology, 1969. (a)

Kalish, R. A. The old and the young as generation gap allies. *Gerontologist*, 1969, *9*, 83–89. (b)

Kalish, R., & Johnson, A. Value similarities and differences in three generations of women. *Journal of Marriage and the Family*, 1972, *34*, 49–55.

Kamin, L. J. *Heredity, intelligence, politics, and psychology*. Paper presented at the Eastern Psychological Association Convention, May 5, 1973.

Kandel, D. B., & Lesser, G. S. Parental and peer influence on educational plans of adolescents. *American Sociological Review*, 1969, *34*, 213–223.

Kanner, L. Autistic disturbances of affective contact. *Nervous Child*, 1943, *2*, 217–250.

Kanter, R. M. Communes. *Psychology Today*, 1970, *4*(2), 53–57.

Kaplan, E., & Kaplan, G. The prelinguistic child. In J. Eliot (Ed.), *Human development and cognition*. New York: Holt, 1971.

Kapp, F. T., Hornstein, S., & Graham, V. T. Some psychologic factors in prolonged labor due to inefficient uterine action. *Comprehensive Psychiatry*, 1963, *4*, 9–18.

Karel, F. (Ed.). *Special Report: Regionalized Perinatal Services*. Princeton, N.J.: Robert Wood Johnson Foundation Communications Office, 1978.

Kasl, S. V., & Cobb, S. Blood pressure changes in men undergoing job loss: A preliminary report. *Psychosomatic Medicine*, 1970, *32*, 19–38.

Katz, E., Blau, P. M., Brown, M. L., & Strodbeck, F. L. Leadership stability and social change: An experiment with small groups. *Sociometry*, 1957, *20*, 36–50.

Katz, J. J., & Fodor, J. A. The structure of semantic theory. *Language*, 1963, *39*, 170–210.

Katz, J. J., & Postal, P. M. *An integrated theory of linguistic descriptions*. Cambridge, Mass.: MIT Press, 1964.

Keightey, G. An instrument for measurement of vibration sensation in man. *Milbank Memorial Fund Quarterly*, 1946, *24*, 36–48.

Kellaghan, T., & MacNamara, J. Family correlates of verbal reasoning ability. *Developmental Psychology*, 1972, *7*, 49–53.

Kessner, D. M. (Project Director). *Infant death: An analysis by maternal risk and health care*. Washington, D.C.: Institute of Medicine, 1973.

Kety, S. S. Disorders of the human brain. *Scientific American*, 1979, *241*, 202–218.

Kety, S., Rosenthal, D., Wender, P., Schulsinger, F., & Jacobsen, B. *Mental illness in the biological and adoptive families of adopted individuals who have become schizophrenic*. (Paper presented at the annual meeting of the American Psychopathological Association, March 7, 1973.)

Keys, A. *Seven countries: A multivariate analysis of deaths and coronary heart disease*. Cambridge: Harvard University Press, 1980.

Kimble, G. A. *Hilgard and Marquis' conditioning and learning*. New York: Appleton, 1961.

Kimmel, H. D. Instrumental conditioning of autonomically mediated behavior. *Psychological Bulletin*, 1967, *67*(5), 337–345.

Kimura, D. Speech lateralization in young children as determined by an auditory test. *Journal of Comparative and Physiological Psychology*, 1963, *56*, 899–902.

Kimura, D. Functional asymmetry of the brain in dichotic listening. *Cortex*, 1967, *3*, 163-178.

King, J. A. Species specifity and early experience. In G. Newton and S. Levine (Eds.), *Early experience and behavior*. Springfield, Ill., Charles C. Thomas, 1968.

King, J. A., & Eleftheriou, B. B. Effects of early handling upon adult behavior in two subspecies of deermice. In S. Ratner & M. R. Denny (Eds.), *Comparative psychology*. Homewood, Ill.: Dorsey, 1964.

Kinney, D. K., & Kagan, J. Infant attention to auditory discrepancy. *Child Development*, 1976, *47*, 155-164.

Kinney, D. K., & Matthysse, S. Genetic transmission of schizophrenia. *Annual Review of Medicine*, 1978, *29*, 459-473.

Kinsey, A. C., Pomeroy, W. B., & Martin, C. E. *Sexual behavior in the human male*. Philadelphia: Saunders, 1948.

Kinsey, A. C., Pomeroy, W. B., Martin, C. E., & Gebhard, P. H. *Sexual behavior in the human female*. Philadelphia: Saunders, 1953.

Klaiber, E. L., Broverman, D. M., & Kobayashi, Y. The automatization cognitive style, androgens, and monoamine oxidase. *Psychopharmacologia*, 1967, *11*, 320-336.

Klaiber, E. L., Broverman, D. M., Vogel, W., Abraham, G. E., & Cone, F. L. Effects of infused testosterone on mental performances and serum LH. *Journal of Clinical Endocrinology and Metabolism*, 1971, *32*, 341-349.

Kleemeier, R. W. (Ed.). *Aging and leisure*. New York: Oxford University Press, 1961.

Klein, R. C. Age, sex, and task difficulty as predictors of social conformity. *Journal of Gerontology*, 1972, *27*, 229-236.

Klein, R. L., & Birren, J. E. Age, perceived self-competence and conformity. *Proceedings, 81st Annual Convention, American Psychological Association*, 1973, 779-780.

Kniep, E. H., Morgan, W. L., & Young, P. T. Studies in affective psychology. XI. Individual differences in affective reaction to odors. XII. The relation between age and affective reaction to odors. *American Journal of Psychology*, 1931, *43*, 406-421.

Kohlberg, L. Development of moral character and moral ideology. In M. L. Hoffman & L. W. Hoffman (Eds.), *Review of child development research* (Vol. 1). New York: Russell Sage, 1964.

Kohlberg, L. A cognitive-developmental analysis of children's sex-role concepts and attitudes. In E. E. Maccoby (Ed.), *The development of sex differences*. Stanford, Calif.: Stanford University Press, 1966.

Kohlberg, L. Stage and sequence: The cognitive-developmental approach to socialization. In D. A. Goslin (Ed.), *Handbook of socialization theory and research*. Chicago: Rand McNally, 1969.

Kohlberg, L. Stages and aging in moral development—Some speculations. *Gerontologist*, 1973, *13*, 497-502. (a)

Kohlberg, L. Continuities in childhood and adult moral development revisited. In P. B. Baltes & K. W. Schaie (Eds.), *Life-span developmental psychology: Personality and socialization*. New York: Academic, 1973. (b)

Kohlberg, L. The cognitive-developmental approach to moral education. *Phi Delta Kappa*, 1975, *46*(10), 670-677.

Kohlberg, L. The meaning and measurement of moral development. Heinz Werner Memorial Lecture, 1980.

Kohlberg, L., & Kramer, R. Continuities and discontinuities in childhood and adult moral development. *Human Development*, 1969, *12*, 93-120.

Kolata, G. B. Prevention of heart disease: Clinical trials at what cost? *Science*, 1975, *190*, 764-765.

Kolata, G. B. Gonorrhea: More of a problem but less of a mystery. *Science*, 1976, *192*, 244—247.

Kolata, G. B. Scientists attack report that obstetrical medications endanger children. *Science*, 1979, *204*, 391-392.

Koop, C. E. Separating the Siamese twins: The surgeon's story. *Modern Medical World News*, November 8, 1974, 90-98.

Kretschmer, E. *Physique and character*. New York: Harcourt Brace, 1925.

Kron, R. E., & Brackbill, Y. Toxic prescription for babies. *American Journal of Obstetrics and Gynecology*, 1980, *136*, 819-820.

Kuhn, C. M., Butler, S. R., & Schanberg, S. M. Selective depression of serum growth hormone during maternal deprivation in rat pups. *Science*, 1978, *201*, 1034-1036.

Labouvie, E. W., & Schaie, K. W. Personality structure as a function of behavioral stability in children. *Child Development*, 1974, *45*, 252-255.

Labouvie-Vief, G., & Gonda, J. N. Cognitive strategy training and intellectual performances in the elderly. *Journal of Gerontology*, 1976, *31*, 327-332.

Labov, W. *The study of nonstandard English*. Urbana, Ill.: National Council of Teachers of English, 1970.

Laidlaw, R. W., & Hamilton, M. A. A study of thresholds of apperception of passive movement among normal control subjects. *Bulletin of the Neurological Institute of New York*, 1937, *6*, 268-273.

Laird, D. A., & Breen, W. J. Sex and age alterations in taste preferences. *Journal of the American Dietetic Association*, 1939, *15*, 549-550.

Langworthy, O. R. Development of behavior patterns and myelinization of nervous system in human fetus and infant. *Contributions to Embryology*, 1933, *24*, 1-13.

Laslett, P. Societal development and aging. In R. Binstock & E. Sharas (Eds.), *The handbook of aging and the social sciences*. New York: Van Nostrand Reinhold, 1976.

Lassigne, M. W. *The influence of peer and adult opinion on moral beliefs of adolescents*. Unpublished doctoral dissertation, Indiana University, 1963.

Lawrence, M. M., & Feind, C. Vestibular responses to rotation in the newborn infant. *Pediatrics*, 1953, *12*, 300-306.

Leaf, A. Getting old. *Scientific American*, September 1973, 44-53.

Leary, T. *Interpersonal diagnosis of personality*. New York: Ronald, 1957.

Lecours, A. Myelogenetic correlates of the development of speech and language. In E. H. Lenneberg & E. Lenneberg (Eds.), *Foundations of language development* (Vol. 1). New York: Academic, 1975.

Lehman, H. C. *Age and achievement*. New York: Oxford University Press, 1953.

Lenneberg, E. H. A biological perspective of language. In E. Lenneberg (Ed.), *New directions in the study of language*. Cambridge, Mass.: MIT Press, 1967. (a)

Lenneberg, E. H. The biological foundations of language. *Hospital Practice*, 1967, *2*, 59-67. (b)

Lenneberg, E. H. *Biological foundations of language*. New York: Wiley, 1967.

Lenz, W., In *Proceedings of the Second International Conference on Congenital Malformations*. London: International Medical Congress Ltd., 1964, p. 270.

Lenz, W. Epidemiology of congenital malformations. *Annals of the New York Academy of Science*, 1965, *123*, 228.

Levendusky, P. G. Effects of social incentives on task performance in the elderly. *Journal of Gerontology*, 1978, *33*, 562-566.

Levi-Montalcini, R. The nerve growth factor. *Annals of the New York Academy of Science*, 1964, *118*, 149-168.

Levi-Montalcini, R. Revoltella, R., & Calissano, P. Microtubule proteins in the nerve-growth-factor-mediated response: Interaction between the nerve growth factor and its target cells. *Recent Progress in Hormone Research*, 1974, *30*, 635-664.

LeVine, R. A. Cross cultural study in child psychology. In P. Mussen (Ed.), *Carmichael's manual of child psychology*. New York: Wiley, 1970.

Levine, S. Sex differences in the brain. *Scientific American*, 1966, *214*, 84-90.

Levitin, T. E., & Chananie, J. D. Responses of female primary school teachers to sex-typed behaviors in male and female children. *Child Development*, 1972, *43*, 1309-1316.

Levy, A. The thalidomide generation. *Life*, July, 26, 1968, pp. 42-62.

Levy, J. Possible basis for the evolution of lateral specialization of the human brain. *Nature* (London), 1969, *224*, 614-615.

Lewin, K. *Dynamic theory of personality*. New York: McGraw-Hill, 1935.

Lewin, K., Lippitt, R., & White, R. K. Patterns of aggressive behavior in experimentally created "social climates." *Journal of Social Psychology*, 1939, *10*, 271-299.

Lewis, D. Wind, wave, star and bird. *National Geographic*, December 1974.

Lewis, M. Individual differences in the measurement of early cognitive growth. In J. Hellmuth (Ed.), *Exceptional infant: Studies in abnormality* (Vol. 2). New York: Brunnel/Mazel, 1971.

Lewis, M. What do we mean when we say "infant intelligence scores"? A socio-political question. In M. Lewis (Ed.), *Origins of intelligence*. New York: Plenum, 1976.

Lieberman, M. A. Some issues in studying psychological predictors of survival. In E. Palmore & F. C. Jeffers (Eds.), *Prediction of life-span*. Lexington, Mass.: Heath, 1971.

Lifton, R. J. *Death in life: Survivors of Hiroshima*. New York: Random House, 1967.

Light, R. J., & Smith, P. V. Choosing a future: Strategies for designing and evaluating new programs. *Harvard Education Review*, 1970, *40*, 1-28.

Lipsitt, L. P. The study of sensory and learning processes in the newborn. *Symposium on Neonatal Neurology: Clinics in Perinatology*, 1977, *4*, 163-186.

Lipsitt, L. P., Engen, T., & Kaye, H. Developmental changes in the olfactory threshold of the neonate. *Child Development*, 1963, *34*, 371-376.

Livson, N., & Peskin, H. Prediction of adult psychological health in a longitudinal study. *Journal of Abnormal Psychology*, 1967, *72*, 509-518.

Loehlin, J. C. Empirical methods in quantitative human behavior genetics. In K. W. Schaie, V. E. Anderson, G. E. McClearn & J. Money (Eds.), *Developmental human behavior genetics*. Lexington, Mass.: Heath, 1975.

Longstreth, L. E. *Psychological development of the child*. New York: Ronald, 1968.

Lopata, H. Z. *Widowhood in an American city*. Cambridge, Mass.: Schenkman, 1973.

Lorenz, K. *King Solomon's ring*. New York: Crowell, 1952.

Lorenz, K. *Evolution and modification of behavior*. Chicago: University of Chicago Press, 1965.

Lorenz, K. The evolution of behavior. In *Psychobiology: The biological bases of behavior*. San Francisco: Freeman, 1967.

Lott, A. J., Lott, B. E., & Matthews, G. N. Interpersonal attraction among children as a function of vicarious rewards. *Journal of Educational Psychology*, 1969, *60*, 274-283.

Lovaas, O. I., Berberich, J. P., Perdoff, B. F., & Schaeffer, B. Acquisition of imitative speech by schizophrenic children. *Science*, 1966, *151*, 705-706.

Lovaas, O. I., Koegel, R., Simmons, J. Q., & Long, J. S. Some generalizations and follow-up measures on autistic children in behavior therapy. *Journal of Applied Behavior Analysis*, 1973, *6*, 131-166.

Lowenthal, M. F., & Haven, C. Interaction and adaptation: Intimacy as a critical variable. *American Sociological Review*, 1968, *33*, 20-30.

Lowenthal, M. F., & Robinson, B. Social networks and isolation. In R. H. Binstock & E. Shanas (Eds.), *Handbook of aging and the social sciences*. New York: Van Nostrand Reinhold, 1976.

Lowenthal, M. F., Thurnher, M., & Chiriboga, D. *Four stages of life: A psychosocial study of women and men facing transition*. San Francisco: Jossey-Bass, 1975.

Lozoff, B. Brittenham, G. M., Trausse, M. A., Kennell, J. H., & Klaus, M. H. The mother-newborn relationship: Limits of adaptability. *Journal of Pediatrics*, 1977, *91*, 1-12.

Luckey, E., & Nass, G. A. A comparison of sexual attitudes and behavior in an international sample. *Journal of Marriage and the Family*, 1969, *31*, 364-379.

Luria, A. R. *The role of speech in the regulation of normal and abnormal behavior*. New York: Liveright, 1961.

Luria, A. R. [*The working brain*] (B. Haigh, Trans.). Middlesex, England: Penguin, 1973.

Lusk, D., & Lewis, M. Mother-infant interaction and infant development among the Wolof of Senegal. *Human Development*, 1972, *15*, 58-69.

Lynn, R. *Attention, arousal, and the orientation reaction*. New York: Macmillan, 1966.

Maas, H. S., & Kuypers, J. A. *From thirty to seventy*. San Francisco: Jossey-Bass, 1974.

Maccoby, E. E. Role-taking in childhood and its consequences for social learning. *Child Development*, 1961, *30*, 239-252.

Maccoby, E. E. Differential socialization of boys and girls. Paper presented at the annual meeting of the American Psychological Association, Hawaii, September 1972.

Maccoby, E. E., & Feldman, S. Mother-attachment and stranger-reactions in the third year of life. *Monographs of the Society for Research in Child Development*, 1972, *37* (No. 146).

Maccoby, E. E., & Jacklin, C. N. *The psychology of sex differences*. Stanford, Calif.: Stanford University Press, 1974.

MacFarlane, A. *The psychology of childbirth*. Cambridge: Harvard University Press, 1977.

MacRae, J. M. Retests of children given mental tests as infants. *Journal of Genetic Psychology*, 1955, *87*, 111-119.

Maddox, G. L. Disengagement theory: A critical evaluation. *Gerontologist*, 1964, *4*, 80-83.

Maddox, G. L. Retirement as a social event in the United States. In J. C. McKinney & F. T. deVyver (Eds.), *Aging and social policy*. New York: Appleton-Century-Crofts, 1966.

Maddox, G. L., & Eisdorfer, C. Some correlates of activity and morale among the elderly. *Social Forces*, 1962, *40*, 254-260.

Madison, P. *Personality development in college*. Reading, Mass.: Addison-Wesley, 1969.

Margolies, R. On community building. In R. Buckhour (Ed.), *Toward social change*. New York: Harper & Row, 1971.

Marmot, M. G., & Syme, S. L. Acculturation and coronary heart disease in Japanese-Americans. *American Journal of Epidemiology*, 1976, *104*, 225-247.

Marmot, M. G., Syme, S. L., Kagan, A., et al. Epidemiological studies of coronary heart disease and stroke in Japanese men living in Japan, Hawaii and California: Prevalence of coronary and hypertensive heart disease and associated risk factors. *American Journal of Epidemiology*, 1975, *102*, 514-525.

Marquis, D. P. Learning in the neonate: The modification of behavior under three feeding schedules. *Journal of Experimental Psychology*, 1941, *29*, 263-282.

Marsh, G. Talk presented at the Psychology Department, University of California, Los Angeles, 1977.

Martin, W. C., Bengtson, V. L., & Acock, A. A. Alienation and age: A context-specific approach. *Social Forces*, 1974, *53*, 266-274.

Marx, J. L. Drugs during pregnancy: Do they affect the unborn child? *Science*, 1973, *180*, 174-175.

Maslow, A. H. Self-actualizing people. A study of psychological health. In W. Wolff (Ed.), *Personality symposium*. New York: Grune & Stratton, 1950.

Maslow, A. H. *Motivation and personality*. New York: Harper & Row, 1954.

Maslow, A. H. Self-actualization and beyond. In J. F. T. Bugental (Ed.), *Challenges of humanistic psychology*. New York: McGraw-Hill, 1967.

Maslow, A. H. *Toward a psychology of being* (2nd ed.). New York: Van Nostrand Reinhold, 1962, 1968.

Masters, W. H., & Johnson, V. E. *Human sexual response*. Boston: Little, Brown, 1966.

Masters, W. H., & Johnson, V. E. *Human sexual inadequacy*. Boston: Little, Brown, 1970.

McCandless, B. R. *Children and adolescents*. New York: Holt, 1961.

McCandless, B. R. *Children: Behavior and development*. New York: Holt, 1967.

McCandless, B. R. Cognition in sex roles: Dependence-independence. Paper presented at meeting on Piagetian Theory and Application sponsored by SUNY and New York State Education Department, Ellenville, New York, 1975.

McCary, J. L. *Human Sexuality*. New York: Van Nostrand, 1973.

McClearn, G. E. Genetic influences on behavior and development. In P. H. Mussen (Ed.), *Carmichael's manual of child psychology*. New York: Wiley, 1970.

McClearn, G. E. Behavioral genetics. *Behavioral Science*, 1971, *16*, 64-81.

McClearn, G. E., & DeFries, J. C. *Introduction to behavioral genetics*. San Francisco: Freeman, 1973.

McClelland, D. C., Atkinson, J. W., Clark, R. A., & Lowell, E. L. *The achievement motive*. New York: Appleton, 1953.

McDonald, R. L., Gynther, M. D., & Christakos, A. C. Relations between maternal anxiety and obstetric complications. *Psychosomatic Medicine*, 1963, *25*, 357-363.

McFarland, R. A. The sensory and perceptual processes in aging. In K. W. Schaie (Ed.), *Theory and methods of research on aging*. Morgantown: West Virginia University Press, 1968.

McFarland, R. A., & Fisher, M. B. Alterations in dark adaptation as a function of age. *Journal of Gerontology*, 1955, *10*, 424-428.

McGraw, M. B. Swimming behavior of the human infant. *Journal of Pediatrics*, 1939, *15*, 485-490.

McGraw, M. B. Development of rotary-vestibular reactions of human infants. *Child Development*, 1941, *12*, 17-19. (a)

McGraw, M. B. Neural maturation as exemplified in the changing reactions of the infant to pin prick. *Child Development*, 1941, *12*, 31-42. (b)

McGraw, M. B. *The neuromuscular maturation of the human infant*. New York: Columbia University Press, 1943.

McGuire, W. J. The nature of attitudes and attitude change. In G. Lindsey & E. Aronson (Eds.), *The handbook of social psychology* (Vol. 3, 2nd ed.). Reading, Mass.: Addison-Wesley, 1969.

McKee, J., & Leader, F. The relationship of socioeconomic status and aggression to the competitive behavior of preschool children. *Child Development*, 1955, *26*, 135-142.

McNeil, T. F., & Kaij, L. Obstetric factors in the development of schizophrenia: Complications in births of preschizophrenics and in reproductions by schizophrenic parents. In L. Wynne, R. Cromwell, & S. Matthysse (Eds.), *Nature of schizophrenia*, New York: Wiley, 1978.

McNeill, D. Developmental psycholinguistics. In F. Smith & G. A. Miller (Eds.), *The genesis of language*. Cambridge, Mass.: MIT Press, 1966.

McNeill, D. The development of language. In P. H. Mussen (Ed.), *Carmichael's manual of child psychology* (Vol. 1, 3rd ed.) New York: Wiley, 1970. (a)

McNeill, D. *The acquisition of language: The study of developmental psycholinguistics*. New York: Harper & Row, 1970. (b)

Mead, M. *Coming of age in Samoa*. New York: Morrow, 1928.

Medawar, P. B. *The uniqueness of the individual*. London: Methuen, 1957.

Medinnus, G. R. The development of a parent attitude toward education scale. *Journal of Educational Research*, 1962, *56*, 100-103.

Mednick, S. Breakdown in individuals at high risk for schizophrenia: Possible predispositional perinatal factors. *Mental Hygiene*, 1970, *54*, 50-63.

Mednick, S. Perinatal conditions and infant development in children with schizophrenic parents. *Social Biology*, 1972, *18* (Supplement), S103-113.

Mercer, J. R. *Labelling the mentally retarded: Clinical and social system perspectives on mental retardation.* Berkeley: University of California Press, 1973. (a)

Mercer, J. R. The pluralistic assessment project: Sociocultural effects in clinical assessment. *School Psychology Digest*, 1973, *2*, 10-18. (b)

Meredith, H. V. Somatic changes during human prenatal life. *Child Development*, 1975, *46*, 603-610.

Messenger, J. C. In D. S. Marshall & R. C. Enggs (Eds.), *Human Sexual Behavior.* Englewood Cliffs, N.J.: Prentice-Hall, 1972.

Miles, C. C. Influence of speed and age on intelligence scores of adults. *Journal of General Psychology*, 1934, *10*, 208-210.

Miller, G. A., & Isard, S. Some perceptual consequences of linguistic rules. *Journal of Verbal Learning and Verbal Behavior*, 1963, *2*, 217-228.

Miller, N. Can blood pressure be self-controlled? *Esquire*, 1978, *90*, 91-94.

Miller, O. L., Jr. The visualization of genes in action. *Scientific American*, 1973, *228*(3), 34-49.

Milner, B. Memory disturbances after bilateral hippocampal lesions. In P. Milner & S. Glickman (Eds.), *Cognitive processes and the brain.* Princeton, N.J.: Van Nostrand, 1965.

Minton, C., Kagan, J., & Levine, J. Maternal control and obedience in the two-year-old. *Child Development*, 1971, *42*, 1873-1894.

Mischel, W. Father-absence and delay of gratification: Cross-cultural comparisons. *Journal of Abnormal and Social Psychology*, 1961, *62*, 116-124.

Mischel, W. Continuity and change in personality. *American Psychologist*, 1969, *24*, 1012-1018.

Mischel, W. Sex-typing and socialization. In P. H. Mussen (Ed.), *Carmichael's manual of child psychology* (Vol. 2). New York: Wiley, 1970.

Moberg, D. O. Spiritual well-being. *White House Conference on Aging Background Papers.* Washington, D. C.: U. S. Government Printing Office, 1971.

Moncrieff, R. W. *The chemical senses.* London: Leonard Hill, 1951.

Money, J. Sex hormones and other variables in human eroticisms. In W. C. Young (Ed.), *Sex and internal secretions* (Vol. 2). Baltimore: Williams & Witkins, 1961.

Money, J. Sexually dimorphic behavior, normal and abnormal. In N. Kretchmer & D. N. Walcher (Eds.), *Environmental influences on genetic expression: Biological and behavioral aspects of sexual differentiation.* Washington, D.C.: U.S. Government Printing Office, 1971.

Money, J., & Ehrhardt, A. A. *Man and woman, boy and girl.* Baltimore: Johns Hopkins University Press, 1972.

Money, J., Hampson, J. G., & Hampson, J. L. Imprinting and the establishment of gender role. *American Medical Association, Archives of Neurological Psychiatry*, 1957, *77*, 333-336.

Monge, R. F. Experimental tests from the Syracuse Adult Development Study. Unpublished manuscript, 1971.

Moore, P. Not by medicine alone. *APA Monitor*, 1975, *6*, 1; 24.

Moore, W. M., Silverberg, M. M., & Read, M. S. In W. M. Moore, M. M. Silverberg, & M. S. Read (Eds.), *Nutrition, Growth, and Development of North American Indian Children.* DHEW Publication No. (NIH) 72-26, 1972.

Morton, R. S. *Venereal diseases.* Baltimore: Penguin, 1972.

Moss, H. A. Sex, age, and state as determinants of mother-infant interaction. *Merrill-Palmer Quarterly*, 1967, *13*, 19-36.

Mowrer, O. H., & Kluckhohn, C. Dynamic theory of personality. In J. McV. Hunt (Ed.), *Personality and the behavior disorders.* New York: Ronald, 1944.

Murray, H. A. *Explorations in personality.* New York: Oxford University Press, 1938.

Mussen, P. H., Conger, J., & Kagan, J. *Child development and personality.* New York: Harper & Row, 1974.

Mussen, P. H., & Jones, M. C. Self-conceptions, motivations, and interpersonal attitudes of late- and early-maturing boys. In M. C. Jones, N. Bayley, J. W. McFarlane, & M. P. Honzik (Eds.), *The course of human development.* Waltham, Mass.: Xerox College Publishing, 1971.

Myers, R. E. Lactic acid accumulation as a cause of brain edema and cerebral necrosis resulting from oxygen deprivation. In R. Korobkin & C. Guille-minault (Eds.), *Advances in perinatal neurology.* New York: Spectrum, 1978.

Myers, R. E. Reply to Drs. Kron and Brackbill. *American Journal of Obstetrics and Gynecology,* 1980, *136,* 819-820.

Myers, R. E., & Myers, S. E. Use of sedative, analgesic, and anesthetic drugs during labor and delivery: Bane or boon. *American Journal of Obstetrics and Gynecology,* 1979, *133,* 83-104.

Nardi, A. H. Person-perception research and the perception of life-span development. In P. B. Baltes & K. W. Schaie (Eds.), *Life-span developmental psychology: Personality and socialization.* New York: Academic, 1973.

Nash, J. The father in contemporary culture and current psychological literature. *Child Development,* 1965, *36,* 261-297.

Navrat, M. L. Color tint matching by children. *Perceptual and Motor Skills,* 1965, *21,* 215-222.

Neel, J. V., & Schull, W. J. Cited in I. M. Lerner, *Heredity, environment and society.* San Francisco: Freeman, 1968.

Nelson, P. D. Similarities and differences among leaders and followers. *Journal of Social Psychology,* 1964, *63,* 161-167.

Nesselroade, J. R., & Baltes, P. B. Adolescent personality development and historical change: 1970-1972. *Monographs of the Society for Research in Child Development,* 1974, *39,* 1-80.

Neugarten, B. L. A new look at menopause. *Psychology Today,* 1967, *1,* 42-45.

Neugarten, B. L. Toward a psychology of the life cycle. In B. L. Neugarten (Ed.), *Middle age and aging: A reader in social psychology.* Chicago: University of Chicago Press, 1968. (a)

Neugarten, B. L. (Ed.). *Middle age and aging.* Chicago: University of Chicago Press, 1968. (b)

Neugarten, B. L. Adaptation and the life cycle. *Journal of Geriatric Psychiatry,* 1970, *4,* 71-87.

Neugarten, B. L., & Datan, N. Sociological perspectives on the life cycle. In P. B. Baltes & K. W. Schaie (Eds.), *Life-span developmental psychology: Personality and socialization.* New York: Academic, 1973.

Neugarten, B. L., Havighurst, R. J., & Tobin, S. S. Personality and patterns of aging. In B. L. Neugarten (Eds.), *Middle age and aging.* Chicago: University of Chicago Press, 1968.

Neugarten, B. L., & Weinstein, K. K. The chang-ing American grandparent. *Marriage and Family Living,* 1964, *26,* 199-204.

Neugarten, B. L., Wood, V., Kraines, R. J., & Loomis, B. Women's attitudes toward menopause. *Vita Humana,* 1963, *6,* 140-151.

Newcombe, N., Rogoff, B., & Kagan, J. Developmental changes in recognition memory for pictures of objects and scenes. *Developmental Psychology,* 1977, *13,* 337-341.

Newman, B. M., & Newman, P. R. *Development through life: A psychosocial approach.* Homewood, Ill.: Dorsey, 1975.

Newman, H. W., & Corbin, D. B. Quantitative determination of vibratory sensibility. *Proceedings of the Society of Experimental Biology and Medicine,* 1936, *35,* 273-276.

Newson, J., & Newson, E. *4 year old in an urban community.* London: G. Allen, 1963.

Newsweek. VD: The epidemic. 1972, pp. 46-50.

Newsweek. New science of birth. 1976, pp. 55-57.

Nichols, R. C. The resemblance of twins in personality and interests. In M. Manosevitz, G. Lindzey, & D. Thiessen (Eds.), *Behavioral genetics: Method and research.* New York: Appleton-Century-Crofts, 1969.

Nuckolls, K. B., Cassel, J., & Kaplan, B. H. Psychosocial assets, life crisis and the prognosis of pregnancy. *American Journal of Epidemiology,* 1972, *95,* 431-441..

Oberlander, M., Jenkins, N., Houlihan, K., & Jackson, J. Family size and birth order as determinants of scholastic aptitude and achievement in a sample of eighth graders. *Journal of Consulting and Clinical Psychology,* 1970, *34,* 19-21.

Oden, M. H. The fulfillment of promise: 40-year follow-up of the Terman gifted group. *Genetic Psychology Monographs,* 1968, *77,* 3-93.

Odom, L., Seeman, J., & Newbrough, J. R. A study of family communication patterns and personality integration in children. *Child Psychiatry and Human Development,* 1971, *1,* 275-285.

Olds, J. Self-stimulation of the brain. *Science.* 1958, *127,* 315-324.

Olds, J. Hypothalamic substrates of rewards. *Physiological Review,* 1962, *42,* 354-404.

Oliver, D. B. Career and leisure patterns: Middle-aged metropolitan out-migrants. *Gerontologist,* 1971, *11,* 13-20.

The open generation. *Look,* September 20, 1966, p. 52.

Ordy, J. M., & Kaack, B. Neurochemical changes in composition, metabolism, and neurotransmitters in the human brain with age. In J. M. Ordy & K. R. Brizzee (Eds.), *Neurobiology of aging.* New York: Plenum, 1976.

Orma, E. J., & Koskenoja, M. Postural dizziness in the aged. *Geriatrics,* 1957, *12,* 49–50.

Ornstein, E. *The psychology of consciousness.* New York: Penguin, 1972.

Orton, S. T. Some studies in language function. *Research Publications Association for Research in Nervous and Mental Disease,* 1934, *13,* 614–632.

O'Sullivan, M., Guilford, J. P., & DeMille, R. *Measurement of social intelligence.* Psychological Laboratory Report No. 34, University of Southern California, 1965.

Owens, W. A. Age and mental abilities: A longitudinal study. *Genetic Psychology Monographs,* 1953, *48,* 3–54.

Packard, V. *The sexual wilderness.* New York: McKay, 1968.

Palermo, D. Research on language acquisition: Do we know where we are going? In L. Goulet & P. D. Baltes (Ed.), *Life-span developmental psychology: Research and theory.* New York: Academic, 1970.

Palmore, E. B. The effects of aging on activities and attitudes. *Gerontologist,* 1968, *8,* 259–263.

Palmore, E., & Whittington, F. Trends in the relative status of the aged. *Social Forces,* 1971, *50,* 84–91.

Papalia, D. E. The status of several conservation abilities across the life span. *Human Development,* 1972, *15,* 229–243.

Parens, H., McConville, B. J., & Kaplan, S. M. The prediction of frequency of illness from the response to separation. A preliminary study and replication attempt. *Psychosomatic Medicine,* 1966, *28,* 162–176.

Parsons, T., & Bales, R. F. *Family, socialization, and interaction process.* Glencoe, Ill.: Free Press, 1955.

Parsons, T., & Platt, G. M. *The American university.* Cambridge: Harvard University Press, 1973.

Pasamanick, B., & Knobloch, H. Brain damage and reproductive casualty. *American Journal of Orthopsychiatry,* 1960, *30,* 298–305. (a)

Pasamanick, B., & Knobloch, H. Epidemiologic studies on the complications of pregnancy and the birth process. In G. Caplan (Ed.), *Prevention of mental disorders in children.* New York: Basic Books, 1960. (b)

Pasamanick, B., & Knobloch, H. Retrospective studies on the epidemiology of reproductive casualty: Old and new. *Merrill-Palmer Quarterly,* 1966, *12,* 7–26.

Pavlov, I. P. [*Conditioned reflexes*] (G. V. Anrep, Trans.). London: Oxford University Press, 1927.

Pavlov, I. P. *Lectures on conditioned reflexes.* New York: International, 1928.

Pearlman, C. K. Frequency of intercourse in males at different ages. *Medical Aspects of Human Sexuality,* November 1972, pp. 92–113.

Pearson, G. H. J. Effect of age on vibratory sensibility. *Archives of Neurology and Psychiatry,* 1928, *20,* 482–496.

Penfield, W., & Roberts, L. *Speech and brain mechanisms.* Princeton: Princeton University Press, 1959.

Pepys, S. *The diary of Samuel Pepys* (Vol. 3). Los Angeles: University of California Press, 1976. (P. Lathan & W. Matthews, Eds.) (Originally published, 1662.)

Peskin, H. Multiple prediction of adult psychological health and preadolescent and adolescent behavior. *Journal of Consulting and Clinical Psychology,* 1972, *38,* 155–160.

Pfeiffer, E. Psychopathology and social pathology. In J. E. Birren & K. W. Schaie (Eds.), *Handbook of the psychology of aging.* New York: Van Nostrand Reinhold, 1977.

Pfeiffer, E., Verwoerdt, A., & Wang, H. S. Sexual behavior in aged men and women. In E. Palmore (Ed.), *Normal aging.* Durham, N.C.: Duke University Press, 1970.

Phoenix, C. H., Goy, R. W., Gerall, A. A., & Young, W. C. Organizing action of prenatally administered testosterone proponate on the tissue mediating mating behavior in the female guinea pig. *Endocrinology,* 1959, *65,* 369–382.

Phoenix, C. H., Goy, R. W., & Resko, J. A. Psychosexual differentiation as a function of androgenic stimulation. In M. Diamond (Ed.), *Reproduction and sexual behavior.* Bloomington: Indiana University Press, 1969.

Piaget, J. *The language and thought of the child.* New York: Harcourt, 1926.

Piaget, J. *The psychology of intelligence.* London: Routledge, 1950.

Piaget, J. [*The origins of intelligence in children*] (M.

Cook, Trans.). New York: International University Press, 1952.

Piaget, J. [*The construction of reality in the child*] (M. Cook, Trans.). New York: Basic Books, 1954.

Piaget, J. *Psychology of intelligence.* Totowa, N.J.: Littlefield, Adams, 1966.

Piaget, J. *Six psychological studies.* New York: Random House, 1967.

Piaget, J. [*The child's conception of movement and speed*] (G. E. T. Holloway & M. J. Mackenzie, Trans.). New York: Basic Books, 1970.

Piaget, J. Intellectual evolution from adolescence to adulthood. *Human Development*, 1972, *15*, 1-12.

Piaget, J. Quoted in interview, in Richard Evans' *Jean Piaget, the man and his ideas.* New York: Dutton, 1973. (a)

Piaget, J., & Inhelder, B. *Memory and intelligence.* New York: Basic Books, 1973. (b)

Plummer, G. Anomalies occurring in children exposed in utero to the atomic bomb in Hiroshima. *Pediatrics*, 1952, *10*, 687.

Pollack, R. H. Hue detectability as a function of chronological age. *Psychonomic Science*, 1965, *3*, 351-352.

Pollack, R. H. Ontogenetic changes in perception. In D. E. Elkind & J. H. Flavell (Eds.), *Studies in cognitive development.* New York: Oxford University Press, 1969.

Pollack, R. The carpentered world: Or biology stay away from my door. Paper delivered at City University Graduate School and University Center, New York, December 1972.

Pontius, A. A. Neurological aspects in some types of delinquency, especially among juveniles. *Adolescence*, 1972, *7*, 289-308.

Pontius, A. A. Basis for a neurological test of frontal lobe system functioning up to adolescence—A form analysis of action expressed in narratives. *Adolescence*, 1974, *9*, 221-232.

Pope, B. Socio-economic contrasts in children's peer culture prestige values. *Genetic Psychology Monographs*, 1953, *48*, 157-220.

Porter, R. B., & Cattell, R. B. *Handbook for the Children's Personality Questionnaire.* Champaign, Ill.: Institute for Ability and Personality Testing, 1960.

Pratt, K. C., Nelson, A. K., & Sun, K. H. The behavior of the newborn infant. *Ohio State University Study, Contributing Psychology*, 1930, *10*, 1-237.

Preyer, W. *The mind of the child.* Leipzig: Fernau, 1882.

Purpura, D. P. Dendritic spine "dysgenesis" and mental retardation. *Science*, 1974, *186*, 1126-1128.

Quetelet, M. A. *Sur l'homme et le développement de ses facultés* (2 vols.). Paris: Bachelier, 1835. (English translation. Quetelet, M. A. *A Treatise on Man, and the Development of his Faculties.* Edinburgh: 1842.)

Quinn, R., Staines, G., & McCullough, M. *Job satisfaction: Is there a trend?* (U.S. Department of Labor, Manpower Research Monograph No. 30). Washington, D.C.: U.S. Government Printing Office, 1974.

Rabbin, M. Sex role identity in young children in two diverse social groups. *Genetic Psychology Monographs*, 1950, *42*, 81-158.

Rabkin, L. Y., & Rabkin, K. Children of the kibbutz. *Psychology Today*, 1961, *3*(4), 40-46.

Rader, N. Department of Psychology, University of California at Los Angeles, personal communication, 1977.

Radke-Yarrow, M., Trager, H. G., & Davis, H. Social perceptions and attitudes of children. In R. G. Kuhlen & G. G. Thompson (Eds.), *Psychological studies in human development* (3rd ed.). New York: Appleton-Century-Crofts, 1970.

Rank, O. *The trauma of birth.* London: Routledge, 1929.

Rappaport, L. *Personality development: The chronology of experience.* Glenview, Ill.: Scott Foresman, 1972.

Ray, W. S. A preliminary report on a study of fetal conditioning. *Child Development*, 1932, *3*, 175-177.

Rebelsky, F., & Hanks, C. Fathers' verbal interaction with infants in the first three months of life. *Child Development*, 1972, *42*, 63-68.

Reese, H. W., & Lipsitt, L. P. *Experimental child psychology.* New York: Academic, 1970.

Reichard, S., Livson, F., & Petersen, P. G. *Aging and personality.* New York: Wiley, 1962.

Renne, K. S. Correlates of dissatisfaction in marriage. *Journal of Marriage and the Family*, 1970, *32*, 54-67.

Richter, C. P. A behavioristic study of the activity of the rat. *Comparative Psychological Monographs*, 1922-1923, 1.

Richter, C. P., & Campbell, K. H. Sucrose taste thresholds of rats and humans. *American Journal of Physiology*, 1940, *128*, 291-297.

Riegel, K. F. Dialectic operations: The final period of cognitive development. *Human Development*, 1973, *16*, 346-370.

Riesen, A. H., & Aarons, L. Visual movement and intensity discrimination in cats after early deprivation of pattern vision. *Journal of Comparative and Physiological Psychology*, 1959, *52*, 142-149.

Riley, M. W., & Foner, A. *Aging and society: An inventory of research findings*. New York: Russell Sage, 1968.

Riley, M. W., Foner, A., Hess, B., & Toby, M. L. Socialization for the middle and later years. In D. A. Goslin (Ed.), *Handbook of socialization theory and research*. Chicago: Rand McNally, 1969.

Rivers, W. H. R. Primitive color vision. *Popular Science Monthly*, 1901, *59*, 44-58.

Roberts, E., & Matthysse, S. Neurochemistry: At the crossroads of neurobiology. *Annual Review of Biochemistry*, 1970, *39*, 777-820.

Robinson, H. G., & Robinson, N. M. *The mentally retarded child: A psychological approach*. New York: McGraw-Hill, 1965.

Robson, K. S. The role of eye-to-eye contact in maternal-infant attachment. *Journal of Child Psychology and Psychiatry and Allied Disciplines*, 1967, *8*, 13-25.

Roffwarg, H. P., Muzio, J. N., & Dement, W. C. Ontogenic development of the human sleep-dream cycle. *Science*, 1966, *152*, 604-619.

Rogers, C. R. Some observations on the organization of personality. *American Psychologist*, 1947, *2*, 358-368.

Rogers, C. R. A theory of therapy, personality, and interpersonal relationships as developed in client-centered framework. In S. Koch (Ed.), *Psychology: A study of a science* (Vol. 2). New York: McGraw-Hill, 1959.

Rogers, C. R., & Skinner, B. F. Some issues concerning the control of human behavior: A symposium. *Science*, 1956, *124*, 1057-1066.

Roman, P., & Taietz, P. Organizational structure and disengagement: The emeritus professor. *Gerontologist*, 1967, *7*, 147-152.

Ronge, H. Altersveranderungen des Beruhrungssinnes. I. Druckpunktscjwellem und Druckpunktfrequenz. *Acta Physiologica Scandinavica*, 1943, *6*, 343-352.

Rorvik, D. M., & Shettles, L. B. *Your baby's sex: Now you can choose*. New York: Dodd, Mead, 1970.

Rose, P. *They and we* (2nd ed.). New York: Random House, 1974.

Rosen, B. C. Family structure and value transmission. *Merrill-Palmer Quarterly*, 1964, *10*, 59-76.

Rosen, B. C., & D'Andrade, R. G. The psychosocial origin of achievement motivation. *Sociometry*, 1959, *22*, 185-218.

Rosenberg, G., & Adams, A. Effect of age on peripheral vibratory perception. *Journal of the American Geriatrics Society*, 1958, *6*, 471-481.

Rosenkrantz, P. S., Vogel, S. R., Bee, H., Broverman, I. K., & Broverman, D. M. Sex role stereotypes and self-concepts in college students. *Journal of Consulting and Clinical Psychology*, 1968, *32*, 287-295.

Rosenthal, D. *Genetic theory and abnormal behavior*. New York: McGraw-Hill, 1970.

Rosenthal, R. *Experimenter effects in behavioral research*. New York: Irvington, 1976.

Rosenthal, R., & Jacobson, L. *Pygmalion in the classroom: Teacher expectations and pupils' intellectual development*. New York: Holt, 1968.

Rosenthal, R., & Rosnow, R. L. (Eds.). *Artifact in behavioral research*. New York: Academic, 1969.

Rosenweig, M. R., Bennett, E. L., & Diamond, M. C. Brain changes in response to experience. In *The nature and nurture of behavior: Development psychobiology*. San Francisco: Freeman, 1973.

Rosow, I. Long concentrations of aged and intergenerational friendships. In P. F. Hansen (Ed.), *Age with a future*. Philadelphia: Davis, 1964.

Rosow, I. Status and role change through the life span. In R. H. Binstock & E. Shanas (Eds.), *Handbook of aging and the social sciences*. New York: Van Nostrand Reinhold, 1976.

Rotter, J. B. *Social learning and clinical psychology*. Englewood Cliffs, N.J.: Prentice-Hall, 1953.

Rotter, J. B., Chance, J. E., & Phares, E. J. (Eds.). *Applications of a social learning theory of personality*. New York: Holt, 1972.

Rovee, C. K., Cohen, R. Y., & Shlapack, W. Life-span stability in olfactory sensitivity. *Developmental Psychology*, 1975, *11*, 311-318.

Rowell, J. A., & Renner, V. J. Personality, mode of assessment and student achievement. *British Journal of Educational Psychology*, 1975, *45*, 232-236.

Ruebsaat, H. J., & Hull, R. *The male climacteric*. New York: Hawthorn Books, 1975.

Rugh, R., & Shettles, L. B. *From conception to birth.* New York: Harper & Row, 1971.

Runner, M. N. Comparative pharmacology in relation to teratogenesis. *Federation Proceedings,* 1967, *26*(4), 1131–1136.

Ryans, D. G. Some relationships between pupil behavior and certain teacher characteristics. *Journal of Educational Psychology,* 1961, *52,* 82–90.

Sackett, G. P. Monkeys reared in isolation with pictures as visual input: Evidence for an innate releasing mechanism. *Science,* 1966, *154,* 1468–1473.

Salk, L. The role of the heartbeat in the relationship between mother and infant. *Scientific American,* March 1973.

Salmon, P. Differential conformity as a developmental process. *British Journal of Social and Clinical Psychology,* 1969, *8,* 22–31.

Sampson, E. E., & Hancock, F. T. An examination of the relationship between ordinal position, personality, and conformity: An extension, replication, and partial replication. *Journal of Personality and Social Psychology,* 1967, *5,* 398–407.

Sargart, W. *A mind possessed.* New York: Lippincott, 1974.

Sargent, S. S. The humanistic approach to personality. In B. B. Wolman (Ed.), *Handbook of general psychology.* Englewood Cliffs, N.J.: Prentice-Hall, 1973.

Savage-Rumbaugh, E. S., Rumbaugh, D. M., & Boysen, S. Symbolic communication between two chimpanzees (*Pan troglodytes*). *Science,* 1978, *201,* 641–644.

Savin, H. B., & Perchonock, E. Grammatical structure and the immediate recall of English sentences. *Journal of Verbal Learning and Verbal Behavior,* 1965, *4,* 348–353.

Scarr, S., & Winberg, R. A. I.Q. test performance of black children adopted by white families. *American Psychologist,* 1976, *31,* 726–739.

Schaefer, E. S. A circumplex model for maternal behavior. *Journal of Abnormal and Social Psychology,* 1959, *59,* 226–235.

Schaffer, H. R., & Emerson, P. E. The development of social attachments in infancy. *Monographs of the Society for Research in Child Development,* 1964, *29,* 1–77.

Schaie, K. W. A field-theory approach to age changes in cognitive behavior. *Vita Humana,* 1962, *5,* 129–141.

Schaie, K. W. A general model for the study of developmental problems. *Psychological Bulletin,* 1965, *64,* 92–107.

Schaie, K. W. Reflections on papers by Looft, Peterson, and Sparks: Intervention towards an ageless society? *Gerontologist,* 1973, *13,* 31–35.

Schaie, K. W. Translations in Gerontology—From lab to life: Intellectual functioning. *American Psychologist,* 1974, *29,* 802–807.

Schaie, K. W. Toward a stage theory of adult cognitive development. *Aging and Human Development,* 1977–1978, *8,* 129–138.

Schaie, K. W. The Primary Mental Abilities in adulthood: An exploration in the development of psychometric intelligence. In P. B. Batles & O. G. Brim, Jr. (Eds.), *Life-span development and behavior* (Vol. 2). New York: Academic, 1979.

Schaie, K. W., Anderson, V. E., McClearn, G. E., & Money, J. (Eds.), *Developmental human behavior genetics.* Lexington, Mass.: Heath, 1975.

Schaie, K. W., Baltes, P. B., & Strother, C. R. A study of auditory sensitivity in advanced age. *Journal of Gerontology,* 1964, *19,* 453–457.

Schaie, K. W., & Gribbin, K. The impact of environmental complexity on cognitive development. Paper presented to the International Society for the Study of Behavioral Development, Guilford, England, 1975.

Schaie, K. W., & Gribbin, K. Adult development and aging. *Annual Review of Psychology,* 1975, *26,* 65–96.

Schaie, K. W., & Labouvie-Vief, G. Generational versus ontogenetic components of change in adult cognitive behavior: A fourteen-year cross-sequential study. *Developmental Psychology,* 1974, *10,* 305–320.

Schaie, K. W., & Marquette, B. W. Personality in maturity and old age. In R. M. Dreger (Ed.), *Multivariate personality: Contributions to the understanding of personality in honor of Raymond B. Cattell.* Baton Rouge, La.: Claitor, 1972.

Schaie, K. W., & Parham, I. A. Social responsibility in adulthood: Ontogenetic and sociocultural change. *Journal of Personality and Social Psychology,* 1974, *30,* 483–492.

Schaie, K. W., & Parham, I. A. Stability of adult personality traits: Fact or fable? *Journal of Personality and Social Psychology,* 1976, *34,* 146–158.

Schaie, K. W., & Parham, I. A. Cohort-sequential analyses of adult intellectual development. *Developmental Psychology,* 1977, *13,* 649–653.

Schaie, K. W., & Strother, C. R. A cross-sequential study of age changes in cognitive behavior. *Psychological Bulletin*, 1968, *70*, 671–680.

Schaie, K. W., & Strother, C. R. Cognitive and personality variables in college graduates of advanced age. In G. S. Talland (Ed.), *Human aging and behavior: Recent advances in research and theory.* New York: Academic, 1968.

Schaie, K. W., & Willis, S. L. Life-span development: Implications for education. *Review of Research in Education*, 1978, *6*, 120–156.

Scheibel, A., & Scheibel, M. Some structural and functional substrates of development in young cats. *Progress in Brain Research*, 1964, *9*, 6–25.

Schoenfield, R. K. Melatonin: Effect on punished and non-punished operant behavior of the pigeon. *Science*, 1971, *171*, 1258–1260.

Scholz, A. T., Horrall, R. M., Cooper, J. C., & Hasler, A. D. Imprinting to chemical cues: The basis for home stream selection in salmon. *Science*, 1976, *192*, 1247–1249.

Schonfield, D., & Robertson, A. B. Memory storage and aging. *Canadian Journal of Psychology*, 1966, *20*, 228–236.

Schoonover, S. M. The relationship of intelligence and achievement to birth order, sex of sibling, and age interval. *Journal of Educational Psychology*, 1959, 143–145.

Schusky, E. L., & Weiss, G. Scientific concept of culture. *American Anthropologist*, 1973, *75*, 1377–1413.

Schwartz, A. N., Campos, J. J., & Baisel, E. J. The visual cliff: Cardiac and behavioral responses on the deep and shallow sides at five and nine months of age. *Journal of Experimental Child Psychology*, 1973, *15*, 86–99.

Schwartz, G. E. Biofeedback, self-regulation and the patterning of physiological processes. In I. L. Janis (Ed.), *Current trends in psychology: Readings from American Scientist.* Los Altos, Calif.: William Kaufman, 1977.

Scott, J. P. Critical periods in behavior development. *Science*, 1962, *138*, 949–958.

Scott, J. P. *Early experience and the organization of behavior.* Monterey, Calif.: Brooks/Cole, 1968.

Scott, M. The absence of interference effects in preschool children's picture recognition. *Journal of Genetic Psychology*, 1973, *122*, 121–126.

Sears, R. P., Maccoby, E. E., & Levin, H. *Patterns of child rearing.* New York: Harper, 1957.

Sears, R. R., Rau, L., & Albert, R. *Identification and child rearing.* Stanford, Calif.: Stanford University Press, 1965.

Seaver, W. B. Effects of naturally induced teacher expectancies. *Journal of Personality and Social Psychology*, 1973, *28*, 333–342.

Sechrest, L. Studies of classroom atmosphere. *Psychology in the Schools*, 1964, *1*, 103–118.

Segal, J., Boomer, D. S., & Bouthilet, L. (Eds.). *Research in the service of mental health.* (Document No. ADM 75-237). Washington, D.C.: U.S. Government Printing Office, 1975.

Segall, M. H., Campbell, D. T., & Herskovits, M. J. *The influence of culture on visual perception.* New York: Bobbs-Merrill, 1966.

Seitz, V., Abelson, W. D., Levine, E., & Zigler, E. Effects of place of testing on the Peabody Picture Vocabulary Test scores of disadvantaged Head Start and non-Head Start children. *Child Development*, 1975, *46*, 481–486.

Seligman, M. E. P. On the generality of the laws of learning. *Psychological Review*, 1970, *77*, 406–418.

Selye, H. *The stress of life.* New York: McGraw-Hill, 1978.

Shanas, E., Townsend, P., Wedderburn, D., Friis, H., Milhoj, P., & Stehouwer, J. *Old people in three industrial societies.* New York: Atherton, 1968.

Shapira, A., & Madsen, M. C. Cooperative and competitive behavior of kibbutz and urban children in Israel. *Child Development*, 1969, *40*, 609–617.

Shashoua, V. E. Brain metabolism and the acquisition of new behaviors. III. Evidence for secretion of two proteins into the brain extracellular fluid after training. *Brain Research*, 1979, *166*, 349–358.

Shashoua, V. E. Harvard Medical School and McLean Hospital, personal communication, 1980.

Sheldon, J. H. The effect of age on the control of sway. *Gerontologica Clinica*, 1963, *5*, 129–130.

Sheldon, W. H. *The varieties of temperament: A psychology of constitutional differences.* New York: Harper, 1942.

Shepard, R. N. Recognition memory for words, sentences and pictures. *Journal of Verbal Learning and Verbal Behavior*, 1967, *6*, 156–163.

Shirley, M. N. *The first two years* (Institute of Child Welfare Monograph, No. 7). Minneapolis:

University of Minnesota Press, 1933.

Shuttleworth, F. K. The adolescent period: A pictorial atlas. *Monographs of the Society for Research in Child Development*, 1949 (No. 14).

Sigman, M., Kopp, C. B., Littmann, B., & Parmelee. Infant visual attentiveness in relation to birth condition. *Developmental Psychology*, 1977, *13*(5), 431-437.

Simon, N., & Volicer, L. Neonatal asphyxia in the rat: Greater vulnerability of males and persistent effects on brain monoamine synthesis. *Journal of Neurochemistry*, 1976, 76, 893-900.

Sinclair-DeZwart, H. Developmental psycholinguistics. In D. Elkind & J. H. Flavell (Eds.), *Studies in cognitive development*. New York: Oxford University Press, 1969.

Skeels, H. M. Adult status of children with contrasting early life experiences: A follow-up study. *Monographs of the Society for Research in Child Development*, 1966, *31* (No. 105).

Skinner, B. F. *The Behavior of Organisms*. New York: Appleton-Century, 1938.

Skinner, B. F. *Walden Two*. New York: Macmillan, 1972, 1948.

Skinner, B. F. How to teach animals. *Scientific American*, 1951, *185*(6), 26-29.

Skinner, B. F. *Science and human behavior*. New York: Macmillan, 1953.

Skinner, B. F. *Verbal behavior*. New York: Appleton-Century-Crofts, 1957.

Skinner, B. F. *Beyond freedom and dignity*. New York: Knopf, 1971.

Skinner, B. F. *About behaviorism*. New York: Vintage, 1976.

Slataper, F. J. Age norms of refraction and vision. *Archives of Opthalmology, Chicago*, 1950, *43*, 466-481.

Slobin, D. I. The acquisition of Russian as a native language. In F. Smith & G. A. Miller (Eds.), *The genesis of language*. Cambridge, Mass.: MIT Press, 1966.

Slobin, D. I. Universals of grammatical development in children. In G. B. Flores d'Arcams & W. J. M. Levelt (Eds.), *Advances in psycholinguistics*. New York: American Elsevier, 1970.

Smith, A. D. Age differences in memory as influenced by qualitatively different types of processing. Paper presented at the annual meeting of the Gerontological Society, Washington, D.C., November 1979.

Smith, C. R., Williams, L., & Willis, R. H. Race, sex, and belief as determinants of friendship acceptance. *Journal of Personality and Social Psychology*, 1967, *5*, 127-137.

Smith, O.W., & Smith, P. C. Developmental studies of spatial judgments by children and adults. *Perceptual and Motor Skills*, 1966, *22*, 3-73.

Snow, C. P. *The two cultures*. Cambridge: Cambridge University Press, 1969.

Solomon, D., Bezdet, W. E., & Rosenberg, L. Dimensions of teacher behavior. *Journal of Experimental Education*, 1964, *33*, 23-40.

Sontag, L. W. The significance of fetal environmental differences. *American Journal of Obstetrics and Gynecology*, 1941, *42*, 996-1003.

Sontag, L. W. War and fetal maternal relationships. *Marriage and Family Living*, 1944, 6, 1-5. (a)

Sontag, L. W. Differences in modifiability of fetal behavior and physiology. *Psychosomatic Medicine*, 1944, 6, 151-154. (b)

Sorensen, B. Dependability of wind energy generators with short-term energy storage. *Science*, 1976, *194*, 935-937.

Sorenson, R. C. *The Sorensen report: Adolescent sexuality in contemporary America*. Cleveland: World, 1973.

Spelt, D. K. The conditioning of the human fetus in utero. *Journal of Experimental Psychology*, 1948, *38*, 338-346.

Sperry, R. W. Lateral specialization of cerebral function in the surgically separated hemispheres. In F. J. McGuigan & R. A. Schoonover (Eds.), *The psychophysiology of thinking*. New York: Academic, 1973.

Spielberger, C. D., Lushene, R. E., & McAdoo, W. G. Theory and measurement of anxiety states. In R. M. Dreger & R. B. Cattell (Eds.), *Handbook of modern personality theory*. New York: Hemisphere, 1976.

Spinelli, D. N., Hirsch, H. V. B., Phelps, R. W., & Metzler, J. Visual experience as a determinant of the response characteristics of cortical receptive fields in cats. *Experimental Brain Research*, 1972, *15*, 289-304.

Spitz, R. A. Hospitalism: An inquiry into the genesis of psychiatric conditions in early childhood. In O. Fenichel (Ed.), *The psychoanalytic study of the child* (Vol. 1). New York: International Universities Press, 1945.

Spitz, R. A. Hospitalism: A follow-up investigation. *The Psychoanalytic Study of the Child*, 1946, *2*, 113–117.

Spitz, R. A., & Wolf, K. M. Anaclitic depression: An inquiry into the genesis of psychiatric conditions in early childhood, II. *The Psychoanalytic Study of the Child*, 1946, *2*, 313–342.

Spock, B. *Baby and child care.* New York: Pocket Books, 1957.

Staats, A. W., & Staats, C. K. *Complex human behavior,* New York: Holt, 1963.

Stafford, R. E. Sex differences in spatial visualization as evidence of sex-linked inheritance. *Perceptual and Motor Skills*, 1961, *13*, 428.

Stagner, R. *Psychology of personality.* New York: McGraw-Hill, 1974.

Stechler, G. Newborn attention as affected by medication during labor. *Science*, 1964, *144*, 315–317.

Stedman, T. L. *Stedman's medical dictionary.* Baltimore: Williams & Wilkins, 1972.

Stein, A. H., & Friedrich, L. K. Impact of television on children and youth. *Review of Child Development Research*, 1975, *5*, 183–256.

Stellar, E. Brain mechanisms in hunger and other hedonic experiences. *Proceedings of the American Philosophical Society*, 1974, *118*, 276–282.

Stewart, W. A. Urban Negro speech: Sociolinguistic factors affecting English teaching. In R. W. Shuy (Ed.), *Social dialects and language learning.* National Council of Teachers, 1964.

Stone, J., & Norris, A. H. Activities and attitudes of participants in the Baltimore longitudinal study. *Journal of Gerontology*, 1967, *21*, 575.

Stoodley, B. H. Mother role as a focus of some family problems. *Marriage and Family Living*, 1952, *14*, 13–16.

Stott, D. H. Follow-up study from birth of the effects of prenatal stress. *Developmental Medicine and Child Neurology*, 1973, *15*, 770–787.

Stoyva, J., University of Colorado Medical School, personal communication, 1967.

Streib, G. F., & Thompson, W. E. The older person in a family context. In C. Tibbitts (Ed.), *Handbook of social gerontology.* Chicago: University of Chicago Press, 1960.

Streissguth, A. P., Landesman-Dwyer, S., Martin, J. C., & Smith, D. W. Teratogenic effects of alcohol in humans and laboratory animals. *Science*, 1980, *209*, 353–361.

Stricker, E. M., & Zigmond, M. H. Recovery of function after damage to central catecholamine-containing neurons: A neurochemical model for the lateral hypothalamic syndrome. In J. M. Spragues & A. N. Epstein (Eds.), *Progress in psychobiology and physiological.* New York: Academic, 1976.

Sullivan, H. S. *The interpersonal theory of psychiatry.* New York: Norton, 1953.

Sussman, M. B., & Burchinal, L. Kin family network: Unheralded structure in current conceptualizations of family functioning. *Marriage and Family Living*, 1962, *24*, 231–240.

Sutton-Smith, B., & Rosenberg, R. G. Sibling consensus on power tactics. Paper presented at the annual meeting of American Psychological Association, New York, 1966.

Sutton-Smith, B., Rosenberg, B. G., & Landy, F. Father-absence effect in families of different sibling compositions. *Child Development*, 1968, *38*, 1213–1221.

Syme, S. L., Hyman, M. M., & Entoline, P. E. Some social and cultural factors associated with the occurrence of coronary heart disease. *Journal of Chronic Diseases*, 1964, *17*, 277–289.

Szafran, J., & Birren, J. E. Perception. In J. E. Birren (Ed.), *Contemporary gerontology: Concepts and issues.* Los Angeles: Gerontology Center, University of Southern California, 1969.

Tanner, J. M. *Growth at Adolescence* (2nd ed.). Oxford: Blackwell Scientific; Philadelphia: Davis, 1962.

Tanner, J. M. Physical growth. In P. Mussen (Ed.), *Carmichael's manual of child psychology.* New York: Wiley, 1970.

Tanner, J. M. *Foetus into man: Physical growth from conception to maturity.* Cambridge: Harvard University Press, 1978.

Tanner, J. M., Whitehouse, R. H., & Takaishi, M. Standards from birth to maturity for height, weight, height velocity, and weight velocity: British children, 1965. *Archives of Diseases in Childhood*, 1966, *41*, 454–471; 613–635.

Tanzer, D. *Why natural childbirth?* New York: Schocken Books, 1976.

Tarler-Benlolo, L. The role of relaxation in biofeedback training: A critical review of the literature. *Psychological Bulletin*, 1978, *85*(4), 727–755.

TenHouten, W. D., Thompson, A. L., & Walter, D. O. Discriminating social groups by performance on two lateralized tests. *Bulletin of the Los Angeles Neurological Societies*, 1976, *41*, 99–108.

Terman, L. M. In symposium: Intelligence and its measurement. *Journal of Educational Psychology*, 1921, *12*, 127-133.

Terman, L. M., & Merrill, M. A. *Measuring intelligence.* Boston: Houghton Mifflin, 1937.

Terman, L. M., & Oden, M. H. *The gifted child grows up: Twenty-five years follow-up of a superior group.* Stanford, Calif.: Stanford University Press, 1947.

Terman, L. M., & Oden, M. H. *The gifted group at midlife: Thirty-five years follow-up of the superior child, genetic studies of genius.* Stanford, Calif.: Stanford University Press, 1959.

Theorell, T., & Rahe, R. H. Life change events, ballistocardiography and coronary death. *Journal of Human Stress*, 1975, *1*, 18-24.

Thomae, H. Theory of aging and cognitive theory of personality. *Human Development*, 1970, *13*, 1-16.

Thomae, H. The "developmental-task-approach" to a theory of aging. *Zeitschrift fuer Gerontologie*, 1975, *8*, 125-137.

Thomas, A., Chess, C., & Birch, H. The origin of personality. *Scientific American*, 1970, *223*(2), 102-109.

Thomas, E. L. Family correlates of student political activism. *Developmental Psychology*, 1971, *4*, 206-214.

Thompson, A. L., Bogen, J. E., & Marsh, J. F., Jr. Cultural hemisphericity: Evidence from cognitive tests. *International Journal of Neuroscience*, 1979, *9*, 37-43.

Thompson, L., & Joseph, A. *The Hopi way.* Chicago: University of Chicago Press, 1945.

Thompson, W. R. The inheritance and development of intelligence. *Research Publications of Nervous Mental Disorders*, 1954, *33*, 209-331.

Thompson, W. R., Watson, J., & Charlesworth, W. R. The effects of prenatal maternal stress on offspring behavior in rats. *Psychological Monographs*, 1962, *78*(38).

Thorndike, E. L. *The measurement of intelligence.* New York: Teachers College, Columbia University, Bureau of Publications, 1926.

Thorpe, W. H. The learning of song patterns by birds, with a special reference to the song of the chaffinch. *Fringilla coelebs, Ibis*, 1958, *100*, 535-570.

Thurlow, L. C. Myth of the American economy. *Newsweek*, 1977, Vol. 89, p. 11.

Tinbergen, N. *The study of instinct.* Oxford: Oxford University Press, 1951.

Tinbergen, N. *The study of instinct.* New York: Oxford University Press, 1969.

Toffler, A. *Future shock.* New York: Random House, 1970.

Torrance, E. P. *Guiding creative talent.* Englewood Cliffs, N.J.: Prentice-Hall, 1962.

Torrance, E. P. *Role of evaluation in creative thinking, Revised summary report.* Minneapolis: Bureau of Educational Research, University of Minnesota, 1964.

Torrance, E. P. Peer influences on preschool children's willingness to try difficult tasks. *Journal of Psychology*, 1969, *72*, 189-194.

Treas, J., & VanHilst, A. Marriage and remarriage rates among older Americans. *Gerontologist*, 1976, *16*, 132-136.

Trehub, S. E., & Chang, H. Speech as reinforcing stimulation for infants. *Developmental Psychology*, 1977, *13*, 170-171.

Triandis, H. C. Cultural influences upon cognitive processes. In L. Berkowitz (Ed.), *Advances in experimental social psychology* (Vol. 1). New York: Academic, 1964.

Troll, L. E. The family of later life: A decade review. *Journal of Marriage and the Family*, 1971, *33*, 263-290.

Troll, L. E. *Early and middle adulthood.* Monterey, Calif.: Brooks Cole, 1975.

Tryon, R. C. Genetic differences in maze-learning ability in rats. *39th Yearbook Nat. Soc. Stud. Educ.* (Part 1). Bloomington, Ill.: Public School Pub. Col., 1940.

Tuddenham, R. D. The constancy of personality ratings over two decades. In M. C. Jones, N. Bayley, J. W. McFarlane, & M. P. Honzik (Eds.), *The course of human development.* Waltham, Mass.: Xerox College Publishing, 1971.

Tulkin, S. R. Race, class, family and school achievement. *Journal of Personality and Social Psychology*, 1968, *9*, 31-37.

Tylor, E. B. *Primitive culture: Researches into the development of mythology, philosophy, religion, language, art and custom* (Vol. 1). London: John Murray, 1871.

U.S. Department of Health, Education, and Welfare. *Health, United States, 1975* (DHEW Pub. No. (HRA) 76-1232). Rockville, Md.: National Center for Health Statistics. 1975.

U.S. Department of Health, Education, and Welfare.

National health survey: Hearing levels of adults by age and sex, U.S. 1960-1962. Washington, D.C.: 1965.

U.S. Department of Health, Education, and Welfare. *Health, United States, 1978.* Rockville, Md.: National Center for Health Statistics, 1978.

U.S. Department of Health, Education, and Welfare. National Institute of Child Health and Human Development. *Perspectives on Human Deprivation: Biological, Psychological, and Sociological.* Washington, D.C.: Public Health Service, 1968.

U.S. Department of Health, Education, and Welfare, Public Health Service, 1973. Cited in *Newsweek,* January 29, 1973, p. 46.

U.S. Department of Health, Education, and Welfare, Public Health Service, Office of Smoking and Health. *Smoking and health: A report of the surgeon general* (DHEW Pub. No. (PHS) 79-50066), 1979.

Utech, D. A., & Hoving, K. L. Parents and peers as competing influences in the decisions of children of different ages. *Journal of Social Psychology,* 1969, *78,* 267-274.

Uzgiris, I. C. Patterns of vocal and gestural imitation. In F. J. Monks, W. W. Hartup, & J. Dewit (Eds.), *Determinants of behavioral development.* New York: Academic, 1972.

Vaillant, G. E. *Adaptation to life.* Boston: Little, Brown, 1977.

Van Dusen, R. A., & Sheldon, E. B. The changing status of American women. A life cycle perspective. *American Psychologist,* 1976, *31,* 106-116.

Van Lawick-Goodall, J. The behavior of free-living chimpanzees in the Gombe Stream Reserve. *Animal Behavior Monographs,* 1968, *1,* 161-311. Cited in Wilson, E. O. *Sociobiology.* Cambridge: Harvard University Press, 1975.

Vandenberg, S. G. Multivariate analysis of twin differences. In S. G. Vandenberg (Ed.), *Methods and goals in human behavior genetics.* New York: Academic, 1965.

Vandenberg, S. G. Human behavior genetics: Present status and suggestions for future research. *Merrill-Palmer Quarterly of Behavior and Development,* 1969, *15,* 121-154.

Vernon, P. E. Recent investigations of intelligence and its measurement. *Eugenics Review,* 1951, *43,* 125-137.

Vernon, P. E. Psychological studies of creativity.

Journal of Child Psychology and Psychiatry, 1967, *8,* 153-165.

Vernon, P. E. *Intelligence: Heredity and environment.* San Francisco: Freeman, 1979.

Veroff, J., & Feld, S. *Marriage and work in America: A study of motives and roles.* New York: Van Nostrand Reinhold, 1970.

Vogel, S. R., Broverman, I. K., Broverman, D. M., Clarkson, F. E., & Rosenkrantz, P. S. Maternal employment and perception of sex roles among college students. *Developmental Psychology,* 1970, *3,* 384-391.

Vogler, R. E., Masters, M. M., & Merrill, G. S. Shaping cooperative behavior in young children. *Journal of Psychology,* 1970, *74,* 181-186.

Vygotsky, L. S. [*Thought and language*] (E. Hanfmann & G. Vakar, Trans.). Cambridge, Mass.: MIT Press, 1962.

Waber, D. P. Sex differences in cognition: A function of maturation? *Science,* 1976, *192,* 572-573.

Wada, J. A., Clarke, R., & Hamm, A. Cerebral hemispheric asymmetry in humans: Cortical speech zones in 100 adult and 100 infant brains. *Archives of Neurology,* 1975, *32,* 239-246.

Waddington, C. H. *The strategy of the genes.* New York: Macmillan, 1957.

Waldron, I. Why do women live longer than men? *Social Science and Medicine,* 1976, *10,* 349-362.

Waldrop, M. F., Bell, R. Q., & Goering, J. D. Minor physical anomalies and inhibited behavior in elementary school girls. *Journal of Child Psychology and Allied Disciplines,* 1976, *17,* 113-122.

Walk, R. D. The development of depth perception in animals and human infants. In H. W. Stevenson (Ed.), *Concept of development. Monographs for the Society of Research in Child Development,* 1966, *31,* 82-108.

Walk, R. D., & Gibson, E. J. A comparative and analytic study of visual depth perception. *Psychological Monographs,* 1961, *75*(15, Whole No. 519).

Walker, D., Grimwade, J., & Wood, C. Intrauterine noise, a component of the fetal environment. *American Journal of Obstetrics and Gynecology,* 1971, *109,* 91-95.

Walker, W. B. The alcids, birds threatened by man and by oil spills. *Boston Sunday Globe, New England Magazine,* November 28, 1976, pp. 8ff.

Walters, J., & Stinnett, N. Parent-child relationships: A decade review of research. In C. Broderick (Ed.), *A decade of family research and* action. Minneapolis: National Council of Family Relations, 1971.

Wang, H. S., Obrist, W. D., & Busse, E. W. Neurophysiological correlates of the intellectual function of elderly persons living in the community. *American Journal of Psychiatry*, 1970, 126, 1205-1212.

Warr, P. B., & Knapper, C. *The perception of people and events*. New York: Wiley, 1968.

Warren, J. R. Birth order and social behavior. *Psychological Bulletin*, 1966, 65, 38-50.

Watson, J. B. Psychology as the behaviorist views it. *Psychological Review*, 1913, 20, 158-177.

Watson, J. B. *Psychology from the standpoint of a behaviorist*. Philadelphia: Lippincott, 1919.

Watson, J. B., & Rayner, R. Conditional emotional reactions. *Journal of Experimental Psychology*, 1920, 3(1), 1-15.

Watson, J. D. *The molecular biology of the gene* (3rd ed.). New York: Benjamin-Cummings, 1976.

Watson, J. D. *The double helix*. New York: Atheneum, 1968.

Wattenberg, W. W. *The adolescent years* (2nd ed.). New York: Harcourt Brace Jovanovich, 1973.

Weale, R. A. On the eye. In A. T. Welford & J. E. Birren (Eds.), *Behavior, aging and the nervous system*. Springfield, Ill.: Charles C Thomas, 1965.

Wechsler, D. *The measurement of adult intelligence* (3rd ed.). Baltimore: Williams & Wilkins, 1944.

Weiss, A. D. Sensory functions. In J. E. Birren (Ed.), *Handbook of aging and the individual*. Chicago: University of Chicago Press, 1959.

Wender, P. H. *Minimal brain dysfunction in children*. New York: Wiley, 1971.

Werner, E. E., Bierman, J. M., & French, F. E. *The children of Kauai*. Honolulu: University of Hawaii Press, 1971.

Werner, H. *Comparative psychology of mental development*. New York: International Universities Press, 1957. (a)

Werner, H. The concept of development from a comparative and organismic point of view. In D. B. Harris (Ed.), *The concept of development*. Minneapolis: University of Minnesota Press, 1957. (b)

Whalen, C. K., & Henker, B. Psychostimulants and children: A review and analysis. *Psychological Bulletin*, 1976, 83(6), 1113-1130.

Whipple, G. M. *Manual of mental and physical tests*. Baltimore: Warwick and York, 1914.

White, J. R., & Froeb, H. F. Small-airways dysfunction in nonsmokers chronically exposed to to-bacco smoke. *New England Journal of Medicine*, 1980, 302, 720-723.

White, R. Motivation reconsidered: The concept of competence. *Psychological Review*, 1959, 66, 297-333.

White House Conference on Aging. *Toward a national policy on aging* (Vol. 2). Washington, D.C.: U.S. Government Printing Office, 1973.

Whiting, J. W. M., & Child, I. *Child training and personality*. New Haven: Yale University Press, 1953.

Whorf, B. *Language, thought and reality*. Cambridge, Mass.: MIT Press; New York: Wiley, 1956.

Wiggins, N., & Wiggins, J. S. A typological analysis of male preferences for female body types. *Multivariate Behavioral Research*, 1969, 4, 89-102.

Wilentz, J. S. The senses of man. New York: Crowell, 1968.

Wilkie, F., & Eisdorfer, C. Intelligence and blood pressure in the aged. *Science*, 1971, 172, 959-962.

Wilkie, F., & Eisdorfer, C. Systemic disease and behavior correlates. In L. Harvick, C. Eisdorfer, & J. E. Blum (Eds.), *Intellectual functioning in adults*. New York: Springer, 1973.

Willerman, L. Biosocial influences on human development. *American Journal of Orthopsychiatry*, 1972, 42, 452.

Willerman, L., Broman, S. H., & Fiedler, M. Infant development, preschool IQ, and social class. *Child Development*, 1970, 41, 69-77.

Williams, R. J. *Biochemical individuality*. New York: Wiley, 1963.

Wilson, E. O. *Sociobiology*. Cambridge: Harvard University Press, 1975.

Wilson, R. S. Synchronies in mental development: An epigenetic perspective, 1978, 202, 939-948.

Winick, M. *Malnutrition and brain development*. New York: Oxford University Press, 1976.

Winick, M., Meyer, K. K., & Harris, R. C. Malnutrition and environmental enrichment by early adoption. *Science*, 1975, 190, 1173-1175.

Winn, M. *The plug-in drug*. New York: Viking, 1977.

Wintrob, R. M. An inward focus: A consideration of psychological stress in fieldwork. In F. Henry & S. Saberwol (Eds.), *Stress and response in fieldwork*. New York: Holt, 1969.

Wolf, E. Glare and age. *Archives of Ophthalmology*, 1960, 64, 502-514.

Wolf, R. M. *The measurement of environments*.

Princeton: Educational Testing Services, 1964.

Wolhwill, J. F. The development of "overconstancy" in space perception. In L. P. Lipsitt & C. Spiker (Eds.), *Advances in child development and behavior.* New York: Academic, 1963.

Wong, R. *Motivation.* New York: Macmillan, 1976.

Woodruff, D. S. Brain electrical activity and behavior relationships over the life span. In P. B. Baltes (Ed.), *Life span and development and behavior* (Vol. 1). New York: Academic, 1978.

Woodruff, D. S. *Can you live to be 100?* New York: New American Library, 1978.

Woodruff, D. S., & Birren, J. E. Age changes and cohort differences in personality. *Development Psychology,* 1972, *6,* 252-259.

Woodruff, D. S., & Birren, J. E. (Eds.). *Aging: Scientific perspectives and social issues.* New York: Van Nostrand, 1975.

Woodworth, R. S., & Marquis, D. G. *Psychology* (5th ed.). New York: Holt, 1947.

Wylie, R. C. *The self-concept.* Lincoln: University of Nebraska Press, 1961.

Yakovlev, P. I., & Lecours, A. The myelogenetic cycles of regional maturation of the brain. In A. Minkowski (Ed.), *Regional development of the brain in early life.* Oxford: Blackwell Scientific, 1967.

Yang, R. K., Zweig, A. R., Douthitt, T. C., & Federman, E. J. Successive relationships between maternal attitudes during pregnancy, analgesic medication during labor and delivery, and newborn behavior. *Developmental Psychology,* 1976, 12, 6-14.

Yerkes, R. M., & Morgulis, S. The method of Pavlov in animal psychology. *Psychological Bulletin,* 1909, *6,* 257-273.

Zajonc, R. B. Family configuration and intelligence: Variation in scholastic aptitude scores parallel trends in family size and the spacing of children. *Science,* 1976, *192,* 227-236.

Zax, M., Sameroff, A. J., & Farnum, J. E. Childbirth education, maternal attitudes, and delivery. *American Journal of Obstetrics and Gynecology,* 1975, *123,* 185-190.

Zeaman, D., & House, B. J. The role of attention in retardate discrimination learning. In N. R. Ellis (Ed.), *Handbook of mental deficiency.* New York: McGraw-Hill, 1963.

Zigler, E., Abelson, W., & Seitz, V. Motivational factors in the performance of economically disadvantaged children on the Peabody Picture Vocabulary Test. *Child Development,* 1973, *44,* 294-303.

Zubin, J., & Money, J. (Eds.) *Contemporary sexual behavior: Critical issues in the 1970's.* Baltimore: Johns Hopkins University Press, 1973.

NAME INDEX

SUBJECT INDEX

SOME MAJOR STAGE THEORIES

Approximate Chronological Age	Some Physiological Milestones	Cognitive Development (Piaget)
Infancy (0–1)	Birth Rapid brain growth	Sensorimotor period
Early childhood (1–5)	Mobility Language acquisition	Preoperational period
Late childhood (5–11)		Period of concrete operations
Adolescence (11–18)	Puberty Physical growth spurt Sexual maturity	Period of formal operations
Early adulthood (18–25)	Peak physical condition	Consolidation of formal operations
Middle adulthood (25–50)	Menopause	Verbal intelligence may increase in healthy adults
Later adulthood (50–75)	Physical decline (depending on habits)	Decline in speed of information processing For some, increased mastery of life tasks
Old age (75 and up)	Increasing risk of illness/disability Death	Decline in intelligence with terminal illness For some, wisdom and transcendence of limitation